The Rule of Law in the Islamic Republic of Iran

After Iran's 1979 Revolution, Ayatollah Khomeini denounced the secular legal system of the Pahlavis and pledged his commitment to *distinctly* Islamic conceptions of law and justice: The application of both the shari'a and the rule of law (*hākemiyat-e qānun*) became major ideological pillars of the Islamic Republic. This precipitated the Islamization of the legal system, the judiciary, and the courts, a process that continues to this day and is the subject of intense ideological and political contestation. *The Rule of Law in the Islamic Republic of Iran* is the first comprehensive analysis of the judicial and legal institutions of the Islamic Republic of Iran in their social, political, and historical contexts. Scholars and practitioners of law, several with experience as defendants or defenders in Iranian courts of law, shed light on how the rule of law has fared across a variety of areas, from criminal law to labor law, family law, minority rights, policing, the legal profession, the visual and performing arts, trade law, and medicine.

Hadi Enayat is the author of *Law, State and Society in Modern Iran* (Palgrave Macmillan, 2013), winner of the biennial Mossadegh Prize 2013, and *Islam and Secularism in Post-Colonial Thought: A Cartography of Asadian Genealogies* (Palgrave Macmillan, 2017). He teaches at the Institute for the Study of Muslim Civilisations of the Aga Khan University and is a research fellow at the Foreign Policy Centre in London. He has worked as an expert witness for UK courts in Iranian asylum cases.

Mirjam Künkler is Research Professor at the Netherlands Institute for Advanced Study. Her recent books include *Female Religious Authority in Shi'i Islam: Past and Present* (Edinburgh University Press, 2021) and *A Secular Age beyond the West* (Cambridge University Press, 2018), among others. She is a principal investigator of the Iran Data Portal, and sits on the editorial boards of journals in Iranian studies, Middle Eastern studies, law, and the sociology of religion.

The Rule of Law in the Islamic Republic of Iran

Power, Institutions, and the Limits of Reform

Edited by

Hadi Enayat
Aga Khan University

Mirjam Künkler
Netherlands Institute for Advanced Study

Shaftesbury Road, Cambridge CB2 8EA, United Kingdom

One Liberty Plaza, 20th Floor, New York, NY 10006, USA

477 Williamstown Road, Port Melbourne, VIC 3207, Australia

314–321, 3rd Floor, Plot 3, Splendor Forum, Jasola District Centre, New Delhi – 110025, India

103 Penang Road, #05–06/07, Visioncrest Commercial, Singapore 238467

Cambridge University Press is part of Cambridge University Press & Assessment, a department of the University of Cambridge.

We share the University's mission to contribute to society through the pursuit of education, learning and research at the highest international levels of excellence.

www.cambridge.org
Information on this title: www.cambridge.org/9781108481427

DOI: 10.1017/9781108630603

© Hadi Enayat and Mirjam Künkler 2025

This publication is in copyright. Subject to statutory exception and to the provisions of relevant collective licensing agreements, no reproduction of any part may take place without the written permission of Cambridge University Press & Assessment.

First published 2025

A catalogue record for this publication is available from the British Library

Library of Congress Cataloging-in-Publication Data
Names: Enayat, Hadi, editor. | Künkler, Mirjam, 1977– editor.
Title: The rule of law in the Islamic Republic of Iran : power, institutions, and the limits of reform / edited by Hadi Enayat, Aga Khan University, London; Mirjam Künkler, Netherlands Institute for Advanced Study.
Description: Cambridge, United Kingdom ; New York, NY : Cambridge University Press, 2025. | Includes bibliographical references and index.
Identifiers: LCCN 2023033731 | ISBN 9781108481427 (hardback) | ISBN 9781108630603 (ebook)
Subjects: LCSH: Rule of law – Iran. | Law reform – Iran. | Justice, Administration of – Iran. | Shīʿah – Iran – Doctrines. | Joint Comprehensive Plan of Action (2015 July 14) | Iran – History – Revolution, 1979.
Classification: LCC KMH2020 .R85 2025 | DDC 349.55–dc23/eng/20231002
LC record available at https://lccn.loc.gov/2023033731

ISBN 978-1-108-48142-7 Hardback

Additional resources for this publication at www.cambridge.org/Enayat-Kunkler

Cambridge University Press & Assessment has no responsibility for the persistence or accuracy of URLs for external or third-party internet websites referred to in this publication and does not guarantee that any content on such websites is, or will remain, accurate or appropriate.

Contents

List of Figures, Maps and Tables	*page* vii
List of Contributors	viii
Acknowledgments	xiii
Note on Transliteration	xiv
Chronology	xv
List of Abbreviations and Glossary	xxxi

1 Governing the Law in the Islamic Republic of Iran 1
   MIRJAM KÜNKLER

2 The Islamic Penal Code of 2013: Traditions and Innovations 45
   SILVIA TELLENBACH

3 The Administration of Criminal Justice in Iran: Ideology, Judicial Personalism, and the Cynical Manipulation of Security 66
   DREWERY DYKE AND HADI ENAYAT

4 Shi'i Family Law under the Rule of Law? The Iranian Model and Current Approaches in the Shi'i World 104
   HANNAH L. RICHTER

5 Rule of Law or Rule by Law? Iran's Bar Association as a Pawn in Islamic–Republican Contestations 135
   MIRJAM KÜNKLER

6 Law Enforcement and the Judiciary in Postrevolutionary Iran 159
   SAEID GOLKAR

7 The Problem of Overcrowded Prisons in the Islamic Republic of Iran 187
   ANNA ENAYAT AND HADI ENAYAT

8 Legal Barriers to Accessing Vital Medical Services and Creative Responses to Overcoming These 236
   ARASH ALAEI AND KAMIAR ALAEI

v

9	Reform from Within? *Hākemiyat-e Qānun* from the Reformist Era to 2022 MIRJAM KÜNKLER	260
10	Iran's Religious and Ethnic Minorities in the Eyes of the Judiciary and the Security Apparatus SHAHIN MILANI	289
11	Labor Rights in Postrevolutionary Iran M. STELLA MORGANA	331
12	The Effects of the Joint Comprehensive Plan of Action (JCPOA), and Subsequent US Withdrawal, on Iranian Law FAEZEH MANTEGHI AND SEYED EMADEDDIN TABATABAEI	357
13	Multilayered Mechanisms of Control and Censorship of Arts and Culture in the Islamic Republic of Iran ROOZBEH MIREBRAHIMI AND AZADEH POURZAND	386
14	The Legal Situation Regarding Assisted Reproduction in Iran: Current Developments and Concerns SHIRIN NAEF	414
15	Conclusions: Regressions and Progressions in the Rule of Law of the Islamic Republic of Iran HADI ENAYAT AND MIRJAM KÜNKLER	444
Index		463

Figures, Maps and Tables

Figures

6.1	Police and judiciary	page 163
6.2	Authority structure of the police (Niruhā-ye Entezāmi Jomhuri-ye Eslāmi, NAJA)	164
6.3	Police structure: A vertical view	180
6.4	Police structure: A horizontal view	181
8.1	Epidemic estimates in Iran, 2005–2021	237
8.2	HIV testing and treatment cascade in Iran, 2020	246
8.3	Estimated number of people living with HIV, new HIV infections, and AIDS-related deaths, 1990–2020	252
8.4	HIV population by mode of contraction, 2010–2017	252
12.1	Inflation of the Iranian rial, 2018–2020	372
12.2	Development of consumer price index in Iran, 2005–2021	379

Maps

10.1	Geographic distribution of religious and ethnic minorities in Iran	313

Tables

7.1	Iran: Permanent prison population, selected years between 1979 and 2019	230
7.2	Prisoners by category for selected years between 1989 and 2018	232
9.1	Heads of the Judiciary, 1989–2022	279
9.2	Prosecutors general, 1979–2022	280
10.1	Minorities in the Iranian census of 2016	291
12.1	State intervention, the Joint Comprehensive Plan of Action (JCPOA), and sanctions	373

Contributors

ARASH ALAEI is Director of the Institute for International Health and Education. He has been a senior consultant for the United Nations Children's Fund, the United States Agency for International Development/President's Emergency Plan for AIDS Relief, the Centers for Disease Control and Prevention, the Joint United Nations Programme on HIV and AIDS, and the Tajikistan Ministry of Health. He served as the Associate Vice Provost for International Education at the State University of New York at Albany (SUNY Albany), as well as Clinical Associate Professor and the cofounding Director of the Global Institute for Health and Human Rights at the same university. He has authored and coauthored several peer-reviewed journal articles. Among several awards, the Alaei brothers – Arash and Kamiar – have received the Heinz R. Pagels Human Rights of Scientists Award from the New York Academy of Science, the Jonathan Mann Award for Global Health and Human Rights from the Global Health Council, the Human Rights Award from the Pan American Health Organization/World Health Organization, and the inaugural Elizabeth Taylor Award from the International AIDS Society/Foundation for AIDS Research.

KAMIAR ALAEI is the Chair and Professor of Department of Health Science at California State University, Long Beach. He was a visiting academic at the University of Oxford and a distinguished global health scholar at Drexel University. He was the founding Director of the Global Institute for Health and Human Rights at SUNY Albany. He studied medicine, epidemiology, international health, health policy, and international human rights law at universities such as Harvard and Oxford, gaining several degrees, including an MD, MPH, MS, DrPH, and MSt. He has authored and coauthored numerous peer-reviewed journal articles in prestigious publications including *The Lancet Global Health*, the *British Medical Journal*, and *AIDS*. He has been featured and interviewed by major academic journals such as *Nature*, *Science*, and *The Lancet*.

List of Contributors

DREWERY DYKE is a human rights policy analyst and advocate. He is a senior fellow at the UK's Foreign Policy Centre and, between 1999 and 2017, served as a researcher at Amnesty International, where he led work on Iran, Afghanistan, and several Gulf Cooperation Council countries. In June 2020, the Ceasefire Centre for Civilian Rights and Minority Rights Group published his report, "In the Name of Security: Human Rights Violations under Iran's National Security Laws." His published work on Iran deals with the administration of justice, including the issues of "knowledge of the judge" and *gozinesh* (discriminatory selection criteria), as well as the rights of ethnic and religious minorities, notably in the criminal justice system.

ANNA ENAYAT was a lecturer in sociology at the Faculty of Economics of Tehran University where she taught the sociology of economic life and the sociology of development. She is a Senior Common Room member of St Antony's College, Oxford, and from 1993 to 1998 was Editorial Director at I. B. Tauris publishers. She has been a recognized expert on the social, political, and human rights backgrounds of Iranian refugee cases heard by the UK Immigration Appeal Tribunal, where her reports have covered a range of topics, including the political situation in Iran, and the position and treatment of political dissidents and of various social groups, including women and religious ethnic and sexual minorities.

HADI ENAYAT is a political sociologist teaching at the Institute for the Study of Muslim Civilizations at Aga Khan University in London. His book *Law, State and Society in Modern Iran: Constitutionalism, Autocracy and Legal Reform, 1906–1941* (Palgrave Macmillan, 2013) won the biennial Mossadegh Prize (2013) for distinguished scholarship in Iranian studies. His most recent book is *Islam and Secularism in Post-Colonial Thought: A Cartography of Asadian Genealogies* (Palgrave Macmillan, 2017). He has worked in UK courts as an expert witness in Iranian asylum cases.

SAEID GOLKAR is a UC Foundation Associate Professor in the Department of Political Science and Public Service at the University of Tennessee at Chattanooga, and, concurrently, Nonresident Senior Fellow on Middle East Policy at the Chicago Council on Global Affairs and the Institute for Global Change in the UK. His research focuses on comparative politics of authoritarian regimes in the Middle East. A former postdoctoral fellow at Stanford University's Center on Democracy, Development, and the Rule of Law, Golkar received a PhD from the Department of Political Science at Tehran

University in June 2008. His book *Captive Society: The Basij Militia and Social Control in Post-Revolutionary Iran* (Columbia University Press, 2015) was awarded the 2016 Washington Institute Silver Medal Prize. His recent articles have been published in *Middle East Journal*, *Armed Forces & Society*, *Politics, Religion & Ideology*, and *Middle East Policy*.

MIRJAM KÜNKLER is Research Professor at the Netherlands Institute for Advanced Study. Her recent books include *Female Religious Authority in Shi'i Islam: Past and Present* (Edinburgh University Press, 2021) and *A Secular Age beyond the West* (Cambridge University Press, 2018). She lived in Iran in 2002 and 2003 as a visiting scholar to the Department of Sociology and Demography of the University of Tehran and is a founder and principal investigator of the Iran Data Portal. She sits on the editorial boards of journals in Iranian studies, Middle Eastern studies, law, and the sociology of religion. Her books have been translated into Arabic and Persian. In 2023, she was elected President of the Association for the Study of Persianate Societies (ASPS).

FAEZEH MANTEGHI holds a PhD in criminal law and criminology from the Faculty of Law and Political Science of the University of Tehran, Iran. Her research focuses on the role of political groups in the codification of criminal law in Muslim-majority countries. She received her Bachelor of Laws and her Master of Criminal Law and Criminology degrees from the University of Tehran in 2012 and 2014, respectively. She writes about law and politics, legal theory of criminal law, and Iranian legal history. She is also passionate about human rights education for young people and has taught and worked with high school students in Iran. She is licensed to practice law in Iran.

SHAHIN MILANI is the Executive Director of the Iran Hunan Rights Documentation Center. He obtained his JD from Howard University School of Law and his LLM from Vermont Law School. Milani is the principal author of several International Human Resources Development Corporation reports, including "The 1980 Cultural Revolution and Restrictions on Academic Freedom in Iran" (2020), "Access to Justice for Victims of Sexual Violence in Iran" (2020), "Extreme Inequality: The Human Rights Situation of Iran's Baluch Minority" (2019), "Excluded from the Public Sphere"(2018), "Controlled and Pursued: Labor Activism in Contemporary Iran" (2018), "Restrictions on Freedom of Expression in the Islamic Republic of Iran" (2016), "Apostasy in the Islamic Republic of Iran" (2014), and "Denied Identity: Human Rights Abuses against Iran's LGBT Community" (2013).

List of Contributors

ROOZBEH MIREBRAHIMI is Head of Research of Impact Iran, a US-based coalition of fourteen nongovernment organizations (NGOs) working to advance human rights in Iran. He has written more than ten books about Iran and his experiences as a censored, imprisoned, and exiled journalist, among them *Āzādi va Digar Hich* [*Freedom and Nothing Else*], about the life and works of Iranian intellectual Ehsan Naraghi (Resanesh Novin Publisher, 2016); and *Kheshte-e Aval [The First Brick]*, a look at the 1979 Revolution through the eyes of the postrevolutionary generation (Non-Stop Media, 2019). Mirebrahimi is the recipient of the Arthur L. Carter Journalism Institute of New York University's Visiting Scholarship (2010–2011), the City University of New York Graduate School of Journalism's first International Journalist in Residence Fellowship (2007–2008), and the Human Rights Watch Hellman/Hammett International Prize (2006). He has been a member of the expert jury for the Freedom in the World Index of Freedom House and has been an Iran consultant for Human Rights Watch. Mirebrahimi is featured in the exhibition *Who Is Like Me: The Human Rights Movement* at the National Center for Civil and Human Rights in Atlanta, Georgia.

M. STELLA MORGANA is a British Academy postdoctoral fellow at the University of Liverpool. Previously, she was a lecturer in Middle Eastern history and politics at the University of Amsterdam and in the history of Iran at Leiden University. Her latest publications include "'Produce and Consume' in the Islamic Republic: The 1990s Myth of the Winner in the Iranian Public Sphere and Its Impact on Workers," *International Journal of Middle East Studies*, 2020; "Talking to Workers: From Khomeini to Ahmadinejad, How the Islamic Republic's Discourse on Labor Changed through May Day Speeches (1979–2009)," *Iranian Studies*, 2019; and "The Islamic Republican Party of Iran in the Factory: Control over Workers in Posters," *IRAN – British Journal for Persian Studies*, 2018.

SHIRIN NAEF is Lecturer at the Department of Social Sciences, University of Fribourg, Switzerland, where she teaches on the relationship between law and religion. Her research interests focus on the history of ideas, law, religion, and ethics in modern Iran, with particular focus on the Shi'i legal tradition. An examination of regulation and practice of reproductive technologies in Iran was the subject of her doctoral thesis. From October 2018 to June 2019, she was a fellow at the Käte Hamburger Center for Advanced Study in the Humanities "Law as Culture," working on her second area of study on legal and cultural dimensions of charitable giving in Iran.

AZADEH POURZAND is the Executive Director of the Siamak Pourzand Foundation, dedicated to the promotion of freedom of expression in Iran. A PhD candidate at the School of Oriental and African Studies University of London's Global Media and Communications Department, she is a graduate of Harvard University's Kennedy School of Government with a master's degree in public policy. A human rights advocacy officer at Impact Iran, Azadeh has spent the past decade contributing to the design, implementation, and impact evaluation of civil society, strengthening media development, education, and human rights programs for marginalized communities in the Middle East and South Asia through organizations such as the International Research & Exchanges Board, the Small Media Foundation, the Asian University for Women, Gateway House: Indian Council on Global Relations, and the Open Society Foundation.

HANNAH L. RICHTER has a PhD in Islamic Studies from a German University and is currently working at a German research institute. Richter has chosen to write under a pseudonym due to being under a protection order. Richter has published on Islamic family law in both modern Shi'i and Sunni contexts.

SEYED EMADEDDIN TABATABAEI holds an LLM (summa cum laude) from Albert Ludwig University, Freiburg (2010) and a LLB (magna cum laude) from the University of Tehran (2003) and for several years he was a member of the International Max Planck Research School for Comparative Criminal Law. He is an Of Counsel to the European law firm association ADVANT, which is established by three founding members: Altana in France, Beiten Burkhardt in Germany, and Nctm in Italy. He is the contact point for Middle East countries and deals mainly with corporate and commercial law.

SILVIA TELLENBACH completed her studies of law in 1976 and earned her doctorate in Islamic studies with a dissertation on the constitution of the Islamic Republic of Iran in 1984. From 1984 until 2015 she held the position of Head of the Research Section for Turkey, Iran, and the Arab States at the Max Planck Institute for Foreign and International Criminal Law (now: Max Planck Institute for the Study of Crime, Security and Law). She has published more than 200 books and articles in the field of criminal and constitutional law in Germany and abroad and given over 160 lectures in 17 countries. She is a member of the managing committee of the Society for Arab and Islamic Law and a member of other associations in the field of Near and Middle Eastern law.

Acknowledgments

As editors we have benefited from multifarious support by colleagues and friends in the preparation of this volume. We thank the Institute for the Study of Muslim Civilizations at the Aga Khan University in London for funding a conference where early drafts of many of the chapters of this volume were first presented. During the conference we were fortunate to have an exceptionally well-informed audience, who helped sharpen and refine the arguments made in the conference papers.

We thank the artist Shiva Ahmadi for her generous permission to reproduce her painting *The Knot* on our book's cover. Shiva's intricate style, alluding to the classical tradition of Persian miniature painting, combined with her acute sense of the political and social violence that is embedded in many of the scenes her paintings depict, made her art particularly relevant for our purposes. We are honored she has given us permission to reproduce her work.

We further thank the known and anonymous reviewers of chapters in this volume who commented wisely and competently.

Finally, we thank our colleagues in Iran and beyond for generously helping us with resources and data that are often difficult to acquire or to access. While putting this volume together, several of our authors faced severe challenges, hostility, or even defamation due to their legal or academic work on the law and politics of Iran. We are grateful for the wise counsel they and we received, legal and otherwise, from CUP and colleagues. We dedicate this volume to all those inside and outside the country who struggle to improve the rule of law and make the government accountable to the people. Too many have paid a terribly high price in this endeavor.

Hadi Enayat and Mirjam Künkler
London, October 2023.

Note on Transliteration

The book adopts the *Iranian Studies* journal rules of transliteration in both spoken and written Persian. For the proper names of public figures and places (e.g., Khamenei, Shiraz), common English-language spelling is used where available. For Arabic terms, a modified version of the transliteration scheme of the *International Journal of Middle East Studies* is used. In words accepted in the *Oxford English Dictionary*, such as ayatollah, Qur'an, hejab, and fatwa, macrons and diacritics are omitted. Where an Arabic phrase appears in Persian speech, or a technical term has the same meaning in both Arabic and Persian, one or the other transliteration style is used depending on the context.

Chronology

1979

February 1 – After fourteen years in exile in Iraq and France, Ayatollah Ruhollah Khomeini returns to Iran.

February – The Islamic Revolutionary Courts are established to try the Shah's officials and later all those accused of political crimes. More than 500 are sentenced to death in the courts' first year in operation.

March – The Family Protection Law of 1968 is abolished. This law had denied men the right to unilateral divorce and put women on an equal footing with men with regard to divorce and child custody.

March 30–31 – A referendum asks voters to approve or not approve the creation of an Islamic republic.

June 14 – First official draft of the constitution is published.

November 15 – The Constituent Assembly adopts the constitutional text.

December 1–2 – A second referendum asks voters to approve the new constitution. The new constitution goes into effect in early December. Khomeini becomes Supreme Leader.

1980

February 23 – Mohammad Beheshti is appointed head of the judiciary.

March–May – The first parliament is elected. Akbar Hashemi Rafsanjani is elected Speaker of Parliament.

March 21 – The Cultural Revolution is proclaimed. The "Islamization" of the educational system begins in June.

June 26 – Formation of the Judicial Police (*polis-e qazā'i*).

September 22 – Iraq invades Iran. The war lasts until August 1988.

1981

June 28 – Abdul-Karim Mousavi Ardebili is appointed the new head of the judiciary after Mohammad Beheshti is assassinated. Ardebili remains in this role until August 1989.

October 2 – Ayatollah Ali Khamenei is elected president for the first of two four-year terms.

October 31 – Mir-Hossein Mousavi is appointed prime minister.

1982

October 30 – The Civil Code is amended to expand women's access to divorce by introducing into divorce law the concept of ʿosr va haraj (inflicting hardship and suffering).

Autumn – Islamic penal laws are promulgated (*hodud, qesās,* and *diyāt*).

December – After protests by women's groups, new marriage contracts are introduced that contain a stipulation by which the husband authorizes his wife to sue for divorce provided that she can prove to the court that one of the contractual conditions, according to which she may execute this right, is fulfilled. For these stipulations to become effective, the husband has to accept them.

December 15 – Ayatollah Khomeini issues an eight-point human rights platform, seemingly strengthening individual rights in arrests, searches, and seizures.

December 28 – The Tehran and Qom prosecutors are dismissed.

1983

January 1 – Further purges of revolutionary tribunals are undertaken.

January – Ayatollah Khomeini issues a directive to streamline the process of selecting candidates for government employment. It is meant to restrain the massive purges that were taking place in the aftermath of the 1979 Revolution.

August – The Taʿzirāt law (discretionary punishments) is introduced.

December 8 – Ayatollah Ali Montazeri, later to become Ayatollah Khomeini's heir apparent, urges government reforms, criticizing the revolution for lacking "a certain moral courage."

1988

February 6 – Khomeini establishes the Expediency Discernment Council to mediate conflicts between the Guardian Council and the parliament, and to advise the Supreme Leader.

April – The third parliamentary elections are held; leftists win the majority of seats.

July 19 – Following an order by Khomeini to execute members of the People's Mojahedin Organization of Iran as *mohārebs* (those who wage war against God) and leftists as *mortads* (apostates from Islam), special "death commissions" are formed that draw up lists on the basis of which mass executions against political prisoners are carried out across Iran, amounting to thousands of deaths.

October 25 – Anti-Drug Law introduced. It mandates the death penalty for anyone found trading in, or in possession of, more than 5 kg of opium or more than 30 g of heroin, and sets out a hierarchy of penalties for lesser amounts. These lesser penalties consist of a combination of fines, lashes of the whip, and prison sentences. The law also criminalizes drug addiction.

1989

March 28 – Khomeini dismisses his heir apparent, Ayatollah Montazeri.

June 3 – Ayatollah Khomeini dies.

June 4 – Ayatollah Ali Khamenei is elected the new Supreme Leader by the Assembly of Experts (an eighty-six-member council of directly elected clerics).

July 28 – The 1979 constitution is amended, eliminating the office of prime minister, putting the Expediency Discernment Council on a constitutional footing, and expanding the Supreme Leader's power, among other changes. Leadership of the judiciary is reduced from a three-member council to a single individual.

August 3 – Rafsanjani is elected president for the first of two four-year terms.

August 15 – Mohammad Yazdi is appointed the new head of the judiciary.

1990

June 22 – The parliament approves a law that integrates various police forces, specifically, the municipal police, gendarmerie, Islamic Revolutionary Committees, and judicial police, into one force, the NAJA.

November 20 – The Islamic Labor Code is introduced, reducing working hours from forty-eight hours to forty-four hours a week and to thirty-six hours for dangerous jobs. Annual paid leave is increased to thirty days and the minimum working age is raised to 15.

1991

February – The Supreme Council of Cultural Revolution issues a secret memorandum, signed by Khamenei, that instructs officials to enforce the exclusion of Bahá'ís from mainstream Iranian life and suppress the practice of their faith.

July – Books I–IV (General Part, *hodud, qesās, diyāt*) of the Islamic Penal Code are ratified.

1992

April–May – In the fourth parliamentary elections, the Guardian Council for the first time extensively vets candidates and disqualifies thirty incumbents from running again. Ali Akbar Nategh-Nouri is elected Speaker.

– In family law, the requirement to obtain a certificate of "Impossibility of Reconciliation" issued by a court in order to register divorce, which had been part of the abandoned Family Protection Law, is reinstated and arbitration proceedings are made obligatory. Moreover, the wife is henceforth entitled to claim compensation for her past housework (*ojrat al-methl*) if the divorce is not initiated by her.

1994

July – The Office of Public Prosecutor is abolished and the functions of investigator, prosecutor, and adjudicator are henceforth vested in a single case judge.

Chronology   xix

1996

March–April – In the fifth parliamentary elections, the conservative Society of Combatant Clergy and technocrats allied with President Rafsanjani win most seats. Nategh-Nouri is reelected as Speaker.

May 14 - The *gozinesh* (selection) law is passed. While recognized religious minorities can be hired by state agencies under this law, they are still required to abstain from practices that would openly violate Islamic norms. Belief in and acceding to *velāyat-e faqih* is also required of all state employees, whether or not they are Muslim. As such, the *gozinesh* law creates an impediment for employment of religious minorities, particularly because the public sector makes up a large part of the Iranian economy.

May 22 – Book V of the Penal Code on discretionary punishments (*taʿzirāt*) is ratified.

1997

May – Mohammad Khatami wins the presidency in a landslide with 70 percent of the vote. The reformist era begins. A coalition of eighteen organizations and parties identified as reformist form the Second Khordad Front, named for the Persian calendar date of Khatami's election.

– Amendment to the anti-drug law of 1988 effectively decriminalizes addiction. Although the law states that addiction is a crime, it states that addicts will be exempt from criminal prosecution so long as they voluntarily seek treatment at an officially recognized clinic.

1998

"Triangular Clinics" are set up to cater to the health needs of the key populations at risk of HIV infection. These clinics work in the three fields of sexually transmitted infections (STIs), HIV/AIDS, and drug-addiction programs, offering a comprehensive harm-reduction approach. This includes needles, methadone, condoms, treatment for STIs, antiretroviral therapy, and other medical services for people living with HIV/AIDS.

1999

May 29 – The first countrywide municipal elections are held; the candidates of the reformist Second Khordad Front outperform conservatives.

July 8 – Iran sees the greatest student demonstrations since the early 1980s, after the judiciary forces the reformist *Salām* newspaper to close. Protests continue for six days. More than 1,000 students are arrested; dozens die.

August 14 – Mahmoud Hashemi Shahroudi is appointed the new head of the judiciary.

September 19 – The Code of Criminal Procedure for the General and Revolutionary Courts is introduced for a trial period.

2000

February–May – In the sixth parliamentary elections, the reformist Second Khordad Front wins 65 percent of the 290 seats. Reformist cleric Mehdi Karroubi is elected Speaker.

April – The judiciary bans sixteen reformist newspapers in a widening crackdown on the burgeoning independent press.

June 27 – The appointment of Brigadier General Mohammad Baqer Qalibaf as commander of NAJA.

2001

June 8 – Khatami is reelected president.

2002

The Foreign Investment Promotion and Protection Act is passed, which means the law no longer distinguishes between domestic and foreign investments in rights, protections, and facilities, and capital market transactions.

September – The Office of Public Prosecutor is partially restored.

– The Civil Code is amended in the area of *'osr va haraj* (inflicting hardship and suffering). The amendment defines "hardship" more clearly, reducing the judges' discretion in accepting or rejecting its fulfilment.

December – Head of the Judiciary Ayatollah Shahroudi announces the suspension of executions by stoning.

Chronology

2003

June 10 – Students lead protests against university fees and the privatization of universities that grow into wider prodemocracy demands. They also condemn President Khatami for failing to support them against the crackdown by the security services.

July 30 – The Act Concerning Embryo Donation to Infertile Couples (known as "the embryo donation law") is ratified. This legalizes embryo donation.

October 10 – Shirin Ebadi, human rights activist and lawyer (and Iran's first female judge prior to the revolution), wins the Nobel Peace Prize.

– Harm-reduction (instead of punitive) measures are introduced in prisons to combat HIV/AIDS. This includes a needle-exchange program (to prevent needle sharing) and methadone treatment.

December 28 – Blood money (*diyeh*) for Muslims and non-Muslims is equalized.

2004

February – In the seventh parliamentary elections, conservatives take control after the Guardian Council disqualifies thousands of reformist candidates, including eighty incumbents.

May – The Law to Respect Legitimate Freedoms and Citizens' Rights is ratified by parliament, which prohibits the use of torture after the Guardian Council has refused to ratify the international Convention Against the Use of Torture, arguing it violates Islamic penal law.

2005

January – Head of the Judiciary Shahroudi issues a decree explicitly endorsing increased access to needles, syringes, and methadone "and other material used individually by drug addicts and AIDS patients," thereby embracing a rehabilitation approach rather than exclusive criminalization.

June 22 – The appointment of Brigadier General Ismail Ahmadi-Moghaddam as commander of NAJA.

June 24 – Mahmoud Ahmadinejad is elected president.

2006

September 10 – Sakineh Mohammadi Ashtiani is sentenced to death by stoning (despite Head of the Judiciary Shahroudi's moratorium against stoning in 2022) for having an extramarital relationship. Three of the five judges presiding found her guilty on the basis of ʿelm-e qāzi ("knowledge of the judge"). Her sentence is eventually commuted to death by hanging and, after nine years on death row, she is pardoned and released in 2014.

2007

June 27 – Protests erupt after the government imposes fuel rationing.

2008

March – In the eighth parliamentary elections, conservatives retain control after extensive disqualification of reformist candidates by the Guardian Council. Ali Larijani is elected Speaker of Parliament.

2009

June 12 – Ahmadinejad is reelected. Allegations of massive voting fraud lead to the largest demonstrations since the revolution. Under the banner of the so-called Green Movement, millions turn out on the streets for two weeks with banners declaring "Where is my vote?"

August 1 – The judiciary launches televised trials of well-known reformers and former government officials of the most popular reform parties who are accused of fomenting unrest and other anti-government activities. Five trials last into the fall.

August 14 – Sadegh Larijani is appointed the new head of the judiciary.

September 18 – On Qods Day (Jerusalem Day), thousands demonstrate across Iran in support of opposition candidate Mousavi in an attempt to redefine Qods Day as a day of justice at home.

December – Leading dissident cleric Ayatollah Montazeri dies, sparking widespread protests across Iran, including in the holy city of Qom.

2010

January – The parliament and the Guardian Council approve a plan for subsidy reform.

July 21 – Ayatollah Khamenei issues a fatwa declaring that the Supreme Leader's rule is a direct succession to the Prophet Mohammed and the Shi'ite imams.

2011

January – The Anti-Drug Law of 1988 is amended further to suspend the prosecution of addicts who did not voluntarily seek treatment. These are henceforth sent "by judicial order" to a compulsory rehabilitation center for one to three months, renewable for another three months, after which, if the treatment is successful, prosecution is to be dropped.

February 14 – Inspired by protests in the Arab world, violent clashes with security forces ensue, leading to 1,500 arrests.

February 28 – Reformist leaders Mir-Hossein Mousavi and Mehdi Karroubi are placed under house arrest for supporting the widespread demonstrations.

2012

October 3–5 – Following the plummeting value of the rial, demonstrations ensue and the Tehran bazaar closes for three days.

November 9 – Iran announces a ban on over seventy types of foreign luxury goods.

2013

January – Iran arrests eleven journalists accused of working with foreign Persian-language media organizations, such as the BBC.

January 28 – The Guardian Council approves amendments to Iran's Election Law that significantly limit the elected government's role in running elections and allow for greater interference by the Guardian Council.

February 19 – A new Family Protection Law is ratified. This provides for the establishment of new specialized family courts and family counselling centers. The law also prescribed that a female counselling judge is to be next to the presiding male judge at each family court; her opinion has to be considered in the judgments. Temporary marriages henceforth have to be officially registered.

February 26 – Tehran Prosecutor Saeed Mortazavi is put on trial for the torture and death of at least three detainees who had protested against the disputed elections of 2009. He is eventually acquitted of the charges in 2015.

April – New Islamic Penal Code is ratified. The punishment of stoning is no longer contained in the code but the code also does not prohibit its application.

June 15 – Hassan Rouhani wins the presidential election with just over half of the votes.

October 2 – The Guardian Council approves the new adoption law, entitled the Act of Protection of Children and Adolescents Without Guardians or With Irresponsible Guardians to facilitate the conditions of adoption in Iran, giving, for example, Iranian couples living abroad and single Iranian women over 30 years of age the right to adopt a child (in the latter case only a female child to whom the name of the adoptive mother is given).

2014

August 20 – Parliament dismisses Science Minister Reza Faraji-Dana for his support of students involved in the 2009 demonstrations. The science minister's decision to allow students previously expelled for their involvement in protests to return to classes had angered many conservatives.

2015

February 20 – Brigadier General Ashtari is appointed to command the NAJA.

March 10 – Ayatollah Mohammad Yazdi is elected chairman of the Assembly of Experts following the death of the previous chairman, Ayatollah Mohammad Reza Mahdavi-Kani.

June 22 – New Code of Criminal Procedure (CCP) is ratified.

July 14–20 A nuclear deal (the Joint Comprehensive Plan of Action [JCPOA]) is agreed on by Iran and the five permanent members of the United Nations Security Council, plus Germany. In exchange for sanctions relief, the deal requires Iran to eliminate its stockpile of medium-enriched uranium, cut its stockpile of low-enriched uranium by 98 percent, reduce by about two-thirds the number of its gas centrifuges for thirteen years, and to enrich uranium up to only 3.67 percent in the next fifteen years.

2016

January 20 – The Guardian Council disqualifies more than 600 candidates for the parliamentary and Assembly of Experts elections, including a grandson of Ayatollah Ruhollah Khomeini.

April 30 – Reformists, centrists, and moderate conservatives, known as the "List of Hope," gain a plurality of seats, forming the largest bloc.

2017

May 20 – President Rouhani wins reelection over hardliner Ebrahim Raisi, with 57 percent of the vote.

May 29 – Reformist candidates outperform conservative candidates in municipal elections.

June 7 – Islamic State of Iraq and al-Sham terrorists attack the mausoleum of Ayatollah Khomeini and parliament, killing eighteen people and injuring fifty.

October 9 – The Court of Administrative Justice suspends a Zoroastrian member of the Yazd city council, following a Guardian Council decision that the election of non-Muslims in Muslim-majority districts is a violation of shari'a. A jurisdictional battle between parliament and the Guardian Council ensues.

December 27 – The Girls of Revolution Street protest movement against the mandatory hejab (head covering) begins. Female protesters record videos of themselves without a hijab, or waving their hijabs on street corners and in other public places.

December 28 – Protest over economic hardship break out in Mashhad, spreading to more than eighty cities and lasting for two weeks. At least 20 people are killed and more than 3,000 arrested. The demonstrations are the largest challenge to the government since the 2009 Green Movement.

2018

February 11 – Following protests in January, President Rouhani uses the day commemorating the revolution to (unsuccessfully) call for a referendum on Iran's future.

February 28 – Saeed Mortazavi, the ex-prosecutor of Tehran, is sentenced to two years in prison for his complicity in the deaths of several protestors who died under suspicious circumstances in Kahrizak prison after having been detained for taking part in protests against the contested 2009 elections. In August 2021, the Supreme Court acquits Mortazavi of the charges.

April 7–9 – The rial hits an all-time low against the dollar. In response, the government unifies the free-market exchange rate and the official exchange rate.

April 18 – Kaveh Madani, deputy head of Iran's Organization of Environmental Protection, resigns and leaves Iran for the United Kingdom, following a crackdown on environmental activists.

May 8 – President Trump announces the US withdrawal from the JCPOA and the reimposition of nuclear-related sanctions on Iran.

June 25 – Tehran sees its largest demonstration since 2012 in response to the devaluation of the rial.

July 29 – Iran's currency hits another record low. The economy continues a downward spiral in anticipation of the reimposition of US sanctions in August.

August 8 and 26 – Parliament impeaches the ministers of labor and the economy for Iran's economic deterioration.

September 3 – Iran's rial hits another record low, having lost 70 percent of its value over the year.

September 22 – Gunmen attack a military parade in the southwestern Iranian city of Ahvaz, killing at least twenty-nine people and wounding seventy, including Islamic Revolutionary Guard Corps (IRGC) soldiers and civilians. Arab separatists claim responsibility.

2019

January 5 – The Expediency Council approves an anti-money-laundering bill that was one of four reforms required to keep Iran off the blacklist of the Financial Action Task Force (FATF), an international watchdog.

February – A prisoner amnesty marks the 40th anniversary of the revolution. A total of 100,000 prisoners are either pardoned or have their sentences reduced, and another 70,000, who have not yet entered prison, have their sentences converted to fines.

February 14 – A suicide bombing in Sistan and Baluchistan province kills twenty-seven IRGC soldiers.

Chronology

March 7 – Khamenei appoints Ebrahim Raisi as the new head of the judiciary, hoping he will bring about a "transformation" in the judiciary and be "with the people, the revolution and against corruption."

March 11 – Nasrin Sotoudeh, Iran's most prominent human rights lawyer, is sentenced to 38 years in prison and 148 lashes for 9 charges. She receives twelve years for allegedly encouraging "corruption and prostitution." The charge is likely connected to Sotoudeh representing a woman who was arrested for peacefully protesting the compulsory hejab imposed after the 1979 Revolution.

Late March–early April – Flash floods kill dozens across Iran and destroy at least 25,000 homes. Head of the Judiciary Ebrahim Raisi uses the floods to threaten the elected government, suggesting it is not handling the environmental catastrophe properly: "Any shortcomings regarding the handling of the floods, failure to provide relief and aid to the survivors will be investigated."[1]

April 21 – Supreme Leader Khamenei appoints Major General Hossein Salami, previously responsible for Iran's missile program, as new IRGC commander.

October 1 – President Rouhani's brother, Hosseini Fereydoun, is sentenced to five years in prison for corruption, according to state media.

December 2019–January 2020 – Protests against a rise in fuel prices throughout the country lead to a violent crackdown by security forces, who kill up to 1,500 people.

2020

February 20 – The Guardian Council disqualifies more than 9,000 of the 14,000 candidates registered to run in the February parliamentary elections.

February 21 – Conservative and hardline factions, including candidates closely aligned with the Revolutionary Guards, win 221 of the 290 seats in the parliamentary elections, more than doubling their presence in parliament.

July 13 – The Anti-Drug Law of 1988 is amended further to reduce prison sentences for a number of crimes, including drug trafficking, and ensure that judges impose only the

---

[1] Parisa Hafezi, "Floods Kill at Least 18 in Southern Iran, Provinces on Alert," Reuters, March 25, 2019: www.reuters.com/article/iran-floods-casualties-idINKCN1R61D4/

minimum sentence of the range laid down in the relevant code, unless there is a justifiable reason for a higher sentence. The amendment is expected to lead to a significant reduction in the prison population.

December 1 – Parliament passes a bill requiring the government to immediately resume enriching uranium to 20 percent and to stockpile 120 kg (265 lb.) of it annually. Uranium must be enriched to 90 percent or above to fuel a weapon.

2021

June 18–19 – Ebrahim Raisi wins the presidential election with 62 percent of the vote.

July – Gholam-Hossein Mohseni Eje'i is appointed the new head of the judiciary.

July 15 – Nearly a fourth of all municipalities face water shortages caused by a drought while several major cities, including Tehran, are also hit by rolling power blackouts caused by soaring temperatures and rising demand on crumbling infrastructure. The twin crises trigger protests in major cities and the provinces across several days, during which eight protesters and bystanders are killed by security forces in Khuzestan province.

November 1 – The Guardian Council approves the Rejuvenation of the Population and Protection of the Family Bill, which restricts women's access to reproductive health services and contraceptives.

December 22 – The national police force NAJA is elevated to the FARAJA (Law Enforcement Command of the Islamic Republic of Iran) at cabinet level.

2022

September 16 – Mahsa Jina Amini dies in custody after having been arrested for violating hijab provisions. Following her death, countrywide protests break out under the slogan "Woman Life Freedom." In the following months, some 20,000 demonstrators are arrested, and at least 500 people are killed by the security forces.

September 30 – Iranian security forces kill more than 90 protestors and injure hundreds in what becomes widely known as the "Bloody Friday" of Zahedan

Chronology   xxix

December 22 – Khamenei appoints Brigadier General Radan as Commander of FARAJA

2023

January 7 – Iran executes two men arrested in connection with anti-government protests. The two men, Mohammad Mehdi Karami and Seyed Mohammad Hosseini, had been convicted for allegedly killing a paramilitary volunteer during a protest.

January 10 – Iran sentences Faezeh Hashemi, the daughter of former President Akbar Hashemi Rafsanjani, to five years in prison on the charge of "propaganda against the system".

January 14 – Iran executes Alireza Akbari, a former deputy defense minister (2000–2004), after he was convicted of spying for Britain and "corruption on earth."

January 18 – Judiciary spokesman Masoud Setayeshi announces that 5,200 people – 98 percent of detained protesters in Tehran province – have been released.

January 23 – The United States, Britain, and the European Union sanction Iran for its crackdown on protesters. U.S. sanctions largely target the Islamic Revolutionary Guard Corps (IRGC). Britain imposes sanctions on five individuals and two entities. The European Union targets 30 Iranians, including IRGC officials.

January 30 – Iran and Russia sign an agreement to connect their interbank communication and transfer systems in an effort to evade international sanctions. Both Iran and Russia had been disconnected from the international SWIFT financial messaging service by U.S. sanctions.

February 1 – A protester sentenced to death is granted a stay of execution. Mohammad Ghobadlou had been convicted of "corruption on earth" for allegedly killing a security official by running over him with a car in November 2023.

February 5 – Supreme Leader Ayatollah Ali Khamenei pardons or reduces the sentences of tens of thousands of prisoners, including some protesters, to mark the 44th anniversary of the Islamic Revolution. The pardons are heavily conditioned on good behavior, a formal apology, and a pledge not to engage in protests or other activities "undermining the regime".

April 8 – The police announces the installation of public cameras to monitor women violating the mandatory hejab law.

May – Iran executes at least 142 people, the most in one month since 2015, according to Iran Human Rights (IHR).

July 8 – Jaish al-Adl, a militant Sunni and Baluch group, kills two police officers at a police station in Zahedan, the capital of southeast Sistan and Baluchistan province. The militants claimed the attack was in retaliation for the police station's involvement in "Bloody Friday," a massacre of protestors by security forces on Sept. 30, 2022.

July 16 – Police Spokesperson Saeed Montazer al-Mahdi announces that Iran would resume vehicle and foot patrols to enforce the country's mandatory hejab laws.

October 6 – Narges Mohammadi – an imprisoned Iranian human rights activist – wins the Nobel Peace Prize. The Norwegian Nobel Committee commends "her fight against the oppression of women in Iran and her fight to promote human rights and freedom for all."

October 28 – Armita Geravand, a 16-year-old Iranian student, dies in the hospital after suffering a severe head injury during an encounter with Iran's morality police over hejab rules on October 1st.

November 13 – Iran's judiciary executes three members of Jaish al-Adl, an armed Sunni Baluch group, for a 2019 bombing that had killed 27 Revolutionary Guard members.

All authors in this book contributed to this timeline and we thank Iran Primer for permission to adopt selected entries.

Abbreviations and Glossary

ʿādel	Righteous; possessing ʿedālat
ʿaql	Reason; the mental faculties; mental sanity. In jurisprudence, it refers to reason, which in Shiʿism is considered a valid source of law.
ahkām (sing. hokm)	Commandments or legal directives
Armed Forces General Staff	(AFGS or Setād-e Koll-e Niruhā-ye Mosallah)
ayatollah (lit. "sign of God")	Title given to high-ranking Shiʿi *mojtahed*s. Higher-ranking titles are *āyatollāh al-ʿozmā'* (grand ayatollah) and *marjaʿ-e taqlid* (source of emulation); a lower-ranking title is *hojjat al-eslām* ("proof of Islam")
āyin-nāmeh	Regulations
bakhshesh	Forgiveness/clemency
CAT	United Nations Convention against Torture and Other Cruel, Inhuman or Degrading Treatment or Punishment
CCP	Code of Criminal Procedure, passed in April 2014 and entered into force in June 2015
CEDAW	Convention on the Elimination of All Forms of Discrimination Against Women
CIC	Iran's Council for Intelligence Coordination, which oversees more than sixteen separate governmental intelligence agencies
CRC	United Nations Convention on the Rights of the Child

xxxii   List of Abbreviations and Glossary

Dādsarā	A public prosecutor's office
dādsetān-e 'omumi	Office of the General Prosecutor
dhimmi	Member of a recognized religious minority ("people of the Book": Jewish, Christian, Sabian, or, in Iran, Zoroastrian) in Muslim lands, protected and potentially eligible for Heaven (Qur'an 2:62, 5:69, 22:17) but lacking some rights
diyeh (pl. *diyāt*)	"Blood money" which injured parties, or their heirs can claim for injuries or murder if they waive *qesās* (retributive justice)
efsād, efsād-e fel 'arz	Vice, corruption; offence of "corruption on earth"
'elm-e qāzi	Knowledge of the judge
FARAJA (Farmāndehi-ye Entezāmi Jomhuri-ye Eslāmi)	The Law Enforcement Command of the Islamic Republic of Iran
FATA	*Polis-e fazā-ye towlid va tabādol-e ettelā'āt* (lit. police of the virtual space and information exchange)
fatwa	A (nonbinding) religious ruling issued by an Islamic jurist
FPL	Family Protection Law (Iran) of 1967 (amended)
gasht-e ershād	Guidance patrols
gozinesh	lit. selection, relevant in the 1996 *gozinesh* law that enshrines discrimination in hiring on the basis of ideology. Belief in and acceding to *velāyat-e faqih* is required of all state employees, even religious minorities.
hadd (pl. *hodud*, lit. "limit," "boundary")	A crime for which a fixed punishment is derived from the Qur'an or the hadith. In current Iranian law, these crimes are adultery, fornication, sodomy, pimping, lesbianism, alcohol consumption, theft, "insurrection and corruption on Earth," and false accusations

List of Abbreviations and Glossary

	of adultery/fornication/sodomy. Punishments for these crimes by nature cannot be attenuated, commuted, bargained down, or in any way altered.
hākemiyat-e qānun	Rule of law (lit. the governance of law) The governance of law
haqq (pl. *hoquq*)	Right(s)
hokm (pl. *ahkām*)	Commandment, legal directive
hokumat-e qānun	Rule of law (lit. government of law)
ICCPR	International Covenant on Civil and Political Rights
ICESCR	International Covenant on Economic, Social and Cultural Rights
ICPPED	International Convention for Protection of all Persons from Enforced Disappearances
ijtihād (lit. "effort")	A qualified jurist's independent reasoning to extrapolate laws and principles from the Qur'an and hadith. A person qualified to perform *ijtihād* is a "*mojtahed*."
Iran CC	Iranian Civil Code (amended)
Iran Const	Constitution of the Islamic Republic of Iran of 1979 (amended)
Kānun-e Vukalā-ye Dādgostari	Iran Bar Association
Komiteh-ye Enqelāb-e Eslāmi	Islamic Revolutionary Committees
KoP (*Kalāntari o Pāsgāh*)	Urban and rural police forces
Majles	Iran's national parliament
Majma'-e Tashkhis-e Maslahat-e Nezām	Council for discerning the benefits of the state; in short, Expediency Council
Markaz-e tahqiqāt-e fiqhi	Center for Studies of Fiqh (Qom)
Masāleh-e mursaleh	Benefits for which there is no authoritative divine text (*nass*). The idea that when the divine law is silent on a particular point, it is licit to use the benefit of the community (*maslahat*) as a source of law.
mohārebeh	Offence of "enmity against God"

xxxiii

mosavvabeh	Resolutions (e.g., resolution of the Supreme Council of the Cultural Revolution)
mutʿa (nikāh al-mutʿa)	Temporary marriage (lit. "pleasure marriage")
NAJA	*Niruhā-ye Entezāmi-ye Jomhuri-ye Eslāmi* (Law Enforcement Forces of the Islamic Republic of Iran)
NOPO	*Niru-ye Vizheh-ye Pād-vahshat* (NAJA's Counterterrorism Special Force)
Office for Drafting Judicial Bills	(*Edāreh-ye tadvin-e lawāʾeh-e qovveh-ye qazāʾiyeh*)
ʿosr va haraj (inflicting hardship and suffering)	A principle that can be invoked to justify divorce
Polis-e Āgāhi (*Edāreh-ye āgāhi-ye niruhā-ye entezāmi*)	The Criminal Investigations Office of the Law Enforcement Forces
Polis-e Amniyat-e Akhlāqi	Moral security police, a subbranch of PAVA
Polis-e Amniyat va Ettelāʿāt ʿOmumi (PAVA)	General Public Security and Intelligence Police
Polis-e Nezārat bar Amāken-e ʿOmumi	(Police for the Supervision over Public Facilities and Locations), a subbranch of PAVA
Polis-e Pishgiri va ʿAmaliyāt	Prevention and Operation Police
qāʿedeh-ye darʾ	Principle of reasonable doubt
qānun	(Usually codified) law
qesās	Punishment of retribution in kind. *Qesās* belongs to a category of law known in Shiʿi jurisprudence as "*haqq al-nās*" (punishment which is the "right of the people" as opposed to the "right of God"). Thus, murder is treated as a "private" matter and a charge of murder must be brought, not by the state but by the immediate relatives of the victim (known as "owners of the blood"/heirs), who must initiate proceedings by lodging a formal complaint with the Prosecutor's Office.

List of Abbreviations and Glossary

Sāzmān-e Hefāzat-e Ettelā'āt-e Qazā'i	Judiciary's Intelligence Protection Organization
Sāzmān-e Tablighāt-e Eslāmi	Lit. Islamic Propaganda Organization; officially translated as Islamic Development Organization
SCC	Special Court for the Clergy (*dādgāh-e vīzheh-ye ruhāniyat*)
Sepāh	Islamic Revolutionary Guard Corps (IRGG)
siyāsat-hā	Policies
talāq	Unilateral divorce or repudiation pronounced by the husband according to Islamic law
ta'zir (pl. *ta'zirāt*)	Discretionary punishment for crimes for which fixed penalties are not provided in Islamic law. Iranian law, however, does stipulate a maximum and minimum sentence between which the judge can choose. *Ta'zir* is the residual category of crimes and punishment that are not part of *hodud*, *qesās*, or *diyāt*.
UDHR	Universal Declaration of Human Rights
velāyat-e motlaqeh-ye faqih	Absolute rule of the guardian jurist

1 Governing the Law in the Islamic Republic of Iran

Mirjam Künkler

The Islamic Republic of Iran is a legalist system par excellence. It prides itself on the extent to which it has codified Islamic law, and it bases its entire legal system, not only constitutional or family law, but ostensibly all realms of law, on legal codes in which Islamic notions of justice have been translated into concrete statutes. As such, the Islamic Republic sees itself as the prototype of a modern state based extensively on Islamic law: one where the positivization of Islamic norms has progressed much further than in other states assuming the title of Islamic republic or Islamic state, such as Pakistan, Saudi Arabia, or the Maldives.

Arguments in favor of the codification of Islamic law frequently invoke its effects on improving the rule of law: Codification minimizes the risks associated with judge-made law and improves on the law's predictability and consistency. Iran then presents a formidable case to probe this hypothesis. How has the rule of law fared in Iran since the 1979 Revolution set in motion the most comprehensive process of Islamizing and codifying religious law seen in the twentieth century?

This introduction will provide a theoretical, historical and legal background to the chapters in this volume. Section 1 provides a brief survey of the various uses and connotations of the concept of rule of law. Section 2 gives an overview of the evolution of the modern legal system in Iran, while Section 3 describes the Islamization of the legal system following the 1979 revolution and constitutional amendment in 1989. Section 4 discusses three key innovations with which Islamic law, as codified in the Islamic Republic, has been reformed and revised. Section 5 presents the main outlines of the legal and judicial system of Iran, Section 6 provides an overview of the chapters of the book, and Section 7 outlines some of the main challenges to the rule of law in Iran today.

1 The Rule of Law

Rule-of-law conceptions range from the most minimalist "thin" conceptions to more substantive "thick" ones. The antithesis of rule of law is arbitrary power. Yet the absence of arbitrary power can take many shapes and degrees of legal protection (Krygier 2012). Continental legal traditions distinguish between "formal" (procedural) and "material" (substantive) rule of law.[1] The former is a commitment to ruling qua formal procedures without a normative commitment to human rights, while the concept of "material rule of law" refers to a constitutional state with human rights and other liberal commitments. In Anglophone literature this distinction is also referred to with the notions of "rule by law" versus "rule of law," whereby the former characterizes an abiding by formal procedures without normative commitments, whereas the latter implies a substantive commitment to fundamental rights and democratic procedures.

While binaries in the rule-of-law literature are quite pervasive, Brian Tamanaha (2004: 91f.) has categorized the continuum of notions of law along a six-point scale which allows for more fine-grained differentiations between differences in degree and kind. Whereas the first three constitute rather formal or procedural notions of the rule of law, the last three are of substantive nature.

The first, most minimalist, notion is what he calls "rule by law," where law is simply an instrument of government action, which does not imply that it needs to be general, prospective, clear, and certain. This first notion is thus little more than a descriptive reference to abiding by what a given regime may call "law" and it does not require the presence of legal limitations on government. The second, slightly more ambitious, notion is that of formal legality. Here law needs to be general, prospective, clear, and certain. There is no concern here, however, that the source of this law lies in those who will be subject to it. In other words, rule of law in the sense of formal legality can be established in a nondemocratic regime where legal norms may not reflect the preferences of those who are governed, but is at least general, prospective, clear, and certain. The third notion includes all the aforementioned criteria, plus it fulfils the requirement that consent determines the content of law. The third notion thus combines the criteria of legality with direct or indirect democracy. There is no sense of individual rights here yet, which brings us to the fourth notion. This requires that the rule of law safeguard and guarantee individual rights, in particular the right to property, security of contract, the right to privacy, and autonomy.[2]

---

[1] For a detailed account of conceptual demarcations between *Rechtsstaat*, rule by law, and rule of law, see Meierhenrich (2021a).
[2] Here lies also the minimum condition of a rule of law state for Böckenförde (1969): "The Rechtsstaat is aimed at the demarcation and restriction of state power in the interest of the freedom of the individual."

Many liberal democratic systems around the world feature rule of law of this type, where property rights are guaranteed, but which do not provide for the right to dignity (the idea that a rule of law-based system must provide the conditions where one can live a dignified life), which is the content of the fifth notion. States aiming to provide this high level of the rule of law do not stop at ensuring rule by democratically legitimated procedures and the safeguarding of property rights, but also provide infrastructures and welfare provisions, where necessary, to ensure every citizen can live a dignified life. This includes at least access to water, electricity, a well-functioning health system, an insurance system that covers cases of accident and illness, a pension system, and access to free or affordable education. Countries of the European Union (EU) all aspire to this level of the rule of law. Finally, the sixth notion is that of a social welfare-based rule-of-law state where the state is understood to have a duty to enable citizens' self-determination, including to ensure all the material conditions for citizens to do so. The Scandinavian countries represent this maximalist notion of the rule of law, but the German Basic Law bears elements of this too (Böckenförde 1974), for example, although the legal reality in Germany is closer to the fifth notion. Theorists such as Friedrich Hayek have argued that the social welfare state is not compatible with the rule of law because of the threats it may pose to the security of private property. Others have argued, by contrast, that the conditions of security and predictability of the rule of law may very well be guaranteed and abided by in a social welfare system and that it is only a planned economy that is not compatible with the rule of law (Max Weber, Brian Tamanaha, Martin Krygier). In addition, some insist that the formal rule of law means little if the existential conditions for citizens to enjoy their rights are not fulfilled – these scholars argue that for the rule of law to mean something in most cases necessitates the state provide the kind of social services that social welfare states typically offer (Böckenförde 1974).

Where does the rule of law in the Islamic Republic fall along this continuum? Readers of this volume will likely conclude that the answer depends very much on the realm of the law under scrutiny. In the realm of criminal law, and especially if one takes legal practice into account, one might be hard pressed to find that the law is general, prospective, clear, and certain, thus falling short of anything more ambitious than the most minimalist notion. If one looked at reproductive rights, where the Islamic Republic has some of the most advanced forms of regulation in the world, the rule of law fulfils many of the requirements of the fifth notion, and indeed, Shirin Naef in this volume argues that discussions around human dignity are a key facet driving the Islamic Republic's regulatory regime around assisted reproductive technologies (ART). The reader will also likely conclude that the area of reproductive rights is the exception in this matter, and that in labor and commercial law Iran leans closer to the third or fourth notions, and in constitutional, criminal, and family law, the letter of the law and legal practice in the early 2020s render Iran closer to the minimalist end of the rule-of-law continuum. This has not always been the case, and while this volume seeks to demonstrate variation with regard to different areas of the law in Iran, it also aims to show progression and regression from 1979 onward.

The World Justice Project (WJP) ranks countries on an annual basis in according to the strength of their rule of law. In doing so, the WJP considers not only the letter of the law but also legal practices. Its results are based both on the experiences of ordinary citizens, as well as the evaluations of legal experts. It breaks down its ranking into eight dimensions, which are in turn made up of three to eight variables each. The eight dimensions comprise: (1) constraints on government powers, (2) absence of corruption, (3) open government (which includes publicized laws and government data, complaints mechanisms, and the right to information), (4) fundamental rights, (5) order and security, (6) regulatory enforcement, (7) civil justice, and (8) criminal justice.

Iran in 2023 ranks in the third quartile, which puts it at the lower or weaker end of this comparative rule-of-law index. In its income group of upper middle-income countries, it ranks at the bottom of the group, together with Turkey and Venezuela. Within the eight countries included from the region of the Middle East, it ranks second from the bottom, with only Egypt performing worse. Among the eight indicators, Iran ranks highest (or less badly) on the provision of order and justice, meaning that the state generally has a low intensity of crime as well as civil conflict. It also ranks high (or not so badly) with regard to impartial and effective alternative dispute resolutions. Its weakest performances are in the areas of fundamental rights and criminal justice. Iran falls short of providing and securing freedom of expression, freedom of religion, the right to privacy, freedom of association, and labor rights. It falls short in the realm of criminal justice, particularly in terms of discrimination and government influence on court cases. In certain areas, constraints on the government are also weak: Sanctions for official misconduct are seldom implemented and complaint mechanisms do not work well.

This very weak performance has not always been the case. In 2011, the year Iran was first included in the WJP, it was ten ranks higher than Turkey and Venezuela, which were at the bottom of the upper middle-income group. At that time, Iran also ranked higher than Malaysia,

Mexico, and EU member state Romania. Documenting the variations in the degree and quality of Iran's rule of law is a core task for this edited volume. As readers will see, there have been periods in the history of the Islamic Republic when legal reforms were undertaken that increased the autonomy or independence of the legal profession and that improved citizens' access to justice. However, many of these reforms were later superseded by legislative, regulatory, and institutional changes that diminished the quality of the rule of law.

Overall, we hope with this volume to go beyond a criterial study of the rule of law, which, as Judith Shklar (1987: 1) has warned, at times risks being shorn of contact with its political, social, and historical context. The tendency to think of the rule of law as a discreet entity that is either present or absent necessarily occludes the wider context which makes the rule of law intelligible in a particular society (Meierhenrich 2021b: 577). Thus, alongside the criterial approach to the rule of law sketched above, the chapters in this volume try to throw light on the discursive construction of law and the political struggles to establish the rule of law as part of the "social imaginary" of contemporary Iran (Taylor 2004).[3] The rule of law has been part of the "social imaginary" of the liberal tradition in Iran from the constitutional movement of the early twentieth century to the premiership of Mohammad Mossadegh (1951–1953) and then later, under the Islamic Republic, to the premiership of Mohammad Khatami (1999–2005), the Green Movement of 2009, and the Woman Life Freedom protests of 2022 and 2023.[4] Consequently, the chapters in this volume do not focus purely on "procedural" or "substantive" dimensions of the rule of law but on a wider range of legal and political domains, which hopefully give the reader a more contextual and richer understanding of the ideology *and* practice of the law, and the struggles surrounding these.

---

[3] Charles Taylor (2004: 23) defines the "social imaginary" as "that common understanding that makes possible common practices and a widely shared sense of legitimacy" relating to the ways people imagine their social existence, the expectations of common practices that are normally met and the deeper normative notions that underlie these expectations (Taylor 2004: 29).

[4] As Charles Taylor has argued, social imaginaries are never just ideology; rather, they are both factual and normative – "that is we have a sense of how things usually go but that is interwoven with an idea of how things ought to go, of what missteps would invalidate the practice" (Taylor 2004: 24). Thus, "social imaginary" is a useful heuristic trope for thinking about the rule of law in modern Iran because it has not played a purely ideological role but has helped to constitute the political, discursive, and institutional context in which struggles for political liberation, between the two revolutions of 1906 and 1979 and up to the present day, have unfolded. For further discussion of the rule of law as "social imaginary," see Meierhenrich (2021b).

2 The Emergence of a Modern Legal System: From the Qajars to the Islamic Republic

The modern legal system of Iran emerged in the aftermath of the Constitutional Revolution (1905–1911), the first revolution "from below" in the Muslim world, which resulted in the promulgation of a constitution limiting the powers of the shah, and the creation of a parliament, the Majles. It was only in the aftermath of the Constitutional Revolution that a system of codified state law was gradually developed, although it would take another twenty years for the first permanent criminal and civil codes to be promulgated, and for a state judiciary capable of applying these codes to be built up. Prior to the establishment of the modern legal and justice system, the formal administration of justice during the Qajar dynasty was characterized by a duality of sharʿ (religious) and ʿurf (state) courts. Generally speaking, the sharʿ courts dealt with matters of personal status, property, and some types of commercial contracts, while most criminal offenses were dealt with by the ʿurfi authorities. The lack of any formal demarcation of their jurisdiction led to repeated conflict between the state and Shiʿi authorities.

Jurisprudence was not standardized, and opposing parties could choose between judges (i.e. engage in "forum shopping"), which proved fertile ground for corruption and led to frequent complaints, particularly among merchants, for whom predictability and consistency was vital. Justifying their stance with reference to the courts' arbitrariness and corruption, foreign authorities were able to negotiate capitulations which shielded their subjects from prosecution in Persian courts, thus effectively giving them legal immunity.

Beyond the formal realm, a pluralism of different actors was involved in the administration of justice, including clerics, state officials, local elders, landowners, and tribal leaders. Most disputes were resolved informally and according to local custom within families, guilds, and other corporate groups, as well as village and tribal communities. The non-Muslim religious minorities, principally Jews, Christians, and Zoroastrians, had autonomy in resolving intracommunal disputes, and in matters of personal status they were subject to their own religious laws.

Under Nāṣer-al-Din Shah (r. 1848–1896), several judicial and legal reforms were initiated, partly to respond to the conditions that had forced the shah to agree to foreign capitulations. In most cases, these reforms were not implemented systematically and not across the entire territory, so that informal dispute resolution remained the norm. From 1860 onwards, people could file complaints about administrative and state officials with the *mazālem* courts (in a way a precursor to today's

Administrative Court of Justice) and drop petitions in complaint boxes (*sanduq-e ʿedālat*) that had been set up in all major towns. This led to a very vibrant petitioning regime among the populace which significantly influenced political consciousness and public mobilization for years to come. From 1871 on, the verdicts of the religious courts had to be confirmed by the justice ministry, and six years later, a first attempt was made to codify the shariʿa, although it was soon aborted. Further reform attempts largely failed, partly due to the weakness and corruption of the Qajar dynasty and partly because of the opposition of local governors and *ʿulamāʾ* (Islamic scholars) who generally opposed any attempts that might undermine their power (Adamiyat 1963).

This failure to reform helps to explain the centrality of "law" in the discourse of the Constitutional Revolution (1905–1911), epitomized in the most important oppositional journal of the day, *Qanun* (The Law, 1890–1900). The revival of the *mazālem* court and the introduction of the justice boxes had fanned ever louder growing denunciations of the nepotism of the Qajar monarchy, the corruption and unaccountability of public officials, and calls for the adoption of legal rationality in a *ʿedālatkhāneh* (house of justice), a system of state courts which would function on the basis of positive law.

The Constitutional Revolution triggered a process of institutional transformation and secularization which was driven by a struggle between three competing, though not mutually exclusive, conceptions of law, and the social groups behind them: Islamic (with an emphasis on clericalism and the shariʿa), liberal (with an emphasis on separation of powers, civil and political rights, and property rights), and *étatiste* (with an emphasis on legal positivism, centralism and a clear hierarchy of norms). The promulgation of the constitution (1906) and the Supplementary Law (1907) introduced new concepts of governance, law, and state, involving conceptual shifts, which, however weakly instituted at the time, were to have far-reaching implications. First, the establishment of a parliament meant that for the first time there was a lawmaking institution independent of both the will of the ruler and the shariʿa. However, the constitution also granted the *ʿulamāʾ* unprecedented powers in the new order, most importantly in Article 2 of the 1907 Supplementary Law, which provided for a clerical board to vet all legislation (an institutional model for the later Guardian Council). Second, a process of "juridification" of the state set in during this period: the increasing formalization and writing of regulations defining public office and the rules of governance (Marin 2004). A concept of public law emerged (*hoquq-e ʿomumi*), which was distinct from the shariʿa, from custom, and from the tradition of *mazālem* justice (administrative justice): now the ruler himself was to be bound by law. Third, concomitant with the "juridification" of the state, the judicial clauses of the 1907 Supplementary Law marked the first steps in the "étatisation" of the law and the introduction of novel legal procedures derived from European models. The provision in the Supplementary Law for a state court system with state judges was an important step in this direction. New courts were established (principally in the realms of crime, property and financial claims), effectively limiting the jurisdiction of the shari'a courts to family matters and *waqf* (religious endowments). Codes were drawn up and introduced on a preliminary, non-permanent basis to avoid lengthy discussions with the 'ulamā' over their compatibility with the shari'a. Thus, in 1911 the Provisional Code of Judicial Organization and the Provisional Code of Civil Procedure were promulgated. On the one hand, these reforms limited the power of Shi'i authorities by integrating the shari'a courts into the state judiciary and making all judges state appointees. On the other hand, since most legal training was still undertaken in the Shi'i seminaries, many judges even of the secular courts tended to be recruited from among seminary graduates and so in the short to medium term, the religious establishment gained more control over the judiciary than it had before.

The details of the post-constitutional legal and judicial reforms owed much to the French legal advisor Adolphe Perny, who stayed in Iran from 1911 until 1926 and chaired the weekly meetings in the ministry of justice during which draft laws and codes were prepared. Perny had penned the 1911 Code of Civil Procedure and he was instrumental in the opening of the *Madreseh-ye Hoquq* (Judicial School) in 1920, which was staffed mainly by French judicial personnel to train future lawyers and judges.

The buildup of a mostly secular, state-administered judiciary came to a preliminary end with the coup d'état of February 1921 that marked the end of the Qajar dynasty. Codes and statutes were abrogated with the consequence that the newly created state courts had no law on the basis of which to adjudicate. In some regions the old religious courts were reestablished. When Reza Pahlavi assumed the throne in 1925, one of his chief objectives was to present to Western powers new permanent codes in order to put an end to the undignified capitulations, which reserved foreign countries the right to try their citizens for crimes committed in Iran in their own rather than Iranian courts. Between 1925 and 1928, several permanent laws were passed, among them a new commercial code (*Qānun-e tijārat*) in February 1926 and a new criminal code later that year, also penned by Perny, based on the French code (Marin 2004). The Code of Civil Procedure (*Qānun-e ā'in-e dādrasi-ye madani*) and the first book of a new civil code (*Qānun-e madani*) were passed in 1928. The latter consisted of the codification of shari'a following the format of the French Code Civil (the Code Napoléon). Meanwhile, on May 10, 1927, diplomatic missions were quietly informed that the capitulatory rights of their nationals would be revoked in twelve months' time and assured that Iran intended to continue reforming its legal and justice system. (Amanat 2011; Enayat 2011: 125–143).

The establishment of a Bar Association (Kānun-e Vukalā) in 1930 was a key instrument in instilling a strong belief in constitutionalism and in nurturing a culture of liberal legality in the legal profession. By the 1950s, bar associations had been established in two more Iranian cities, although it was not until 1953 that they had gained their full independence from the Ministry of Justice. This independence was maintained under Mohammad Reza Shah and the 1970s saw the heyday of the professionalization of lawyers and judges and the crystallization of public support for an independent judiciary (see Chapter 5). By this time, lawyers and legal professionals more generally had become the backbone of the liberal opposition to the Pahlavi regime (Arjomand 1988: 109).

After the 1979 Revolution, Khomeini denounced the secular legal system of the Pahlavi era and pledged his commitment to a distinctly Islamic system of law on which the new order would be based. Once the postrevolutionary power struggle ended with complete victory for him and his supporters, Khomeini declared his commitment to the rule of law, having established in his 1971 classic work on Islamic government that "the rule of Islam is neither arbitrary, nor absolutist .... It is the rule of law" (Khomeini 1971: 43) and declaring that "all the Prophets since the beginning of the world have come for the establishment of the law (*qānun*) and Islam has come for the establishment of the law." Characteristically, once the revolution consolidated its power, the Persian New Year 1360 (1981/1982) was celebrated as the "year of the rule of law" (*sāl-e hokumat-e qānun*). On December 15, 1982, Khomeini issued a decree in eight clauses, guaranteeing all Iranian citizens security from arbitrary arrest and confiscation of property and promising the restoration of law and order. Khomeini's concept of *velāyat-e faqih* (guardianship of the jurist) was enshrined in the new constitution and the shari'a was transformed from being a jurist's law into the law of the state.

3 Islamization of the Legal System

Following the 1979 constitution, all realms of the law were to be re-Islamized. But, interestingly, this did not mean a return to the legal practices prior to the codification of law in the 1930s and 1940s. Instead, the parliament, with oversight by the Guardian Council, re-Islamized the codes of law from the Pahlavi era. As such, the fundamentally French civil law-type structure of the legal system was largely retained, as well as the organization of law. Piece by piece, the parliament, guided by drafts drawn up by committees from inside the judiciary, would consider certain spheres of law, such as family law, labor law, or criminal law, and seek to Islamize them. Unlike the prerevolutionary criminal code, civil and contract laws were deemed sufficiently Islamic not to require great changes. Overall, the Islamization process took several decades, and most codes of law were initially promulgated as temporary until a more systematic reform was achieved.

By the late 1980s, gridlock characterized the "Islamization of law" process, which was to a large extent due to the standoff between the parliament, which by and large championed a strong state with a far-reaching redistributive mandate, and the Guardian Council, a twelve-member council made up of six Islamic jurists (*mojtahed*s) and six constitutional law experts, which aimed to limit the state (not least in order to reserve competencies for the *'ulamā*) and safeguard private property rights, especially of the landed clergy. No law could pass without approval by the Guardian Council and the council repeatedly vetoed legislation, most prominently land reform and the labor law (the subject of Chapter 11).

Beside the conflict between parliament and the Guardian Council, other constitutional institutions created deadlock or institutional conflict. Iran's 1979 constitution had been modelled on the French 1959 constitution and had adopted several of its institutional features, including the French system of semi-presidentialism, which features both a prime minister and a president. Iran thus featured a dual executive, that of prime minister and president, who often clashed over policy, but, unlike the French system, featured an additional third force that occasionally functioned as an executive power – that of the Supreme Leader, Ayatollah Khomeini, who had the power to declare war and peace and in general assumed the highest political authority. A further institutional conflict stemmed from the fact that the judiciary was led by a council of five, rather than one person, which caused contradictory policies and inconsistencies. The judiciary regularly turned to the Supreme Leader for guidance and requests to resolve tension. The institution of the Supreme Leadership was itself in crisis by the late 1980s, as Khomeini had dismissed his designated successor, Ayatollah Montazeri, in 1987 over the latter's criticism of the Islamic Republic's dismal human rights record, and an alternative successor was not easily found. The constitution required that the Supreme Leader be the highest Shi'i authority in the country at the same time, but none of the high-ranking *mojtahed*s supported the Islamic Republic – for a variety of reasons. Most did not agree with Khomeini's particular reinterpretation of the notion of *velāyat-e faqih* on which the Islamic Republic was founded.

Thus, at the end of the costly Iran–Iraq War (1981–1988), Iran found itself in dire political and economic straits. The constitutional crafters of 1979 had deliberately omitted an amendment clause from the constitution and eliminated one that was part of an earlier draft. This omission was due to their confidence that the constitution codified the best possible polity with the most effective institutional design, reflecting Khomeini's vision of an Islamic Republic, which future generations should not alter. Yet, de facto violating that very constitution, Khomeini called together a committee of twenty in 1989 to outline various amendments addressing the institutional deadlocks and inefficacies created by the 1979 constitution. With the 1989 amendment, the only amendment to date, the office of the prime minister was eliminated and the council directing the judiciary replaced by a single head of the judiciary. A national security council was created, ensuring that the Ministries of Intelligence and Defense, and the various security services, coordinated their actions and no longer acted in competition on major security issues. The two most important changes concerned the office of the Supreme Leader and the relationship between parliament and the Guardian Council. To ease the succession of Khomeini, the requirement that the Supreme Leader be the highest Shi'i authority in the country was dropped. At the same time, the office of the Supreme Leader received an upgrade as it was now described as absolute: The guardian jurist at the helm of the Islamic Republic henceforth had absolute authority (*velāyat al-faqih al-amr*). Institutionally, the Ministry of Intelligence was no longer primarily answerable to the president but to the Supreme Leader and no longer had to report to parliament. To address the deadlock between parliament and the Guardian Council, a powerful mediation council – known as the Expediency Council, created in 1988 – was now constitutionally recognized. The Expediency Council was also given guideline competency and was to advise the Supreme Leader on all major policy issues. The council began with seventeen members and over time grew to more than forty-five. All members are appointed by the Supreme Leader and it includes ex officio the six *mojtahed*s of the Guardian Council.

4   Revolutionary Innovations in Shi'i Law

In its founding and in subsequent developments, the Islamic Republic reinterpreted Shi'i legal conceptions in its governmental theory to an extent that amounts to nothing short of a revolution in Shi'i legal theory. At the core stands the concept of *velāyat-e faqih*, which literally means guardianship of the jurist. Up until the last third of the twentieth century, it referred to the legal representation in court and law by a member of the clergy of those who do not have standing – the legal minor (*saghir*), for example, or the cognitively challenged (*mahjur*). In his Najaf lectures of

1972, Khomeini extended the meaning of this concept in three significant ways. First, he reinterpreted it to apply to the sphere of government, not only courts of law. As such, he argued that representation extended to the political sphere. Second, he extended the concept of those to be represented to the citizenry at large – it was now the entire citizen population, not only those who lacked standing in court, who required representation. Third, he reinterpreted it to mean that the highest Shi'i authority ought to undertake the representation, not the clergy at large. The result of this tripartite reinterpretation, any one of whose elements was without precedent in 1,200 years of Shi'i legal thought, was the notion that the citizenry at large required legal representation by the highest authority of the Shi'i clergy. This was enshrined as the central concept of government in the final draft of the constitution in 1979, and even though Khomeini was not the highest Shi'i authority at the time, being the prevailing revolutionary leader he was elevated to the position of *vali-e faqih*, Guardian-Jurist of the people. (Earlier drafts of the constitution had not contained the notion of *velāyat-e faqih* and once the concept was enshrined, high-ranking members of the Shi'i clergy voiced their vigorous resistance against it – for a variety of reasons; see Randjbar-Daemi 2013; Saffari 1993.)

The next revolution in Shi'i legal doctrine took place in the standoff between parliament and the Guardian Council over land reform and labor law reform, both of which hinged on competing understandings of Islamic property law and the scope of its jurisdiction. Parliament, where redistribution-oriented leftist Islamists enjoyed a majority throughout the 1980s, had passed a number of land reform bills early in the decade, which were repeatedly vetoed by the Guardian Council. The council argued that Shi'i property law defines land ownership as a legal relationship between the owner and the property, which outside parties – including the state – lacked the power to disturb. After months of standoff, Ali Akbar Rafsanjani, then Speaker of Parliament (later president of the country), suggested that land reform was a matter of national emergency that necessitated resort to administrative law – specifically, emergency rules (*qā'edeh-ye zarurat*) – implying that the situation of the national emergency afforded disregarding, for the moment, the requirements of Islamic property law. He further argued that emergency regulations did not require review with regard to their congruence with Islamic law. Rafsanjani thus introduced a distinction between ordinary legislation (which was constitutionally required to cohere with Islamic principles) and temporary legislation passed due to practical necessity (*zarurat*), which would be exempt from veto by the *mojtahed*s on the Guardian Council. Following this new understanding – under which Article 4 of the constitution ("all law must be based on Islamic principles") would not apply to temporary legislation and which required review only with an eye to questions of constitutionality but not congruence with Islamic law – the land reform eventually passed. Other bills that had been held up due to the Guardian Council veto passed with similar emergency provisions: rent law, foreign trade law, and divorce law. In all cases, this meant, however, that their nature was temporary, and the issues would need to be taken up again by the Majles after three or five years.

The other key piece of legislation that led to a major reinterpretation in Shi'i legal doctrine concerned the labor law (see Chapter 11). While the parliament worked toward strengthening workers' rights, the Islamic jurists on the Guardian Council saw the property rights of factory owners and merchants potentially threatened by the bill. Prerevolutionary trade unions had been banned in 1979 and replaced by state-run Islamic labor councils that functioned on the basis of Islamic contract law without enforcing unitary social standards regarding pay, retirement benefits, health benefits, and accident insurance. Since Shi'i jurisprudence did not offer guidance for the state to set conditions on private businesses, labor standards de facto eroded following the revolution. With the new labor law, parliament sought to address the issue; yet, again, the Guardian Council argued that the state had no jurisdiction to regulate labor contracts.

This time, it was the minister of labor who found a way out of the impasse. He elevated a legal principle that existed in Shi'i private law, "contractual conditions" (*shart-e zemn-e 'aqd*), to the level of public law by proposing a category of "obligatory contractual conditions" (*shurut-e elzāmi*). He argued that the state, acting as a third party, had the power to impose obligatory contractual conditions on existing bilateral or multilateral relations between and among contracting parties. His argument was supported by jurists, who argued that the sanctity of contractual freedom may hold only to the extent that contractual conditions meet certain social standards which the state may impose because it also provides services such as electricity, telephone, and water to the private sector (Ansari and Taheri 2009). Khomeini accepted the argument and declared that the state could issue "obligatory conditions" applicable to all private contracts (Khomeini 1987). The upshot of this legal innovation was that a state ministry could now regulate vast swathes of private activity by formulating obligatory contractual conditions that private contracts had to abide by.

The Guardian Council, meanwhile, protested this interpretation and argued that the state's power to issue obligatory contractual conditions ought to be lawful only in services that are under the "exclusive supervision" of the state. In a letter to then President Khamenei, who sought clarification on the matter, Khomeini insisted that the scope of the obligatory contractual conditions was not limited to matters of government, but could apply to all matters, even the primary ordinances of Islam. Thus, he suggested that if the pilgrimage or daily prayer were found to violate the public interest, the Islamic government had the right to abrogate these ("I would explicitly pronounce that this is the prerogative of the state" [*Keyhān*, January 7, 1988; *Ettelā'āt*, January 9, 1988]). Khomeini legitimized this new legal theory with a notion current in Sunni legal theory that had been rejected by Shi'i jurists for twelve centuries: *maslahat*, best translated as expediency, or public interest.

What is the significance of all of this for the rule of law? On the one hand, the evolution of Shi'i fiqh in the first decade of the Islamic Republic to adapt to the necessities of political circumstance shows great creativity and flexibility in the application of religious law. Each innovation had to be carefully legitimated, but in the end, it was often possible to circumvent stricter interpretations of Shi'i fiqh in order to either address socioeconomic challenges in ways still seemingly justified by religious law or to broaden the scope of Shi'i public law. But on the other hand, and particularly so once the Expediency Council was created, it also meant the increasing political instrumentalization of fiqh discourse in order to justify political ends. Once Khomeini had declared that the principle of *maslahat* could even justify the abrogation of the primary imperatives of Islam, all doors were opened to render as law whatever the Supreme Leader decrees it to be. Supreme Leader Khamenei has increasingly used the concept of *maslahat* to rule by executive decree (*hokm-e hokumati*) and other agencies and institutions have emulated the practice. As such, the intelligence services, the Revolutionary Guard Corps, and the representatives of the Supreme Leader in all administrative and judiciary bodies frequently invoke *maslahat* when opportune to circumvent prior legal or normative commitments.

5 Organization of the Judiciary

According to Article 156 of the constitution, "the judiciary is an independent power, the protector of the rights of the individual and society, responsible for the implementation of justice." Following Article 61, the functions of the judiciary are to be performed by courts of justice, which are to be formed "in accordance with the criteria of Islam," and are vested with the authority to examine and settle lawsuits, protect the rights of the public, dispense and enact justice, and implement "God's punishments" (*al-hudūd al-Ilāhiyya*).

5.1 Courts

Iran has five principal types of courts, three of which are constitutional: the civil courts, criminal courts, and the military courts (Article 172). The latter deal with crimes committed in connection with law enforcement, the regular army (*artesh*), and the Revolutionary Guard Corps (*sepāh*). The unconstitutional courts are the revolutionary courts and the special courts for the clergy.

The vast majority of cases are dealt with in the civil courts, including civil disputes, divorces, and custody cases. The criminal courts are distinguished between those dealing with *hodud* crimes (*dādgāh-e keifari-e yek*) and those dealing with *taʿzir* and other crimes (*dādgāh-e keifari-e do*).[5] Permission to work at the courts for *hodud* crimes requires higher qualifications from judges and lawyers than work at courts dealing with other crimes.

Two types of courts are not constitutional, and there have been efforts, particularly in the 1980s, to phase these out. The first are the Islamic Revolutionary Courts, set up in 1979 by decree of the Revolutionary Council (but initiated by Ayatollah Khomeini) to adjudicate offences regarded as threatening to the Islamic Republic, including crimes against national security, narcotic crimes, economic crimes, and financial crimes.[6] An appeals procedure in these courts was not instituted until 1988. In 1994, the revolutionary courts were formally incorporated into the judiciary through the Act of Establishment of General and Revolutionary Courts. Revolutionary courts are the foremost courts to prosecute political crimes.

The second type of unconstitutional courts are the Special Courts for the Clergy. These were established in 1980 to try and punish misdeeds by Shi'i clergymen. The courts were endowed with a code of procedure in 1991 and an expanded code in 2005, establishing an appeals procedure (Künkler 2012). While the constitutional courts and the revolutionary courts are under the administration of the judiciary, the Special Courts for the Clergy are under the direct jurisdiction and financing of the office of the Supreme Leader.

---

[5] As part of the 2001 Development Plan (Article 187), three-member dispute-resolution councils were created, responsible for the settlement of minor civil and criminal cases. These concern civil cases with damages of up to about 1,500 USD but also higher values if both parties agree. Dispute-resolution councils may also decide criminal cases for which the maximum penalty is ninety-one days imprisonment or fines of up to about 600 USD. The councils are not bound by the Codes of Civil and Criminal Procedure. Their decisions may be appealed in the general courts.

[6] Official Gazette, No. 10018, 25/4/1358 [July 16, 1979].

Members of the Bar Association have called numerous times, but to no avail, for the revolutionary courts and the Special Courts for the Clergy to be closed and for their jurisdiction to be transferred to the ordinary courts. Both types are today the most politically powerful courts in the Islamic Republic, and nearly all political activists are tried in one of the two.

There is another type of court which evolved as a special court over time: the Press Courts. As per Article 168 of the constitution, crimes relating to journalists and other members of the media must be tried in front of a jury. It states: "Investigation of political and press offenses is conducted openly in the courts of the Ministry of Justice before a jury. The manner and conditions of jury selection and their authorities and the definition of political offenses are defined by the law on the basis of Islamic criteria." The clause was initially meant to protect the press against a vengeful state. The Press Law of 1986 further regulated the establishment of dedicated press courts. During the reformist era, Khatami's administration activated these courts, whose juries were appointed by a committee dominated by the Ministry of Culture and Islamic Guidance. However, the Supreme Leader imposed a draconian judge on the Tehran Press court, Saeed Mortazavi, who turned it into a major instrument for the suppression of the burgeoning press. In 2002, the press law was amended, and the selection of the jury henceforth regulated in a manner so as to ensure dominance by members of institutions close to the Supreme Leader rather than the Ministry.[7] Since Sadegh Larijani assumed the head of the judiciary in 2009, journalists have most frequently been tried again in revolutionary courts, which means that trials are not open to the public and are not held in front of a jury.

There are two national high courts, the Supreme Court and the Court of Administrative Justice (CAJ). The Supreme Court serves as the highest court of appeal for *hodud* crimes. It also supervises the implementation of laws by the courts and should ensure uniformity in judicial procedures. The Supreme Court has several administrative branches with its headquarters based in Tehran. The CAJ investigates any complaints made against government officials, organs, and statutes. It also is under the supervision of the head of the judiciary. In addition, in 1991 a Judges' Disciplinary Court was established (see Section 5.3).[8]

---

[7] Per Article 36 of the Press Law, amended in 2002, the juries consist of twenty-one members in Tehran and fourteen in the provinces who are selected by the chief of the judiciary, the Minister of Culture and Islamic Guidance, the chief of the city's Islamic Council, the chief of the Organization of Islamic Propaganda, and a representative of the Association of Friday Prayer Leaders.

[8] In addition, there is the State Inspectorate Organization, a division of the judiciary that is charged with auditing and investigating state institutions accused of alleged contraventions.

Litigants may appeal court decisions on procedural grounds. In such cases, the Supreme Court will review the case and if it accedes to the appeal, send the case for retrial to the Appellate Courts of the province in which the case was first tried. In cases involving offenses with the legal punishments of death, stoning, amputation, or imprisonment for over ten years, in other words for *hodud* crimes, the Supreme Court will affirm the lower court decision, or order a retrial, usually by the same court. In the case of drug offenses, these are tried in the revolutionary courts, where a single judge decides the case in a trial that is not public. Until 2015, drug-related sentences could not be appealed, but this has changed with the new Code of Criminal Procedure (CCP) of 2015 (see Chapter 3).

The CAJ was created by the Majles in 1982 and in the absence of a constitutional court in the Islamic Republic, the CAJ has often taken on the role of defending citizens' basic rights (Jalali and Roshan 2016): it has defended free access to information, the right to choose and be represented by a lawyer, minority language rights, women's rights, the freedom to choose an occupation, and prisoners' rights (Sangri 2017; Mansouri Nia 2021). Thus in 2004, for example, the CAJ found that the executive bylaws of the Prisons Organization, which included "solitary confinement of up to one month," violated Article 39 of the constitution, under which "All affronts to the dignity and repute of persons arrested, detained, or imprisoned, …, whatever form they may take, are forbidden and liable to punishment." The court also has occasionally succeeded in protecting the separation of powers. In 2000, it ruled that the enactments of the Supreme Council of Cultural Revolution (SCCR) are administrative rules and regulations rather than laws and hence are not exempt from the CAJ's power of judicial review. In the relevant case, the SCCR had passed a regulation aiming to preclude citizens from bringing rights violations committed by the SCCR to the CAJ. Partly prompted by confrontations such as the 2000 case, the Guardian Council and Expediency Council have over time forced the Majles to limit the CAJ's jurisdiction. In 2006, the Expediency Council changed the Majles draft amendment to its 1982 law with a note (19) which excluded, from the CAJ's review, judicial decisions of the judicial branch; and decisions and enactments of the Guardian Council, the Expediency Council, the Assembly of Experts, the Supreme National Defense Council, and the SCCR.[9] This has had the consequence that the CAJ can henceforth only review decisions made by elected officials, but no longer of the councils predominantly appointed by the Supreme Leader.

---

[9] The Expediency Council followed an interpretation by the Guardian Council of November 2004 to the same effect. Interestingly, the exemptions were justified with

5.2 The Head of the Judiciary and the Minister of Justice

The head of the judiciary is directly chosen and appointed by the Republic's Supreme Leader for a five-year term. Nearly all heads of the judiciary so far have served two terms each (Ebrahim Raisi is the exception as he was elected president during his first term as head of the judiciary). The head of the judiciary, in consultation with the judges of the Supreme Court, nominates the chief of the Supreme Court and the prosecutor general. According to the constitution (Articles 157 and 162), the head of the judiciary, the chief of the Supreme Court, and the prosecutor general must all be *mojtahed*s. The head of the judiciary also draws up the list of candidates from which the parliament must choose six jurists for the Guardian Council (with the other six, all *mojtaheds*, being directly appointed by the Supreme Leader).

Per Article 158 of the constitution, the head of the judiciary appoints, promotes, suspends, and dismisses judges.[10] According to Article 164, judges can be removed and transferred "where public interest [*maslahat*] necessitates or requires it ..." This occurs by decision of the head of the judiciary after consultation with the prosecutor general and the head of the supreme court (both of whom he appoints).

The role of the head of the judiciary is separate from the far less powerful role of minister of justice; the latter is responsible for matters concerning the relationship between the judiciary on the one hand and the executive and legislative branches on the other hand. The minister of justice is appointed by the president, who, however, has to choose from a list of nominees proposed to him by the head of the judiciary. Further, it is the head of the judiciary, not the minister of justice, who drafts bills concerning the judiciary. The competencies of the minister depend largely on the head of the judiciary in so far as "The head of

---

reference to a distinction between *hokumat* and *dowlat*, concepts that can be translated as "government" and "state." The Guardian Council argued that *dowlat* referred to the executive branch, and the latter's decisions would indeed fall into the CAJ's jurisdiction. But institutions such as the Guardian Council, the Expediency Council, and the SCCR were all *hokumati* institutions and thus not in the CAJ's jurisdiction. Quite by design, the Guardian Council's distinction coincided with the division of republican versus theocratic institutions in the Islamic Republic. The 2006 exemptions (https://qavanin.ir/Law/TreeText/116481 accessed May 2, 2019) were reconfirmed in a 2011 Majles law on the Court of Administrative Justice as revised by the Expediency Council in 2013. See https://qavanin.ir/Law/TreeText/205259 accessed May 4, 2019.

[10] This excludes the judges of the Special Court for the Clergy, because the court is not under the jurisdiction of the judiciary. Its judges and prosecutors are directly appointed by the Supreme Leader.

the judiciary may delegate full authority to the Minister of Justice in financial and administrative areas and for employment of personnel other than judges, in which case the Minister of Justice shall have the same authority and responsibility as those possessed by the other ministers in their capacity as the highest-ranking government executives" (Article 160). In the original 1979 constitution, the minister of justice was responsible for all courts throughout the country. After the 1989 amendment, this responsibility shifted to the head of the judiciary, who could delegate that power back to the minister.

Even though the head of the judiciary's powers could effect complete (forced) cohesion inside the judiciary and promote the subordination of lower-ranking judges to higher-ranking ones, there are examples of judges defying the head of the judiciary. When Mahmoud Shahroudi, head of the judiciary from 1999 to 2009, decreed a moratorium on stoning, his decree was ignored at least seven times and stoning sentences were carried out (stoning being the lethal punishment for adultery).

Further, there are clear signs of the judiciary's ultimate subservience to the security forces, as Shahroudi was not – despite several decrees (along with two parliamentary acts) – able to integrate the security forces' detention centers into the Prison Organization, which is a branch of the judiciary (Chapter 9). The judiciary also acquiesces regularly to the intervention of military and security forces to quell public protests through the use of mass arrests, arbitrary detention, and torture.

5.3   Judges

Following the Law on the Qualifications for the Appointment of Judges, of May 4, 1982, all judges must have reached the level of *ijtihād* (being capable of independent reasoning regarding Islamic law), usually as a result of reaching the highest degree of learning from Shi'i seminaries. While it is possible to specialize in Islamic law in the religious seminaries (as opposed to theology, for example), judges are not required to have focused on Islamic law in their studies. Neither do judges need to have law degrees from the secular universities of the country. They must be committed to the principles of Islam and the Islamic Revolution. If, at any time, there is an insufficient number of *mojtahed*s (those who have reached the level of *ijtihād*), judges can be recruited from among the graduates of law schools, faculties of theology, or from graduates of seminaries who have not yet reached the level of *ijtihād*. In 2020, there were about 11,000 judges employed by the judiciary.[11] How many of these are indeed *mojtahed*s is difficult to ascertain but one source puts the percentage at 22 (Jalali-Karveh 2006: 443f.).

According to Article 164 of the constitution, judges cannot be removed from a post "except by trial and proof of guilt" and cannot be transferred without their consent (amended 1989 constitution). Yet, the same article adds "except in cases when the public interest [*maslahat*] necessitates it," and it is on the basis of this exception that the head of the judiciary moves judges when politically opportune. Then deputy Head of the Judiciary Hadi Marvi, stated in 2000 that "judges must obey the Supreme Leader and have no independence in judgment" (Cumaraswamy 2001, para. 116). It is questionable whether his own superior, Mahmoud Shahroudi, would have uttered such a statement, but it nevertheless gives insight into the mindset of many judicial officials.

Women had been full judges prior to the 1979 revolution (indeed, the 2003 Nobel Peace Prize Laureate Shirin Ebadi was Tehran's first female judge) but were barred from serving as judges after the revolution (Ebadi was demoted to be the scribe in the very court over which she had previously presided). Since 1992, women have been permitted to work as legal advisors and advisory judges in family courts, but the final judgment may only be made by a male judge. Despite these restrictions, women make up almost 70 percent of law students in Iran, most of whom become lawyers.

Parallel to the Guardian Council, which screens all legislation as to its compatibility with Islamic law, Article 170 stipulates that judges are "obliged to refrain from executing statutes and regulations of the government that are in conflict with the laws or the norms of Islam or lie outside the competence of the executive power." This has allowed judges to defy directives by the minister of justice when they have deemed it opportune. When the 1979 constitution was amended in 1989, the following clause was added to Article 170: "Everyone has the right to demand the annulment of any such regulation from the Court of Administrative Justice," but in 2006 the Expediency Council passed a law exempting judgments and decisions of the judicial branch from CAJ review (see section 5.1).

In October 1991, a law was passed by the Expediency Council establishing the Disciplinary Court of Judges (DCJ), which may

---

[11] See www.isna.ir/news/96092413086/۹-۹۶-%سال-تا-پایان-قضائیه-قوه-انسانی-منابع-معاونDB%B0۸-دستگاه-نفر-ه accessed May 24, 2022. In total, the judiciary employs around 88,000 people. Non-senior judges are paid between 8 and 20 million tomans (between USD 348 and 870) a month, and, according to the judiciary, they review and issue verdicts for between 100 and 120 cases each month.

dismiss judges at the recommendation of the head of the judiciary.[12] The court is made up of five individuals: the head of the judiciary, the head judge of the DCJ, the prosecutor of the DCJ, the head of the Supreme Court, and the prosecutor general. Once the head of the judiciary recommends a judge's dismissal, a three-person investigatory committee, made up of the prosecutor of the DCJ, the deputy minister of justice in legal and parliamentary affairs, and the deputy of the prosecutor general, will examine the case. After the investigation, the committee will send its recommendations to the court, which will issue a ruling based on majority vote, but subject to veto by the head of the judiciary.

The Bar Association has criticized the apparent lack of independence of the DCJ, given that the head of the judiciary initiates the process, appoints most members of the court, has veto power over its decision, and decides on the action to be taken afterwards, that is, whether, if proven guilty, the accused shall be dismissed, forced into retirement, or transferred.[13] Further, reformist parliamentarians have criticized the DCJ for not increasing accountability to the public or tackling corruption on the part of judges, as it was designed to do. The Majles has aimed to investigate reports into corrupt judicial practices, but these investigations have failed due to a lack of cooperation on part of the judiciary.[14]

A particularly interesting constitutional article with regard to the judiciary is Article 167, according to which if a case cannot be decided on the basis of codified law, the judge has to deliver his judgment "on the basis of authoritative Islamic sources [Qur'an and hadith] and

---

[12] Law on the Formation of the High Tribunal for Judicial Discipline, December 1991: www.adalatgazaee.com/index.php?option=com_mtree&task=viewlink&link_id=75&Itemid=0 accessed May 20, 2022.

[13] The numbers of dismissals and disciplinary action are difficult to ascertain as different offices issue different proclamations in this regard and the judiciary does not publish unified statistics on the matter. To illustrate, in May of 2017, for example, Ahmad Tavakoli, a Tehran MP, mentioned the dismissal of 170 judges due to economic or moral violations. One month later, on June 20, 2017, Gholam-Hossein Mohseni-Eje'i, spokesman of the judiciary at that time and vice chief justice of Iran, announced that fifty judges had been disciplined, while on July 9, 2017, the judiciary intelligence office announced the suspension of seventy-eight judges and sixty-four judicial experts.

[14] One of the most high-profile cases in this regard was that of Saeed Mortazavi, who served as the Tehran prosecutor general. After countrywide protests against the reelection of President Ahmadinejad in 2009, four detainees died in the Kahrizak Detention Center. An investigation by the Article 90 Commission of the Majles held Saeed Mortazavi personally responsible. Mortazavi was also suspected of direct involvement in the murder of Zahra Kazemi, an Iranian Canadian photojournalist, in Evin Prison in 2003. Despite the parliamentary investigation, the judiciary undertook no disciplinary action against him at the time.

authentic fatwas."[15] On the one hand, the article clearly establishes that Islamic (noncodified) law is ranked secondary to any codified law. But the article also means that a judge has relatively large leeway in determining a verdict in the absence of codified law, as there is great diversity in Islamic scholarly opinion and fatwas on a given matter. A Research Centre in Jurisprudence (Markaz-e tahqiqāt-e fiqh), set up by Mahmoud Shahroudi in the early 2000s, keeps a registrar of the most important fatwas of those *marāje'* (sources of emulation, the highest religious authorities in Shi'i Islam) that are officially recognized by the regime and which judges ought to consult.

Beyond fatwas by the most outstanding living religious authorities, the same Article 167 permits judges to apply their own insight, *'elm-e qāzi* (lit. knowledge of the judge), but without specifying the methodology with which *'elm-e qāzi* shall be derived, in which areas of law it is permissible proof, and who may apply it. Critics of this particular clause allege that judges use Article 167 to ignore codified law. Partly in response to the criticism, the 2013 Penal Code requires a judge who invokes *'elm-e qāzi* to describe how he has derived it in a given decision and to name the evidence that lies at its basis (such as expert reports). But the same code also explicitly allows *'elm-e qāzi* to be based on invalid evidence and to override other legally sanctioned forms of evidence. Critics point out that following classical fiqh, only *mojtahed* judges are permitted to invoke *'elm-e qāzi*, and that most judges in Iran are not trained *mojtahed*s (up to 80 percent). Even Khomeini and Shahroudi took this position. Some critics go further and state that *'elm-e qāzi* can only be applied by those who are infallible (*ma'sum*) and that this applied only to the Prophet and the Imams (see Chapter 9).

5.4 Trials

The 1979 constitution requires all trials to be open to the public (Article 165) unless the court determines that an open trial would be detrimental to public order, or, in cases of private disputes, if both parties request that open hearings not be held. This does not apply to the Special Court for the Clergy, whose hearings are always closed to the public. In addition, the hearings of the revolutionary courts usually take place behind closed doors.

A 1994 reform of the court system combined, in the revolutionary and general courts, the functions of the judge, the investigator,

---

[15] Khomeini's *Tahrir al-Vasila* is extensively used in trials.

and prosecutor in one. In the face of a great deal of domestic and international criticism of this flagrant violation of the separation of functions in the court, the reformist-dominated parliament of 2000–2004 passed a bill to reestablish the role of prosecutor. The bill was blocked, however, by the Guardian Council. In 2006, the office of public prosecutor was finally reinstated, but only for lower-level criminal courts.

Until the 1993 Appeals Law, court decisions could not be appealed, reflecting Shi'i juristic opinion that forbids appeals unless judges are proven incompetent or their rulings contain errors of fiqh. This was also Khomeini's position. Since 1993, appeals have been permitted and appellate courts were established in each provincial capital. A Province Court of Appeal is composed of a three-judge panel. Appeals that concern *hodud* are directly sent to the Supreme Court.

Convicts may also apply for pardons, and all death sentences except those for murder can be pardoned by the Supreme Leader. Pardon petitions are considered by the Pardon and Clemency Commission (Komision-e 'Afv va Bakhshudegi), which consists of five legal experts chosen by the head of the judiciary. A Procedural Code for the Pardon and Clemency Commission regulates its proceedings. Rejected pardon requests can be resubmitted if the reason for rejection ceases to exist (see Chapter 3).

6   This Volume

When conceiving this volume, we aimed to recruit authors working on diverse areas of the law and taking a range of positions with regard to the quality of the rule of law in Iran. The group of authors assembled is trained in various disciplines, from Islamic studies to the anthropology of law, to constitutional law, commercial law, criminal law, sociolegal studies, political science, medicine, human rights law, and Iranian studies. All authors work in the primary languages and have undertaken fieldwork in Iran; some have had personal experience with Iranian law, as defenders or defendants.

Shining a light on the legal, judicial, penal, and carceral institutions of any authoritarian context is bound to reveal much that is disturbing, and this volume is no exception in this regard. But the volume is not intended to underline any kind of exceptionalism in connection with the repressive nature of the institutions of the Islamic Republic of Iran, which have sometimes been depicted as an almost inevitable expression of Islamic law, of Shi'ism, or of Iranian culture and history. Instead, we hope that the chapters convey the contingencies and discontinuities at work in the processes of law enforcement, lawmaking, and legal reform in contemporary Iran. We also hope that the volume is a modest contribution to understanding the political, legal, and cultural context in which ordinary citizens have struggled, often with great bravery, for political emancipation.

First, a note on the cover art. "The Knot" by the artist Shiva Ahmadi evokes manifold associations. Do we witness a royal audience, a court hearing, or a discussion at a religious seminary? Who presides? A shah? A mujtahid? A judge? And, who listens? Subjects? Citizens? Or, "just" monkeys?[16] At the center, is what we see the *zamzam* of the desert, a well of justice, or a furnace, channeling a destructive fire? Are the lines floating across the painting decorative calligraphy, are they the words of the law, or shackles that bind? At the top, against a seemingly shifting, elusive background, do we see archangel Gabriel delivering a new life, do we see an angel of justice? What is being knotted to whom and how is the knot constituted? Ahmadi's intricate style, alluding to the classical tradition of Persian miniature painting, combined with her acute sense of political and social violence that is embedded in her painting, seemed to make it particularly relevant for our book cover.

Speaking directly to those binds and knots, Chapters 2, 3 and 4 provide insight into the challenges arising from codified Shi'i fiqh, the first in penal law, the second in criminal procedure, the third in family law. Silvia Tellenbach discusses the postrevolutionary Penal Code of Iran, highlighting the enormity of the codification and re-codification project. The code itself is divided into five books, organized around key concepts of Islamic penal law. Only the most general principles of criminal law, laid out in Book I, are now in permanent form, while the other four books are still in force only as temporary statutes that have to be re-validated by parliament every three to five years. But even Book I took about thirty years to be finalized and was only promulgated as a permanent code in 2013. In other words, it took the Islamic Republic no less than twenty-four years to thoroughly Islamize the *general principles* of its criminal law, while the vast majority of the *specific* elements of criminal law are yet to be permanently codified. Tellenbach focuses in particular on the theory and practice of the principle of legality, the

---

[16] To those following human rights adjudication in Iran, the scene evokes a famous court case of the early 2000s, when in 2002, the Iranian history professor Hashem Aghajari was accused of heresy for stating in a public speech that people should not follow their religious leaders like monkeys. The court case, which overall lasted into mid-2004, was widely publicized as Aghajari refused to ask the Supreme Leader for a pardon after having been sentenced to death. The Supreme Court, which de jure needs to confirm all death sentences even if the defendant has not asked for a pardon, had the case twice retried by lower courts until the sentence was commuted to five years imprisonment (and ultimately to three years imprisonment and two years' probation).

system of sanctions, juvenile criminal law, and rules of evidence. She notes that while rules in the areas of *hadd*, *qesās*, and *diyeh* are regarded as divine law that cannot be altered or abolished, Iranian legislation on penal law occasionally relies on minority opinions in legal justification if deemed opportune. Furthermore, the texts of *hadd*, *qesās*, and *diyeh* are sometimes embedded in other rules of substantive or procedural law in such a way so as to diminish the harshness of punishments while formally still upholding Islamic law. This was done, for example, concerning the criminal responsibility of juveniles, and in the law of evidence.

Drewery Dyke and Hadi Enayat then analyze the nature and evolution of the administration of criminal justice with a particular view to the innovations brought about with the new 2015 Code of Criminal Procedure. As the authors show, the code further solidified the politicization of the judiciary, for example by removing the right of the accused to choose their own defense counsel in cases involving charges of national security (a frequent charge in politically motivated cases). The new code also did little to place limits on the very wide discretion in the conduct and outcome of cases that judges enjoy, often justified with reference to *'elm-e qāzī* (lit. knowledge of the judge).

Hannah L. Richter discusses how Iranian family law was codified following the Shi'i (*Ja'farī*) school of jurisprudence and how Shi'i fiqh relates in practice to other sources of law, such as the Civil Code and the Family Protection Act. The author asks how independent legal reasoning (*ijtihād*) by qualified scholars as a main concept of Shi'i legal thought can or cannot be aligned with the idea that codified law reigns supreme over noncodified law, asking "should Shi'i family law be codified at all," and if so, who is qualified to legitimately do so? Discussing different approaches to the question, the chapter compares the Iranian situation with recent approaches in other parts of the Shi'i world, notably Bahrain, Afghanistan and Iraq, where different, exclusively Shi'i, personal status draft laws have been put forward, occasionally meeting strong objections by government officials or religious scholars. Analyzing specific aspects of these drafts in comparison with Iranian family law, Richter concludes that orientation along rule-of-law aspects is stronger in Iranian Shi'i family law than its cognates elsewhere.

The next two chapters deal with the status of the legal profession and the labyrinthian system of law enforcement in the Islamic Republic respectively.

In Chapter 5, Mirjam Künkler sheds light on the professional associations of lawyers in the country, the bar associations. Following the 1979 Revolution, the bar associations were dismantled but rose from the ashes during the reconstruction period under President Rafsanjani (1989–1997) when they attempted to reassert themselves as the primary institutions for the licensing of lawyers. Unsurprisingly, this attempt met with fierce resistance from officials inside the judiciary, who in the meantime had built up alternative training and recruitment programs for future lawyers. But as leading rights activists argued, the bar associations and their independence from the judicial branch of power are a key pillar of any rule-of-law state. The independence of lawyers and their professional integrity hinges on training and licensing programs that are shielded from political interference and instrumentalization. Künkler argues that ever since the early 2000s, the bar associations have been a pawn not only between the legal profession and the judiciary, but also between those aiming to strengthen the independence of the judiciary and those insisting that the Islamic character of the regime demands the judiciary's subservience to the authority of the Supreme Leader and his appointees.

Saeid Golkar in Chapter 6 discusses the various law enforcement agencies and their proliferation during the tenure of Supreme Leader Khamenei (1989–). While presenting the different mandates and goals of the police units, Golkar argues that the security mission has, since the 1990s, expanded alongside the police's disciplinary and religious morality mission, and especially so since the countrywide protests following the disputed 2009 elections, after which the police has heavily focused on anti-protest strategies. To maintain social and political order, the Islamic Republic has taken several measures, such as the establishment of several special forces for crowd control and anti-riot missions, and heavy investment in the training and equipment of these forces. To ready its personnel for security missions, the police force has also dramatically intensified its ideological programs for the indoctrination of its members. Recruitment has shifted toward more conservative parts of society, especially from amongst the voluntary reserve force, the Basij-e Mostaż'afin. Golkar argues that these two elements combined have led to increasing estrangement between the police and society and heightened societal resentment toward the police. He also suggests that despite some attempts at reform, Iran's various police forces are by and large shielded from disciplinary action.

The next two chapters touch on the problematics arising from the carceral regime in the Islamic Republic and drug addiction. Most accounts of prisoners in Iran over the past thirty years have focused on political prisoners. The chapter by Anna Enayat and Hadi Enayat instead focuses on the status and conditions of ordinary prisoners, that is, those incarcerated for crimes ranging from drug offences and minor moral offences to theft, murder, or grievous bodily harm. The authors observe that the 1979 Revolution led to the establishment of a penal system that placed an emphasis on restitutive (and to a lesser extent restorative) justice rather than incarceration. This was tied to an Islamic philosophy of punishment articulated by Khomeini and other senior clerics about the swift and "efficient" nature of Islamic penal justice, with its emphasis on corporeal punishments as opposed to the socially detrimental effects of imprisonment. Despite this ideological approach, the incarceration rate has overall been consistently high since 1979 – higher than under the Pahlavi monarchy – and often at the higher end of the scale in global comparative terms. At the same time, the Islamic Republic has not managed to maintain the requisite prison capacity to accommodate such high numbers of prisoners, leading to severe problems with overcrowding.

The chapter by Arash and Kamiar Alaei directly connects to the issue of incarceration, as it deals with Iran's policy toward drug addiction, which is tightly related to the former. The two doctors, who are now living outside Iran, recount their efforts, at times successful, of creating an alternative approach to meeting the medical needs arising from the HIV/AIDS epidemic. The majority of those who contract HIV/AIDS in Iran (ca. 60,000 in a given year) are drug addicts, men who have sex with men, and sex workers. These three groups officially do not exist in Iran as their behavior is strictly prohibited and warrants the death penalty. As such, there are no official channels for these populations to access rehabilitation and health services. Only 19 percent of those living with HIV/AIDS are in treatment and in only 13 percent is the disease virally suppressed (whereas the Joint United Nations Programme on HIV and AIDS [UNAIDS] target is 90 percent in both cases). In the early 2000s, the Alaei brothers developed a "triangular" approach to dealing with the epidemic as they worked in the three fields of sexually transmitted infections (STIs), HIV/AIDS, and drug-addiction, offering a comprehensive harm-reduction approach, including needles, methadone, condoms, treatment for STIs, antiretroviral therapy, and other medical services for people living with HIV/AIDS in their hometown. Under reformist president Khatami, this approach was met with approval and allowed to expand across several provinces. In particular, while the phenomenon of drug addiction had been flatly denied under Khatami's predecessors, addressing it was now considered "humanitarian," "Islamic," and part of the government's "redefined responsibility toward vulnerable citizens." Once Ahmadinejad replaced Khatami, however, the program was rolled back and the Alaei brothers arrested for allegedly seeking to overthrow the government. They spent two and three years respectively in prison and eventually left Iran to work in the United States. The authors explain the variation in the approach taken by the government as predominantly dependent on the president in office at a given time but point out that it also coincides with whether the Revolutionary Guards or the Ministry of Intelligence is in charge of formulating drug policy. When the former is the case, the approach is rather ideology-driven – criminalizing addiction, enforcing drug bans – when the latter is in charge, the approach – in this particular area of dealing with the social effects of drug addition – is one of relying more on expert counsel.

Picking up on the theme of progressions and regressions in the quality of the rule of law depending on which official or agency is in charge of making relevant policy, Mirjam Künkler in Chapter 9 provides an overview of the tenures of the heads of the judiciary in the post-Khomeini period and of major reform initiatives since. Mahmoud Shahroudi stands out as a head of the judiciary (1999–2009), under whose aegis the most far-reaching reforms were initiated to enhance if not the rule *of* law, then at least the rule *by* law. These included proposals to amend the criminal code and the CCP, and to stipulate precise rights standards for prisoners and those standing trial. His successors, by and large, have failed to pursue similar projects, instead blocking the implementation of his reforms or reversing them altogether. It was also during Shahroudi's tenure that the judiciary enjoyed the greatest degree of independence from the Supreme Leader's office. The last three heads (Larijani, Raisi, and Mohseni-Eje'i) have administered the judiciary essentially as a prolonged arm of the security state.

The next two chapters focus on the rights of particular populations: Iran's ethnic and religious minorities, and workers respectively. Shahin Milani in Chapter 10 notes that Iran's discriminatory policies against religious minorities are rooted in the Islamic Republic's foundational ideology and institutionalized in its constitution. With respect to ethnic minorities, government-sanctioned discrimination has a different quality from that committed against religious minorities. Unlike its approach to religious minorities, the Islamic Republic's ideological framework is not based on racial or ethnic supremacy. In practice, however, ethnic discrimination overlaps with religious discrimination to a large extent because Iran's Sunni citizens are overwhelmingly ethnic minorities as well. Furthermore, when ethnic identity fosters political dissent, ethnicity can also be the basis for invidious state action on its own. Numerous sympathizers of ethnic opposition groups and activists advocating for the rights of ethnic minorities have received harsh sentences, including the death penalty, after trials that do not meet the criteria of due process.

Milani notes that all state institutions are in some ways responsible for the Islamic Republic's discriminatory policies. The intelligence and security apparatus intimidate and arrest members of minority groups, and the judiciary usually issues harsh sentences against them. The executive branch also engages in discriminatory action, such as denying higher education and public sector employment to minorities. The parliament, having passed discriminatory laws, does not hold other state organs accountable for extralegal actions against minorities. Nor has it conducted investigations necessary to determine the extent of discriminatory practices in the country.

Courts have reacted to minority cases in diverse ways, often validating discrimination but in some cases also protecting defendants against rights abuses. Milani suggests that if this diversity in court rulings indicates anything, it is that not all courts are completely in agreement with the government but retain some modicum of political independence. Revolutionary courts tend to be stacked by regimist judges, but some (very few) revolutionary courts have delivered judgments that are sensitive to the plight of religious minorities. In the general courts, minority status tends to matter much less. The bigger picture is, however, that minority cases are often treated as politically sensitive irrespective of the nature of the case and therefore tried in the revolutionary rather than the general courts.

In no other law did the early ideological struggles between different visions of an Islamic economics crystallize more clearly than the labor law. It defined the standoff between the parliament and the Guardian Council throughout the 1980s, which eventually led to the creation of the Expediency Council, arguably the most powerful legislative institution in the Islamic Republic today. In Chapter 11, Stella Morgana recounts why – even though economic justice was one of the three key demands of the revolutionaries in 1979 – workers' rights have not been at the core of the Islamic Republic's social policies, especially from the 1990s onward. She notes that the labor law offers far-reaching exemptions and loopholes that make it possible to circumvent minimum legal standards. Further, from Rafsanjani's neoliberal turn to Rouhani's presidency, a process of labor casualization and job insecurity has gradually – and systematically – undermined workers' rights, exposing them to severe exploitation and failing to provide legal protection. The policies of the different presidents have not been equally detrimental, as the values behind every administration as well as the general economic context profoundly influenced different governments' choices: From Rafsanjani's market-oriented rhetoric to Khatami's participative narrative of civil society, from Ahmadinejad's conservative populism to Rouhani's business-friendly pragmatism. Yet on the whole, one would be hard-pressed to argue that the rule of law goes beyond Tamanaha's second most minimalist definition of formal legality, oscillating between that and the more minimalist notion of mere rule by law.

Chapter 12 examines the rule-of-law effects of the Joint Comprehensive Plan of Action (JCPOA), the multilateral agreement reached between Iran and the five permanent members of the United Nations (UN) Security Council plus Germany in 2015. The JCPOA limited Iran's enrichment activities and implemented enhanced monitoring of the country's nuclear program in exchange for relief from all UN and EU nuclear-related economic and financial sanctions. As a result of the agreement, from "Implementation Day" (January 16, 2016) onward, financial transactions and a whole range of other associated service sectors in Iran were opened up for international trade. These included banking and insurance; oil, gas, and the petrochemical sector; shipping, shipbuilding, and transport sectors; gold, other precious metals, banknotes, and coinage; and software. Some restrictions remained in force, however, including restrictions on the transfer of sensitive goods, arms, and ballistic missiles, as well as restrictive measures against certain listed persons and entities. Faezeh Manteghi and Emad Tabatabaei, two lawyers working in international trade law, recount the many changes undertaken by the Iranian parliament and other institutions to prepare the legal environment for the economic liberalization to come. A prominent strand in the rule-of-law literature holds that creating economic security, ensuing property rights, and creating a safe investment climate can be steps toward achieving more ambitious standards of the rule of law beyond the realm of business. To some extent, the authors suggest, this was achieved in 2016 and 2017, as the state undertook a great number of legal reforms to ensure security and predictability in business and opened up avenues for the expansion of the private sector (and the retreat of parastatal companies) in Iran's key energy sector. (Scholars such as Saïd Amir Arjomand have argued that Iran's accession to the World Trade Organization – to achieve such the significant expansion of the private sector would be a component – would invariably lead to the political demise of the current regime, as this would, in the medium term, withdraw from it its political economic foundation.) The initial expansion of the private sector came to a sudden halt, however, with the unilateral withdrawal of the United States from the agreement and the reactivation of US sanctions. This, the authors suggest, has led the Iranian government to reorient its regulatory framework toward increased trade with China, and, overall, resolidified the state's hold on the economy.

The last two chapters in the volume address areas of the law that are particularly dynamic and multi-faceted, although in the first case this does not render the regulatory regime less repressive. In Chapter 13,

Roozbeh Mirebrahimi and Azadeh Pourzand examine the elaborate censorship apparatus at play with regard to visual arts and culture in Iran. They ask why, while freedom of expression is restricted and the rights of artists are frequently and systematically violated in theory and practice, Iranian artists and writers remain known internationally for their resilience and vibrant creativity, many being thought of as high-end producers of film and the visual arts around the world. The authors show that a multilayered system of monitoring and control mechanisms not only regulates and routinely stifles, but at the same time also promotes art. It is not the case, as it is in many other non-democratic regimes, that particular artists are courted by the regime while others are generally suppressed. Rather, the regime oscillates in its policies toward a given individual, alternating between support and repression. The authors do not argue that this necessarily reflects a deliberate policy. Instead, the practice of oscillation is to some extent the result of the myriad institutions tasked with monitoring arts and culture at all stages of the process. Thus, successfully completing the licensing processes and obtaining official permits does not guarantee freedom from post-expression ordeals with the judiciary. Even when they have obtained all necessary licenses for a given piece, artists and writers live with the legitimate fear of facing heavy criminal charges under the pretext of security crimes such as "promoting propaganda against the Islamic Republic." Depending on who staffs the presidency, there are at times varying degrees of censorship at the level of the Ministry of Culture and Islamic Guidance (MCIG), some of which can be intensified or minimally relaxed within the realm of the authority of the president of the Islamic Republic and his appointed minister. But more serious limitations on the freedom of expression are usually imposed by the Supreme Council of Cultural Revolution (SCCR), the Islamic Revolutionary Guards Corps (IRGC), the Basij (paramilitary organization), the judiciary, and intelligence entities whose control is completely outside the scope of the authority of the president of the country.

The chapter by Shirin Naef, discussing Iran's regulations of Assisted Reproductive Technology (ART), illustrates the dynamism and adaptability of Shi'i fiqh, where socially and scientifically so desired. Iran's regulatory regime regarding ART is uniquely permissive in the Muslim world. Surrogacy and the use of egg and embryo donation are all permitted in Iran, and the Supreme Leader even considers sperm donation permissible, an opinion that places him in the minority of Shi'i religious scholars in this matter. Naef shows that a combination of Iranian state law, Shi'i rulings, and national, medical, and clinical guidelines govern access to ART and related ethical questions, such as the rights of surrogates. In 2003, the Iranian parliament enacted a law allowing the use of embryo donation for treating infertility in Iranian married couples. The law also implicitly recognizes the permissibility of embryo-carrying agreements and surrogacy arrangements. In recent years, surrogacy regulation has enhanced the rights of both parents and surrogates and standardized the processes for issuing birth certificates. Examining "family" as a legal concept, Naef argues that Iranian family beliefs and values play a crucial role in shaping Iran's permissive reproductive policy. The legal production of genealogical continuity and of parenthood are central to these beliefs and values.

In the concluding chapter, Hadi Enayat and Mirjam Künkler address regressions and progressions in the rule of law throughout the history of the Islamic Republic. The authors highlight diversity in quality of the rule of law across different areas of the law, and the struggles that have characterized legal and judicial politics in the post-Khomeini period. They suggest that the early 2000s saw the strongest policies to move from mere rule by law toward formal legality where the law is at least general, prospective, clear, and certain (Tamanaha), but that a significant and unintended side effect of the reformist project was the highlighting of opportunities for reform from within, especially in constitutional and criminal law, which the conservatives successfully closed up in subsequent years.

7 Five Major Challenges to Strengthening the Rule of Law

Many challenges remain toward deepening the rule of law in Iran, and, if anything, they have increased since 2009. A notable improvement regarding the clarification of competencies and increased standards of professionalism took place under the leadership of Mahmoud Shahroudi, head of the judiciary from 1999 to 2009. But, if anything, since his tenure the politicization of the judiciary has returned to the levels of the 1980s (Chapter 9), so have torture and illegal detention (Chapter 3), and the independence of the legal profession has been further undermined (Chapter 5). The period of deepening rule of law in the 2000s was due to no small extent to the burgeoning reformist press which openly addressed corruption, lawlessness, abuses of power, and named state officials acting with impunity. But the period also coincided with the tenure of the only head of the judiciary to date who had been a jurist of outstanding learning and, in his career, relatively independent from the Supreme Leader. Yet, as Chapter 9 documents, many of his initiatives, too, were stifled, most frequently by interference from the Ministry of

Intelligence or the Supreme Leader's Office, or, if implemented, they were later reversed or watered down. Five areas in particular stand out in which severe challenges remain or have reemerged with regard to strengthening the rule of law.

7.1 The Political Subservience of Parts of the Judiciary

The first factor relates to the judiciary's lack of independence, as it is structurally subordinated to the Supreme Leader in several significant ways. First, he appoints the head of the judiciary, who in turn appoints all senior judges and may move and remove any judge.[17]

The internal hierarchy in the judiciary is very strong, an element exacerbated further when the 1989 amendment to the constitution replaced the five-member body at the summit of the institution by just one person. The head of the judiciary became the "judge of the judges" with broad powers: he appoints, promotes, suspends, and dismisses judges. He can transfer and dismiss judges after consultation with the prosecutor general and the head of the Supreme Court, both of whom he appoints.

The other branches of power cannot exercise any checks on the judiciary. The parliament and the presidency have no "power of interpellation" over the head of the judiciary or any official of the judiciary. Even though the parliament has a commission (the so-called Article 90 commission) to which citizens may report their grievances about members of the judiciary (as well as any other state institution), the committee has no power to sanction or even to force the judiciary to be accountable.[18] Neither can the executive exercise any checks on the judiciary, as the power and competencies of the minister of justice are stipulated by the head of the judiciary (see Section 5.2).

Partly connected to the subservience of the judiciary to the Supreme Leader are widespread allegations of corruption and bribery.[19] Ebrahim

---

[17] The Supreme Leader also has the power to create or renew special tribunals, as, for example, the Special Court for Economic Corruption, a subbranch of the revolutionary court. The Supreme Leader regularly renews the existence of this court, as last undertaken in September 2020.

[18] The Article 90 Commission of Parliament is constitutionally mandated to address private complaints against the three branches of power. The commission has no effective powers of enforcement but has been used to some effect to bring grievances to light. For an account, see Human Rights Watch (2004: 60–63).

[19] Iran ranks 149th among 180 countries in Transparency International's Corruption Perceptions Index, with a score of 25 out of 100, indicating that the Islamic Republic is among the most corrupt countries in the world. By comparison, the average score of countries in the Middle East is 39.

Raisi, head of the judiciary from 2019 till 2021, embarked on an elaborate program of "judicial development" to address them. His fight against corruption, however, targeted in particular affiliates of his political opponents rather than corrupt officials in general (Chapter 9).

Complaints against judges may be reported to the DCJ and the mentioned Article 90 Commission of Parliament. According to the judiciary, on average 3,000 complaints are filed against judges each year, and judges are regularly dismissed. In 2017, different sources put the number of dismissed judges at between 60 and 170. In June 2020, a spokesperson for the judiciary indicated that "the number of offenders within the judiciary, especially in the judges' community, is low, and less than one percent [equivalent to less than about 110 per year]."[20] Judges were dismissed due to either economic or moral violations.

In lawsuits where the government has a role, processes are perceived to be highly biased toward the state. Occasionally, lawyers have even been accused of "propaganda against the regime" when pointing out mistakes or inconsistencies in the judicial procedures. The accusations reveal that the judiciary itself is perceived by hardliners as a branch of the state and to criticize its procedures is to criticize the Islamic regime at large. With such a mindset, any independence of the judiciary is impossible to achieve. Characteristically, the text of the judges' oath also includes a pledge of allegiance to the *velāyat-e faqih* (guardianship of the Islamic jurist).

At the same time, a differentiation is called for between the political courts on the one hand (the revolutionary and special courts) and the regular courts on the other. When processes take place in the latter courts without the direct interests of any employee, official, or government department at stake, the judiciary has a reputation of broadly following the letter of the law.

7.2 The Death Penalty, Grievous Bodily Harm, Torture, and Prison Conditions

The Islamization of criminal law led to the passing of the Law of Qesās in 1982, which provided that in cases of violent crime, families of the victims could demand retribution, up to and including death (see Chapter 3). Punishments prescribed in these laws include public floggings, amputations, and blinding.

Islamic penal law also means that the age of criminal responsibility is tied to maturity (*bolugh*), which is 8 ¾ years (nine lunar years) for

---

[20] See www.mehrnews.com/news/4945327/آمار دقیق قضات متخلف از زبان سخنگوی قوه قضاییه, accessed January 21, 2021.

girls and 14 ½ years (fifteen lunar years) for boys. After reaching *bolugh*, children were treated until recently as bearing adult criminal responsibility and were eligible for all punishments, including death. The 2013 Penal Code retained these ages in Article 146, but in Article 90 allowed for the factor of mental maturity to play a role in the sentencing. Critics point out that this has merely shifted the issue to ʿ*aql*, which was already necessary for criminal responsibility, irrespective of age.

The low age of criminal responsibility explains why Iran leads the world in harsh punishment and executions of minors – because, in the eyes of Iranian law, girls between 8 ¾ and 18 and boys between 14 ½ and 18 are not juveniles, but adults. In 2013, eleven individuals were executed for crimes committed while they were under 18, in 2014, thirteen, and in 2019, four. In 2020, Iran passed a law to protect children and adolescents, but it failed to change the age of criminal responsibility.

Executions are usually carried out by hanging, but in few cases also by firing squad. The sentence of death by stoning, reserved for adulterers, is still on the books. It has not been officially carried out since 2003 when the then head of the judiciary placed on it a moratorium in exchange for negotiations over sanctions relief with the EU, but there are several reports of judges defying the moratorium and enforcing stoning based on Article 170 of the constitution, according to which they must not enact directives that are contrary to Islamic law.

Iran has consistently the highest number of executions of any country proportional to its population.[21] Executions have risen from the early 2000s until 2015,[22] then stagnated for five years around 300–500 per year (largely due to changes in sentencing for drug users and amnesties granted during the pandemic) and have risen again from 2021 to 2023. A total of 333 people were executed in 2021, 582 in 2022, and more than 800 in 2023.[23]

Verdicts are often based on "confessions" extracted during interrogations, even though forced confessions are not admissible according to Islamic law. Proceedings that violate due process also include summary trials and show trials. The latter often include televised confessions.

Once those convicted are imprisoned, they are often denied access to essential medical care, and not few prisoners have lost vital organs, such as a kidney, as a result.

---

[21] See https://iranhr.net/fa/articles/4311 accessed January 4, 2023.
[22] The country executed ninety-four individuals in 2005, 402 in 2009, 676 in 2011, 753 in 2014, and 977 in 2015. See https://iranhr.net/en/reports/5 (accessed January 21, 2021) and Report of the Special Rapporteur on the situation of human rights in the Islamic Republic of Iran, Ahmed Shaheed, March 12, 2015.
[23] See World Coalition against the Death Penalty, *Annual Report on Iran*.

Sentences that include grievous bodily harm are not only a consequence of Iran's criminal law, which, together with the CCP in fact frequently offers ways out of strictly applying corporal punishments, but rather of the principle of ʿelm-e qāzi, which, according to Iran's constitution (Article 167), allows judges to apply their own reasoning or insight in the absence of codified law. In practice, judges often invoke ʿelm-e qāzi even where the law is clearly applicable and unambivalent in its wording. Fraser Fujinaga (2013: 274), who has produced one of the most thorough accounts of the theory and application of criminal law in the Islamic Republic to date, identified ʿelm-e qāzi "as probably the greatest obstacle to lenience in hudud … judges use it with utmost discretion, interpreting it in many cases as licence to disregard legal strictures including those governing evidence. Several, even Supreme Court judges, characterize ʿelm as ineffable intuition which resides only in the judge's mind and therefore cannot be questioned by anyone." Thus, for example, judges have based their reasoning on pretrial confessions, which are de jure inadmissible in court and therefore invalid, claiming these gave them "insight" into the crimes. Fraser Fujinaga (2013: 274) notes that "[m]ost of the death and amputation sentences observed throughout [my study] would have been impossible without ʿelm, because ʿelm was used to overcome the ordinary strictures of the law such as the invalidity of pre-trial confession or the ability of repentance to preclude the hadd in certain circumstances."

7.3   Lack of Independence of the Legal Profession

The Iranian bar associations have been in a long battle with the regime to (re)establish their independence, a battle they eventually lost in 2023. In 1997, the Central Bar Association was for the first time since the revolution allowed to hold internal elections again and to aim at establishing its autonomy, but the regime soon interfered to only permit handpicked candidates. In 2000, following an addendum (Article 187) to the five-year economic development plan (in full: the Third Economic, Social and Cultural Development Plan), which otherwise had no bearing on judicial matters, the judiciary established its own accreditation system for lawyers. This new mechanism, through the newly established Center for the Affairs of Advisors, Judges, and Experts of the Judiciary (Markaz-e omur-e mushāvirān, vokalā va kārshenāsān-e qovveh-ye qazāʾiya), should have ceased to exist when the relevant law expired in 2005, but the judiciary retained the mechanism regardless and further increased the number of legal advisors trained and accredited on the basis of Article 187. De facto, the new accreditation process was instituted for graduates of the religious seminaries and students of the social sciences who did not have sufficient legal training to pass the Bar, as well as for law graduates who had failed to pass it. The so-called Article 187 legal advisors need to seek reaccreditation with the judiciary every year and are thus highly dependent on their superiors. While the bar associations have a rigorous recruitment and examination scheme, the Art. 187 legal advisors merely undergo a six-month training program designed by the judiciary, then pass an exam and take an oath. They may file claims and defend cases in any court throughout the country.

By contrast, in the bars' accreditation process, candidates need to be at least 25 years of age; be a regular resident of the location for which the license is applied for; have a clear record and a reputation for honesty and integrity; have completed legal studies in one of the Iranian or foreign recognized universities; have rendered legal services for at least eighteen months under the supervision of a professional lawyer approved for such purpose by the Bar; and have successfully passed the Bar examinations.

Beside the creation of a parallel accreditation system, a draft law of 2023 (which had been in the making since the early 2010s and became a battleground between the parliament and the Guardian Council) would force the bar associations into "supervision" by the Ministry of Economy and Finance, with the ministry taking over all of the bars' functions, most importantly the accreditation of lawyers. If approved by the Guardian Council, the law will transform the bar associations into an arm of the government rather than independent, self-governing associations that protect the rights and interests of Iranian lawyers, and, by extension, Iranian citizens.

Beyond the establishment of the parallel accreditation process and the incorporation of the bar associations into a governmental ministry, lawyers have seen numerous obstacles placed in their path, especially when they represent those accused of political crimes. Judges can refuse to permit individual lawyers entry into court houses and access to relevant files. When lawyers are given access at all to the results of the investigation in criminal cases, it is often so late that they have little time to thoroughly prepare the defense. What is more, lawyers are repeatedly arrested and occasionally accused of the same charges against which they defend their clients.[24]

---

[24] Among the most prominent are Mohammad Najafi, Nasrin Sotoudeh, Payam Derafshan, Qasem Shole Sadi, Arash Keikhosravi, Masoud Javadieh, and Amirsalar Davoodi.

7.4 The Revolutionary Courts and the 2016 Political Crimes Act

Most political cases are dealt with in the revolutionary courts. The courts are de jure overseen by the judiciary, but in practice, many of their personnel come from the Intelligence Ministry, the Revolutionary Guard Corps, and other security institutions. Despite repeated attempts by the judiciary to assert exclusive control over all detention and incarceration facilities in the country (see Chapter 9), political prisoners are usually held in detention centers run by the Revolutionary Guard Corps or the Intelligence Ministry and thus beyond the judiciary's control.

Typical crimes dealt with in the revolutionary courts are *mohārebeh* (war against God and the state), *baghy* (armed insurrection against the government), and insulting the leadership, as well as drug-related crimes.

The relevant crimes, as named in Iran's Islamic Penal Code (IPC), are so vaguely worded that they can often be very broadly interpreted. For example, the crime of "corruption on earth" (*efsād-e fel 'arz*) includes "spreading lies," "aiding and abetting in corruption and prostitution," and "felony against the bodily entity of the people." The Penal Code also prohibits "acts of propaganda" against the Islamic Republic, "espionage," and "collusion" with foreign states. How precisely these must be proven is not specified, while the penalty for such crimes may be death.

An amended CCP of 2015 further undermined the rights of those accused of national security crimes, when it withdrew (in Article 48) their right to choose their own lawyer, directly contravening the constitutional guarantee of legal representation, as well as the 2004 Law to Respect Legitimate Freedoms and Citizen Rights.[25] This means that those potentially facing the death penalty no longer have recourse to their own defense counsel during the crucial pre-trial investigation. Evidence may be fabricated without the accused being able to effectively challenge it, and interrogations may take place without a third party ensuring the accused are fully aware of their rights.

Political crimes in general are dealt with in the revolutionary courts, but it was not until the Political Crimes Act of 2016 that such crimes were clearly defined. Up until that point officials frequently claimed that there were "no political prisoners" in Iran. This was because citizens

---

[25] Although criticized as a severe blow to the right of defendants in criminal proceedings, similar provisions had already existed beforehand in a note to Article 128 of the 1999 CCP, which was routinely employed by prosecutors to exclude defense lawyers from the investigative stage of proceedings. As discussed in Chapter 9, Head of the Judiciary Shahroudi issued a decree insisting that the accused have access to a lawyer from the time of arrest. The 2004 Law to Respect Legitimate Freedoms and Citizen Rights reiterated this right.

targeted by the state for political reasons were instead frequently charged with crimes against "national security."[26]

For many years, activists and opposition figures had argued that peaceful opposition to the regime must be protected by the law and shielded against accusations of violations of either Islam or national security. The reformist Islamic legal scholar Mohsen Kadivar (2021) argued that the dominant view in Shi'i Islamic law neglects the possibility of legitimate political opposition by conceptualizing opposition as either insurgency (*baghy*) or "warring against god" (*mohārebeh*). Even Shahroudi had acknowledged in a 1996 article that the two concepts of *baghy* and *mohārebeh* do not include peaceful political opposition, and that the latter could not be subsumed under the former. After many years of lobbying, which began during the Khatami years and was driven by both human rights and fiqhi approaches to the issue, the Political Crimes Act was passed in 2016 in order to establish a legitimate category of a political crime as any act "against the administration, political bodies and domestic and foreign policies and with the aim of reforming the country's affairs." This covers insults toward any of the heads of the three branches of power, members of the parliament, the chairman of the Expediency Council, members of the Guardian Council, vice presidents, ministers, and members of the Assembly of Experts. The same law qualifies as a political crime any message in a publication, or any gatherings or activities by political parties, civil society organizations, trade unions, and Islamic associations that violate "the legitimate freedoms of others" or engage in "slander, defamation and spreading rumors."

The 2016 Political Crimes Act also reiterates the right of those accused of political crimes to remain "separate from ordinary criminals during detention and imprisonment." Further, political prisoners have the right to not be extradited (similar to the Extradition Act of 1961, Paragraph 2 of Article 8), are exempt from wearing prison uniforms, and must not be placed in solitary confinement (except in tightly defined cases of exceptions in which case solitary confinement must not exceed fifteen days). They have the right to meet and correspond with first-degree relatives during detention, and the right to access books, journals, radio, and television during detention.[27] The formulation of the political crimes act was a major breakthrough as it differentiated political crimes from security and religious crimes, and accorded those found guilty of political crimes more rights than other criminals.

---

[26] See https://iranwire.com/en/features/7235 accessed January 16, 2021.
[27] Ahmad Momeni Rad, a spokesman for the Press and Political Crimes Jury, speaking to Tasnim News Agency on Monday, October 12, 2019.

7.5 Lengthy Litigation Timelines

A fifth aspect undermining the rule of law has been the slowness of the judicial administration in dealing with cases. This is mainly due to three factors.

First, there is a high level of cases per capita in Iran. On the one hand, this attests to the fact that Iranians do have some level of trust in the ability of courts to settle their disputes and it supports those who argue that while the revolutionary courts are considered corrupt and arbitrary, the general courts enjoy some respect among the public. According to the head of the judiciary, there were between 15 and 20 million cases in the judiciary in 2020, with 46 percent of court cases ending at the first instance. Considering that only few cases involve children, more than a quarter of Iranians are believed to be involved in litigation at any given time. The number, however, also needs to be read against the background of long litigation timelines which mean even relatively simple court cases may drag on for three to seven years. Documentation during the 2000s suggests that while most civil cases take one to two years, some last as long as twelve years when moving through all appeals procedures. Data from 2008 suggests that in that year 8–9 million new cases were brought to the courts. National media in the same year claimed that 20 million Iranians were in court in any given year, while judges only reviewed and issued verdicts of between 100 and 120 cases each month.[28]

Second, there is a systematic shortage of judges. As of 2020, about 11,000 judges were employed in the judiciary, whereas twice the amount are needed. Overall, about 88,000 employees work in the judiciary. The shortage of judges is partly explained by the relatively low salaries they receive. Average judges (not at the highest courts) are paid between 8 and 20 million tomans a month (between USD 350 and 870).

Third, even though there is a law on mandatory representation in courts, this law is not consistently implemented, with the consequence that ordinary citizens rather than professionals often prepare the paperwork used in lawsuits, frequently making procedural and bureaucratic mistakes. Such mistakes may take months to resolve and further extend the overall time cases take until closure.

Ebrahim Raisi, who assumed the position of head of the judiciary in the fall of 2019, addressed the issue of long litigation timelines in

---

[28] Data from the deputy justice minister, November 8, 2008, cited in Maranlou (2015: 102).

January 2020 by reminding judicial officials of Article 3 of the CCP, according to which "judicial authorities must, with impartiality and complete independence, investigate the charges attributed to persons, take appropriate action and decide as soon as possible and refrain from any action that interferes with or prolongs the criminal proceedings." He instructed judicial officials take note of Clause D of Paragraph 113 of the Sixth Development Plan Law, which outlines specific time limits for the processing of cases.

8   Where to in the Rule of Law in Iran?

Much remains to be researched regarding the rule of law in Iran, especially considering those spheres of the law which have seldom been subjected to scrutiny in legal and sociolegal studies, such as the regulation of censorships and the arts, the role of women advisory judges, alternative dispute-resolution mechanisms including arbitration and mediation councils, and more generally the work and quality of lower-level courts. When doing so, it will be important both to connect Iran to the relevant literature in comparative rule-of-law studies and to represent the nuances of local rule-of-law debates and initiatives. Studies tend to portray the latter as purely a matter of interest to civil society and reformist politics, with the judiciary and the Guardian Council consistently blocking all reform proposals, but the picture is far more complex. Even inside the Iranian judiciary fierce disagreements exist over the interpretation of Islamic legal principles, their application, and their openness to adaptation in changing social circumstances (see Chapter 9). Opinions among Islamic law scholars regarding the rule of law in Islamic law are as diverse and diverging as they are among secular law scholars regarding the rule of law in secular law, and numerous law journals affiliated with Iran's clerical seminaries attest to the diversity and vibrancy of the debate. As Mohsen Kadivar, the country's leading voice for reform within the Islamic legal tradition, has established, Islamic legal principles can be reinterpreted and their application designed in ways that are consistent with the rule of law (Kadivar 2021), and, as chapters in this book show, Mahmoud Shahroudi, as head of the judiciary in the 2000s, took important steps in this direction. But as the analyses across different areas of law in this book also document, voices resistant to such adaptations usually win. That is, they win the power struggles, but as many Iranians would argue, they have already lost the debate.

Bibliography

Adamiyat, Fereydun. *Andishe Tarāqi va Hokumate Qanun: 'Asr-e Sepāhsalar* Tehran: Sherkat-e Sehāmi-ye Enteshārāt-e Ḫwārazmi, 1963.

Amanat, Abbas. Constitutional Revolution i. Intellectual background. *Encyclopædia Iranica*, vol. VI, Fasc. 2, 1992/2011, pp. 163–176.

Ansari, Masud and Mohammad 'Ali Taheri. *Dāneshnāmah-ye hoquq-e khosusi* (3 vols.), Tehran: Mehrāb-e Fekr, 2009.

Arjomand, Saïd Amir. *The Turban for the Crown: The Islamic Revolution in Iran*, Oxford: Oxford University Press, 1988.

Böckenförde, Ernst-Wolfgang. "Fundamental Rights: Theory and Interpretation [1974]," in Ernst-Wolfgang Böckenförde, *Constitutional and Political Theory: Selected Writings*. Oxford University Press, 2017, pp. 266–289.

Böckenförde, Ernst-Wolfgang. "The Origin and Development of the Concept of the Rechtsstaat [1969]," in Ernst-Wolfgang Böckenförde, *State, Society and Liberty*, Berg Publishers, 1991, pp. 47–70.

Cumaraswamy, Dato Param. *Report of the UN Special Rapporteur on the independence of judges and lawyers*, U.N. Doc. E/CN.4/2001/65, February 1, 2001.

Enayat, Hadi. *Law, State and Society in Modern Iran: Constitutionalism, Autocracy and Legal Reform 1906–1941*, London: Palgrave Macmillan, 2011.

Fraser Fujinaga, Antonia. *Life and Limb. Irreversible hadd penalties in Iranian criminal courts and opportunities to avoid them*. Doctoral Dissertation, Islamic Studies, University of Edinburgh, 2013.

Fraser Fujinaga, Antonia. "Islamic Law in Post-Revolutionary Iran," in Anver M. Emon and Rumee Ahmed (eds.), *The Oxford Handbook of Islamic Law*. Oxford: Oxford University Press, 2016.

Gazette of the Revolutionary Council, No. 10018, 25/4/1358 (June 1979).

Ghaemi, Hadi. "The Islamic Judiciary," in *The Iran Primer*. Washington, DC: United States Institute of Peace, 2010.

Hāshemi, Mohammad. *Hoquq-e asāsi-ye jomhuri-ye eslāmi-ye Irān* ("Iranian Constitutional Law"), Vols. I and II, Tehran: Mizan Publishers, 1382–1383 (2002–2003).

Hirschl, Ran. *Towards Juristocracy: The Origins and Consequentialism of the New Constitutionalism*, Boston, MA: Harvard University Press, 2004.

Human Rights Watch, *"Like the Dead in Their Coffins": Torture, Detention, and the Crushing of Dissent in Iran*, Vol. 16, No. 2(E), June 2004.

Iran Bar Association News. *Ejrā-yi ahkāmi mesl-e sangsār bāyad banā bar salāhdid-e riasat-e qovv-e qazā'iyya anjām shavad*. 21 Khordād 1386 (21 June 2007).

Jalali, Mohammad and Hamida Saeedi Roshan. "Nefash-e divān-e 'edālat-e edāreh-ye dar siānat az qanun-e asāsi," *The Judiciary's Law Journal*, Vol. 80 (94), 2016/1395, pp. 117–140.

Jalali-Karveh, Mahmoud. "Theory and Practice of Arbitration as a Peaceful Means of Dispute Settlement in the Iranian Legal System," in Hans-Jörg Albrecht, Jan- Michael Simon, Hassan Rezaei, Holger-C. Rohne, and Ernesto Kiza (eds.), *Conflicts and Conflict Resolution in Middle Eastern Societies – Between Tradition and Modernity*, Berlin: Duncker & Humblot, 2006, pp. 429–446.

Kadivar, Mohsen. *Human Rights and Reformist Islam*, Edinburgh: Edinburgh University Press, 2021.

Khomeini, Ruhollah Mousavi. *The Velāyat-e Faqih* (Governance of the Jurist) or *Islamic Government*, The Institute for Compilation and Publication of Imam Khomeini's Works (International Affairs Division). Translator and Annotator: Hamid Algar. Tehran, Islamic Republic of Iran, 1971.

Khomeini, Ruhollah Mousavi. *Sahifeh-ye Nūr*, vol. 20, pp. 170f. Reprinted in Persian and translated into English by the Iran Data Portal: https://irandataportal.syr.edu/admonition-to-ayatollah-khamenei-on-the-limits-of-the-valiye-faqihs-authority-and-the-course-of-its-stages.

Krygier, Martin. "Rule of Law," in Michel Rosenfeld and András Sajó (eds.), *Oxford Handbook of Comparative Constitutional Law*, Oxford: Oxford University Press, 2012, pp. 233–249.

Künkler, Mirjam. "The Special Court of the Clergy (dādgāh-e vīzhe-ye rūḥānīyat) and the Repression of Dissident Clergy in Iran," in Said Amir Arjomand and Nathan Brown (eds.), *The Rule of Law, Islam, and Constitutional Politics in Egypt and Iran*, Albany: SUNY Press, 2012, pp. 57–100.

Künkler, Mirjam. "Rule of Law or Rule by Law? Iran's Bar Association as a Pawn in Islamic–Republican Contestations," in Silvia Tellenbach and Thoralf Hanstein (eds.), *Beiträge zum Islamischen Recht XII*. Reihe: Leipziger Beiträge zur Orientforschung, 2017, pp. 133–153.

Mansouri Nia, Zainab. "*Aṣle hākemiyat-e qānun dar sāzmānhā-ye 'edāre dar partaw ārā'-e divan-e adālat-e 'edāri*" [The Principle of the Rule of Law in Administrative Organizations in the Light of the Opinions of the Administrative Justice Court]," *Scientific and Legal Quarterly Journal of Law*, Vol. 5 (17), spring 2021.

Maranlou, Sahar. *Access to Justice in Iran: Women, Perceptions, and Reality*, Cambridge: Cambridge University Press, 2015.

Marin, Soudabeh. "La Réception Mitigée des Codifications Napoléoniennes en Iran (1911–1935)," *Droit et Cultures (Jus et le Code Civil)*, Vol. 48 (2), 2004, pp. 107–131.

Mehrpour, Hossein. "The Islamic Concept of Political Crime and the Jury in Iran," *Islamic Studies on Human Rights and Democracy*, Vol. 2 (2), 2019, pp. 21–32.

Meierhenrich, Jens. "Rechtsstaat versus the Rule of Law," in Jens Meierhenrich and Martin Loughlin (eds.), *The Cambridge Companion to the Rule of Law*, Cambridge: Cambridge University Press, 2021a, pp. 39–67.

Meierhenrich, Jens. "What the Rule of Law Is ... and Is Not," in Jens Meierhenrich and Martin Loughlin (eds.), *The Cambridge Companion to the Rule of Law*, Cambridge: Cambridge University Press, 2021b, pp. 569–621.

Meierhenrich, Jens and Martin Loughlin (eds.). *The Cambridge Companion to the Rule of Law*, Cambridge: Cambridge University Press, 2021.

Najafi, A. "Jaygāh-ye kānun-e vukalā-ye dādgostarī va vakīl dar jāmi'a-ye ḥoquqī va-qānun-e ā'īn-e dādrasī-ye kayfarī-ye Irān," in, Ḥ. Gholāmī (ed.), *'Olum-e jināyī-ye taṭbīqī dar partu-ye hamkārīhā-ye bain al-milalī. Majmu'a-ye maqālāt-e nikudāsht-e doktor-e Sīlvīyā-ye Tillinbākh*, Tehran: Mizan Legal Foundation, 2017, pp. 458–478.

Rahmani, Tamineh and Nader Mirzadeh Kooshahi. "Introduction to Iran's Judicial System," *Journal of Law, Policy and Globalization*, Vol. 45, 2016, p. 47.

Randjbar-Daemi, Siavush. "Building the Islamic State: The Draft Constitution of 1979 Reconsidered," *Iranian Studies*, Vol. 46 (4), 2013, pp. 641–663.

Saffari, Saïd. "The Legitimation of the Clergy's Right to Rule in the Iranian Constitution of 1979," *British Journal of Middle Eastern Studies*, Vol. 20 (1), 1993, pp. 64–82.

Salehi Taeblo, Feizolla, Manoucher Tavassoli Naini, and Mohamad Mahdi Ghamami. "Defendant's Rights in the Iranian High Disciplinary Court of Judges and Human Rights Instruments," *Criminal Law Research*, Vol. 10 (2), Winter 2020, pp. 113–136.

Sangri, Koresh Astvar. "Siānat az āzādihā dar ārāye divān-e ʿedālat-e ʿedāri [Protection of Freedoms in the Decisions of the Court of Supreme Administrative]," *Quarterly Journal of Public Law Essays*, Vol. 1 (1), summer 2017.

Shahroudi, Mahmud Hashemi. *Bāyestehāye Feqh-e Jazā'*, Tehran: Nashr-e Mizan, 1378 AP (1999/2000).

Shahroudi, Mahmud Hashemi. "Who is a *muhārib* and what is *muhāraba?*" *Fiqh ahl al-bayt Quarterly Journal*, Qom, Vols. 11–12, fall and winter 1996, pp. 143–200; and Vol. 13, spring 1997, pp. 3–82.

Shklar, Judith N. "Political Theory and the Rule of Law," in Allan C. Hutchinson and Patrick Monahan (eds.), *The Rule of Law: Ideal or Ideology?* Toronto: Carswell, 1987, pp. 1–16.

Special Rapporteur on the situation of human rights in the Islamic Republic of Iran, Ahmed Shaheed, Report of 12 March 2015.

Tabari, Keyvan. "The Rule of Law and the Politics of Reform in Post-Revolutionary Iran," *International Sociology*, Vol. 18 (1), 2003, pp. 96–113.

Tamanaha, Brian Z. *On the Rule of Law: History, Politics, Theory*, New York: Cambridge University Press, 2004.

Tavassolian, Nargess. *The Future of Iran: Judicial Reform*, Legatum Institute, 2012.

Taylor, Charles. "What Is a 'Social Imaginary'?," in Dilip Parameshwar Gaonkar, Jane Kramer, Benjamin Lee, and Michael Warner (eds.), *Modern Social Imaginaries*. New York: Duke University Press, 2004, pp. 23–30. https://doi.org/10.1515/9780822385806-004.

WJP (World Justice Project). *Rule of Law Index 2020*, Washington, DC: World Justice Project, 2020.

World Coalition against the Death Penalty. *Annual Report on the Death Penalty in Iran*. Multiple years. https://worldcoalition.org/.

Zubaida, Sami. *Law and Power in the Islamic World*, London: I. B. Tauris, 2000.

2 The Islamic Penal Code of 2013
Traditions and Innovations*

Silvia Tellenbach

1 Introduction

In the summer of 2013, a new Penal Code came into force in Iran. It is already the third reform since the establishment of the Islamic Republic in 1979. After the revolution, the Penal Code of 1926 in the amended version of 1973 was abolished because it had been strongly influenced by French law and, according to Article 4 of the new 1979 constitution, all law had to be in line with Islamic criteria. In 1982 and 1983, four separate laws came into force that were to function together as a Penal Code (Tellenbach 1989). The first of these laid down general principles (the "general part") that continued to be influenced by Western law. The other laws followed the categories of Islamic criminal law that are characterized by the types of punishment provided for offences, namely *hadd* (pl. *hodud*), *qesās*, *diyeh* (pl. *diyāt*), and *ta'zir* (pl. *ta'zirāt*). *Hodud* (corporal) punishments apply to the most egregious offences (including, for example, enmity against God, corruption on earth, rebellion, theft, sex outside marriage, and the consumption of alcohol); *qesās* are punishments in retaliation for homicide and bodily injury; *diyeh* refers to blood money; and *ta'zirāt*, which apply in the vast majority of criminal cases, are discretionary punishments originally laid down by a judge but today set out in law. While most of the *hodud* are considered to be punishments for crimes against God, *ta'zirāt* are thought of as punishments for behavior that is regarded as worth punishing according to the circumstances of a certain time and place in the frame of general Islamic principles.

The structure of Iranian criminal law reflecting these types of punishments was more or less retained in the Islamic Penal Code (IPC) of 1991/1996 and the IPC of 2013. The latter, which came into force after

---

* In memory of Professor Dr. Mansour Rahmdel, Tehran, whose life was cut short by COVID-19 at the age of 51 on May 2, 2021.

many years of debate, comprises 728 articles in four books, namely Book I: *General Part*; Book II: *Hodud*; Book III: *Qesās*; Book IV: *Diyāt*. Book I was drafted by the Office for Drafting Judicial Bills (Edāreh-ye tadvin-e lawā'eh-e qovveh-ye qazā'iye), which is part of the judiciary. In addition, professors from Iran's faculties of law familiar with the newest developments in international and foreign law, particularly in French law, were consulted. Books II–IV, on *hodud*, *qesās*, and *diyāt*, were drafted at the Center for Studies of Fiqh (Markaz-e tahqiqāt-e fiqhī) in Qom. The 1996 fifth book however – on offences to be punished under the category of *ta'zirāt* – remained in force and was not replaced by a new version.

This chapter analyzes some characteristic features of the new 2013 code, particularly with regard to their sources and their effects.

2   General Part

Book I refers to general concepts that may play a role in all offences, for example territorial jurisdiction, attempt, co-perpetration, and accessoryship. Islamic law historically does not recognize principles corresponding to these general concepts, but instead foresees special regulations for every category of offences and punishments. Thus, the general part of the Iranian IPC has, strictly speaking, no roots in Islamic law, and as a consequence every provision has to be examined as to whether the IPC prescribes that it has to be applied to all offences or only to *ta'zir* offences (i.e., the crimes contained in Book V that are neither punished by a *hadd* nor *qesās* or *diyeh* penalties). This may be expressed clearly in Book I or there may be special provisions for *hodud*, *qesās*, or *diyāt* in one of the other books.

2.1   *The Principle of Legality*

One of the core questions of criminal law relates to the principle of legality (Tellenbach 2013), that is, the idea that an accused may not be prosecuted for an act that has not beforehand been declared a crime in that jurisdiction. It is not only recognized in Western law, but contemporary Islamic jurists also recognize its validity based on verses 17/15 and 65/7 of the Qur'an. According to Article 2 of the IPC, every action or omission for which a punishment is foreseen in the law is regarded as an offence. Based on Article 36 of the constitution, Article 12 of the IPC reads as follows: "Imposing and executing a punishment or security and correctional measures (*eqdām-e ta'mini va tarbiati*) shall be carried out by a competent court and in accordance with the law and subject

The Islamic Penal Code of 2013

to conditions and requirements specified in the law."[1] Furthermore, according to Article 13 of the IPC, a sentence of punishment or security and correctional measures must not exceed the type or extent of the sanction provided by the law.

In spite of these provisions, there are certain problems regarding the principle of legality. They do not result from the *ta'zirāt* offences that originally caused concern because of their vagueness. This vagueness is no longer an issue as offences and punishments of the category of *ta'zirāt* must be specified in the law today (Article 18 IPC). But there is a tension between, on the one hand, Articles 36, 166, and 169 of the constitution that provide for the principles of legality and nonretroactivity, and, on the other, Article 167, which reads as follows:

> The judge is bound to endeavor to judge each case on the basis of the codified law. In case of the absence of any such law, he has to deliver his judgement on the basis of authoritative Islamic sources and authentic fatwas. He, on the pretext of the silence of or deficiency of law in the matter, or its brevity or contradictory nature, cannot refrain from admitting and examining cases and delivering his judgement.[2]

It had always been a matter of scholarly debate whether this rule applies only to cases of civil law, whether it is only applicable to the interpretation of codified legal provisions, and whether it can actually be the basis for offences and punishments not provided for in the codified law. There were, however, some laws that led to the conclusion that Article 167 of the constitution allowed the judge to punish a person without referring to the basis of a law, for example Article 214 in the Code of Criminal Procedure (CCP) of 1999. The IPC of 2013 brought this debate to an end with Article 220, which is contained in the second book, on *hadd* punishments. This article states: "Regarding the *hadd* punishments that are not mentioned in this law, article one hundred and sixty-seven (167) of the Islamic Republic of Iran's Constitution shall be applicable."

This is clarification of the fact that in the domain of *hodud* punishments (but only in this category), the judge may punish conduct that, in authoritative sources and fatwas, is regarded an offence to be punished with a *hadd* punishment even if it is not mentioned in Iranian codified law. This may be relevant in the case of apostasy. In classical Shi'i law, male apostates have to be sentenced to death and female apostates to imprisonment, which will only end when they convert to Islam again.

---

[1] For the English translation of this article and the following articles of the Islamic Penal Code of 2013, see https://iranhrdc.org/english-translation-of-books-i-ii-of-the-new-islamic-penal-code/#2 accessed October 4, 2020.
[2] See www.iranonline.com/iran/iran-info/government/constitution.html accessed November 17, 2016.

Though apostasy is not mentioned in the IPC, a judge may refer to Article 167 of the constitution to rule it a punishable offense.

2.2 Punishment

2.2.1 The System of Sanctions

In the major Islamic schools of law, *hodud*, the harshest corporal punishments, which apply only to a limited number of offences, include stoning, crucifixion, other ways of execution, amputation, flogging, and banishment. In the Shi'i Ja'fari school of jurisprudence, the crimes deserving of these punishments are unlawful sexual intercourse (*zenā'*), homosexual and lesbian acts, procuring, false accusation of unlawful sexual intercourse (*qadhf*), drinking alcohol, theft, enmity against God (*mohārebeh*) and corruption on earth (*efsād-e fel 'arz*), rebellion (*baghy*), and apostasy (*ertedād*).[3]

Retaliation (*qesās*) is the punishment for homicide and bodily injury. It may consist of capital punishment, amputation, or other types of bodily injury akin to the principle of an eye for an eye and a tooth for a tooth. The execution of the judgment depends on the decision of the victim's family. Blood money (*diyeh*) has to be paid for nonintentional homicide and bodily injury and for intentional homicide and bodily injury in cases in which *qesās* is not applied for whatever reason.

All other conduct regarded as punishable, according to the circumstances of time and place, is punished by discretionary punishment/chastisement (*ta'zir*, pl. *ta'zirāt*). *Ta'zirāt* (a concept rarely discussed in Islamic law) refers to the pragmatic decisions of judges, which have to remain, nevertheless, within the general framework of Islamic principles. *Ta'zir* offences constitute the vast majority of all offences. *Ta'zirāt* is defined in Article 18 of the IPC as "a punishment which does not fall under the categories of *hadd*, *qesās*, or *diyeh* and is determined by law for commission of prohibited acts under shari'a or violation of state rules." For this reason, Islamic criminal law is very flexible with regard to offences punished under *ta'zir*. This principle also makes it possible for Iranian *ta'zirāt* law to continue to be influenced by French law and to be open to developments in international law.

The *ta'zirāt* law of 1996 is the main but not the only law to regulate *ta'zirāt* offences. Many other pre- and postrevolutionary laws specify *ta'zirāt* offences,[4] such as, for example, the Anti-Drug Law of 1988, which systematically dealt with drug-related offences to be punished under *ta'zir*.

---

[3] In the Iranian Penal Code, however, apostasy is not mentioned.
[4] The collection of laws by Mohammed Reza Khosravi (1393/2014), containing the provisions of penal law and the law of criminal procedure, totals 1,532 pages.

The IPC contains very detailed regulations on *ta'zir* punishments (Article 19). The only corporal punishment mentioned in Article 19 is flogging, which can be applied in cases of mid-level crimes and petty offences. The most important *ta'zir* punishments are imprisonment and fines, along with complementary punishments, such as being required to undergo vocational training or prohibited from carrying arms. Certain punishments, such as suspended sentences with probation (Articles 46–55) and conditional release (Articles 58–63 IPC), which had already existed for decades, were, in 2013, supplemented by other alternative punishments, such as community service (Article 84 IPC) or even the postponement of a sentence (Articles 40, 41 IPC).

2.2.2   Terminating or Expunging Punishments

The 2013 Penal Code contains detailed provisions of the grounds for terminating or expunging criminal liability. To mention only some of them, pardon is not granted by the president of the Republic but by the Supreme Leader (*rahbar*) himself, upon the proposal of the head of the judiciary, and within the framework of Islamic criteria (Article 96). The implication of the latter is that pardon is always possible for *ta'zir* offences, but only in exceptional cases for *hadd* offences. Furthermore, amnesty may be granted by parliament, but only for *ta'zir* offences (Article 97). Parliamentary amnesty is not rare and has been deployed as a way of avoiding the overcrowding of prisons (see Chapter 7 in this volume). Thus, it is common to grant amnesty to many prisoners on the occasion of high religious holidays (Ghassemi 2013: 122–126). Furthermore, a complainant or private claimant may forgive those *ta'zir* offences classified as "forgivable" (this is not a matter of Islamic law but an influence of European law ["withdrawal of the criminal complaint"]); prosecution or execution will be halted in such cases (Article 100).

Two grounds for terminating or expunging criminal responsibility that stem from classical Islamic law have been inserted into the new 2013 code, namely repentance (*towba*) and the principle of reasonable doubt (*qā'edeh-ye darʾ*).[5] In the field of offences punished by *hodud*, repentance is accepted, with the exception of false accusation of unlawful sexual intercourse (*qadhf*) and with certain limitations in the case of "enmity against God" (*mohārebeh*). The perpetrator has to prove their repentance through self-improvement. In this case, there will be no *hadd* punishment but, where applicable, a *ta'zir* punishment (Article 114 IPC). For serious

---

[5] As for both institutions, see, in detail, Shams et al. (2014: 257–263).

50 *Silvia Tellenbach*

taʿzir offences, repentance will lead to a lighter *taʿzir* punishment; for petty *taʿzir* offences, the punishment will be dropped altogether (Article 115 IPC). In the domain of offences punished with *qesās* or *diyeh*, repentance does not have any effect.

The principle of reasonable doubt (*qāʿede-ye darʾ*) is one of the most important principles in Islamic law. If there is any doubt (*shobheh*), any uncertainty (*tardid*), regarding an element of the offence or the responsibility of the perpetrator, and if this uncertainty or doubt cannot be removed, the element has to be regarded as missing and a *hadd* punishment must not be handed down (Article 120). This principle is similar to the Latin *in dubio pro reo* principle ("when in doubt, rule for the accused" – the presumption of innocence) but, as will be outlined in Section 5, is even broader in the IPC.

3   The Offence

3.1   Offence and Perpetrator

A general principle of most systems of law (not only Islamic law) is that an offence is an offence only if committed by a natural person. The IPC, however, also accepts the punishability of legal entities in the context of private law, following the French model, if its legal representative commits an offence in its name or for its benefit (Article 20).

Primarily, an offence is committed by means of active conduct. But in some cases, an omission may be punishable too, for example the violation of the maintenance obligation toward one's wife (Article 642 *taʿzirāt* law of 1996). Islamic law also recognizes cases of "commission by omission," for example the classic case of the mother who lets her baby starve. Secular contemporary scholars in Iran are often hesitant to recognize "commission by omission,"[6] although it is expressly recognized in the IPC in cases of homicide and bodily injury (Article 295).

Attempt to commit a crime was regulated in the former code only in a very general manner. This may be a consequence of the fact that "attempt" has not been properly worked out in Islamic jurisprudence. In fact, an attempted offence was regarded as a complete *taʿzir* offence, following the principle that the way to a forbidden end is also forbidden. Thus, in the IPC of 1991, an attempt was to be punished if it fulfilled the elements of an offence in itself. If the severely injured victim survived, the perpetrator was punished for complete bodily injury, not for attempted

---

[6] This is also influenced by French criminal law, which is very hesitant to recognize commission by omission.

homicide. The IPC of 2013 has clarified this offence by defining attempt as a criminal act that is started willfully but could not be completed for reasons beyond the control of the perpetrator (Article 122 IPC). The punishment for an attempted offence is now in a fixed relation to the punishment for the completed offence: For example, life imprisonment instead of capital punishment, fixed-term imprisonment instead of life imprisonment, and so on. If the perpetrator abandons the execution of an offence voluntarily, s/he is not punished, except if the act(s) already completed constitute offences in themselves.

As a rule, the text of the IPC refers to a perpetrator acting alone. But, as the code acknowledges, it is possible that more than one perpetrator is involved (Article 125). Additionally, co-perpetration is one of the cases in which the provisions of Book I of the 2013 IPC are not applicable to all offences; on the contrary, special rules apply for offences to be punished under *hadd*, *qesās*, or *diyeh*.

3.2   Responsibility for an Offence

The requirements for criminal responsibility are sound mental health, age of criminal responsibility (*bolugh*), and acting of one's own free will (Articles 140, 149 IPC). A person who commits an offence when asleep or unconscious will not be punished, except if s/he causes this state intentionally knowing that s/he would commit an offence in this situation (Article 153). A person who willingly consumed alcohol, drugs, or psychedelic substances will be punished, except if s/he proves that s/he completely lost the ability to control her/himself. If s/he consumed these substances knowing that s/he would commit an offence or having the intention to do so, s/he will be punished for two offences: For drinking alcohol and for the offence committed under the influence of alcohol (Article 154).

Criminal responsibility is personal; only in exceptional cases can a person be held responsible for the criminal act of another person (Articles 141, 142 IPG), for example, if they are a member of the *'āqeleh* that has to pay blood money in certain cases.[7]

As to responsibility, the question of the responsibility of juveniles and the appropriate sanctions for them has been one of the most intensely discussed topics among legal scholars and legal practitioners in Iran in the last several years. A specific juvenile criminal law was abolished after the revolution. According to the IPC of 1991/1996, young people were regarded as fully responsible as soon as they had

---

[7] A solidarity group according to the law of *diyāt*, consisting of the male relatives who would inherit.

reached the *bolugh*, namely sexual maturity, according to Islamic law. The Iranian Civil Code fixed the age of *bolugh* at 15 lunar years for boys (= approx. 14 years, 7 months in solar years) and 9 lunar years for girls (= approx. 8 years and 9 months). Apart from the fact that that there is such a difference in the age for responsibility for boys and girls, the age is very low for both sexes – all the more as *bolugh* means full responsibility; there was no transitional phase of limited responsibility.[8] In practice, judges could mitigate punishments for juveniles by applying Article 22 of the IPC of 1991, which allows milder punishments, for example if there are special circumstances related to the person of the perpetrator. In general, Iranian lawyers regarded this situation as unfortunate and tried to find solutions that took social and psychological factors into account.

The respective amendments in the new IPC of 2013 are a good example of how to reform a law that is based on elements considered immutable because they are divinely sanctioned. Such elements are embedded in other provisions of substantive and procedural law that, as a whole, ensure that the aim of the reformers will be realized without touching upon such fundamental rules. To begin with, the general rule concerning criminal responsibility of juveniles in the chapter on criminal responsibility remained the same: Boys are fully responsible at the age of 15 lunar years, girls at 9 lunar years (Article 147). The chapter on punishments, however, now contains a special section on "Punishments and Measures of Security and Education for Children and Juveniles" (Articles 88–95 IPC). This chapter is divided into provisions for offences to be punished with *taʿzir* and for offences to be punished according to the other categories. *Taʿzir* punishments are again subdivided into two groups: Children under 15 (solar) years are punished with educational measures; only in special cases may they be punished with sanctions, such as placement in an educational center for three months to one year (Article 88). Juveniles between 15 and 18 years may be placed in an educational center for up to five years; other sanctions are fines or community service. As to offences punished with *hadd* and *qesās*, there are quite interesting rules: If a perpetrator who has already reached the *bolugh* and is not yet 18 years old (solar years) has not yet grasped the meaning of the offence, or if doubts arise as to her/his physical or mental maturity, s/he is punished by the sanctions provided in this section, not with *hadd* or *qesās* (Article 95). The court may get an expert opinion from a public health officer about

---

[8] Therefore, Western criticism as to executions of death penalties against minors is not appropriate in the eyes of Iranian law, as the executed persons in most of these cases are boys of 16 or 17 years who are already regarded as fully criminally responsible.

the maturity of the juvenile perpetrator. But it may also use any other appropriate means to assess the juvenile's level of criminal responsibility. This provision allows the judge to collect information by asking family members, teachers, neighbors, and other persons in the social environment of the perpetrator and to base his decision on this information. This provision grants the judge quite a broad discretion in his decision-making and gives him the possibility of avoiding applying the severe *hadd* and *qesās* punishments to juveniles.[9]

4 Defense

4.1 Duress

As a rule, nobody who commits an offence under duress is punished (Article 151). For offences punishable with *ta'zir*, the coercer will be punished as the perpetrator instead (Article 151 IPC); for offences punishable with *hadd* or *qesās*, the relevant provisions will apply. As to the famous problem of Carneades,[10] which has been a subject of discussion among philosophers and jurists for centuries, Islamic law has a clear position: Nobody may kill another person to save his or her own life. Therefore, the IPC also provides that nobody may kill another person and escape punishment even if s/he is forced to do so (Article 375 IPC).

4.2 State of Necessity

A person who acts in a state of necessity (*ezterār*) will not be punished (Article 152 IPC). In Islamic law, the principle of nonpunishability for a conduct in a state of necessity is based, inter alia, on Sura 2:173, which allows the consumption of pork if it is the only means to survive (Ardebili 2014: 250).

4.3 Self-Defense

Self-defense is known in Western law as well as in Islamic law. Whereas, in Western law, it is regarded as a right of the person unlawfully attacked,

---

[9] For juvenile justice in Iran, see, for more detail, Abachi (2015).
[10] The ancient Greek philosopher Carneades posed the following thought experiment: Two shipwrecked men, A and B, see a plank which, however, can only support one of them. Both swim toward it. A reaches it first, but B, who gets to it later, pushes A from the plank. A drowns, B is later saved. The question is whether B has to be punished for murder or whether he would be exempt from punishment because he acted in order to save his own life.

in Islamic law, it is a duty (Ardebili 2014: 286). Self-defense is regarded as a ground of justification if an offence was committed to defend the life, honor, property, or physical liberty of the perpetrator him/herself or of a third party against present or imminent unlawful attack. Furthermore, the act of defense must be necessary; this is not the case, however, if there is the possibility of being helped by the authorities in time. Other grounds of justification are, for example, acting on the basis of a law or official permission, executing a higher-ranking law, or executing the legal order of a competent authority. Consent is not mentioned as a ground of justification; in many cases, the lack of consent is regarded as an element of the offence, and, if there is consent, there is no offence. The person who takes away a book with the consent of its owner has not committed a theft. It should be mentioned that a person can only consent to the violation of rights over which s/he can dispose. This rule has two important consequences in the criminal law of an Islamic state (Ardebili 2014: 273). First, a human does not have the right to dispose of his or her own life. Therefore, suicide is a sin, and nobody has the right to consent to his or her own killing. Second, sexual contact is not only a matter of the person(s) involved but of society as a whole and, therefore, its legitimacy does not depend on the will of the individuals involved in the sexual act only.

4.4   Mistake of Law

For the first time in Iranian criminal law, the new code contains a general provision on mistake of law (Article 155 IPC). The degree to which a mistake of law is taken into account in Islamic law is rather different from Western law. In the latter, a mistake of law is only taken into consideration if it is unavoidable – but the unavoidability of the mistake of law is very rarely accepted; it is expected that persons inform themselves about the law. In Islamic law, however, mistake of law is accepted much more easily, as is shown in the provisions in the category of offences punished with *hodud* (see Section 3.1).

5   **Evidence**

The last chapter of Book I deals with the law of evidence. This is rather unexpected for European lawyers who regard law of evidence as part of the law of criminal procedure. In Islamic penal law, the law of evidence is so closely intertwined with the substantive law of offences punishable with *hadd*, *qesās*, and *diyeh* that they are treated together with substantive law, although there is a separate law of criminal procedure. Article 160 enumerates the evidence admitted in Shiʿi penal law: Confession, witnesses, oath, *qasāmeh* (oath of a group),[11] and the knowledge of the judge (*ʿelm-e qāzi*). In all the cases in which the guilt of the defendant has to be proven by one of these means of evidence, the judge will base his judgment on this evidence, except if he definitely knows that the offence was committed another way (Article 161). This means that he is not bound to judge against his better knowledge even if *sharʿi* evidence is furnished. Conversely, if a means of evidence does not fulfil the requirements of a *sharʿi* evidence, for example if a witness is not a Muslim, it does not mean that it has no value at all in the proceedings. The judge may consider it a kind of circumstantial evidence which, together with other circumstantial evidence, may be taken to conclude that the act under consideration occurred in a certain way. In the 2013 IPC, the result of this procedure (which resembles the free assessment of evidence by a judge in Western law) is regarded as a means of evidence in itself, namely knowledge of the judge (*ʿelm-e qāzi*) (Article 162).

A confession can only be made by the confessing person him/herself. The confessing person must be adult and mentally sane; s/he must have the intention to make a confession and act of her/his own free will (Article 168). A confession made under pressure, torture, or physical or psychological maltreatment may not be used (Article 169). As a rule, the judge will base his judgment on a confession, but if he has reason to suppose that the confession is not in accordance with the facts, he will investigate further (Article 171). Normally, it is sufficient if a confession is made once, but there are special rules as to the number of confessions for offences punishable with *hadd*, *qesās*, and *diyeh*. Confessions of offences punishable with *hadd* can only be made before the judge; a confession made before the police or before the prosecutor does not have any effect (legal explanation no. 2 to Article 218). If the confession of an offence punishable with stoning or capital punishment as a *hadd* punishment is withdrawn, the offender will be exempted from *hadd* punishments. It does not matter whether the confession was true or not. This does not, however, mean that a perpetrator goes unpunished. Depending on the offence, he or she can be sentenced to flogging or a *taʿzir* punishment (Article 173 IPC).

---

[11] Under special circumstances, a crime punished with *qesās* or *diyeh* may be proven by a number of oaths made by the complainant's relatives and dependents. The accused may clear themselves by compurgation (trial by oath) if they can gather enough witnesses to swear the number of oaths required. If the number of witnesses is not enough, every witness may swear more than one oath – as much as necessary to have the number of oaths required. In the case of premeditated murder, however, the complainant has to present fifty witnesses, whereas the accused may take up to fifty oaths her/himself to be acquitted (Articles 336, 338, 455–458 IPC).

Offences relating to the core of Islamic criminal law (offences punishable with *hadd*, *qesās*, *diyeh*) can be proven by witnesses only if the witnesses fulfil the requirements of the shari'a. A witness must be adult, mentally sane, and a faithful Muslim; in Iranian law, the implication of the latter is that he/she must be a Shi'i Muslim. Furthermore, he/she must be honest (*'ādel*) and born in wedlock, may not draw any profit from the matter, and may not be the enemy of one of the parties. Finally, he/she may not be either a beggar or a vagrant (Article 177 IPC). Witnesses who do not fulfil these requirements may still be questioned, however, and their statements may be used as circumstantial evidence (Article 176). As regards offences punished with *hadd*, *qesās*, and *diyeh*, according to Article 199 each offence has its own requirements as to the number and sex of admissible witnesses. In most of these cases, the offence can be proven by two honest male witnesses and the statement of one man may be replaced by the statement of two women, but *hadd* punishments cannot be based on the testimony of female witnesses alone. In practice, however, testimony of women is used as circumstantial evidence that may lead to the knowledge of the judge (*'elm-e qāzi*) being applied.

A very important feature of Shi'i law is acceptance of the knowledge of the judge (*'elm-e qāzi*)[12] as a means of evidence for offences punishable with *hadd*, *qesās*, and *diyeh*. Whereas in the IPC of 1991, it was only admitted as evidence for theft, illegal sexual intercourse, and homicide (Articles 199, 105, and 231), now it is admitted as evidence for all offences. Therefore, types of evidence, such as expert opinions, visual inspection, police reports, may form the basis of the knowledge of the judge (Article 211). Thus, all modern methods of securing evidence and types of evidence, such as DNA analysis, may be used.

6   Books II–IV

6.1   Hadd

As mentioned, whereas the general principles of criminal law are laid out in Book I of the 2013 IPC, Books II–IV deal with *hadd*, *qesās*, and *diyeh* respectively. The first chapter of Book II, dealing with *hadd* punishments, comprises some general rules for all the individual offences dealt with in this book (Articles 217–220). They show the tendency of Islamic law to avoid *hadd* punishments. First of all, offences punished with *hadd* punishments are always intentional offences; unintentional offences are not subject to this category of offences. The perpetrator must know and

---

[12] This concept is rejected in Sunni law.

must be conscious of the fact that his/her conduct is prohibited by the shariʿa at the moment of the commission of the offence (Article 217). If the perpetrator claims that s/he did not know about the prohibition or claims the existence of a justification or excuse and it seems that his or her statement is true, this statement is accepted without taking further evidence; an oath by the perpetrator is not even required (Article 218). The perpetrator will not be punished with a *hadd* punishment. The same holds true if s/he claims to have made the confession under threat, intimidation, or torture (Article 218). In these cases, the court proceedings are stopped. Only in cases of enmity against God, corruption on earth, and sexual offences that have been committed by pressure, force, or deception is *hadd* not automatically removed and the court obliged to investigate further (legal explanation no. 1 to Article 218).

As described,[13] apostasy is not expressly mentioned in the law, but the IPC contains a provision proscribing swearing at the Prophet, the twelve Shiʿi Imams, and at Fatima, the daughter of the Prophet (Article 262 IPC). Here also, the law contains provisions by which the death penalty can be evaded for this offence. The perpetrator is not punished if s/he claims to have committed such swearing under coercion, due to negligence, by mistake, in a state of drunkenness, out of anger, by a slip of tongue, without thinking about the meaning of their words or by repeating the words of another person (Article 263).

In Islamic law, all sexual intercourse between a man and a woman outside a valid marriage (*zenāʾ*) is punishable and both are sentenced to 100 lashes. This includes sex before marriage as well as adultery and homosexuality, but the latter two carry additional sentences. A married person who commits adultery has to be sentenced to stoning if s/he is *mohsen/mohseneh* (Article 225),[14] which means the following factors have to be met: The perpetrator must be in a permanent marriage, not in a temporary marriage (*mutʿa*);[15] s/he must have had vaginal sexual intercourse with her husband/his wife and have the possibility to have such an intercourse whenever s/he wishes (Article 226). The law enumerates some cases that exclude the quality of being *mohsen/eh*: Husband or wife are traveling or in prison or have contracted a disease that makes sexual intercourse impossible or at least dangerous. As examples, the law expressly names syphilis and AIDS (Article 227). It is notable that

---

[13] See Section 2.1.
[14] In 2002, the head of the judiciary announced a moratorium on stoning. Nonetheless, according to Amnesty International's annual reports on Iran in 2007, 2008, and 2009, stoning has taken place in rare cases, and also more recently.
[15] In Shiʿi law, temporary marriage is permitted, whereas in Sunni law it is strictly prohibited.

Islamic law makes no difference between men and women in these provisions.[16] Only if all of these criteria apply (permanent marriage, availability of vaginal intercourse, etc.) does the punishment of stoning apply to the crime of adultery.

Homosexuality and lesbianism are also dealt with by law (Articles 233–240). It is not the sexual orientation that is punished but the sexual act. In the case of homosexuality, the punishable conduct consists of sexual intercourse (Article 233). There is a difference between active and passive partners. The passive partner is sentenced to death. The active partner is sentenced to death if he acts with force, if he is a non-Muslim and the passive partner a Muslim, or if he is *mohsen*, which means that he in a permanent marriage despite his sexual orientation (Article 234 IPC). In all other cases, the punishment is 100 lashes for the active partner. In the case of lesbianism, both women are punished with flogging (Article 239). There is no death penalty for lesbian women, as they cannot have sexual intercourse in the legal sense for physical reasons.

Apart from the difficulties of proving *zenā'*, homosexuality, and lesbianism, the Iranian law tries to restrict punishment for such conduct by means of procedural regulations. According to Article 241 IPC, no investigation may be conducted into such cases if the perpetrator contests the allegation of the offence and no evidence is presented, except in cases of force or deception as mentioned in the law. According to the CCP, investigations of sexual offences are only admissible if the offenses were committed in public or if there is a plaintiff (Article 102 CCP). If there is no plaintiff and the perpetrator wishes to confess to such an offence, the judge has to counsel him or her not to do so (legal explanation to Article 102 CCP). In practice this means that – if conducted in private and with mutual consent – homosexual relations and sex outside marriage should not be subject to criminal prosecution.

The *hadd* punishment for false accusation of unlawful sexual intercourse (*qadhf*) consists of eighty lashes and is intended to stop gossip about sexual behavior in a society that is very sensitive to any real or presumed violations of sexual norms. The implication of this is, however, that women who were victims of sexual attacks and cannot present the necessary evidence to the court run the risk of being punished for *qadhf*, or even for committing illegal sexual acts themselves.

---

[16] It should be noted that, according to Article 630 of the *ta'zir* law of 1996, the husband who catches his wife *in flagranti* and kills or injures her and/or her lover remains unpunished. This provision, however, does not have an Islamic but a French origin (Article 324 of the French Penal Code of 1810).

The Quranic verse 5:38 "cut the hands of the male thief and the female thief" is the basis of the *hadd* punishment for theft. This case, however, also shows the way in which Islamic scholars have tried to limit the application of this rule as much as possible. They developed a large number of requirements that have to be fulfilled in order to punish a person for theft in this way. Today, this development is reflected in Article 268 IPC, which, apart from general requirements (mental sanity and so on), enumerates fourteen requirements that have to be met, for example, a stolen good must have a minimum value and must have been kept in a container that is suitable for its protection (*herz*). The thief must have broken open this container and taken the item out of it. If the object was the property of the state or of a religious foundation, there is no *hadd* punishment because the perpetrator might have been a beneficiary of these institutions. The perpetrator is likewise not punished with a *hadd* punishment if s/he became the legal owner of the stolen object after the offence, by buying it, inheriting it, receiving it as a present from the victim, or if the object belongs to a descendant of the perpetrator. It must be noted, however, that exemption from *hadd* punishment does not mean that the perpetrator remains unpunished. S/he is punished according to Articles 651–662 of the *ta'zir* law of 1996.

A Muslim who consumes alcohol will be punished with eighty lashes (Articles 264, 265 IPC). A non-Muslim, however, will only be punished if s/he consumes alcohol in public or if s/he is drunk in public (Article 266).

The crime of "enmity against God" (*mohārebeh*) is based on the Quranic verse 5:33. It punishes the use of weapons in order to frighten people. The offence has to be committed at a place where the victim is particularly helpless. In former times, this often happened in rural areas. This is the reason why this offence is often referred to as highway robbery (*qat' at-tariq*). Today, the lack of a relationship between the perpetrator and the victim is seen as the characteristic feature of this offence; in other words, the victim is a random victim. There are four possible punishments for this offence, namely crucifixion, the death penalty, amputation of the right hand and the left foot, or banishment. Sunni criminal law and part of the Shi'i doctrine (e.g., Shaykh Tusi, d. 1067) strictly combine certain modalities of an offence with certain punishments. Robbery with murder is to be punished with crucifixion, murder with the death penalty, robbery with the severing of a hand and a foot, and frightening people without murder or robbery with banishment. Another opinion in the Shi'i doctrine, shared for example by Allama al-Hilli (d. 1325), al-Shahid al-Thani (d. 1558), and Khomeini, opposes such strict connections and would prefer to leave the choice of the appropriate punishment to the judge.[17] This opinion is followed by the Iranian legislator (parliament and Council of Guardians) (Articles 282, 283) and has meant that crucifixion has never been applied in the Islamic Republic.

The punishment for corruption on earth (*efsād-e fel 'arz*) is the death penalty. According to Article 286 IPC, this offence includes all offences against bodily integrity, internal and external security of the state, spreading lies, economic offences, arson, destruction, spreading toxic/microbic/other dangerous substances, or running brothels if these acts have such an effect that the public order is disturbed to a considerable degree or that they cause uncertainty or considerable damages to persons or public or private property. It remains uncertain, however, what "a considerable degree" means, thus leaving a broad discretion to the court that may be used arbitrarily.

Finally, Article 287 punishes rebellion (*baghy*), which is defined as an armed insurgency against the order of the Islamic Republic. A group that is arrested after already having used weapons against the state is punished with the death penalty under the crime of "enmity with God"; if weapons have not yet been used, such groups are punished with a *ta'zir* punishment (Article 288).

6.2 Qesās *and* Diyeh

The types of offences which fall under the categories of *qesās* and *diyeh* are closely related.[18] They comprise offences against life and bodily integrity. Generally speaking, *qesās* is the punishment for intentional offences and *diyeh* for unintentional offences against life and bodily integrity. Whereas offences are only divided into intentional and negligent offences in Book I (Articles 144, 145 IPC), there is a tripartite division in the categories of *qesās* and *diyeh* into intentional, semi-intentional, and unintentional offences. An intentional offence exists if the perpetrator acted with the intention (*'amd*) to kill a person, or if s/he acted in a way that usually has fatal consequences, and was conscious of this fact, even if s/he did not want to kill the victim. It also applies if the act had fatal consequences because of certain facts about the victim that were known to the perpetrator (Article 290), for example if the victim was a hemophiliac. Semi-intention (*shebh-e 'amd*) means that the perpetrator had the intention to act against the victim but not to kill; or if there was in *error in objecto*, for example if the perpetrator thought that the target of his or her act was

---

[17] See, for details, Shambayati (2009: 83–84).
[18] In Sunni law, they are in fact considered one category for this reason.

an animal; and lastly if the perpetrator acted imprudently or negligently (Article 291). The third category is mere fault (*khatā-ye mahz*). It consists of acts committed by a perpetrator who was unconscious, sleeping, a minor, mentally ill, or if s/he did not have intent to perform an act against the victim at all (Article 292). This category is a collection of circumstances in which the perpetrator is not criminally responsible in a strict sense but in which the victim should receive compensation. Therefore, mere fault may be regarded as a kind of strict liability.

As mentioned, only intentional offences can be punished with *qesās* (retributive justice where the punishment is decided by the victim or his/her kin). But there are additional requirements for the application of *qesās*. A basic principle of *qesās* is the equivalence of perpetrator and victim as to sex, religion, and, to a certain degree, also state of health as far as members or organs of the body are concerned. There are, however, some exceptions to this principle. If perpetrator and victim are both men or both women, *qesās* is possible. If the perpetrator is a man and the victim a woman, the blood avengers of the woman may execute *qesās* against the perpetrator, but they have to pay half the blood money to the perpetrator in advance (Article 382).[19] If the perpetrator is a woman and the victim a man, *qesās* is possible. If the perpetrator and victim are both Muslims or both followers of a religion recognized in Article 13 of the constitution (Judaism, Zoroastrianism, Assyrian Christianity, or Armenian Christianity), *qesās* is likewise possible (Article 301). The same holds true if the perpetrator is a non-Muslim man and the victim a Muslim man (legal explanation to Article 301). If a non-Muslim man kills a Muslim woman, *qesās* is again possible (Article 382). But if the perpetrator is a Muslim and the victim a non-Muslim follower of a religion recognized in the constitution, no *qesās* will take place. In that case, the perpetrator has to pay *diyeh*.

Qesās for taking a life is normally hanging (in a prison, as opposed to in public),[20] as in other cases of capital punishment. *Qesās* for bodily injury is very rare today.[21]

If the offence was committed unintentionally or *qesās* did not take place after an intentional offence for whatever reasons, blood money has to be paid. Though Islamic law and the IPC of 1991 specify a catalogue of objects that can be paid as blood money (for example camels or

---

[19] The reason for that is that traditionally the value of the life of a woman has been estimated at half of the value of that of a man.
[20] See, for details, https://iranhrdc.org/english-translation-of-regulatory-code-on-sentences-of-qisas-stoning-crucifixion-execution-and-flogging/.
[21] See, for example, the annual reports of Amnesty International.

dresses), the new IPC only refers to Islamic law in a general way, and, in practice, blood money is paid in money, the amount of which is fixed every year by the head of the judiciary in order to adapt it to inflation. A detailed catalogue stipulates the amount of blood money that has to be paid for specific injuries, amounting to fractions of full blood money (Articles 549–717).

According to traditional Islamic law, the amount of blood money for women and for non-Muslim followers of heavenly religions (in Iran, members of religions recognized by Article 13 of the constitution, that is, Judaism, Zoroastrianism, Assyrian Christianity, and Armenian Christianity) is half the amount of blood money for men and for Muslims respectively. But modern Iranian law has created rules that result in equal payment of blood money to non-Muslims and women. The methods of bringing about these results deserve mention. A decision of the Tehran Appeals Court that favored the same blood money for non-Muslims was based on three fatwas from high-ranking clerics,[22] who stated that there is no obstacle in Islamic law to paying non-Muslims and their blood avengers the same amount of blood money as for Muslims. With the help of these fatwas it was possible to gain a majority in favor of such a law in parliament, that was also approved by the Guardian Council (Showrā-ye Negahbān). Thus, since 2004, followers of the non-Muslim religions recognized in the Iranian constitution have received the same amount of blood money as Muslims (legal explanation no. 2 to Article 297 IPC 1991; Article 554 IPC 2013). The alignment of blood money for women with the blood money paid for men turned out to be more difficult. The first step was completed in 2008 outside the sphere of penal law, namely in insurance law. Since that year, insurance companies have been obliged to pay female traffic accident victims the difference between the blood money for men and the blood money for women (with the rest being paid by the offender). This solution solved the problem in many cases, as traffic accidents account for a considerable percentage of women who are killed or injured. The new IPC maintains the rule that blood money for women is half the amount of the blood money for men as the general principle (Article 550) but provides that the second half of the blood money has to be paid by a fund (legal explanation no. 1 to Article 551). This payment is no longer limited to deaths in traffic accidents and is now applicable to all cases in which women are killed or suffer bodily harm. The punishment for the perpetrator may still be less than the punishment

---

[22] Grand Ayatollahs Naser Makarem Shirazi, Hossein Nouri Hamedani, and Yousef Sanei, see Goldouzian (2003).

for having killed or injured a man, but the female victim or her blood avengers have a right to the full amount of blood money equal to that paid to male victims in the end.

The responsibility of a person suspected of homicide or bodily injury has to be proven before the judge, and it is the judge who renders the judgment against the accused. The execution of a judgment of *qesās* was originally in the hands of the blood avengers. They decided whether to execute the judgment, to take blood money instead, or to pardon the convicted. This was still the situation in the first decades after the revolution. In the meantime, the state has tried to limit the full power of decision of private persons for the execution of punishment in such severe offences as homicide. On the one hand, the blood avengers have to ask the special permission of the Supreme Leader (Khamenei) or his representative if they wish to execute *qesās* (Article 417 IPC). On the other hand, even if the blood avengers pardon the perpetrator, s/he will not remain unpunished as was possible before 1991. If, in the case of an intentional homicide (for which *qesās* would be possible), *qesās* does not take place for whatever reasons but public security, public order, or considerations of deterrence require a punishment, the judge will sentence the perpetrator to a *ta'zir* punishment of three to ten years' imprisonment (Article 612 IPC 1991/1996).

7   Concluding Remarks

Qua the constitution, criminal law in the Islamic Republic of Iran has to be in line with Islamic criteria. Though a limited number of rules in the areas of *hadd*, *qesās*, and *diyeh* are regarded as divine law and therefore cannot be altered or abolished, the texts of *hadd*, *qesās*, and *diyeh* are not isolated rules. They have been the subject of interpretation for centuries, and Islamic legal scholars have often restricted the applicability of *hadd*, as becomes apparent, for example, in the crime of theft (where the punishment of cutting off the thief's hand is very seldom reported and appears to have been applied only very rarely). Furthermore, the scholarly doctrine of Islamic law is multivocal, with a variety of different, even contrary, opinions. Today, one can observe how Iranian legislation on penal law has benefited from this diversity and has even relied on minority opinions in legal justification if deemed opportune, for example in leaving the choice of the most appropriate of four possible punishments for "enmity with God" to the discretion of the judge.

Furthermore, the texts of *hadd*, *qesās*, and *diyeh* can be embedded in other rules of substantive or procedural law in such a way that the aims of limiting the harshness of punishments can be realized while formally remaining true to Islamic legal traditions. This method seems to be rather frequently used. It was chosen, for example, to reform the system of criminal responsibility of juveniles, to create an additional claim supplementing blood money for female victims, to create a *taʿzir* punishment for certain cases of homicide, and to develop the law of evidence.

The largest group of criminal offences, meanwhile, systematically belongs to the category of *taʿzirāt*, which leaves a lot of room to develop the law according to the requirements of time and space. This makes it possible for the current Iranian criminal law to continue to be influenced by French law, and to be open to international developments in penal law, as is shown, for example, in the very detailed system of *taʿzir* sanctions. It is also interesting to observe that, in many cases, Islamic law and Western law similarly evaluate a problem, for example that victims of unlawful attacks may defend themselves, with the notable difference that in Western law this is a right while in Islamic law it is a duty. Sometimes the differences in evaluation are greater: In Western law, a "mistake of law" is only recognized as an excuse if it was unavoidable. Islamic law, which deals with this question particularly in the context of *hodud*,[23] is more generous than European law in recognizing "mistakes of law" as grounds for exculpation.

A last comment: Today, a certain pragmatism is also accepted in Iranian penal law, and norms are tacitly regarded as being consistent with Islamic principles as long as nobody contests them.

Bibliography

Abachi, Maryam. The Modern System of Juvenile Justice in Iran, *Zeitschrift für die gesamte Strafrechtswissenschaft* 127, 2015, pp. 822–841.

Ardebili, Mohammad Ali. *Hoquq-e jazā-ye ʿomumi* [*Criminal Law: General Part*], vol. 1, 21st ed. Tehran 2014.

Ghassemi, Ghassem. *Criminal Policy in Iran Following the Revolution of 1979*, Berlin: Duncker & Humblot, 2013, pp. 122–126.

Goldouzian, Iradj. "L'arrêt récent de la cour d'appel iranienne modifiant la jurisprudence discriminatoire entre les musulmans et les minorités religieuses à propos de l'indemnisation de la victime dans l'infractions contre l'intégrité corporelle," *Revue pénitentiaire et de droit pénal*, 2003, pp. 205–208.

Khosravi, Mohammed Reza. *Majmuʿeh-ye kāmel-e qavānin va moqarrarāt-e jazāyi*, Tehran, 1393/2014.

---

[23] See Article 217 IPC: "In cases of offenses punishable by hadd, the offender shall be liable only if, in addition to having knowledge, intention, and meeting the requirements for criminal responsibility, [he/she] is aware of the prohibition of the conduct committed under shariʿa rules."

Shambayati, Houshang. *Hoquq-e keifari-ye ekhtesāsi*, 3 vols., 7th ed. Tehran 1388/2009, pp. 83–84.

Shams Nāteri, Mohammed Ebrahim, et al. *Qānun-e mojāzāt-e eslāmi dar nazm-e hoquqi-ye kununi* [*The Islamic Penal Code in Modern Legal Order*], Tehran 1393 (2014), pp. 257–263.

Tellenbach, Silvia. "Zur Re-Islamisierung im Strafrecht in der Islamischen Republik Iran," *Zeitschrift für die gesamte Strafrechtswissenschaft*, 101, 1989, pp. 188–205.

Tellenbach, Silvia. "The Principle of Legality in the Iranian Constitutional and Criminal Law," in Said Amir Arjomand and Nathan J. Brown (eds.), *The Rule of Law, Islam and Constitutional Politics in Egypt and Iran*, Albany: SUNY Press, 2013, pp. 101–122.

3 The Administration of Criminal Justice in Iran

Ideology, Judicial Personalism, and the Cynical Manipulation of Security

Drewery Dyke and Hadi Enayat

> In the judicial realm, it must be explicitly stated that the judicial power of the Islamic Republic is a manifestation of injustice and tyranny, a violator of human rights. The independence of the judicial branch is impossible when the head of this branch is directly appointed by the Supreme Leader and revolutionary courts are under the control of security and military institutions. What is not achievable in this judicial system, is justice.
>
> Narges Mohammadi, Nobel Prize Lecture 2023.[1]

This chapter will analyze the nature and evolution of the administration of criminal justice in the Islamic Republic of Iran.[2] Although current Iranian law incorporates a range of provisions intended to protect the rights of the accused in criminal prosecutions, in practice these provisions are routinely violated.[3] It is argued that the violations of due process in the Islamic Republic of Iran are the result of three factors. Firstly, the criminal justice system in Iran has been securitized, with disastrous implications for the rule of law. "Securitization" here refers to the process of framing issues as existential threats in order to justify taking extraordinary measures to deal with them (Mabon and Kapur

---

[1] The lecture is available at: www.nobelprize.org/prizes/peace/2023/mohammadi/lecture/ accessed 15th March 2024.

[2] We thank Anna Enayat for providing some of the material for this chapter.

[3] Article 32 of the constitution calls for the immediate presentation of charges to persons arrested in accordance with criminal procedures. The rules that govern criminal procedure also prohibit arbitrary detention and require that families of the detained be informed. The law guarantees access to and representation by legal counsel, and prohibits temporary detention for nonviolent crimes, unless there is a flight risk. Moreover, Article 38 of the constitution prohibits torture and states that confessions solicited by coercive actions "have no validity whatsoever." Furthermore, Article 14 of the International Covenant on Civil and Political Rights (to which Iran is a signatory) provides for due process and fair trial guarantees, including the right of all persons to a fair and public hearing by a competent, independent, and impartial tribunal established by law.

The Administration of Criminal Justice in Iran 67

2019: 21).[4] This securitization has found expression in the criminal justice system, which has been configured to deal with political opposition as an existential threat to the state, resulting in frequent interference in the judicial process and secretive and arbitrary trials in revolutionary courts which continue to be used over forty years after the 1979 Revolution. Secondly, the structural subordination of the judiciary to the effective power of the Supreme Leader and the agencies under his control, facilitating their interference in hundreds of security related criminal cases over the past 40 years.[5] This is a function of the ideology of *velāyat-e faqih*, which, especially after the 1989 constitutional reforms described in the introduction to this volume, concentrated considerable judicial as well as executive power in the hands of the Supreme Leader. Thirdly, the ideological imperative to Islamize the judicial system after the 1979 Revolution has led to the adoption of shari'a modes of punishment and judicial procedure, which have given judges very wide scope in the conduct and outcome of cases, notably in criminal law. This "judicial personalism," which seems to be particularly pronounced in the Shi'i legal tradition, historically gave judges the ability to rule according to the exigencies of particular cases. Under the Islamic Republic of Iran, however, it has often led to the inconsistent application of the law and been used to enforce cruel and arbitrary punishments. This is not to argue that shari'a is by definition incompatible with the rule of law but rather that the particular modalities of its adoption in Iran after the revolution have generally had negative consequences for the rule of law in the sphere of criminal justice.

The long-standing character of human rights abuse has meant that the administration of justice in Iran has been the subject of domestic and international scrutiny since before the 1979 Revolution. Critical reports by academics and international nongovernmental organizations (INGOs) in the 1970s continued into the postrevolutionary era in the 1980s and 1990s, supplemented by the growing number and scope of reports issued by intergovernmental organizations (IGOs), notably the United Nations' (UN's) Treaty Bodies and thematic Special Procedures, whose global reach and impact have grown from the late 1970s, along with those of

---

[4] On the impact of securitization on civil and political rights in various countries, especially since 9/11 see: United Nations, General Assembly, and Human Rights Council, "Impact of Measures to Address Terrorism and Violent Extremism on Civic Space and the Rights of Civil Society Actors and Human Rights Defenders: Report of the Special Rapporteur on the Promotion and Protection of Human Rights and Fundamental Freedoms while Countering Terrorism" (UN index A/HRC/40/52), March 1, 2019: www.ohchr.org/en/issues/terrorism/pages/annual.aspx, accessed June 15, 2020.

[5] "Effective" used in the legal sense, that is, if not "formally" responsible for the conduct of, for example, the judiciary and the Ministry of Intelligence there is often, we argue, effective oversight by the Supreme Leader.

INGOs, in the field of human rights. Iran's international human rights obligations notwithstanding, for at least sixty years many such reports have been consistently critical of the Iranian criminal justice system and have repeatedly pointed to chronic due-process violations which have undermined fair trial rights.[6] Some of these are quoted extensively throughout this chapter which also draws from the work of Iranian lawyers, jurists, activists and journalists working both inside and outside Iran.

The chapter begins by discussing how the criminal justice system was transformed in Iran after the 1979 Revolution, focusing on the attempts to Islamize the system. The chapter then goes on to evoke the administration-of-justice "journey," that is, the basis of arrest and who may conduct it, through to detention, trial adjudication, and then appeal and/or retrial. This "journey" shows, step by step, the challenges impeding the delivery of justice in Iran today. Thus, this chapter concentrates mainly on criminal procedure, the judicial process, and aspects of criminal law, and aims to complement Silvia Tellenbach's jurisprudential analysis of the 2013 Penal Code (Chapter 2 in this volume).

1 The Trajectory of Criminal Procedure under the Islamic Republic

This section describes the broad trajectory of criminal procedure reform under the Islamic Republic of Iran, forming a backdrop for the rest of the chapter. Today's criminal justice system springs from a long-term emphasis on national security and an idiosyncratic interpretation of *Shi'ism* inspired by Ayatollah Khomeini and the writings and pronouncements of other leading thinkers. After the 1979 Revolution, the new authorities' national security imperative placed the preservation of the new Islamic Republic over considerations of due process. This is often the case in postrevolutionary situations. Militant supporters of the new government killed thousands of people following summary, grossly unfair "trials" held in the weeks and months after the revolution, including in regions, such as Kurdistan, where armed opposition emerged. According to Ervand Abrahamian (2008: 181), between February 1979 and June 1981 revolutionary courts executed 497 political opponents as "counter revolutionaries" and "sowers of corruption

---

[6] Iran acceded to the following international conventions: The Convention on the Elimination of All Forms of Racial Discrimination (CERD) in 1968; the Covenant for Civil and Political Rights (CCPR) and on the Covenant of Economic, Social and Cultural Rights (CESCR) in 1975. After the 1979 Revolution, in 1994 the government acceded to the Convention on the Rights of the Child (CRC). In 2007, Iran acceded to the Optional Protocol to the Convention on the Rights of the Child on the Sale of Children, Child Prostitution and Child Pornography (CRC-OP-SC). Iran after 1979 did not withdraw from the human rights treaties to which previous governments had acceded and these remain binding.

on earth." This number rose to 8,000 from June 1981 until June 1985, following, in every known case, unfair trials. The securitization of the criminal justice system paved the way for a severe regime of criminal law involving revolutionary courts with little or no due process, still in use today, as well as the enfeebling of the once independent legal profession and the frequent use of torture and forced confessions.

Moreover, after the 1979 Revolution the moral and ethical sources of law and legal procedure were transformed. Ayatollah Khomeini sought to tear down the tāghuti (idolatrous) secular judiciary of the Pahlavi era and rebuild an Islamic judiciary under the "Government of God." Whilst the 1979 Revolution's leaders did not dismantle the core of the Pahlavi-era judiciary's administrative structure, it facilitated an Islamization of the legal system and administrative elements of its operation. From 1982, an Islamic Penal Code (IPC) was introduced, which replaced the secular codes promulgated under the Pahlavi monarchy, transforming large areas of (public) criminal law into private law again (see Section 2.2 below on *qesās* and *bakhshesh*).

As described in Chapter 9 of this volume, a number of attempted judicial reforms aimed at improving the rule of law in the sphere of criminal justice, took place under the tenure of Ayatollah Hashemi Shahroudi from 1999 to 2009. Shahroudi, though appointed by Khamenei, managed to navigate Iranian politics with some degree of independence from the Supreme Leader and initiate a reform program within the judiciary. In 1999, a new code of criminal procedure, deemed more suitable to the postrevolutionary circumstances, replaced the 1911 Law of the Principle of Trials. The Code of Criminal Procedure for the General and Revolutionary Courts (*Qānun-e dādresi-ye keyfari-ye dadgāhāh-ye omumi va enqelābi* – heretofore referred to as the CCP) was passed into law for a trial period of three years in 1999. As we shall see, the code had significant flaws and fell far short of international fair trial standards. In 2000, a year after the introduction of the CCP, Shahroudi initiated a process for drafting a new CCP. This new law was to address the "ambiguities and mistakes of existing laws" and ensure consistency with "scientific developments" (quoted in Amnesty International 2016: 19). The draft bill, which was prepared by the judiciary, was delayed by the review process between parliament and the judiciary. Meanwhile, the trial period of the 1999 CCP was repeatedly extended. The code remained operational until the promulgation of a new CCP in 2014, which was amended in 2015 (discussed more in Section 4 below).

2 Tension between Premodern Authenticity and the Challenges of Modernity

The tension between premodern, seemingly authentic, notions of justice informed by a particular theological perspective and the challenge of running a modern justice system is almost uniquely manifested in the Iranian context. The Islamization of the Penal Code from 1982 onward – and its most recent iteration in 2013 – is the most striking manifestation of this ideological proclivity to Islamize the legal system after the revolution. In this section we discuss aspects of criminal law and procedure which have been reformed as part of the project of the Islamicizing the legal and judicial system. It is in this realm that the 'judicial personalism' identified in the introduction to this chapter is most evident. We focus on three features: methods of proof – specifically a concept known as "knowledge of the judge" (*'elm-e qāzi*) – retaliation (*qesās*) and forgiveness/clemency (*bakhshesh*), and the unification of the offices of the judge and the prosecutor.

2.1 Evidence Used in Court: "Knowledge of the Judge" ('elm-e qāzi)

The Islamic Penal Code of 2013 identifies four evidentiary requirements needed to prove guilt in criminal cases. These are confession (*eqrar*), witness testimony (*shāhadat*), sworn oaths (*qāsameh* and *sogand*), and, finally, knowledge of the judge (*'elm-e qāzi*).[7] This last form of evidence is a controversial feature of Iranian criminal law which is perhaps unique to Iran, though it bears some resemblance to the procedures used in medieval European chanceries.[8] Rooted in Shi'i jurisprudence, *'elm*, meaning "knowledge" or "insight," is a form of knowledge defined as higher than *zann* (conjecture) on the scale whose apex is *qat'* or *yaqin* (certainty). Notably, since it is called *'elm*, a word associated with reliable insight, some jurists and judges claim that *'elm-e qāzi* is by definition more authoritative than the mere *zann* deriving from other forms of proof (Dadashi-Niaki and Feez 2011: 93; Fraser Fujinaga 2013: 388; Quddusi 2019: 62).[9]

However, there has been a great deal of disagreement amongst Shi'i scholars as to whether the principle is valid as regards "the rights of God" (*haqq allāh*) or the "rights of people" (*haqq al-nās*) or both or neither (Arjomand 1988: 187). Crimes which violate the former category are usually deemed to be *hodud* crimes. But Ayatollah Sanei, for example, holds *'elm* to be inapplicable in *hodud* cases because scripture clearly requires sufficient numbers of confessions or witnesses in *hudud*, so although fewer confessions or witnesses could give a judge *'elm*, they

---

[7] Articles 211–213 of the Islamic Penal Code regulate the principles of *'elm-e qāzi*.
[8] See Macnair (2007: 674–676) on medieval European chanceries.
[9] Dadashi and Feez (2011: 93) identify three views on the nature of "knowledge" in *'elm-e qāzi* in Islamic jurisprudence: (1) *'elm-e qāzi* is certain and logical (*yaqini va manitiqi*); (2) *'elm-e qāzi* is ordinary certainty (*ādi itmināni* – as opposed to extraordinary certainty based on dreams, visions, divine inspiration, magic, etc.); (3) *'elm-e qāzi* is conjectural (*zann*).

cannot justify the *had* (Fraser Fujinaga 2013: 57). Moreover, some jurists define *ʿelm* as the Imam's firsthand knowledge after personally seeing a crime, attributing his right to rule by *ʿelm* from the fact that he is infallible (*maʿsum*), or that he is God's representative on Earth, or both. Some jurists transfer this right to the Imam's "representative," without specifying who this is. However, the Penal Code under the Islamic Republic has transferred the right of *ʿelm* to all judges, who are neither infallible nor the Imams' vicegerents (Fraser Fujinaga 2013: 58). Authorization to use this method of proof was first contained in the 1991 Penal Code in four articles: Article 105, part of the section on adultery; Article 120, concerning methods of proof in homosexual and lesbian relationships; Article 231, concerning cases of theft where the punishment is amputation; and Article 305, concerning methods of proving murder under the law of retribution (*qesās*). Article 105 reads:

In both divine right (*haqq allāh*) and people's right (*haqq al-nās*) cases, the judge may rule on the basis of his own knowledge (*ʿelm-e khod*) and may impose the *hadd* penalty [on that basis]. It is necessary [in such cases] for the judge to state the sources of his knowledge.

The basis of Article 105 was Ayatollah Khomeini's book of jurisprudence – *Tahrir al-Vasila* – which was used as the principal reference in the post-1979 codification of Islamic criminal law and which, according to Arjomand, transformed what had been an ancillary principle in Shiʿi jurisprudence into "an independent means for establishing evidence and issuing a verdict" (Arjomand 1988: 187). The relevant passage in *Tahrir al-Vasila* reads as follows:

The judge is permitted to [issue a verdict] on the basis of his own knowledge [of *ʿelm*] without needing [formal] proof or confession or oath, be it concerning "the rights of God" [*haqq allah*] or "the rights of the people" [*haqq al-nās*]. (Khomeini, quoted in Arjomand 1988: 187)

An explanation of how the knowledge of the judge may be applied in Khomeini's jurisprudence is provided in an authorized 1980 commentary to another of Khomeini's books on law (*Resāleh-ye Novin*) which states that:

If the judge acquires knowledge and certainty concerning the facts of the case through the reliable modern means and instruments such as fingerprinting, medical examination, the infra-red camera which photographs the past and other instruments for the detection of the crime, this knowledge is more valid for him than … proofs of the Sacred Law such as confession, witnesses and oath which are of the next [i.e., lower] order. (Khomeini, quoted in Arjomand 1988: 189)

Thus, circumstantial and forensic evidence, not traditionally recognized in Islamic law, could be used alongside the judge's intuition about a defendant's guilt to reach a verdict. Despite the continuing dispute over its meaning and application, the "knowledge of the judge" clause has led to the passing of death sentences and executions, including *hodud* punishments such as stoning, often overriding the strict evidentiary requirements in Islamic law in connection with such cases. The government itself publishes no statistics about these executions and indeed, until the early 2000s, made great efforts to hide cases of stoning from public view. But data assembled by various human rights groups indicates that between 1986 and 2010 a number of stonings were carried out, sometimes secretly in prisons. Amnesty International, for example reported that in 1986 at least eight people were stoned to death and that in 1995 as many as ten people were stoned to death (Woolridge 2010). There were apparently no stonings in the year 2000, leading some international commentators to conclude, prematurely, that the practice had fallen into disuse. But executions of this kind were resumed in 2001 amid much publicity in Tehran's main prison, Evin.[10]

In December 2002, following considerable domestic and international pressure, Ayatollah Shahroudi, as head of the judiciary, announced the suspension of executions by stoning. Moreover, Shahroudi denounced the use of *ʿelm-e qāzi* which was used to overcome the ordinary strictures of the law such as the invalidity of pretrial confession or the ability of repentance to preclude *hadd* in certain circumstances. Indeed, Shahroudi even wrote a detailed essay arguing that scripture does not support the permission of *ʿelm* in criminal matters for ordinary judges, but only for the Imams or their representative, the *vali-ye amr* (Fraser Fujinaga 2013: 56). Shahroudi's views on *ʿelm-e qāzi* are discussed in more detail in Chapter 9.

For a few years, after Shahroudi's moratorium in 2002, no one was sentenced to stoning. But *ʿelm-e qāzi* continued to be used as a basis for handing down stoning as punishment. The most well-known case of this, widely covered in the international media, was the case of Iranian-Azerbaijani Turkic-speaker Sakineh Mohammadi Ashtiani. Arrested in 2005, Ashtiani was convicted by a lower court in May 2006 for having an "illicit relationship" with two men. A judge reportedly sentenced her to receive ninety-nine lashes and this sentence is believed to have been carried out. The court then convicted her of "adultery while being married" and handed down the mandatory sentence of death by stoning. In court she retracted a "confession" she had made during interrogation, stating

---

[10] For example, the stoning to death of Maryam Ayubi on July 11, 2001. See Abdorrahman Boroumand Center, "One Person's Story," https://perma.cc/7B6W-AZPQ, accessed February 4, 2021.

The Administration of Criminal Justice in Iran

that it was made under duress. However, she was convicted by a majority of three out of five trial judges on the basis of *ʿelm-e qāzi*.[11] Her sentence was eventually commuted to death by hanging and, after nine years on death row, she was pardoned and released in 2014.

From 2007 onward substantial additional information about the use of *ʿelm-e qāzi* in such cases came to light through research conducted by the Tehran-based "Stop Stoning Forever" campaign, which was established following reports of an execution by stoning in Mashhad on May 7, 2006. A small group of human rights activists and members of the Iranian Bar set out to determine whether there were others who were awaiting execution by this method. They uncovered nine cases up and down the country and the six lawyers involved with the group volunteered pro bono representation in the appeal process. On or around October 21, 2006 these lawyers wrote to Ayatollah Shahroudi about the cases they had discovered and to demand that the punishment of stoning be removed from the statute books. On their website they recall this episode:

> Although it is apparently very difficult to provide evidence in the court to prove adultery (testimonies by four fair male witnesses, or four confessions to the offense by the accused), Article 105 of the Islamic Penal Code leaves the judge's hands open to issue a subjective and arbitrary ruling based on his own understanding, or knowledge, of the case. As has been stated by the lawyers of five women sentenced to stoning in a letter to the head of the judiciary, in most of the cases these women have been sentenced solely based on the judge's knowledge despite the lack of evidence. Thus, the difficulty of presenting evidence is not an issue when the judge can rely on his own knowledge.[12]

The Minister of Justice at the time, Jamal Karimi-Rad, responded to this letter by claiming that stonings do not happen in the Islamic Republic of Iran and that when a stoning sentence is handed down it never obtains final approval.[13] However, the group refuted this claim, pointing out that in six of the nine cases they had discovered the stoning sentence had been approved by the high court.[14]

In 2013 a new Islamic Penal Code was promulgated which in its first draft no longer contained the punishment of stoning. The government touted the revision as an improvement on the previous Penal Code and

---

[11] Amnesty International, "Let Me Go," September 28, 2010: https://perma.cc/394W-DPFU, accessed June 10, 2021.
[12] Iran: "Stop Stoning Forever" Campaign, June 12, 2006: https://perma.cc/FCW9-WWZR, accessed June 15, 2021.
[13] Ibid.
[14] Ibid. For more examples of how *ʿelm-e qāzi* has been used to override the high evidentiary rules of shariʿa as well as other exculpatory evidence leading to the sentences of stonings, death, and amputations, see Fraser Fujinaga (2013, especially pp. 142–145 and 246–249).

one that broadly complies with international human rights standards. But though explicit reference to punishments like stoning were removed in reality, the new code employed a great deal of sophistry and vaguely worded articles to retain and even enhance many of the negative features of the old code. For example, the code allows judges to refer to noncodified law in the form of Shi'i jurisprudence (which prescribes stoning for adultery) to issue their verdicts. In April 2013, a few months after it was initially promulgated, the Guardian Council reinserted the clauses which prescribed stoning for adultery into the code – a move which reflected the religious and ideological importance that stoning holds for the conservative clerical ruling elite.

Since 2009 there have been no records of stoning sentences passed in the courts, but the possibility that these might be imposed again in the future is certainly there. This is exacerbated by the fact that the 2013 Penal Code retained the concept of *ʿelm-e qāzi*. Article 210 states that "knowledge of the judge comprises certainty derived from presentable evidence in connection with an issue before the judge." In the absence of confessions or other available testimony by eyewitnesses, a judge may enter a conviction for certain crimes based on his "knowledge." The law requires, however, that rulings based on a judge's "knowledge" derive from evidence, including circumstantial evidence, and not merely personal belief that the defendant is guilty of the crime.

Despite marginally enhanced conditionality under the 2013 Penal Code, such provisions remain problematic for several reasons. The existence and practice of this provision continues to violate the right to a fair trial by, in effect, making the judge a witness for the prosecution and therefore able to introduce evidence against the defendant. Moreover, as Human Rights Watch have noted, it "is not clear whether new provisions defining 'knowledge of the judge' in the new code prohibit the use of non-codified law to determine culpability."[15]

By increasing the scope of judicial discretion, *ʿelm-e qāzi*, could be seen as an expression of the "historical openness that the shariʿa ideally possesses by allowing judges to tailor their decisions to the exigencies of individual cases" (Osanloo 2020: 85). But, as we have seen, it has in practice often led to highly arbitrary decisions and the uneven and inconsistent application of the law.[16] Moreover, whilst there might be some scope for judges to use *ʿelm* to reduce punishments by erring on

---

[15] Human Rights Watch, "Codifying Repression: An Assessment of Iran's New Penal Code," August 28, 2012: https://perma.cc/N3PF-LPKU, accessed June 15, 2021.

[16] See Fraser Fujinaga (2013) for numerous examples of these inconsistencies.

the side of caution, and even deliberately getting some cases wrong to save the defendant, there is little or no evidence that this has happened. On the contrary, it seems to have been used primarily as a way of enforcing *hodud* punishments such as stoning by overcoming the ordinary strictures of the law that have traditionally been used in Islamic jurisprudence to avoid applying these punishments. As we have seen, the status of this principle is highly contested within Shi'i jurisprudence especially in connection with *hadd* cases. It could thus be reformed without controversy or even abolished through legislation based on a different reading of the Shi'i sources, which are the law's ostensible origin – something the 2013 Penal Code failed to do (Fraser Fujinaga 2013: 282).

2.2 Qesās *(Retaliation) and* Bakhshesh *(Forgiveness and Clemency)*

Qesās (retaliation) is often portrayed in Western media as the "eye-for-an-eye law." It is frequently used in Iran in "ordinary" (nonpolitical) cases of criminal law involving homicide and bodily harm. For example, during 2019, most executions for murder took place under this provision.[17] *Qesās* provides for a range of cruel, inhuman, and degrading (CID) punishments under *qesās-e 'ovz* (retaliation for injured limbs or body parts). Articles 386 to 416 of the IPC contain regulations providing for *qesās-e 'ovz*. According to Article 386, causing intentional bodily harm carries the penalty of *qesās-e 'ovz* upon the request of the victim or their guardian. The offence is defined as causing severe harm short of murder, such as severing a body part or impairing the function of an organ. Penalties provided for include amputation of limbs, cutting of body parts such as lips, tongue, ears, eyelids, and nose, removal of teeth, and blinding (Articles 390 and 402–416).[18] As in other areas of the criminal justice system, there are reports of due-process violations, including the use of torture to extract "confessions" and hasty trials without sufficient time to investigate the evidence.[19]

Alongside *hodud*, *qesās*, and *diyeh*, the law also provides for the possibility of clemency or forgiveness (*bakhshesh*) by the plaintiff for the defendant, thus introducing an important element of restorative justice

---

[17] Iran Human Rights, "Iran Executions 2019: *Qesās* and Forgiveness," April 7, 2019: https://perma.cc/88QG-D962, accessed June 17, 2021.

[18] For an example of this, see Dehghan (2015).

[19] Iran Human Rights, "Iran Executions 2019: *Qesās* and Forgiveness," April 7, 2019: https://perma.cc/2U2W-HTMS, accessed November 19, 2020.

into the system. This is based on Quranic principles of mercy, compassion and forgiveness.[20] Evidence suggests that a majority of criminal cases involving *qesās* are concluded by the victim's family forgiving the defendant or agreeing to commute the punishment (Osanloo 2020: 28). This is sometimes achieved through encouragement by judicial officials, but more often is the result of civil society initiatives and alternative dispute resolution, which constitute a space for negotiation, bargaining, and reconciliation. Indeed, the option to forgive, without however having recourse to meaningful guidelines on how to do so, has produced "an informal cottage industry of advocacy, one that is populated by diverse actors and which produces numerous avenues for negotiating forbearance by forging reconciliation and settlement" (Osanloo 2020: 3).

Over the years, Iranians have mobilized in different ways against the death penalty and have tried to convince the families of the victims to forgive as a means of last resort. Since the early 2010s, these efforts have increased, leading to at least 200 cases of forgiveness each year from 2015 to 2019 (Sepehri Far 2019). In 2018, the organization Iran Human Rights reported an increase in the movement to encourage forgiveness or clemency, recording 272 such cases – almost the same as the number of recorded executions for that year. Whilst acknowledging the role of judicial officials in encouraging forgiveness, the report identifies the main forces behind this movement as activists, journalists, and charity organizations, such as the Imam Ali Society. These organizations support prisoners and have worked across the country to mediate between families of victims and the accused in informal settings to convince the victims' heirs to forego executions.[21] Instead, families often ask for *diyeh*, which many of the accused's families cannot afford. This has led charity workers and activists to join forces with celebrities such as football players and actors to raise the money. Every year, activists organize fundraising events in which celebrities – and in exceptional cases, government officials – participate. For example, Shahindokht Molaverdi, the former vice president for women and family affairs, participated in fundraising efforts for *diyeh* payments when she was in office.[22] In December 2018, Asghar Farhadi, the Oscar-winning film

---

[20] For example, the Quranic verse: "And the recompense of evil is punishment like it, but whoever forgives and amends, he shall have his reward from Allah; surely He does not love the unjust" (42:40).

[21] The website of the Imam Ali Society is available at: https://perma.cc/V6BW-NUSD, accessed June 15, 2020.

[22] (In Persian): Iran Student News Agency (ISNA), "Can You Let Me Live?" Khordad 23 1395/ June 12 2016: https://perma.cc/9XCG-T5MP, accessed June 16, 2020.

director, and Rakhshān Banietemad, another respected film director, organized an event to raise funds for two people on death row for crimes they allegedly committed when they were children.[23] Iranian journalists have also contributed to this movement by reporting on the devastating harm executions cause to families, particularly in the cases where children were the offenders. Newspapers have also featured interviews with families who have chosen not to ask for the death penalty.[24] Many efforts have been focused on women who have been accused of killing their husbands and those who offended while children. Despite these efforts, at least 180 people were executed for murder in 2018 and Amnesty International estimated that 90 people were on death row that year for crimes they committed when they were children.[25]

This element of restorative justice within the system is not without its drawbacks. For example, it puts a severe psychological burden onto the victims or their families to decide the appropriate punishment. Moreover, it can lead to the early release of prisoners who have committed serious crimes without proper rehabilitation and probation. Conversely (as discussed in Chapter 7 of this volume on prisons), it can sometimes lead to long delays whilst families decide on the outcome – which means people are held in jail for a long time for sometimes relatively minor crimes.

2.3   The Office of Public Prosecutor (dādsetān-e ʿomumi)

Finally, in this consideration of attempts to institute "authentic" forms of shariʿa criminal procedure, we will consider the question of prosecution. The office of public prosecutor was first introduced in Iran in 1907 and was part of a package of reforms which gradually transformed large areas of criminal law – especially murder and bodily harm – from private to public law. This new institution faced some opposition from conservative ʿulamā' during the post-constitutional period but nevertheless became accepted and institutionalized fairly quickly (Enayat 2013: 72, 74). After the 1979 Revolution, the office was initially retained, but in 1994 it was abolished and the functions of investigator, prosecutor, and adjudicator were vested in a single case judge. This reform sought to institute a traditional, authentic model of

---

[23] (In Persian): Iranian Labor News Agency, "Farhadi and Banietemad Campaign to Free Two Youths Sentenced to Qesās," Dey 10 1397/December 31 2018: https://perma.cc/2YGQ-PFBD, accessed June 18, 2020.

[24] (In Persian): Islamic Republic News Agency (IRNA), "A Smile after the Confusion of the Jehoon Tragedy Khordād 17 1396/June 7 2017:" https://perma.cc/J8ND-RKDY, accessed June 15, 2020.

[25] Amnesty International, "Stop Imminent Execution of Three Prisoners Arrested as Teenagers," February 22, 2019: https://perma.cc/88U4-JMK2, accessed June 18, 2020.

shariʿa justice in which the *qāzi* assumed all of these functions (Zubaida 2003: 201). Thus, it ended the adversarial tension and inbuilt check between the role of the prosecutor and judge: the internationally accepted principle of the separation of powers.[26] Over this period, according to Amnesty International, "cases were tried in a manner that is incompatible with the norms guaranteeing the right to due process, including the essential norm of the impartiality of the judge."[27] A 2003 report of the UN Working Group on Arbitrary Detention (WGAD) makes similar observations.[28] In light of these criticisms, complaints from judges themselves, as well as pressure from Iranian human rights activists and lawyers, the office of public prosecutor was gradually restored from 2002 onward but many problems have persisted. The restoration only applied to the lower-level criminal courts and not to special tribunals such as the military, clerical, and revolutionary courts. Moreover, the office of prosecutor remained institutionally under the same roof as the judgment and sentencing, which is a violation of due process. The two stages of the criminal indictment process should be undertaken by separate institutions to ensure the neutrality of the court.

3   Politicization: Consequences of a Nonindependent Judiciary

As we have seen in the introduction to this volume, the judiciary has been increasingly subordinated to the powers of the Supreme Leader and the agencies under his control and judges lack security of tenure. Moreover, whilst the head of the judiciary has some room for maneuver in terms of instituting reforms – as is discussed in Chapter 9 with reference to Mahmoud Shahroudi – the structural subordination of the judiciary to the Supreme Leader means that it serves the interests of the system (lit.: *nezām*, or "order") as defined by the Supreme Leader. This mirrors the tensions or tradeoffs of his office between national security imperatives and justice. As an institution under the formal control of the Supreme Leader, its conduct cannot be checked by the other constitutional "powers" since they have no "power of interpellation" over the head of

---

[26] Amnesty International, "Iran: A Legal System That Fails to Protect Freedom of Expression and Association," December 2001: https://perma.cc/QJU9-RS2W, accessed August 5, 2020.
[27] Ibid., 22.
[28] United Nations, "Civil and Political Rights, Including the Question of Torture and Detention: Report of the Working Group on Arbitrary Detention. Addendum: Visit to the Islamic Republic of Iran, 15–27 February 2003" (E/CN.4/2004/3/ Add.2), June 27, 2003, Paragraph 62.

The Administration of Criminal Justice in Iran 79

the judiciary or any judiciary officials.[29] This has resulted in the effective politicization of the judiciary since the founding of the Islamic Republic and this is, in part, the reason for the conduct – and gross human rights violations – of the criminal justice system that have occurred since 1979. Apart from individual cases, this includes mass killing in prisons in 1988; waves of arbitrary arrests in the early 1990s; and brutal responses to student protests in 1999, to the protests after the disputed election in 2009, mass killing with impunity by security forces after unrest following energy price rises in 2019 and again after the death of Mahsa Jina Amini in 2022. This trend has sometimes been commented upon in the Majles. In 2014, for example, a parliamentarian stated that "we have witnessed the security apparatus, from the position of strength, putting the judge under pressure to steer the trial in the direction that they want."[30]

It is likewise the structural subordination of the security forces, and the effective, if not formal, control exerted by the office of the Supreme Leader over bodies that have the power of arrest that necessarily results in the alignment of purpose between those institutions and the judiciary. Indeed, the lines between the judiciary and various agencies of the executive branch and the security apparatus are similarly blurred, including the Revolutionary Guard, the Basij, the police, and the Ministry of Intelligence (Khalaji 2009; Ebadi 2019). Overt and covert interference of these agencies in the judicial process is commonplace, as discussed in Section 4.2 below, under the role of judicial officers (*zābetān-e qazā'i*).

3.1 The Tehran Prosecutor's Office

As we have seen, the office of the prosecutor was abolished in 1994 and, until its gradual restoration between May 2003 and 2005,[31] in both the public and revolutionary court systems the functions of the investigative judge (*bāzpors*) and the prosecutor were vested in the trial judge. Over this

---

[29] That is to say, parliament has no power to supervise the activities of the judiciary or dismiss the head of the judiciary (see Arjomand 2008). The partial exception is the Article 90 Commission of Parliament, which is constitutionally mandated to address private complaints against the three branches of government. The commission has no effective powers of enforcement but has been used, to some effect, to bring grievances to light. See, for an account, Human Rights Watch, "'Like the Dead in Their Coffins': Torture, Detention, and the Crushing of Dissent in Iran" (Vol. 16, No. 2(E)), June 2004, pp. 60–63: https://perma.cc/9VN4-HCWL, accessed May 5, 2018.

[30] United Nations, General Assembly, Sixty-Ninth Session, Item 69 (c) of the provisional agenda: Promotion and protection of human rights: human rights situations and reports of special rapporteurs and representatives – Situation of human rights in the Islamic Republic of Iran: Note by the Secretary-General (UN reference A/69/356) August 27, 2014: https://perma.cc/4FBK-U2Q8, accessed September 18, 2020.

[31] By legislation approved in November 2002.

period, according to Amnesty International, "cases were tried in a manner that is incompatible with the norms guaranteeing the right to due process, including the essential norm of the impartiality of the judge."[32] The report of the WGAD makes similar observations.[33] These criticisms, as well as pressure from Iranian human rights activists and lawyers, led the head of the judiciary Ayatollah Shahroudi to restore the office of public prosecutor in 2002. But the process by which the office was restored drew much criticism, largely owing to the appointment of Saeed Mortazavi as chief prosecutor for Tehran with powers to supervise the reform throughout the country. Of his appointment, the WGAD, in a coda on developments since its visit to Iran in February 2003, commented:

> [T]he recent appointment, questionable and questioned, of judge Saeed Mortazavi, a judge at the Administrative Court for the Press, as Attorney General [sic Chief Prosecutor] of Tehran, with the task of reforming the prosecution service [...] was seen as a provocation by the [domestic] press. In that connection, the Commission on Human Rights will recall, on reading the most recent report by the UN Special Representative, Mr. Copithorne (E/ CN.4/2002/42, Paragraphs 11, 22, and 40), that this judge was responsible for the mass closure in 2000 of newspapers (12 were banned) and for the wave of arrests of journalists and editors, several of whom were visited by the Working Group in Evin. He is also responsible for the sentencing of academics and intellectuals who on 7 and 8 April 2000 participated in a conference in Berlin on the subject of "Iran after the elections," including Akbar Ganji and Ali Afshari, visited by the Group in Evin, and of attorneys Mohammad-Ali Dadkhah and Abdul Soltani (sic), visited by the Group after their sentencing for events relating to the legitimate exercise of their functions as defense counsel.[34]

In fact, there is a consensus that Mortazavi was appointed because he was favored by the Supreme Leader precisely for his combination of ruthlessness and absolute commitment to the interests of the system. From the end of 2003 to August 2009 when he was removed from his post, under Mortazavi the Tehran prosecutor's office accumulated much power and was described as "the jugular vein of the judiciary of the Islamic Republic."[35] Though responsible for the conduct of ordinary criminal prosecutions as well as political/security cases, after his appointment Mortazavi continued to play a high-profile, often "hands-on," role in the suppression of dissent,

---

[32] See note 26, p. 22.
[33] United Nations, "Civil and Political Rights, Including the Question of Torture and Detention: Report of the Working Group on Arbitrary Detention. Addendum: Visit to the Islamic Republic of Iran, 15–27 February 2003" (E/CN.4/2004/3/ Add.2), June 27, 2003, Paragraph 62.
[34] WGAD, Paragraph 63.
[35] Radio Free Europe/Radio Liberty (RFE/RL), "Tehran's Hard-Line Prosecutor Moved to State Role, But Little Changes," Iran Report, August 31, 2009: www.rferl.org/a/Tehrans_HardLine_Prosecutor_Moved_To_State_Role_But_Little_Changes_/1811597.html, accessed December 22, 2020.

The Administration of Criminal Justice in Iran 81

and he was implicated in a series of gross human rights abuses which clearly left their stamp on the overall culture of the institution.[36] These violations are well documented and include the extrajudicial murder of Canadian-Iranian photojournalist Zahra Kazemi in 2003,[37] the arbitrary detention of more than twenty bloggers and internet journalists in the fall of 2004,[38] and the torture and death of arrested demonstrators at Kahrizak Prison after the contested 2009 elections.[39] After a number of investigations into Mortazavi's role in these abuses he was removed from office in 2009, and in 2018 he received a two-year sentence for his complicity in the death of three protestors who died after being tortured in Kahrizak.[40] The leniency of this sentence was commented on by Siamak Modir Khorasani who was the presiding judge of Branch 76 of Tehran Criminal Court for close to twelve years. In an interview in 2017 published by the Mashregh News Agency, Khorasani revealed that in the Kahrizak case, where he was the presiding judge, the parents of Amir Javadifar – one of the victims - withdrew their complaint against Mortazavi. "My own feeling was that this letter of withdrawal had been obtained beforehand and was then introduced during the trial," says Khorasani. "This was my personal impression … By the way it was written I gathered that the family of the victim had written it under coercion." In other words, Khorasani had concluded that the letter of withdrawal had been obtained from the victim's family by force and, as a result, the charge of accessory to murder against Mortazavi was dropped. "I believed he was an accessory to murder and wrote this in my opinion but three members of five-member panel of judges voted against it," he said. "I along with another colleague voted for a sentence of 15 years in prison for being accessory to murder but the other three colleagues did not believe so and, as a result, the court acquitted him on the charge of accessory to murder."[41] Mortazavi served seventeen months in prison for

---

[36] See also, on Mortazavi, Human Rights Watch, "'Like the Dead in Their Coffins': Torture, Detention, and the Crushing of Dissent in Iran" (Vol. 16, No. 2(E)), June 2004, pp. 43–60: www.hrw.org/reports/iran0604.pdf, accessed December 22, 2020.

[37] Iran Human Rights Documentation Center, "Impunity in Iran: The Death of Photojournalist Zahra Kazemi," November 2006: https://iranhrdc.org/impunity-in-iran-the-death-of-photojournalist-zahra-kazemi/, accessed December 15, 2010.

[38] Human Rights Watch, "Iran: Judiciary Uses Coercion to Cover Up Torture," December 19, 2004: www.hrw.org/news/2004/12/20/iran-judiciary-uses-coercion-cover-torture, accessed December 22, 2020.

[39] "Iran's Parliament Exposes Abuse of Opposition Prisoners at Tehran Jail," *The Guardian*, January 10, 2010: www.guardian.co.uk/world/2010/jan/10/iran-prisoners-abuse-jail, accessed January 10, 2010.

[40] "Notorious 'Butcher' Prosecutor Sentenced to Two Years," *Iran Farda*, March 2, 2018: https://en.radiofarda.com/a/iran-mortazavi-prosecutor-sentenced/29072990.html, accessed March 15, 2022.

[41] "Fact Check: Iran's Judiciary Is Not and Has Never Been Independent," *Iran Wire*, September 24, 2020: https://iranwire.com/en/features/67655/, accessed March 16, 2022.

his role in the killings, after which he was released for "good behaviour." In August 2021 the Supreme Court acquitted him of all charges.[42]

Mortazavi's career and the conduct of the cases against him showed that where the interests of the state are involved, in whichever type of court a trial is held, judicial officials easily and readily construct proceedings so as to ensure a "positive" outcome for the state and its officials. The biased structure of the judiciary, notably in respect to whom it is accountable – not to the people, nor even to the state, but rather to one individual/institution – frames the selection of judges, the legal options of those wishing to complain and procedures that lawyers may or may not be allowed to deploy.

4 Challenges at Every Stage of the Criminal Justice System

We now turn to the criminal justice "journey" from arrest to prosecution and appeal/retrial. Specific procedural shortcomings exist at every stage of the criminal justice process, from the very basis of arrest to pretrial detention (PTD), access to legal representation of one's choice; to trial and issues relating to due process and conviction/imprisonment exacerbating the overriding structural flaws discussed.

4.1 Flawed Basis for Arrest

UN human rights experts, nongovernmental organizations (NGOs), and commentators have, for decades, pointed out that constitutional guarantees notwithstanding, the specific laws upon which the authorities make arrests are often extremely vaguely worded, flawed, and do not constitute internationally recognizable criminal offences.[43] Such laws form parts of Book V of the Penal Code on *taʿzīrāt* (discretionary punishments). For example, Articles 498 and 499 of Book V state that whoever forms or joins a group or association either inside or outside the country, which seeks to "disturb the security of the country" will be sentenced to between two and ten years' imprisonment, yet there is no definition of "disturb" or "security of the country" in the code itself.[44] Articles 500 and 610 deal with national security and are

---

[42] "Tehran's 'Butcher of the Press' Saeed Mortazavi Is Acquitted of Murder," *Iran Wire*, August 10, 2021: https://iranwire.com/en/features/70120/, accessed March 15, 2022.

[43] Article 23 of the constitution states that "The investigation of individuals' beliefs is forbidden" and that "no one may be molested or taken to task simply for holding a certain belief." Article 24 also provides for freedom of expression in press and publications.

[44] Some of these examples are taken from, inter alia, Amnesty International; see note 26.

similarly vaguely worded. Article 500 states that "anyone who undertakes any form of propaganda against the state ... will be sentenced to between three months and one year in prison." Under Article 610, two or more persons who conspire to commit or facilitate a nonviolent offence against the internal or external security of the nation will be imprisoned for between two and five years. Again, "security" and "propaganda" are not defined in the Penal Code.

4.2 Legal and Judicial Flaws which Enable Arbitrary Detention and the Use of Torture

As Golkar discusses in greater detail in Chapter 6 of this volume, judicial officers (*zābetān-e qazā'i*) are officials authorized to arrest and investigate a crime under the supervision of a judicial authority, such as a judge. The CCP also empowers the police and the nonuniformed Basij and Revolutionary Guards to make arrests.[45] In addition, Iran's Supreme National Security Council may empower other bodies or agencies to do so as well. While Ministry of Intelligence personnel do not appear in law to have the power of arrest, under these conjunctural provisions they may well have been given it. Therefore, organizations whose officials possess power of arrest may include:[46]

i) The Criminal Investigations Office of the Law Enforcement Forces (Edāreh-ye āgāhi-ye niruhā-ye entezāmi) informally known as the "Agahi police,"
ii) The Basij (a paramilitary organization under the command of the Revolutionary Guard).
iii) The Ministry of Information and Security (the "Intelligence Ministry"). Along with other agencies, the Intelligence Ministry has played a significant role in investigating economic crimes.[47]
iv) The Intelligence Division of the Islamic Revolutionary Guards Corps (IRGC).

In respect to arrests made following the disputed 2009 presidential election, Amnesty International noted that:

---

[45] Ibid., p. 29.
[46] Article 28 CCP 2015.
[47] Economic offences are investigated and tried at a dedicated judicial complex, the Special Judicial Complex for Economic Affairs (Mojtama'-ye Qaza'i Omur-e Eqtesādi). The complex consists of specialized prosecutors' offices and a range of courts, including a revolutionary court and a branch of the Provincial Criminal Court, thus drawing together several jurisdictions, often overlapping, under a single roof.

The lack of transparency of this system gives rise to abuse of the power of arrest, reinforcing the practice of arbitrary arrest, which is facilitated by flawed provisions in the Penal Code. The lack of transparency and oversight mechanisms also allows the various forces, particularly the Basij militia, to commit human rights violations with impunity.[48]

While carrying out their investigations, "officers of court" are theoretically subject to the authority of the investigating judge.[49] In practice, however, the relationship has often been the other way round.

In addition to the lack of clarity over authorities with powers of arrest, due process in Iran's criminal justice system is undermined by the routine practice of torture or ill-treatment in pre-trial detention.[50] Despite Article 38 of the 1979 constitution, which provides that "All forms of torture for the purpose of extracting confession or acquiring information are forbidden," substantial evidence that torture is used is available in multiple accounts in Iran's prison memoir literary genre.[51] Moreover, reports from political, student, and human rights groups dating from the early 1980s indicate that arbitrary and unfair arrest, followed by torture or ill-treatment in pretrial custody has been endemic in prisons and detention centers of the Islamic Republic since the inception of the state.[52]

In connection with confessions, moreover, the Penal Code states:

Article 166 – Confession must be made by [saying the] words or in writing; and, if [the above-mentioned ways] are not possible, it can be made by an act such as a gesture; and in any event it should be clear and unambiguous.

Article 167 – Confession must be incontrovertible; a conditional and suspended confession shall not be considered.

Article 168 – A confession shall be admissible only if, at the time of confession, the confessor is sane, pubescent, intended [to make the confession] and free.

Article 169 – A confession which is taken under coercion, force, torture, or mental or physical abuses, shall not be given any validity and weight and the court is obliged to interrogate the accused again.[53]

---

[48] Amnesty International, "Iran: Election Contested, Repression Compounded," December 2009, p. 29: https://tinyurl.com/25ya2s9u, accessed December 22, 2020.

[49] Article 28 CCP 2015.

[50] See also Devraj (2009) and Abdorrahman Boroumand Foundation, "Coerced Confessions in the Islamic Republic of Iran," August 15, 2007: https://perma.cc/8Z3A-UWHA, accessed December 22, 2020.

[51] For a recent example of this genre, see Mohajer (2020).

[52] The article also states that "compulsion of individuals to testify, confess, or take an oath is not permissible; and any testimony, confession, or oath obtained under duress is devoid of value and credence. Violation of this article is liable to punishment in accordance with the law."

[53] Taken from the English translation of Books I and II of the new Islamic Penal Code, Iran Human Rights Documentation Center, April 4, 2014: https://perma.cc/CPZ3-R6GT, accessed December 15, 2018.

Despite this, there are no detailed provisions on the inadmissibility of unlawfully obtained confessions or other evidence (at the time of writing), and Article 360 of the CCP "allows the court to issue a verdict on the basis of confessions if there exists no doubt about their accuracy or that they have been voluntarily given by the accused person."[54] Neither the nature of a "confession" nor procedures about their expression are further set out in the Penal Code, which fails to "specify procedures that must be followed by judges and prosecutors to establish whether a statement is lawful and admissible, including automatic and immediate medical examination where the accused alleges that a statement has been extracted under torture or other ill-treatment."[55] Such matters are left to the trial judge.

The use of flawed legislation by unaccountable bodies to conduct arbitrary arrest and long-term detention beyond the reach of the judiciary, when the authorities deploy torture or ill-treatment in order to coerce "confessions," grossly erodes the presumption of innocence.

4.3 Examples of Torture and Ill-Treatment

The following, chronologically ordered, examples – not intended to be exhaustive – reflect emblematic facets of Iran's conduct in relation to the administration of justice. Specialist organizations that have assembled documentation from victims of torture who have fled abroad include the respected London-based Medical Foundation for the Care of Victims of Torture (now Freedom from Torture). In 2003, the Foundation published figures showing that of 2,101 new referrals in that year, Iranians, with 230, were third on the list by country of origin (after Turkey, with 407, and Congo with 293).[56] In June 2012 the director of Freedom from Torture, announcing the Foundation's plans to publish its data on Iran in the near future, remarked that:

Since we opened our doors 25 years ago, Freedom from Torture has documented the injuries and provided therapeutic care to thousands of people in the UK who have been subjected to torture and other ill treatment at the hands of the Iranian authorities. Last year, nearly 20 percent of the individuals referred to us for help were from Iran. When you consider that we receive referrals from people from over 80 different countries around the world, this is a staggering amount.[57]

---

[54] Amnesty International, "Flawed Reforms: Iran's New Code of Criminal Procedure," February 11, 2016, p. 72: https://perma.cc/54JJ-JYCP, accessed December 15, 2018.
[55] Ibid.
[56] For statistics on torture in Iran and several other countries, see the Freedom from Torture website: https://perma.cc/BN9C-AASL, accessed March 15, 2021.
[57] Keith Best, chief executive of Freedom from Torture, quoted in "Campaigners Designate 20th June as 'International Day in Support of Political Prisoners in Iran,'" June 19, 2012: www.freedomfromtorture.org/news-blogs/6405, accessed January 2, 2013.

Commonly reported methods of torture included prolonged solitary confinement,[58] sensory deprivation such as blindfolding and sleep deprivation, white torture,[59] severe and repeated beatings, often with cables or other instruments, the suspension of detainees by the arms and legs, threats of execution and mock executions, burning with cigarettes, and rape.[60]

In order to address the prevalence of torture in Iran's criminal justice system, parliamentary advocates of rule of law and legal reform during the early 2000s sought to introduce legislation to curtail abuses. In April 2004 the Citizens Rights Law was promulgated.[61] Its scope was, however, limited: Reporting on its enactment, then UN Special Rapporteur on Iran, in 2017, Asma Jahangir, stated that "[I]in key areas such as women's rights and the rights of ethnic and religious minorities, the Charter offers almost no new rights protection" and noted concerns "about [its] non-binding legal nature."[62] The continuing, direct involvement of the judiciary in the practice of torture, further neutralized the potentially positive impact of the legislation.

[58] The UN WGAD noted in its 2004 report on Iran (Paragraph 54) that: "Solitary confinement covers the generalized use of 'incommunicado' imprisonment. The Working Group, for the first time since its establishment, has been confronted with a strategy of widespread use of solitary confinement for its own sake and not for traditional disciplinary purposes, as the Group noted during its truncated visit to sector 209 of Evin prison. This is not a matter of a few punishment cells, as exist in all prisons, but what is a 'prison within a prison,' fitted out for the systematic, large-scale use of absolute solitary confinement, frequently for very long periods." It appears to be an established fact that the use of this kind of detention has allowed the extraction of "confessions" followed by "public repentance" (on television); besides their degrading nature, such statements are manifestly inadmissible as evidence. The WGAD noted that "such absolute solitary confinement, when it is of a long duration, can be likened to inhuman treatment within the meaning of the Convention Against Torture": https://tinyurl.com/2ucr2aw6, accessed March 15, 2019.

[59] 'White torture' is a form of psychological torture aimed at total sensory deprivation and isolation in which everything the prisoner sees is white including their food.

[60] See, among other sources, Freedom from Torture, June 2012: www.freedomfromtorture.org/news-blogs/6405, accessed January 12, 2013; and Amnesty International, "We Are Ordered to Crush You," February 2012, p. 21: https://perma.cc/YQ2A-7VMU, accessed April 3, 2013.

[61] The Law on Respect of Lawful Liberties and Protection of Citizenship Rights, ratified by the Majles on April 19, 2004, was amended and ratified by parliament April 21, 2004. Prior to this, between 2001 and the end of 2003 three successive attempts had been made by the advocates of legal reform in the sixth parliament to pass legislation on the issue. Although limited in scope, the Guardian Council vetoed all of the bills. The Citizen's Rights Bill, which simply made into law an earlier directive of the head of the judiciary, was rushed through under emergency procedural rules in May 2004 when parliament was at the end of its term, putting the Guardian Council in an impossible position.

[62] United Nations, General Assembly, Seventy-Second Session, "Promotion and Protection of Human Rights: Human Rights Situations and Reports of Special Rapporteurs and Representatives – Situation of Human Rights in the Islamic Republic of Iran" (A/72/322), August 14, 2017, Paragraphs 7–9: http://undocs.org/A/72/322, accessed March 22, 2020.

Addressing an October 2004 case, Dr. Nemat Ahmadi, a professor of law at Tehran University and a prominent defense counsel, set out evidence on the Agahi police's practice of torture to extract forced confessions. In an open letter to the head of the judiciary on the subject of due process, Ahmadi wrote:

> Excellency I can give you case file numbers (if your office cares to ask me for them) in which a confession has been extracted by breaking teeth or even by the use of a soft drink bottle [through instrumental rape] and however loudly a complaint was made in court the judge ignored it. More important, the confession bore absolutely no relationship to what actually happened in the incident. Interestingly, as soon as the accused went in front of a judge, they denied any guilt and said, "if you send us again to the Law Enforcement Forces [LEF, or police] we will confess to anything they ask." Excellency, I wish you would ask to see these files. They have simply obtained the signatures of the accused under all kinds of torture (including hanging from the wrists) the accused has declared "[...] I'll say whatever you ask or sign the interrogation sheet. Fill it out yourself."[63]

In response to these criticisms, in 2004 Head of the Judiciary Shahroudi issued a fifteen- point circular directed at the judiciary, police, and intelligence officials banning torture.[64] For a short while reports of torture receded but following the mid-2005 election to the presidency of Mahmoud Ahmadinejad, international human rights bodies documented a deterioration of the human rights situation, signaled by arbitrary arrests based on vaguely worded provisions relating to national security.[65] After the contested 2009 elections, some 300 protesters were killed in the crackdown, and rape and torture in Kahrizak Detention Center have been widely documented.

In late December 2013, the owner of a garage located in Karaj, which specialized in changing oil for motor vehicles, faced execution for murder. In 2007, the courts had wrongfully convicted him for the murder of his apprentice who slept in the garage and whose body was discovered by the owner the morning after the murder. The owner immediately reported the death, only to find himself arrested by the Agahi police. They accused him of murder and tortured him to confess. Six years on,

---

[63] Nemat Ahmadi, blog: www.nematahmadi.ir/default.aspx?page=blog&blogid=54, accessed August 20, 2008.

[64] "Human Rights Groups Welcome Move to Ban Torture," *The New Humanitarian*, May 3, 2004: https://perma.cc/JW3T-CDEL, accessed August 22, 2008.

[65] According to a 2006 report by Amnesty International, there were signs of further harsh repression and newly reported cases of torture during the first six months of the Ahmadinejad presidency. Amnesty International, "Iran: New Government Fails to Address Dire Human Rights Situation," February 16, 2006: https://perma.cc/C8CF-EGUL, accessed August 22, 2008.

just forty-eight hours before the scheduled execution of the owner, an impoverished drug addict was arrested for a robbery in Gilan and confessed to the 2007 murder, leading to fast action by a conscientious prosecutor to stay the execution in light of new evidence which exonerated the garage owner.[66]

In early January 2014 an eminent legal scholar, broadly protected from state harassment on account of his close relationship to the late Ayatollah Khomeini, Ayatollah Mostafa Mohaqqeq-Damad,[67] used this case to illustrate a point he made in a lecture on the criminal justice system about the role of "confession" as a method of proof in criminal trials. Mohaqqeq-Damad argued that while "confession" could be regarded as decisive in civil proceedings (contrary to the practice of the courts) in criminal proceedings a confession can never be viewed as decisive. In quoting the example, Mohaqqeq-Damad mistakenly reversed the identity of victim and murderer in the case under discussion, but made no mistake over essential points, including the statement of the apprentice who was suddenly acquitted (which exactly follows the December reports):

> Just 48 hours before the [scheduled] execution, a man was arrested in Gilan and confessed to this murder. When they asked why he had confessed to the crime the apprentice of the oil seller [sic] replied "The Āgāhi police were beating me so hard that I said to myself I will be killed under this torture; it's better that I confess and die by execution so that I will suffer fewer blows." When they asked him, "why then did you confess in court?" he replied that "I knew that if I didn't confess when I returned from the court, I would be beaten again."[68]

In light of these problems the new CCP of 2015, a reform largely initiated by Shahroudi but brought to completion under his successor Sadegh Larijani, introduced changes. These required law enforcement personnel with arrest, detention, and investigation powers to undergo training and carry special identification cards, and restricted the law enforcement

---

[66] The news of this acquittal was reported in detail by the domestic press on December 21, 2013. See, for example (in Persian), Bashgah-e Khabarnegaran-e Javan (Young Journalists Club), "An Innocent Man Tells of the Beatings by Police Officers," Azar 31, 1392/December 21, 2013: https://perma.cc/UW9Z-8HFW, accessed March 3, 2018.

[67] Ayatollah Mostafa Mohaqqeq-Damad is a professor of Islamic jurisprudence and philosophy and currently director of the Department of Islamic Sciences of the Academy of Sciences of Iran. He is a former head of the State Inspectorate (a division of the judiciary charged with auditing, and, where there is an alleged contravention, investigating state institutions).

[68] Mohaqqeq-Damad's speech was reported in the mainstream domestic press by *Khabaronline*, Dey 16, 1392/January 6, 2014: https://tinyurl.com/ybqxzltf, accessed December 22, 2020.

agencies that can exercise judicial powers.[69] However, these reforms were undermined by provisions in the code that continued to grant an array of intelligence and security forces wide-ranging powers of arrest and detention without effective oversight. For instance, the new CCP explicitly includes Ministry of Intelligence officials as "judicial officers" who can make arrests, ending years of debate on whether they were legally allowed to act in this capacity, but fails to restrict the scope of crimes these officials can deal with as "judicial officers."[70] Such flaws erode the rule of law and allow state agents to arbitrarily deprive people of their liberty with almost total impunity (Amnesty International 2016: 9). Indeed, reports of torture continued to emerge. In early 2019, the UN's Special Rapporteur on the situation of human rights in the Islamic Republic of Iran reported on the use of torture with respect to alleged crimes committed by children.[71] He noted that:

> The inherent vulnerability of children is further increased because if they are charged with crimes involving the death penalty, they cannot choose their own lawyer during the initial investigation phase. They are instead limited to a lawyer approved by the head of the judiciary. Information received indicates that numerous children have been convicted on the basis of confessions compelled during this phase. In 2018 for example, Zeinab Sekaanvand was reportedly coerced into confessing that she had killed her husband when she was 17 years old. She recanted her confession but was nevertheless executed. Alireza Tajiki was executed in 2017, after confessing to murder at the age of 15 after reportedly being tortured. He also later recanted his confession, but no investigation was undertaken into his claims […].

In the aftermath of the November 2019/2020 demonstrations over fuel prices there was also evidence of tortured confessions.[72] The continuing practice of torture by police and security forces was also recently highlighted in October 2020 after a video went viral on social media showing police beating up detainees in pickup trucks in the middle of the street. Despite the existing laws against such treatment, the head of the judiciary ordered a ban on torture, the use of "forced confessions,"

---

[69] Article 29 CCP 2015.
[70] Ibid.
[71] See Section (3) "Circumstances of Children Sentenced To Death," Paragraph 57, in United Nations, General Assembly/Human Rights Council, 40th Session, February 25–March 22, 2019, "Human Rights Situations that Require the Council's Attention – Situation of Human Rights in the Islamic Republic of Iran: Report of the Special Rapporteur on the Situation of Human Rights in the Islamic Republic of Iran" (A/HRC/40/67), January 30, 2019: https://perma.cc/U8RM-ZTYD, accessed March 2020.
[72] Amnesty International, "Iran Detainees Flogged, Sexually Abused and Given Electric Shocks in Gruesome Post-Protest Crackdown: New Report," September 2, 2020: https://perma.cc/CR8G-ELWE, accessed July 1, 2021.

solitary confinement, illegal police detentions, and other violations of defendants' rights.[73] The practice of arbitrary arrest as well as torture and ill treatment, including pre-trial detention, looks set to continue for the forseeable future.

4.4 Limiting Access to Legal Counsel

This section, supplemental to Chapter 5 of this volume on the legal profession, discusses the authorities' efforts to prevent access to legal counsel, including counsel of one's choosing. Iran's constitution guarantees the right of people arrested or detained to access legal counsel (Article 35). In practice, however, the authorities have long denied individuals this right during the investigative stage. Before the introduction of the new CCP in 2015, this was justified with reference to Article 128 of the 1999 CCP, which gave the judiciary discretion to exclude counsel during the investigative phase of a prosecution. The text states:

> In cases when the subject has a confidential nature, or if the presence of anyone other than the accused can cause corruption, and also in the case of crimes against national security, presence of attorney in the investigation phase will be with court permission only.

Prosecutors repeatedly invoked Article 128 in political cases and nonpolitical cases alike, as noted by the UN WGAD.[74] A passage from a May 27, 2004 speech by death-penalty opponent Emadeddin Baghi at a seminar on counsel, defense, and preliminary investigation,[75] points to the exclusion of counsel during the investigative phase in ordinary criminal cases:

> We [the ODPR] have seen many cases where, because of the absence of a lawyer and failure to observe the rights of the accused during interrogation and investigation, and the latter's ignorance of their rights, people have confessed to a crime they did not commit – even to planting a bomb, or to committing murder. Only a few weeks ago an individual who had been sentenced to death for a murder was freed from prison. Some three years after he was first imprisoned, quite by accident, one of a gang who were arrested for robbery referred in his confessions to a murder that happened three years ago although the murderers did not know that another person had borne the sentence for an act they had committed.[76]

---

[73] Al Jazeera, "Iran: Judicial Authority Bans Torture," October 15, 2020: https://perma.cc/WJ5K-QBFU, accessed July 1, 2021.
[74] WGAD, Opinion No. 14/2006, May 11, 2006: https://perma.cc/WVL9-QNQL, accessed March 14, 2010.
[75] Baghi was president of the now banned Organization for the Defense of Prisoner's Rights (ODPR), which concentrated on the situation of ordinary as opposed to political prisoners.
[76] (In Persian): Keynote speech by Emadeddin Baghi at the Seminar "Counsel, Defense and Preliminary Investigation," Shahid Beheshti University, Khordad 7, 1383/May 27, 2004: https://perma.cc/UUW3-VB64.

Iranian and international bodies have frequently called for the removal of this provision from the CCP (or its revision).[77] The note to Article 128 was also used in some instances to forbid a lawyer access to the case file during the investigative stage of the proceedings. But even when access was granted once an investigation was complete, attorneys were often not permitted to makes copies of documents or papers in the case file. As a result, they were compelled to make multiple visits to the court, each time facing the possibility of nonadmission (Daraeizadeh, 2010: 13).[78] Some lawyers for political detainees complained that they were only given access to their clients' file at the last minute, and sometimes not at all. Farideh Gheirat, a former vice president of the Bar Association (and one of several prominent women lawyers who have defended politically motivated criminal cases), commented on the case of her client Emadeddin Baghi in May 2010:

The courts established at Evin Prison are courts which were previously located in the Revolutionary Courts [building]. When they were at the Revolutionary Courts, people and lawyers had easier access to them. During the interrogation stage, lawyers are not allowed any involvement with the case, but [inside the Revolutionary Courts] it was possible for the lawyers to go and find information about the cases. But now, after the Ashura events and even before that during the [post] elections events, they have set up the courts inside Evin Prison and with the exception of one or two court branches which remain inside the Revolutionary Courts [building], all the other courts are now at Evin. These courts specifically review the cases of those detained. Accessing these courts for us lawyers is not possible at all, as lawyers and others are not allowed inside. As a result, we cannot even have access to what little and incomplete information we used to gain about [our] cases, as this is no longer possible. For example, [there are instances where] the investigations have been completed and the case file has been sent to the Revolutionary Courts, but we have not yet been informed so that we may present our power of attorney documents and there is no way for us to gain such information. Of course, changing the location of a court is within

---

[77] Examples of the many references on this subject are: United Nations, "Report of the Working Group on Arbitrary Detention: Visit to the Islamic Republic of Iran" (E/CN.4/Sub.2/2003/3/Add.2), June 27, 2003, Paragraph 18; (E/CN.4/2004/3/ Add.2): "The active involvement of counsel must be provided for, whatever the nature of the case, starting with the custody, or, the very least, the investigation phase, throughout the trial and the appeals stage." Daraeizadeh, "Legal Commentary," p. 10. Amnesty International, "Addicted to Death: Executions for Drugs Offences in Iran," December 15, 2011: https://perma.cc/ABH7-GDVW, accessed November 15, 2018, p. 31: "In Amnesty International's view, repeal of this note would reduce the high numbers of arbitrary arrests, help protect individuals from torture or other ill-treatment, and make trials fairer in Iran."

[78] Footnote 45 reads: "Aside from the fact that many political cases are discussed in provincial courts, access to the revolutionary court and meeting judicial officials in those courts is a difficult task. For example, in Tehran, after entering the revolutionary courts building that is under heavy security and requires bodily searches, the relevant branch is contacted through the administrative officers and if permission is received, attorneys are given a sheet to enter the court and study the case file."

the powers of the Judiciary and we cannot ask why a court has been set up in a particular location, but lack of access for lawyers and the public has become problematic for essential follow-up.[79]

In January 2010, Dr. Mohammad Sharif, lawyer for the political activist and blogger Abdollah Momeni, reported that during a first instance trial he had been denied all access to both his client and the case file and had been unable to defend him in court. Finally, after seven months he received permission to read the file in preparation for the appeal of the case at Branch 36 of the Appeals Court.[80]

The new CCP, as adopted in 2014, enhanced the right to access a lawyer by removing some of the previous restrictions but did not fully guarantee the right from the time of arrest, as it permitted the judicial authorities to delay access to a lawyer in the case of some offences (Amnesty International 2016: 41). Moreover, the amendments approved by the Guardian Council in June 2015 failed to bring provisions of the new code in line with international law and standards with regards to the right to access a lawyer from the time of arrest. Instead, they replaced the relevant provision of the new code, which allowed access to legal counsel to be delayed for up to a week, with a provision that denies individuals facing national security-related charges the right to access an independent lawyer of their own choice for the investigation phase, which can last for months. According to the final text of the code, such individuals may only select their lawyers from a list of lawyers approved by the head of the judiciary. The same condition was introduced for individuals accused of involvement in organized crimes that are subject to such punishments as the death penalty, life imprisonment, or amputation (Amnesty International 2016: 11).

At the time of writing, despite international standards that provide for the right to choose one's own legal counsel, suspects are required to choose their defense counsel from a judiciary-approved list of lawyers rather than being able to make their own choice.

4.5 Procedural Flaws during Investigation and Trial

Iran's revolutionary court is the court many think of when discussing Iran's judicial system. It carried out thousands of summary trials and hasty executions in the months following the revolution. These courts, in which leading revolutionary figures assumed a pivotal role, organized ad hoc processes to

---

[79] International Campaign for Human Rights in Iran, "Farideh Gheirat: Even Baghi's Lawyer Can't Access His File," April 21, 2010: https://perma.cc/M4LC-BRTQ accessed May 15, 2017.

[80] Committee of Human Rights Reporters, "Lawyer to Access Client's File after Seven Months," January 19, 2010: http://persian2english.com/?p=4596, accessed March 14, 2015.

try to hold to account and exact revenge against, many of those associated with the Pahlavi regime. None of these constituted fair trials but over time, the revolutionary courts were formalized and procedures improved, at least on paper. They nevertheless depart from the principle that ordinary courts should have primacy, that is, deal with as wide a range of crimes as possible, to ensure standards of uniformity and accountability. Despite periodic calls for its phasing out (especially since it is extraconstitutional), the authorities have chosen to keep it as a specialized criminal court in order to prosecute allegations – often very vaguely worded in the Penal Code – relating to national security, the identity and character of the state, and acts that impact on the national economy. These are designated in the CCP as:

- Crimes against national and external security; *mohārebeh* (enmity against God); *efsād-e fel ʿarz* (corruption on earth), *baghy* (armed rebellion against the state), gathering and colluding against the Islamic Republic, armed activities, arson, and "destruction and plunder of resources with the purpose of opposing the system." These crimes usually carry a death sentence.
- Anyone not considered to be a *mohāreb* but who is nevertheless deemed to be a threat to national security is prosecuted under the vaguely worded Article 498 of Book V of the Law of Islamic Punishments (on *taʿzirāt*) which is often used against political activists in Iran. The article states: "Anyone, whatever his or her belief, who forms or administers a group, an association, or a branch of an association with a membership of more than two persons, inside or outside of the country, under whatever name or heading, the objective of which is to undermine national security, and who is not considered to be a person 'at war with God' (*mohāreb*) will be sentenced to a term of 2–10 years imprisonment."
- Insulting the founder of the Islamic Republic and the Supreme Leader.
- All drug-related offences as well as trafficking of arms and ammunition and other restricted items (insofar as these constitute a deprivation of state income).
- Other offences whose prosecution is assigned to the revolutionary courts on the basis of special, usually temporary, laws.

Revolutionary court trials are "notorious for their disregard of international standards of fair trial," and in the early 1980s, trials were brief – often lasting for no more than a few minutes, at which neither the accused, nor their lawyer (if at all present), were able to make a meaningful oral defense (although they could and can submit a written defense).[81] Writing in 2010, lawyer Behnam Daraeizadeh observed that

---

[81] For the early 2000s see, for example, International Commission of Jurists, "Iran Attacks on Justice 2002": https://perma.cc/U87K-49EW, accessed May 3, 2008: "Trials in these

judges are often merely left to determine the sentence, while the Ministry of Intelligence has often already prepared the verdict:

> In the political/prisoners of conscience cases, Agents of the Ministry of Intelligence prepare a report called "final circulation." In this report or "circulation," the manner of the formation of the case and selected confessions of the accused are noted, while the judge or court magistrate of the case are given the options of designated punishments and even recommendations regarding increasing or decreasing the level of punishment (Daraeizadeh 2010: 5.)

Besides those conducted by the revolutionary courts, other trials involving a political or state interest take place in the military courts (if the accused is an officer of the police, armed forces, or security forces), the Special Courts for the Clergy, or the press courts.

4.6 Procedural Flaws at the Appeal Stage

The 2014 CCP states that the right to appeal a verdict resulting from an error in law or a breach of rights is guaranteed. Article 427 provides for a wide scope for appeal, save for a few very minor, lower court convictions.[82] Appeals, the basis of which can be wide-ranging, as specified by other provisions in the CCP, go to provincial courts of appeal or, ultimately, to the Supreme Court.

In connection with the right of appeal, a 2016 Amnesty International report suggests:

> courts are notorious for their disregard of international standards of fair trial. In addition to those shared by the Islamic Revolutionary Courts with courts in general, these courts have the following deficiencies: the judges are chosen in part based on their ideological commitment; defendants are detained for prolonged periods without access to a lawyer and the right to confront their accusers; secret or summary trials take place; defendants are often indicted for vaguely defined offences such as 'insulting Islamic tenets', 'insulting the Supreme Leader', 'anti-revolutionary behavior', 'moral corruption' and 'propaganda against the state'. The abuses associated with the Islamic Revolutionary Courts appear to be so numerous and so entrenched as to be nearly beyond reform." For the situation in early 2012, see Amnesty International, "'We Are Ordered to Crush You': Expanding Repression of Dissent in Iran," February 2012, pp. 23–24: https://perma.cc/69JX-JJ6F, accessed December 22, 2020.

[82] Article 427 states: "The decisions of the criminal courts, except in the following cases, which are considered final, may be appealed in the provincial court of appeal of the same jurisdiction or to the Supreme Court, as the case may be: A – *Ta'zir* crimes should be eighth degree; B – Crimes requiring the payment of *diyeh* or *arsh*, if the amount or sum of them is less than one tenth of the full *diyeh* – Note 1 – In the case of alternative punishments to imprisonment, the criterion for appeal is the same as the initial legal punishment. – Note 2: The appeals can be appealed, whether it is a conviction, acquittal, or prohibitions and suspension of prosecution, postponement and postponement of the issuance of the sentence. The rejection of an appeal or appeal is subject to this ruling if the decision on the substance of the case can be appealed." The original Persian text of the 2014 CCP is available at: https://perma.cc/8P4R-MEAP, accessed May 5, 2018.

While the CCP provides for the right to appeal before a higher tribunal, the appeal proceedings, in particular before the Supreme Court, are of concern on various grounds. Firstly, those convicted of crimes punishable by serious and irreversible punishments such as the death penalty and amputation have access to just one level of appeal conducted in writing. This is because there is no intermediary tribunal between the court of first instance and the Supreme Court, and the appeal request on such cases must be lodged directly with the Supreme Court. A panel of one judge and two associate judges may then uphold the sentence in the absence of the parties to the case.[83]

As discussed in Section 4.7 below, June 2015 amendments to the CCP reduced to two the number of judges whose presence is required for the court to convene. In a context in which the judiciary is not independent, this is an important factor in respect to due process.[84] Even where a higher court overturns a lower court's verdict, the lower court may nevertheless reimpose the same verdict. There are also a variety of instances at the appeal stage in which the CCP does not expressly provide for the presence of the accused at appeal court sessions, leaving it to the discretion of the court itself, thus favoring the prosecution and undermining an effective right to appeal.[85] The 2014 CCP, in Articles 474, 475, and 477, also reduced the scope for retrial. Finally, it should be noted that there exists a route by which the Head of the Judiciary can intervene in cases which have been finalized and instruct the Supreme Court to overturn them and issue a new verdict. According to Article 477 of the CCP, the Head of the Judiciary is authorized to exercise this power if he thinks that the verdict is "in contravention with Shariʿa". In such instances, the Head of the Judiciary refers the case to branches of the Supreme Court which are specially allocated to handle them. These special branches "shall overturn the sentence, try the case both on merit and procedural grounds, and issue a verdict". Thus, the Head of the Judiciary is effectively authorized to indirectly overturn verdicts they deem to be in conflict with Shariʿa. Whilst the authority granted to the Head of the Judiciary in such cases provides an opportunity to reverse unjust decisions it can also facilitate miscarriages of justice. This is because, as we have seen, the Head of the Judiciary is directly appointed by the Supreme Leader and will most often enforce his will in political cases. Moreover, the ambiguous phrase of "in contravention of Shariʿa" allows the Head of the Judiciary to resort to uncodified laws to order that a judgement be overturned.

---

[83] See note 52.
[84] See the *Official Gazette* (in Persian), issue dated Tir 14, 1394/July 5, 2015: https://perma.cc/49H8-8D36, accessed May 5, 2018.
[85] See, inter alia, Amnesty International (2016), Chapter 7.9, "Right to be Present during Hearing and Appeal."

4.7 The Flawed Structure of Adjudication

The factors undermining the independence of the judiciary, especially its subordination to the Supreme Leader, have been described in section 7.1 of the introduction of this volume. These concerns regarding the structure of the judiciary have heightened concerns with respect to adjudication. Alongside flaws such as the unified authority of both prosecuting and judging functions that undermines the independence of the latter; the flawed basis of arrest, including by those who conduct arrests, as well as trial practices that fall short of international standards, notably arbitrariness, another concern relates to the training, capacity and number of judges deciding a case. Rather than a panel of judges, in which a majority adjudication will determine the case, the Iranian courts only have a small number of judges. Reforms implemented in 2014 and 2015 reduced the number of judges. For example, in the revolutionary courts only one presiding judge is present – unless the possible sentence is death, life imprisonment, amputation, payment of half or more of a full *diyeh*, and punishments prescribed for serious *ta'zir* crimes, when there will be a presiding judge and one associate judge. Under the 2015 amendments, both the provincial courts of appeal as well as the various branches (it is not one sole body) of the Supreme Court may sit with only two judges. Despite its pivotal role in respect to setting precedent and maintaining broad, judicial cohesion in adjudication, the Supreme Court consists of separate branches, in Tehran, Qom, Mashhad, and other places, and their approaches and decisions may differ, even in terms of broadly analogous issues. We should also mention that the independence of judges, already compromised in various ways discussed above and in the introduction to this volume, is further undermined by the fact that judges are held personally liable, according to Article 171 of the Constitution, to reach a verdict and not dismiss a case due to evidential or procedural deficiencies. This puts further pressure on them to comply with the will of security officials or judicial officers who may be interfering with a case.[86]

5 The 2019–2020 Protests: Whither Accountability?

In late November 2019, the government used excessive and frequent lethal force in response to spontaneous and generally unorganized nationwide protests that erupted in reaction to a sudden increase in fuel prices. On May 20, 2020, Amnesty International stated:

> The organization has found the security forces' use of lethal force against the vast majority of those killed to be unlawful. In almost all protests that took place

---

[86] The General Board of the Supreme Court oversees binding precedent and cohesion by issuing guidance called *ra'y-e vahdat-e raviye*, meaning a "unified opinion of procedure" or "verdict of unified precedent."

The Administration of Criminal Justice in Iran 97

between 15 and 19 November, there is no evidence that people were in possession of firearms or that they posed an imminent threat to life that would have warranted the use of lethal force, according to extensive research, including video analysis, conducted by Amnesty International. The organization is aware of two exceptions in one city on 18 November where gunfire was exchanged between a number of protesters and security forces [...].[87]

In the overwhelming majority of cases, the security forces directly targeted protesters who posed no threat to life; all in all, at least 300 people (and possibly up to 1500 people) were killed, and thousands injured. A further 7,000 were detained.[88] In its February 2020 assessment of the events, human rights group Justice for Iran (JFI) reported:

[Our] review and analysis of official statements confirm that the main body involved in decision-making with regards to the November protests was the National Security Council, headed by the Minister of Interior, Abdolreza Rahmani Fazli. According to Article 3 of the 1993 Law on the Establishment and Responsibilities of the National Security Council, the Council consists of the General Commander of Iran's Police forces, one of the Supreme Leader's advisors from the Defence Council, the Head of Joint Staff of the Islamic Republic of Iran Army, the General Commander of the IRGC, and the Intelligence Minister. However, according to Rahmani Fazli's live interview with the State television, broadcast on the 26th of November, the Head of the Islamic Republic of Iran Broadcasting (IRIB) also participated in the Council's sessions.[89]

A few years on from the atrocities, under the Supreme Leader's direction, the authorities have refused to initiate judicial investigations or criminal proceedings. Instead, the families of the victims have had to settle for monetary compensation and have been threatened by the authorities if they tried to speak out. In response, Iranian human rights groups led by the lawyers Hamid Sabi and Shadi Sadr, organized the Aban Tribunal held in London in November 2021 and February 2022. This was a people's tribunal modeled on the tribunal established by Jean-Paul Sartre and Bertrand Russell which investigated US military intervention in Vietnam. The tribunal included a panel of international lawyers and judges and took testimonies from people inside and outside Iran who had witnessed the shooting of protesters.[90] The tribunal formally invited

---

[87] Amnesty International, "Details of 304 Deaths in Crackdown in November 2019 Protests," May 20, 2020: https://perma.cc/R345-X2DV.

[88] An Amnesty International Report gives the figure as 304: www.amnesty.org/en/latest/news/2020/05/iran-details-released-of-304-deaths-during-protests-six-months-after-security-forces-killing-spree, accessed February 15, 2021. Later accounts have reported a much higher figure.

[89] Justice for Iran, "Shoot to Kill: Preliminary Findings of Justice for Iran's Investigation into the November 2019 Protests," February 2020: https://perma.cc/X6VX-HYU8, accessed February 15, 2021.

[90] For more information on the Aban Tribunal, see: https://abantribunal.com/about-us, accessed February 15, 2022.

the Iranian government to take part but never received a response. It found that "beyond a reasonable doubt that the Iranian security forces launched an attack against the civilian protesters across several provinces in Iran, which included the commission of the crimes of murder, enforced disappearances, imprisonment, sexual violence, torture and ill-treatment and, as found by the Majority, [...] persecution."[91]

6 The Crackdown on the 2022–2023 Protests

On September 16, 2022, a unit of Iran's *Gasht-e ershād* ('guidance patrol') detained 22-year-old Mahsa Jina Amini for alleged irregularities in her mandatory clothing. Following her death in custody, nationwide protests – many led by women – erupted across Iran. These events tragically underline many of the themes discussed in this chapter. By December 2022 over 500 people were killed by security forces – forty-four of them children[92] – overwhelmingly in the non-Shiʻi areas of Baluchistan and Kurdistan; less in Persian and Azeri/Shiʻi areas – but there too. At least 19,000 protestors were arrested. On October 30, 2022, after weeks of trying to quell the protests through lethal violence, the judiciary announced that a thousand protestors arrested in Tehran and a thousand others outside the capital would be put on trial. Since then, a number of hasty trials – with little or no due process – have been held, mainly in the revolutionary courts in which protestors have faced charges ranging from the crime of 'illegal association' (carrying a sentence of two to ten years) to the crime of *mohārebeh* (enmity against God), which can carry a death sentence. So far, eleven have been sentenced to death. In at least one of these trials, the concept of *ʻelm-e qāzi*. has been invoked to arbitrarily sentence a protestor to death.[93] At least seven demonstrators have been executed for the crime of *mohārebeh*. The evidence presented was often opaque, sometimes relying on grainy video footage. Rights groups and families of the executed say that in some cases there are accounts and evidence of torture.[94]

---

[91] One panel member dissented on the point of persecution.
[92] Amnesty International, "Iran: Killing of Children during Youthful Anti-Establishment Protests," December 9, 2022: www.amnesty.org/en/documents/mde13/6104/2022/en/, accessed January 15, 2023.
[93] [In Persian] "In the Court, What Happened to One of the Accused for Setting Fire to the Qarchak District Building?" (see video, especially from 4.35 onward), *Mizan Online News Agency*', Aban 8 1401= October 30, 2022: https://tinyurl.com/bdhnnst8, accessed November 2, 2022.
[94] Farnaz Fassihi and Cora Engelbrecht, "Three More Executed in Iran over Protests," *The New York Times*, May 22, 2023: www.nytimes.com/article/iran-protests-death-sentences-executions.html, accessed June 18, 2023.

Moreover, at least forty-four lawyers were arrested after representing protestors. Some of these were released on bail and others received prison sentences.[95]

In March 2023, Head of the Judiciary Mohseni-Eje'i announced that the authorities had pardoned 22,000 protestors.[96] The amnesty did not apply to dual nationals, those deemed to have cooperated with foreign agents, or those charged with committing acts of arson against government buildings. Furthermore, those "affiliated with groups hostile to the Islamic Republic" were also excluded, suggesting that the authorities were only interested in releasing those with minimal political motives who could be portrayed as naïve youth swayed by emotion or foreign propaganda.[97] The conditional nature of the amnesties was greeted with skepticism by many Iranians, who viewed it as a superficial act of reconciliation. Moreover, there are reports that some of the pardoned protestors have been resummoned by the revolutionary courts.[98] The amnesty may also have been partly motivated by Iran's overcrowded prisons (see Chapter 7 by Enayat and Enayat in this volume).

7 Conclusion

The crackdown on the protests following Mahsa Jina Amini's death in September 2022 brutally highlighted the cruelty and arbitrariness of Iran's criminal justice system. Nevertheless, as this chapter has tried to show, the system has evolved since 1979 and despite its glaring inadequacies, the training and capacity of many judges, including in respect to international fair trial standards, has improved. Indeed, in cases where a political interest is not involved, there is evidence to indicate that the basis of reasonably fair trials has been achieved. This marks an improvement in the administration of justice after a sharp deterioration immediately following the 1979 Revolution when thousands of people were arbitrarily detained, imprisoned, tortured and summarily executed with little or no regard for due process. Since then, relative order and a clear structure to

---

[95] "More than 40 Iranian Lawyers Detained So Far during Protests," *Radio Free Europe*, December 22, 2022: www.rferl.org/a/iran-protests-40-lawyers-detained/32189170.html, accessed December 24, 2022.

[96] [In Persian] "Iran Pardons 22 000 Protestors," *Deutsche Welle*, "Esfand 22 1401/March 13 2023" https://tinyurl.com/7htyzzhr, accessed May 15, 2023.

[97] Patrick Wintour, "Iran's Supreme Leader to Pardon Some Detained Anti-Government Protestors," *The Guardian*, February 5, 2023: www.theguardian.com/world/2023/feb/05/irans-supreme-leader-pardons-tens-of-thousands-of-prisoners, accessed March 18, 2023.

[98] [In Persian] "A Big Lie in the Name of Amnesty," *Iran Wire*, Esfand 23/1301/March 14 2023: https://tinyurl.com/2fszkupb, accessed May 15, 2023.

the system has been imposed. Yet the overall administration of criminal justice in the Islamic Republic of Iran still falls woefully short of the international standards to which the authorities are legally committed. The various legal reforms discussed in this chapter, such as the partial restoration of the office of public prosecutor in 2004, the introduction of a new Islamic Penal Code in 2013, and of a new Code of Criminal Procedure of 2015, constitute some improvements on the previous codes and procedures. However, they also contain many shortcomings, which hinder Iran's compliance with international human rights law and severely undermine the right to a fair trial, especially in cases involving political prisoners. These flaws include the frequent interference by security bodies and officials under the ultimate control of the Supreme Leader, the frequent use of special courts in which rule of law standards are severely curtailed, the continued absence of lawyers during interrogation, torture, forced confessions and arbitrary judicial decisions facilitated by ʿ*elm-e qāzi*.

These flaws are largely the result of the securitization of the criminal justice system, which has become primarily an instrument of regime preservation rather than the rule of law. Whilst Iran's security doctrine has evolved significantly since 1979, it has throughout this time been shaped by a deep distrust of Western powers (Tabatabai 2020: 298). These fears about security, though exaggerated and manipulated by the regime, are not baseless. Ever since its inception as a modern nation-state, Iran has experienced threats and intervention from foreign powers. These include the Russian and British occupation of Iran after the Constitutional Revolution of 1906, the occupation of Iran by the allies in 1941, the 1953 coup against Mohammed Mossadegh engineered by the CIA, and the invasion of Iran by Iraq in 1980, leading to eight years of war. Today, the government of the Islamic Republic of Iran believes that it faces an existential threat from the United States and its allies in the Middle East. The presence of US military forces in the region, the US sanctions regime against Iran, the January 2020 killing of Quds Force Commander Qasem Soleimani near Baghdad Airport and Israel's strike on the Iranian Consulate in Damascus in April 2024 all serve to ground the regime's fear of survival. Internally, Iran also continues to face significant security threats, including the trade in narcotics and acts of terrorism such as the assassination of the nuclear scientist Mohsen Fakhrizadeh, probably at the hands of Mossad.[99]

To be sure, Iran's security concerns are legitimate but its response to these concerns is not. Whilst all governments have a responsibility to

---

[99] "Iranian Nuclear Scientist Killed by One-Ton Automated Gun in Israeli Hit: *Jewish Chronicle*," *Reuters*, February 10, 2021: www.reuters.com/article/us-iran-nuclear-scientist-idUSKBN2AA2RC, accessed March 18, 2022.

maintain public order and security, measures to safeguard these should be necessary, proportionate, and lawful. Instead, the national security imperative has been manipulated by the Iranian government to turn on many of its own people, committing grave and widespread human rights violations in the name of security and combating terrorism. Indeed, "security" is often cynically invoked to justify harsh crackdowns on protesters, human rights activists, and lawyers who are often accused of working for foreign powers bent on destroying the Islamic Republic. As a result, many tens of thousands of Iranians have suffered arbitrary imprisonment, torture, and execution, including members of ethnic and religious minorities and other vulnerable communities such as migrants. As we have seen, the Iranian authorities continue to employ vaguely worded national security and anti-terrorism laws to conduct trials whose procedures do not meet minimum international due-process standards.

The deleterious effects of this securitization are exacerbated by the structural subordination of the judiciary to the power of the Supreme Leader and the frequent interference of agencies under his control in the judicial process. This is a function of the highly personalistic mode of governance deriving from Khomeini's doctrine of *velāyat-e faqih*. As we have seen in the introduction to this chapter, this personalism is mediated by a dense and complex web of institutions such as the Guardian Council, the National Security Council, and the Maslahat Council. Nevertheless, most power is ultimately concentrated in the hands of the Supreme Leader and the institutions under his control, including the judiciary. Personalism has also found expression at lower levels of the judicial system, which has featured traditionalist, though contested, modes of *qāzi* judicial procedures such as *'elm-e qāzi* and the temporary abolition of the public prosecutor, which, by giving judges excessive judicial discretion to decide cases, have undermined the rule of law.

Finally, what does this partial, eclectic overview of aspects of the administration of justice in today's Islamic Republic of Iran reveal about the system? The legislative basis and operation of a criminal justice system, including in relation to its use in holding officials to account, constitute an expression of the norms to which that state – or, at any rate, its rulers, aspire. As an expression of real power and political purpose, responding to the question "whom does the criminal justice system serve?" – from the development, formulation and ratification of law, to their implementation, prosecution, and adjudication – the answer can only be the same as the vision set out in the preamble of the constitution: that of the rulership of an unelected ideologically determined leader and a small number of powerful institutions intended to support the regime itself. Ultimately, Iran's criminal justice system is not about supporting or directing the moral and ethical conduct of Iran's peoples, but the maintenance of a specific order and a small number of people at the core of that order. It is about maintaining a national security posture in which those indifferent to or opposed to that order are seen, equally, as threats to the very existence of that order and, by extension, the very survival of the state. Insofar as the criminal justice system has been the subject of ongoing conflict and political dissent, it has, like other aspects of the Islamic Republic, shown an ability to change. Nevertheless, its detractors would argue that this has been too little, too late, resulting in the delay and outright denial of justice, prioritizing, and indeed manipulating, a narrow conception of national security over justice.

Bibliography

Abrahamian, Ervand. *A History of Modern Iran*. New York: Cambridge University Press, 2008.

Amnesty International. *Flawed Reforms: Iran's New Code of Criminal Procedure*, Amnesty International, 2016. https://perma.cc/6WRJ-HN2T.

Arjomand, Said Amir. *The Turban for the Crown: The Islamic Revolution in Iran*, Oxford: Oxford University Press, 1988.

Arjomand, Said Amir. "Islam and Constitutional Democracy," *Foundation for Iranian Studies*, Nowruz Lecture, George Washington University, March 17, 2008: https://perma.cc/5P4K-ZWRS.

Dadashi-Niaki, Mohammad Reza and Zahra Feez. "The Nature of Knowledge of the Judge," [in Persian], *Research in Fiqh and Islamic law*, 8 (14), Spring/Summer, (1390/2011), pp. 91–112.

Daraeizadeh, Behnam. "A Look at Criminal Procedure in Iran," *Iran Human Rights Documentation Centre*, 2010. https://perma.cc/LTY5-BMHP.

Dehghan, Saeed Kamali. "Eye for an Eye: Iran Blinds Acid Attacker," *The Guardian*, Thursday, March 5, 2015: https://perma.cc/DR83-T9AT.

Devraj, Ranjit. "Damaging Forced Confessions," *IPS News*, May 4, 2009: https://perma.cc/KY5H-VGZR.

Ebadi, Shirin. "The Judiciary is a 'Branch of the Intelligence Ministry,'" *Centre for Human Rights in Iran*, April 5, 2019. https://perma.cc/472W-FW36.

Enayat, Hadi. *Law, State and Society in Modern Iran: Constitutionalism, Autocracy and the Legal Reform 1906–1941*, New York: Palgrave Macmillan, 2013.

Fraser Fujinaga, Antonia. "Life and Limb Irreversible *hadd* penalties in Iranian criminal courts and opportunities to avoid them," Unpublished PhD thesis, University of Edinburgh, 2013.

Khalaji, Mehdi. "The Judiciary and the Rule of Law," [in Persian], BBC Persian, August 16, 2009. https://perma.cc/2WMN-9KF8.

Mabon, Simon and Saloni Kapur (eds.). *Securitisation in the Non-West*, London: Routledge, 2019.

Macnair, Mike. "Equity and Conscience," *Oxford Journal of Legal Studies*, 27(4), 2007, pp. 659–681.

Mohajer, Nasser (comp. and ed.). *Voices of a Massacre: Untold Stories of Life and Death in Iran, 1988*. London: Oneworld Books, 2020.

Odabaei, Milad. "The Slip of a Philosopher and the Sinking of the Ship, Translation, Protest, and the Iranian Travails of Learned Politics," *Journal of Ethnographic Theory*, 10 (2), 2020, pp. 561–578.

Osanloo, Arzoo. *Forgiveness Work: Mercy, Law and Victims' Rights in Iran*, Princeton: Princeton University Press, 2020.

Quddusi, Zahra. "Knowledge of the Judge," [in Persian], *Bi-Quarterly Journal of Jurisprudential Studies*, 2 (2), Spring/Summer, 1398/2019, pp. 62–80.

Sepehri Far, Tara. "Forgiveness: A Growing Anti-Death Penalty Movement in Iran," *Atlantic Council*, April 26, 2019. https://perma.cc/J4CG-6SB2.

Tabatabai, Ariane. M. *No Conquest, No Defeat: Iran's National Security Strategy*. London: Hurst Publishers, 2020.

Woolridge, Mike. "Iran's Grim History of Stoning," BBC, July 9. 2010: https://perma.cc/M7XJ-VL2B.

Zubaida, Sami. *Law and Power in the Islamic World*. London: I. B Tauris, 2003.

4 Shi'i Family Law under the Rule of Law? The Iranian Model and Current Approaches in the Shi'i World

Hannah L. Richter

1 Introduction

The discussion of the rule of law is usually located in the realm of public law rather than private law,[1] as it mainly takes into view constitutional principles, governmental and judicial acts, and the scope of their subjection to the law. A number of aspects associated with the rule of law, however, can be discussed with regard to private law, including family law.

Family law is the area of law which in Muslim-majority countries today is usually more strongly based on Islamic law than any other area of law. In nearly all these countries, family law is – to different degrees – codified. However, a closer look shows that, for some countries, this does not, or only since recent years, hold true for the whole population. While there are family law codifications for the Sunni (and sometimes non-Muslim religious communities), Shi'i family law is applied by Shi'i courts or court chambers,[2] and is not based on codified law but on Shi'i jurisprudence (fiqh),[3] in countries such as Saudi Arabia,[4] Lebanon,[5] and, until very recently, Kuwait and Bahrain.[6]

Until 2009, the only country where Shi'i family law was codified, that is, put into codes of law which in form are inspired by European Civil

---

[1] Concerning private law, the rule of law is mostly discussed with regard to (international) business and trade law.
[2] This chapter deals only with the Twelver Shi'is, who follow the Ja'fari School of Law.
[3] Technical terms of Islamic law are given in Arabic in this chapter. Persian is used when referring to Iranian or Afghan sources.
[4] See Louër (2008: 248–249).
[5] In Lebanon, there are currently fifteen PSLs, each for a different religious community. The Ja'fari courts do not base their rulings on codified law but on Ja'fari fiqh. There are, however, handbooks and treatises compiling established fiqh opinions on practical law, which are consulted frequently; see Clarke (2014: 34–36, 38).
[6] For Kuwait, see An-Na'im (2002:124) and al-Maghāmis, July 07, 2019; www.moj.gov.kw; Kuwaiti PSL of 1984, Article 346; Kuwaiti Code of Civil Procedure of 1980, Article 34.

Shi'i Family Law under the Rule of Law? 105

Codes, was Iran, where codified family law was first introduced in the 1930s. In recent years, however, there have been attempts to introduce Shi'i family law codes or personal status laws (PSLs) in other countries of the region as well. In Afghanistan, a Shi'i PSL came into force in 2009. Iraq has witnessed attempts to make possible the application of Shi'i family law since 2003, so far without success. In Bahrain, a mostly unified Family Law, containing a number of special provisions for Sunnis and Shi'is, was enacted in 2017. In Kuwait, a draft for a Shi'i PSL was presented to parliament in 2017 and came into force in its final version in August 2019.[7] While in some countries Shi'i family law codes introduce codified family law for the Shi'i population for the first time (such as Bahrain and Kuwait, where family law was previously uncodified or codified only for the Sunni population), in other places such codification attempts aim at replacing existing unified (applicable to all Muslims) family law codes with Shi'i law for the Shi'i population (such as Afghanistan and Iraq). Shi'i family law codification therefore occurs in very different contexts and with different purposes. The question of family law codification can be considered a current issue in significant parts of the Shi'i world.

Codification of Islamic legal norms was first initiated by the Ottoman Empire in the early nineteenth century, with family law being codified only in the early twentieth century (Anderson 1966: 245–246). Classical Islamic law is not based on binding codes of law but was practiced on the basis of the religious sources of law and the jurisprudential methodology and works of legal scholars, developed in jurisprudential literature and in form of legal opinions (fatwa) issued by scholars. Islamic law has therefore been referred to as "jurists' law," for example by Wael Hallaq, a characterization which other scholars of Islamic law, such as Irene Schneider, have criticized as reductionist (Hallaq 2002: 1708; Schneider 2008: 180–182). Its transformation from "jurists' law" into statutory or codified law has been considered as depriving the law of its traditional flexibility.[8]

Family law has been called the "last bastion" of Islamic law (Mir-Hosseini 1993: 12). Here, the Muslim identity and the family as the basic unit of Muslim society come into play, "traditional" and "modern" gender roles are negotiated, and the question of Western influences repeatedly becomes the object of debate. Therefore, maintaining,

---

[7] *Qānūn raqm (124) li-sanat 2019 bi-isdār qānūn al-aḥwāl al-shakhṣiyya al-ja'fariyya* (*Official Gazette*, No. 1459, August 25, 2019).

[8] Implications and consequences of transforming the shari'a from "jurists' law" to "statutory law" have been discussed by Tucker (2008: 223–225), Layish (2004), and Peters (2002).

reintroducing, or reducing the Islamic or specifically Shi'i character of family law are demands often accompanied by very emotional and controversial debates.[9]

When, in the mid-twentieth century, the codification of family was debated in Iraq, Shi'i scholars were especially vocal and rejected the law introduced in 1959 not only because of what they perceived as contradictions with and deviations from substantive Islamic family law but also on a more fundamental level: They rejected codification of (Shi'i) family law per se. Muhammad Bahr al-Ulum,[10] the author of an extensive critique of the 1959 law, wrote in 1963: "It is not proper to legislate a Code of Personal Status [...]. Such Code would be [...] an expression of the closure of the gate of ijtihād."[11] *Ijtihād* denotes independent legal reasoning by qualified Islamic legal scholars and is a central concept in Shi'i law. Due to their competence to practice *ijtihād*, that is, to deduce legal rulings from the sources, these scholars came to play a very prominent role in Shi'i religious law, religious life, and sometimes politics. Bahr al-Ulum considered codification to be contrary to *ijtihād* because it would be "binding on the judges of all times" and "constitute a departure from the open-ended nature [of personal status matters]" (Bahr al-Ulum 1963: 26; Mallat 1993: 79–80).

Bahr al-Ulum's statement raises the question of whether this opposition of *ijtihād* and codification plays a role in developments of Shi'i family law in Iran and its codification in other countries today.

One difference between other Shi'i environments and Iran is that the latter self-identifies not only as an "Islamic" state (Islamic Republic) but also as a Shi'i state, in the sense that, first, the Iranian constitution in Article 12 declares Islam – according to the Ja'fari or Twelver Shi'i school of law – to be the official religion of the state and that, second, Shi'i legal scholars are integrated into the constitutional system and the process of legislation.

This chapter argues that codification in principle is closely connected to the rule of law. The chapter aims to look at how the rule of law (in this

---

[9] On the special role of family law and its connection to identity, see Kinninmont (2011: 53, 56–57) and Hélie-Lucas (1994: 393–400).

[10] Bahr al-Ulum, born on 1927 in Najaf and coming from a family of Shi'i scholars, belonged to the circle of the influential Ayatollah Muhsin al-Hakim in the 1960s. Like other oppositional Iraqi Shi'i scholars, he went into exile, leaving Iraq in 1969. See Mallat (2003: 28–29) and Mallat (1993: 71–72).

[11] Bahr al-Ulum, *Adwā' 'alā qānūn al-ahwāl al-shakhsiyya al-'irāqī* [*Lights on the Iraqi Law of Personal Status*], Najaf: Matba'at al-Nu'mān 1963, 26; translation cited in Mallat (1993: 79). See also Hamoudi (2016: 337).

case the rule of codified law) and the concept of *ijtihād* are dealt with in contexts of contemporary Shi'i family law in Iran, Afghanistan, Bahrain, and Iraq. Does Iran, with its decades of experience in applying codified Shi'i family law, serve as a model for others? In which aspects do these laws differ and how does this connect to the rule of law?

The approach to dealing with these questions will be twofold: Following some general remarks on the concepts of *ijtihād* and the rule of law and their role in the Iranian constitutional system (Section 2), the first step will be to look at the general context of the different (draft) laws as specifically Shi'i laws and their development in Iran, Afghanistan, Iraq, and Bahrain (Section 3). The second step will be to look at selected areas of Shi'i family law – substantive and procedural. These selected areas are temporary marriage, women's access to divorce, and the judicialization of unilateral divorce by the husband (*talāq*) (Section 4). These examples serve to illustrate the different extents to which codification can contribute to the rule of law and to show where the laws differ from or might be inspired by each other (Section 5). The question of the actual application of these laws cannot be addressed in detail.

2 *Ijtihād*, the Rule of Law, and the Iranian Constitutional Context

2.1 Ijtihād *in Shi'i Islam*

The Arabic word *ijtihād* literally means "exertion" or "effort." As a legal term, it refers to independent legal reasoning with the aim of deducing legal rulings from the sources, first and foremost of the Qur'an and the traditions of the Prophet and – in the Shi'i case – the twelve Shi'i Imams narrated in the hadiths. *Ijtihād* is practiced by a qualified Islamic legal scholar (*mujtahid*). The understanding and relevance of *ijtihād* went through different developments in Sunni and Shi'i legal thought.[12]

---

[12] When it comes to Sunni *ijtihād* the prominent but today contested expression of the "closure of the gate of *ijtihād*" cannot be left unmentioned. While *ijtihād* was accepted in Sunni Islam from the beginning, a number of reasons were given as to why the *ijtihād* was no longer practiced in Sunni Islam since about the tenth century and why therefore the "gate of *ijtihād*" was closed. This closure, however, has been disproved in recent decades. Research on this issue is most prominently tied to Wael Hallaq (1984). Within Shi'i doctrine, *ijtihād* was rejected in the early centuries of Islam – when the Imams as authorities on religious and legal matters were still present – and started to gain recognition in the thirteenth century, until it became one of the most important characteristics of Shi'ism. See Momen (1985: 95, 185–188, 203–207) and Gleave (2007: 64–66).

The current importance *ijtihād* enjoys in Shi'i Islam goes back to developments in the eighteenth century when the school of the *usūliyya* (referring to the sources or principles of Islamic jurisprudence, the *usūl al-fiqh*[13]) prevailed over the school of the *akhbāriyya* (traditionalists), who rejected *ijtihād*. The *usūli* school, which has since been dominant in most Shi'i environments, divides the community of believers into two groups: The *mujtahid*s, qualified to deduce legal rulings, that is, to practice *ijtihād*, and the *muqallid*s, laypeople who have to choose a *mujtahid* whom they follow or "imitate." This practice of following a *mujtahid* is called *taqlid* (emulation).[14] Shi'i *ijtihād* is based on two important principles: One is the general prevalence of living *mujtahid*s over their predecessors. The other is the concept of fallibility, according to which *mujtahid*s are fallible and can therefore be incorrect in their deductions. These deductions, however, if based on valid *ijtihād* practiced to the best of the *mujtahid*'s abilities, are considered valid and applicable. Differing and contradicting opinions and conclusions are therefore accepted, as there is no ultimate authority available (Halm 1988: 84–89; Damad 2020: 10–24). This contributes to what Bahr al-Ulum called the "open-ended nature" of Shi'i jurisprudence. High-ranking Shi'i *mujtahid*s who gained the reputation of excelling all or most others in learning and knowledge have been, since the nineteenth century, referred to as *marja' al-taqlid* (Pers. *marja'-e taqlid*, lit. "source of emulation"). These *mujtahid*s often enjoy followings across state borders and have largely maintained (financial) independence from the state.[15]

2.2 The Rule of Law and Family Law Codification

The "rule of law" is often contrasted with the "rule of men," the latter standing for arbitrary rule and unrestricted power. The rule of law, therefore, according to a very basic definition, means "that government officials and citizens are bound by and abide by the law" (Tamanaha 2012: 233). From this definition follow some basic requirements such as the law being "set forward in advance," "stated in general terms," "generally known and understood," "applied equally to everyone according to their terms," and having mechanisms or institutions present to enforce it (Tamanaha 2012: 233). These requirements – which partly overlap with and strongly

---

[13] According to Shi'i doctrine, these are the Qur'an, hadith, consensus (*ijmā'*), and reason (*'aql*).
[14] On the *usūli* dominance and its effects, see Momen (1985: 127–128, 186, 222–225).
[15] As emphasized recently, this ideal type of Shi'i scholarly authority is necessarily always reflected by actual practice; see Clarke and Künkler (2018: 8–15) and other articles in the same special issue "De-Centring Shi'i Islam" of the *BJMES*, 45 (1).

relate to the principle of legal certainty (Maxeiner 2008: 28–32) – are often found in definitions following a formal understanding of the rule of law, while other definitions include substantive elements such as democracy and human rights as well.[16] In this chapter, it is the formal and procedural elements of the rule of law which are of interest since this is where codification as such connects to the rule of law. From the perspective of substantive elements of the rule of law, such as human rights, especially women's and children's rights, the laws and drafts discussed in this article are to a different extent all problematic as they maintain unequal rights for men and women. It will be argued here that codification is more amenable to the rule of law than noncodified law. While codification is *not necessary* to implement the rule of law, as the long-standing tradition of the rule of law in common law systems shows,[17] and while codification also does *not necessarily* contribute to the implementation of the rule of law, as reflected in the distinction between rule *of* law and rule *by* law,[18] it *can* be a suitable means (and in many places is) to contribute to the implementation of formal or procedural elements of the rule of law such as clarity, publicity, generality of the laws, and access to justice.

The rule of law not only has the function to protect citizens from the state but also to protect citizens from one another (Bedner 2010: 51–52). Such protection is not only relevant as protection against crime, it is also relevant in the realm of the family. Questions of marriage and divorce, which often have far-reaching economic implications, are of utmost importance in the life of the individual person. Codifying family law strengthens the rule of law (in the formal sense) and can contribute to protecting the weaker parties in a marriage or family, who, in all countries discussed in this chapter, tend to be women and children.[19] Moreover, codified law can facilitate the layperson's knowledge of having certain rights and the knowledge of how to claim these in court.[20] Codification also creates clear rules which can serve as a starting point for formulating concrete demands and reform proposals.

---

[16] On different definitions and different categorizations of definitions and elements of the rule of law, see Bedner (2010: 51–54), Fallon (1997: 1–3), and Radin (1989: 781–791).

[17] On the rule of law in common law systems, see Nedzel (2010: 62–64, 66–77).

[18] While the rule *of* law subjects the government itself to the law, the rule *by* law emphasizes the state ruling by law as opposed to arbitrary rule. The rule *of* law therefore requires the rule *by* law, whereas the rule *by* law alone is less restrictive on state power; see Bedner (2010: 56–58).

[19] As Kinninmont (2011: 60) points out, family law codification does not necessarily improve women's legal position; this depends on the intentions of the legislator.

[20] Osanloo (2006: 195) describes how women in Iran learned how to claim their rights at court and how they emerged "as rights-bearing subjects with greater knowledge than laypersons of both the laws and the procedural mechanisms involved in petitioning for divorce."

2.3 Ijtihād *and the Rule of Law in the Iranian Constitution*

Turning to Iran – where the rule of law is known as *hākemiyat-e qānun*[21] – one thing is quite striking: It very soon became clear that the Islamic Revolution would not lead to the abolishment of codified law nor to its replacement with uncodified "jurists'" or "*mujtahid*s'" law. The Islamic Republic of Iran had a constitution which came into force in 1979 and clearly envisaged a legal system based on codified law. The fact that no law could become effective without the Guardian Council's confirmation of its conformity with Islam and the constitution does not change this basic commitment to codified law.[22] The prominent position of Shi'i legal scholars, characteristic of Shi'i Islam, was incorporated into the system of the Islamic Republic nonetheless. The concept of *velāyat-e faqih* (guardianship or governance of the Islamic jurist, which is neither a traditional nor an uncontested concept), as formulated by Revolutionary Leader Ayatollah Khomeini and then put into effect in the constitution, provides for the *vali-ye faqih*, the Supreme Jurist or *rahbar* (Leader) to be the head of state and to stand above the three branches of government. He determines the general policy of the state and appoints or confirms numerous holders of important governmental positions.

Ijtihād as concept is explicitly enshrined in the Iranian constitution in Article 2 as a general principle as well as by making the rank of a *mujtahid* a requirement for certain positions, such as the head of the judiciary (Article 157). At the same time, the constitution stipulates the supremacy of codified laws (*qavānin-e modavvane*). If, however, the law is silent, the judge may in this case refer to authentic Islamic sources and fatwas (Article 167). The constitution therefore includes both concepts, that of *ijtihād* as well as that of the (formal) rule of law. What this constitutional frame means for Shi'i family law will be discussed in Section 3.

3 Shi'i Family Law in Current Legislation and Draft Laws

3.1 Iran

When Reza Shah Pahlavi (1925–1941) began his modernization program, legal reform played a major role and family law was not left out. Family law codification started in 1931 with the Marriage and Divorce

---

[21] The idea of *hākemiyat-e qānun* gained prominence when the former President Khatami (1997–2005) made the promotion of the rule of law one of his central goals; see Künkler in this volume (Chapter 8) and Arjomand (2000).

[22] Six of the Guardian Council's twelve members are Islamic legal scholars (*foqahā*), appointed by the Supreme Leader, who review laws passed by parliament regarding their conformity with Islam. Conformity to the constitution is checked by all twelve members.

Law, which required the registration of every marriage and divorce in a civil bureau.[23] Codification of substantive family law followed in 1935 with Articles 1034–1206 of the newly introduced Civil Code. Most of these stipulations reflect the majority opinion (*mashhur*) of Shi'i fiqh.[24]

Major changes occurred under Mohammed Reza Shah (1941–1979) with the Family Protection Law (FPL) of 1967, which was amended in 1975. The FPL significantly broadened women's rights in marriage and divorce, among other things by limiting men's right to unilateral divorce (*talāq*) while expanding women's access to divorce. The latter was obtained by making mandatory a stipulation in the marriage contract by which the husband authorizes his wife to perform *talāq* herself. Such a stipulation is permitted but is purely optional in classical law. In addition, divorce had not only to be registered, but also required in all cases the involvement of the newly established family courts.

The situation again changed drastically with the 1979 Islamic Revolution and the subsequent establishment of the Islamic Republic. The FPL was declared to be unIslamic and was implicitly abolished when a return to the shari'a-based provisions of the Civil Code was declared; the courts established under the FPL's regime were replaced with Special Civil Courts. As a result, the rights women had just gained were again curtailed. Protest against the new legal situation and court practices led to the introduction of new standard marriage contracts in 1982 containing a stipulation by which the husband authorizes his wife to pronounce *talāq*, provided that she can prove to the court that one of the contractual conditions according to which she may execute this right is fulfilled. For these stipulations to become effective, the husband needs to accept them.

In the same year the Civil Code was amended to further expand women's access to divorce by introducing into divorce law (Article 1130 Iranian Civil Code) the concept of *osr va haraj* (hardship and suffering). The parliamentary bill first was met with rejection by the majority of the members of the Guardian Council and was approved only after Ayatollah Khomeini gave his support. Further changes in divorce law occurred

---

[23] These and the following developments are described by Mir-Hosseini (2012: 67–76), Mir-Hosseini (2007: 113–124), Mir-Hosseini (1993: 23–25, 54–58), and Osanloo (2006: 196–202).

[24] The Civil Code departed from the dominant opinion in prohibiting the marriage of girls under 13 and widening women's options to obtain judicial divorce (i.e., divorce officiated by a judge, as opposed to *talāq*, which in classical law is conducted as a "private divorce" that becomes effective without the involvement of a judge); see Mir-Hosseini (2012: 67).

in 1992. The requirement to obtain a certificate of "Impossibility of Reconciliation" issued by a court in order to register divorce, which had been introduced under the FPL, was reinstated and arbitration proceedings were made obligatory (Ansaripour 2011: 38–40, 42). Moreover, the wife was entitled to claim compensation for her housework (*ojrat al-methl*) if the divorce was not initiated by her.

In 1999, new family courts were established. In the same year, the issue of *osr va haraj* made it back onto the legislative agenda. The Women's Commission of the Parliament aimed to define "hardship" more clearly by law, reducing the judges' discretion in accepting or rejecting its fulfillment. Even though the bill was passed by parliament after overcoming conservative opposition, it received its final approval only in 2002, after having been sent back and forth several times between parliament and the Guardian Council, with the latter rejecting it repeatedly. A modified version was finally approved by the Expediency Council.[25]

The most recent comprehensive family law reform was initiated in 2007, when the first draft for a new FPL was presented by the Ahmadinejad cabinet. The draft went through a number of changes before coming into force in April 2013 (Ansaripour 2013: 71–72; Bøe 2015: 58–78). This law, like its predecessors, is understood to be of a procedural nature, while the Civil Code remains the source for substantive law in family matters (Ansaripour 2013: 71–72. See also Mir-Hosseini 2012: 68). Among the changes and innovations introduced by the 2013 FPL are the establishment of new specialized family courts and of family counselling centers. These counselling centers, in line with the law's title, are to protect the family and prevent divorce. Also, based on the new FPL, at each family court, alongside the presiding male judge, there is to be a female counselling judge, whose opinion has to be considered in the judgments. One of the most controversial questions addressed by the 2013 FPL was the registration of temporary marriage, as will be seen in Section 4.1.

3.2   Afghanistan

Family law in Afghanistan is mostly regulated by the 1977 Civil Code (Afghan Civil Code), which is based on Sunni (mostly Hanafi) law. Afghan Shi'is make up only about 10–15 percent of the population, and most belong to the ethnic minority of the Hazara. After the US-led

---

[25] This council was established in 1988 by Khomeini in order to overcome the paralysis of the legislative procedure, which had repeatedly emerged due to disagreement between the parliament and the Guardian Council. The Expediency Council was integrated into the constitutional system with the 1989 amendment to the constitution; see Arjomand (2013: 33–40).

overthrow of the Taliban in 2001, they received special recognition in the 2004 Afghan constitution. Article 131, in accordance with long-standing demands from Afghan Shi'is, provides that courts shall apply Shi'i law (*ahkām-e madhhab-e tashayyo'*) to Shi'is in cases involving personal matters. This was generally considered a positive step for Shi'i minority rights and Sunni–Shi'i relations. Ayatollah Asef Mohseni (d. 2019), a Shi'i cleric belonging to the biggest (and mostly Sunni) ethnic group in Afghanistan, the Pashtuns,[26] and his (Afghan) students, who were reportedly residing in the Iranian shrine city of Mashhad, spent the following years compiling a draft for a Shi'i PSL, which in its first submitted version was comprised of some 750 articles.

As the draft made its way through procedures of reviews by the Ministry of Justice, parliament and other institutions, it was reduced to less than 250 articles. Some provisions were omitted due to protests from Afghan women's rights activists and the international community (Oates 2009: 20–22; Rastin-Tehran 2012: 127). The final version of the Shi'i PSL (Afghan PSL) was promulgated in July 2009.[27] The law is applied by the general courts as, to date, no Shi'i courts have been established. While the status of the Shi'i law following the Taliban's return to power in 2021 remained unclear for some time, it was reported to have been abolished by summer 2023 (BBC Persian 2023).

3.3   Bahrain

While Bahraini Shi'is constitute the majority of Bahraini nationals, the ruling family, Al Khalifa, adheres to Sunni (Maliki) Islam. Bahrain is a constitutional monarchy with a bicameral parliament, half of whose members are elected (forming the Council of Representatives), and half of whom are appointed by the King (making up the Consultative Council). Until 2009, the only laws governing family matters in Bahrain were of procedural nature.[28] Sunni and Shi'i courts applied family law according to the judges' interpretation and understanding of the classical sources. At the beginning of the 2000s, the idea of the codification of substantive family law was put forward by the government, while women's rights

---

[26] Mohseni was a controversial figure among Afghan Shi'is, due to his *mojāhedi* past, his political ambitions, and his supposed close links to Iran. He studied and stayed, among other places, in Najaf and Qom. On his biography, see Crews (2015: 293–300).

[27] *Qānun-e ahval-e shakhsiyye ahl-e tashayyo'* (*Official Gazette*, No. 988, July 27, 2009).

[28] These include Decree No. 45 from 2007, issued by the Ministry of Justice, which effectively raised the minimum marriage age for men to eighteen years and for women to fifteen years. In 2016, the minimum marriage age was set at sixteen years for both sexes (Decree No. 1, Article 12, *Official Gazette*, January 7, 2016).

activists had been demanding codification since the 1980s. Especially among the Shi'is, there was strong opposition against this form of state intervention into what is perceived a domain of the Shi'i clerics. In 2009, the government attempted to enact a Family Law Code consisting of two parts, a Sunni and a Shi'i part. As Shi'i opposition continued, only the Sunni part was put into force.[29] In 2017, this law was replaced with a mostly unified Family Law, which on certain matters contains separate provisions for Sunnis and Shi'is.[30] The government's efforts to codify family law were connected to the general goal of legal harmonization and modernization as well as the implementation of the United Nations (UN) Convention on the Elimination of Discrimination against Women (CEDAW). The law is, furthermore, considered to consolidate the rule of law in Bahrain (Ebert 2011: 123; Abdulhadi 2016; Gulf News 2017), which increasingly seems to be considered of importance by the government.[31] The 2017 law however, as well as any earlier attempt to enact Shi'i family law codification by the government and the parliament, was rejected by many Bahraini Shi'i scholars, whose major representative is the Islamic Council of Scholars (ICS), which was banned in 2014 (Russel Jones 2007: 36).[32]

In a number of different statements, the ICS gave the following reasons for their position: The provisions for family law, just like those for prayer (*al-salāt*), fasting (*al-siyām*), and pilgrimage to Mecca (*al-hajj*), belong to the shari'a provisions of worship (*ahkām shar'iyya ta'abbudiyya*)[33] Such provisions cannot, according to the ICS, be defined or limited by parliament, they can only be deduced from the divine sources by qualified legal scholars (*al-fuqaha*). The ICS therefore rejects the interference of

---

[29] These developments are described in more detail by Russel Jones (2007: 33–39) and Kinninmont (2011: 55–56, 58–67).
[30] *Qānūn raqm (19) li-sanat 2017 bi-isdār qānūn al-usra* (*Official Gazette*, July 20, 2017).
[31] The Bahrain Ministry of Foreign Affairs (www.mofa.gov.bh) dedicates a whole website to the rule of law in Bahrain, both in English and Arabic. However, this prominent presentation does not necessarily reflect the actual implementation of the rule-of-law principle.
[32] Also see Bahrain Mirror (2017).
[33] These provisions are those for which the determining reason cannot be accessed or explained by human reason but has to be accepted as a divine commandment (see Poya 2003: 96–97). The ICS's position that family law as a whole belongs to the *ahkām ta'abbudiyya* is controversial. Shari'a provisions are divided into two categories: *'ibādāt* (worship and religious rituals) and *mu'āmalāt* (interpersonal and contractual relations). Family law generally belongs to the *mu'āmalāt* (see Rohe 2015: 15), which mostly do not count as *ahkām ta'abbuddiyya* (see al-Rumayli 2016: 245). Thus, while certain family law provisions are considered to be *ta'abudiyya* (see Rubah 2013: 117), family law as a whole is not generally seen as provisions of worship and thus inaccessible by reason. The distinction between *ahkām ta'abbudiyya* and *'ibādāt*, however, is itself contested (cf. Rohe 2015: 19; Rubah 2013: 117).

parliament into areas they would otherwise regulate. The parliament, argued the ICS, is not allowed to define the times of prayer (*awqāt al-salāt*) or the number of the pillars of Islam (*'adad arkān al-islām*) and the same goes for family law provisions. The council also argues that the existence of codified (*maktūb*) legal codes for civil, trade, and criminal law does not provide more justice or bring an end to problems in these areas. The reason for the problematic situation in Shi'i courts, which is criticized by supporters of codification for being chaotic, discriminating against women, and for overlong proceedings, according to the ICS, lies not in the lack of codified law but in the lack of enough qualified judges for whose appointment the government is responsible.[34] The ICS also rejects any imposition of Sunni law on Shi'i believers.[35]

Furthermore, the ICS rejected the idea that Iranian law could be used as a model for family law codification in Bahrain, based on three reasons: First, while the Iranian parliament is based on elections and can therefore be viewed as representing the people,[36] the Bahraini parliament is half-appointed, and as such cannot be viewed as representing the will of the people. Second, in Iran, the Guardian Council ensures that no law is contrary to the shari'a. Such an organ does not exist in Bahrain. And third, whereas in Iran the shari'a is the only source of legislation, in Bahrain it is only one major source besides others (cf. Article 2 Bahrain Constitution and Articles 4 and 72 Iran Constitution). The ICS's critical position toward attempts to codify Shi'i law is therefore at least partly based on its criticism of the Bahraini constitutional system, which is not designed to ensure that laws do not deviate from the shari'a. The ICS repeatedly made clear that it would accept family law codification only when three conditions are met: The drafters must be shari'a scholars, the law must be approved by the highest Shi'i religious authority (*al-marja'iyya al-diniyya al-'ulyā li-l-shī'a*, which for the ICS is Grand Ayatollah al-Sistani who resides in the Iraqi shrine city of Najaf), and a constitutional amendment must guarantee that the law cannot be changed without this authority's prior approval (Russel Jones 2007: 38).[37]

The ICS's criticism of the government's attempt to codify Shi'i family law mainly draws on who should be allowed to draft the law and who should be allowed to amend it. In their view, the lawmaking should be in the hands of Shi'i scholars of Islamic law. The ICS's rejection of parliament's interference with "God's law" is directed specifically at the

---

[34] See ICS (n.d.a).
[35] See ICS (n.d.b).
[36] The statement makes no mention of the Guardian Council's vetting of all candidates for parliamentary elections.
[37] Also see ICS (n.d.a).

Bahraini parliament but also makes reference to the experience of other Muslim countries where such "parliamentary interference" occurred. The Iranian model seems to be more acceptable due to its constitutional commitments to ensure that no law is contrary to shari'a and that the Guardian Council has veto power over all legislation. A somewhat different position was taken by Al-Asfour, the Shi'i judge and critic of the Shi'i courts' way of working, who published his own draft in 2002, of which he presented a first version to the King in 2000.[38] Apparently, he did not share (all) of the ICS's concerns, as his main concern was a widespread insufficiency in knowledge of the shari'a among court judges, which is why he proposed his draft to the government in order to improve court practice. At the same time, he remained critical of any Western or secular-inspired demands for legal reform.[39]

3.4　Iraq

In Iraq, the main law governing family matters for Iraqi Muslims is the PSL of 1959. As mentioned, it has been opposed by Shi'i scholars both on general grounds – for making the practice of *ijtihād* and *taqlid* impossible for believers – as well as on particular grounds regarding specific provisions. Only after the end of the Ba'athist regime in 2003 were the Iraqi Shi'is, as the country's largest religious community, in a position in which changing the status quo on family law matters became possible. A first and ultimately unsuccessful attempt as early as December 2003 aimed at replacing the 1959 law with "shari'a" and therewith allowing the application of family law according to Shi'i fiqh for Shi'i Iraqis. Resolution No. 137,[40] issued by the Interim Governing Council (of which Muhammad Bahr al-Ulum was a member, Stilt 2004: 751–754), stipulated that from then on, matters of family law were to be adjudicated according to the shari'a while all laws contrary to it were to be abolished. This resolution, which would have "uncodified" Iraqi family law, was met with public protest and vetoed by Paul Bremer, the head of the US-led Coalition Provisional Authority in Iraq.

A major milestone in the direction of Shi'i family law application was the adoption of the new Iraqi constitution in 2005, guaranteeing Iraqis the freedom to adhere to their belief, religion, sect (*madhhab*),

---

[38] The draft was entitled "Aḥkām al-aḥwāl al-shakhṣiyya wafqa al-madhhab al- ja'farī" (Provisions of Personal Status according to the Ja'fari School).

[39] See Russel Jones (2007: 35) and the interview with Al-Asfour in Akhbar al-Khalij (June 13, 2003): www.al-asfoor.org/edara/print.php?id=85&tab=4.

[40] The full text of Resolution 137 in Arabic is available on the website of the Kurdistan Regional Government: https://perma.cc/QS3X-KBCZ, accessed April 1, 2021.

or choice in matters of PSL, but stipulating that this was to be regulated by law (Article 41). In 2014, finally, the justice minister, who at that time belonged to the Shiʿi Islamic Virtue Party, presented drafts of two laws: A Jaʿfari PSL and a Law on the Jaʿfari Judiciary. The first draft contained regulations on family matters as well as on inheritance and *waqf* (endowments). The second draft was to establish a Shiʿi shariʿa court system for the application of the first draft. Both drafts were approved by the Council of Ministers but not passed by parliament. Furthermore, the draft on the Jaʿfari PSL provoked much public protest and was criticized for its content as well as for technical flaws. While not opposing the general idea of a Jaʿfari PSL, Grand Ayatollah al-Sistani did not support this draft. The rise of the Islamic State of Iraq and Syria (ISIS) and the parliamentary elections in April 2014, which led to a new justice minister taking office, contributed to the draft's disappearance from the agenda (Hamoudi 2016: 333, 340–343).[41]

In 2017, an amendment to the 1959 law was proposed, which was to give Iraqis in matters of PSL the right to request from the court the application of shariʿa provisions according to their madhab.[42] This draft was rejected by parliament after being strongly criticized for representing a major setback for women's and girls' rights (*The New Arab* 2017). Neither the parliamentary elections in 2018 nor those in 2021 led to the presentation of new drafts or a revival of old ones.

3.5 *Summary: Shiʿi Family Law and Codification Today*

This survey indicates that major representatives of many of the region's Shiʿi communities do not reject Shiʿi family law codification per se and therefore do not consider family law codification contrary to Shiʿi legal principles.[43] In fact, in Afghanistan and Iraq, it was Shiʿi parties and scholars who demanded and prepared such laws. In Bahrain, the leading clerical body rejects any law imposed on them by the government but does not oppose the idea of codifying Shiʿi family law as such. Nonetheless, the Bahraini ICS does not consider codified law necessary to improve Shiʿis' lives, arguing that the existing codes of civil and trade law have not provided better justice. A different position was taken

---

[41] Hamoudi (2016: 341) described the draft as "atrociously drafted as a technical matter."
[42] *Qānūn taʿdīl qānūn al-aḥwāl al-shakhsiyya raqm 188 li-sanat 1959* [Law to Amend the Personal Status Law No. 188 of 1959]; see http://ar.parliament.iq/2017/09/14/ /قانون-تعديل-قانون-الأحوال-الشخصية-رقم-.
[43] Another major case one could discuss here is the 2019 Kuwaiti law.

by the Shi'i judge and cleric Al-Asfour who criticized the "chaos" in Bahraini Shi'i family courts and put forward his own draft of codified law (Russel Jones 2007: 35).

To what extent was safeguarding and establishing the rule of law perceived and presented as a goal of codification and legislative reform?

Especially in the Iraqi case, there has been speculation that the main motive behind the drafts was to win Shi'i votes. The draft in this case, and against the background of an existing PSL, can be seen more as an attempt to establish the Islamic Virtue Party as a representative of Shi'i interests. This was reflected in the criticism of the draft by its opponents, who accused those behind it not only of violating women's rights but also of deepening the sectarian divisions in Iraqi society (alhayat.com 2014; Hamoudi 2016: 342). Likewise, in Afghanistan, the support former president Hamid Karzai granted to the Shi'i law was assumed to be tied to his hope for political and electoral support from Shi'i communities and Shi'i leaders (Oates 2009: 7).

As for Bahrain on the other hand, the Supreme Council for Women, a government agency, argued that family law codification would help make court proceedings fair and efficient and ensure "secure families" (Russel Jones 2007: 34–37; Kinninmont 2011: 63). However, the government's actions, as well as the Shi'i opposition's reactions, have to be seen in the light of identity politics within Bahrain and the power struggle between the government and the Shi'i clergy. As Kinninmont points out, the debate on family law has been strongly colored by other interests and motivations on both sides.[44]

In Iran, the most recent reforms were explained to be necessary because "certain parts of the laws concerning rights of the family have been found incompatible with the shari'a and the legal vacuum arising therefrom, in view of the confusion in the rules in this sphere, lack of clarity as to which of those rules are outdated and which are not, leading to harmful effects and numerous problems."[45] This statement implicitly refers to formal elements of the rule of law, such as laws being clear and rules being known and understood by those to whom they apply.

The following sections focus on substantive and procedural law examples in order to specify how these codification and codification attempts do or do not enhance the rule of law in family matters and to what extent developments in Iran are reflected in more recent codes.

---

[44] Kinninmont (2011: 55–67) has analyzed how strongly identity politics shaped the debate on family law codification in Bahrain.
[45] Introduction to the 2007 FPL draft, translation from Bøe (2015: 61).

4 Shi'i Family Law under the Rule of Law: A Comparison

4.1 Temporary Marriage

Temporary marriage (often referred to as *nikāh al-mutʿa* – "pleasure marriage" – in Arabic and *sigheh* in Persian) constitutes one of the major differences between Shi'i and Sunni (family) law, which is why it is a particularly relevant to study in Shi'i codification attempts. It is based on a contract which determines the duration of the marriage and the amount of the dowry paid by the husband to the wife. A man may have an unlimited number of temporary wives at the same time, a woman only one husband. The marriage may last for less than an hour or many years; the duration is to be agreed on by the couple. The contract can be concluded in private. Children emanating from temporary marriage are considered legitimate and are entitled to inherit.[46] While temporary marriage is strongly rejected and considered prohibited in Sunni law, it is permitted or even recommended in (Twelver) Shi'i law (Gribetz 1994: 78ff.). The issue of temporary marriage has been the subject of sectarian polemics over the centuries and it is still brought up in the context of Sunni–Shi'i tensions.[47]

Even though temporary marriage is perfectly acceptable according to Shi'i legal doctrine, social acceptance is a different issue. In some Shi'i societies a certain ambivalence and sometimes even embarrassment or rejection is attached to it (Gribetz 1994: 80–83).[48] Today, temporary marriage is practiced by Shi'is in all the countries discussed in this chapter. There is, however, no reliable data as to how widespread the practice actually is. Some reports indicate an increase of temporary marriages in Afghanistan and Iraq, as well as in Bahrain.[49] In Iran, small numbers of temporary marriages are registered, but the practice is usually frowned upon (ISNA.ir 1393). Moreover, as registration is obligatory only in certain cases, the extant numbers are not reliable as they do not include unregistered cases.

So far, the only place where Shi'i temporary marriage is regulated by law is Iran, even though not in great detail. Substantive regulations

---

[46] On temporary marriage in general, see Haeri (2014: 51–60) and Yassari (2005: 557–567).
[47] See, for example, from Bahrain, where reference to temporary marriage is used to insult Shi'is: Reuters (2011) and The Independent (2011).
[48] The collection of hadith cited here shows a "sense of embarrassment" felt by early Shi'is, sometimes shared by the Imams, toward the practice of *mutʿa*. For a modern example from Iran, see Haeri (2014: 6–7, 105ff).
[49] For Iraq and Afghanistan, the increase is widely considered to be an outcome of violent conflicts and deteriorated economic conditions. See, for example, BBC Persian (2006); Elaph.com (2008) and *The Arab Weekly* (2016).

on temporary marriage are mostly found in Articles 1075–1077 of the Civil Code. Explicit regulations in procedural law were introduced with the FPL of 2013 for the first time, according to which temporary marriage is to be registered if both parties agree on it being registered, or if the registration has been stipulated in the contract, or if the wife becomes pregnant (Article 21) (Ansaripour 2013: 81). Only with the introduction of the first draft of the new FPL in 2007 did the issue of temporary marriage emerge "as a legal debate on its own terms" (Bøe 2015: 123).[50] Some members of the Iranian parliament even demanded the registration of temporary marriage be made obligatory (Ansaripour 2013: 80).[51]

The Afghan Shi'i PSL of 2009 mentions and implies temporary marriage in a side note in two articles (Articles 86 and 124) – thereby recognizing the practice – but does not provide for any substantive regulations, such as a contract form or a dowry. A glance at the drafting history of the law, however, indicates that such regulations did exist in the first draft, prepared under Ayatollah Mohseni's leadership, and remained even in later versions of the draft, but were removed when the law was being discussed in parliament, mainly due to Sunni objections. In fact, omitting temporary marriage seems to have greatly contributed to Sunni MPs de facto supporting the law and taking a position of non-interference in Shi'i legal issues (Wimpelmann Chaudhary et al. 2011: 109–110).

In the Bahraini case, the 2009 draft and the 2017 law do not make any mention of temporary marriage at all. It is a question of interpretation if the mention of "permanent marriage" at one point in the 2017 law implies the law's recognition of nonpermanent or temporary marriage (Article 88). The earlier draft prepared by the Shi'i judge Al-Asfour, in contrast, contained stipulations on the main questions connected to temporary marriage. Interestingly, a statement by the ICS, listing a number of differences between Sunni and Shi'i family law, abstains from mentioning temporary marriage at all (ICS, *mawqifunā*). It can only be assumed that this is to avoid drawing attention to the politically sensitive issue in the first place.

The Iraqi draft of 2014 implies recognition of temporary marriage by stipulating that *permanent* marriage between a Muslim man and a non-Muslim woman is unlawful (Article 63). This clause has been interpreted as to indirectly allow temporary marriage (Hamoudi 2016: 355).

---

[50] Temporary marriage has been the subject of intense public debate before, following its recommendation in a Friday sermon in 1990 by the then president Hashemi Rafsanjani; see Haeri (1992: 203, 205–207).
[51] On debates and developments regarding temporary marriage, see also Bøe (2015: 50–57, 123–133).

In all cases, with the exception of Iran, those laws or drafts written or revised by governmental or political actors do not contain any substantive regulation of temporary marriage and only mention or imply it once or twice, or are completely silent on the subject. Even though it is difficult to confirm the motivation behind this for each case, two factors are likely connected to it, namely the widespread rejection of temporary marriage within Shi'i communities and its rejection by the Sunnis, which has to be seen in the context of current Sunni–Shi'i tensions. As to the first factor, Hamoudi has provided some insight for the Iraqi case, observing that the idea of temporary marriage is contrary to the values of Iraq's conservative Shi'is (Hamoudi 2016: 353–354). The second factor is exemplified by the position of Sunni MPs in Afghanistan on this matter as well as by expressions such as "child of *mut'a*" being used by Sunnis to insult Shi'is in Bahrain, especially in the context of political tensions.

The silence on temporary marriage – a gap in the law which judges might fill by references to uncodified fiqh[52]– can result in difficulties for women and children, who usually are in a more vulnerable position. In the face of the legal uncertainty of temporary marriage – which is allowed religiously and implied legally (it is not prohibited) but remains uncodified – women and children might find themselves subject to the "rule of men" rather than the "rule of law." Affected children may suffer from social and legal disadvantages, especially when the temporary husband's paternity is not documented. Reports indicate that widows and other women in precarious economic conditions are especially ready to agree to temporary marriage. Some critics blame men for taking advantage of the weak position of these women, as the latter risk social stigma by marrying temporarily.

In Iran, the issue has been discussed more openly and has also been addressed and even recommended by state officials in earlier years, sparking controversy (Haeri 1992; Safai and Emami 2015: 34–36). As mentioned, the 2013 law made obligatory the registration of temporary marriages that result in a wife's pregnancy; this guarantees the child's rights and prevents the mother being left as solely responsible for the child. In other words, temporary marriage was subjected to the rule of law to a larger extent than before.[53]

It needs to be added that this form of marriage is criticized in all mentioned countries from a women's rights perspective. Critics' demands

---

[52] As provided for in Article 2 Afghan PSL and Article 3 Bahrain Family Law.
[53] In practice, the number of registered temporary marriages is only a few hundred each year, see Oates (2009: 7).

range from total abolishment on the one hand to clear legal regulations providing women and children with more legal certainty on the other hand (e.g., Elaph.com 2008; Bøe 2015: 123–133). Therefore, while the Iranian legal regulation can be considered to subject temporary marriage to the rule of law by providing a legal framework, this codification of temporary marriage can at the same time be seen as anchoring unequal rights for women in law.

4.2 Access to Divorce for Women

Access to divorce in classical Islamic law is granted unequally: While a husband has the right to unilaterally divorce his wife without giving any reason at all (*talāq*), a wife's access to divorce is much more limited, especially when her husband does not agree to divorce.[54] In such a case, she has to prove to the judge that certain conditions are met, which allow the judge to compel the husband to pronounce *talāq* or to impose the divorce himself. The grounds on which a woman can demand divorce differ from school to school. Modern legislation often combines teachings from different schools or reinterprets and applies existing concepts to broaden women's access to divorce. This was also the case with the Iranian Civil Code, which in Articles 1129 and 1130 grants women access to divorce where classical Shi'i *fiqh* does not (Mir-Hosseini 2007: 111).

Access to divorce has been one of the main issues which (substantive) family law reform dealt with since the establishment of the Islamic Republic in Iran. Of great importance here is the aforementioned concept of *osr va haraj* (hardship and suffering), a concept of Islamic jurisprudence which "allows the suspension or removal of a rule (*hukm*) when its compliance produces hardship in general (i.e. for all) or for an individual (i.e. one person)" (Mir-Hosseini 2007: 111). The concept first found its way into Article 1130 of the Civil Code in 1982 (Mir-Hosseini 2007: 117–119). Henceforth the wife could demand divorce based on *osr va haraj*, that is, if she could prove that the continuation of marriage would cause hardship and suffering to her. In 2002, the article was amended by adding five instances of what constitutes hardship and suffering, while not limiting the application of this concept to these five examples.

---

[54] The wife can sue for divorce through *khul'* or *mubāra'a*. Both types of divorce require the wife to waive financial claims against her husband or pay him a certain amount and in return, the husband – if he agrees to divorce – pronounces *talāq*. In classical law, the husband needs to consent to such divorce. Modern (Sunni) legislation, for example in Egypt, introduced judicial *khul'*, which can be carried out without the husband's consent.

Given that these reforms predated all other Shi'i (draft) laws discussed here, the question arises whether legal developments in Iran are reflected in later Shi'i family law outside of Iran.

With regard to the Afghan PSL, this clearly is the case. The section entitled "Judicial Divorce" (*talāq tavassot-e mahkame*) of the Afghan Shi'i PSL starts with Article 141, which explicitly invokes the concept of *osr va haraj* as well as that of *zarar* (harm or injury):[55] "Whenever the continuation of the marriage causes harm or hardship and suffering unbearable for the wife, she can request divorce from the court"[56] (Article 141 (2)). The formulation so far is very close to the Iranian Civil Code, with only slight changes, such as including *zarar* as well. The Afghan PSL then lists the same examples for what constitutes *osr va haraj* but not without also making some slight changes. These five instances are:

1. The husband's unexcused absence from the family home (the laws differ on the necessary duration of his absence).
2. The husband's alcohol and drug addiction (the Iranian Civil Code demands the addiction be "detrimental to marriage").
3. The husband being sentenced to a prison term (the laws differ on the length of the term).
4. Beating or any kind of maltreatment that is intolerable to the wife, given custom and her situation (the Iranian Civil Code requires this to occur repeatedly or to be ongoing [*mostamarr*], the Afghan PSL does not).
5. The husband being "afflicted by an incurable or contagious disease disrupting marital life," to which the Iranian Civil Code adds "or any other affliction disrupting marital life."

In addition to this list, the Iranian Civil Code stipulates that the court can divorce a couple based on the wife's hardship and suffering caused by other instances than those given in the law. Such a clause is not included in the Afghan PSL, which therefore limits hardship and suffering to the five instances given by the law. Interestingly, an earlier draft of the Afghan PSL (2008/2009) did not include *osr va haraj* as grounds for judicial divorce of a permanent marriage but did invoke the concept with regard to temporary marriage (however, without providing any specifications on what constitutes *osr va haraj*). In following the Iranian reforms, the final Afghan Law of 2009 therefore provides women with a wider access to divorce than the drafts did.

---

[55] *Zarar* as grounds for judicial divorce is a Maliki concept that was integrated into many Family and Personal Status Law Codes (Tucker 2008: 120), among them the Afghan Civil Code (Articles 183–190).

[56] This and following translations are based on Mir-Hosseini (2007: 123).

The Bahraini Law of 2017 does not differ much from the 2009 Shiʻi draft and the 2009 Sunni Law on the substantive level. Article 98 provides the (Sunni and Shiʻi) wife with the right to demand divorce on the grounds of *zarar* or her husband abandoning her. The wife may furthermore request divorce if the husband is absent or missing (Article 107), sentenced to a term of imprisonment by which the wife is affected (Article 111), or if he abuses drugs or alcohol, in which case she can request divorce on the grounds of *zarar* (Article 112). A husband being infected by a contagious disease is not mentioned explicitly, nor are beating nor maltreatment. Aside from these exceptions, the divorce grounds are largely the same as those stipulated in the Iranian Civil Code and the Afghan PSL as instances of *osr va haraj* but are placed in a different order. The 2017 law is clearly based on its 2009 predecessor and the mentioned provisions on divorce and their order can be assumed to be in the result of the Bahraini codification of Sunni (Maliki-based) law.

While Al-Asfour listed in his draft fourteen examples for separation and/or dissolving the marital bond in Article 129,[57] he did not include *osr va haraj* or harm. From among the possible grounds on which the wife may request judicial divorce, he only includes the husband's absence and lack of providing maintenance to his wife (the latter being included in the Afghan and Iranian laws as well but not as an instance of *osr va haraj*).

The Iraqi 2014 draft, like the 2002 Bahraini draft, provided comparably less access to divorce for Shiʻi women. It includes separate sections on *khulʻ* (Articles 163–167) and *mubāraʼa* (Article 168),[58] but does not have any section on judicial divorce. There are some instances, found in different sections, in which the wife can request divorce from the judge: When the husband does not fulfill certain rights of the wife (Articles 102, 103, 104, 108), rejects the request for divorce and refuses to pay her maintenance (Article 147), and when he has left her and does not provide for her (Article 162). The husband may, as is the case in all the aforementioned laws, authorize his wife to perform *talāq* on herself (Article 145). The concepts of *osr va haraj* or *zarar* are not found in the draft, neither are the specific grounds of divorce for women that were included in the other laws as described, such as the husband's imprisonment or his addiction to drugs. Instead, grounds for divorce are treating the wife unfairly without legal reason, abstaining from intercourse with her for more than four months, or not giving her a due share of his time in cases where he has more than one wife.

---

[57] Including *talāq*, *khulʻ*, and *mubāraʼa* as well as annulment (*faskh*) for different reasons, which in principle can be found in all (draft) laws.
[58] See note (68).

Interestingly, the Iraqi draft includes a provision which is not found in any of the other laws or drafts: Article 146, being the last article of the first section of the chapter on *talāq*, declares that the law has in mind "the just man" (*al-rajul al-ʿadl*), who is "righteous on the path of the holy sharīʿa." This article, one can argue, implicitly confirms two things: First, there are just and unjust men (otherwise mentioning the just man in this context would be unnecessary) and these unjust men might use their legal rights in an unjust way. And second, women's agency is very restricted, which is why there is no invocation of the "just woman." A woman's justness or unjustness seem to be irrelevant to the drafter, because, due to her restricted ability to act independently, her justness or unjustness would not have any considerable impact. The question is, what would Article 146, if effective, mean in practice? It states that the rules put down in the draft are based on the assumption of men being just. What then does this mean when men are not just? Can a woman claim at court that certain provisions are inapplicable because her husband is unjust and therefore cannot base his claims on the law? This seems very unlikely. The provision probably was not intended to have any enforceable legal meaning. The clause rather sounds like an attempt to absolve the draft from unjustness arising from its application and blaming this on the unjustness of men. Perplexingly, the draft seems to concede the possibility that its application might be unjust, however without providing any means of protection against such unjustness for those who have to face it. This article, due its lack of clarity, is a clear example of a codified provision which, if put into force, would not enhance the rule of law in either the substantive nor the formal sense.

4.3 *Judicializing* Talāq

As mentioned, Article 146 of the 2014 Iraqi draft is found in the chapter on *talāq* and not, for example, among the general provisions, which indicates that it is especially connected to *talāq*. *Talāq* allows a husband to (even arbitrarily or unjustly) divorce his wife and, in many cases, to take her back afterwards without her consent as long as he does so within her waiting period (of usually three months).[59] *Talāq* in classical Islamic law is a form of extrajudicial divorce. No involvement of a

---

[59] During this period, the woman is not allowed to remarry. After the expiration of this period, the *talāq* becomes irrevocable. Under certain conditions, such as the marriage not having been consummated, the *talāq* becomes irrevocable immediately and the waiting period does not have to be observed. On revocable and irrevocable *talāq*, see Rohe (2015: 118).

judge is needed, as the divorce becomes effective by the husband's pronouncement. Today, this legal institution has been, in most places, put into a framework of formal and procedural regulations requiring at least the registration of the *talāq*.[60]

In Iran, these regulations require the involvement of a court in every case of *talāq* or any other form of divorce. In case filing for divorce is not based on the spouses' mutual agreement, the court initiates arbitration proceedings.[61] If reconciliation cannot be reached, the court issues an "Impossibility of Reconciliation" certificate. This certificate is submitted to the registrar at the place where the divorce is executed (that is, the *talāq* is pronounced in the presence of two witnesses) and registered (final registration occurs for revocable *talāq* after the expiration of the waiting period). Nonregistration is punishable. The process is different when the wife files for divorce. In this case, the judge, instead of issuing a certificate, issues a ruling for divorce.[62] In the Iranian case, *talāq* therefore has been clearly judicialized. It not only needs to be registered, it also needs to be brought to court. Even though the husband, in accordance with Islamic law, does not have to give any reasons for divorce, he has to submit to arbitration proceedings.

The Afghan Civil Code, by contrast, requires marriage registration but does not require the registration of divorce or any involvement of the court (Schneider 2005/2006: 232; Yassari and Rastin-Tehrani 2012: 77).[63] The Afghan PSL neither demands marriage registration nor divorce registration explicitly. Following Shi'i law, it does, however, require two male and just witnesses for *talāq* (Articles 142, 146). Furthermore, according to Article 141 (4), whenever *talāq* is requested by the husband or the wife, the court has to appoint two arbitrators for a reconciliation attempt. This seems to imply that *talāq* cases have to be brought to court even when initiated by the husband. Thus, a Shi'i husband has to undergo court and arbitration proceedings in order to carry out his right to *talāq*, while a Sunni husband in Afghanistan does not. Legal practice, though, might be different.

According to Article 89 of the 2017 Bahraini Law, the judge has to try to reconcile the couple before *talāq* is pronounced. Furthermore, the husband has to pronounce *talāq* in front of the judge (*amāma al-qādī*), out-of-court *talāq*s may, however, be registered. Also, two just witnesses

---

[60] For example, for such restrictions, see Tucker (2008: 116–117).
[61] The 2013 FPL also established family counselling centers which attempt to reach reconciliation in cases where the spouses request divorce based on mutual consent (Article 25).
[62] For details, see Ansaripour (2013: 84–89).
[63] As of 2005, most marriages were not registered in Afghanistan; see MPI (2005: 19).

are required for *talāq* according to Shi'i *fiqh* (Article 86). The details on marriage and divorce registration have been determined by law since 2007, before substantive family law was codified.[64]

The 1959 Iraq PSL makes it mandatory for the husband to initiate court proceedings in order to obtain a court issue for *talāq*. However, extrajudicial divorce may simply be registered during the woman's waiting period (Article 39). The 2014 Ja'fari draft law neither mentions marriage registration nor divorce registration. It solely demands two just male witnesses for *talāq* (Article 136). The draft law on the Ja'fari judiciary (which would establish Shi'i courts) provides a list of instances to be registered by the Ja'fari shari'a courts, which includes marriage contracts (Article 32 (6)) but does not mention *talāq* or any form of marriage dissolution. It therefore seems plausible to assume that the drafters wanted *talāq* to remain an extrajudicial form of divorce with no procedural or formal impediments to the husband's right to divorce whenever he wishes.[65] As with women's access to divorce, the Iraqi draft follows classical law more closely, with the result that much power is placed in men's hands and the role of the judiciary and the options of women to terminate marriage are restricted.

5 Contemporary Shi'i Family Law, *Ijtihād*, and the Rule of Law: Conclusions

The foregoing analysis shows that Shi'i family law – like Sunni family law – can be interpreted and codified in multiple different ways. The Iranian divorce law does deviate from classical Shi'i substantive provisions, but at the same time makes use of existing concepts and principles, such as *ijtihād* and *osr va haraj* to bring about legal reforms, which, in a number of ways, strengthened the formal and procedural elements of the rule of law. The Afghan and the Bahraini law follow this method to some extent, but there still remain differences. While, for example, the Afghan, Bahraini, and Iraqi (draft) laws seem to implicitly recognize temporary marriage without providing any legal framework for it, the Iranian legislator provides for substantive and, since 2013, also for

---

[64] See Ansaripour (2013: 71–72) and also Mir-Hosseini (2012: 68). Currently, effective provisions on marriage and divorce registrations are stipulated in Articles 6–20 of Decree No. 1 of 2016.

[65] In Shi'i law, the husband is restricted with regard to when he can divorce his wife in so far as a declaration of *talāq* is only allowed while the wife is in the state of purity (*tuhr*). She is not in a state of purity during her menstruation and during postpartum bleeding. A *talāq* pronounced in a phase of purity during which intercourse took place is likewise invalid.

procedural regulations on temporary marriage. Temporary marriage also is an example of political and other considerations being given priority over codifying pure doctrine, as the Afghan and Iraqi cases show.

Regarding the husband's right to *talāq*, the Iranian, Afghan, and Bahraini laws aim at judicializing *talāq*, thereby restricting its arbitrary character. Iranian law, however, provides for far more detailed stipulations on registration, arbitration, and court proceedings than the Afghan law. In Bahrain, marriage and divorce registration have been regulated in detail for Sunnis and Shi'is alike since 2007. According to the Iraqi draft, *talāq* can be extrajudicial. The Iraqi draft also keeps women's access to divorce considerably limited while the Afghan PSL very clearly took the Iranian Civil Code as a model for this issue. The introduction of *osr va haraj* or *zarar*, also common in Sunni legislation, indicates that codification need not bring an end to the flexibility associated with Islamic law. Legislative organs may and do respond to social needs and changes. The examples also show how formal aspects can have a quite substantive impact, as in all described cases the outcomes of (non)codification may affect women's rights significantly.

The fact that in most of the presented cases it was Shi'i clerics who drafted or supported codes of Shi'i family law clearly shows that, contrary to Bahr al-Ulum's rejection of such codification efforts, codification is no longer perceived to be contrary to Shi'i legal principles. A crucial question, however, is who has the competence to draft the law. Bahraini Shi'i scholars emphasize that the parliament (half-appointed by the king) is not qualified to do so and therefore demand that codification be in the hands of Shi'i scholars. In Afghanistan, the draft presented by Shi'i scholars has been altered considerably by parliament and governmental institutions. An amendment to the Afghan PSL would, however, probably need the support of Shi'i clerics.[66] As for the Iraqi draft law of 2014, it is unclear who wrote it. The Islamic Virtue Party which presented it, however, is linked to Ayatollah al-Yaqoubi. The draft law on the Ja'fari judiciary, in addition, intended to include the leading Shi'i *mujtahid*, Ayatollah al-Sistani, in the Ja'fari shari'a court system (Article 2, speaking of the highest authority of the Ja'fari school in Iraq),[67] thereby maintaining clerical authority over Shi'i family law to a certain degree.

---

[66] This was stated by a Kabuli judge who asked not to be named (personal email correspondence, June 3, 2018).

[67] According to this article, a Supreme Council for the Ja'fari Judiciary was to be established and associated with the supreme *marja'*, who should have selected the council's members. The council was to appoint the judges for the Ja'fari Courts of First Instance and the Ja'fari Supreme Court.

Thus, the motivation behind these codes might not be that different from Bahr al-Ulum's back in the 1960s. Bahr al-Ulum intended to preserve Shi'i clerical authority over family law, just as much as some Shi'i parties and clerics today want to gain or maintain authority over Shi'i family law (and possibly Shi'i electoral support) by codifying it. Identity politics in the context of sectarianism played a major role, especially in Bahrain and Iraq. Therefore, in most cases, the rule of law as such did not seem to be the main motivation, even though it did play a role in Bahrain in the campaign of the Supreme Women's Council for codification and the government's efforts to modernize the law. In Iran, the need for family law reform was based on existing laws being unclear and inconsistent, which shows that the reforms were to some extent aiming at enhancing what can be labeled formal elements of the rule of law. In Iraq, the 2014 draft would have limited the rule of law in comparison to the existing Iraq PSL by, for example, placing *talāq* again completely into the private sphere. As for Afghanistan, after nearly ten years since the Afghan PSL has been enacted, information on its actual implementation and on how in practice it does or does not contribute to subjecting issues of marriage and divorce to court supervision are very scarce.

In Iran, the question of *ijtihād* played a more prominent role in debates around family law reform than in the other three countries. In general, the practice of *ijtihād*, taking into account "the conditions and needs of the present time,"[68] have been emphasized by leading state officials in Iran. Also, a connection between using the concept of *ijtihād* and enhancing the rule of law has been made (Kar and Pourzand 2016: 200).[69] With regard to family law reform, women's rights activists claimed that not only *mujtahid*s but *any* Muslim, male or female, with knowledge of Islam may practice *ijtihād* (Bøe 2015: 86–90, 152). With reference to these views on *ijtihād*, codification and *ijtihād* do not have to be mutually exclusive, as Bahr al-Ulum suggested. Rather, the setting of *ijtihād* can be a different one: *Ijtihād* need not be practiced by the judge,[70] or an authoritative individual, but instead can be practiced by the legislator, who might be informed by the expert opinions of *mujtahid*s (and potentially even by others who enter the "*ijtihādi* discourse").

---

[68] This expression, for example, was used during a gathering of members of the Guardian Council and the Expediency Council on the issue of *ijtihād* in 2008 by the chairman of the Expediency Council at that time and former president, Rafsanjani; for a full translation of the statement see Kar and Pourzand (2016: 207).
[69] On *ijtihād* and the Guardian Council, see Kar and Pourzand (2016: 206).
[70] On judicial *ijtihād* and the question to what extent judges should or should not practice *ijtihād*, see Schneider (1990: 202–227).

In Iran, Shiʿi family law codification and reform take place within a consolidated system of Shiʿi legislation. It is not identity politics and sectarianism that impact the discourse surrounding family law; rather, it is questions of women's rights and gender roles that are more dominant. The political and constitutional context is very different from Iraq and Afghanistan, where Shiʿi family law codification emerged in the process of state-(re)building and the formation of new power structures. While Bahrain did not experience a turning point comparable to Afghanistan in 2001 and Iraq in 2003, the majority and minority ratios and tensions between Sunnis and Shiʿis strongly affect the question of how to deal with Shiʿi family law codification.

Thus, experience in legislation and enforcement can be seen as the main factors as to why, in Iran, Shiʿi family law is subjected to the rule of law – in the formal sense – to a larger extent than elsewhere.

Bibliography

Abdulhadi, Khalaf. "Qānun ahkām al-usra fi-l-bahrayn" [The Family Law in Bahrain], November 25, 2016. arabi.assafir.com, https://perma.cc/LGH2-BC4N, accessed April 1, 2021.

alhayat.com. "*Mashruʿ qānun al-aḥwāl al-shakhsiyya al-jaʿfari fi-l'-irāq. Istiʿāra lubnāniyya li-ʿawda ilā al-ṭā'ifiyya*" [The Draft for Jaʿfari Personal Status Law in Iraq: A Lebanese Borrowing for the Return to Sectarianism]. March 10, 2014. www.alhayat.com/m/story/1022429#sthash.HHSCtMbQ.dpbs, accessed June 12, 2018, not available any longer, on file with author.

Anderson, J. N. D. "Codification in the Muslim World," *Rabels Zeitschrift für ausländisches und internationales Privatrecht*, 30, 1966, pp. 241–253.

Ansaripour, M. A. "Arbitration in Divorce Proceedings under Islamic and Iranian Law," *Yearbook of Islamic and Middle Eastern Law*, 15 (1), 2011, pp. 37–52.

Ansaripour, M. A. "A Brief Analysis of the 2013 Family Protection Act," *Yearbook of Islamic and Middle Eastern Law*, 17 (1), 2013, pp. 70–101.

The Arab Weekly. "'Marriages of pleasure' take Iraq by storm," May 8, 2016, p. 19.

Arjomand, Said. "Civil Society and the Rule of Law in the Constitutional Politics of Iran under Khatami," *Social Research*, 76 (2), 2000, pp. 283–301.

Arjomand, Said. "Shiʿite Jurists and the Iranian Law and Constitutional Order in the Twentieth Century," in S. Arjomand and N. Brown (eds.), *The Rule of Law, Islam, and Constitutional Politics in Egypt and Iran*, Albany: State University of New York Press, 2013, pp. 15–56.

Bahrain Mirror. "*4 min kibār ʿulamāʾ al-dīn al-shīʿī fi-l-Baḥrayn: raʾy al-ʿulamāʾ wa-l-madhhab lā yataghayyur bi-iqrār qānūn aḥkām al-usra*" [Four Great Shiʿi Religious Authorities in Bahrain: the Opinion of the Religious Scholars and the Law School Does Not Change with the Adoption of the Family Law], July 16, 2017 https://perma.cc/AD5S-LQEZ, accessed April 1, 2021.

BBC Persian. "*Ezdevāj-e movaqqat dar Afghānistān roshd mi-konad*" [Temporary Marriage Spreads in Afghanistan], April 23, 2006. www.bbc.com/persian/iran/story/2006/04/060424_mj-afghan-short-marriage.shtml, accessed July 27, 2023.

BBC Persian. *"Qānun-e ahvāl-e shiʿayān-e afghān tasvib shod"* [Personal Status Law for Afghan Shiʿis Approved], February 7, 2009. www.bbc.com/persian/afghanistan/2009/02/090207_a-afghan-shiite-law.shtml?print=1, accessed May 24, 2018.

BBC Persian. *"Negāh-e hokumat-e tālebān beh shiʿayān-e; hasrat-e gozashteh va āyandeh-ye mobham"* [The Taliban Government's View on the Shiʿis; Regrets of the Past and an Uncertain Future], July 28, 2023. www.bbc.com/persian/articles/c3gdpky5wxwo accessed August 27, 2023.

Bedner, Adriaan. "An Elementary Approach to the Rule of Law," *Hague Journal on the Rule of Law*, 2, 2010, pp. 48–74.

Bøe, Marianne. *Family Law in Contemporary Iran: Women's Rights Activism and Shariʿa*, London, New York: I. B. Tauris, 2015.

Clarke, Morgan. "Shariʿa Courts and Muslim Family Law in Lebanon," in E. Giunchi (ed.), *Adjudicating Family Law in Muslim Courts*, London and New York: Routledge, 2014, pp. 32–47.

Clarke, Morgan and Mirjam Künkler. "De-centring Shiʿi Islam," *British Journal of Middle Eastern Studies*, 45 (1), 2018, pp. 1–17.

Crews, Robert D. *Afghan Modern: The History of a Global Nation*, Cambridge, MA: Belknap Press, 2015.

Damad, Seyyed Mostafa Mohaghegh. "The Reception of Factuality (taṣwīb) Theories of Ijtihād in Modern Uṣūlī Shīʿī Thought," in A. Bhojani, L. de Rooij, and M. Bohlander (eds.), *Visions of Sharīʿa. Contemporary Shīʿī Legal Theory*, Leiden: Brill, 2020, pp. 10–25.

Ebert, Hans-Georg. "Rechtsreformen in Bahrain am Beispiel des Familienrechts," *GAIR-Mitteilungen*, 3, 2011, pp. 123–129.

Elaph.com. *"Zijāt al-mutʿa fi-l-bahrayn bi-7 dulār wa-taṣil li-nisf sāʿa"* [Temporary Marriages for 7 Dollars and Half an Hour], December 23, 2008. elaph.com/Web/Politics/2008/12/393720.htm, accessed July 27, 2023.

Fallon, Richard H. Jr. "The Rule of Law as a Concept in Constitutional Discourse," *Columbia Law Review*, 97 (1), 1997, pp. 1–56.

Gleave, Robert "Conceptions of Authority in Iraqi Shiʿism: Baqir al-Hakim, Ha'iri and Sistani on Ijtihād, Taqlid and Marja'iyya," *Theory, Culture and Society*, 24 (2), 2007, pp. 59–78.

Gribetz, Arthur. *Strange Bedfellows: mutʿat al-nisā' and mutʿat al-ḥajj: a study based on Sunnī and Shīʿī sources of tafsīr, ḥadīth and fiqh*, Berlin: Klaus Schwarz Verlag, 1994.

Gulf News. "Bahrain's Shura approves unified family draft law," July 19, 2017. https://gulfnews.com/world/gulf/bahrain/bahrains-shura-approves-unified-family-draft-law-1.2061301, accessed July 17, 2023.

Haeri, Shahla. "Temporary Marriage and the State in Iran: An Islamic Discourse on Female Sexuality." *Social Research*, 59 (1), 1992, pp. 201–223.

Haeri, Shahla. *Law of Desire: Temporary Marriage in Shiʿi Iran*, rev. edn. Syracuse, NY: Syracuse University Press, 2014.

Hallaq, Wael B. "Was the Gate of Ijtihād Closed?" *International Journal of Middle East Studies*, 16 (1), 1984, pp. 3–41.

Hallaq, Wael B. "'Muslim Rage' and Islamic Law," *Hastings Law Journal*, 54 (6), 2002, pp. 1705–1720.

Halm, Heinz. *Die Schia*. Darmstadt: Wiss. Buchgesellschaft, 1988.

Hamoudi, Haidar A. "Resurrecting Islam or Cementing Social Hierarchy? Reexamining the Codification of 'Islamic' Personal Status Law," *Arizona Journal of International & Comparative Law*, 33 (2), 2016, pp. 329–382.

Hélie-Lucas, Marie-Aimée. "The Preferential Symbol for Islamic Identity: Women in Muslim Personal Status Laws," in V. Moghadam (ed.), *Identity Politics and Women. Cultural Reassertion and Feminism in International*, Boulder: Westview Press, 1994, pp. 391–407.

ICS. *Mawqifunā min qānun "ahkām al-usra"* [Our Position on the Family Law], (n.d.a). www.olamaa.cc/?p=9750, accessed May 29, 2018, not available any longer, on file with author.

ICS. *Mulāhazāt hawla taqnīn al-ahwāl al-shakhsiyya* [Remarks on the Codification of Personal Status Matters], (n.d.b). www.olamaa.cc/?p=5113, accessed May 29, 2018, not available any longer, on file with author.

The Independent. "Poet jailed in protests claims she was beaten by Bahraini royal," July 18, 2011. www.independent.co.uk/news/world/middle-east/poet-jailed-in-protests-claims-she-was-beaten-by-bahraini-royal-2315431.html, accessed May 16, 2018.

ISNA.ir. "*Roshd-e thabt-e ezdevāj-e movaqqat*" [Increase in Registrations of Temporary Marriage], Ordibehesht 4, 1393. www.isna.ir/news/93020201013/, accessed August 8, 2018.

Kar, Mehrangiz and Azadeh Pourzand. "The Rule of Law and Conflict in the Reform Era," in Daniel Brumberg and Farideh Farhi (eds.), *Power and Change in Iran: Politics of Contention and Conciliation*, Bloomington: Indiana University Press, 2016, pp. 195–223.

Kingdom of Bahrain Ministry of Foreign Affairs. *Rule of Law*, www.mofa.gov.bh/AboutBahrain/RuleofLaw/tabid/125/language/en-US/Default.aspx, accessed July 2, 2020.

Kinninmont, Jane. "Framing the Family Law: A Case Study of Bahrain's Identity Politics," *Journal of Arabian Studies*, 1 (1), 2011, pp. 53–68.

Layish, Aharon. "The Transformation of the Sharīʿa from Jurists' Law to Statutory Law in the Contemporary Muslim World," *Die Welt des Islams*, 44 (1), 2004, pp. 85–113.

Louër, Laurence. *Transnational Shia Politics: Religious and Political Networks in the Gulf*, London: Hurst Publishers, 2008.

al-Maghāmis, Turkī. "'Al-ahwāl al- shakhsiyya al-jaʿfariyya'… malaʾa al-farāgh al-tashrīʿī li-atbāʿ al-madhhab fī dawāʾir al-qadāʾ" [The Jafari Personal Status… Filled the Legislative Gap for Followers of the Madhhab in Court Chambers], alraimedia.com, July 7, 2019. https://perma.cc/7UYS-RMY5, accessed August 27, 2023.

Mallat, Chibli. "Shi'ism and Sunnism in Iraq: Revisiting the Codes," *Arab Law Quarterly*, 8 (2), 1993, pp. 141–159.

Mallat, Chibli. *The Renewal of Islamic Law: Muhammad Baqer as-Sadr, Najaf and the Shi'i International*. Cambridge: Cambridge University Press, 2003.

MPI (Max Planck Institute for Foreign Private Law and Private International Law). *Family Structures and Family Law in Afghanistan*, 2005.

Maxeiner, James R. "Some Realism about Legal Certainty in the Globalization of the Rule of Law," *Houston Journal of International Law*, 31 (1), 2008, pp. 27–46.

Mir-Hosseini, Ziba. *Marriage on Trial: A Study of Islamic family law; Iran and Morocco compared*, London: I.B. Tauris, 1993.

Mir-Hosseini, Ziba. "When a Woman's Hurt becomes an Injury: 'Hardship' as Grounds for Divorce in Iran," *Hawwa*, 5 (1), 2007, pp. 111–126.

Mir-Hosseini, Z. "The Politics of Divorce Laws in Iran: Ideology versus Practice," in Rubya Mehdi, Werner Menski, and Jorgen S. Nielsen (eds.), *Interpreting Divorce Laws in Islam*, Copenhagen: DJØF Publishing, 2012, pp. 65–83.

Momen, Moojan. *An Introduction to Shi'i Islam: The History and Doctrines of Twelver Shiism*, New Haven: Yale University Press, 1985.

An-Naʿim, Abdullahi A. *Islamic Family Law in A Changing World: A Global Resource Book*. London: Zed Books, 2002.

Al-Najafī, Muḥammad ḥasan. *Jawāhir al-kalām fī sharh sharāʾiʿ al-islām* [*The Jewels of Discourse in Elucidation of the Prescriptions of Islamic Law*], Vol. 31, Qom: Muʾassasat al-nashr al-islāmi, 1422/2012 [1266/1850].

Nedzel, Nadia E. "The Rule of Law: Its History and Meaning in Common Law, Civil Law, and Latin American Judicial Systems," *Richmond Journal of Global Law & Business*, 10 (1), 2010, pp. 57–109.

The New Arab. "Iraq withdraws controversial 'child marriage law'," November 23, 2017. www.alaraby.co.uk/english/news/2017/11/23/iraq-withdraws-controversial-child-marriage-law, accessed December 19, 2017.

Oates, Lauryn. *A Closer Look: The Policy and Lawmaking Process Behind the Shiite Personal Status Law*. Afghanistan Research and Evaluation Unit Issues Paper Series, 2009.

Osanloo, Arzoo. "Islamico-Civil 'Rights-Talk': Women, Subjectivity, and Law in Iranian Family Court," *American Ethnologist*, 33 (2), 2006, pp. 191–209.

Peters, Rudolph. "From Jurists' Law to Statute Law or What Happens When the *Shariʿa* is Codified," *Mediterranean Politics*, 7 (3), 2002, pp. 82–95.

Poya, Abbas. *Anerkennung des Iğtihād – Legitimation der Toleranz: Möglichkeiten innerer und äußerer Toleranz im Islam am Beispiel der Iğtihād-Diskussion*, Berlin: Klaus Schwarz Verlag, 2003.

Radin, Margaret J. "Reconsidering the Rule of Law," *Boston University Law Review*, 69 (4), 1989, pp. 781–819.

Rastin-Tehrani, Kabeh. *Afghanisches Eherecht: mit rechtsvergleichenden Hinweisen*. Frankfurt am Main: Metzner, 2012.

Rastin-Tehrani, Kabeh and Nadjma Yassari. *Max Planck Manual on Family Law in Afghanistan*, 2nd ed., Heidelberg: Max Planck Institute, 2012.

Reuters. "Sectarian divide widens after Bahrain unrest," June 9, 2011. https://uk.reuters.com/article/uk-bahrain-sectarianism/sectarian-divide-widens-after-bahrain-unrest-idUKTRE7581OO20110609, accessed March 7, 2018.

Rohe, Mathias. *Islamic Law in Past and Present*, Leiden: Brill, 2015.

Rubāh, Suʿād. "Al-ahkām al-sharʿiyya wa-qāʿidat al-taʿlil wa-l-taʿabbud [The Provisions of the *Shariʿa* and the Basis of Interpretation and Worship]," *Majallat- al-sharīʿa wa-l-iqtisād*, 2 (3), 2013, pp. 111–140.

Al-Rumayli, ʿAbd al-hakīm. *Taghayyur al-fatwā fi-l-fiqh al-islāmi* [The Transformation of the Fatwa in Islamic Fiqh], Beirut: Dar Al-Kotob Al-ilmiyah, 2016.

Russel Jones, Sandy. "The Battle over Family Law in Bahrain," *Middle East Report*, 242, 2007, pp. 33–39.

Safai, Sayyed Hossein and Asadollah Emami. *Mokhtasar-e hoquq-e khānevādeh* [A Concise Summary of Family Law], Tehran: Mizan Foundation, 2015.

Schneider, Irene. *Das Bild des Richters in der adab al-qāḍī-Literatur*. Frankfurt am Main: Lang, 1990.

Schneider, Irene. "Registration, Court System and Procedure in Afghan Family Law," *Yearbook of Islamic and Middle Eastern Law*, 12, 2005/2006, pp. 209–234.

Schneider, Irene. "Islamisches Recht zwischen göttlicher Satzung und temporaler Ordnung? Überlegungen zum Grenzbereich zwischen Recht und Religion," in C. Langenfeld and I. Schneider, (eds.), *Recht und Religion*, Göttingen: Universitätsverlag Göttingen, 2008, pp. 138–191.

Stilt, Kristen. "Islamic Law and the Making and Remaking of the Iraqi Legal System," *The George Washington International Law Review*, 36, 2004, pp. 695–756.

Tamanaha, Brian Z. "The History and Elements of the Rule of Law," *Singapore Journal of Legal Studies*, 2012, pp. 232–247.

Tucker, Judith E. *Women, Family, and Gender in Islamic Law*, Cambridge and New York: Cambridge University Press, 2008.

Wimpelmann Chaudhary, Torunn, Orzala Ashraf Nemat, and Astri Suhrke. "Promoting Women's Rights in Afghanistan: The Ambiguous Footprint of the West," in S. Campbell, D. Chandler, and M. Sabaratnam (eds.), *A Liberal Peace? The Problems and Practices of Peacebuilding*, London and New York: Zed Books, 2011, pp. 106–120.

Yassari, Nadjma. "An Islamic Alternative: Temporary Marriage," in N. Yassari and J. Scherpe (eds.), *Die Rechtsstellung der nichtehelichen Lebensgemeinschaften – Legal Status of Cohabitants*, Tübingen: Beck, 2005, pp. 557–567.

5 Rule of Law or Rule by Law? Iran's Bar Association as a Pawn in Islamic–Republican Contestations

Mirjam Künkler

1 Introduction

The institution of the Bar Association and its independence from the judicial branch of power is a key pillar of any rule-of-law state. Bar associations design and conduct the licensing examinations for future lawyers, and their boards are usually instrumental in screening prospective parliamentary legislation for its compatibility with the constitution and the rule of law (IBA 2016; Künkler 2022). The independence of lawyers and their professional integrity hinges on training and licensing programs that are shielded from political interference and instrumentalization. Independent bar associations that oversee the training and certification of future lawyers are therefore indispensable to guaranteeing the rule of law. Conversely, where political elites have the power to interfere with the certification of lawyers and inject political considerations into the decision-making process of who can and who cannot join the Bar, the legal profession is at risk of becoming subservient to political power and, ultimately, of becoming a tool of authoritarian rule.[1]

The development of the Bar Association of Iran (Kānun-e Vokalā-ye Dādgostari) is intricately bound up with the development of a modern legal system in the course of the twentieth century. After the parliament and the constitution itself, it is one of the important institutional outcomes of the Constitutional Revolution of 1906/1907, often credited with signifying and further instilling in twentieth-century Iran a strong

---

Parts of this chapter have previously been published in Künkler (2017). I thank the publisher for the permission to reprint them. I further thank Ehsan Hosseinzadeh for valuable comments on an earlier draft of this chapter.

[1] On rule-of-law conceptions, see Chapter 1 in this volume, based on Tamanaha (2004). The Islamic Republic of Iran generally falls into type a (and thus the thinnest) of Tamanaha's six conceptions of the rule of law ("Rule-by-Law: law is instrument of government action"), although reformists and human rights activists generally, but with limited success, fight for type b ("Formal Legality: general, prospective, clear, certain").

belief in constitutionalism and with fertilizing a rule-of-law-oriented legal culture.[2] By mid-century, a professional bar association had been established, although it took until 1953 for it to become completely independent from the Ministry of Justice.[3] The 1960s and 1970s saw the heyday of the professionalization of lawyers and judges and the crystallization of public appreciation for an independent legal profession and an independent judiciary. During the 1979 Revolution, lawyers made up the backbone of the human rights movement that called for fundamental political reform. Contrary to the movement's campaigns in favor of democratization and the rule of law, the revolution quickly degenerated into lawlessness, where standards of due process were abrogated. In the aftermath of the systemic transformation of the legal system that followed the establishment of the Islamic Republic, the bar associations were effectively neutralized in the 1980s but rose from the ashes during the post-Iran–Iraq War reconstruction period under President Rafsanjani (1989–1997) when they attempted to reassert themselves as the primary institutions for the licensing of lawyers. Unsurprisingly, this attempt met with fierce resistance from officials inside the judiciary who had built up alternative training and recruitment mechanisms for future lawyers. Nevertheless, they were not able to replace the bar associations entirely and to date no head of the judiciary has succeeded in closing them down once and for all. Ever since the early 2000s, they have been a pawn in the internal contestations between those forces aiming to strengthen the independence of both the legal profession and the judiciary, and those insisting that the Islamic character of the regime demands the subservience of both lawyers and judges to the executive (which, in their view, is led by the highest Islamic legal authority of the country).[4]

This chapter offers an overview of the history of the bar associations in modern Iran, with particular focus on the regulation of the Tehran-based Central Bar Association following the 1979 Revolution. Although the bar associations are among the most important nonstate institutions capable of strengthening the rule of law, they have received only scant

---

[2] On the concept of "legal culture," see Nelken (2004, 2016).

[3] Beside the Tehran-based bar, two more associations were set up in subsequent years, in Fars and Azerbaijan provinces. These bar associations were and are legally independent from one another. In the Islamic Republic, the Tehran bar functions as the Central Bar Association and the National Bar Associations Union is the umbrella organization for all independent bar associations. When officials refer to "the Bar" in the singular, they usually refer to the broader idea of independent bar associations and thus not a particular one. The Central Bar Association runs a newsletter and website at http://icbar.ir/.

[4] Technically, the president heads the executive, but the Supreme Leader stands above all three branches of power and in the eyes of conservative officials is the highest executive authority in the country.

academic attention so far.[5] The chapter will first offer a brief history of the establishment of the modern judiciary in the first part of the twentieth century and the development of the Tehran Bar Association as part of it. It will then turn to an overview of the justice system and the Islamization process that the judiciary underwent as a result of the 1979 Revolution, and examine how the consolidating revolutionary regime dealt with the Central Bar Association as the most important body that could present a counterweight to a politically controlled legal profession. It will be suggested that over time the judiciary has succeeded in creating a parallel institution that fulfils the functions of the bar, and allows it to control the training and certification of lawyers. This process is representative of two larger trends in the institutional development of the Islamic Republic: (1) the subordination of law and the legal profession to political considerations; and (2) the creation of regimist institutions parallel to those beyond the regime's purview, in order to tighten spaces over which it could otherwise not exert full control.

Methodologically, the research for this chapter is based on textual analysis of decrees, ordinances, bills, laws, and regulations, and the documentation of judicial appointment decisions. It also incorporates ethnographic work consisting of interviews with Tehran-, Isfahan- and Tabriz-based lawyers and with judges in a high court. A third type of source consists of domestic and international news coverage and reports by human rights organizations.

2   Popular Sovereignty and Clerical Veto Actors

The Islamic Republic presents a unique hybrid of a republican regime that on the one hand seeks to maximize participation and – with recourse to revolutionary rhetoric – legitimacy, but which, on the other hand, concentrates political power in the office of the Supreme Leader (Rahbar) with virtually no checks and balances vis-à-vis other branches of power and nearly full executive control over the judicial and security system (see Chapter 1 in this volume). A key institution of legislation and judicial review is the Guardian Council (Shorā-ye Negahbān), which is made up of six jurists trained in Shi'i law (*mojtahed*s) and six jurists trained in Iranian public law.[6] The entire council screens draft legislation for consistency with the constitution. Only the six *mojtahed*s check the congruence

---

[5] For notable exceptions, see Mehrpour (1989: 17) and Najafi (2017: 458–478). Banakar and Ziaee (2018) was published after an earlier version of this chapter was published in 2017. See note 1.

[6] For an overview, see Saffari (1993: 64–82).

of draft legislation against (their interpretation of) Shi'i Ja'fari law. As the Supreme Leader appoints half of the Guardian Council and as he also appoints the head of the judiciary who in turn proposes the other half of the Guardian Council, his preferences are decisive in the makeup of this institution. If the Guardian Council decides that the draft legislation violates constitutional or Shi'i law, it can veto it and send it back to the parliament (Majles) for revision. The parliament then has the choice of either revising the draft legislation in line with the Guardian Council's demands, or to vote with a two-thirds majority in favor of forwarding it on to the Council for the Discernment of the Expediency of the System (Majma'-e Tashkhis-e Maslahat-e Nezām), hereafter Expediency Council.

The Expediency Council, which is entirely appointed by the Supreme Leader and on which the Islamic jurists of the Guardian Council also sit *ex officio*, may then decide to pass the bill with the changes recommended by the Guardian Council or pass its own version, which may substantively deviate from the original.[7] Due to these inbuilt mechanisms of potential clerical veto, a parliament committed to a reform agenda may not get very far, unless the Supreme Leader has appointed into the Guardian Council and the Council of Expediency individuals committed to the same reform agenda.

Set up as a body to advise the Supreme Leader, the Expediency Council also passes its own budget, despite the fact that budgetary power is constitutionally assigned to the parliament. The council can thereby endow certain institutions with independent or additional funding. These include those courts that lie outside the official judiciary, such as the Special Courts for the Clergy (Künkler 2013).

The *rahbar* is also commander in chief of the regular army and the revolutionary guards. He has personal representatives in all ministries, and appoints the chairmen of the country's *bonyād*s, major economic institutions that often consist of conglomerates of economically powerful parastatal enterprises.[8] He has personal representatives in all embassies and consulates around the world, as well as in all major centers of Shi'i learning in the region, extending beyond the Middle East to Africa and

---

[7] For the internal bylaws of the council, see the bylaws and translation available on the Iran Data Portal: https://irandataportal.syr.edu/http-www-maslahat-ir-index-jspfkeyidsiteid3pageid409, last accessed June 6, 2019.

[8] A three-part *Reuters* series provides powerful insight into the dual economic and political functions of these parastatal institutions: "Assets of the Ayatollah." Land Grab: www.reuters.com/investigates/iran/#article/part1; National Champion: www.reuters.com/investigates/iran/#article/part2; Rough Justice: www.reuters.com/investigates/iran/#article/part3, last accessed July 3, 2019.

South and Southeast Asia, where his office funds religious seminaries and thousands of their students (Lob 2020; Künkler 2019).

The judiciary is under the supervision of the Supreme Leader who, in accordance with Article 158 of the constitution amended in 1989, appoints the head of the judiciary for a five-year term. The office of the head of the judiciary is responsible for the appointment, dismissal, suspension, and promotion of all judges, and it often makes requests for certain cases to be tried in specific courts. While it is independent from the other branches of power, that is, the parliament and the presidency, it is not independent from the *rahbar*.

Thus, on the one hand, the process of legislation is highly dependent on individuals who are directly or indirectly appointed by the Supreme Leader. On the other hand, the Islamic Republic features regular elections for the parliament and the presidency, and, since 1999, also the municipal councils. The highest political office, the *rahbar*'s, is itself the product of an election, that is, that of the Assembly of Experts, a clerical council of now eighty-eight members (previously eighty-six), which is directly elected by the people for eight-year terms and could theoretically depose the Supreme Leader if it found he had violated the law or was otherwise unfit to rule (this, however, has never happened). Electoral competition is limited by virtue of the fact that the Guardian Council has the power to screen and disqualify all candidates intending to run for political office beforehand, a mandate the council has interpreted in maximalist ways and has made use of extensively since 1992.

On paper, the elected institutions are not powerless. The parliament's most important mandate is its budgetary power, while the president's primary purview is in designing economic policy. Foreign and security policy, by contrast, is the mandate of the National Security Council and not that of an elected body. Given the long-standing economic sanctions against Iran, and also given that economic policy is highly dependent on security policy, the president's powers are de facto limited even in the realm of economic policy. Further, given that all major reforms, in favor of privatization for example, must pass not only parliament but also the clerical councils, the president is unable to work toward economic reform unless he is also backed in this by the Guardian and Expediency Councils.

The institutional design of the polity encourages political contestation and, to a limited degree, open political discourse *qua* a constitution that guarantees a range of civil liberties. For example, the principle of the presumption of innocence is specified in Article 37, and Article 169 stipulates the non-retroactivity of new laws. Article 32 recognizes the right of arrested individuals to know the reason of their detention within twenty-four hours, and Article 34 their right to call on justice. According to Article 35, the accused have a right to legal representation in court. Article 36 lays out that only competent courts have the right to pass sentences. Articles 165 and 166 assert that courts are open to the public and that verdicts can be passed only after the examination of evidence.[9] The severe limitations of the justice system notwithstanding, the 1979 constitution thus does recognize several key rights that might facilitate a rule-of-law state, if they were immutable.[10]

As will be shown, the institutions of the bar associations, with independent recruitment of future lawyers, could be primary tools in holding potential abuses of power at bay, but the associations' struggle to reassert their place after 1979 has continuously been met with strong resistance by judicial officials.

3 History of the Modern Judiciary and the Tehran Bar Association

The Tehran Bar Association was established as a consequence of the Constitutional Revolution 1906/1907 and apart from the constitution itself and the parliament, was one of the revolution's long-term institutional achievements. The revolution ushered in a period of state formation with the gradual buildup of a state-run legal system, increasingly taking the administration of justice out of the hands of the *'ulamā'* (Mohammadi 2008; Enayat 2013). New civil courts were established, although in the absence of any codified law, the courts continued to follow shari'a and those that were recruited as judges had still overwhelmingly been trained in the religious schools (madrasas). The court decisions on similar cases could vary widely from place to place and as no formal appeals procedure existed, claimants would often turn to religious authorities outside the courtroom to resolve their cases, thereby undermining the legitimacy of the new state-run system.

In 1911, a major justice reform was enacted through the passing of the Provisional Code of Judicial Organization (Qānun-e movaqqati-e tashkilāt-e ʿadliya) and the Provisional Code of Civil Procedure (Qānun-e movaqqati-ye osul-e muhākamāt-e hoquqi). The latter stipulated that lawyers licensed by the Ministry of Justice be present during court proceedings (Matin-Daftari 1945: 263f.). It was thus a first step toward the

---

[9] See the 1979 constitution (as amended in 1989): https://irandataportal.syr.edu/wp-content/uploads/1368-persian.pdf, last accessed June 20, 2019. For an excellent overview of the process of constitution-making and key ideas in the drafting process, see Schirazi (1997).

[10] Among the most detailed analyses in Persian is Hashemi (1996/1375).

state-run certification of lawyers, although the dearth of applicants for certification meant that this guideline was de facto seldom followed.

The 1911 codes were passed as temporary (*muvaqqatī*) laws in order to circumvent a discussion with the '*ulamā*' in parliament about the laws' compatibility with shari'a. It was hoped that the laws and regulations were more likely to meet approval for their permanent adoption after they had been shown to withstand the test of time, had been put into practice, and, in some cases, had been improved through legal reform.

In the same year, 1911, the first Code of Civil Procedure was promulgated, again on a temporary basis. It had been drafted by Adolphe Perny, a French jurist, who worked as a legal advisor to the parliament and the Ministry of Justice for fifteen years (1911–1926). Perny had also been instrumental in the opening of the *Madreseh-ye Hoquq* (Judicial School) in 1920, which was staffed mainly by French judicial personnel with the primary function of training future lawyers and judges.[11]

The coup d'état of February 1921 that marked the end of the Qajar dynasty also put a preliminary end to the recent buildup of a mostly secular, state-administered judiciary. In many regions of the country the entire judicial personnel were dismissed after the coup, and in some regions the old religious courts were reestablished. When Reza Pahlavi assumed the throne in 1925, one of his chief objectives was to present to Western powers new permanent codes in order to put an end to Western capitulations, which reserved Western countries the right to try their citizens for crimes committed in Iran in their own rather than Iranian courts. These capitulations had been justified with reference to the absence of permanent codes and the general weakness of Iran's justice system, effectively immunizing foreign citizens from criminal prosecution in Iran. Between 1925 and 1928, several permanent laws were passed, among them a new commercial code (*qānun-e tijārat*) in February 1926 and a new criminal code later that year, also penned by Perny, based on the French code (Daftari 1935; Marin 2004). A permanent Code of Civil Procedure (Qānun-e ā'in-e dādrasi-ye madani) and the first book of a civil code (Qānun-e madani) were passed in 1928. The latter consisted of the codification of shari'a following the format of the French Code Civil (the Code Napoléon). The new Judicial Organization Act (Qānun-e tashkilāt-e 'adliya) of 1928 provided that in order to practice, lawyers had to have either a law degree, a certificate

---

[11] Gulshā'iyān 1998, Vol. 1, 52–54. The school was later expanded and renamed the Faculty of Law, Political Science, and Economics (Dāneshkadeh-ye hoquq va 'olum-e siyāsi va eqtesādi). On the school, see Kasravi 1944, especially pp. 146–148.

from the Ministry of Justice, or previous experience as a judge. A disciplinary court for judges was established, which would impose stricter disciplinary regulations.

The law of 1911 had established that professional lawyers (*vakil-e rasmi*) had to be Iranian, at least 30 years of age, of good conduct, and not in the employ of the government. To be certified, they had to pass a special examination in the Ministry of Justice. While the 1911 law still allowed "occasional" (as opposed to professional) lawyers to serve in court from time to time, the new Judicial Organization Act allowed only professional lawyers to represent clients in a court of law. A law of 1930 once again reversed this, due to a shortage of lawyers, and stipulated that sub-provincial courts could authorize certain competent persons to act as lawyers, but only in courts that had given such permission. A 1936 law then created a three-tiered (*pāyeh*) system, whereby first-grade lawyers could appear in any court; second-grade lawyers in provincial, sub-provincial, and district courts; and those of the third grade only in sub-provincial and district courts. Each tier had standardized examinations, and official dress became obligatory at court appearances.

As per the law of 1911, appointment of judges to the Supreme Court, courts of appeal, and as chiefs of the courts of first instance occurred by imperial decree at the proposition of the minister of justice. The religious judge (*hākim-e sharʿ*), appointed by the Shah, had to agree to the appointment of the public prosecutors of the Supreme Court and the courts of appeal. All candidates had to be Iranian citizens and Muslim, and at least 25 years of age for the lowest ranks and 40 years of age for the highest ranks. Candidates were generally *madrasa*-trained or, after the opening of the law school, increasingly law school graduates. After the 1936 law that further reformed the organization of the judiciary, those who were *madrasa*-trained could rise only to a certain level (grade six out of eleven) while law school graduates could attain the upper echelons (Matin-Daftari 1945). A 1955 law then stipulated that only law school graduates were eligible for judgeships.

A first professional association of lawyers, the Bar Association (Kānūn-e Vūkalā-ye Dādgūstarī), was founded in 1930. One of its founders remarked during the opening:

> There is no doubt that court proceedings cannot rest on the dossier alone, the judge cannot rule on the dossier by itself. Other elements exist, and of these the most important is defence lawyers who should not allow a judge to deviate from the law in the proceedings or in his judgment. Throughout the civilized world those acquainted with legal affairs know that without the provision of good lawyers, justice is impossible. (Matin-Daftari 1945: fn. 8, pp. 33, 103–108)

Initially functioning as an organization under the auspices of the judiciary, the Bar Association was formally recognized as the sole institution certifying future lawyers in 1937, although it was still not independent from the Ministry of Justice at this point. During the brief period of parliamentary democracy (1941–1953) after Reza Shah Pahlavi was deposed by the Allied Powers, a law was passed under Prime Minister Mossadegh in 1953 that secured the independence of the Bar Association from the state, the Independence of the Bar Act (Lāyiha-ye Qānuni-ye Istiqlāl-e Kānun-e Vokalā-ye Dādgostari).

From 1954 on, when the law came into effect, lawyers were no longer licensed subject to Ministry approval nor any other state institution. They were certified in the now independent (Tehran-based) Bar Association and only the disciplinary court of the Bar could try lawyers for professional transgressions and offenses.

The Bar, now an autonomous authority vested with an independent legal identity, consisted of four sub-entities: a board of directors, a disciplinary investigation bureau, a disciplinary tribunal, and a legal aid section.[12] Its main tasks included to grant (and extend) licenses to qualified persons to practice law; to administer the Bar examinations; to discipline lawyers in breach of professional ethics; to provide legal aid to represent those who are financially unable to hire a lawyer of their choice; and to assist the Ministry of Justice in the preparation of legal rules and regulations.

Despite all other interferences of the state into societal matters and the authoritarian character of Mohammad Reza Pahlavi's reign, the regime did respect the autonomy of the Bar Association, and the latter remained independent until its purging during the 1979 Revolution. At the height of its activities in the late 1970s, the Bar was composed of around 7,000 members. As Saïd Arjomand has pointed out, the Bar Association and legal scholars and professionals associated with it constituted the backbone of the liberal-nationalist opposition during the 1960s and 1970s (Arjomand 1988: 109). As "guardians of the fundamental laws," lawyers had been instrumental in denouncing the violations of the constitution by the Pahlavi regime. The 1977 creation of the Association of Iranian Jurists (Jam'iyat-e Hoqūq-danān) and the Iranian Committee for the Defense of Freedom and Human Rights (Jam'iyat-e Irāni-ye Difāʿ az Hoqūq-e Bashar), headed by Mehdi Bazargan and set up to monitor prison conditions and publicize abuses of the intelligence services SAVAK

---

[12] Members of the board of directors, which consisted of twelve full-time and six substitute members and whose task was to manage the Bar and oversee the conduct of its various responsibilities, were elected in free elections by lawyers for two-year terms.

(Sāzmān-e Ettelāʿāt va Amniyat-e Keshvar – Organization of Intelligence and Security of the Country), constituted a decisive movement toward a liberal extraparliamentary opposition. When, in the summer of 1977, the Bar Association demanded the abolition of all extraconstitutional tribunals, including military courts, the episode seriously damaged the legitimacy of the Pahlavi regime.[13]

4 Islamization of the Justice System after 1979

In the aftermath of the revolution, the Iranian justice system underwent a far-reaching Islamization process. As the Islamic Republican Party (IRP) sought to Islamize the legal system and redraw the country's statutes in accordance with (an interpretation of) Jaʿfari jurisprudence in the 1980s and 1990s, it also needed to replace secular trained lawyers and judges with those trained in the "new law" – a law consisting, in theory, of positivized Shiʿi law and prerevolutionary codes that had been transformed to bring them in line with Jaʿfari jurisprudence. The new and transformed laws required a new class of lawyers and reformed curricula in the country's law schools, a process complicated by the fact that the initial phase of the Islamization of the legal system was not completed until the mid-1990s and that even the most important codes, such as the penal law, have since undergone repeated changes and reforms (see Chapters 2 and 3 in this volume).

Judges appointed prior to the revolution continued to enforce the prerevolutionary laws and regulations until, on August 22, 1982, Ayatollah Khomeini ordered all such laws null and void and threatened criminal prosecution to those who continued to enforce them. He further decreed that in those areas not yet covered by postrevolutionary legislation, judges should render decisions based on their own knowledge of Islamic law (in line with Article 167 of the 1979 constitution) and existing fatwas. As new legislation only very gradually filled the space voided by the August 1982 decree, individual judges were granted wide discretionary powers (ʿĀqili 1990).

After the marginalization of Prime Minister Bazargan's liberal-nationalist faction as the internal power struggles of the revolution intensified, the Central Bar Association was purged in June 1980.[14] The revolutionary prosecutor (dādsetān-e enqelāb) and the chief religious judge (hākim-e sharʿ), both appointed by Khomeini, successively drew up lists

---

[13] "The Iranian Bar Association headed by Hasan Nazih and Hedayatollah Matin-Daftari (a grandson of Mosaddeq) was particularly audible in its call for free elections and the release of political prisoners" (Green 1980: 13).

[14] The 1980 Law by the Revolutionary Council on Purging the Bar Association.

of lawyers to be expelled from the Bar,[15] and their names were published in *Kayhān* newspaper.[16] Shortly after the purge, lawyers were barred from defending those accused in the revolutionary courts, the main courts at the time. The offices of the Bar, located in the Ministry of Justice, were occupied in May 1981, and archives, documents, and funds seized (Lahidji 2000). Eight months later, those sitting on the board of directors were arrested, unless they had gone into hiding or exile beforehand. In 1984, the association was deprived of the right to hold its own elections and was put under the supervision of an appointed official (a *sarparast*, "supervisor") from the judiciary. The offiical was no other than Gholam-Hossein Mohseni-Eje'i, who ejoyed a long career in the Ministry of Intelligence and later became Head of the Judiciary. The exclusion of lawyers from the revolutionary courts meant that many closed their offices and retrained or went into exile. In addition, a number of lawyers had been Jews and Bahá'ís who already left Iran in the early years of the revolution due to the discrimination they suffered on religious grounds.

Faced with a dearth of legal professionals familiar with the new legal environment, the judiciary often awarded judgeships ad hoc to leading revolutionaries without closely probing their jurisprudential credentials. An Islamized justice system, it was argued, would function best with *mojtahed*s in the seats of judges, but little attention was paid initially as to whether a *mojtahed* had actually specialized in *fiqh* during his training, or had instead focused on theology (*kalām*), ethics (*akhlāq*), mysticism (*tasawwuf*), or some other branch of Islamic knowledge. Numerous courts therefore came to be presided over by individuals who had spent years in the religious seminaries but had little idea of the legal profession, let alone of the positive law according to which they were expected to adjudicate. Incidentally, until today, no regulation requires a *hojjatoleslām* (mid-ranking Shi'i cleric, literally "proof of Islam") to have specialized in *fiqh* in order to qualify for a judgeship (Lawyers Committee for Human Rights 1993: 43–44).

In order to justify legal reform after laws had been "Islamized" and to allow for greater responsiveness of Islamic law in rapidly changing times, Khomeini introduced, toward the end of the Iran–Iraq War in 1988, the principle of *maslahat*, "expediency." In essence, the introduction of *maslahat* suggested that contextual considerations could overrule strict adherence to Ja'fari jurisprudence. The principle found its institutional home in the newly established Expediency Council (1988) which could now overrule the clerical Guardian Council. It was therefore no longer guaranteed that legislation would be strictly in line with

---

[15] The first purge banned fifty-seven lawyers, the second thirty-two, and the third fifty-two.
[16] Kayhān, June 20, 1983 and August 30, 1983.

Islamic jurisprudence. From now on, the decision of a potentially non-clerical Expediency Council could outweigh that of the clerical Guardian Council. Sami Zubaida aptly commented on the introduction of *maslahat* with the remark that twelve centuries of legal and jurisprudential thinking could not achieve what eight years of Islamic governance had done to Shi'i jurisprudence: The Shi'i adoption of a principle at the heart of Sunni jurisprudence in order to justify deviation from the tradition (Zubaida 2003: 210ff.; see also Amanat and Griffel 2009).

With the increasing normalization of politics after the Iran–Iraq War (1980–1988) and as a period of reconstruction began, the leadership signaled greater adherence to the constitution and the rule of law from then on. In a letter to the parliament, Khomeini asked for the extrajudicial court systems (the revolutionary courts and the Special Courts for the Clergy) to be integrated into the judiciary or else be abolished. Lawyers and litigants started to demand the reestablishment of the Bar Association. A 1990 draft bill by parliament reaffirmed: "The parties of a lawsuit have the right to appoint an attorney at law, and all the courts ... are obliged to receive the attorney at law ..."(Special Representative of the Commission on Human Rights 1990: Paragraph 213). The final version that passed the Expediency Council, however, replaced "attorney at law" (*vakil-e dādgostari*) simply with "attorney" (*vakil*), thus opening up the possibility for anyone who had not passed the Bar to be accepted in court (Expediency Council 1369). The resultant article of the Law of Appointment of Attorney by Parties to a Lawsuit read: "The parties of a lawsuit have the right to appoint any attorney [not attorney at law], and all the prosecution offices and courts including the civil, penal, revolutionary, military, and the special courts for the clergy are obliged to receive the attorney in all stages of interrogation and court process" (Expediency Council 1369). With the change from *vakil-e dādgostari* to *vakil* the law was neither congruent with Article 35 of the constitution on the rights of the accused to *legal* counsel, nor was it in line with Article 9 of the United Nations' (UN) Basic Principles on the Role of Lawyers, which requires that "Governments, professional associations of lawyers ... shall ensure that lawyers have appropriate education and training and be made aware of the ideals and ethical duties of lawyers and of human rights ... recognized by national and international law."

After a visit by the UN Representative for Human Rights in 1991, new assurances were made that the Central Bar would be revived and elections held for it in October 1991. However, one day before the scheduled election, a new law was passed whose first article read: "In order to reform the Bar Association of the Islamic Republic of Iran, a Revitalization Board of the Bar Association, comprising of six attorneys at law and three practicing judges, chosen by the head of the judiciary, is appointed for a one-year period to implement and enforce this act." As a result of this 1991 Law of Correction of the Bar Association, a further 133 attorneys were purged from the Bar and the elections were indefinitely postponed (Special Representative of the Commission on Human Rights 1993).

As the 1990 bill solidified the possibility for those who had not passed the Bar to serve as recognized legal counsel, more and more graduates of the religious seminaries moved into the legal profession (Kashani 1992). Still, by the mid-1990s only about 2,500 trained judges were available for over 10,000 positions, and the newly recognized study programs of law produced only 600 graduates a year.[17] The status of *hojjatoleslām* now became useful for all sorts of jobs and few were more lucrative than those in the court system. Incidentally, the demand for *mojtahed*s to serve in positions of the state bureaucracy in the aftermath of the revolution contributed to the inflation of clerical titles the regime has witnessed since.

In 1994, a new judicial reform was drawn up (the 4 June 1994/15 Tīr 1373 Law of General and Revolutionary Courts) under the head of the judiciary Mohammad Yazdi (1989–1999) that combined the civil, criminal, and family courts into so-called general courts. With devastating consequences for due process, the roles of investigator, prosecutor, and judge were merged in one.

When Ayatollah Sayyed Mahmud Hashemi Shahroudi took over the judiciary in 1999, he declared the judiciary to be a wreck (*virāneh*).[18] With the support of the Expediency Council, he reintroduced in 2002 the division of courts into criminal (*keifari*), family and personal status (*madani*), civil and commercial (*hoquqi*) courts, and reinstated an appellate system.[19] He also passed separate laws of procedure (*dādrasi*) for each, and reintroduced, in most but not all courts, the differentiation of the offices of judge and prosecutor.[20]

---

[17] According to the Iranian representative appearing before the 46th Session of the UN Human Rights Committee in New York, April 7, 1993, in April 1993, there were 2,661 registered lawyers in Iran, including 185 women.

[18] *Ettelā'āt*, November 23, 1999.

[19] *Ettelā'āt*, July 10, 2000.

[20] *Manshur-e tawsi'a*, 3: 52. In theory, the office of the public prosecutor was reestablished in October 2002 for general and revolutionary courts (in the Amendment to the Law of Formation of General and Revolutionary Courts [1994], dated Mehr 28, 1381), but in practice, even as late as 2008, it was not in place everywhere. According to Article 3 of the 2002 reform (http://mellat.majlis.ir/archive/1382/MOSAVABAT/MOSAVABAT1 .HTM#48), an office of prosecution (*dādsarā*) should be established in every urban jurisdiction, but according to the *Official Gazette* (*Ruznāmeh-ye Rasmi*), No. 16823, November 7–9, 2002/ Ādhar 1381, the prosecution was only reestablished for the lower criminal courts.

In order to deal with questions arising from the new Islamic Penal Code (IPC), Shahroudi instituted regular sessions of expert judges in towns and provincial capitals to answer questions and requests for guidance by the courts under jurisdiction. He also strengthened the Legal Office of the Judiciary (Edāreh-ye hoquqi) and instituted a Research Center in Jurisprudence (Markaz-e tahqiqāt-e feqh) that would answer inquiries from the courts and provincial branches of the Ministry of Justice, and keep a registrar of the most important fatwas of those *marāje'* (sources of emulation, the highest religious authorities in Shi'i Islam) that are officially recognized by the regime. A given judge might then compare the fatwas of the highest Shi'i authorities in the country and if no positive law existed to be applied on a given case, invoke one of the *marāje''s* fatwas.

5 Revival in 1997 and Threatened Closure Thereafter

It was not until the early years of the Khatami administration (1997–2005), that the Bar experienced a revival. Under the influence of the reform movement, bar associations were (re)established in all major jurisdictions across the country.[21] The Central Bar Association in Tehran was given the right to (re)establish subcommittees, such as a legal aid committee and a human rights commission, and to position delegates in the Ministry of Justice and in the Foreign Ministry (Musavi-Bujnurdi 1376). In 1997, during the visit of the UN human rights envoy, promises were made that the bars would be reauthorized to hold elections for their boards – something they had not been permitted to do for nearly two decades. In tandem with that promise, however, the conservative-dominated parliament passed a law in the same year allowing the judiciary to vet candidates running for the boards of directors.[22] While it

---

[21] The Ardabil Bar Association, serving Ardabil province; the East Azerbaijan Bar Association in Tabriz (one of the oldest in the country); the Fars Bar Association in Shiraz, also one of the oldest, covering attorneys in Fars, Bushehr, Kohgiloyeh, and Boyerahmad provinces; the Gilan Bar Association located in Rasht; the Golestan Bar Association for Golestan province; the Hamedan Bar Association, the Isfahan Bar Association for Isfahan and Markazi provinces; the Kermanshah and Ilam Bar Association, for Kermanshah and Ilam provinces; the Khuzestan and Lorestan Bar Association, located in Ahwaz; the Khorasan Bar Association, Mashhad, for Khorasan province; the Kurdistan Bar Association, Sanandaj; the Mazandaran Bar Association, Sari; the Qazvin Bar Association; the Qom Bar Association; the West Azerbaijan Bar Association; the Central Bar Association in Tehran covering the attorneys in Tehran. The Iran Bar Associations Union based in Tehran was established to coordinate between the twenty-two region-based Iranian bar associations. See for example: www.iranbar.org (Persian), www.iranbar.org/pltren.php (English), www.iranbar.org/pltrfr.php (French), www.centralbar.ir, www.azarbar.org, and www.khoozestanbar.org.

[22] The Law on the Requirements for Obtaining a Lawyer's License (*Qānun-e nahveh-ye akhz-e parvāneh-ye vikālat*) 1376 (1997) also stipulated the admissions

was internationally signaled that the bars would be revived and their autonomy reinstated, internally the electoral rules for the bars' boards were changed in a manner that the judiciary could now cherry-pick its candidates. Specifically, per the new Law on Conditions for Obtaining the Attorney's Licence, candidates had to be confirmed by the Supreme Disciplinary Court for Judges, satisfy, among other requirements, "commitment to the revolution," and prove they had not ever been members of or "cooperated with" organizations deemed politically oppositional. As Mohammad H Nayyeri correctly notes, "it would be true to say that until 1997 the independence of the Bar Associations was denied in practice, while in 1997 it was attacked in law" (Nayyeri 2012).

An interview with one of the members of the Tehran Bar Association's Human Rights Commission reveals the internal tensions the Bar faced at that time, where the work of relatively independent commissions often failed to receive approval from the Bar's own board, whose candidates had been vetted by the judiciary:

[During the violent repression of student protests in the summer of 1999] we informed the International League of Human Rights of the abuses and violent acts of the [Revolutionary Guards]. When demonstrators were shot in different cities, we recorded the complaints of the families and wrote reports to the UN. We demanded the release of political prisoners and the freedom of expression. Our present activities are very limited. Even if internal elections took place for the first time after the revolution in 1997, we are under close scrutiny, given the pre-selection of our candidates. A candidate who would write against the *qesās* [retributive justice] or the *lex talionis* will never be admitted by the judiciary apparatus. [...] We receive many complaints and we cannot cope. For example, we have received many testimonies of members of the Bahá'í community whose graveyards have been sacked and their graves turned upside down. We denounced these acts of violence. But the Bar's [board of directors] refused to sign our protest letter. Actually, it does not sign half of the letters of its own Human Rights Commission. When the members wrote an official request demanding an inquiry about the conditions of Zahra Kazemi's murder

---

requirements: Candidates would need to have Iranian citizenship; be at least twenty-five years of age; be a regular resident of the location for which the license is applied; have a clear record and a reputation for honesty and integrity; have completed legal studies in one of the Iranian or foreign recognized universities; have rendered legal services at least for eighteen months under the supervision of a professional lawyer approved for such purpose by the Bar; have successfully passed the Bar examinations. In addition, Article 2 of said law states that candidates must fulfil the following conditions: "A. Profess belief in and practical devotion to Islam and its precepts; B. Profess belief in the Islamic Republic, *velāyat-e faqih* [guardianship of the religious jurisprudent] and loyalty to the Constitution. [...]; D. Not having been a member of or active in atheist groups, 'misguided' denominations and groups opposed to Islam as well as groups whose manifesto is based on negating divine religions; E. Not having the record of being an associate of the defunct Pahlavi regime or strengthening the foundations of the former regime; F. Not having been a member of or supported outlawed groups opposed to the Islamic Republic of Iran."

[an Iranian-Canadian who, while visiting Iran, was arrested for political activism and died under torture in Evin Prison in spring 2003], this letter did not receive the signature of the Bar's representatives.[23]

In subsequent years, the judiciary repeatedly intervened in the internal affairs of the Bar. Abdul Fattah Sultani, lawyer of the dissident journalist Akbar Ganji and of the family of journalist Zahra Kazemi, was excluded from the board despite his election to it in February 2005.

Apart from human rights advocacy, the Bar also fulfilled an important cultural role when it emerged as a defender of cultural and historical heritage during the first Khatami administration (1997–2001). When construction permits were issued for towers in Isfahan that would have imperiled the historical site of the Safavid Naqsh-e Jahān, the city's central square of exceptional beauty, and a United Nations Educational, Scientific and Cultural Organization (UNESCO) World Heritage Site, the Bar Association issued several letters of protest. In another instance, when media in February 2004 uncovered the extent of human-trafficking rings between Iran, the United Arab Emirates, and other countries bordering the Persian Gulf, the Bar issued an official letter to the Minister of Interior and demanded the inception of a commission of inquiry on human trafficking in the region. The regime denied the existence of the phenomenon.

As was the case with most civil society organizations and media in the early years of the Khatami presidency, the bar associations' revival was short-lived. When the third five-year plan for economic and social development (2000–2005) was passed by the outgoing conservative parliament in 2000, the judiciary attained the power to make its own selection and to confer, per Article 187 of the law,[24] the title of 'legal advisor' to applicants who had not been admitted to the Bar.[25] This was done through the creation of a new institution, the Center for the Affairs of Advisors, Judges, and Experts of the Judiciary (Markaz-e Omur-e Moshāvirān, Vukalā Va Kārshenāsān-e Quwwa-ye Qazā'iya). The step to institutionalize an additional accreditation process for lawyers through the judiciary was legitimized with reference to the high levels of unemployment at the time. In other words, in order to fight unemployment, the regime claimed, it would certify more lawyers through a less transparent certification process rather than expanding upon and improving on the training opportunities for future lawyers who would then be independently certified by the bars. De facto, the new accreditation process

---

[23] Interview with Dr. I., May 2005, cited in Farkhondeh (2006).
[24] The 2000 Law of the Third Economic, Social and Cultural Development Plan.
[25] At this point, the membership of the Bar had increased to about 6,000 attorneys at law as well as over 2,500 trainees.

was instituted for graduates of the religious seminaries and students of the social sciences who did not have sufficient legal training to pass the bar exam, as well as for law graduates who had failed to pass it.[26]

A key function which the Bar had fulfilled for nearly thirty years between 1953 and 1979, that is, to exclusively certify lawyers through a comprehensive and demanding training and examination program, had thus been stripped from it. Its role in guarding the professionalism of future lawyers, judges, and judicial officials was thereby officially neutralized.

The new parallel accreditation process was also less challenging in terms of the training required. Unlike those seeking accreditation through the bars, applicants to the judiciary do not need to have a BA degree in law, nor do they need to take an entrance exam, and in contrast to the bars' eighteen-month training schemes, their training lasts for only six months. Moreover, their license to practice needs to be renewed with the judiciary on an annual basis, which de facto ensures that such applicants do not take on politically delicate cases for fear of not getting their license renewed in the following year (Nayyeri 2012).

While the bars through their disciplinary boards used to be able to take disciplinary actions against lawyers who had compromised the integrity of the profession, this function was now undertaken in the Judges' Disciplinary Court run by the judiciary. The latter is known to discipline lawyers and judges who are not in line with the politics of the Supreme Leader's office. For example, a judge of Iran's Supreme Court was called before the Judges' Disciplinary Court for having advocated the eradication of the extraconstitutional and extrajudicial courts for the clergy.[27]

After Mahmoud Ahmadinejad assumed the presidency in 2005, the Iranian state showed remarkable efficacy in rolling back the political and civil liberties societal actors had succeeded in carving out from the state's legal and judicial apparatus in the previous years (see Chapter 9 in this volume). Especially in the aftermath of the contested June 2009 presidential elections and the subsequent anti-governmental demonstrations that were brutally suppressed, the government further limited the space of civil and political engagement. Societal organizations were forced to accept governmental appointees on their boards, which discredited

---

[26] In order to be accredited, applicants undergo a six-month training program designed by the judiciary, then pass an exam and take an oath. The judiciary then assigns those who are accredited as legal advisers to a specific city, where they have to establish their own law firms or join an extant one. Those accredited may file claims and defend cases in any court throughout the country. Accreditations need to be renewed with the judiciary on an annual basis.
[27] Personal interview, 2009.

their legitimacy in the eyes of the public and compromised their political autonomy. The (limited) ties that civil society organizations were able to build during the first and second Khatami presidencies (1997–2001 and 2001–2005) with foreign and international organizations were effectively outlawed, with the result that domestic organizations lost important sources of funding and were often compelled to accept parastatal subsidies, or to cease operating officially altogether.

Although Mahmud Hashemi Shahroudi, who headed the judiciary from 1999 to 2009, made some improvements to the efficacy of the judiciary by reconstituting the office of the prosecutor in many courts and by partly reestablishing the appeals procedure, his position vis-à-vis the Bar Association was ruinous. Despite the fact that the 2000 law that had established the parallel accreditation process in Article 187 expired in 2005 with the end of the five-year development plan, the new institutional structures for certifying lawyers inside the judiciary were retained – illegally as the bar associations argue. When the Tehran Bar Association issued a critical assessment on the eve of Shahroudi's second term in the spring of 2009, he responded with a draft amendment to the Executive Regulations of the Law of the Bar Associations on June 17, 2009 (that is, five days after the consequential presidential elections which many observers called rigged) that would have effectively dissolved the associations by stripping them of any rights, functions, and responsibilities.[28] The proposed amendment would de facto eradicate the external certification process (through the bars) by moving the mandate to certify lawyers and apprentice-lawyers to a new "selection committee" appointed entirely by the judiciary. The amendment would also give the Ministry of Intelligence the right to surveil the defense lawyers of political activists and to pull their credentials if deemed "necessary."[29] The draft amendment also comprised a catalogue of "professional ethics" that compromised the defense counsel in criminal cases by suggesting, per Article 44, that lawyers would abet a sin if they endorsed the plea of a client they knew to be false.

In 2011, in an astounding act of defying the judiciary, 153 members of parliament introduced a new bill according to which the merger envisioned by the 2009 draft would bring the judiciary's accreditation process under the control of the bar associations (rather than the other way

---

[28] *E'temād*, July 5, 2009/Tir 14, 1388.
[29] Compare the open letter by Mostafa Mohaqqeq-Damad, an ayatollah and well-known scholar of Islamic law, to Hashemi Shahroudi, published in *Ettelā'āt* newspaper on August 2, 2009, "Kāsh dar hawza māndeh budid." ["I wish you had stayed in the hawza"].

around). Unsurprisingly, the bill did not see the light of day and the judiciary instead introduced its own bill for a merger under reverse conditions. After rejection by the plenary in November 2016, the judiciary's bill was returned to the Legal and Judicial Commission of the Parliament for modification.[30] In July 2017, the latter commission dismissed the bill and decided not to amend the existing law. The parallel structure of the Bar Association and separate recruitment and certification of legal advisors through the judiciary per Article 187 henceforth continued unchanged.[31] However, the judiciary scored a consequential goal with the new Code of Criminal Procedure (CCP) of June 2015, which came into force after having been in the making for almost a decade, replacing a temporary 1999 code, whose validity had to be extended by parliament every three years. In a note added last minute to Article 48 of the new code, it was stipulated that in cases involving serious charges, such as those carrying the death penalty or imprisonment for more than five years, only lawyers from a list approved by the head of the judiciary could henceforth be chosen by the accused for the crucial pretrial investigative phase. This applies for example to crimes against national security, which is a frequent accusation made against political opposition activists.[32] The note to Article 48 met with strong objections from the Tehran Bar Association, but to no avail. Since the promulgation of the new code in 2015, those accused of serious crimes no longer have access to independently certified lawyers. What is more, recent years have brought the harshest forms of repression against defense attorneys, who are often charged with creating disorder and given long jail terms for the sole reason of having dared to take on the cases of political dissidents. Thus, the last decade has seen the imprisonment of human rights lawyers to a previously unknown degree, particularly in the aftermath of the 2018, 2019, and 2022/2023 protests.[33]

In May 2020, the bill on the independence of the bar associations was tabled once again. Following the new version of the bill, proposed by Mohammad Mossadegh, judiciary deputy in legal affairs, the executive body of the Bar Associations would be replaced by a "Supreme

---

[30] See www.isna.ir/news/95082417104/, last accessed June 25, 2021 ("Judicial Commission rejecting the comprehensive attorney bill" [in Persian]).

[31] See www.irinn.ir/fa/news/510111/, last accessed June 23, 2021 ("The comprehensive attorney bill is rejected" [in Persian]).

[32] The changes to the code are reviewed article by article by the Iran Human Rights Documentation Center: https://iranhrdc.org/amendments-to-the-islamic-republic-of-irans-code-of-criminal-procedure-part-1/; see also Chapter 3 in this volume.

[33] Among these Mohammad Najafi, Nasrin Sotoudeh, Payam Derafshan, Qasem Shole Sadi, Arash Keikhosravi, Masoud Javadieh, Saeed Sheikh, Mohammad Hadi Erfanian, Hossein Bayat, Soheila Hejab, Giti Pourfazel, Mostafa Nili, Leila Heidari, Mohammad Reza Faghihi, Farzaneh Zilabi, Mohammad Hadi Erfanian-Kaseb, and Amirsalar Davoodi.

Council for the Coordination of Lawyers' Affairs," with seven members appointed by the government, two of whom, the chairman of the Central Bar Association and the chairman of the National Bar Associations Union, would sit on the council ex officio. Out of the seven members, only these two would legitimately represent the interests of independently certified lawyers. More than 12,000 legal professionals, among them 180 former judges, signed a letter of protest, in which they called on Head of the Judiciary Ebrahim Raisi to revoke the proposed bill and end the "illegal interference" into the affairs of the bar associations, which violates Article 22 of the Bar Associations Independence Law. In 2020, a General Office for the Supervision of Lawyers was set up in the judiciary, and provincial administrations were invited to submit reports of transgressions by legal professionals to it as part of an expansion of a "security umbrella" over practicing attorneys.

Throughout the 2010s and early 2020s, the lawyers had successfully effected a delay in the passing of a new bill regulating the bar associations. A complete replacement of the bar by a judiciary-dominated Supreme Council for the Coordination of Lawyers' Affairs was never achieved. But by 2023, officials had an ingenious idea. In August that year, parliament passed a bill that forces the bar associations to be treated in law similar to private companies and to register with the Ministry of the Economy and Finance. The bill would also mean that the power to issue, renew, suspend, and revoke licenses for legal practice would be withdrawn from the bar associations and handed over to a Regulatory Task Force operated by the ministry. The decisions of the task force cannot be challenged in the Administrative Court of Justice. The Guardian Council has yet to agree to the legislation.

6 Conclusions

Despite the fact that the 1979 constitution grants all political rights and civil liberties political scientists consider fundamental for electorally competitive politics, civil liberties are frequently and systematically curtailed in the Islamic Republic. After the reform era of 1997–2001, civil liberties and the rule of law were systematically undermined by the mass closures of critical newspapers and magazines; the ban on individual political parties and the persecution of their members; the rejection by non-elected clerical councils of a third of legislative proposals of the elected parliament; and the widespread disqualifications of political candidates wishing to run in elections. The bar associations experienced a brief revival in the 1990s, when they were permitted to (re)open offices across the country and when their right to internal autonomy was reinstated by permitting them to hold elections once again and to resume their work in various internal committees. As soon as a date for internal elections was announced in 1997, however, the judiciary asserted its right to screen candidates, thereby compromising the associations' autonomy and curtailing their legal aid and human rights work. The bar associations were further compromised when, in 2000, at the height of the reform era, a parallel accreditation process for lawyers was created inside the judiciary, allowing those not trained in the professional law schools and those who failed the Bar exam to seek certification through this alternative channel. Importantly, it allows the judiciary to cherry-pick its own candidates for a pool from which it can recruit future high court judges. And as certification by the judiciary needs to be renewed every year, these so-called 'Article 187 legal advisors' are unlikely to take on politically sensitive cases or to pass down judgments that are likely to be overruled in an appeals procedure. With the creation of this alternative recruitment, training, and certification mechanism, the number of lawyers/legal advisors in the country rose from 20,000 in 2005 to 60,000 within a decade.

The regulation of the recruitment of lawyers and the status of the bar associations in the postrevolutionary period exhibit two larger trends in regime–societal contestations: The regime's attempt at controlling electoral outcomes and the creation of institutions paralleling those that hardliners do not control, with the aim of replacing the latter in the long run. In the case of the legal profession, the first dynamic was at play when conservatives in 1997 started to exert the same control mechanism on the bar associations that is applied to popular elections in the country: Electoral candidates can be disqualified if found to lack "revolutionary credentials." Elections thus become a farce where only *khodi* (insiders) and those from whom no political contra is to be expected are permitted to toss their hats into the ring. The second dynamic manifested itself when the judiciary established its parallel accreditation process for legal advisors and henceforth attempted to blur public distinctions between lawyers accredited independently by the Bar on the one hand, and those trained and accredited with lower professional standards inside the judiciary, on the other. Instead of being eliminated altogether, the bar associations became marginalized, with the goal of making them superfluous in the long term.

In 2009, a draft bill was first tabled which would have effectively closed the associations. That bill underwent various instantiations throughout the 2010s and was repeatedly brought to a vote, but failed to pass thanks to resistance by reform-oriented parliamentarians and the legal profession, which argued that its independence would be undermined if recruitment and training were to take place exclusively inside the judiciary. In 2023, a strongly revised version of the reform was passed by the parliament, which forces the bar associations to register with the Ministry of the Economy and Finance, which will appoint a Regulatory Task Force to take over key functions of the bar, including the power to issue, renew, suspend, and revoke licenses for legal practice. Decisions of the Task Force cannot be challenged in the Administrative Court of Justice.

At the time of writing, the bill has yet to pass the Guardian Council to become law. But the fact that the struggle to replace the bars once and for all with regime-appointed boards has continued for fourteen years testifies to the continued pockets of contestation and the work of some decisive members in the Iranian polity to work toward a more robust notion of the rule of law and the independence of the judiciary. While legal practice in Islamic Iran broadly falls into Tamanaha's thinnest notion of the rule of law as merely "rule by law," where law, by and large, is used as an instrument of government action, there are recurring attempts, by reform-minded parliamentarians, individual judicial officials, civil servants, lawyers, and rights activists, to work toward a more expansive notion of the rule of law, approximating Tamanaha's concept of formal legality, where the law is general, prospective, clear, and certain, even though it still falls short of delivering a more robust understanding of a rule of law that would include political equality and individual rights.

Bibliography

Amanat, Abbas and Frank Griffel (eds.) *Shari'a: Islamic Law in the Contemporary Context*, Stanford: Stanford University Press, 2009.

'Āqili, Bāqir. *Dāvar wa 'adliya*, Tehran: Elmi Publishers, 1990.

Arjomand, Saïd Amir, *The Turban for the Crown: The Islamic Revolution in Iran*, Oxford: Oxford University Press, 1988.

Banakar, Reza and Keyvan Ziaee. "The Life of the Law in the Islamic Republic of Iran," *Iranian Studies*, 51 (5), 2018, pp. 717–746.

Daftari, Ali Akbar. *Geschichte und System des iranischen Strafrechts*, Bonn: L. Röhrscheid, 1935.

Enayat, Hadi. *Law, State, and Society in Modern Iran: Constitutionalism, Autocracy, and Legal Reform 1906–1941*, London: Palgrave, 2013.

Expediency Council. *Majmu'a-ye mosavvabāt-e Majma'-e Tashkhis-e Maslahat-e Nezām az tārikh-e 1369* [Collection of Approvals by the Expediency Council in the year 1369]. https://web.archive.org/web/20170619073606/http://81.91.157.27/DocLib2/Approved%20Policies/Noncompatabilities.aspx.html

Farkhondeh, Sepideh. *Rule of law, authoritarianism and theocracy in Iran: the role of secular specialists of law*. Paper presented at Sciences Po, Paris, November 2006.

Government of India. *The Persian Gulf Administration Reports: 1873–1947*, 10 vols., n.p., Archive Editions, 1986.

Gulshā'iyān, 'Abbasgholi. *Gozashtehā va andishehā-ye zendegi yā khātirāt-e man*, 2 vols., Tehran: Entesharāt-e Aynshtayn, 1998.

Green, Jerrold D. "Pseudoparticipation and Countermobilization: Roots of the Iranian Revolution," *Iranian Studies*, 13 (1–4), 1980, pp. 31–53.

Hashemi, Mohammad. *Hoquq-e asāsi-ye jomhuri-ye eslāmi-ye Īrān*, 2 vols. (Qom, Mujtamaʿ-e Āmuzesh-e ʿAlī), 1996/1375.

International Bar Association. *Findings from the Directory of Regulators of the Legal Profession*. London: IBA, 2016. www.ibanet.org/MediaHandler?id=1ecea440-9157-4a78-b4b5-6559c7d2876c.

Iran Bar Association News. *Ejrā-ye ahkām mesl-e sangsar bāyad banā bar salāhdid-e riyāsat-e qovveh-yr qazā' 'āye anjām shavad*, 21 June 2007.

Kashani, Mahmud. *Barrasi-ye qānun-e nahva-ye eslah-e kānūnhā-ye vokalā-ye dādgostari*, Tehran, 1992.

Kasravi, Ahmed. *Zandagānī-yi man yā dah sāl dar ʿadliya*, Tehran, 1944.

Künkler, Mirjam. "The Special Court of the Clergy (dādgāh-e vīzhe-ye rūhānīyat) and the Repression of Dissident Clergy in Iran," in Saïd Arjomand and Nathan Brown (eds.), *The Rule of Law, Islam, and Constitutional Politics in Egypt and Iran*, Albany: SUNY Press, 2013, pp. 57–100.

Künkler, Mirjam. "Rule of Law or Rule by Law? Iran's Bar Association as a Pawn in Islamic–Republican Contestations," in Silvia Tellenbach and Thoralf Hanstein (eds.), *Beiträge zum Islamischen Recht XII*. 2017, pp. 133–153.

Künkler, Mirjam. "The Bureaucratization of Religious Education in the Islamic Republic of Iran," in Arif A. Jamal, Jaclyn L. Neo, and Daniel Goh (eds.), *Regulating Religion in Asia: Norms, Modes, and Challenges*, Cambridge: Cambridge University Press, 2019, pp. 187–206.

Künkler, Mirjam. "Lawyers in the Muslim World: Between Social Transformation, Judicial Control, and Feminisation," in Rick Abel, Ole Hammerslev, Hillary Sommerlad, and Ulrike Schultz (eds.), *Lawyers in 21st-Century Societies: Comparisons and Theories*, Oxford: Hart, 2022, pp. 73–97.

Lahidji, Abdollah. *La justice Islamique*, Vincennes: Khavaran Editions, 2000.

Lawyers Committee for Human Rights, "The Justice System of the Islamic Republic of Iran," May 1993.

Lob, Eric. *Iran's Reconstruction Jihad: Rural Development and Regime Consolidation after 1979*. Cambridge: Cambridge University Press, 2020.

Marin, Soubabeh. "La réception mitigée des codifications napoléoniennes en Iran (1911–1935)," *Droit et cultures* [online], 48 | 2004-2, http://droitcultures.revues.org/1723, accessed 21 August 2017.

Matin-Daftari, Ahmad. *Ā'in-e dādrasi-ye madani va bāzargāni*, 2 vols., Tehran: Chāpkhāneh Melli, 2002 [1945].

Mehrpour, Hosein. "Aṣl-e chahārum-e qānun-e asāsi va-qalamru-ye shumul-e ān," *Majalla-ye Kānun-e Vokalā*, 146–147 (1989), 15–31.

Mohammadi, Majid. *Judicial Reform and Reorganization in 20th Century Iran: State-Building, Modernization and Islamicization*. New York: Routledge, 2008.

Mohaqqeq-Damad, Mostafa. "Khatāb be Shahroudi: Kāsh dar hawza māndeh budid." *Ettelāʿāt*, August 2, 2009. Retrieved 7 December 2016.

Musavi-Bujnurdi, Muhammad. "Naqsh-e Zamān va Makān dar taghyīr ahkām," *Majalleh-ye Kānun-e Vukalā-ye Dādgustari,* No 10 (1376/1996/97).

Najafi A. "Jaygāh-ye kānun-e vokalā-ye dādgostari va vakil dar jāmiʻa-ye hoquqī va qānun-e āʾin-e dādrasi-ye keifari-ye Irān," in H. Gholāmi (ed.), *ʻOlum-e jenāyi-ye tatbiqi dar partu-ye hamkārihā-ye beyn al-milali. Majmʻa-ye maqālāt-e nekudāsht-e doktor-e Silviyā Tillinbākh,* Tehran, 2017, pp. 458–478.

Nayyeri, Mohammad H. *Iranian Bar Associations. Struggle for Independence.* New Haven: Iran Human Rights Documentation Center, 2012: www.iranhrdc .org/english/english/publications/legal-commentary/1000000211-iranian-bar-associations-struggle-for-independence.html?p=12, accessed 31 August 2017.

Nelken, David. "Using the Concept of Legal Culture," *Australian Journal of Legal Philosophy,* 29, 2004, pp. 1–26.

Nelken, David. "Comparative Legal Research and Legal Culture: Facts, Approaches, and Values," *Annual Review of Law and Social Science,* 12, 2016. pp. 45–62.

Saffari, Said. "The Legitimation of the Clergy's Right to Rule in the Iranian Constitution of 1979" in *British Journal of Middle Eastern Studies,* 20 (1) (1993), 64–82.

Schirazi, Asghar. *The Constitution of Iran: Politics and the State in the Islamic Republic.* London: I. B. Tauris, 1997.

Special Representative of the Commission on Human Rights (Mr. Reynaldo Galindo Pohl), "Report on the human rights situation in the Islamic Republic of Iran" (UN Doc. No. E/CN.4/1990/24), February 12, 1990.

Special Representative of the Commission on Human Rights (Mr. Reynaldo Galindo Pohl), "Final report on the situation of human rights in the Islamic Republic of Iran," E/CN.4/1993/41, January 28, 1993.

Tamanaha, Brian Z. *On the Rule of Law: History, Politics, Theory.* New York: Cambridge University Press, 2004.

Tellenbach, Silvia. Zum Strafgesetzbuch der Islamischen Republik Iran von 2013, *Zeitschrift für die gesamte Strafrechtswissenschaft,* 126, (2014), 775–801.

Zubaida, Sami. *Law and Power in the Islamic World.* London: I. B. Tauris, 2003.

6 Law Enforcement and the Judiciary in Postrevolutionary Iran

Saeid Golkar

1 Introduction

The principle of the rule of law is closely associated with democracy and has been identified as one of the main elements of a modern political order, along with state-building and accountability (Fukuyama 2014). In this framework, the modern state is understood as an impersonal territorial and functional state, accountability refers to the responsiveness of the rulers to the people, and the rule of law relates to restrictions and constraints on power.

But the rule of law is more than just a procedural concept; it is a principle of good governance by which every person, organization, and institution should be accountable under just laws – laws which are aligned with international human rights norms and applied equally to all citizens (Fukuyama 2014: 248). According to a United Nations' (UN) report, the principle of the rule of law involves "adherence to the principles of supremacy of law, equality before the law, fairness in the application of the law, and avoidance of arbitrariness and procedural and legal transparency" (Report of the UN Secretary General 2004: 40).

Four key state institutions, which have been identified as critical for establishing the rule of law are the judiciary, the police, the military, and regulatory agencies (Bellin 2014). To achieve the rule of law, the existence of an independent judiciary, a civilian-controlled and depoliticized military, professional police, and strong regulatory agencies are vital. Among these institutions, an independent judiciary is the most important because not only can it constrain the power of the state agencies, police, and the military, but it can also make sure these institutions are accountable (Diamond 1999: 111).

In terms of the contribution of the police to upholding the rule of law, the police should be committed to a mission of service to the people, to protecting people's rights and public order. Police agencies must work in accordance with the law and should not use fear to enforce the law. To achieve these goals, the police should be professional and monitored by the elected bodies and civil society. Professional police officers should also be taught to respect international human rights standards. To combat corruption, and as part of the professionalization, police salaries should be in accordance with their responsibilities (Bellin 2014).

The close and internal relation between democracy and rule of law has been widely accepted (Habermas 1995). In fact, there are only a few authoritarian regimes that respect the rule of law, such as Singapore. According to the World Justice Project (WJP), in 2021 Iran's overall rule-of-law performance was ranked 119th out of 139 countries, and the country sat at rank 7 out of the 8 countries that are included from the Middle East and North Africa (WJP 2021).[1] While Iran is *the* worst country in terms of respecting fundamental rights (139th out of 139) according to the WJP, its criminal and civil justice performances were ranked, respectively, 98th and 65th out of 139. As the Introduction to this volume shows, Iran does not comply with long-established rule-of-law principles such as an independent judiciary, separation of powers, right to a fair trial, equal protection and due process of the law, as well as individual freedoms such as the rights to freedom of expression and association.

According to the WJP, Iran's best performance in the sphere of the rule of law is in "maintaining order and security" (66th out of 139), meaning Iran's security and military apparatuses are able to control the country and enforce the law. But many questions remain. To what extent are the various Iranian police forces professional and accountable to the people? Why and how does the police help the clerical regime maintain political order? This chapter will explain the transformation and structure of Iran's police forces, most importantly, the Law Enforcement Command of the Islamic Republic (Farmāndehi-ye Entezāmi Jomhuri-ye Eslāmi/ heretofore referred to as FARAJA) in postrevolutionary Iran, as well as to what extent it is aligned with the principle of the rule of law.

2 Islamization of the Judiciary and the Police: 1979–1988

After the 1979 Revolution, which eventually led to the consolidation of clerical rule, Islamization of state and society became the main policy of the new Islamic Republic. One of the main goals of this policy was the Islamization of the judiciary, as the revolutionaries believed "the monarchical justice system was the primary channel for spreading corruption, inefficiency, and foreign political and cultural domination of

---

[1] See the WJP website. https://worldjusticeproject.org/rule-of-law-index/country/2021/Order%20and%20Security/, accessed January 30, 2022.

the country" (Entessar 1988: 91). Under the leadership of Ayatollah Mohammad Beheshti, who was appointed by Ayatollah Khomeini as the first head of the judiciary in 1980, the drafting of new civil and criminal codes based on Shi'i fiqh began. The Islamic Penal Code (IPC) replaced the secular one (see Chapter 2 in this volume), high-ranking female judicial employees were fired, and secular civil court judges were replaced by inexperienced clerics and seminarians, many of whom had not specialized in jurisprudence and had often completed only lower levels of theological training. Beside the public courts, special courts were created: The Revolutionary Courts, the Press Courts, and the Special Courts for the Clergy (Künkler 2013). While general courts were responsible for dealing with civil and criminal cases, revolutionary courts were created to quickly discipline officials of the Pahlavi regime and antirevolutionaries (Entessar 1988: 100). The press and clergy courts were established to deal with "transgressions" of the press and the clergy respectively.

In 1979, Islamic Revolutionary Committees (Komiteh-ye Enqelāb-e Eslāmi) were established to arrest the revolution's enemies, maintain order, and ultimately guard the newly established regime. These committees consisted mainly of religious and conservative youth and were established in neighborhoods and cities based around mosques. Each committee was headed by a cleric, and they soon became powerful, independent forces that began undermining the police's authority within the respective neighborhoods and cities. The committees soon began to broaden their sphere of influence in public matters, such as protecting government buildings and suppressing protests across the country, as well as private matters, such as raiding private homes in which people were suspected of holding illegal parties and consuming alcohol, or arresting women for not wearing a proper head covering (*hejab*).

According to some reports, the postrevolutionary era witnessed the creation of up to 1,500 revolutionary committees in Tehran alone. These committees were eventually consolidated into fifteen large committees, with Hojjatoleslam Mahdavi Kani appointed as the director in Tehran (Torabi and Rahmani 2007: 121). Tehran's central committee soon became the headquarters for all committees across the country. The well-established organizational structure of the committees, however, did not facilitate the smooth functioning of power for long, and soon a struggle broke out between the clerics, which eventually led to the resignation of Mahdavi Kani in 1981. This subsequently led to the appointment of Hojjatoleslam Nateq-Nouri as the minister of interior in 1982 by Ayatollah Khomeini, Iran's Supreme Leader at that time. Through this appointment, the committees were now brought under the control of the Ministry of Interior.

In an attempt to highlight the duties of the disciplinary forces, Iran's parliament passed a new charter for the revolutionary committees in 1986. According to this law, the committees were to become more involved in surveillance and intelligence gathering in collaboration with the Ministry of Intelligence. Additionally, they were expected to help identify and arrest dissidents, or "counterrevolutionaries," while partnering with the Islamic Revolutionary Guard Corps (IRGC) to protect the borders alongside other disciplinary forces.

While the Islamic Revolutionary Committees worked as the main judicial officers for the revolutionary courts, the *Shahrbāni* (municipal police) and Gendarmerie (rural police) worked mainly as judicial officers for the regular courts. As disciplinary forces, the *Shahrbāni* and Gendarmerie worked under the Interior Ministry as law-enforcement bodies throughout the country, and, while the *Shahrbāni* were responsible for policing and enforcing law within the borders of the city, the Gendarmerie worked in smaller cities and on intercity roads to maintain security and order.

Created in the Qajar era and molded into modern disciplinary forces under the Pahlavi dynasty, the *Shahrbāni* and Gendarmerie were not trusted by the Islamic Republic and its revolutionary cadres. That is why, as part of the policy of Islamization, both forces underwent a series of rigorous screenings and purges to ensure a police force with an Islamic identity and strong loyalties to the new republic. Many personnel were fired in the process. Furthermore, like other security and military establishments in Iran, an ideological political bureau dominated by the clergy was established at both the *Shahrbāni* and Gendarmerie level to indoctrinate and survey the personnel.

In addition to these forces, in 1981, a new body called the Judicial Police (*polis-e qazā'ī*) was created by the order of the "Council of the Revolution" to enforce Islamic laws. The Judicial Police became officially subordinate to the *Shahrbāni* (and thus under the Ministry of Interior), despite the vision of its founders, Ayatollah Beheshti (head of the judiciary 1980–1981), and his successor, Ayatollah Mousavi Ardebili (head of the judiciary 1981–1989), who tried to bring the new force under the control of the judiciary. Judicial officers (*zābetān-e qazā'i*), trained by the judiciary and the IRGC, became the main judicial police personnel. They were responsible for performing prejudicial operations, such as conducting early investigations, collecting and saving criminal evidence, delivering documents, organizing detention, and executing judicial decisions (Figure 6.1).

Despite the efforts to increase cooperation between these forces (the revolutionary committees, the *Shahrbāni*, the Gendarmerie, and the Judicial Police), tensions persisted, especially concerning budgetary

Law Enforcement and the Judiciary

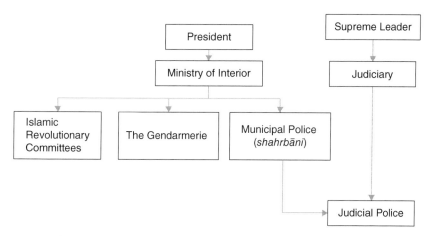

Figure 6.1 Police and judiciary

issues. Interagency competition further undermined effective coordination between the various police forces. The boundaries of the different jurisdictions between the four forces were often not made clear, and there were also frequent reports claiming that the revolutionary committees had abused their authority, which led to widespread resentment and dissatisfaction among the other forces and the public.

3 Judiciary and Law Enforcement from the end of the Iran–Iraq War to the Reformist Era (1989–1999)

After the death of Ayatollah Khomeini in the summer of 1989, Ayatollah Ali Khamenei was elected by the Assembly of Experts as the new Supreme Leader on June 4, 1989. He appointed Ayatollah Mohammad Yazdi, a rightwing cleric, as the new head of the judiciary. Under Ayatollah Yazdi's leadership (1989–1999), Iran's judiciary underwent extensive structural change. In 1994, a new law entitled the Law of General and Revolutionary Courts was introduced in order "to regularize the revolutionary courts and integrate them into the judiciary system". As part of this law, the office of public prosecutor (*dādsarā*) was removed from the criminal justice system to give judges full control over investigation, prosecution, and judgment in criminal cases in an attempt to revert to the qadi court model prescribed by the shariʿa (Arjomand 2013: 44). Many prosecutors and interrogators were appointed as judges to fill the vacuum (Mohammadi 2008: 237).

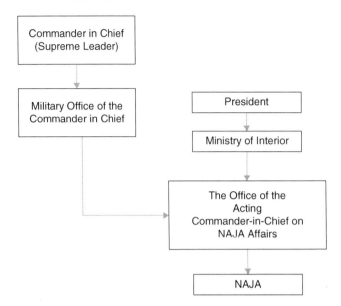

Figure 6.2 Authority structure of the police (Niruhā-ye Entezāmi Jomhuri-ye Eslāmi)

Another development was the dissolution of the Judicial Police which was merged with the *Shahrbāni*, the Gendarmerie, and the Islamic Revolutionary Committee. The goal was to form a centralized police force called the Niruhā-ye Entezāmi-ye Jomhuri-ye Eslāmi (Law Enforcement Forces of the Islamic Republic or NAJA), which became operational in April 1991.

According to NAJA's charter, the organization was described as an armed force subordinated to Ayatollah Khamenei and affiliated to the Interior Ministry. The minister of interior's sole responsibility was to tackle logistical issues, such as equipping and supporting NAJA. Although Ayatollah Khamenei usually made the minister of interior his representative regarding NAJA's affairs, the head of NAJA was (and is) directly appointed by the Supreme Leader in his capacity as chief of staff. The head of NAJA then appoints police officers of higher rank.

Iran's Supreme Leader oversees the NAJA through an office known as Office of the Acting Commander-in-Chief on Police Affairs (Daftar-e janeshini-ye farmāndehi-ye koll-e qovā dar omur-e NAJA). The members of this agency are police officers and citizens selected by the minister of the interior. This office is responsible for coordination between the Ministry of Interior and the Armed Forces General Staff (AFGS or *Setād-e koll-e niruhā-ye mosallah*) (Figure 6.2).

Like other military and security organizations, NAJA consists of three main branches: The police command (*farmāndehi*), the Ideological-Political Organization (*Sāzmān-e 'aqidati va siyāsi*), and the Counterintelligence Organization (*Sāzmān-e hefāzat-e ettelā'āt*). While the Ideological-Political Organization is mainly responsible for indoctrinating the police personnel, the Counterintelligence Organization helps identify foreign spies and corrupt police personnel whilst protecting police intelligence and carrying out other counterintelligence tasks. All these organizations are subordinated to Ayatollah Khamenei and are not accountable to any of the elected bodies.

Since the establishment of NAJA, most of "the regular police forces were side-lined and all influential positions in the NAJA were assigned to former members of the Islamic revolutionary committees" (Buchta 2004: 17). While the head of the Gendarmerie, General Mohammad Sohrabi, was appointed as the first head of NAJA, he was replaced by General Reza Seifolahi, an IRGC commander, in 1992. This paved the way for an increasing number of IRGC commanders being assigned to positions within the Iranian police and the eventual domination of IRGC commanders within NAJA. As a result, the IRGC commanders occupied most of the high and middle levels of management within NAJA (Shemirani 1999: 21).

According to NAJA's charter, the police's core mission is to enforce discipline and maintain security. This includes fighting crime and terrorism, providing security for legal demonstrations, dispersing illegal gatherings, suppressing riots, protecting government buildings, protecting Iranian and foreign politicians, and controlling the country's borders. According to Article 8 of the NAJA charter, the responsibilities of NAJA's judicial officers include combating drug smuggling and dealing, fighting corruption, and moral policing (Qānun Niruhā-ye Entezāmi Jomhuri-ye Eslāmi 1990).

Based on NAJA's charter, all police forces, officers, and conscripted soldiers who spend up to two years of their military service in NAJA, can work as judicial officers, or *zābetān-e qazā'i*, under the supervision of the prosecutor general. Their tasks are to detect crime by gathering and preserving evidence, identifying and locating the accused, preventing the accused from escaping and hiding, conducting early investigations, delivering summons, and implementing judicial orders.

In addition to NAJA, members of the Basij (voluntary reserve army) were permitted to work as judicial officers after a law passed by parliament in 1993. According to this law (1993 Judicial Protection of the Basij Act), members of the Basij militia were allowed to work as judicial agents to enforce law and order alongside the police. It is worth mentioning that, in 1987, when Ayatollah Khomeini was still alive, the judiciary had rejected the use of Basijis as judicial officials (Tamasebi 1999: 65), primarily because their charter did not identify judicial service among their tasks.[2] The new law stipulated that the members of the Basij Resistance Force (BRF), like other judicial officers, have permission to take necessary action whenever a crime is witnessed (*jorm-e mashhud*) and the police are absent or not responding fast enough, or when the police ask for assistance. In these situations, Basij members have to prevent the disappearance of criminal evidence as well as the flight of the accused, and prepare and send a report to the judicial authorities. After the passage of the 1993 law, the Basij became involved even more deeply in imposing Islamic morality by collecting, confiscating, and eliminating satellite dishes and antennas (which are illegal in Iran), to help the police fight against "cultural invasion" (Golkar 2011: 210).

Both the Basij and the police not only work as judiciary officials identifying and combating crimes, they also help the regime to suppress dissidents and impose state control. For example, both forces suppressed the 1993 and 1994 demonstrations throughout Iran, which protested economic hardship, inflation, and unemployment. When NAJA failed to suppress some of the protests, the Basij and the IRGC stepped in to crack down on them.[3] To better prepare for the future, NAJA expanded its crowd-control capacity and established a special unit called NOPO (Niruhā-ye Vizheh-ye Pād-e Vahshat, NAJA's Counterterrorism Special Force) in 1996, to help the Islamic Republic suppress popular uprisings and maintain order. To lead this operation, General Hedayat Lotfian was appointed as the new chief of Iran's police on February 15, 1997.

In addition to these transformations, like other branches of Iran's security and military apparatus, NAJA was encouraged to become involved in the local economy and business sectors in order to generate an independent income. This resulted in the creation of the NAJA Cooperative Foundation (Bonyād-e ta'āvon NAJA), primarily responsible for the social welfare organization of NAJA personnel and for providing housing, medical, educational, and financial support.

---

[2] See (in Persian): "Who is an Officer? And What Justifies a Member of the Basij Being an Officer?" *Māh-nāmeh*, No. 36, Year 6, 1, Esfand 1371 (February 20, 1993): https://tinyurl.com/3ccejzpb, particularly page 4, paragraph 3. Interestingly, the charter was not changed in 1993, but the interpretation of the parliament, dominated by the conservatives, changed. Ayatollah Khamenei was very supportive of the Basij and pushed for more Basiji involvement in society.

[3] NAJA was caught off-guard by the protests, mainly because the Islamic Republic conceived of itself as a popular and legitimate regime. It was shocked by the scope of the unrest and dissatisfaction among a sizable percentage of its citizens.

4 The Judiciary, the Police, and the Containment of Reform (1999–2004)

After May 1997, when the reformist candidate Mohammad Khatami won the presidential election, the police and the judiciary became the two main political forces mobilized by Ayatollah Khamenei and his conservative allies to block reform and suppress its support. During Khatami's presidency (1997–2005), the press court systematically closed many reformist newspapers, while political trials frequently targeted activists and intellectuals to repress the reform movement (Shambayati 2010: 301).

In addition to the judiciary, which tried to silence critics, NAJA became a tool of the conservatives and the Supreme Leader with which to harass and prosecute the reformists. The members of the Counterintelligence Organization of NAJA, who, according to the law, are not judiciary officers, began working as judicial officers confronting reformists between 1997 and 1998. For example, the police incarcerated and tortured the mayor of Tehran, Gholam-Hossein Karbaschi, alongside other Tehran district mayors who supported Khatami's 1997 presidential campaign (Golkar 2018). In addition, some high-ranking NAJA commanders became more involved in illegal acts, such as carrying out physical attacks on Khatami's ministers, including hojjatoleslam Abdollah Nouri, the minister of interior, and Ataollah Mohajerani, minister of culture and Islamic guidance, in 1998.

NAJA's special counterterrorism force NOPO was also used to suppress student uprisings, such as the one in July 1999, when NOPO attacked students at Tehran University as they protested the closure of the reformist daily *Salām* as well as parliament's approval of a highly restrictive press law. When *Salām* was closed by the Special Court for Clergy, the ensuing student protests seriously shook the Islamic Republic for the first time since 1979 (Künkler 2013). The police, along with hardline vigilantes, attacked a student dormitory, resulting in in the killing of at least three students and the arrest and injury of hundreds of others. There was a paltry attempt to hold the police accountable for the violence. In a subsequent show trial, only one conscript soldier was convicted, and as such for the minor misdemeanour of stealing an electric razor. The conviction was perceived by many students as humiliating and a mockery of the law (Iran: The Revenge 2009). The convicted soldier joined the police as an officer, and was later promoted to the head of a police station in southeast Tehran (Midān 2018).

This and other incidents where police suppressed dissidents resulted in widespread disapproval of the police forces and the judiciary, especially amongst the youth, further deteriorating the legitimacy of the police, which had already been on the decline for the past three decades (Kalki and Doustar 2009: 248). Additionally, the judicial reforms implemented by Ayatollah Yazdi since 1994 had chaotic results (see the Introduction to this volume). In particular, his reform that combined the role of judge and prosecutor in one office and person had disastrous effects on the neutrality of the courts. Both the head of the judiciary and of the NAJA were replaced by the Supreme Leader in 1999.

In 1999 Ayatollah Mahmoud Shahroudi, the new head of the judiciary, reinstated the separation of courts into criminal, family, civil, and commercial courts, passed distinct laws of procedure for each of these courts, and revived the public prosecutor's office (see Chapter 9). Shahroudi also pushed for the reintroduction of a judicial police force (*polis-e qazā'i*). Even before the parliament approved the bill, the judiciary started creating and training the Judicial Services Police, which was supposed to be subordinate to the judiciary like its predecessor in the 1980s. According to former Tehran's chief prosecutor, Saeed Mortazavi, the Judicial Services Police units would be based in police stations and tasked with carrying out the orders issued by judiciary officials (Iran Focus 2006). However, the judiciary's bill was rejected by a conservative-dominated parliament on the grounds that it violated the principle of the separation of powers.

Additionally, Ayatollah Khamenei replaced the head of NAJA, General Hedayat Lotfian, with General Mohammad Baqer Qalibaf, the head of the IRGC air force. Many police commanders were removed or replaced as a result, including the head of the Tehran police, General Farhad Nazari, who was subsequently involved in the suppression of student uprisings in 1999. General Mohammad Reza Naqvi, who was the head of the NAJA counterintelligence organization, was also replaced by hojjatoleslam Gholam Hossein Ramezani in September 2000.

During his term as head of NAJA, Qalibaf made several attempts to improve the police's reputation. He tried to rebuild the organization as a "society-centered police" (*polis-e jāmeh-ye mehvar*) and popularized concepts such as *jāmeh-ye mas'ul* ("responsible society") and *polis-e pāsokhgu* ("accountable police") (Golkar 2018: 3).[4] In a further attempt to improve police legitimacy, the position of "social deputy" was established to collaborate with writers, intellectuals, and academics to improve police–society relations and, consequently, create a more positive image of the police. The establishment of a new operational

---

[4] Historically, the police were only answerable to the Shah or the Supreme Leader, not to the people. However, a change was made to ensure that the police are accountable to the people (at least in theory).

unit, Police 110, was also set up as an emergency hotline (like 911 in the United States). This hotline aimed to allow rapid police response to criminal activities and the dispersal of gatherings perceived as dangerous to public order. The number of police stations increased from 311 in 2000 to 784 throughout the country in 2003. In addition to maintaining public order, the expansion of police stations enabled the Islamic Republic to successfully control guild strikes and corporate crises in big cities between 2001 and 2005 (Vatankhah 2010: 144).

One of the main popular grievances amongst the civilians had been police corruption. To make the police more accountable and oversee the police forces, a new office, the Office of Public Surveillance (Daftar-e nezārat-e hamegāni sāmānah 197) was established. The bureau allocated a telephone number (197) by which the general public could report complaints and comments about the police forces.

Another major initiative was the inclusion of women in the Iranian police force. In 1998, Iran's parliament approved the amendment of the NAJA charter, permitting it to recruit and train women for administrative work, enforce rules related to women, and suppress female gatherings deemed dangerous to social and political order. Subsequently, the Kowsar Academy for Police admitted female candidates to work and study as police officers for bachelor and associate degree courses from 1999 onward.

The police also set up the Bureau of Social Work and Consultation (Edāreh-ye koll-e madadkāri *va moshāvere* NAJA) and hired social workers to work in police stations to promote the police's social crime prevention policy: crime prevention through interaction with people and the education of people. The police established a news agency and published a weekly newsletter to better communicate with the public. The NAJA filmmaking institute (NAJA-ye Honar) was also created to produce movies and TV programs to educate people and improve the police's social prestige and public relations. During this era, the police also began to privatize some of its service sectors. To achieve several disciplinary service offices, the Police Electronic Services Offices (Daftar-e khadamāt-e elektronik-e entezāmi), or *Polis-e beʿalāveh* 10, were established in February 2004.[5] Some of the responsibilities of these offices, which were usually staffed by retired police officers, entailed issuing drivers' licenses and passports, doing military service paperwork, issuing fuel cards, and so on.

However, despite all the initiatives taken to improve the legitimacy of the police, the police continued to suppress dissident intellectuals.

---

[5] Polis-e +10 uses information and communication technologies to improve police activities and efficiency, for example, in the issuing of passports.

One such example was the brutal suppression of student protests concerning the privatization of universities in July 2003. But more importantly, police and judiciary worked hand in hand to arrest several journalists and writers on accusations of "cultural degeneracy" by a new body under NAJA, called Edāreh Amāken ʿOmumi (Department of Public Places). Many intellectuals, students, and activists were arrested and interrogated by this force and were secretly held in detention outside of the judiciary's jurisdiction and the state prison organization (Human Rights Watch 2004:18).

Like the police, the judiciary continued to impose political control by summoning, trying, and punishing reformists. It attempted to suppress people participating in dissident activities, such as students, members of parliament, political opponents, and scholars. Although, according to the IPC, torture and abuse are illegal, torture was used frequently in the police detention centers (Tavassolian et al. 2015: 42). The extensive allegations of torture by police and other security forces made Ayatollah Shahroudi issue a special order in January 2005 banning all forms of abuse and torture (Center for Human Rights in Iran 2009).

To further undermine the reformists and put pressure on their social constituencies, the judiciary established the Department for Social Prevention and Protection (Edāreh-ye hefāzat va pishgiri-ye ejtemāʿi) in 2004 to enforce Islamic codes. Controlled by conservatives, this department was given the responsibility for extending regime control over society. According to its regulations, regime devotees (*isārgarān*) were recruited to form a group in every mosque and neighborhood to work as the eyes and ears of the judiciary by gathering intelligence, fighting crime, providing religious guidance, and identifying suspected criminals. The plan was approved by the judiciary while the reformists were in power, but the conservatives shelved the plan when Ahmadinejad became president in 2005.

5 The Judiciary and the Police in Ahmadinejad's Era

The head of police, General Qalibaf, resigned to run for president in 2005, but he was defeated by the populist hardliner, Mahmud Ahmadinejad. After the defeat, General Qalibaf was appointed as the mayor of Tehran in 2005 with the help of hardliners in Tehran city councils. This led to increased involvement of NAJA in the economy. As the head of police and former commander of the IRGC, General Qalibaf opened doors for many military personnel, including police commanders, to join the Tehran municipality, and assigned many projects to the NAJA economic foundation. According to one of the members of the Tehran city council, more than 600 police and IRGC commanders had entered the Tehran municipality since the year 2005. This helped the economic arm of the police, the Bonyād-e- ta'āvon-e NAJA, to gain access to more businesses and construction projects within Tehran. Furthermore, NAJA's financial institution, Qavamin, which was originally established in 2000 to provide support for police personnel, was upgraded to a bank and expanded throughout the country.

Ayatollah Khamenei appointed Brigadier General Esmail Ahmadi-Moghaddam, the former head of the Basij militia in Tehran, as the new commander of NAJA in 2005, who encouraged hiring Basij members as police officers. According to the police chief, more than 75 percent of the new police forces hired in 2006 were from the Basji, and, in 2007, this percentage had increased to 80. He stressed that "in that upcoming year, 100 percent of the new forces of the police should be from the Basij." (Golkar 2012: 467). After 2005, the "Basijification" of the police meant that they became more conservative. Since members of the Basij are often from more religious and conservative backgrounds, by hiring them NAJA became more ideological, and the cultural gap between the police forces and many Iranians increased. In addition to the Basij, the police usually recruit from particular social groups, including families of martyrs (for example, martyrs of the Iran–Iraq War) and children of military personnel, including the IRGC (Fars News Agency 2012).

To advance reforms, the police purged some of its own forces who were accused of being corrupt and, in some cases, not completely loyal to the Islamic Republic. In fact, according to the head of the police, in 2005 more than 2,000 policemen were fired (Parsine 2013). According to the head of police counterintelligence, hojjatoleslam Ramazani, in 2004, about 600 policemen were fired monthly (Sharif News 2006). Under Ahmadi-Moghaddam's leadership, between 2005 and 2015, 50 percent of police personnel had been changed.

Additionally, NAJA has been involved in implementing the Public Safety Plan (Tarh-e amniyat-e ejtemā'i). The 2005 Public Safety Plan was an initiative that entailed a series of morality plans in urban areas whilst confronting drug dealers, thieves, and other criminals. Part of the plan was to arrest thugs (arāzel va obāsh), drug addicts, and other criminals who endangered public safety and morality. The goal was not only to increase public security and remove criminals from the street but also instill fear and terrorize the general public. The Public Safety Plan was illegal, according to twenty independent lawyers, who took a complaint against the police to the Divān-e 'edālat-e edāri, the highest administrative court in Iran (Khatam 2010: 221). Ignoring the law, the police special units would violently raid homes at night to arrest alleged criminals and humiliate them in public spaces in front of cameras to set an example. For instance, in some cases, they would publicly humiliate the criminals "by hanging watering cans used for lavatory ablutions around their necks" (Yousefi 2007). Shahram Khosravi explains how the police encouraged people to watch and participate in the humiliation of the arrestees by "performing mob justice," for example by throwing tomatoes (delivered by the police) at the person in handcuffs (Khosravi 2017: 112).

Many of these people were imprisoned in Kahrizak Detention Center, which was under the control of NAJA, where they were tortured and treated inhumanely by being beaten regularly by police guards. According to a report by the Committee of Human Rights Reporters, Kahrizak was built as an underground facility, aiming to deprive detainees of access to fresh air and sunlight. According to some testimonies, the former police chief of Greater Tehran, Brigadier General Ahmad Reza Radan, threatened the detainees in Kahrizak Prison: "You will be tortured and kept without food and water to such an extent that you will become as thin as mice able to walk through cell bars of the detention centre. And only then, that is if you are still alive, will you be taken to court and transferred to another prison" (Memorial 2014). The result was the severe torture of detainees, even before being sent to court, and the death of some of the detainees between 2007 and 2008. While Kahrizak camp was identified as substandard and illegal by the judiciary, which had recommended its closure in 2007, it continued to serve the police until 2010 (Amnesty International 2009: 45).

Kahrizak was only one of many substandard NAJA detention centers. NAJA has about 1,400 detention centers, according to the former head of Iran's police, General Ahmadi-Moghaddam. Some of these detention centers *(taht-e nazergāh)* are for detaining suspects for twenty-four hours when a crime is witnessed *(jorm-e mashhud)* and are based in the urban police stations *(kalāntari)* and rural police stations *(pāsgāh)*. According to General Ahmadi-Moghaddam, anti-narcotic, intelligence, and anti-criminal police have about 290 detention centers, which, he claimed, are standardized.

One part of the Public Safety Plan is the Morality Safety Plan, or moral policing, in which NAJA also became excessively involved. Gasht-e ershād (guidance patrols) was a branch of the police that had been responsible for monitoring and arresting people who did not conform to Islamic dress codes and the strict prohibition against male–female "fraternization." Consisting of both male and female personnel, the force created a menacing environment for youth in particular, who were frequently threatened with arrest due to "improper clothing" or socializing with the opposite sex. According to the national police commander, during a single year, the *Gasht-e ershād* gave more than three million oral guidance or verbal warnings (*tazakkor-e lesāni*) to people who behaved improperly or immodestly, whilst also arresting many of them (Golkar 2016: 144). Many reports show police forces have been violently imposing moral control. In one case, which became public, female police brutally beat a woman for "improper" hejab (Jalili 2018). While NAJA pushed for enforcing morality plans, some of its high-ranking commanders were arrested for moral crimes, including General Reza Zarei, a former IRGC member and the head of Tehran police, who was arrested in a brothel with a group of prostitutes (Fathi 2008: 1).

6 The Suppression of the 2009 Green Movement

With the announcement of the results of the June 2009 presidential election, hundreds of thousands of people poured into the streets to protest the perceived fraudulent result in what become known as the Green Movement. But they were brutally suppressed by the regime's coercive apparatuses, including the judiciary, police, and Basij militia forces.

Based on Iran's internal security doctrine, NAJA and its special forces (NOPO) are the first line of Iran's coercive apparatus to deal with any threat to public order, such as worker strikes and other protests (Golkar 2018). Thus, after the ignition of the Green Movement, the special unit or NOPO forces, alongside the Basij, immediately poured into the streets to suppress the protesters. Moreover, police brutality and the suppression of students in the dormitories of Tehran University in June 2009 led to eight months of demonstrations in which 300 people were killed and thousands were arrested. Levels of violence were so shocking that, according to a reformist, even the paramilitary forces "were screaming at them [the police] not to beat the students anymore" (Al-Monitor 2014).

Many of the protestors, especially the youth, who were arrested, were detained in the infamous Kahrizak Detention Center, which was notorious for its appalling conditions. The police beat, tortured, and raped some of the detainees in Kahrizak, and several people died in detention. As the result of the brutal suppression of the Green Movement, many of the leading police and judiciary personnel were sanctioned by American and European countries, including having property and bank accounts that were located in these countries seized, and being banned from entering (Kahn 2018).

174 Saeid Golkar

In addition to police and other security agencies, the judiciary, and especially the revolutionary courts which are responsible for prosecuting acts against national security, became one of the main instruments for intimidating and suppressing the Green Movement. A series of show trials were televised that included confessions conducted by the revolutionary courts, in which many activists received harsh punishments and were sentenced to long prison sentences (Ghaemi 2010).

The suppression of the Green Movement subsequently led to dramatic structural changes in NAJA, including the expansion of police stations, the creation of cyber police, and a renewal of police equipment. Following the protests, the Islamic Republic expanded and renewed its crowd-control equipment whilst establishing new police districts, offices, and stations throughout the country. Police headquarters were also established in the city borders to increase control in suburban areas. For example, ten new police stations were created on the west side of the city of Tehran, where westernized middle classes live, to further enhance political control over these areas and improve security, according to Morteza Tamaddon, Tehran's governor (Mehr News Agency 2013).

During this time, NAJA also sought to further increase police special units by creating a separate branch for the judiciary and criminal police. In 2013, NAJA Special Forces established new units including a female anti-riot unit, a mounted police unit, and a police canine unit to help quell social unrest. Police also established a special Cyberspace Police (FATA, Polis-e fazā-ye towlid va tabādol-e ettelāʿāt, lit. "police of the virtual space and information exchange"), which is responsible for monitoring online user activity and investigates and identifies cyber activists.[6] Since 2010, FATA has arrested many activists, at least one of whom, Sattar Beheshti, died under torture while in police custody (Internet in Chains 2014).

The successful subjugation of the Green Movement by the Basij militia convinced the Islamic Republic to create a volunteer police force and use them to police society. As a result, in 2010 the police were ordered to recruit and organize volunteers into police volunteer units. The goal was to hire and recruit about 300,000 voluntary police in five years.[7] The

---

[6] In September 2009, Chief Police Commander Ismail Ahmadi-Moghaddam announced the creation of the Cyberspace Police: https://nligf.nl/v1/upload/pdf/Structure_of_Irans_Cyber_Operations.pdf.

[7] See (in Persian) "25 000 Police Volunteers Will Be Recruited," *Borna News Agency*, July 25, 2015. https://tinyurl.com/mma23nhs, accessed January 18, 2019. There are no official statistics available to trace the extent to which the policy was fully deployed, but we know that in Mazandaran province 1,200 persons were recruited in 2018. See (in Persian) "1200 Volunteer Police Recruited in the Province of Mazandaran," *DEFA Press. IR*, August 18, 2018. https://tinyurl.com/62nkdatc accessed June 25, 2019. Further, 4,000

plan became operational in 2013, when NAJA established Volunteer Police Units to cooperate with the police in preventing crime. These forces are recruited on two levels. The first level consists of people older than 18 who work as judiciary officers (*zābetān-e qazā'i*). The second level consists of people aged 15–18 who collaborate with the police to educate the people and enhance their public awareness. The volunteer police functions under a separate branch of NAJA and is responsible for traffic policing, moral policing, and anti-narcotic policing. Their list of duties ranges from enhancing people's knowledge about policing to gathering intelligence in their respective neighborhoods.

Members of the voluntary police enjoy special benefits such as the option of serving compulsory military service in their hometown and getting first hiring preference at military organizations. Sometimes, cash prizes are granted to the voluntary police members for carrying out their duties. However, while the option to join the voluntary police units is open to all, precedence is given to members of the Basij, retired members of the police, other armed forces, and the families of martyrs.

The police also created "protection units" (*yegānhā-ye hefāzat*) to help NAJA maintain order, especially when the internal and external challenges to the regime intensified. The regulation for the establishment of protection units for government organizations was initially approved in 2000 by the general staff of the armed forces, but it was only in 2012 that the plan became operational after the approval of Iran's Supreme Leader. According to this regulation, all ministries, bureaus, and governmental organizations can request NAJA to establish special protection units for their institutions. These units were put under the control of NAJA and tasked to follow police orders.

Based on this order, in 2013 the judiciary created a judiciary protection unit, which consisted of 25,490 personnel under the control of the judiciary's own counterintelligence security unit or protection of intelligence unit (*sāzmān-e hefāzat-e ettelā'āt-e quwwa-ye qazā'iya*) (Fars News Agency 2014). In each judicial district, the unit is responsible for the protection of the judiciary buildings and equipment, as well as gathering news and intelligence alongside the implementation of moral policing plans. Although the primary responsibility of the protection units is to provide physical protection and law enforcement within the organizations, they are also tasked with helping NAJA control society and maintaining order.

people were recruited in Sistan and Baluchistan. See (in Persian) "4000 Volunteer Police Recruited in Sistan and Baluchistan," *Seda va Sima* (Sistan and Baluchistan Center), n.d. https://tinyurl.com/2yucwcus, accessed April 5, 2019.

The Ahmadinejad presidency (2005–2013) witnessed NAJA's increased involvement in international oil trading. According to some reports, the government gave NAJA at least two oil cargos to sell to provide for a shortfall in funding for the police budget. In fact, the NAJA Cooperation Foundation is currently the fifth largest holding company in Iran, and its influence extends to every sector of the economy, from construction and real estate, marine and oil industry, to the stock market. Some of NAJA's economic offshoots include the Mehregān Investment Company, NAJI Pushesh (Clothing), Pars Hotels, and the *Sāzeh-ye pāydār-e qarn* Housing and Construction Group.

7 Police and Law Enforcement in the Rouhani Era (2013–2021)

Involvement in the economy led to pervasive corruption among police commanders. At least twelve high-ranking police commanders were fired in 2015, among them the head of the police General Ahmadi-Moghaddam, who was replaced by Brigadier General Hossein Ashtari in 2015. Like his predecessor, General Ashtari was an IRGC member and a former head of the Public Security and Intelligence Police. General Ashtari was the man behind the implementation of several security plans within Iran, including the Public Safety Plan. His appointment as the new commander was indicative of the further securitization of the police forces.

NAJA's involvement in moral policing continued with, for example, the deployment of seven thousand undercover personnel to enforce Islamic rules on Tehran's streets (Dehghan 2016). NAJA's violent involvement has been criticized by many Iranians, including President Hassan Rouhani (2013–2021), who stated that the police's duty is to enforce the law, not Islam (Reuters 2016). Parallel to this trend, the process of police modernization and privatization of NAJA's activities has continued under Ashtari. For example, police personnel have been equipped with body cameras to monitor their interactions with citizens.

Like the police, the judiciary underwent a transformation after the Green Movement of 2009. When his two terms were completed as head of the judiciary, Ayatollah Shahroudi was replaced by a more radical cleric, Ayatollah Sadegh Larijani. During Larijani's tenure, Iran's judiciary continued to act as the regime's coercive apparatus to maintain social control by silencing dissidents. In 2011, Ayatollah Larijani pushed for the reintroduction of the Judicial Police. Ahmadinejad's administration had initially ignored the bill for creating the Judicial Police because of political conflict between the president and the head of the judiciary. President Rouhani's administration later approved the bill. However, as in the past, it was again rejected by the parliament.

Law Enforcement and the Judiciary   177

The parliament, however, approved a new Code of Criminal Procedure (CCP) for the Public and Revolutionary Courts in 2014, which went into effect in 2015. According to this law, only police officers who pass special judicial training and receive a judiciary officer certificate will be recognized as judicial officers. According to the new code, judicial officers are divided into two groups, "general judicial officers" (*zābetān-e qazā'i 'āmm*) and "special judicial officers" (*zābetān-e qazā'i khāss*). General judicial officials are those who have the authority to prosecute all offenses, except for those that are officially referred to other authorities. "Special judicial officers", such as the Basij members, are also permitted to perform the duties outlined in Article 28 of the CCP, provided that they are "within their designated responsibilities on the grounds of specific laws" (Amnesty International 2016: 27–28).[8]

The law also authorizes prosecutors to visit the police stations and temporary detention centers under the control of NAJA every two months. Article 33 was added to the new CCP, mainly because, on numerous occasions, police commanders had not let the judges and prosecutors visit detention centers, arguing that the police were under the interior minister's control. In the past three decades, the Court of Administrative Justice (Divān-e 'edālat-e edāri), which is responsible for solving disputes of competencies between various state and administrative organs, has cancelled the police orders for not allowing the judges to visit the police stations, but the conflict between police and judiciary has continued in some cases.[9] The relationship between police and judiciary has not always been straightforward and has often depended on the personalities involved in the case.

The winter of 2017–2018 saw another wave of police involvement in political suppression. The protests initially began over economic and environmental issues, but eventually evolved to encompass political and social concerns. Despite their dramatic spread to more than eighty-six cities in January 2018, the protests were suppressed quickly by the coercive apparatus – most notably by the police forces. In contrast to 2009, when the Iranian police were insufficiently prepared to put down the mass uprising, the police in 2017–2018 were able to quash the protest

---

[8] Article 28 of the new CCP states: "Judicial officers are officials who, under the supervision and training of the Prosecutor and under the law, act in order to uncover crimes, preserve and gather proof and evidence of the crime, identify and locate the accused, prevent the accused from escaping and hiding, conduct early investigations, deliver summons and implement judicial orders."

[9] See, for example (in Persian), "The Decision of the Administrative Justice Court: The Annulment of the Circular regarding the Permission of Judicial Officials to Visit Police Stations," May 7, 2012. www.khoshyaran.com/print.php?ToDo=ShowArticles&AID=6836 and http://rc.majlis.ir/fa/law/show/129185, accessed November 5, 2019.

movements quickly, effectively, and without the help of either the paramilitary militia (the Basij) or the IRGC.

As in the past, the police applied violent measures to suppress the unrest and restore order. In an apparent act of psychological warfare, police broke the windows of closed shops and hit parked motorcycles with batons (Kurubas 2018). The police have frequently applied these tactics to instill fear of chaos and delegitimize the protests.

In November 2019, after the announcement of subsidy cuts, a new wave of protests spread rapidly across Iran to twenty-nine of Iran's thirty-one provinces, with ten of them experiencing major clashes between protesters and security forces. The protests featured people from a wide range of social backgrounds, although most could be described as young and working class. The brutality of police and other repressive bodies led to the death of 1,500 people as well as at least 8,600 arrests in just a few days (Golkar 2020: 13).

In the medium term, the November 2019 protests led to an expansion of the police's security role. In late 2021, NAJA national police force underwent restructuring and expansion. It was renamed FARAJA, or the Law Enforcement Command of the Islamic Republic of Iran (Farmāndehi-ye Entezāmi Jomhuri-ye Eslāmi). This change resulted in the police holding an equivalent organizational position as the IRGC and Artesh (Iran's conventional army). As a result, the police force commander now holds the same rank as the commanders of the army and the IRGC. As part of this, the intelligence police department was elevated to the Police Intelligence Organization. The aim was to enable the regime to allocate additional resources and personnel to monitor and control protest movements (Toumaj 2022).[10]

In October 2022, another wave of mass unrests (perhaps unprecedented in their ideological challenge to the republic) was triggered by the death of a young Iranian woman in police custody, Mahsa Jina Amini, on September 16, 2022. Chanting "women, life, and freedom," women across Iran took off their hejabs and burned their scarves, even in small and traditionally conservative towns. The police, along with the Basij and the IRGC, violently suppressed the protests, leading to the death of more than 500 people and the arrest of more than 20,000 (Golkar 2023).

The Iranian people have become increasingly dissatisfied with their government, and the regime has responded with increased repression. Since 2009, Iran has seen an escalation in mass protests, leading to the

---

[10] Amir Toumaj, "Iran's Law Enforcement Shuffle Reflects Concern about Protests," The Washington Institute, 2022. www.washingtoninstitute.org/policy-analysis/irans-law-enforcement-shuffle-reflects-concern-about-protests, accessed 15th March 2023.

replacement of Police Commander General Ashtari with a more hardline figure, General Ahmad Reza Radan. Believing in the iron fist, Radan was involved in the 2009 ultra-violent repression of the Green Movement. This has further eroded the regime's legitimacy.

8   Police Structure and Personnel

Having analyzed the trajectory of the multiple and overlapping police and security forces in Iran, this final part of the chapter will focus on the vertical and horizontal structure of the various police forces and their interrelations. The vertical structure of the police begins at a national police commandership level (*farmāndehi-ye entezāmi-ye* NAJA). There is one police provincial command (*farmāndehi-ye entezāmi-ye ostān*) in each province that controls all the police stations in that province. A level below that is a disciplinary district command located in each city that manages and controls the police stations in that city (*farmāndehi-ye entezāmi-ye shahrestān*). Police stations (*kalāntari*) and disciplinary stations (*pāsgāh-ye entezāmi*) are the lowest executive levels in the police structure, with *kalāntari*s located in urban areas, *pāsgāh*s in rural areas. According to the head of Iran's Prevention and Operation Police, General Mohmmad Sharfi, there are about three thousand *pāsgāh*s in Iran (Young Journalists Club 2016). The structure of the police stations, regardless of district, is the same. Each police station is usually manned by a deputy of prevention, a deputy of intelligence, a deputy of inspection (*tajassos*), a deputy of operations, and the judiciary services police (Mir Azim 2011: 61).

Police personnel in the *kalāntari*s and *pāsgāh*s are known as general police and are the main connections to the judiciary and the prosecutor's office (*dādsarā*). When somebody files a complaint in the prosecutor's office, the prosecutor asks the police to collect the evidence, initially interrogate the suspect, and then send all the evidence to his office (Figures 6.3 and 6.4).

Another specialised police unit, the Public Security Police (Polis-e amniyat-e omumi), is tasked with identifying and arresting violent criminals. It is also involved in the confiscation of illegal satellite dishes and the arrest of members of pyramid schemes. The Moral Security Police (Polis-e amniyat-e akhlāghi) is a subbranch of General Public Security Police (Polis-e amniyat-e ʿomumi), which is responsible for arresting women with inappropriate hejabs or those engaging in mixed gatherings. The Guidance Patrols (gasht-e ershād) are subordinate to the Moral Security Police and are responsible for patrolling streets and issuing warnings to those dressed inappropriately or engaged in un-Islamic conduct. The Police for the Supervision over Public Facilities

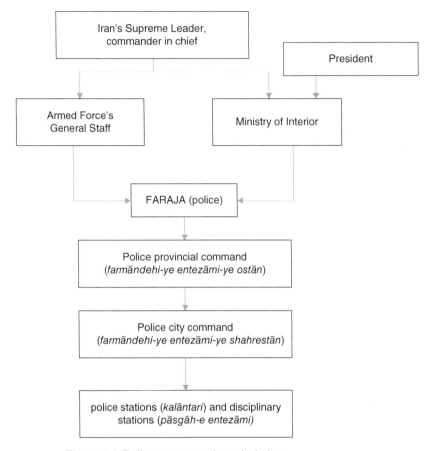

Figure 6.3 Police structure: A vertical view

and Locations (Polis-e nezārat-bar amāken-e ʿomumi) is another branch of the Public Security Police. This body is responsible for regulating and controlling businesses such as shops, restaurants, hotels, public transportation companies, and photo galleries, through issuing and revoking work permissions for people in these businesses.

The Police Intelligence Organization (Sāzemān-e ettelāʿāt-e FARAJA) was created in 2022, aimed at monitoring and controlling protest movements by allocating additional resources and personnel. This organization provides intelligence support for the police, trains personnel, maintains preparedness, and generates intelligence in border areas. It monitors guild activities, and runs a network of local informants (*mokhber mahali*) to collect information, news, and rumors; it also conducts research and compiles specialized documents.

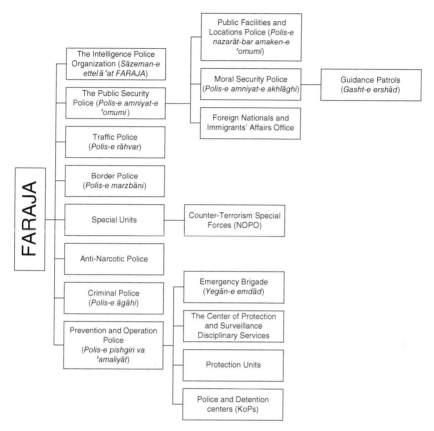

Figure 6.4 Police structure: A horizontal view

The Criminal Investigation Police (Polis-e āgāhi) is composed of the main special judicial officers who work closely with the judiciary and the prosecutor's office. It has several bureaus for combating criminals, armed robbery, and economic crimes, and its police have frequently been accused of using torture to extract "confessions," claims which have always been denied.

FARAJA also has several operational units, including Police 110, Helper Brigades (yegān-e emdād), and Special Units (yegān-e vizheh). Helper Brigade forces support other police branches by confiscating illegal DVDs and conducting moral policing. They also help with anti-narcotic missions, crowd control, and the suppression of protests. Special Units (or NOPO) are another operational police force responsible for crowd control, riot suppression, and special weapons and tactics (SWAT).

A special unit was set up in each province, and ultimately works under the headquarters in Tehran. Although NOPO was originally created as a counterterrorism unit, it later developed into a more complex structure with different brigades fulfilling different functions, one of which is focused on counterterrorism and hostage rescue, while others are focused on anti-riot actions and SWAT.

Currently, police personnel consist of cadres (*pāyvar*), who are recruited as full-time employees, and conscript soldiers who spend two years mandatory military service in FARAJA. Though there are no official statistics on police personnel, in the 2000s such personnel amounted to about 100,000 to 120,000 men (Buchta 2004), including all police, FARAJA officers, noncommissioned officers, and employees. My estimate is that the police had 300,000 personnel in 2023, approximately 50 percent of whom were conscripts. Out of the total number of police cadres (150,000), about 60,000 are judicial officers.

According to Ahmadi-Moghaddam, in addition to official police personnel, more than 100,000 people work in FARAJA-affiliated organizations, such as the Police +10 Entezām Center (Markaz-e Entezām-e Polis Pishgiri FARAJA).[11] Within this group, 41,000 people work in protection and surveillance companies, which provide security for more than 4,600 neighborhoods. Policing in Iran has historically been stigmatized as a disreputable rather than an honorable profession because it is regarded as being pursued by men of low socioeconomic status unfit for high office (Kusha 2013: 171). This remains true even after the revolution, as many police officers recruited in the Islamic Republic's early years came from lower, or lower middle-class families with a Basij affiliation.

There has been growing criticism of the Iranian judiciary for its lack of independence from security organizations, and in particular its inability to reign them in. When he was head of the judiciary, Shahroudi tried repeatedly, but in vain, to force the security organizations to give up their extra-judicial detention centers and relinquish control over their detainees, including political prisoners, to the Prisons Organization (Künkler, Chapter 9 this volume). He also issued a circular instructing the police forces to no longer refer detainees to the country's special courts and sought to dissolve the latter, only to find himself overruled by the Minister of Intelligence (Künkler 2013).

---

[11] The center is named Police +10 because the initial goal was to provide ten of the services previously provided by the FARAJA. Police +10 is under the supervision of the Prevention Police but is staffed by civilians.

9   Conclusions

The transformation of the police forces since 1979 is indicative of the police's security mission that has expanded alongside its disciplinary mission. The police, for example, have heavily focused on anti-protest activities since 2009. To maintain social and political order, the Islamic Republic has taken several measures, such as the expansion of its law enforcement forces, the creation of police stations throughout the country, the establishment of several special forces for crowd control and anti-riot missions, and heavy investment in the training and equipping of these forces. The creation of special women's units, mounted police, and canine units, and the subsequent expansion of these forces in each province have further enhanced the regime's ability to exert and maintain control over the country's population.

To enforce the law and deal with increasing crime rates, the police also recruited volunteers as honorary police personnel and privatized several service branches for smoother, more effective functioning. By creating quasi-private security and protection centers, the police not only engaged a large group of people in maintaining social order but also tied their economic and ideological interests to the survival of the regime. This helped the police shift their focus from disciplinary missions to more important security missions.

To prepare its personnel for security missions, the police force has dramatically intensified its ideological programs for the indoctrination of its members. The authorities have also changed the police's hiring policies by shifting the focus toward recruiting from more conservative parts of society, especially from amongst Basij militia members. These two trends combined have led to increasing estrangement between the police and society.

Overall, despite some progress toward the rule of law during President Khatami's term (such as creating the "Office of Public Surveillance" through which people could report police misconduct to the authorities), Iran's police forces are not accountable to elected institutions or citizens. Instead, they are politicized and compete with one another in repressive activities to "prove" their raison d'être to the regime. Moreover, police brutality, especially in the suppression of political and social protests, is a pervasive reality.

Bibliography

Al-Monitor. "Iranian police commander concedes mistakes in 2009 protests," September 2, 2014. https://perma.cc/2L93-URDV.

Amnesty International. *Flawed Reforms: Iran's New Code of Criminal Procedure.* 2016. https://perma.cc/X9V9-T3LF, accessed July 3, 2019.

Amnesty International. *Iran: Election Contested; Repression Compounded.* December 2009. www.amnesty.org/en/documents/mde13/123/2009/en/, accessed March 2, 2019.

Arjomand, Said Amir. "Shiite Jurists and the Iranian Law and Constitutional Order in the Twentieth Century," in Said Amir Arjomand and Nathan J. Brown (eds.), *The Rule of Law, Islam and Constitutional Politics in Egypt and Iran*, Albany: State University of New York Press, 2013, pp. 15–56.

Bellin, Eva. "The Road to Rule of Law in the Arab World: Comparative Insights," *Middle East Brief*, 84, 2014. https://perma.cc/Q5DT-8MDA.

Buchta, Wilfried. "Iran's Security Sector: An Overview," Paper presented at the Workshop on *"Challenges of Security Sector Governance in the Middle East,"* 2004, Geneva 12–13 July.

Center for Human Rights in Iran. *Four Journalists Sentenced to Prison, Floggings*, February 10, 2009. https://perma.cc/AU8F-962D.

Dehghan, Saeed Kamali. "Influx of morality police to patrol the streets of Tehran," *The Guardian*, April 19, 2016, https://perma.cc/862Z-UZY4.

Diamond, Larry. *Developing Democracy: Toward Consolidation*, Baltimore: Johns Hopkins University Press, 1999.

Entessar, Nader. "Criminal Law and the Legal System in Revolutionary Iran," *Boston College Third World Law Journal*, 8(1), 1988, pp. 91-102.

Fars News Agency. "Goftogu-e Ekhtesasi-e Fārs bā Moʻaven-e Niru-ye Ensāni-ye NAJA" ["An inclusive interview with the NAJA deputy of human resources"], Tehran, February 4, 2012. https://perma.cc/U4VG-ELMP.

Fars News Agency. "Tasvib-e Jadhb-e 25 hezār nafar niru barāy-e sāzeman-e Yegān-e Hefāzat-e quwwa-yi qazā'iya" ["Approval of hiring 25,000 troops for the judiciary Protection Units"]. August 28, 2014. https://perma.cc/J4KJ-Y7J2.

Fathi, Nazila. "Chief of Police for Tehran Was Arrested, Iran Confirms Top of Form Bottom of Form," *New York Times*, April 16, 2008, https://perma.cc/6TTX-Z3ME.

Fukuyama, Francis. *Political Order and Political Decay: From the Industrial Revolution to the Globalization of Democracy*, New York: Farrar, Straus and Giroux, 2014.

Ghaemi, Hadi. "The Islamic Judiciary," *Iran Primer*, 2010, https://perma.cc/S75V-NCL4.

Golkar, Saeid. "Politics of Piety: The Basij and Moral Control of Iranian Society," *The Journal of the Middle East and Africa*, 2 (2), 2011, pp. 207–219.

Golkar, Saeid. "Manipulated Society: Paralyzing the Masses in Post-revolutionary Iran," *International Journal of Politics, Culture, and Society*, 29 (2), 2016, pp. 135–155.

Golkar, Saeid. "Organization of the Oppressed or Organization for Oppressing: Analysing the Role of the Basij Militia of Iran," *Politics, Religion & Ideology*, 13 (4), 2012, pp. 455–471.

Golkar, Saeid. "Iran's Coercive Apparatus: Capacity and Desire," *Policy Watch*, 2909, 2018. https://perma.cc/6JW9-65T6.

Golkar, Saeid. "The Evolution of Iran's Police Forces and Social Control," *Middle East Brief*, 120, 2018. https://perma.cc/CBK9-35ML.

Golkar, Saeid. "Protests and Suppression in Post-Revolutionary Iran," *Policy Notes 85*, The Washington Institute for Near East Policy, October 2020.

Golkar, Saeid. "The Mahsa Amini Protests and the Defeat of Islamism in Iran," *Current Trends in Islamist Ideology*, April 18, 2023, pp. 94–111.

Habermas, Jürgen. "On the Internal Relation between the Rule of Law and Democracy," *European Journal of Philosophy*, 3(1), 1995, pp. 12–20.

Human Rights Watch. *Like the Dead in Their Coffins: Torture, Detention, and the Crushing of Dissent in Iran*, June 6, 2004. https://perma.cc/69TV-LZRK.

"Internet in Chains; The Front Line of State Repression in Iran," *International Campaign for Human Rights in Iran*, 2014. https://perma.cc/3BMT-ARMZ

Iran Focus. "New Judicial Police launched in Iran capital," August 31, 2006. https://perma.cc/TU2C-S5NK.

"Iran: The Revenge." *The New York Review of Books*, November 5, 2009. https://perma.cc/A6VX-QDYM.

Jalili, Saeed. "Anger in Iran as 'morality police' scuffle video goes viral," *Aljazeera*, April 20, 2018. https://perma.cc/8HWM-GCN9.

Kalki, Hasan, and Reza Doustar. "Barrasi Manzelat-e Shoghli va Ejtemāʿi Polis-e Irān," ["The study of social and occupational prestige of police forces"], *The Quarterly of Disciplinary Management Studies*, 4 (2), 2009, pp. 229–251.

Khan, Tzvi. "Meet the Iranian Police Who Enforce Iran's Islamist Ideology", *Washington Examiner*, June 20, 2018. www.washingtonexaminer.com/weekly-standard/meet-the-iranian-police-who-enforce-irans-islamist-ideology.

Khatam, Azam. "Struggles over Defining the Moral City: Islam and Urban Public Life in Iran," in Linda Herrera and Asef Bayat (eds.), *Being Young and Muslim: New Cultural Politics in the Global South and North*, New York: Oxford University Press, 2010, pp. 207–223.

Khosravi, Shahram. *Precarious Lives: Waiting and Hope in Iran*. Philadelphia: University of Pennsylvania Press, 2017.

Künkler, Mirjam. "The Special Court of the Clergy (*dādgāh-e vīzhe-ye rūḥānīyat*) and the Repression of Dissident Clergy in Iran," in Said Amir Arjomand and Nathan Brown (eds.), *The Rule of Law, Islam, and Constitutional Politics in Egypt and Iran*, Albany: SUNY Press, 2013, pp. 57–100.

Kurubas, Saim. "Strikes against economic conditions in Iran pile pressure on government," *TRT World*, June 27, 2018. https://perma.cc/Z5QR-RTVS, accessed September 12, 2019.

Kusha, Hamid Reza. "Impediments to Police Modernisation in Iran, 1878–1979," *Policing and Society*, 23 (2), 2013, pp. 164–182.

Mehr News Agency. "Erteqā-e Shakhesehā-ye Amniyati Gharb-e Tehrān" ["Increasing the security measures of west of Tehran city"], February 18, 2013. https://perma.cc/SCT6-7LU6, accessed April 12, 2019.

Memorial. "One Person's Story: Ramin Purandarjani," *The Abdorrahman Boroumand Center in Iran*, 2014. https://perma.cc/4WXE-YH4Q, accessed April 12, 2019.

Midān. "Sāreq-e Rish-tarāsh dar Ku-ye Dāneshgāh, Sarhang Shodeh Ast" ["The burglar in the college's dormitory became a colonel"], Maydān September 4, 2018. https://perma.cc/7XNQ-NYHZ, accessed April 12, 2019.

Mir Azim, Qavam. "Naqesh-e *Polise dar* Hemāyat *az* Bezehdideh" ["The police's role in supporting delinquent victims"], Tehran: Hadis-e Kosar Publisher, 2011.

Mohammadi, Majid. *Judicial Reform and Reorganization in 20th Century Iran State-Building, Modernization and Islamicization*, Abingdon-on-Thames: Routledge, 2008.

Nayyeri, Mohmmad, Ronda Cress, and Catherine Kent. *Rule of Law in Iran: Independence of the Judiciary, Bar Association, Lawyers and Iran's Compliance with*

International Human Rights Obligations. University of Essex – Human Rights in Iran Unit (2014) https://perma.cc/D5WK-HZLC, accessed March 3, 2019.

Parsine Website. "Sardār Esmaeil Ahmadi-Moghaddam; Vorud beh Sefārat-e Engelis-e Dām Bud" ["General Esmaeil Ahmadi-Moghaddam; Entering the British Embassy was a Trap"], Tehran, May 13, 2013. https://perma.cc/UZD3-7TS3, accessed April 12, 2019.

Qānun Niruhā-ye Entezāmi Jomhuri-ye Eslāmi [The Act of the Islamic Republic's Law Enforcement Forces]. Research Center of the Islamic Consultative Assembly, July 17, 1990. https://perma.cc/3649-N89S, accessed May 4, 2019.

Report of the UN Secretary General. "The rule of law and transitional justice in conflict and post-conflict societies," UN Security Council. 23 August, 2004. https://perma.cc/RFY7-3DFC, accessed April 12, 2019.

Reuters. "Rouhani clashes with Iranian police over undercover hijab agents," Reuters, April 20, 2016. https://perma.cc/7SX9-N2YR.

Shambayati, Houtan. "Courts in Semi-Democratic/Authoritarian Regimes: The Judicialization of Turkish (and Iranian) Politics," in Tamir Moustafa and Tom Ginsburg (eds.), *Rule by Law: The Politics of Courts in Authoritarian Regimes*, New York: Cambridge University Press, 2010, pp. 283–303.

Sharif News. "Sāzemān-e hefāzat va Ettelā'āt-e NAJA har māh 600 polis rā dastgir mikonad" ["The NAJA counterintelligence arrest 600 policemen every month"], February 10, 2006. http://sharifnews.ir/?3089.

Shemirani, Kasra Nouri. "Āsibshenasi Niruhā-ye Entezāmi Irān" ["The Pathology of Iran's Law Enforcement Force"], *Gozaresh Magazine*, October, No. 104, 1999, pp. 19–23.

Tamasebi, Javad. "Zābet Kist va, Niruhā-ye Moqāvemat basij dar cheh Mavāredi Zābet Hastand" [Who is a Judiciary Officer: And Under Which Circumstances are Members of the Basij Resistance Force Judiciary Officers], *A'ine Dādrasi Magazine*, 36, 1999, pp. 64–69.

Tavassolian, Narges, Mohmmad Hedayati-Kakhki, Alexandra Harrington, Kamiar Alaei. "Iran – The Interrogation of Suspects," in David Walsh, Gavin Oxburgh, Allison Redlich, and Trond Myklebust (eds.), *Contemporary Developments and Practices in Investigative Interviewing and Interrogation: International Perspectives*. Abingdon-on-Thames: Routledge, 2015, pp. 34–48.

Torabi, Yosef and Seyed Ehsan Rahmani. "Islamic Revolutionary Committee, an Important Experience in the Sphere of Society Center and Popular Police (1979–1983)," *Dānesh-e Entezāmi*, Fall 9 (3), 2007, pp. 112–130.

Vatankhah, Hamid Reza. "Barrasi Naqsh-e *Kalāntarihā-ye* Tehrān-e Bozorg dar Kontorol-e Bohranhā-e Senfi az sāl-e 1380–1384" ["Investigation of the Role of Tehran's Police Stations in Controlling Corporate Crises, 2001–2005"], *Studies of Crime Prevention* 5 (15), 2010, pp. 115–146.

World Justice Project (WJP). Rule of Law Index 2021. https://perma.cc/3K9A-4EA8.

Young Journalists Club. "Fa'āliyat-e seh hezār kalāntari va pāsgāh dar keshvar" ["The activities of three thousand kalantaris and pasgahs in the country"], *Bāshgāh-e Khabarnegarān-e Javān* (Young Journalists Club), December 21, 2016. https://perma.cc/662R-JXYH, accessed April 4, 2019.

Yousefi, Nader. "Thug Crackdown Operation under Way in Iran," *Rooz Online*, June 21, 2007. https://perma.cc/34KT-P32U, accessed April 12, 2019.

7 The Problem of Overcrowded Prisons in the Islamic Republic of Iran

Anna Enayat and Hadi Enayat

1 Introduction

As we have seen in Chapters 2 and 3 of this volume, the 1979 Revolution led to the construction of a penal system ostensibly based on Islamic principles, which put an emphasis on retributive justice (*hodud* and *qesās*) and restorative justice (*diyeh* and *bakhshesh*) rather than incarceration. This new penal system was to be based on an Islamic vision of justice, articulated by Khomeini and other senior clerics in the Islamic Republic of Iran, which extolled the virtues of the swift and efficient nature of Islamic penal justice. This was contrasted with the laborious, inefficient, and corrupt nature of penal justice in the *ancién regime* as well as the dehumanizing effects of imprisonment under the vast carceral archipelago established by the Pahlavis (Newman 1982: 577; Rejali 1994: 62–83).[1]

But despite attempts to Islamize the system, Iran is still very much a carceral state and, far from receding to the margins, custodial sentences have been used extensively since 1979. Indeed, rates of imprisonment have been consistently high, higher than under the Pahlavi dynasty on the eve of the 1979 Revolution,[2] and often well above the median in global terms (discussed in Section 2). This is despite the fact that the level of violent crime has been relatively low by international standards.[3] At the same time, the government has been unable (or unwilling) to generate the necessary prison capacity to accommodate the high

---

[1] According to Khomeini, Islamic criminal justice is free of bureaucracy. "These foreign laws caused the Muslim society numerous problems ... a proficient lawyer can keep a case in the courts all [his] life .... The case on which the shariʻa judge used to make a decision in two or three days now takes twenty years to settle [under Western law]" (quoted in Newman 1982: 577). The concept of a "carceral archipelago" was first used by Michel Foucault (1979) in his classic study *Discipline and Punish* (1979) to refer to the technologies, mechanisms, and knowledge systems related to modern prisons.

[2] Based on the permanent prison population, the incarceration rate in 1978, just before the 1979 Revolution, was 25 per 100,000 (Madani 2006); in the 2000s, it averaged 230 per 100,000.

[3] In 2015, Iran ranked ninety-second in terms of the homicide rate. See https://perma.cc/EN7U-ZXTV, accessed April 12, 2017.

number of prisoners, leading to severe problems with overcrowded prisons, appalling living conditions, and attendant health problems, such as the spread of hepatitis, HIV/AIDS, and COVID-19 in the prisons. Indeed, as we shall see, the IRI has consistently had some of the most overcrowded prisons in the world and understanding the causes of this problem is the main focus of this chapter.

The causes of prison overcrowding lie at the intersection of several factors. These include the budget provided for prisons and prison construction, the rates of serious crimes committed, the rates of pretrial detention and the definition of what constitutes a "crime," in particular crimes punishable with prison sentences. Other factors include cultural attitudes to punishment amongst the population as well as among police and judicial officials. This chapter will focus on four policy/legal areas in connection with the problem of overcrowding: (1) the prison budget and lack of capacity, (2) imprisonment for non-intentional (*gheir-e 'amdi*) crimes, (3) pretrial detention (PTD), and (4) narcotics prisoners. We will also discuss some of the responses by Iranian civil society to this problem, as well as the strategies of decarceration employed by the government, and look at how successful these have been.

Since the founding of Iran's modern prison system in the 1920s and 1930s under Reza Shah, prisoners have been divided into two distinct categories by the state: the "ordinary prisoners" (*zendāniān ādi*), who make up the vast majority of Iran's incarcerated population, and a smaller but significant number of political prisoners who are referred to as "security prisoners" (*zendāniān amniyati*). Most academic accounts of prisons and prisoners in the Islamic Republic of Iran have focused on political prisoners. This is partly due to the prominence of accounts given by dissident activists fleeing repression during the 1980s and early 1990s, which highlighted the plight of political prisoners. The waves of arrests after the 2009, 2019, and 2022 uprisings, widely covered in the international media, has further highlighted this issue. Indeed, the number of political prisoners in Iran has metastasized since 2022 after the crackdown on the protests triggered by the death of Mahsa Jina Amini in the custody of the *gasht-e ershād* (guidance patrols).[4] With media attention and academic analysis mainly focused on the issue of the status and

---

[4] The figures are somewhat disputed, but up to 30,000 were arrested for taking part in the protests after Mahsa Amini's death in October 2022. Human Rights Activists News Agency, March 18, 2023: www.en-hrana.org/statistical-report-on-human-rights-in-iran-for-the-year-1401-hijri/, accessed June 15, 2023.

plight of political prisoners, this chapter concentrates on ordinary prisoners who have been largely absent from general accounts of penal history since the 1979 Revolution, though, as we shall see, the distinction between these two categories is not clear-cut.[5]

There was little information about the ordinary criminal justice system until a 2003 analysis by the United Nations (UN) Working Group on Arbitrary Detention, which posed questions about the standards of justice in the ordinary as well as the revolutionary court system.[6] The UN Working Group was given rare but nonetheless limited access to Iran's prisons and was able to conduct interviews on detention conditions. It touched briefly on conditions for what it called "ordinary law prisoners," pointing out that a factor leading to prison overcrowding was a lack of proportionality in sentencing, particularly where the imprisonment of destitute people on account of a usually minor debt was concerned (see Section 6 on this issue and Table 7.2). The most extensive and reliable reports on the conditions for "ordinary law prisoners" were compiled and published by the Iran-based Society for Defense of the Rights of Prisoners (SDRP), covering the period March 2005–March 2008 (1384–1386 in the Iranian calendar).[7] The SDRP was founded in July 2004 by Emadeddin Baghi, a prominent Islamic reformist intellectual and journalist respected for his investigation of controversial episodes in the history of the Islamic Republic through meticulous factual documentation, and his outspoken positions on civil rights. The society's board of directors consisted of senior lawyers and well-known reformist professionals. This was a rare example of a nongovernmental organization (NGO) in the IRI to attempt, indeed insist upon, an open, legal, and independent existence. Probably for this reason, but also because the organization's reports reflect the evidence-based approach of Baghi and his staff, SDRP's reports may be described as "ultra-scrupulous" in that they only recorded matters that could be verified through the society's professional associates or through statements by relevant government officials. As such, these reports are a uniquely reliable source on the state

---

[5] Golnar Nikpour, "All Prisoners are Political Prisoners: Rethinking the Campaign to #Free Them All Beyond Borders and Beyond Covid 19," *Jadaliyya*, March 25, 2020: www.jadaliyya.com/Details/40865, accessed May 18, 2022.

[6] UN Commission of Human Rights, "Civil and Political Rights, Including the Question of Torture and Detention," Report of the Working Group on Arbitrary Detention. Addendum: Visit to The Islamic Republic of Iran, February 15–27, 2003: https://perma.cc/2MJ8-D5Y6, accessed May 1, 2015.

[7] Emadeddin Baghi, "Report on the Conditions of Prisoners of the Country," Tir 8, 1386/ June 29, 2007: https://perma.cc/S2YE-6VW3, accessed March 14, 2015.

of prisons in Iran in the mid-2000s.[8] This chapter has supplemented these accounts with an extensive analysis of Iranian press reports, human rights reports, legal blogs by Iranian lawyers and activists, prison memoirs as well as the existing academic literature on Iranian prisons and related issues such as narcotics and family law. We will begin with an analysis of the incarceration rate in the IRI before addressing the various causes of overcrowding and the attempts to reduce prison numbers.

2 The Incarceration Rate in the Islamic Republic of Iran

Discussing the incarceration rate in the IRI warrants a preliminary note on figures and data. The most common, and relatively standardized, method of measuring a country's rate of incarceration is to calculate the number of people imprisoned as a proportion of 100,000 individuals in the total population. Most figures cited in the following originate with the National Prisons Organization (NPO), which is a branch of the judiciary. That figures for the same year can sometimes be seen as slightly conflicting is due to the fact that the NPO maintained a running tally of prisoners which, throughout the second half of the 2000s to 2011, could be accessed on its website.[9] As far as we are aware, there are no publicly available end-of-year-statistics. Figures reported in the Iranian press, by senior NPO or judiciary officials, or by the World Prison Brief (WPB) are therefore usually correct at or around the date of their statement but can vary considerably within the same calendar year. For this reason, we have based Table 7.1 in the Appendix on NPO figures quoted by the WPB for alternate years from 2001 to 2013 and historic figures quoted by prison officials for 1980 and 1993. The figures for 2015–2019 are from a summary provided by *E'temād* newspaper and probably stem from the judiciary's annual reports. We should note here that there are

---

[8] The society did not last long. By 2004, Baghi had already spent two years in prison for his newspaper and his writings on the chain murders (*qatlhā-ye zanjireh-'e*), only to be arrested again and charged with spreading anti-state propaganda on account of a new book he published, titled *The Tragedy of Democracy in Iran*. He was sentenced to another year in prison, but the sentence was suspended. He was again arrested in October 2007, at the height of President Ahmadinejad's campaign against NGOs, and imprisoned for a year. *Reporters Sans Frontiers*, "A Journalist Arrested and Sent to Evin Prison, Another Gets Three-Year Sentence," August 1, 2007: https://perma.cc/6KTE-7SZZ, accessed April 4, 2018. He would serve a further two years as a prisoner of conscience in 2010/2011. In December 2004, Baghi was awarded the French government's Human Rights Prize and on April 8, 2008 he was named International Journalist of the Year by the British Press Awards. See "Civil Courage Prize: Emadeddin Baghi 2004": https://perma.cc/3LC3-39EG, accessed January 22, 2014, and *The Guardian*, "British Press Award Winners," Wednesday April 9, 2009: https://perma.cc/98WJ-PX7J, accessed January 22, 2014.

[9] See the NPO website: www.prisons.ir/, accessed March 15, 2017.

The Problem of Overcrowded Prisons   191

sometimes discrepancies between the statistics issued by NPO officials in the Iranian press and statistics given to the WPB (discussed in more detail in the next section).

In light of this, we begin this analysis of prison numbers with a statement by the head of Iran's Prisons Organizations, Asghar Jahangir, who in May 2017 underlined the growing problem of overincarceration: "In 1358 (1979) with a population of 37 million we had 8,557 prisoners, in 1360 (1981) with a population of 40 million we had 34,590 prisoners. In 1395 (2016) with a population of 78 million we have 223,000 prisoners. While the population has increased [in this period] by 66.95 per cent, the number of prisoners has increased by 300 per cent." In other words, the incarceration rate increased some elevenfold from circa 25 per 100,000 in 1979 to 283 in 2016. As Jahangir goes on to observe, by 2016 the incarceration rate of the IRI was 223 per 100,000, well above the international average of 168, giving Iran the 41st highest per capita incarceration rate in the world (out of 220 countries).[10] It was also the second highest among Muslim-majority countries, lower than Turkey (268) but considerably higher than other Middle Eastern states such as Bahrain (234), Saudi Arabia (197), Kuwait (157), Jordan (197), Iraq (126), and Lebanon (126). These rates were dwarfed, however, by the figure for the United States, which had the world's highest incarceration rate at 655 prisoners per 100,000.[11]

The development of the prison population since the late 1990s shows three trends. There was a spike in 1999 when 190,000 prisoners were recorded, followed by a slow but notable reduction till 2005 when there were 134,000. The upward trend resumed in 2006 and by April 2010 numbers had reached 184,000. From there numbers spiraled to 204,000 in August 2010,[12] 220,000 in March 2011, and reaching over 250,000

---

[10] Iranian Students News Agency (ISNA), "Head of the Prison Organization: Building a Prison is Not an Art," Khordad 1, 1396/May 22, 2017: https://perma.cc/93VF-A6LE, accessed June 1, 2020.

[11] International Centre for Prison Studies, "World Prison Population List," 12th ed., 2018: www.prisonstudies.org/sites/default/files/resources/downloads/wppl_12.pdf, accessed June 1, 2020. Note that, according to the WPB, the IRI's incarceration rate had risen considerably to 284 by 2018.

[12] *Khabar Online*, "Unprecedented Increase in the Number of Prisoners," Mehr 9, 1398/October 1, 2010: https://perma.cc/6KHP-ZK2S; *Zamaneh*, "Iranian Judiciary Wants Number of Prisoners Reduced," March 3, 2011: https://perma.cc/3RJ8-2BKR, accessed October 3, 2012. For October 2011, see (quoting various state news agencies), Inside of Iran, "Iran: Number Imprisoned Grows Exponentially," October 10, 2011: https://web.archive.org/web/20111012023753/http://insideofiran.org/en/human-rights/2793-iran-number-imprisoned-grows-exponentially.html, accessed October 15, 2015. *Mehr News*, "America is the World's Largest Prison Guard," Mehr 17, 1390/October 9, 2011: www.mehrnews.com/fa/NewsDetail.aspx?NewsID/1423300, accessed March 18, 2015.

in October 2011.[13] From 2012 on, various measures (to be discussed in Sections 4 and 7) produced a temporary reduction, but renewed pressures soon took the figure up again to 230,000 in 2017 and 240,000 in 2018.[14] With a simultaneously growing population the incarceration rate dropped from circa 300 per 100,000 in 1999 to 192 in 2005 and rose above 250 per 100,000 in 2011. From 2011 to 2019 the figure was between 280 and 295 per 100,000 (see Table 7.1 in the Appendix). At the time of writing (2023) the incarceration rate is 228 according to the WPB.[15] This reduction may be down to changes in the anti-narcotics laws, which will be discussed further in Section 7.

2.1 Prison Capacity

In the early 2000s, leading state officials did not seek to deny the problem of overcrowded prisons and bad prison conditions. Indeed, in 2001, Iran's head of the judiciary, Ayatollah Hashemi Shahroudi, told his audience that "every year we take 600,000 people to prisons that are full of filth, crime, moral depravity and evil." He compared imprisonment to "putting fresh water into a sewer pipe and expecting fresh water to come back out."[16] Similarly, in May 2007 Prosecutor General Ayatollah Dorri-Najafabadi declared that: "The situation in some of the country's prisons is so bad that prison officials themselves have difficulty in tolerating it."[17] And to take a more recent example, in 2017, a judge described conditions in Iran's prisons as "*asafbār*," the strongest way of expressing "deplorable" or "terrible" in Persian.[18] Through the early and mid-2000s, officials repeatedly put the capacity of the Iranian prison system at 60–65,000 inmates in total. In 2006, according to Ali Akbar Yesaqi, the NPO head for much of the 2000s, this was made up of 234 units – 175 prisons, 25 juvenile detention centers, 23 camps, and 11 temporary detention centers.[19] There were, he added, about a hundred other

---

[13] *Mehr News*, "America is the World's Largest Prison Guard"; see note 14.
[14] "A Look at the Condition of the Number of Prisoners over the Last Five Years," *E'temād Online*, Tir 13, 1398/July 4, 2019: https://perma.cc/ZZ5S-C5M4, accessed August 2, 2020.
[15] See World Population Review: https://worldpopulationreview.com/country-rankings/incarceration-rates-by-country, accessed July 28, 2023.
[16] Quoted in *Faslnameh-ye Majalleh-ye Hoquq-e Dādgostari* (the judiciary's quarterly law journal), No. 80, Fall 2001, no page number.
[17] Najafabadi 1386/2007.
[18] "Population Explosion in the Prisons," *Magiran*, Azar 28, 1396/December 19, 2017: www.magiran.com/article/3678303, accessed March 5, 2018.
[19] ISNA, "Head of the Prisons Organization: Each Prisoner has a Daily Cost of 8000 Tomans," Khordad 23, 1385/June 13, 2006: https://perma.cc/U25P-GDXS, accessed

The Problem of Overcrowded Prisons

detention centers administered by the security forces and the police. These centers, notorious for rights violations, are not under the authority of the NPO and very little is known about their size or the numbers who pass through them. Of the 175 official prisons, as many as 130 were (by 2008) 30 years old or more, and in a state of "extreme decay" according to Yesaqi. Accommodation for 60,000 prisoners meant that at the turn of the century the system held around three times more than its capacity, and for the next five years from just under to just over two and a half times its capacity.[20]

A start was made on the construction of several new prisons in response to the 1999/2000 crisis, and in 2001 a planning law provided for the removal of twenty major prisons from the center of cities to new premises on the outskirts. But by 2006 there had been scant progress only, causing the NPO head to comment that "if the trend of reconstruction proceeds at its present pace, it will take another half century for the renovation of those prisons to be completed."[21] It was not until 2009 that Yesaqi was able to announce that the construction of thirty-four new prisons was underway and the budget for thirty-nine others had been approved. At the same time, he noted that there had been no progress at all with transferring prisons out of the cities. In the 1386/2007 budget, 150 billion rials had been allotted for preparatory work. But that did not necessarily mean that the money was forthcoming: "we have projects begun 7 years ago (1999/2000) which are still incomplete, and over the past four years at times less than 46 per cent of the planned credit has actually been allocated."[22]

By 2008, official capacity figures as reported to the WPB had risen to 65,000, but so too had the prison population, resulting in an occupancy rate of 243 percent, making Iran's prison system the ninth most

---

July 8, 2015; *Fars News*, Khordad 26, 1387/June 15, 2008: www.farsnews.com/news/8703260477%20%20%20%20/30, accessed June 15, 2010.

[20] Najafabadi 1386/2007. It is not clear what criteria Iranian prison officials use to determine adequate prison capacity, as this can be calculated according to various criteria. For example, the European Committee for the Prevention of Torture and Inhumane or Degrading Treatment or Punishment (CPT) defines the minimal standards of space as: 6 m² of living space for a single-occupancy cell + sanitary facility; 4 m² of living space per prisoner in a multiple-occupancy cell + fully partitioned sanitary facility; at least 2 m between the walls of the cell; at least 2.5 m between the floor and the ceiling of the cell. See Council of Europe, "Living Space per Prisoner in Prison Establishments: CPT Standards," December 15, 2015: https://rm.coe.int/16806cc449, accessed March 12, 2021.

[21] *Iran Daily*, Tir 18, 1385/July 9, 2006: www.iran-daily.com/1385/2605/html/panorama.htm, accessed August 2, 2016.

[22] Ibid.

overcrowded in the world according to WPB data.[23] In May 2011, the WPB put the prison occupancy rate at 258.8 percent, quoting an expanded prison capacity of 85,000, but again a much higher prison population. Prison numbers were expanding rapidly, reaching 250,000 a few months later in December 2011. With an occupancy level of 294 percent, a little less than three times the system's capacity, the Iranian system was at this point ranked by the WPB as the fourth most overcrowded in the world, a hair's breadth behind the Philippines which had an estimated occupancy rate of "circa 300 per cent."[24]

With the country's prisons again in acute crisis, much aired in the domestic press and parliament, for more than a year NPO officials stopped quoting prison population statistics, and access to the relevant page on the NPO website was denied to the public. In 2012 some 25,000 prisoners were released without public record, according to a leak from a highly placed prison official reported by the reformist newspaper *Kalameh*.[25] The release, possibly coupled with the impact of changes in the narcotics law (discussed in more detail in Section 9) which relieved the NPO of responsibility for the detention of drug addicts was reflected in the figures for the prison population for 2013, which, compared to October 2011, show a sudden fall from circa 250,000 to circa 226,000.

In January 2011, Gholam-Hossein Esmaili, the head of the Prisons Organization, announced the launch of a great "movement" (*nehzat*) to expand prison capacity with the construction of 150 new prisons, as well as temporary detention centers in every town with more than 20,000 inhabitants and 28 hard labor camps for narcotics offenders. Additionally, there were plans to hire 2,000 new prison employees and to import 1,000 electronic bracelets and 7 body scanners.[26] Simultaneously an effort was launched by the NPO administration to save face in the international arena by reporting inflated capacity figures to the WPB: 113,000 for 2012, 140,000 for 2014, and 150,000 for 2018. Iran was, in

---

[23] Figure taken from WPB website: www.kcl.ac.uk/depsta/law/research/icps/worldbrief/wpb_stats.php?area/all&category/wb_occupancy, accessed December 12, 2010. According to the *E'temād* newspaper, the capacity figure for 1388/2009–2010 was still 60,000.

[24] See WPB Statistics (Iran): www.prisonstudies.org/info/worldbrief/wpb_stats_print.php?area/all&category/wb_occupancy. For more general prison statistics on Iran up to 2018 from the WPB, see: https://perma.cc/2T8X-4RN8, accessed January 5, 2016.

[25] *Melliyun Iran*, "The Opening of Fashāfuyeh Prison in South Tehran," Shahrivar 24, 1391/September 14, 2012: https://perma.cc/3Q87-VK32, accessed January 6, 2016.

[26] Nikzad 1390/2011. See also, for a repeat announcement from Esmaili two years on: Tasnim News Agency, "Demand for 2000 Prison Guards for the Country's Prisons," Dey 20, 1392/January 10, 2014: https://perma.cc/H7C4-4TLR, accessed January 6, 2016.

this way, moved out of the top ten most overcrowded prison systems in the WPB rankings. Even in 2018, with a prison population of approximately 240,000, an apparently concocted figure of 150, 000 gave Iran a ranking of 51 on the WPB's scale.[27]

Why were Esmaili's figures suspect? Without substantial investment in new prison space in the second half of the 2000s it was, of course, well-nigh impossible for Iran to have suddenly increased capacity by some 20 percent in 2012. To have more than doubled prison capacity vis à vis that of the stagnating prison estate of the 1990s and 2000s would have been impossible without intensive construction activity in the years 2011–2014. Unsurprisingly, in June 2016 when press conferences on the subject of prison numbers resumed, the new NPO head, Asghar Jahangir, told the domestic press that prison capacity stood at 85,000.[28] In May 2017 Jahangir put capacity at 88,000,[29] and in May 2019 again at 85,000.[30] The NPO figure quoted for the Iranian press in 2017 showed the prison system, with 230,000 prisoners and an occupancy level of 263 percent, to have been the 8th most overcrowded in the world (by contrast to 48th with an occupancy level of 161.2 shown in the WPB table for that year).

Jahangir's figures suggest either no expansion of capacity between 2011 and 2016 or, more likely, that official capacity in 2011 was – even at 85,000 – perhaps overstated. Systematic information on actual prison building in the period since 2010 is lacking, but a glance at major innovations recorded in the Iranian press provides some pointers. It is questionable that by the end of 2012 prisons could have provided an additional capacity of much more than 10,000. Two prisons in West Azerbaijan – in Maku and Miandoab – both begun in 2000, were completed in 2010 and 2011 respectively.[31] There is no information about their size, but it is clear that they are relatively small units. A new prison

---

[27] The figure quoted by Esmaili in 2012 as the goal of what turned out to be his entirely imaginary "prison construction movement" was 140,000. Nikzad 2011.
[28] *Radio Farda*, "The Head of the Prisons Organization: Iran's Prisons are Three Times over their Prisoner Capacity," Khordad 15, 1395/June 4, 2016: https://perma.cc/CY64-T24A, accessed March 3, 2020. Jahangir added that while the number in prison is 220,000, there were actually 450,000 prisoners (presumably on leave, on bail awaiting trial, etc.).
[29] *Radio Farda*, "Three Hundred and Thirty-Three Per Cent Rise in Prisoners in 30 Years," Khordad 2, 1390/May 23, 2017: https://perma.cc/22C2-57XK, accessed March 8, 2018.
[30] Islamic Republic News Agency (IRNA), "Jahangir: We Do Not Have a Problem with Majles Deputies Visiting the Women's Prison," Ordibehesht 25, 1398/May 15, 2019: https://perma.cc/KVZ7-K6FJ, accessed September 10, 2020.
[31] *Fars News*, Tir 8, 1389/June 29, 2010: www.farsnews.com/news/8904080824, accessed April 15, 2019.

for women sentenced in Tehran province, Gharchak near Varamin, opened in early 2011 and at the time reportedly housed some 2,000 prisoners. Gharchak was converted – in apparent haste – from a pre-existing building which is reported to have been used for agricultural purposes. Female political prisoners who were transferred there from Evin and Rajai Shahr in April 2011 soon spoke of acute overcrowding, primitive facilities including a lack of drinkable water, and overall inhumane conditions.[32] In September 2011, 6,000 male inmates from Karaj (Rajai Shahr and Qezel Hesar prisons) were moved to the new "Great Tehran Penitentiary," also known as Fashāfuyeh Prison, located in the desert about 25 miles to the south of the capital. The construction of Fashāfuyeh, originally planned as a camp to house 15,000 narcotics offenders, was begun, and abandoned, in 2000, and only resumed in 2009.[33] One of several sections was completed in 2011 and a second section, with a capacity of 2,250, only began to receive transfers from Tehran prisons in the summer of 2015.[34]

There have been further modest additions to the prison estate since 2012. But through 2017, statements by the NPO head Jahangir echoed the same pessimism Yesaqi had expressed in the late 2000s. He lamented that the requirement to build prisons outside the cities had gone nowhere, because it was never properly funded. Indeed the budgets allocated covered no more than the cost of leveling the hilly ground of the desert countryside.[35] Nor had there been any consideration of the scale of problems and complexities involved in the transfer of prisons to the countryside, often 100 kilometers from urban centers: land preparation, provision of services (water, sanitation, electricity), the construction of accommodation for prison personnel – guards and social

---

[32] *Radio Free Europe* (RFE), "A Disturbing Glimpse of Iranian Prison Life," May 10, 2011: https://perma.cc/X975-UQNQ, accessed May 8, 2019.

[33] *Asr-e Iran*, "The Transfer of 6000 Prisoners from Karaj Prison to Greater Tehran Prison," Mehr 30, 1390/September 26, 2011: https://perma.cc/4K8N-TFWC, accessed January 5, 2014. According to a report published in May 2014, "enquiries" confirmed that no more than 6,000 prisoners had been transferred to the facility by that date. See *Khabar Online*, "Did the Incident at Ward 350 of Evin Prison Lead to a Change in the Head of the Prisons Organization?," Ordibehesht 13, 1393/May 3, 2014: https://perma.cc/Z9WM-VSHT, accessed May 15, 2016.

[34] Tasnim News Agency, "Fashāfuyeh, a Camp for the Transfer of Drug Detainees from Tehran's Prisons," Tir 30, 1394/July 21, 2015: https://perma.cc/4HCN-SMQ6, accessed May 17, 2016. *Mehr News*, "The Opening of Number 4 Greater Tehran Rehabilitation Prison," Mordad 6, 1394/July 26, 2015: https://perma.cc/Z86Z-JN8F, accessed May 17, 2016.

[35] *Deutsche Welle Farsi*, "Problems with the Transfer of Evin Prisoners and 20 other Prisoners to other Cities," January 18, 2017: https://perma.cc/JRN2-KM9Y, accessed December 22, 2018.

workers.[36] Furthermore, of the seven hard labor camps for narcotics offenders announced in October 2010, only three incomplete structures had been handed over to the Prisons Organization owing to the failure to provide an adequate budget.[37] In August 2017 Yesaqi remarked that for the past two years the NPO had been given no development budget;[38] in December 2017 he announced that the NPO's budget for the following year had been reduced by 13 percent and the annual rate of prison construction and repair had "fallen to 5 per cent."[39] There were not even sufficient funds to repair the existing prison estate despite the derelict state of buildings which had been in use for twenty to twenty-five years.[40]

Prisoner numbers had meanwhile been increasing and at this point were again nearing the quarter of a million mark. As in 2011, but on a far larger scale, the crisis was addressed through a wide-ranging amnesty, a radical measure announced in February 2019 to mark the 40th anniversary of the revolution. According to the NPO head, by May 2019 the amnesty had applied to about 100,000 prisoners, who were either pardoned or had their sentences reduced, while another 70,000 convicted in the courts had their sentences converted to a fine before they entered prison.[41]

Subsequently, prison numbers fell to 189,500 inmates. One NPO official, quoting what he described as "WPB figures," suggested that the prisons now held no more than 28 percent of their capacity – a comparatively minor level of overcrowding.[42] He was soon corrected by his superior, Asghar Jahangir, who in a May 15 press conference announced, yet again, that the capacity of the prison system was 85,000 and that at the time it held two and a half times its capacity. Prior to the amnesty,

---

[36] Mizan News Agency, "The Dilemmas of Delaying a Law," Azar 8, 1396/November 29, 2017: https://perma.cc/T9QT-AEZE, accessed November 18, 2019.

[37] Mizan News Agency, "The Transfer of Prisons to Outside the Cities Requires the Allocation of Funds," Farvardin 13, 1397/April 2, 2018: https://perma.cc/675J-NFBY, accessed March 15, 2019.

[38] Mizan News Agency, "The Most Important Problem for Us in the Prisons Organization is the Lack of Budget and Equipment," Mordad 18, 1396/August 9, 2017: https://perma.cc/F9V5-8KTU, accessed June 1, 2019.

[39] *Deutsche Welle Farsi*, "The Head of the Prisons Organization: We Do Not Have Enough Money to Feed the Prisoners," December 30, 2017: https://perma.cc/FUU7-M5CR, accessed June 1, 2019.

[40] *Sharq Press*, "With the Decrease in the Budget of the Prisons Organization the Prisoners' Needs for Food Cannot Be Met," Dey 9, 1396/December 30, 2017: https://perma.cc/8E2F-7J5S, accessed June 1, 2019.

[41] Tasnim News Agency, "The Head of the Prisons Organization: We Have 2.5 Times More Than Our Capacity of Prisoners," Ordibehesht 25, 1398/May 15, 2019: https://perma.cc/QVS9-EFH7, accessed June 1, 2019.

[42] *Iran Sputnik*, "Iranian Prisons are Holding 28 Percent More Prisoners than their Capacity," April 30, 2019: https://perma.cc/N8T4-5G7D, accessed June 1, 2019.

the system had held three and a half times its capacity.[43] By December 2019, on the brink of a new crisis – caused by COVID-19 – the number of prisoners had shot back up to 210,000.[44] The protests triggered after the death of Mahsa Jina Amini in October 2022 led to another spike in incarceration, with up to 30 000 people arrested since then – some of whom have been pardoned since (see Section 4 in this chapter and Chapter 2 of this volume).

3 Prison Conditions

In the past our knowledge of prison conditions in Iran stemmed mainly from prison memoirs. More recently, we have come to know much more about contemporary prison conditions because of the extent to which human rights groups such as Amnesty International or Human Rights Watch, and international NGOs and research think tanks have collected witness statements, and images of and statistics about Iran's prisons. Until early 2009, the human reality of the situation of ordinary prisoners was occasionally attested in reports by political prisoners housed in the same wards, often by way of punishment. Many more emerged from prisons around the country following the disputed June 2009 presidential election and the widespread arrests of political activists which followed.[45] A number of recent protests by prisoners over poor conditions also highlight this problem.[46] These speak of prisoners having to sleep on the floor, in corridors, and in courtyards, appalling sanitary facilities, inadequate food, medical neglect, high levels of violence outside the control of, and sometimes with the complicity of guards, sexual abuse, and so on.

Appalling conditions arising from the failure of building new space for prisoners have been exacerbated by inadequate funding for their day-to-day care. The pattern has been evident for years though shortfalls become all the more acute when occupancy figures rise and budgetary

---

[43] See note 39.
[44] IRNA, "Deputy of the Prisons Organization: Increase in the Prison Population is Worrying," Azar 25, 1398/December 16, 2019: https://perma.cc/BET5-3KP7, accessed June 20, 2019.
[45] There have been similar reports for, among others, prisons in Tabriz, Rasht, Qazvin, Boukan, Urumieh, and Saveh. See, for example, Mahjoub (2011).
[46] On recent protests by prisoners over appalling conditions see: *Radio Farda*, "Guards Attack Female Prisoners in Bid to Suppress Protests," February 9, 2019: https://perma.cc/Y4SD-MBSFand, accessed August 22, 2020. Centre for Human Rights in Iran, "Political Prisoner Stabbed to Death in Tehran Penitentiary Three Months After Protesting Unsafe Conditions," June 11, 2019: https://perma.cc/HQY7-P2P9, accessed May 3, 2021.

allocations are squeezed. For example, according to the SDRP (2007), and based on official sources:

> While the Majles set a figure of 85,000 rials per capita for the maintenance of prisoners and the Planning Organisation allocated 60,000 rials, the budget has been reduced to the point that only 25,000 rials are now spent on a prisoner per day. In Khuzestan the budget allocation to prisons in 1386/2007 decreased by 11 per cent ... in some provinces the amount spent on food halved in 2007. For example, in Ilam the budget for food was reduced from 730 million to 400 million tomans, that in Gilan also declined in 1386/2007 compared to 1385/2006 and in some provinces it has halved.[47]

The rapid rise in prisoner numbers over the period 2010–2012 produced an especially harrowing situation, reflected in the statements of the NPO head Esmaili and prison governors around the country over the course of 2011. According to Esmaili, by the NPO's calculation, the daily allocation for food per capita should have been a minimum of 2,400 tomans in 2010–2011 (1389), but in practice, "depending on contributions from provincial budgets" only 577–850 tomans were available (Nikzad 1390/2011). Esmaili also told the press that in the first two months of 1390 (April/May 2011) the NPO budget had not been paid at all, forcing it to take huge sums in credit from the bazaar simply to feed its inmates.[48] Additionally, in early 2011, the Ministry of Health said that it had not been provided with the necessary resources to guarantee health standards and control infectious diseases in prisons.[49]

In a parliamentary debate on the administration's annual budget in April 2011 Younes Mousavi, a member of the Majles Judicial Affairs Committee, admitted that "the annual budget of the Prisons Organization does not even cover the cost of food and clothing," adding: "The prisons are facing so many difficulties that every two prisoners have to share a blanket." Mousavi explained that the removal of government subsidies on energy (from 2010) meant utility bills had surged, so that the annual prison budget was only just enough to cover prisons' water, electricity, and gas needs. He proposed reducing water and electricity

---

[47] SDRP Annual Report, 2007–2008 (1386): www.dprs.ir/ShowNews.php?4468, accessed May 1, 2020.

[48] *Khabar Online*, "The Prisons Have No Space, the Prisons Organization Has No Money," Mehr 30, 1390/October 22, 2011: http://khabaronline.ir/(X(1)S(ykol5lglkv3))/detail/179661/society/84, accessed July 22, 2020.

[49] *Bultan News*, "Ministry of Health Warning on the Consequences of Overcrowding in the Prisons," Farvardin 29, 1390/April 18, 2011: https://perma.cc/ALP5-SWZQ/, accessed May 2, 2019. See also on the impact of overcrowding: "A Prison Population Awaiting a Reduction in the Number of 'Crimes'," *Jam-e Jam*, Mordad 2, 1391/July 23, 2012: www.magiran.com/npview.asp?ID/2546699, accessed August 15, 2018.

tariffs for prisons, but parliament did not agree.[50] A month later another member of the Judicial Affairs Committee, Ezatollah Yousefian, said in a report on the welfare of prisoners published by *Sharq* newspaper that, overall, the country's prisons held four times their capacity while a few held eight times; he advocated an immediate increase in financial allocations. A third committee member added that some prisons were uninhabitable and unhygienic, allowing infectious diseases to flourish. Certain other Majles deputies disagreed, claiming sardonically that Iran's prisons were like "hotels."[51] Nonetheless, leading officials did acknowledge the crisis. For example, the deputy head of the judiciary admitted in October 2011 that overall the system accommodated three times its capacity, a situation which transformed places supposedly devoted to reform into "universities of crime."[52] And no less a figure than Mostafa Pourmohammadi, a regime gatekeeper who at the time was head of the National Inspectorate, accepted that prisons were vastly overcrowded and admitted that the government had neglected to build new prisons.[53] Whether concessions were later made to the prisons budget is unknown because discussion of the subject was suppressed and the immediate problem was defused by large-scale releases (see Section 4).

By 2017, Asghar Jahangir, the head of the NPO, announced in November that he was faced with a 50 percent deficit in his budget and difficulties across the board – with food, health, and prison personnel.[54] Soon afterwards he announced that the prison budget had been reduced by 13 percent for the coming year: "Yet we don't have the means (given the rate of inflation) to provide prisoners in our care with three meals a

---

[50] *Radio Zamaneh*, "Iranian MP Criticizes Prison Conditions," April 30, 2011: https://web.archive.org/web/20160503125910/http://archive.radiozamaneh.com/english/content/iranian-mp-criticizes-prison-conditions, accessed October 2, 2019. See also *Deutsche Welle Farsi*, "The Number of Prisoners in Iran has Increased Twenty-Five-Fold over the Past Three Decades," September 6, 2011: https://perma.cc/VN9X-TA8Y, accessed October 2, 2019.

[51] *Saham News*, "A Majles Deputy: Iranian Prisons are Eight Times over their Capacity," Tir 7, 1390/June 29, 2011: https://web.archive.org/web/20141004233212/http://sahamnews.org/1390/04/54831/, accessed August 15, 2019. Also see *Roozonline*, "31,000 Prisoners in a Prison for 3000," November 8, 2011: https://web.archive.org/web/20111113185427/ www.roozonline.com/persian/news/newsitem/archive/2011/november/08/article/13-3-1.html, accessed December 3, 2015.

[52] *Balatarin*, "The Number of Prisoners in Iran is Three Times the Capacity of the Prisons," no date: https://perma.cc/DVG8-JAF8, accessed December 3, 2015.

[53] *Shargh*, "Pourmohammadi: We Have Three Times More Prisoners than Our Prison Capacity," Aban 1, 1390/October 23, 2011:https://web.archive.org/web/20111026113454/sharghnewspaper.ir/News/90/08/01/14845.html, accessed December 5, 2015.

[54] Islamic Sciences and Culture Academy (ISCA), "Some of the Prison Buildings are Worn Out," Azar 8, 1396/November 29, 2017: https://perma.cc/H24V-CMKK, accessed December 15, 2018.

The Problem of Overcrowded Prisons 201

day or the protein they need, and we owe 80 billion tomans for water, gas and electricity."[55] In May 2019 Jahangir still despaired, lamenting that the prison administration had requested an increase of the daily food ration from 5,000 to 11,500 tomans per capita but was allowed only 7,300 tomans which he said was too little.[56]

Earlier in 2017, faced with criticism of the medical treatment available to inmates, Jahangir had commented that the NPO owed nearly 17 billion tomans to hospitals across the country.[57] It was reported in 2015 that the monthly allocation per prisoner for healthcare was 600 tomans. By way of context, in rural areas the allocation for healthcare was 96,000 tomans per capita and a (badly paid) prison doctor earned 1,300,000 tomans per month.[58] According to another 2015 report, following a February visit to the hugely overcrowded Qezel Hesar Prison in Karaj, the Minister of Health described its condition as deplorable: "the per capita standard for personnel, food, health and many other things is extremely low and this applies not just to this prison but to all prisons in the country." He added that "wards housing 700 to 800 prisoners, whether in this or other prisons, were environments susceptible to the spread of infectious and contagious diseases and something had to be done."[59]

4 Amnesties and Pardons

Stagnating prison capacity and significant shortfalls in the prisons budget, coupled with the rising number of prisoners over the past two decades, have forced the Iranian judiciary to look for remedies. Amnesties granted by the Supreme Leader on religious holidays, conditional releases, and the like have long been a feature of the Islamic Republic's criminal justice system. But such amnesties have historically been in the hundreds and even when high, over a single year did not add up to more than 1,000–2,000.

In 2012, however, the judiciary dealt with the crisis of prison numbers by quietly, without public record, releasing 25,000 prisoners over the year, according to a leak from a highly placed prison official reported by

---

[55] Fars News Agency, Azar 9, 1396/December 30, 2017: www.farsnews.com/news/13961009000580/, accessed March 22, 2018.
[56] See note 28.
[57] Student News Network (SNN), "The Latest Stage of Preparation for Drug Convict Camps," Farvardin 13, 1397/April 2, 2017: https://perma.cc/JLQ3-VU5N, accessed March 8, 2018.
[58] *Deutsche Welle Farsi*, "The Pitiful State of Iranian Prisons in the Words of the Minister of Health," March 2, 2015: https://perma.cc/ZL4D-CFDL, accessed March 8, 2018.
[59] Ibid.

the reformist newspaper *Kalameh*.[60] The release is reflected in the figures for the prison population for 2013 compared to October 2011, which show a sudden fall from circa 250,000 to circa 226,000. In 2016/2017, with the prison population again rising there was another significant release, of 39,791 amnestied prisoners – equivalent to roughly 18 percent of the prison population at the time. Meanwhile, 15,757 inmates left the jails on conditional release.[61]

As we have seen, in February 2019, to mark the 40th anniversary of the revolution, there was a very large amnesty of prisoners. According to the head of the NPO, by May the amnesty had been applied to about 100,000 prisoners who were either pardoned or had their sentences reduced, and another 70,000 convicted in the courts whose sentences were converted to a fine before they entered prison.[62] In March 2023, Head of the Judiciary Mohseni-Eje'i announced that the authorities had pardoned 22,000 of the 30,000 protestors arrested after the death of Mahsa Jina Amini (see more on this in Chapter 3 of this volume).

4.1 Prison Leave

In the period to 2010, a major, though rarely acknowledged, method of managing prison capacity was the generous use of prison leave. There are no systematic figures, but in 2005–2006, according to NPO head Ali Akbar Yesaqi, some 400,000 people were granted prison leave.[63] Another glimpse at just how extensively prison leave was used in the mid-to-late 2000s comes from remarks made in June 2008 by the deputy of the Tehran Prosecutor's Office for Prison Affairs, who said that Evin Prison, with an official capacity of around 1,000, had around 5,300 inmates of whom some 3,000 (56 percent) were on leave at any one time.[64]

The policy was questioned in some quarters, especially by the police, but Yesaqi explained that it was promoted by Ayatollah Shahroudi, the head of the judiciary, who favored the extensive use of leave because, he argued, in Islam prison should only be used in five or six cases (of the

---

[60] See note 23.
[61] *Iran Front Page*, "40,000 Inmates in Iran Granted Amnesty in One Year," June 21, 2017: https://perma.cc/74WN-2HYU, accessed March 5, 2019.
[62] See note 39.
[63] ISNA, "An In-depth ISNA Interview with the Head of the Prisons Organization," Mehr 14, 1385/October 6, 2006: https://perma.cc/HR22-Y7K4, accessed October 6, 2019. The expansion of leave was possibly based on new Executive Regulations of the Prisons Organization introduced on Azar 20, 1384/December 11, 2005.
[64] Quoted in *Mardomak*, "Evin Prison Will Become a Detention Centre," Tir 10, 1387/ June 30, 2008: https://web.archive.org/web/20080828003026/ www.mardomak.org/news/evin_temporary_prison, accessed February 23, 2018.

The Problem of Overcrowded Prisons

most serious crimes) and the extensive use of prison sentences was not right in principle and in some cases was inconsistent with the shariʿa. Yesaqi also dismissed claims that the public was put at risk by the release of criminals because only around 1 percent committed a crime while on temporary release. The benefits of leave far outweighed the drawbacks. Furthermore, he explained that since the country's laws did not allow a rapid reduction of the prison population, authorities were compelled to use other remedies to protect the integrity of the family.[65]

In May 2010 the new judiciary head, the arch-conservative Sadegh Amoli Larijani, brought this relatively "indulgent" policy to a sudden halt on the grounds that it undermined the punitive intent of a prison sentence. Larijani's new regulations redefined leave as a privilege to be earned through a points system, not a right. Prisoners were to become eligible for leave by accumulating at least 200 points for good behavior, assisting with maintaining order, regular attendance at prayers, and so on.[66]

The NPO head at the time, Gholam-Hossein Esmaili counted this change, along with the amended narcotics law, as a major factor in the 2011 crisis of the prison system.[67] Clearly it did not in itself lead to the dizzying rise in the prison population in the course of 2011, but it removed an important safety valve at the disposal of prison administrators. It would soon be modified, though not reversed, in an amendment issued on June 27, 2012, which reduced the number of points a prisoner was obliged to accumulate to earn their leave to 100 and increased the length of leave from 3–5 to 5–10 days.[68] There have been no detailed figures for prison leave since then. Indications are that it has increased but has been by no means as liberal as the policy under Ayatollah Shahroudi.

In light of the coronavirus crisis, in February and May 2020, the Iranian authorities announced that they had pardoned 10,000 prisoners and temporarily released another 128,000 on furlough. According to Amnesty International, however, hundreds of prisoners of conscience

---

[65] ISNA, "An Interview with the Head of the Prisons Organization," Azar 13, 1385/December 4, 2006: www.magiran.com/npview.asp?ID/1301830, accessed May 15, 2018; ISNA, Azar 17, 1385/December 8, 2006: https://perma.cc/GW23-ZARJ, accessed May 15, 2018.

[66] *Iran Human Rights Documentation Center* (IHRDC), "Rights Disregarded: Prisons in the Islamic Republic of Iran," March 18, 2015, Para 3.2.4: https://perma.cc/4H6X-TPTP, accessed May 15, 2018.

[67] See note 46.

[68] Tabnak News Agency, "What Are the Terms and Conditions for Granting Prison Leave?," Esfand 1, 1395/February 19, 2017: https://perma.cc/WDN9-7RHB, accessed March 7, 2019. The amendment was later confirmed in Article 15 of the Head of the Judiciary's Administrative Order of June 23, 2013. See Tasnim News Agency, "The Protocols for Reducing the Prison Population Have Been Issued," Tir 2, 1392/June 23, 2013: https://perma.cc/J5VA-P3H9, accessed May 15, 2018.

were excluded from these measures, including human rights activists, environmentalists, foreign and dual nationals, people held arbitrarily since the November 2019 protests, and people held due to their religious beliefs.[69]

4.2   Alternative Sentences

The use of alternatives to incarceration has been a policy of the judiciary since the mid-2000s, enshrined in the Penal Code in 2013. But many years on, it very largely remains an aspiration stymied by lack of funds and perhaps real commitment by judges and the judicial/prison bureaucracy.

One alternative sentence – corporal punishment, a feature of the post-1979 Penal Codes – should be remarked on from the outset. Whipping is a mandatory punishment, alongside fines and imprisonment, for drug offenders and for certain *hadd* crimes. And it is an alternative sentence, to be used at the judge's discretion, in several other *taʿzir* offences. Throughout his tenure as head of the judiciary (1999–2009), Ayatollah Shahroudi promoted whipping as a divinely sanctioned penalty by which use of the non-Islamic institution of prison, with its negative consequences for society, might be reduced.[70] Nevertheless, Shahroudi did not seek to expand the use of the whip, perhaps because it did not have especially strong support from legal professionals, academics, and students, as reflected in a 2008 study by the lawyer Ghassem Ghassemi (2009: 159–180).[71] The study, based on a survey of 850 members of a range of professional groups from four different Iranian cities, found that the statement "whipping is more humane than imprisonment" was positively endorsed by only 12 percent of lawyers, 20 percent of academics, 22 percent of university students, 23 percent of religious students, and 27 percent of other professions, albeit (the highest count) 33 percent of

---

[69] Amnesty International, "Iran: Leaked Letters Reveal Coronavirus Prisons Crisis Despite 'No Deaths' Claim," Press Release, July 31, 2020: https://perma.cc/8UX5-7DG9, accessed June 18, 2021.

[70] For example, in his 2002 circular (Article 16), Shahroudi insisted that in implementing the recommended protocols judges should not convert a lashing sentence to fines or imprisonment. For examples of his later public interventions on the subject see ISNA, "Hashemi Shahroudi in the Majles: We Will Bring the Rich Tradition of Islamic Jurisprudence into Modern Criminal Procedure, the Benefits of Flogging Outweigh Imprisonment," Aban 10, 1384/November 1, 2005: https://perma.cc/YX2C-5LRZ. Also see *ADN Kroos International*, "Iran: Flogging an Effective Deterrent, Says Senior Official," June 26, 2008: www.corpun.com/irj00806.htm, accessed June 30, 2019.

[71] In Ghassemi's study, 850 questionnaires were completed overall, 740 on the subject of lashes. But see also, on the reasons why Shahroudi, despite his huge influence, did not seek to press his shariʿa-based ideals on prison: Abdi 1397/2019.

police officers. Unexpectedly perhaps, only 20 percent of the 174 judges who completed Ghassemi's questionnaire supported the statement (as opposed to 25 percent who totally disagreed and 37 percent who held an "ambivalent" opinion).

Ghassemi also found that in 2008 prisons enjoyed little legitimacy among Iranian professionals who viewed them as "academies of crime" and supported alternative sentencing such as community service. But although long discussed it was not until 2013 that a systematic legal framework for various alternatives to incarceration was enacted in the revised Book I of the Penal Code (see Chapter 2 by Silvia Tellenbach in this volume).[72] The substitutions include fines, the innovative notion of "daily fines" calculated as a proportion of an offender's earnings, "postponement of the deliverance of judgment," community service, a period of supervision (probation), and deprivation of social rights. With the exception of "security" crimes, and subject to the consent of a private complainant, the law made substitution mandatory for all intentional offences where the maximum sentence is under ninety-one days, and from ninety-one days to six months for offenders without a criminal record in the past five years. In unintentional crimes, substitution became mandatory for all sentences under two years (see Section 6). In practice, the need for the consent of a private complainant undermined the intention of the law and this condition was removed by a ruling of the Supreme Court in July 2016.[73]

The policy of alternative sentencing required a viable administrative and probationary infrastructure, which in turn require an appropriate budget. By January 2019 these remained an ideal – as the head of the NPO remarked, the funds had never been forthcoming.[74] Electronic tagging, floated as a solution to overcrowding at least since 2012, only became a practical option in 2019. Even so, by early 2020 only some eight hundred prisoners had been monitored electronically.[75] Moreover,

---

[72] Articles 64–87. For English translation of the law see IHRDC: https://iranhrdc.org/english-translation-of-books-i-ii-of-the-new-islamic-penal-code/. According to Ghassemi (2009: 165), a draft law on the subject, which had been handed to the Majles in August 2005, was shelved.

[73] *Hamshahri*, "Cancellation of Prison Sentences of Less Than Three Months," Tir 26, 1395/July 16, 2016: www.hamshahrionline.ir/news/340110/. For an instructive background, see *Vekalat Online*, July 21, 2016: http://r-akbari.com/index.php/component/k2/item/45, accessed June 8, 2020.

[74] See note 75.

[75] Iranian Labor News Agency (ILNA), "We Reduced Mehrieh Prisoners By 68%," Khordad 24, 1399/June 13, 2020: https://perma.cc/9F4A-MK48, accessed April 2, 2021.

206 *Anna Enayat and Hadi Enayat*

because those who were tagged had to pay a significant rent to the judiciary for the device, the scheme was criticized both on the grounds of social justice and its practicality as a solution to the overcrowding of prisons whose inmates are overwhelmingly poor.[76]

In the absence of data, it is impossible to assess the impact of the 2013 provisions. But one study of 200 court rulings issued over a three-year period between March 2014 and March 2017 concluded that in order to conform with the 2013 law, the great majority of judges used the "traditional" substitute of a fine and, where appropriate, suspended sentences (Gholami and Khaksar 2019).

4.3 Zendān-zodāyi *(Decarceration): Further Attempts to Reduce the Prison Population*

In 2002 Shahroudi issued an administrative circular (*bakhshnāmeh*) enjoining judges to make generous use of provisions in existing law to help reduce the prison population.[77] This was the first systematic intervention of a policy which became known by the neologism "*zendān-zodāyi*," literally "removing prison" or "decarceration." The circular urged judges to minimize Pre-Trial Detention (PTD) through the maximum use of legal provisions for surety in the 1999 Code of Criminal Procedure (CCP) and enjoined them to use alternative sentences to prison wherever the law allowed. It also set protocols designed to limit the detention of those imprisoned for their inability to pay fines, and rules by which those imprisoned for a debt might be granted temporary release to resolve their affairs.

In 2013 and 2016 Shahroudi's successor as head of the judiciary, Amoli Larijani, issued circulars along much the same lines. But these later circulars additionally reminded judges to observe the provisions of three major reforms in substantive law which, although not part of the judiciary's explicit "*zendān-zodāyi*" agenda, were of greater import in

---

[76] Tabnak News Agency, "Electronic Tagging Scheme for Prisoners Launched," Tir 29, 1398/July 20, 2019: https://perma.cc/TK9M-YMMU, accessed April 3, 2021; Tabnak News Agency, "What are the Conditions for Prisoners Using Electronic Tags?," Bahman 25, 1398/February 14, 2020: https://perma.cc/6CVR-9WF9, accessed April 3, 2021.

[77] Islamic Parliament Research Centre of the Islamic Republic of Iran, "Protocol concerning Penalties for Narcotics, Checks and Debt Offences," Mehr 15, 1381/October 7, 2002: https://perma.cc/FYS2-EQ2S, accessed March 4, 2008; "The Head of the Judiciary Has Issued Protocols," *Shargh*, Tir 2, 1392/June 23, 2013: www.magiran.com/article/2759067, accessed May 15, 2018. "Prospect of 15 Per Cent Reduction of Prisoners with New Circular," *Javan*, Shahrivar 27, 1395/September 17, 2016: https://perma.cc/VZ6Q-K7YN, accessed May 15, 2018.

The Problem of Overcrowded Prisons 207

the tortuous effort to contain the rise of the prison population. These laws were the third-party insurance law of 2008, the 2010 law concerning drug addicts, and provisions introduced in 2015 to expedite bankruptcy proceedings in the case of debt prisoners. We will turn to these issues in Sections 6.1 and 7. In this section we will deal briefly with two key aspects of the head of the judiciary's circulars.

Before proceeding, it is worth noting that as prison numbers have increased in the period since 2013, there have been repeated calls from the press and parliament for a more diligent application of these circulars. The fact is, however, that the circulars do not have the force of law and thus do not override the duty of judges to apply written law. Thus, the circulars do not remove the discretion the law gives to judges (as well as prosecutors and examining magistrates) where PTD and sentencing are concerned.

5 Pretrial Detention

A principle aim of Shahroudi's 2002 circular was to reduce the numbers held in PTD, which had historically been high – reportedly as high as 70 percent of all prisoners at various times in the 1980s and early 1990s (Abdi 1377/1998–1999). The figure declined significantly following the implementation of the 1999 CCP and the gradual restoration of the prosecutorial office after 2002.[78] In 2006 it stood around 40 percent,[79] and by March 2011, according to the NPO, it had dropped to circa 32 percent,[80] still a comparatively high figure internationally. In December 2012 the NPO figure reported to the WPB was 25.7 percent,[81] a significant reduction over a mere eighteen months, resulting in a middle ranking on the international scale. Three years later, when the NPO's own annual reports resumed, the PTD figure was put at 25 percent.[82]

---

[78] Following amendments to the Law on Formation of General and Revolutionary Courts, November 3, 2002. The position of the independent prosecutor was abolished in 1994 when the functions of prosecutor and trial judge were combined in a single person.

[79] According to the Society for Defense of the Rights of Prisoners, quoting the *E'temād* newspaper, Esfand 14, 1396/March 5, 2018. See also Radio Farda, "Report of the Association for the Defense of Prisoners Rights," Khordad 13, 1385/June 10, 2006: https://perma.cc/53NW-NNAH, accessed August 12, 2018.

[80] According to the head of the NPO. Nikzad 1390/2011.

[81] According to WPB, quoted in IHRDC, "Rights Disregarded"; see note 64.

[82] *Shiraze*, "The Head of the Prisons Organization: 25 Per Cent of the Country's Prisoners are in Pretrial Detention," Dey 14, 1393/January 4, 2015: https://perma.cc/QKC2-U2KQ, accessed May 16, 2018.

Subsequent reports showed a decline to 23 percent in January 2017,[83] and to 20 percent in January 2019.[84]

The 1999 CCP specified mandatory PTD for a number of capital and serious noncapital crimes, in circumstances where the freedom of the accused would cause "corruption" (undefined) or where there was a risk of flight, of interference with the evidence, or a threat to public safety. Otherwise, bail could be set at the prosecutor's discretion. Those detained under a temporary order could be held until a trial was completed, but in no case for longer than the minimum sentence for the offence in question (Article 35).[85] There were, however, no other constraints on the permissible length of PTD, allowing virtually unlimited renewals of a temporary detention order.[86] A new CCP, in the making since 2003/2004, and designed to correct this, and other flaws in the 1999 law, was eventually enacted in June 2015. Detention for serious crimes became a matter for the judge's discretion to be exercised if the liberty of the accused involved the risks outlined (although the vague term "corruption" was now excluded). More importantly, it introduced new limits on the permissible length of PTD, adding that, in addition to the minimum sentence for the offence in question, detention for noncapital crimes may not exceed one year and for capital crimes two years.[87]

The remarks of the NPO head, Gholam-Hossein Esmaili, accompanying his announcement of the 2011 figures for PTD at a national convention of prosecutors, illustrate some of the problems of PTD repeatedly raised by commentators.[88] First, he urged prosecutors (often accused of treating all those who came before them as criminals), to remember that many of those held with a temporary arrest warrant prove

---

[83] IRNA, "Forty-Three Percent of the Country's Prisoners are Drug Offenders," Dey 30, 1395/January 19, 2017: https://perma.cc/AK5H-ELA3, accessed May 16, 2018.

[84] *Asr-e Iran*, "What is the Number of Prisoners in Iran?," Dey 18, 1397/January 8, 2019: https://perma.cc/UE5P-A9SY, accessed September 2, 2020.

[85] For an excellent, detailed review see Amnesty International, "Flawed Reforms: Iran's New Code of Criminal Procedure," February 11, 2016: https://perma.cc/THE9-Q9WS, accessed June 6, 2018.

[86] Article 128 of the 1999 CCP also allowed prosecutors/judges to deny detainees access to a lawyer, a provision that has, notoriously, enabled the use of torture by "investigating" organizations. Widely held by civil rights organizations to have been inadequate – there are numerous examples of violations in political, and to an extent ordinary law cases in this period – the 1999 CCP was nonetheless replaced the wholly opaque position in the 1980s and 1990s when judges were able to reject any law dating from the Pahlavi period as "unIslamic."

[87] See note 76.

[88] ISNA, "Head of the Prisons Organization: We Have 220 000 Prisoners throughout the Country, a Person Who Has Been Fined 100 000 Tomans Has Been Imprisoned for 11 Months!," Esfand 1389/March 2, 2011: https://perma.cc/BF77-YJVV, accessed April 8, 2016.

to be innocent. He claimed that over the past year (2011), some 30,000 had been released before charge, and another 35,000 before the matter was sent to court. He went on to say that prison managers continued to encounter inmates who had been on remand for a period longer than the maximum sentence set for their offence. Indeed, he himself had collected fifty or sixty examples in the course of a single inspection. There was also, he argued, a need for better management of cases where the prescribed punishment is a fine or lashes, citing the example of a woman who had been arrested for an immoral relationship and spent 103 days on remand, only to receive a sentence of 30 lashes, and that of a prisoner held for 11 months who was eventually fined the maximum 100,000 tomans. Finally, as many as a quarter of the 400 prisoners held in a small prison claimed that they had arranged bail, but the Prosecutor's Office had not accepted it.

There is no comparable account of PTD from a figure in authority following the introduction of the 2015 CCP. The NPO's statistics indicate a notable decline overall, probably the result of measures to facilitate the swift arrangement of bail (which most often takes the form of property documents), such as the permanent presence of an official from the property registry in prosecutors' offices. But whilst procedures have been improved, there has been at least one report that the provisions of the 2015 CCP concerning the limits of detention are not universally observed. In a May 2019 open letter to the head of the judiciary on the subject of their prolonged PTD, prisoners in Zahedan (Sistan and Baluchistan province) provided a number of examples of inmates who on average had spent three years in PTD, a few of them as many as six years. The authors attribute the delays faced by these detainees to administrative incompetence – frequent changes in the judges responsible for the case, unexplained adjournments, and the large number of cases a single judge must manage (one of them admitted that he had 500 per year).[89]

While the 1999 CCP had its inadequacies, domestic commentaries, largely from lawyers and prison managers, leave little doubt that where ordinary (as opposed to political) prisoners were concerned, defective legal or procedural provisions have not been the root cause of the overuse of PTD. First, as in many other countries, detention is the default option of many examining magistrates and prosecutors. But this seems

---

[89] Human Rights Activists News Agency (HRANA), "Letter from the Prisoners of Zahedan Prison to the Head of the Judiciary: We Have Been in Pretrial Detention for Years," Ordibehesht 22, 1398/May 13, 2019: https://perma.cc/X8Y9-TGPH, accessed June 22, 2021.

to be exacerbated in Iran by a tendency among judicial officials to perceive those who come before them as proven criminals. An Iranian lawyer who defended some of the political prisoners rounded up after the 2009 protests highlighted some of the problems:

> Unfortunately, my personal experience as a trial attorney in Iran has shown that judicial and administrative officials in the Islamic Republic treat the accused as a criminal from the outset. The conditions of detention and interrogation, the tone of voice used by interrogators in questioning, the behaviour of the administrative officers of the detention centres and prosecutor's offices in respect to the accused – these all reflect this wrong and illegal viewpoint ... (Daraeizadeh 2010: 8).

The same issue continues to be raised by lawyers commenting on the subject of temporary arrest who point out that another default strategy used by some prosecutors is to demand very large, and by any measure, disproportionate sums as bail, which the accused party cannot hope to meet.[90] At times, according to one retired lawyer, the refusal to accept a surety boils down to little more than the magistrate's personal interaction with the accused.[91]

Second, the poverty of a large proportion of the prison population means that many of those brought before prosecutors do not have the means to post bail. According to the NPO head, in 2017 poor people made up the lion's share of the remand population.

Third, a major cause of the overuse of PTD is the huge and, since the mid-2000s, rapidly increasing volume of case files (civil and criminal) that have to be processed: 9 million in 2008,[92] and by 2018 "more than" 15 million.[93] Assuming that, at the very least, two people were involved in each case, the 2008 figure meant that one in every eight Iranians was involved in court proceedings.[94] That has meant prosecutors and judges

---

[90] *Borna*, "Attitudes to Crime Have Led to the Proliferation of Pretrial Detention," Mehr 1398/October 16, 2019: https://perma.cc/Q2Z5-4SDB, accessed June 5, 2021.

[91] *Iran*, "Explosion of the Prison Population," Azar 28, 1396/December 19, 2017: www.magiran.com/article/3678303, accessed July 23, 2019.

[92] *Asr-e Iran*, "Alizadeh: One in Eight Prisoners Has a Judicial File, Aban 26, 1387/November 16, 2008: https://perma.cc/6Z5G-ETUK, accessed March 15, 2016.

[93] *Alef*, "An Answer to the Question of the Head of the Judiciary," Ordibehesht 19, 1398/May 9, 2019: https://perma.cc/3LZV-S7QV, accessed June 18, 2020.

[94] See note 83; also *BBC Persian*, "One in Eight Iranians Have a Judicial File," November 25, 2008: https://perma.cc/RVB6-C76K, accessed December 28, 2019. The situation was noted by the International Bar Association in their report on their October 2007 fact-finding mission: Para 4.1 "The delegation heard that a key problem with the Iranian legal system is that every type of dispute has to be resolved in court and as a result, the courts are over-run with cases. At present, the courts are obliged to adjudicate on many different types of subject matter of cases, such as demonstrations at universities, violence towards women, journalists criticising the government and so on. One lawyer told the delegation that three out of every ten people in the Iranian population currently have a proceeding in court. This is an astounding figure and gives

The Problem of Overcrowded Prisons 211

must deal with a very large number of cases on a daily basis, resulting in temporary detention being used as the simplest and safest decision.[95] In 2016 a Majles deputy said that judges were obliged to deal with 100 to 120 files each month by contrast to 30–40 in 'advanced countries'.[96] By 2018, according to an official of the judiciary, the figure had risen to 200.[97]

6 Unintentional Prisoners (*Zendānian-e Gheir-e 'Amd*)

Another cause of overcrowding in prisons is a category of the prison population which figures regularly in public discourse on the reduction of prison numbers. These are so-called "unintentional prisoners" (*zendānian-e gheir-e 'amd*), people who are incarcerated for noncriminal acts but who have been detained on the demand of a private complainant on the basis of laws passed in the 1990s (considered in more detail later in this chapter). They fall into four subgroups: (1) those who, without intent to defraud, have issued a check to guarantee a future payment which in the event they could not honor, (2) those owing *diyeh* or monetary compensation to someone they have unintentionally injured in a car or workplace accident, (3) men unable to pay the *mehrieh* or bride price to their spouse when she legally demands it, and (4) men who have defaulted on maintenance payments (*nafaqeh*) to their spouse.

Overall, these groups have made up a fluctuating proportion of Iran's prison population– from 4 to 8 percent from the late 2000s to date, but a higher proportion, possibly as much as 12–15 percent, in the first half of the decade according to various statements by the heads of the judiciary and Prisons Organization.[98] The relative salience of each group has

---

some context to why the government may have perceived a critical shortage of lawyers." International Bar Association, "Balancing Independence and Access to Justice: A Background Report on the Justice System in Iran," October 2007: http://Users/seyedenayat/Downloads/10_2007_Oct_Balancing_independence_and_access_to_justice_(Iran_report)%20(3).pdf, accessed July 20, 2020.

[95] IRNA, "Organizing Prisoners and Reducing the Criminal Prison Population," Azar 1396/December 2, 2017: https://perma.cc/K2CZ-MJ7A, accessed November 4, 2019.

[96] Islamic Consultative Assembly News Agency (ICANA), "Judicial Cases in Iran Are Twice the Global Standard," Farvardin 20, 1395/April 8, 2016: https://perma.cc/VL3L-KHVX, accessed May 10, 2018.

[97] IRNA, "Each Judge Reviews 200 Cases a Month," Shahrivar 20, 1397/September 11, 2018: https://perma.cc/8FWN-DBDB, accessed March 1, 2019.

[98] *Mehr News*, "Report on Citizen's Rights Relating to Check and Drug Convicts," Mordad 1384/July 25, 2005: www.mehrnews.com/news/210638/, accessed May 6, 2018; BBC Persian, "Iran's Population Has Doubled since the Revolution, But the Prison Population Has Increased Tenfold," February 25, 2006: https://perma.cc/UZ5E-VUMF, accessed July 15, 2020; *Radio Farda*, "The Payment of *Mehrieh* Has Become Conditional on the Financial Capacity of the Husband," Bahman 16, 1385/February 5, 2007: https://perma.cc/M38Z-PA56, accessed July 15, 2020.

varied over the period with revisions in the law and changing economic circumstances, but check prisoners have always been the largest component, followed by drivers involved in road traffic accidents (RTAs) and men owing *mehrieh*.

Postdated checks have long been a common way of doing business in Iran. Before the 1979 Revolution, if such a check bounced creditors could petition a civil court, and prison was automatic if the creditor was willing to pay the prison costs (Keshavarzian 2007: 87–88). The number of bounced checks proliferated after 1988 (Keshavarzian 2007: 75) and new legislation in 1993 turned this issue into a criminal offence for which prosecution was automatic, with no requirement that there should be proof of bad faith or intent of fraud, and irrespective of the amount involved (Nasiri 1997). The practice nonetheless persisted, and the number of check prisoners increased in part because sentences could not be reduced if a convicted offender was able to settle with their complainant. By 2001, the number of prisoners had reached 17,000, second only to narcotics prisoners.[99] With prisoner numbers still rising, in August 2003 the law was again amended to once more make the issuance of bad checks into a civil rather than criminal matter.[100] The amendment also laid down specific prison terms ranging from six months to two years, depending on the sums involved. As intended, it had the effect of allowing offenders to put up collateral or settle with their complainants, drastically reducing the number of incarcerations.[101] In 2008 there were 6,000 as opposed to more than 17,000 in earlier years, and in 2011 there were 4,350. Numbers began to rise again after 2016. In December 2017 the press reported that over the previous month, 1.5 million checks had bounced, representing 22.5 percent of the total number issued,[102] by contrast to 10.7 percent in 2009 (Mazaheri 2010). In 2018, 12,000 check prisoners (4.8 percent of the total) were reported.[103]

There have been regular calls for a major overhaul of the check and bankruptcy laws, and in 2009 the judiciary submitted a draft of a new check law for consideration by the executive and parliament (Mazaheri

---

[99] IRNA, November 27, 2001, quoted in Keshavarzian (2007: 75).
[100] Amendment to the Check Law, August 24, 2003.
[101] *BBC Persian*, "Iran's Population Has Doubled since the Revolution," see note 96.
[102] *Financial Tribune*, "1.5 Million Checks Bounce in One Month," December 11, 2017: https://perma.cc/EQ5P-QGNQ, accessed April 6, 2020.
[103] IRIB News Agency, "Legal Advisor to the Minister of Justice: We Have 12 000 Homeless Check Prisoners," Tir 27, 1397/July 18, 2018: https://perma.cc/VJY9-DUDE, accessed April 6, 2020.

2010). But it was not until December 2018 that the revised legislation finally reached the statute books.[104] This legislation made banks responsible for ensuring that customers who request a checkbook have adequate credit and for providing a mechanism to allow a potential creditor to verify the existence of the funds before a transaction is sealed. If a check cannot be cashed owing to a shortage of credit in the account, without initiating litigation a court can immediately issue a writ for seizure of the assets of the signatory. Punishments include closure of all the issuer's bank accounts and withdrawal of their right to receive bank loans. Furthermore, under the new framework, the courts are obliged to hear the issuer's bankruptcy petition before proceedings to incarcerate them are contemplated. At the time of writing, the outcome of the 2018 provision is uncertain. While the Central Bank reported a substantial reduction in the number of bounced checks by February 2020, the impact on prison numbers is still unknown.[105]

6.1   Car Accident/Diyeh Prisoners

The imprisonment of people in the next category of unintentional offences – those involved in a car accident – snowballed after August 1998 when a law concerning civil indebtedness entitled Law of the Procedure of Enforcement of Financial Sentences (*Qanūn-e nahvehye ejrā-ye mahkumitahā-ye māli, heretofore referred to as the QEMM*) was introduced suddenly, and without explanation, by the ultraconservative fifth Majles (1996–2000).[106] The measure allowed for the open-ended detention of anyone who owed money on the private petition of their creditor. A similar law had been in effect in Pahlavi Iran but with the important caveat that the creditor was obliged to pay the considerable costs of imprisonment. That law was superseded in May 1973 by the Law Forbidding the Detention of Persons on the Basis of Failure to Meet Financial Obligations, which had been introduced by the Pahlavi administration in order to conform to

---

[104] Tabnak News Agency, "The Solution to the Problem of Bounced Checks," Mordad 14, 1397/August 5, 2018: https://perma.cc/WLS2-CBYH, accessed August 15, 2020; also see *Mehr News*, "Reduction of Check Prisoners Awaits Full Implementation of the Law," Esfand 2, 1398/February 21, 2020: https://perma.cc/FM5H-PCA7, accessed August 15, 2020.

[105] *Mehr News*, "Reduction of Check Prisoners"; see note 102.

[106] For commentary by Iranian lawyers on the impact of this law on prison overcrowding see *BBC Persian*, "Significant Increase in Number of Prisoners after the Revolution," February 27, 2006: https://perma.cc/Q5Z3-EEEX, accessed August 15, 2020; Tabatabai 1398/2019.

Article 11 of the International Covenant on Civil and Political Rights to which Iran acceded in June 1975.[107]

One Iranian commentator on the 1998 law has pointed out that besides putting Iran in violation of its international obligations it "sadly" led to many people being imprisoned as a result of family disputes, particularly over the *mehrieh* (see Section 6.3) (Zamani 2006: 85). But more numerous were drivers caught up in RTAs and unable to pay the *diyeh* (compensation) to injured third parties, or in case of death, their families. Iran, famously, has some of the world's most dangerous roads.[108] According to the chief of police, speaking in 2017, in the two decades since 1998, 459,000 have died as a result of RTAs and more than 4.5 million people have been injured.[109] In the ten years from 1998 to 2008 as many as fifty–sixty drivers per day found themselves in prison, whether or not they were guilty of a traffic offence. In 1999 (1378), around 50,000 reportedly went to prison for shorter or longer spells over the year, and in 2003 some 30,200.[110]

In 1984 the concept of *diyeh*, introduced into state law in 1982, was incorporated into the old 1968 third-party insurance law and applied through a bureaucratized system involving an annual assessment of the value of the life of a Muslim man and a schedule for the *diyeh*/compensation due for injury to the main parts of the body and sense organs. This was awarded by the courts on the basis of a medical-legal report (injury to women and recognized minorities was valued at half these rates). Besides the fact that the insurance law was not adequately enforced, a major problem was that the 1968 framework allowed a minimum legal coverage far below the liabilities that could be faced in a serious accident.[111] Such basic policies were common, not least because car manufacturers often included them in their sales packages. However, while the minimum cover in 2008, for example, was 8 million tomans, the

---

[107] Article 11 of the International Covenant on Civil and Political Rights reads: "No one shall be imprisoned merely on the ground of inability to fulfil a contractual obligation." See https://perma.cc/VRT3-AC2A, accessed May 20, 2021.

[108] For an in-depth analysis of law and driving culture in Iran, see Banakar (2016).

[109] *Radio Farda*, "About Half a Million Road Accidents in Iran in Two Decades," October 5, 2017: https://en.radiofarda.com/a/iran-has-high-road-accident-fatality-rate/28776271.html, accessed October 7, 2019. See also *Radio Farda*, October 6, 2018: https://perma.cc/3WF5-RJM4, accessed May 20, 2021.

[110] *Khabar Online*, "Germany Gives 2 Million Tomans in Compensation, We Give 90 Million," Khordad 6, 1390/May 27, 2011: www.khabaronline.ir/news/153753/, accessed August 25, 2020.

[111] This account is based on, among other similar contemporary sources, Tabnak News Agency, "Advantages of the New Third-Party Insurance Law," Bahman 10, 1387/January 20, 2009: https://perma.cc/ELJ4-2G9E, accessed August 25, 2020.

full *diyeh* of a Muslim male in that year was 40 million tomans and 53 million if the accident occurred in one of the four sacred months of the Islamic calendar (Muharram, Rajab, Dhu al-Qaʿda, or Dhu al-Hijja).[112] Even if a crash resulted in injury rather than death, the *diyeh* often outstripped a driver's insurance cover. When the policy holder did not have the resources to pay the difference, they ended up in prison where they remained until the matter was resolved and the complainant no longer had a case.[113]

The large numbers imprisoned on this account in the late 1990s and early 2000s generated pressure for a revision of the insurance law both in the interests of drivers and accident victims, who sometimes had to endure long waits for much needed compensation and frequently got nothing. The reform, several years in the making, was eventually promulgated on an experimental basis on September 21, 2008.[114] The new provisions raised compulsory cover to the value of a whole *diyeh* in the sacred months, included all passengers in the vehicle, and, in a major reform, equalized the *diyeh* for men and women in specific circumstances, and for Muslims and recognized non-Muslim groups (Jews, Christians, Zoroastrians, but not Bahais).[115] It also established a state fund to automatically underwrite compensation where a driver is underinsured or uninsured, or in the case of a hit-and-run accident (proceedings to recover the debt would follow but by the state rather than aggrieved individuals). There were also radical procedural amendments. Because insurance could not be paid without a judicial order, the old law led to very long court cases. Such delays were completely eliminated by cutting out the courts in all but exceptional cases and requiring insurance companies to pay immediate compensation in the case of death and, in the case of injury, up to 50 percent on account pending the Department of Legal Medicine's report. Any disputes were to be adjudicated by a commission established by the insurance company.

---

[112] Months when the faithful must refrain from fighting: Qu'ran 9:36.
[113] See note 108.
[114] On Shahrivar 20, 1387/September 21, 2008, the Law on Compulsory Insurance of Damages Caused by Third Parties as a Result of Accidents Caused by Vehicles was introduced on an experimental basis for five years, and was confirmed by parliament and the Guardian Council with minor procedural adjustments on October 5, 2016.
[115] Using various loopholes, the insurance companies resisted the equalization of the *diyeh* after the promulgation of the law in 2008. The loopholes were closed in the 2016 law. The equalization of *diyeh* was not extended to circumstances other than accident insurance in the case of homicide (i.e., not extending to murder and bodily harm). For an account, see "In Accidents [*diyeh*] Has Become Equalized One to One," *Shargh*, Aban 27, 1394/November 18, 2015: www.magiran.com/article/3266673, accessed August 16, 2020.

The reform had an immediate impact. In September 2008, when the amendment was introduced, about 56 drivers per day were entering prisons and 9,712 were, on that date, held for motor accidents. By May 2011, the number in prison had declined to 1,100, of whom, according to one source, around 80 percent were uninsured.[116] And there were further reductions after 2016 when the reform, with certain refinements, was incorporated into a new, permanent insurance law.[117] By 2018 only around three hundred prisoners were classified as incarcerated owing to an RTA.[118]

The change was all the more remarkable in that the insurance system appears to have absorbed, through progressively raised premiums and perhaps some government subsidies, a sudden reassessment of the material value of a human life ordered in 2011 by Ayatollah Sadegh Larijani soon after he became head of the judiciary. Larijani believed that the current calculation, which was based on an outdated assessment plus the rate of inflation, was inadequate, and delegated a commission to determine the current rate directly from the market price of 100 camels in various provinces. Consequently, on June 6, 2011, the value of the *diyeh* for a Muslim male in the sacred months was increased from 60 to 90 million tomans, much to the dismay of the Majles and the insurance companies.[119]

6.2 *The* Setād-e Diyeh *(*Diyeh *Taskforce)*

In 1980 the judiciary established a division known as the Setād-e diyeh or "*diyeh* taskforce," which in 2007 was turned into a state-sponsored NGO. The purpose of the taskforce was to facilitate negotiations between the perpetrators and victims of injury and to promote the release of prisoners by raising money from the public, and from government bodies, to help pay off the outstanding debt through a loan or a grant. The organization also engaged social workers to help with negotiations between

---

[116] See note 107.
[117] ILNA, "There Are 950 *Diyeh* Prisoners as a Result of Car Accidents in the Country," Azar 24, 1395/December 14, 2016: https://perma.cc/PWR2-QVE2, accessed March 7, 2021.
[118] Fars News Agency, "The Release of 12 'Non-Intentional' Prisoners in Qom," Mordad 11, 1397/August 1, 2018: www.farsnews.com/news/13970510000539/, accessed August 23, 2020.
[119] *Kharbar Online*, "Contradictory News About the Amount of *Diyeh*," Ordibehesht 28, 1390/May 18, 2011: www.khabaronline.ir/news/151779/, accessed August 18, 2020; *Khabar Online*, "Majles in Shock at the Rate of *Diyeh*," Khordad 2, 1390/May 23, 1390: www.khabaronline.ir/news/152795/, accessed August 20, 2020. Also see Tait (2011).

prisoners and their creditors for scheduling payments or even waiving part of the debt.[120]

Apart from workplace accidents, which do not generate a great many imprisonable claims,[121] the taskforce concerns itself with other categories of unintended offenders – *mehrieh* and bounced-check prisoners whose confinement has nothing to do with the shariʿa law of compensation. Those who are imprisoned for intentional bodily harm offences ranging from murder to injuries inflicted in fights, or even domestic violence, do not enjoy its protection.[122]

In 2018 Seyyed Assadollah Julayi, the head of the taskforce, claimed credit for the amendment to the insurance law which meant that no driver would be held in prison on account of *diyeh*. He claimed that without the amendment more than 200,000 drivers would have been imprisoned, but now only 120 were held.[123]

In 1396 (2017–2018) there were about 18,000 prisoners guilty of unintentional crime. Around 11,000 of them, who owed a total of about 10,000 billion rials, were freed by the intervention of the taskforce. About 40 percent of these 10,000 billion rials represented debts waived by the intervention of social workers and the remainder was made up by charitable donations. Over the same period, the taskforce raised 530 billion rials through charitable events and private donations.[124]

6.3 Mehrieh *Prisoners*

All Iranian marriage contracts stipulate a *mehrieh* or *mahr* – usually translated as "marriage portion" – negotiated before a marriage to safeguard the bride's financial security. Although the *mehrieh* can be symbolic, it is more commonly a sum of money today specified in gold coins (known as *Bāhar-e Azādi*) and legally payable to the woman at her request at any time after the marriage is contracted. From 1998, if the husband refused, his spouse could petition the family court to order his imprisonment.

Traditionally, women rarely demanded the *mehrieh* except when a husband exercised his unfettered right to divorce or took a second wife. The shariʿa-based Civil Code also provided a mechanism allowing a woman

---

[120] IRIB News Agency, Tir 27, 1397/July 18, 2018; see note 115.
[121] In 2016 there were ninety *diyeh* inmates imprisoned due to workplace accidents. See note 115.
[122] There is no information about these in the public domain.
[123] IRNA, "The Release of Indebted Prisoners Requires 10 Thousand Billion Rials," Ordibehesht 25, 1397/May 15, 2018: https://perma.cc/4TUV-SQ3L, accessed May 3, 2020.
[124] IRIB, Tir 27, 1397/July 18, 2018; see note 115.

to divorce her husband by repudiating all or part of her *mehrieh* in return for his consent to divorce (known as a *khul'* divorce). In the years since 1979 a number of factors, including the heightened insecurity women have faced as a result of their unequal status in the family, the consequent inflation of the sums negotiated as *mehrieh*, rising gold prices, and much higher divorce rates have led to an increasing number of *mehrieh* disputes. Very often these arise because the woman demands payment as leverage to force an obdurate husband to agree to her request for a *khul'* divorce.[125]

There are no figures for the early 2000s but between March 2010 and March 2012 (1389 and 1390), around 20,000 men spent some time in prison on account of the *mehrieh*, and as of July 2012 there were 3,500 *mehrieh* prisoners.[126] The *mehrieh* became a subject of public controversy in the second half of the 2000s because of proposals to incorporate reforms of the institution into an ultraconservative Family Protection Bill introduced by the Ahmadinejad administration in 2007, but only passed into law, after numerous revisions, in 2013. It was variously suggested during this period that the state should set a ceiling on the value of the *mehrieh*, that the *mehrieh* should be taxed, or that marriage contracts should be amended to allow the husband to meet his financial obligation "when able" instead of "upon the wife's demand." The proposals met with multiple objections from both women's rights defenders and religious conservatives.[127] In the end, the Majles bowed to public opinion over the taxation proposal which was voted down in 2008. However, Article 22 of the Family Protection Law (FPL), which eventually passed in February 2013, limited the amount of the *mehrieh* that a woman could claim on pain of her spouse's imprisonment to 110 gold coins, with the remainder due only when she could prove the man's ability to pay.[128] Around this time 110 gold coins was about a quarter to a fifth of the average *mehrieh*.[129]

---

[125] IHRDC, "Gender Inequality and Discrimination: The Case of Iranian Women," March 8, 2014: https://perma.cc/N7VS-7UP7, accessed April 6, 2020. See Part 2.1.4.1. on the problems created by the inflation of the sums pledged in the *mehrieh* which often bear no relationship to the groom's ability to pay.

[126] *Farāru*, "Announcing a New Circular to Those Sentenced to *Diyeh* and *Mehrieh*," Mordad 9, 1391/July 30, 2012: https://perma.cc/SR9Q-69ZU, accessed January 4, 2018; Tabnak News Agency, "Most of the *Diyeh* Prisoners Are Young," Shahrivar 25, 1390/September 16, 2011: https://perma.cc/NZ9V-956K, accessed April 8, 2020.

[127] For a detailed account of the controversy over *mehrieh* during this period, see Bøe (2015: 93–106).

[128] Text of the law available at: https://perma.cc/Y3WZ-3PCT, accessed June 20, 2021.

[129] *Bartarinhā*, "How Much is the Average *Mehrieh* of Iranian Women?," Mordad 25, 1393/August 16, 2014: https://perma.cc/F6JM-B3FS, accessed July 2, 2021.

The Problem of Overcrowded Prisons 219

A second significant change in the legal framework came in June 2015 with the introduction of a revised law concerning civil indebtedness (QEMM), which involved a thoroughgoing overhaul of the provisions of the December 1934 bankruptcy law and the September 1988 QEMM.[130] By contrast to 1988, the new law explicitly allows debtors to petition for bankruptcy within thirty days of a court order on behalf of the plaintiff. If the court accepts the petition and declares the defendant's inability to meet the debt, it is empowered to arrange a schedule of instalments appropriate to their circumstances. The defendant would only go to prison if it is shown that they have the means to pay and are willfully refusing, or if they are concealing assets.[131] It remains the position, however, that for any sum in excess of 110 gold coins the wife must still prove her husband's ability to pay, not the other way around.

Together these changes resulted in a reduction of *mehrieh* prisoners to some 2,000 in 2017. But numbers increased again in the course of 2018 – to 3,500 in July,[132] and to 4,500 in February 2019, before falling back again to 2,800 by mid-2019.[133] Behind the spike was a sudden, more than fourfold, rise in the price of gold coins, from 900,000 to 4.5 million tomans, which pushed a number of those making scheduled payments into arrears.[134]

Again, the press was full of proposals to solve the "*mehrieh* issue," including reduction of the maximum *mehrieh* that may be enforced to fourteen gold coins, or payment of *mehrieh* at the gold price current at the time of marriage. At the end of the year there was even a proposal in the Majles, widely and erroneously reported as a new law, to exempt *mehrieh* debtors altogether from arrest and imprisonment.[135] More significant was an administrative order (*bakhshnāmeh*) issued in August 2018 by the head of the judiciary, which required the courts to give precedence to petitions for bankruptcy from *mehrieh* prisoners and hear

---

[130] For the text of the law see: https://perma.cc/YN4H-HAFP, accessed May 5, 2021.
[131] For a clear explanation of how the provisions of the 2015 QEMM apply to *mehrieh* disputes, see *Vasael*, "How to Obtain Mehrieh within the Framework of the Law," Bahman 30, 1398/February 19, 2020: https://perma.cc/2TUJ-M3A5, accessed May 5, 2021.
[132] Ana News Agency, "Jahangiri: Society Needs Free Journalists and Independent Newspapers," Mordad 3, 1397/July 25, 2018: www.ana.ir/news/409325, accessed August 20, 2020.
[133] *Khabar Online*, "The Latest Statistics of *Mehrieh* Convicts," Ordibehesht 26, 1398/May 16, 2019: www.khabaronline.ir/news/1260556/, accessed August 28, 2020.
[134] *Independent Persian*, "With the Increase in Price of Gold Coins the Number of *Mehrieh* Prisoners Has Increased," Khordad 22, 1398/June 2, 2019: https://perma.cc/QV4A-3F6J, accessed August 28, 2020.
[135] IRNA, "The Imprisonment of *Mehrieh* Debtors is Prohibited," Azar 4, 1398/November 25, 2019: https://perma.cc/43V5-WQLQ, accessed August 14, 2020.

their cases as a matter of urgency. A similar order was issued by the new head of the judiciary, Ebrahim Raisi, when he succeeded Larijani on March 7, 2019. However, while previous orders for the reduction of the prison population depended on the voluntary consent of prosecutors and judges, Raisi contended that in many cases judges had not properly applied the provisions of "existing law" to *mehrieh* cases, most obviously the revised 2015 QEMM,[136] and he was backed by the formation of dedicated teams tasked with reducing the number of *mehrieh* prisoners.[137] The drive we are told produced the desired result and by August 2019 the number of *mehrieh* prisoners had declined to less than a thousand. According to the NPO head, all those who were able to prove financial embarrassment were released. The men who remained in prison were lawfully detained because they had the necessary assets but refused to pay their wives what they owed.[138]

The reforms of 2011 and 2015 may have resulted in a significant decline in a small, but persistent component of the prison population. But women's rights advocates have pointed out that these measures have been imposed without any balancing attempt to equalize the position of women in the family. For example, according to the lawyer Hoda Amid: "An examination of the changes in laws concerning debt shows that if, on the surface the concern has been over the number of prisoners and poor prison conditions, in practice they have been aimed at litigation for the *mehrieh* and women have been the losers" (Amid 2014). Another lawyer-activist, Shima Ghusheh, has also pointed out that women who depend on the *mehrieh* for post-divorce income (i.e., those unilaterally divorced by their husbands) have faced difficulty because the schedules for repayment ordered by the courts, for example, a single gold coin every eight months, does not cover even minimum needs, besides taking many years to redeem.[139]

7 Narcotic Prisoners

Narcotics prisoners have comprised by far the largest proportion of the prison population in the IRI. The easy availability and relatively low cost

---

[136] Tabnak News Agency, "The Unfortunate Position of *Mehrieh* Debtors in Times of Corona," Esfand 17, 1398/March 7, 2020: https://perma.cc/PKE7-X9TF; ISNA, "Explanation of the Judiciary Spokesman regarding *Mehrieh* Prisoners," Khordad 1398/May 28, 2019: https://perma.cc/2CHV-YW45, accessed August 4, 2020.

[137] *Sahara News* "Sixty Percent Reduction in *Mehrieh* Prisoners in the Country," Khordad 24, 1399/June 13, 2020: https://perma.cc/GF59-7E8E, accessed August 4, 2020.

[138] *Mehr News*, "The Number of *Mehrieh* Prisoners is Now Under a Thousand," Shahrivar 2, 1398/August 24, 2019: https://perma.cc/RSK6-V7HL, accessed August 4, 2020.

[139] Rouydad 24 News Agency, "A Challenge Called *Mehrieh*," Mehr 27, 1398/October 19, 2019: https://perma.cc/QB7E-XK8G, accessed August 5, 2020.

of drugs have helped fuel addiction among the Iranian population. Ever since the outbreak of civil conflict in Afghanistan in the early 1980s Iran has been a major transit route for a swelling trade in smuggled opiates destined for Turkey, Russia, Europe, and for countries in the Persian Gulf. Over the years, opium and heroin from Afghanistan have become a huge business "with an illegal market estimated [by the United Nations Office on Drugs and Crime (UNODC)] in 2009 to be worth $65 billion annually, higher than the gross domestic product of more than 120 countries and 65 times the value of the market for firearms trafficking."[140] Much of it was transited through Iran: UNODC further noted that "by 2009 [Iran] accounted for 89 per cent of all opium seizures worldwide, and 41 per cent of all heroin seizures."[141] Official and unofficial estimates of the number of drug users varied from 1.2 to 3.7 million in the early 2000s (Calabrese 2007: 6),[142] and from 2.8 to as high as 6 million in 2017 when officials announced that the number of users had doubled since an earlier count in 2011.[143] In 2011 it was pointed out that, even by taking the lower figures, the prevalence of opiate use in the population aged 15–64 was 2.26 percent – the second highest in the world.[144]

In the years immediately after the 1979 Revolution, drug addiction and trafficking were largely viewed through the lens of Khomeini's pronouncements on the issue, which declared drugs as "prohibited" and "smuggling" and "trafficking" as *harām* (Ghiabi 2019: 71–74). Prominent clerics also issued official fatwas condemning the use of opium (*taryāk*) – a deviation from traditional jurisprudence, which had traditionally been ambivalent on the issue, maintaining a quietist position on its use. Indeed, drug use was not only deemed immoral but also counterrevolutionary, a practice that had to be stamped out by the Islamic Republic using full force (Ghiabi 2019: 71). This jihad against narcotics was overseen by Ayatollah Khalkhali, who, alongside his appointment as state prosecutor, was also the first head of the bureau of anti-narcotics. Khalkhali's appointment as the IRI's first anti-drugs czar lasted only a year but it set a precedent whose effects were long-lasting (Ghiabi 2019:

---

[140] UNODC, "UNODC Assists in Establishing Iranian Anti-Money-Laundering Unit," February 9, 2010: https://perma.cc/LXR2-3Y9B, accessed August 5, 2020.
[141] US State Department, International Narcotics Control Strategy Report (INCSR), 2010: https://perma.cc/7VZS-SL8Y, accessed August 5, 2020.
[142] See also Nissaramanesh, Trace, and Roberts (2005).
[143] US State Department, INCSR 2016; *BBC News*, "Iran's Drug Problem: Addicts 'More than Double' in Six Years," June 25, 2017: https://perma.cc/3A9Q-2EKM, accessed August 8, 2020; *Radio Goft-o-Gu*, "The Head of the Anti-Narcotics Taskforce Must Change," Tir 4, 1396/ June 25, 2017: https://perma.cc/KT5K-8N4Y, accessed August 5, 2020.
[144] INCSR 2012: https://perma.cc/8WH4-ZCUA, accessed August 8, 2020.

74–76). A zero-tolerance approach was adopted, which included the fining and lashing of addicts, imprisonment for dealers, and the death penalty for drug trafficking. In several cases charges against political opponents were supplemented with charges (often exaggerated or wholly trumped up) of the possession and trafficking of large amounts of narcotics (Ghiabi 2019: 74). As it became clear that this highly punitive approach was not working, it has gradually been softened over the years, with a greater emphasis on rehabilitation and treatment over imprisonment and execution, as we shall see.

It is hardly surprising against such a background that drug offenders crowd the prisons and that their numbers have grown rapidly over the past two decades. As is not uncommon for Iran, there are no systematic figures so estimates are largely reliant on prison and judicial officials' media statements and the occasional compilation.[145] Although not always consistent, these indicate that over the decade 2005–2015 some 45–50 percent of the prison population was incarcerated for drug offences while up to 20 percent more were serving time for crimes committed because of drug abuse, such as theft, murder, bodily harm, or kidnapping.[146] The resulting total of around 70 percent has, over the years, frequently been cited by officials, including the head of the judiciary. After 2015, the proportion held for narcotics offences as such appears to have steadily declined, reaching around 40–43 percent in 2019.[147]

The anti-drug law passed on October 25, 1988 laid down a comprehensive framework for counternarcotics measures and has since

---

[145] *Factnameh*, "Statistics of Drug Prisoners in Iran," Aban 15, 1398/November 6, 2019: https://perma.cc/USM8-7D95, accessed August 15, 2020.

[146] According to the head of the NPO in both 2006/2007 (1386) and 2013/2014 (1392) the proportion of prisoners held for narcotics offences was 47 percent, see *Alef*, "Forty Seven Percent of the Country's Crimes are Drug Related," Ordibehesht 18, 1386/May 5, 2007: https://perma.cc/VHZ2-GNAW, accessed August 18, 2020; *Tadbir*, "Forty Seven Percent of the Country's Prisoners are Drug Offenders," Esfand 4, 1392/February 23, 2014: www.tadbirkhabar.com/news/society/20300, accessed August 23, 2020.

[147] Tasnim News Agency, "Seventy Percent of Inmates Are in Prison for Drug Related Crimes," Tir 20, 1394/June 23, 2015: https://perma.cc/7Q94-Z3EA, accessed August 18, 2020. As the article relates, according to the head of the judiciary, 40 percent of prisoners are charged directly with narcotics crimes while 30 percent are there for offences indirectly linked to narcotics. See also *Iran Online*, "Sixty Percent of Prisoners Are Incarcerated Due to Drug Problems," Shahrivar 17, 1397/September 8, 2018: https://perma.cc/DAY9-GWVA, accessed August 18, 2020. According to this article 40 percent of prisoners were sentenced for narcotics offences and an additional 20 percent for narcotics-related crimes. Also see IRNA, "More than Sixty Percent of the Country's Prisoners are Drug Related," Aban 12, 1396/November 3, 2017: https://perma.cc/LAZ7-WNB2, accessed August 5, 2020, in which a DCHQ official put the proportion of narcotics prisoners at 50 percent with another 10–15 percent there for narcotics-related crimes; *Factnameh*, Aban 15, 1398/June 11, 2019; see note 157.

remained in force, though with significant amendments in 1997, 2010, and 2017.[148] Besides penalties for drug offences, it outlined the powers and obligations of a newly created Drug Control Headquarters (DCHQ) responsible for planning and coordinating the drug-related activities of the police, the Revolutionary Guard, the Intelligence and Health Ministries, and other agencies. The law divided drugs into two categories: (1) opium, together with traditional derivatives, hashish and cannabis, and (2) heroin, morphine, cocaine, codeine, and methadone or their chemical derivatives. It mandated the death penalty for anyone found trading in, or in possession of, more than 5 kg of opium, or more than 30 g of heroin and set out a hierarchy of penalties for lesser amounts. These lesser penalties consisted of some combination of fines, lashes of the whip, and prison sentences. Offences at the bottom end of the scale (less than 500 grams of opium/hashish etc., or less than one gram of heroin etc.) drew fines and lashes. Prison sentences in addition to fines and lashes were mandated on a sliding scale from one to as much as fifteen years, for all offences involving more than 5 grams of opium or cannabis and 1 gram of heroin or morphine.

The law also criminalized drug addiction. According to Articles 15 and 16 all addicts were required to cease consumption within six months. If those under the age of 60 were not clean after this period, they faced enforced residence in rehabilitation camps. Those addicted to heroin, cocaine, methadone, and other substances were punished by a combination of fines and a prison term to which up to fifty lashes were added on the third offence.

Later, in July 1989, the official news agency IRNA reported a major new effort to stamp out drug addiction and claimed that revolutionary committees had rounded up 55,000 addicts who were sent to provincial labor camps.[149] In total, in 1989, almost 100,000 drug *users* were detained (Mokri 2002: 185) and, by July 1990, 1,100 dealers had been executed.[150] A subsequent easing of enforcement meant this figure decreased continuously to around 25,000 by 1992, only to rise again thereafter.

The approach to drug addiction (but not trafficking) was relaxed somewhat during the presidency of the more pragmatic Rafsanjani (1989–1997) and was formally revised in the 1997 amendment to the

---

[148] For the text of the 1988 law, see https://perma.cc/X4A6-V2QL, accessed August 15, 2020.
[149] Y. M. Ibrahimi, "Iran Puts Addicts in its Labor Camps," *New York Times*, July 22, 1989, quoted in Afkhami (2009: 201).
[150] Amnesty International, "Addicted to Death: Executions for Drug Offences in Iran," December 2, 2011: https://perma.cc/XW8U-T65G, accessed September 25, 2020.

anti-drug law.[151] The new Article 15 began by explicitly stating that addiction is a crime, but that addicts would be exempt from criminal prosecution so long as they voluntarily sought treatment at an officially recognized clinic. By Article 16, addicts of any drug who did not seek treatment would no longer be detained in rehabilitation camps but instead be sentenced to a fine of 1 to 5 million rials (USD 112–560) *plus* up to thirty lashes of the whip on the first arrest and on the second and third arrests the same fine but up to seventy-four lashes of the whip. Other parts of the sentencing tariffs were tightened, but the 1988 structure was largely unchanged. The use of prison sentences for the punishment of those involved in opium and related substances was elaborated: 5–20 kilograms meant five to ten years plus lashes and fines with death on the third conviction, and more than 100 kilograms meant life on the first conviction.

The post-1997 situation saw the focus of drug policy in Iran move, gradually, from anti-trafficking to responding to the social and health aspects of domestic consumption, particularly the rise of addictive patterns of heroin use. The amendment of Article 15 in effect legalized medical intervention for drug abusers. Those seeking treatment could refer without fear to registered private practitioners or newly active NGOs, now encouraged by the reformist Khatami government, while the State Welfare Organization began to establish outpatient units for voluntary detoxification, which were free or only incurred low charges. Harm-reduction services were introduced to the prisons in 2003, and, in an effort to curb the spread of HIV/AIDS through needle sharing, came to include needle-exchange programs and methadone treatment (see Chapter 8 by Alaei and Alaei in this volume). This flourishing non-governmental sector with its pragmatic approach to public health and rehabilitation survived the resurgence of populist conservatism after the election of Ahmadinejad to the presidency in 2005.[152] By 2009, 1,596 treatment centers had been established for drug addicts, of which 337 were state run but the vast majority (1,232) were private, mostly sponsored by NGOs, some with government subsidies (Anaraki 2019: 18).

In principle, the punishment of addicts should not have had an impact on prison numbers after 1997 as the law did not prescribe prison sentences either for addicts who did not seek treatment or those found in possession of minor amounts of a drug. However, in practice the addicts

---

[151] For the text of the 1997 law, see: https://perma.cc/NQD7-ZVY5, accessed August 15, 2020.

[152] For an excellent account of this "grassroots" influence on government policy see Nikpour (2018).

ended up, if only briefly, in PTD while the case was being processed (Razzaghi et al., 1999: 35), and frequently served time, simply because they were too poor to pay the fines incurred for addiction or possession of minor quantities of a drug. This pattern was reflected in the head of the judiciary's 2002 administrative circular, which sought to relieve pressure on prisons by stipulating that for petty drug offenders unable to pay their fine, each day in detention would be counted as the equivalent of 50,000 rials (meaning that most would remain in prison for no more than ten to fifty days).[153] In November 2007 the chief of police disclosed that 40,000 were in prison at that time for addiction alone. He added that they were there mostly because they could not afford 50–2,000 tomans fines, and generally spent no more than a month in custody.[154]

It should be noted here that drug addiction cuts across social classes and that those arrested and tried as addicts have mostly been, at least since the mid-2000s,[155] street addicts caught up in periodic police roundups. In November 2006, the NPO head Yesaqi publicly railed against what he called police "maneuvers," "held every six months," and demanded to know why the judiciary should be obliged to issue a temporary arrest order for every "drug-related event."[156]

By the mid-2000s, according to the DCHQ, arrests were running at an annual rate of almost 400,000, "which is a typical level for the last several years," and "twice as many drug abusers were detained as drug traffickers."[157] Figures for 2006–2007 (1385) given in the domestic press under the headline "Startling Narcotics Statistics" provide rare and instructive detail about the penalties this population received. There were in this year 426,808 arrests, of which 68 percent were suspected drug users and 32 percent suspected traffickers. Of the total, 35 percent (149,382) were declared not guilty and "immediately released." Of the 277,394 who were convicted, 20 percent (ca. 55,485) were sentenced to fines of less than 1 million tomans; 66 percent (ca. 183,527) to fines and lashes; 1.5 percent (ca. 4,268) to prison for less than one year;

---

[153] Protocol concerning Penalties for Narcotics, Checks and Debt Offences, Mehr 15, 1381/October 7, 2002: https://perma.cc/E66C-A8GZ, accessed August 26, 2020.
[154] *Kayhan*, "The Police Are Forbidden from Checking People's Mobile Phones," Aban 30, 1386/November 21, 2007: www.magiran.com/article/1524088, accessed August 15, 2020.
[155] Mokri, writing in 2002 observed that "it can be cautiously summarized that, currently, only one quarter of drug users get arrested in their lifetime in Iran" (Mokri 2002: 185).
[156] *Donya-ye Eqtesad*, "Each Prisoner Costs 80 Thousand Rials a Day," Azar 5, 1385/November 26, 2006: https://perma.cc/ZY63-ZJCX, accessed August 15, 2020.
[157] INCSR 2006. The INCSR report is quoting figures supplied by a UNODC, which takes its figures from DCHQ: https://perma.cc/ZJH3-L3CS, accessed August 18, 2020.

4.6 percent (ca. 12,804) to one to five years; 1.5 percent (ca. 4, 268) to over five years to life, and 6.2 percent (17,072) to other (unspecified) punishments.[158]

The publication of these figures followed a statement at the end of November 2007 by the chief of police, who was also secretary general of the DCHQ, General Ismail Ahmadi-Moghaddam, which heralded an important change of policy: "Thirty per cent of the country's prisoners, about 40,000 of them, who have committed no offence other than their use of drugs, will be gradually released beginning next month and henceforth no-one will be imprisoned simply on account of drug addiction."[159]

It is not known whether, or to what extent, the police carried out Ahmadi-Moghaddam's promise over the next two years. But in 2008, DCHQ reported that "almost twice the number of traffickers as drug abusers" had been sentenced to prison, a reversal of the previous pattern.[160] Elsewhere, it stated that there had been 250,000 drug-related arrests in 2008, of which 246,657 were of "distributors," 5,279 were of "drug users," and 3,187 were of "foreigners" – much lower figures than those quoted two years earlier.[161]

A legal basis for the new policy concerning addicts was provided by the amended anti-narcotics law of 2010 (effective from January 2011). Article 16 of the law suspended prosecution of addicts who did not voluntarily seek treatment. These are instead to be sent "by judicial order" to a compulsory rehabilitation center for one to three months, renewable for another three months, after which, if the treatment is successful, prosecution is to be dropped. The rehabilitation camps were to be established under the supervision of the DCHQ and, from 2016, the State Welfare Organization.[162] That is to say, addicts not charged with dealing were removed from the jurisdiction of the NPO and hence from the prison population, although they were still detained in a prison-like setting.

An interview with a police chief in 2012 suggested that the provisions of Article 16 were immediately effective and had indeed been the practice for at least a year before that: Between March 2011 and March 2012 (in 1390) 225,000 addicts were arrested from the streets and taken to rehabilitation centers, "representing a 7 per cent increase on 1389

---

[158] Tabnak News Agency, "Curious Drug Statistics, Half a Million Detainees, Half a Million Homeless," Dey 10, 1386/December 31, 2007: https://perma.cc/SJ3X-K5E9, accessed August 19, 2020.
[159] See note 151.
[160] INCSR 2008 report: https://perma.cc/6XRW-9BTA, accessed August 19, 2020.
[161] See note 147: Amnesty International, "Addicted to Death," p. 16.
[162] ISCA, "Compulsory Drug Treatment Centers for Addiction Are Consolidated," Tir 29, 1395/July 19, 2016: www.iscanews.ir/news/663167, accessed September 15, 2020.

(2010–11)."[163] Also DCHQ reported that in 2011 there had been "a striking 80 per cent reduction in prison admissions for drug users and a concomitant sharp increase in referrals for treatment," suggesting that the transition was not quite complete.[164]

The impact on prisoner numbers of the removal of addicts over this period is hard to assess, because the marked expansion, from circa 2008, of crystal-meth (methamphetamine) use and its underground manufacture in Iran led to numerous arrests of people connected with its trade, especially after January 2011 when the revised narcotics law came into effect. In other words, any space left by the removal of addicts from the prisons was quickly filled by new detentions of dealers, the imposition of heavier sentences, and denial of prison furloughs – a policy adopted by the judiciary in 2011. The intensification of the war on drugs in this period, which from October 2010 saw new measures to speed up the judicial processing of drug trafficking cases, including the referral of all such cases to the Prosecutor General's Office and the denial of the right of appeal for the many sentenced to death also led to a clampdown on information.[165]

According to DCHQ, in 2010/2011 (1389) there was a 38 percent increase over 2009/2010 (1388) in prison admissions of drug cases, and the number of prisoners who remained in the wards in 2010/2011 was 17 percent higher.[166] In 1390/2011, while admissions declined by 4 percent over 2010, 15 percent more were convicted/detained in the longer term. According to DCHQ, the reason was cancellation of prison leave and imposition of heavier sentences for offenders.[167] Another indicator of the pattern is that while the proportion of drugs prisoners declined

---

[163] *Salamat* "A Third of the Volume of Judicial Cases is Related to Drugs," Tir 6, 1391/June 26, 2012: https://perma.cc/27HX-EM49, accessed September 15, 2020.

[164] INCSR 2011 report: https://2009-2017.state.gov/j/inl/rls/nrcrpt/2011/index.htm. Indeed, the transition may not have been completed for some time: It is possible that the police persisted in taking the addicts they rounded up to prisons by manipulating charges. In July 2013 and again in October 2016, reflecting NPO complaints about such practices, the head of the judiciary's administrative circulars instructed prosecutors that "it is forbidden to change a charge from addiction to consumption and this cannot be used as permission to imprison them and the absence of article 16 compulsory camps cannot be a reason to send them to prison." Prosecutors were instead enjoined to devote all their energy to the expansion of centers set out in Articles 15 and 16. See report on Larijani's directive: *Javan Online*, "Probability of a 15% Reduction of Prisoners with New Directive," Shahrivar 27, 1395/September 17, 2016: https://perma.cc/XDA9-ATK8, accessed September 16, 2020.

[165] See note 158.

[166] *Deutsche Welle Farsi*, September 6, 2011, see note 55.

[167] *Tejarat-e farda*, Bahman 21, 1391/February 9, 2013: www.tejaratefarda.com/, accessed October 1, 2020.

from 46 percent in 2006 to 43 percent in June 2011, the numbers had almost doubled from 68,000 to circa 117,000 in June 2011.[168] The sudden sharp drop in the prison population in the second half of 2012 (from 250,000 to 217,000 in April 2013)[169] was due to a series of unannounced releases.[170]

The compulsory treatment camps in theory are staffed by social workers and medical professionals to provide detoxification via systems inspired by Narcotics Anonymous. The reality is, according to a number of reports, somewhat grimmer. Most inmates are homeless street dwellers collected through wide-ranging "purification plans" conducted by the police in the name of medical rehabilitation. But the camps are a large and complex subject which is beyond the scope of this chapter. Suffice to say here, on a point directly relevant to our theme, that there has been no visible evidence of the "judicial supervision" mandated in Article 16 which prescribes "judicial supervision of the arrest, treatment and release process" and requires a judicial dossier to be opened for every referral. Thus, it seems that many street addicts are being taken to the camps illegally and without proper judicial oversight of their treatment program (Ghiabi 2018: 279). Additional evidence stems from the observations of police officers and social workers who report that at least 90 percent of the detainees revert to their previous habits and that some have experienced the vicious circle of arrest, consignment to camp, release, and return to street-addicted lifestyle ten times over.[171]

The share of prisoners incarcerated for drug crimes has stood at about 40–43 percent since 2015 and about 25–30 percent for drug-related crimes, reflecting a steady increase in actual numbers. There has been much discussion amongst professionals, academics, and officials about the sad failure of harsh policies to deter criminals and reduce addiction. The new mood led to an amendment of the drug trafficking law in January 2018 which substantially raised the threshold for the death penalty to more than 50 kg of opium, 2 kg of heroin, and 3 kg of crystal meth, and abolished it for marijuana (Nikpour 2018: 1). As a result, the pending death sentences of most inmates were set for review, with the

---

[168] *Deutsche Welle Farsi*, "Increase in the Number of Prisoners in Iran by 100, 000 in the Last Five Years," June 23, 2012: https://perma.cc/U99T-BPCW, accessed October 1, 2020.

[169] Tasnim News Agency, "America is Number One in Terms of Numbers of Prisoners," Farvardin 21, 1392/April 10, 2013: https://perma.cc/35GP-MXAC, accessed October 2, 2020.

[170] *Kalameh*, Sharivar 24, 1391/September 14, 2012: www.kaleme.org/1391/07/09/klm-114290/, accessed May 18, 2020.

[171] IRNA, "The Vicious Circle in which Drug Addicts Are Caught," Bahman 28, 1398/February 17, 2020: https://perma.cc/8AV9-QDXJ, accessed October 5, 2020.

Majles Judiciary Committee announcing that at least 5,000 people could see their sentences commuted to life imprisonment.[172]

The number of narcotics prisoners was further reduced by the sudden passage on July 13, 2020 of a Law concerning the Reduction of *Taʿzir* Prison Sentences. The law was initially proposed and vigorously promoted by a group of Majles deputies in November 2019. After revision by parliament's Judicial Affairs Committee, it was taken up as a desirable reform and swiftly approved by the Expediency Council. The law reduces prison sentences for a number of crimes, including drug trafficking, by half, and it provides that judges should impose the minimum sentence of the range laid down in the relevant code, unless there is a justifiable reason for a higher sentence. The impact of this measure is likely to be profound. One prominent lawyer believes that if properly implemented, it will lead to a two thirds reduction in the prison population.[173] Judiciary officials interviewed by a journalist believe that 30,000 could be freed in the near future.[174]

8 Conclusion

The problem of overcrowded prisons has been a pervasive problem in the Islamic Republic since its inception. As we have seen, Iranian prison officials have argued that this is primarily a problem of capacity, implying that the answer would be simply to build more prisons. Like many countries around the world, however, the IRI has been unwilling or unable to do this, and indeed it is questionable whether increasing capacity would solve the issue. Other countries have tried to build their way out of this problem by increasing the prison estate only to find that overcrowding remains a stubbornly persistent issue.[175] Indeed, as the foregoing analysis shows, overcrowded prisons in Iran have been caused by overly punitive criminal sentencing policy, especially in connection with drug offenders, but also in the area of "unintentional crimes" as well as problems with delayed justice

---

[172] Dehghan (2018). See also, for the background over rising concerns both at home and abroad over the high number of executions and withdrawal of European funding for the GCHQ, Dehghan (2016).

[173] *E'temād*, "If the Law on Reducing Prisoners Was Applied in This Way Two-Thirds of Prisoners Would Be Released," Mordad 5, 1399/July 26, 2020: https://perma.cc/4YHZ-KD99, accessed October 8, 2020.

[174] Tasnim News Agency, "Release of about 30, 000 Prisoners under the Law of the Reduction of Prisoners," Tir 25, 1399/July 15, 2020: https://perma.cc/WCQ6-R4MM, accessed October 8, 2020.

[175] For example, this was the case in the UK. See Criminal Justice Alliance, "Crowded Out? The Impact of Prison Overcrowding on Rehabilitation," March 2012: https://perma.cc/W8DW-SRX4, accessed September 23, 2020.

and pretrial detainees. Prison protests and riots have put pressure on the authorities to reduce prison numbers and improve conditions. We have also seen that various initiatives from doctors, judicial officials, Majles deputies, and, to a lesser extent, NGOs have tried to deal with the problem of overcrowding and improve prison conditions in various ways: the establishment of drug camps, needle-exchange programs, various strategies of decarceration, like, for example, reducing the number of people imprisoned for unintentional offences, alternative sentencing, and, most importantly, prison furlough schemes and amnesties. These have succeeded in reducing the numbers in prison but not always in a sustained and credible way. For example, the large-scale pardons and amnesties – on paper a humane and progressive policy – need a rehabilitative and probationary infrastructure to support ex-prisoners and prevent recidivism; one for which there is, thus far, scant evidence. Finally, what flows from the foregoing analysis which has focused on "ordinary" rather than "political" prisoners, is that there is no clear-cut distinction between the two categories. Some "ordinary" prisoners may consider themselves "political" (for example, political dissidents held on trumped-up charges of drug possession or women imprisoned for refusing to wear hejab). Moreover, the discursive and ideological processes in which acts such as drug use, sex work, or the failure to pay a debt are defined as "crimes" demanding imprisonment (rather than state investment in public health, education, and welfare) are themselves profoundly political.[176]

APPENDIX

Table 7.1 *Iran: Permanent prison population, selected years between 1979 and 2019*

	Prison Population	Incarceration Rate	Capacity	Occupancy Rate
1979	8,557	23.1%		
1980	10,000	26%		
1981	34,590			
1988	81,000			
1989	66,000			
1993	101,801	172%		
1999	190,000	301%	ca. 60,000	316%
2000	180, 000	272%	ca. 60,000	300%
2001	158,000	237%	ca. 60,000	263%
2003	157,267	229%	ca. 60,000	262%
2005	134,384	192%	ca. 60,000	224%

---

[176] Nikpour 2020. Khalili and Schwedler 2010: 23.

Table 7.1 (*cont.*)

	Prison Population	Incarceration Rate	Capacity	Occupancy Rate
2007	148,843	207%	60,000	248%
2009	168,516	229%	65,000	260%
2010	166,979	222%	80,000	208%
2011	250,000	ca. 231%	ca. 85,000	294%
2013	ca. 226,220	ca. 294%		
2014	217,000		140,000	155%
2015	224,000	290%	85,000	263%
2016	217,043	283%	85,000	243%
2017	224,000	284%	88,000	254%
2018	251,000	294%	88,000	285%
2019	189,000		85,000	222%
2020	228, 000			

Note to the table:
The most common, and relatively standardized, method of measuring a jurisdiction's rate of incarceration is to calculate the number of people imprisoned as a proportion of 100,000 individuals in the total population. Thus, if a nation of 5 million people has 10,000 prisoners, the rate of incarceration is 200 prisoners per 100,000 individuals (i.e., 10,000 divided by 5,000,000 times 100,000). Occupancy rate refers to the capacity of a prison divided by the total number of prisoners in prison. For example, if a prison has a capacity of 60,000 and contains 134,384 prisoners, it has a 224 percent occupancy rate (meaning it is 2.24 times over its capacity). This figure highlights to what extent prisons are overcrowded or not. Figures given to the WPB by the Iranian government are sometimes contradicted by the figures which are reported by Iranian prison officials in the Iranian press. This appears to be the case for the data given to World Justice Project (WJP) in 2014, which differ significantly from those in other years. This is elaborated in the chapter. All figures originate with the NPO. A source of confusion is that the NPO maintains a running tally of prisoners which, throughout the second half of the 2000s to 2011, could be accessed on its website. So far as we are aware, there are no publicly available end-of-year statistics. Figures reported in the Iranian press, by senior NPO or judiciary officials or the WPB, are therefore usually correct at or around the date of their statement but can vary considerably within the same calendar year. For this reason, we have based the table on NPO figures quoted by the WPB for alternate years from 2001 to 2013 and historic figures quoted by prison officials for 1980 and 1993. The figures for 2015–2019 are from a summary provided by *E'temād* newspaper and are probably taken from the judiciary's annual reports.

References to the table by year
1979–1999 – ISNA, Khordad 1st 1396/22 May 2017 (quoting Asghar Jahangir, Head of the National Prisons Organization): https://perma.cc/Y7ZN-A46T, accessed March 2, 2020.
2000 – *Hamshahri*, Azar 6th, 1385/November 27, 2008 (quoting NPO head Ali AkbarYasaqi):www.hamshahrionline.ir/(S(bhyusyrjhu0kae553r4wmi45))/print/9482/ Society/socialnews?model=WebUI.romModels.Details.De, accessed March 16, 2015.
ISNA, 1 Khordad 1396/22 May 2017 (quoting Asghar Jahangir, Head of the National Prisons Organization): https://perma.cc/Y7ZN-A46T, accessed August 15, 2020.
2001 – ISNA, Khordad 1, 1396/May 22, 2017 (quoting NPO head, Asghar Jahangir): https://perma.cc/2K9L-PMKW, accessed August 15, 2020.

2006–NPO, quoted by Ali Akbar Yasaqi. *Mehr News*, Dey 4, 1385/December 25, 2006: www.mehrnews.com/fa/NewsDetail.aspx?NewsID=425657, accessed November 28, 2018.

2007 – NPO head quoted by *Deutsche Welle Farsi*, June 27, 2012: https://perma.cc/3VU3-UW9Y, accessed August 2, 2019.

2009 – Capacity figure of 1,388 quoted in *E'temād*, Bahman 7, 1388/January 27, 2010: www.magiran.com/npview.asp?
ID=2032387, accessed November 25, 2018.

2010 – Deputy head of NPO, quoted Ordibehesht 27, 1390/May 17, 2011: http://iranyar.ir/sayehroshan/25520--90-.html, accessed March 10, 2015; see also *Quds Online*, Shahrivar 25, 1391/September 15, 2012: https://perma.cc/Z6S5-NZT4/, accessed March 10, 2015. Capacity figure for 2010/1389 quoting minister of justice, *Jam-e Jam*, Azar 3, 1389/November 24, 2010: www.magiran.com/npview.asp?ID=2195301, accessed February 15, 2015. *Khabar Online*, Mehr 9, 1389/October 5, 2019: www.khabaronline.ir/news-96668.aspx, accessed December 5, 2020.

2011 – Head of NPO, quoted in *Mehr News*, Mehr 17, 1390/October 9, 2011; *Khabar Online* quoting head of Lorestan judiciary, Mehr 30, 1390/October 22, 2011.

2014 – WPB.

2015–2019 – *E'temād*, Tir 13, 1398/July 4, 2019: https://perma.cc/YCB8-AJJ8, accessed August 5, 2020.

2015 – Tasnim News Agency, Mehr 12, 1395/October 12, 2016 (quoting the minister of justice): https://perma.cc/CU7V-3Y3H, accessed August 5, 2020.

2016 – *Radio Farda*, Esfand 7, 1396/February 26, 2018: https://perma.cc/MWR5-UY6V, accessed August 6, 2020.

2017 – ISNA, Khordad 1, 1396/May 22, 2017 (quoting Asghar Jahangir, head of the Prisons Organization): https://perma.cc/L49R-3QJA, accessed August 15, 2020.

2018 – *Donya-ye Eqtesad*, 16th Khordad 1397/June 6, 2018, https://donya-e-eqtesad.com/بخش-سایت-خوان-62/3397394-خوان-آماری-از-زندان-های-ایران, accessed August 15, 2020.

2019 – NPO, *E'temād*, Tir 13, 1398/July 4, 2019.

2020 – WPB.

Table 7.2 *Prisoners by category for selected years between 1989 and 2018*

Prisoner Category	Check Prisoners	Car-Accident Prisoners	Mehrieh Prisoners	Narcotic Prisoners
1989				100,000
2001	17,000			
2007				40,000
2008	6,000	9,712		38,412
2010			20,000	
2011	4,350	1,100		117,000
2012			3,500	
2017			2, 000	
2018	12, 000	300	3, 500	
2019			4, 500	

Note: Check prisoners are people who have been imprisoned as a result of a bounced check. The sources for all of the data in the table are included in the footnotes of this chapter.

Table 7.2 (*cont.*)

References to the table by year

1989 – Y. M. Ibrahimi, "Iran Puts Addicts in its Labour Camps," *New York Times*, July 22, 1989, quoted in Afkhami 2009: 201. Amnesty International, 'Addicted to Death: Executions for Drug Offences in Iran', December 2, 2011: https://perma.cc/XW8U-T65G, accessed 25th September 2020.

2001 – IRNA, November 27, 2001, quoted in Keshavarzian 2007: 75.

2007 – *Kayhan*, "The Police are Forbidden from Checking People's Mobile Phones," Aban 30, 1386/November 21, 2007: www.magiran.com/article/1524088, accessed August 15, 2020.

2008 – IRNA, November 27, 2001, quoted in Keshavarzian 2007: 75. *Khabaronline*, Khordad 6, 1390/May 27, 2011.

2010 – *Tabnak*, "Announcing a New Circular to Those Sentenced to *Diyeh* and *Mehrieh*," Fararu, Mordad 9, 1391/July 30, 2012: https://perma.cc/SR9Q-69ZU; "Most of the Diyeh Prisoners are Young," Shahrivar 25, 1390/September 16, 2011: https://perma.cc/NZ9V-956K, accessed April 8, 2020.

2011 – *Khabar Online*, Khordad 6, 1390/May 27, 2011, *Deutsche Welle Farsi*, "Increase in the Number of Prisoners in Iran by 100, 000 in the Last Five Years," June 23, 2012: https://perma.cc/U99T-BPCW, accessed October 3, 2020.

2012 – *Tabnak*, Shahrivar 25, 1390/September 16, 2011, op.cit.

2017 – *Khabar Online*, "The Latest Statistics of Mehrieh Convicts," Ordibehesht 26, 1398/ May 16, 2019: www.khabaronline.ir/news/1260556/, accessed August 28, 2020.

2018 – IRIB News Agency, "Legal Advisor to the Minister of Justice: We Have 12 000 Homeless Check Prisoners," Tir 27, 1397/July 8, 2018: https://perma.cc/VJY9-DUDE, accessed April 6, 2023. *Fars News*, "The Release of 12 'Non-Intentional' Prisoners in Qom," Mordad 11, 1397/August 1, 2018: www.farsnews.com/news/13970510000539/, accessed August 23, 2020. *Ana news*, "Jahangiri: Society Needs Free Journalists and Independent Newspapers," Mordad 3, 1397/July 25, 2018: www.ana.ir/news/409325, accessed August 20, 2020.

2019 – *Ana news*, Mordad 3, 1397/July 25, 2018.

Bibliography

Abdi, Abbas (1377/1998). "Taʿsir-e Zendān bar Zendāni," *Noor*, no page numbers.

Abdi, Abbas (1397/2019). "A Problem Called Prison," *Etemād*, Dey 25/January 15: www.magiran.com/article/3883418, accessed June 18, 2020.

Afkhami, Amir Arsalan (2009). "From Punishment to Harm Reduction: Resecularization of Addiction in Contemporary Iran' in Ali Gheissari (ed.), *Contemporary Iran: Economy, Society, Politics*, Oxford: Oxford University Press.

Amid, Hoda (2014). "Do Changes in the Laws Mean that *Mehrieh* is Close to being Abolished?," *Bidār-zani*, January 8: https://bidarzani.com/11093, accessed August 19, 2020.

Anaraki, Nahid Rahimipour (2019). "Prison Subculture and Drug-Related Crimes in Iran," PhD dissertation, Memorial University of Newfoundland: https://perma.cc/4R53-YM9S, accessed June 28, 2020.

Banakar, Reza (2016). *Driving Culture in Iran: Law and Society on the Roads of the Islamic Republic*, London: I. B Tauris.
Bøe, Marianne (2015). *Family Law in Contemporary Iran: Women's Rights Activism and Shari'a*, London: Bloomsbury.
Calabrese, John (2007). "Iran's War on Drugs: Holding the Line?," *Middle East Policy Brief*, No. 3.
Daraeizadeh, Behnam (2010). "A look at criminal procedure in Iran," *Iran Human Rights Documentation Centre*, November: https://perma.cc/ZF6Y-WEVD, accessed June 18, 2018.
Dehghan, Saeed Kamali (2016). "Iran under Pressure to Abolish the Death Penalty for Trafficking," *The Guardian*, June 28: https://perma.cc/W4LB-DN5L, accessed August 17, 2019.
Deghan, Saeed Kamali (2018). "Iran's Easing of Drug Laws Could Halt Execution of 5000 Prisoners," *The Guardian*, January 10: https://perma.cc/R8NK-SAN5, accessed August 22, 2021.
Foucault, Michel (1979). *Discipline and Punish*, New York: Viking Books.
Ghassemi, Ghassem (2009). "Criminal Punishment in Islamic Societies: Empirical Study of Attitudes to Criminal Sentencing in Iran," *European Journal on Criminal Policy and Research*, 15: 159–180.
Ghiabi, Maziyar (2018). "Maintaining Disorder: The Micropolitics of Drugs Policy in Iran," *Third World Quarterly*, 39 (2): 277–297.
Ghiabi, Maziyar (2019). *Drugs Politics: Managing Disorder in the Islamic Republic of Iran*. New York: Cambridge University Press.
Gholami, Hassan and Darius Khaksar, (1398/2019). "Effective Factors on Adjudicating Alternatives to Imprisonment," *Hoquq-e Keyfari*, No. 26, Spring.
Keshavarzian, Arang. (2007). *Bazaar and State in Iran*, New York: Cambridge University Press.
Khalili, Laleh and Jillian Schwedler. (2010). *Policing and Prisons in the Middle East: Formations of Coercion*, London: C. Hurst & Co.
Madani, Sa'id (2006). "The Evolution of Prisoners' Rights from the Constitutional Revolution to the Present Day," *E'temād-e Melli*, November 7.
Mahjoub, Negin (2011). "Conditions in Iranian Prisons," *BBC Persian*, July 18: https://perma.cc/L5VL-9KJY, accessed June 22, 2019.
Mazaheri, Reihaneh (2010). "Iranians Lose Faith in Cheques," *Payvand News*, April 6: https://perma.cc/KTJ8-NHZA, accessed April 6, 2020.
Mokri, Azaraksh (2002). "Brief Overview of the Status of Drug Abuse in Iran," *Archives of Iranian Medicine*, 5 (3): 89–96: https://perma.cc/3JTK-WSD6, accessed May 2, 2010.
Najafabadi, Ayatollah Dari (1386/2007). "The Condition of Prisons in Iran is Not Even Tolerated by Officials," *E'temād*, Ordibehesht 27/May 17: https://web.archive.org/web/20070519041808/www.etemaad.com/Released/86-02-27/213.htm, accessed June 4, 2010.
Nasiri, Morteza (1997). "A Review of Iran's Judicial System" *Iran-nameh*, January 1, Nos. 1–2: https://perma.cc/X6XN-5N48, accessed June 18, 2015.
Newman, Graeme. (1982). "Khomeini and Criminal Justice: Notes on Crime and Culture," *Journal of Criminal Law and Criminology*, 73, (2): 561–588.

Nikpour, Golnar (2018). "Drugs and Drug Policy in the Islamic Republic of Iran," *Brandeis, Middle East Brief*: https://perma.cc/2J8P-HHF6, accessed February 8 2020.

Nikzad, Shahab (1390/2011). "2010: The End of the Humanizing University, the Beginning of the Prison-Building Movement," *BBC Persian*, Farvardin 2/March 22: https://perma.cc/D3EV-SG8L, accessed June 1, 2018.

Nissaramanesh, Bijan, Mike Trace, and Marcus Roberts (2005). "The Risk of Harm Reduction in the Islamic Republic of Iran," Briefing Paper 8: The Beckley Foundation Drug Policy Program: https://perma.cc/MAC8-T6VU, accessed March 18, 2018.

Razzaghi. Emran, Afarin Rahimi, Mehdi Hosseni, Saeid Madani, and Anindya Chatterjee (1999). *Rapid Situation Assessment (RSA) of Drug Abuse in Iran*, Prevention Department, State Welfare Organization, Ministry of Health, I.R. of Iran and United Nations International Drug Control Program: https://perma.cc/DSJ5-ZJAH, accessed May 8, 2015.

Rejali, Darius (1994). *Torture and Modernity: Self, Society and State in Modern Iran*, Boulder, CO: Westview Press.

Samghi, Banafsheh (1388/2010). "Prisons Organization Officials Submit Report," *Etemād*, Bahman 7/January 27: https://web.archive.org/web/20100130174128/www.etemaad.ir/Released/88-11-07/205.htm, accessed September 6, 2018.

Tabatabai, Mahmoud Alizadeh (1398/2019). "Prisons and Criminals: What Should and Should Not Be the Legislation for Financial Debtors," *Sazandegi*, Aban 28/November 19: https://web.archive.org/web/20191207145619/http://sazandeginews.com/News/6545, accessed August 20, 2020.

Tait, Robert (2011). "Iran Gets the Hump over Camel Price Link to Accident Payouts," *The Guardian*, June 3: https://perma.cc/T7CK-F5UY, accessed August 20, 2020.

Zamani, Sadegh (1385/2006). "International human rights standards and the financial prisoners in Iran," *Hoquq-e Beynolmellali*, No. 35, Autumn and Winter.

8 Legal Barriers to Accessing Vital Medical Services and Creative Responses to Overcoming These

Arash Alaei and Kamiar Alaei

1 Overview

In this chapter, we examine the legal challenges to accessing HIV/AIDS services in Iran. In discussing these, we do not focus on HIV positives and carriers themselves. They are already recognized within the Iranian health system and therefore can receive treatment. Instead, we focus on those at risk of becoming infected with HIV/AIDS, the so-called key populations of drug users, MSM (men who have sex with men) and sex workers.[1]

As of 2020, about 54,000 (with an estimated rage between 39,000 and 130,000) adults and children are living with HIV in Iran, with about 3,200 having died from it in 2020, the majority of whom are men older than 15. A total of 2,400 people newly contracted HIV in 2020 (Figure 8.1), of whom three quarters were men and one quarter women (UNAIDS 2021a). Since the Iranian government does not collect data on the key populations (drug users, MSM, and sex workers), it is unclear what percentage of the overall numbers are due to contraction among the key populations, but it is believed that this population makes up the overwhelming majority.

As we will note, providing services to the key populations is met with a number of obstacles. MSM and sex workers engage in behavior considered to be criminal, and the very existence of such populations in Iran is largely denied. Men having sex with men and sex work (as well as adultery) can be punishable by the death penalty, including by stoning. The religious barriers to accepting transgender behavior have been

---

[1] The discussion here is focused on MSM rather than gays: men who have sex with men, which is the terminology used in public health. It should be noted that the transgender condition is considered a disorder by the political authorities and is not viewed in terms of a human rights perspective. Transgender populations are encouraged by the Iranian state to undergo sex-change surgeries.

Legal Barriers to Accessing Vital Medical Services

■ AIDS and sexually transmitted diseases

Islamic Republic of Iran HIV/AIDS country profile 2020

Epidemic estimates

	2020
Adult (15 to 49) HIV prevalence	<0.1 [<0.1–0.2]
Adults and children living with HIV	54 000 [39 000–130 000]
New HIV infections	2400 [1000–11 000]
AIDS-related deaths	3200 [2000–7100]

Epidemic transition

Percentage change in new HIV infections since 2010	–51%
Percentage change in AIDS-related deaths since 2010	–12%

Data on key populations

	Sex workers	Gay men and other men who have sex with men	People who inject drugs
Estimated size of population	138 000	–	90 000
HIV prevalence	1.6	–	3.1
Know their HIV status	67.1	–	52.9
Antiretroviral therapy coverage	–	–	16.7

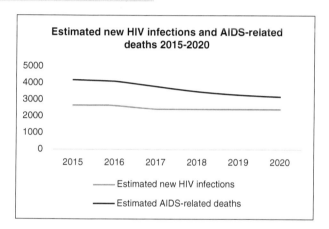

Figure 8.1 Epidemic estimates in Iran, 2005–2021
Source: www.unaids.org/en/regionscountries/countries/islamicrepublicofiran and www.emro.who.int/asd/country-activities/islamic-republic-of-iran.html. Country profile data on AIDS and sexually transmitted diseases is reported by the World Health Organization (WHO) Eastern Mediterranean Regional Office (EMRO) – Islamic Republic of Iran HIV/AIDS country profile 2021.

overcome, but only if transgender people submit to sex reassignment surgery (Najmabadi 2013).

The authors of this chapter are both doctors and together we developed an approach, over time, to ensuring access to for these key populations. The chapter focuses on our efforts in setting up and expanding the primary healthcare clinics in our hometown Kermanshah in the late 1990s, later expanding this program nationwide, being sent to prison in 2009, and being forced into exile since 2010/2011. The chapter significantly draws on our experiences as health professionals, which also led us to become policy entrepreneurs and prison inmates along the way.

In the following, we will outline access to HIV/AIDS services during the last two decades, especially in light of a highly innovative health approach to addressing these barriers in order to enable the target populations to receive treatment. We will discuss how the legal challenges are intertwined with cultural, religious, and political responses to the HIV/AIDS epidemic in Iran. The chapter will also discuss how the contrast between the "national security approach" and the "policing approach" has been the dominant determinant of the extent to which the punishment of the law has been implemented in relation to these key populations, and the political changes that determine which of these approaches dominate.

2 Background

As healthcare professionals based in Iran, in collaboration with Kermanshah medical university, we initiated the establishment of HIV/AIDS services in our hometown of Kermanshah during the late 1990s. Subsequently, we contributed in extending this program to a national scale. However, in 2009, we found ourselves incarcerated due to our involvement in this endeavor. Since 2010/2011, we have been compelled to live in exile. This chapter primarily relies on our healthcare experiences, which not only shaped our paths as healthcare professionals but also led us down the unexpected routes of policy advocacy and incarceration.

Considering the serious crimes with which drug users, MSM, and sex workers may be charged, facilitating their access to health services presented a considerable challenge that we professionally grappled with. Our health and human rights-driven response was developed over years, slowly building up the case for HIV treatment being offered to these key populations through reaching out to extensive networks of support.

The challenges of doing so cannot be overstated. These barriers were legal, political, social, and in policy, reflecting reluctance and prejudices even among health practitioners in Iran. *Legally*, and as expanded on later in this chapter, the criminal penalties faced by the key populations are amongst the most severe. *Politically*, whether at the national, provincial, or local levels, there was initially almost no support for the humane treatment of these key populations. The practices drug users, MSM, and sex workers were assumed to be involved with presented a number of major taboos for which religious arguments were mobilized to justify harsh treatment. *Socially*, too, there was much fear. Discrimination and stigma resulted in, for example, social isolation, loss of employment, denial of medical services, eviction by landlords, abandonment by family members, segregation in prisons, forced divorces, and loss of child custody. In *policy* terms there was very little sympathy for utilizing health budgets and investing in a policy framework to bring the treatment of these populations under the umbrella of existing health provisions.

The considerable severity and weight of these barriers, and the means by which we, along with a number of other individuals and experts, were able to circumvent and overcome them, speak to the gravity of the subject matter. This shared experience – an account of working with these complexities at the grassroots, city, provincial, and national levels in Iran, particularly over the years 1997–2008 – provides insight into the multifaceted issues involved. It highlights the taboos, but also opportunities for grappling with those taboos in the Iranian context through reference to appropriate concepts and collaboration with relevant actors and networks. Each of these will be addressed in the sections that follow.

3   Drug Users, Gays, and Sex Workers before and after the 1979 Revolution

3.1   Before the 1979 Revolution

Drug users, gays, and sex workers were treated very differently before the Revolution of 1979.

Regarding *drug users*, the treatment of narcotics addiction through methadone maintenance treatment was first approved by the US Food and Drug Administration in 1972.[2] The rationale of methadone treatment is best understood within the context of the three main approaches to drugs: Supply reduction, demand reduction, and harm reduction. Iran was the first country in the Middle East and North Africa to implement the methadone maintenance treatment – a *harm-reduction* measure – around 1972/1973.

Methadone maintenance treatment is considered the most human rights-friendly approach to drug users: It allows them to take the lead in the choice and pace of their own treatment. It also has other advantages, such as facilitating continued employment, reducing physical suffering, posing fewer risks in relation to mental health, and promoting the possibility of upholding family connections. There is broad and widely

---

[2] See www.ncbi.nlm.nih.gov/books/NBK64164/pdf/Bookshelf_NBK64164.pdf, p. 22.

accepted evidence that addiction does not increase when methadone maintenance treatment is offered.[3] In addition, the needle and syringe programs that often go along with methadone maintenance treatment can prevent drug users from contracting HIV/AIDS.

Regarding MSM, same-sex relationships were not legal before the revolution, but they were also not criminalized and, in the urban centers, were silently tolerated. A same-sex wedding celebration (without legal effect)[4] was reportedly held at the Commodore Hotel in Tehran around 1973–1975.[5] The adverse reaction to this public event meant that the couple had to leave the country, but despite the social reaction, there are virtually no reports of public attacks on gays before the revolution.

Regarding *sex workers*, prostitutes worked openly in Tehran's Shahr-e No (New Town)[6] red light district from the early 1970s onward. Routine syphilis treatment and condom distribution were publicly and officially available. Social workers offered social and mental support to sex workers, and, since a good number had been trafficked from the villages to the brothels, social workers facilitated their retraining in other careers if they so wished.

3.2   The First Decade after the Revolution

After the revolution, drug addiction, gay sex, and prostitution were thrown into the same basket, as all of them were regarded as symptoms of severe social ills imported from the West. The official policy was the more people embrace Islamic mores and law, the quicker these "social ills" will disappear.

Sexual relations outside legally recognized marriages between a man and a woman were now considered a crime. A "war on drugs" was proclaimed under the first chief justice of the Iranian Revolutionary Courts, hojjatoleslam Khalkhali, which put an end to drug-related facilities and treatments. This meant that all three key populations were deeply impacted legally, politically, and even in terms of access to health services (Small Media 2018: 69–79). The newly passed (provisional) Penal

---

[3] Jafari et al. (2015: 297), for example, note that "Epidemiologic evidence supports that law enforcement policies have not been successful in reducing substance use in Iran. Total number of drug users in Iran has dramatically increased during the last three decades."

[4] Kermanian (2014: 16) describes this as "the first explicit, if not official, gay marriage in the history of modern Iran."

[5] See https://halatnewsdotcom.wordpress.com/2016/06/30/آیا-نخستین-ازدواج-دو-همجنس-در-تهران-اتف.

[6] The following BBC article in Persian discusses three sources that discuss Shahr-e No through a novel, a film, and a collection of photos: www.bbc.com/persian/arts/2013/01/130106_144_shahreno_book_review.shtml.

Code stipulated *hodud* punishments (including the death penalty) for illicit sex, that is, heterosexual sex outside marriage (*zenā'*),[7] sodomy, homosexual acts between men (*livat*) and between women (*musahāqah*), and pimping (*qavvādi*) (Nayyeri 2012: 5).[8] The character of *hadd* punishments is such that "they are regarded as fixed by God and therefore immutable ... there is no possibility of mitigation or replacement of the punishment and it also cannot be waived" (Nayyeri 2012: 6), with penalties to be carried out in public for the deterrence effect, and with strict definitions and evidentiary requirements (see Chapter 2 by Silvia Tellenbach in this volume).

Concretely, this meant the risk of facing the death penalty for sex workers and gays; stoning for MSM, extramarital sex,[9] and sodomy; and mandatory rehabilitation "camp" or prison for drug users.[10] These legal approaches were supported by a political attitude which considered the behaviors associated with the key populations as stemming from Western diseases. AIDS was viewed as a divine punishment for gays, lesbians, and sex workers.

The fact that the Islamic approach to drug use was not as clear cut, due to the absence of any explicit Quranic language on the matter, allowed flexibility. Debates around this and the appropriate responses were to be opened up much later. At this time, Iran saw the introduction of "a harsh anti-drug campaign" which meted out the "death penalty for drug trafficking," amounting to some 10,000 executions per decade (Jafari et al. 2015: 297).

Considering the stigmas involved, it is unsurprising to note that the first case of HIV to be reported by Iran was not related to the key populations. It dated to 1986 and concerned children suffering from hemophilia and thalassemia.[11] This resulted from infected blood products imported from France which infected over 300 people.[12] This too added

---

[7] In specific contexts, the penalty for *zenā'* is stoning. See Nayyeri (2012: 15–17).
[8] For more detail on the treatment of homosexuality in Iran see Justice for Iran and the Iranian Lesbian and Transgender Network, "Diagnosing Identities, Wounding Bodies, Medical Abuses and Other Human Rights Violations Against Lesbian, Gay and Transgender People in Iran," 2014, pp. 55–57, https://justice4iran.org/wp-content/uploads/2014/06/Pathologizing-Identities-Paralyzing-Bodies.pdf.
[9] For one example see *E'temād* newspaper reporting on such a sentencing (in Persian): https://tinyurl.com/p2aazfzf.
[10] For a discussion of what is a "camp" in Iran, see Ghiabi (2018: 279–280).
[11] From 1980 to 1988, there was limited access to blood because of the Iran–Iraq War. Blood was required to support the soldiers. Additionally, some needed it due to diseases such as hemophilia. For that reason, Iran bought and imported blood and blood products from other countries, such as France. Blood was imported and was distributed to people, including children with hemophilia. When HIV tests were carried out, the numbers infected through blood transfusion came to the fore.
[12] BBC News, "AIDS Scandals around the World," August 9, 2001: http://news.bbc.co.uk/1/hi/world/europe/1482021.stm, accessed May 7, 2021.

to the previous widespread association of HIV with a "'sinful' West" (Alaei and Alaei 2007: 49).

3.3 The Second Decade after the Revolution

Since, in Iran, the question of drug policy is not a matter under the purview of the Supreme Leader, the president has always proved very influential on this. The second decade after the revolution saw President Rafsanjani (August 1989–August 1997), known as the Leader of Reconstruction or Sardār-e Sāzandegi, bring in a different approach. Effectively, and on most matters, this meant a continuation of the same overall policy approaches but with less bloodshed and harshness thanks to the stability of the revolutionary government, the end of the Iran–Iraq War, an end to the early revolutionary purges, and fewer political killings.[13]

The approach to drugs was now to "control" them through a Drug Control Headquarters established in October 1989. Muhammad Fallah, formerly head of the Revolutionary Court of Kerman, was appointed the head of its secretariat. He was given the status of deputy president, with the president himself acting as its formal head. The Drug Control Headquarters brought together the Ministries of Intelligence, Health, Education, Ershad (Islamic Culture and Guidance), and the head of law enforcement, the head of national TV and radio, the head of the Tehran Revolutionary Court, the head of Basij, and the attorney general (dādsetān-e koll-e keshvar) to deal with a range of matters including both drug trafficking and treatment.

Who led the Drug Control Headquarters and what did his appointment indicate about the regime's view on appropriate responses to drug addiction? Fallah's appointment meant the Drug Control Headquarters had a former head of a revolutionary court serve as its chief, thus indicating a criminalizing approach to the issue rather than one of rehabilitation.

A human rights perspective would have suggested the appointment of someone with a social care background, not with a background from law enforcement, intelligence, or interior. This would have ensured that social workers took the lead with a treatment approach to the issue. Subunits, such as those concerned with drug trafficking, would play a role, but not take the lead. With the punitive approach, treatment and rehabilitation disappeared from the agenda, whereas a medical approach would require that the treatment aspect led and prevailed over a policing

---

[13] There was, however, a sharp change of approach with regard to family planning – with the introduction of a comprehensive and extensive birth control policy in the early 1990s.

approach to drug trafficking. The human rights and medical rationale for this is clear if drug use is recognized as "a chronic illness" (Claeson 2011: 232) and the "bi-directional correlation between mental disorders and HIV infection" (Shadloo et al. 2018: 25) is recognized.

It is also worth noting that in Iran in the early 2000s "[p]rison inmates between the ages of 19–39 constitute 79 percent of drug related offenders who are serving their sentences in prisons" (Jafari et al. 2015: 297; also see Chapter 7 by Anna Enayat and Hadi Enayat in this volume). Incarceration also impacts the human rights of so many others. As one article observes, it "solves no problem of substance users and their families, but it increases the risk of acquiring HIV/AIDS and makes the already dysfunctional families more dysfunctional. Incarceration brings a mass of economic and psychosocial problems to the families of substance users ... [and] facilitates the transmission of these infections [i.e., HIV/AIDS]" (Jafari et al. 2015: 299).

Fallah's appointment highlighted the fact that drugs were considered a national security matter under President Rafsanjani. In his presidency, the Ministry of Intelligence also gained prominence and played an important role in the war on drugs. His administration's approach, in general, was one of control. By way of example, he started the building of a wall between Iran and Afghanistan to stem the drugs trade (Dahl 2007), to which reportedly more than USD 600 million came to be dedicated (Bjerre 2017: 423).

In 1996, the first prisoner was diagnosed with HIV in Kerman's Ab-e Hayat Prison. This led to 1996–1997 survey carried out by the authorities regarding the AIDS epidemic in three prisons: Kerman (Āb-e Hayāt Prison), Shiraz (Vakil Ābād Prison), and Kermanshah (Dizel Ābād Prison).[14] The results, showing a very high level of prevalence, greatly shocked the authorities. In fact, the report led to the closure of the Kerman Prison and the separation of AIDS patients from other inmates in the Shiraz and Kermanshah prisons. The high prevalence was partly due to the fact that drug users had been sent to prison. The alternative available at the time was to send them to camps, that is, "short-term and medium-term in-patient treatment centres" (Ghiabi 2018: 279) that will be discussed further in Section 4. In Kermanshah, the response took a different turn. Dr. Manouchehr Behnia, member of parliament from March 1996 to March 2000 and also a medical doctor, proposed in the national

---

[14] As reported by Raja News, Azar 11, 1388, IRNA (Islamic Republic News Agency) had an interview with Esmaeili, director of the Prisons Organization, www.rajanews.com. *E'temād*, Bahman 7, 1388/January 27, 2010, p. 8, social report by Banafsheh Samgiss. www.magiran.com/article/2032387, accessed September 3, 2023.

parliament that the first hospital for HIV care be built in Kermanshah. Parliament approved this proposal, and he secured the necessary funds. However, when news of this reverberated through Kermanshah, people took to the streets and objected that their city would become blighted by this association and "no one will marry our girls." The hospital was never built, and the MP lost his seat.

We, the authors, were from the same city, but we took a different approach. We decided that the sustainable way to proceed was to set up a pilot AIDS service within the primary healthcare clinics that already existed in Kermanshah, later to become known as the "Triangular Clinics" (explored in more detail in Section 4.3. This approach became established and well supported, and expanded throughout the country during Khatami's presidency (August 1997– August 2005) – a presidential period which was more socially progressive than the previous presidential periods and less ideologically driven in its policies. However, the Ahmadinejad presidency (August 2005–August 2013), characterized by social conservatism and a desire to return to the revolutionary purity of the Khomeini years, put an end to all this. This period also saw our arrest and sentencing to three and six years in prison respectively, and our forced exile from Iran following the prison terms.

4   The Key Populations in Iran during and after the Khatami Era

4.1   The Khatami Presidency

Khatami's presidency (September 1997–August 2005) marked recognition of the need for more societal openness. This opening of spaces impacted numerous public policy fields, whether in relation to AIDS, journalism, music, dress codes, or publishing. The later reversal of the tightening of pressures led some to comment that the government did not have the capacity to control the consequences of its liberalizations.

4.2   The Treatment Approach to Drug Users

Khatami's presidency also saw the acceptance and spread of the Triangular Clinic methodology and the year 1998, just months into his presidency, marked "a striking change of direction" in the government's approach to drug addiction. It legalized the treatment of drug users, focusing on both harm reduction and demand reduction. Now drug treatment was no longer opposed but considered "humanitarian,"

"Islamic," and part of the government's "redefined responsibilities toward vulnerable citizens" (Christensen 2017: 408).

Regarding drug users, there was now acknowledgment of the failure of the "war on drugs" and the approval of a harm-reduction approach in its place (Ghiabi 2018: 280). It still fell under a policing approach, but services including needle exchanges, and condom promotion and distribution were to be supplied to users. The head of the Drug Control Headquarters was Ali Hashemi from the Ministry of Intelligence. Drug laws were amended in 1999 "to allow drug users to seek treatment from government or licensed private treatment centres" (Jafari et al. 2015 297).

4.3   Setting Up the Triangular Clinics: "Dancing with the Restrictions"

Concurrently, a field experience was emerging from the grassroots, offering timely policy evidence. Described by Behrouzan (2010: 319) as "a dramatic illustration and a model for Iranian health care practitioners and international policy-makers [...] in a highly complex and sensitive political setting," the aim of the Triangular Clinics was to cater to the health needs of the key populations at risk of HIV infection. They were "triangular" as they worked in the three fields of "sexually transmitted infections (STI), HIV/AIDS, and drug-addiction programs," offering a comprehensive harm-reduction approach (Joulaei and Zarei 2018: 33). This included needles, methadone, condoms, treatment for sexually transmitted infections, antiretroviral therapy, and other medical services for people living with HIV/AIDS.

Although the existence of HIV had long been denied, the first outbreak was, as mentioned, officially acknowledged as a result of infected blood imported from France. The second outbreak was acknowledged and traced to three prisons, as discussed, where a high prevalence of infection was found, not least due to the sharing of needles. As Behrouzan (2010: 333) explains, the problem was exacerbated by the fact that "many injecting drug users in prisons choose to share needles, even when clean needles are available, as a gesture of solidarity and collective ritual."[15] The risk of HIV in the wider population was highly evident since Iran had one of the highest per capita rates of opioid users in the world.

The first challenge was that of initiating clinics in the very city that had recently seen vocal public protests to an HIV clinic being established there. We proceeded deliberately and gradually. We started by

---

[15] Khazaei et al. (2019: 357) report that Iran's HIV epidemic "is concentrated among IDUs [intravenous drug users], 68.1% of cases are due to needle-sharing versus 12.7% to sexual transmission."

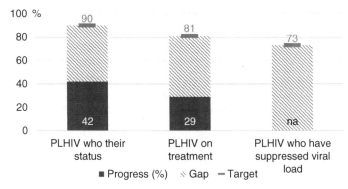

Figure 8.2 HIV testing and treatment cascade in Iran, 2020
Note: As these figures show, the number of people living with HIV who know their status stands at 42 percent, those living with HIV on treatment at 29 percent. There is no data to understand viral suppression among those who started treatment. These stand far lower than the 90–90–90 Joint United Nations Programme on HIV/AIDS (UNAIDS) 2020 target for all countries to ensure: 90 percent of all people living with HIV will know their HIV status, 90 percent of all people with diagnosed HIV infection will receive sustained antiretroviral therapy, and 90 percent of all people receiving antiretroviral therapy will have viral suppression.
Source: UNAIDS (2021a). www.unaids.org/en/regionscountries/countries/islamicrepublicofiran, accessed September 3, 2023

persuading the director of public health in Kermanshah to grant us a small room in the polyclinic of the Medical University of Kermanshah as a base.[16] This allowed the HIV care to become integrated into the regular Iranian health system, one that has been described as "a well-organized health network system at grass root with an eminent role of the community health workers" (Joulaei and Zarei, 2018: 33). It also allowed us to refrain from identifying (and therefore stigmatizing) patients as likely suffering from HIV by calling them to attend an HIV-only clinic or hospital.[17] A further element of the approach was that patients were

---

[16] It should be noted that medical universities in Iran are under the authority of the Ministry of Health, Treatment and Medical Education. As Asadi et al. (2018: 151) note, "Executive tasks of the Ministry of Health have been delegated to Medical Sciences Universities of each province."

[17] For a detailed discussion of why key populations in Iran do not present themselves for HIV testing, see Asadi et al. (2018: 159). The authors note that "patients' information has been disclosed in some cases, and this has caused them to be expelled from work, consequently leading to their distrust in the health care personnel ... but also to the lack of referring again or even concealing their disease in future referrals."

not asked for any personal details such as their names and addresses, and no inquiry was made of how they may have contracted, or why they suspected that they were at risk of contracting HIV. As Behrouzan (2010: 154–157) observed, "the aim of the 'triangular' idea was to diffuse and reduce stigma associated with each of these overlapping populations by avoiding direct reference to HIV and AIDS and to increase the effectiveness of interventions by bringing these three groups together."

We realized that the single main cause of death amongst HIV positive patients in their home province was suicide within a year of diagnosis, usually due to an enormous sense of helplessness, fear of social stigmatization, and social isolation (Alaei and Alaei 2007: 49). We also observed the very high suicide rate of 58 percent amongst HIV patients (Alaei and Alaei 2002).

The clinics therefore started by offering psychosocial and educational counselling to HIV patients and their families, at the clinic during the day and at patients' houses at night. This was seen as crucial to the support of patients and to their adherence to treatment. Patient numbers at the clinic climbed to some eighty patients a day and allowed a gradual expansion of our services from education and counselling to general medical care of HIV patients, including mother and child HIV screening and also non-HIV-related primary care. The Triangular HIV Clinics began to expand into the local Kermanshah prison and focused on drug addiction, HIV/AIDS, and other sexually transmitted infections. All care was provided for free.

The clinic and its success were showcased by the head of the Centre for Disease Control of Iran and chancellor of Kermanshah Medical University at the 2000 Middle East AIDS conference in Beirut. Following this, Iran's Ministry of Health became involved, and this gradually allowed for an expansion of the clinics throughout Iran. Step by step, other authorities were engaged for their support: Prison authorities, the judicial branch, the Ministry of Education,[18] the Ministry of Welfare and Social Security, policymakers, religious authorities, healthcare workers, and, most importantly, civil society. This gradually allowed the provision of HIV/AIDS education, counselling, and medical care for vulnerable drug users outside the prisons in a context where the laws continued to criminalize drug users. Each advantage was leveraged to expand the reach of the Triangular Clinics. The recognition of the clinics by WHO/

---

[18] Dr. Gheyratmand, working in the office of the deputy of health and sports in the Ministry of Education, was approached to create a committee to develop HIV educational materials for schools. The objective was to prevent the spread of HIV/AIDS among the young. This initiative later received support from the United Nations Children's Fund (UNICEF).

EMRO as a "Best Practice Model" in 2003 was particularly helpful in this regard.[19]

By 2006 there were clinics in sixty-seven Iranian cities and fifty-seven prisons (Aman and Maher 2006). Other providers would also visit, learn, and become inspired to set up their own care facilities throughout the country. In time, the methodology came to be reflected in the National Strategic Plan for Fighting HIV and AIDS, effectively acknowledging the provision of care as a positive right, as a government obligation to protect and provide for these key populations.[20]

It is worth drawing specific attention to the engagement of religious leaders. We had already reached out to religious authorities in Kermanshah prior to WHO recognition to gain their endorsement for the activities. The next wave of reaching out to these authorities came in 2004. As the model was spreading, there was concern that there could be a negative reaction from religious leaders. If the leaders were to claim that the Triangular Clinics endangered Islam, all the work could be effectively brought to a standstill overnight. To preempt such a possibility, over fifty fatwas were gradually obtained by stakeholders from a range of religious authorities throughout the country. A booklet of fatwas was even made available to reassure the fearful that their support was not Islamically suspect.

The first thing to note in relation to the significance of this question is, as Ghiabi et al. (2018: 121) note, that Iran is "unique in that it combines religious exegesis with political machination through official channels." In other research, Ghiabi et al. put eight questions on cannabis to nineteen senior religious leaders. Ghiabi et al.'s findings were that the majority did not consider cannabis *harām* or forbidden. Its status was "ambiguous," meaning that there could be a shift from the current "uncompromising ban on drug use" to what the majority of the senior religious leaders suggested: "regulated administration" (Ghiabi et al. 2018: 125). The majority also supported the use of cannabis where "scientific and medical research" justified it "for reasons other than intoxication and inebriation" (Ghiabi et al. 2018: 125).

Returning to the Triangular Clinics, the right of people living with HIV/AIDS, and the right of key populations to access treatment, came

---

[19] WHO EMRO, "Best Practice in HIV/AIDS Prevention and Care for Injecting Drug Abusers: The Triangular Clinic in Kermanshah, Islamic Republic of Iran," September 2, 2004: http://applications.emro.who.int/aiecf/who_em_std_052_e_en.pdf, accessed September 3, 2023.

[20] WHO, "Best Practice for HIV/AIDS Prevention and Care for Re-injecting Drug Users: The Triangular Clinic in Kermanshah, Islamic Republic of Iran," Cairo, 2004: www.who.int/hiv/pub/idu/idu_emro_iran_2004.pdf?ua=1, accessed March 14, 2019.

to enjoy positive recognition in Iran. The approach switched from total denial of the existence of the related phenomena to full recognition. Detection and treatment were fully integrated into the national health system both inside prison and in wider society, to such an extent that there was ready access to Triangular Clinics in most big cities.

4.4   A Change of Approach by the Head of the Judiciary

The unique contribution of the Triangular Clinics was not merely the medical service offered but the stance of equality and respect toward the key populations. This was the prime reason why the Triangular Clinics were able to deeply engage and attract all the key populations and people living with HIV to access services and receive social support. This makes the fact that this approach proved persuasive and contributed to a U-turn in the whole government's approach all the more interesting.

The challenge was now to allow the bottom-up and micro experience of the Kermanshah experience to be scaled up through the national health system itself and be allowed to spread throughout the country. Additionally, the support of the Drug Control Headquarters, at the macro level and in a top-down manner, played an important role. Using our cultural capital – both institutionalized and embodied – we tried to bridge this micro–macro connection, to allow a breakthrough. This breakthrough eventually arrived with an executive order issued by the head of the judiciary, Ayatollah Seyyed Mahmoud Hashemi Shahroudi (1999–2009), explicitly endorsing increased access to HIV services to key populations and those living with HIV/AIDS.

The Executive Order of the Head of Judiciary System stated that the "obligations of the Ministry of Health and Medical Education"[21] included the "implementation of programs necessary for the prevention of transmission of communicable diseases aimed at harm reduction."[22] The order, addressed to "all judicial authorities nationwide," specified interventions such as needles, syringes, methadone, "and other material used individually by drug addicts and AIDS patients"[23] (a subtle endorsement of the distribution of condoms as well). It specifically noted that some judicial authorities "have considered such an intervention as tantamount to a crime, subject to punitive action, thus unintentionally

---

[21] Seyyed Mahmoud Hashemi Shahroudi, Head of the Judiciary, Executive Order to all Judicial Authorities, January 24, 2005, Reference 1-83-14434.
[22] Ibid.
[23] Ibid.

impeding the implementation of health and treatment programs."[24] The order reminds the authorities that such interventions clearly had no "malicious intent" and, in fact, were "motivated by the ... mission of protecting society from the spread of deadly contagious diseases such as AIDS and hepatitis"[25] – hence they should neither be characterized unfairly, nor impeded. In short, Shahroudi's order noted that harm reduction is not only not a crime but is a positive intervention in society. With the order, the head of the judiciary now backed up the presidency, the Drug Control Headquarters, and religious authorities.

4.5 Khāneh-hā ʿEfāf *(Chastity Houses)*

Another of the new approaches under the Khatami administration was the advocacy of Khāneh-hā ʿEfāf or "chastity houses." These had been introduced under the Rafsanjani presidency and he had continued his encouragement of this proposal into the Khatami period. Khāneh-hā ʿEfāf encouraged temporary marriage and provided "a means to avoid allegations of illegal sex work" (Behrouzan 2010: 337); in fact, it was the only possible framework through which to offer some protection to sex workers. When framed as *sigheh* or temporary marriage – "a contractual agreement (as all marriage is according to Islamic jurisprudence) in which the two parties determine beforehand the duration of the marital bond" (Ghiabi 2018: 291) – the women concerned could have access to some protection. For example, they would have recourse to the law in terms of the contractually agreed payment, and resort to the police in cases of violence and abuse – since their behavior would no longer be classified as criminal. This also forced some responsibility on the men engaging in *sigheh* relating to any child that could result and agreement over the terms of the liaison. The relative merits, or otherwise, of this partial protection of rights are best understood in light of the realities of the context.

The particular vulnerabilities of women to HIV in Iran should also be noted. "Unsafe sex and drug injection" are the main routes of HIV transmission to women (Samiei et al. 2016: 5). Female drug users "face greater risk of HIV infection and stigmatization and are harder to reach" (Claeson 2011: 231) than male drug users.[26] In light of the establishment

---

[24] Ibid.
[25] Ibid.
[26] HIV transmission spreads more easily to women due to their physiology, making it even more important to reach them. However, it is harder for HIV/AIDS services to reach women. One reason is due to the stigma of society viewing them as sex workers or injecting drug users, even though they may have been infected from their husbands. Furthermore, sex workers themselves are presumed to have been the source of the spread of HIV/AIDS.

Legal Barriers to Accessing Vital Medical Services 251

of a methadone treatment clinic specifically for women in Tehran, it was observed that women access such services when "there were female staff, a suitable location and facility, including dedicated space for children and reproductive health services, social and psychological support, in addition to harm reduction and methadone maintenance therapy" – in short, "if they can be provided [with a] safe space and services tailored to their needs" (Claeson 2011: 232).

4.6   The Ahmadinejad Presidency

In 2005, the presidency changed from the Khatami administration to the Ahmadinejad administration (August 2005–August 2013) and moved in a more conservative direction. The general social environment saw many changes and these, in turn, each had either a general or targeted impact on the key populations. In terms of the generalized impact, for example, a large number of some 2,000 nongovernmental organizations (NGOs) that had started operating under the Khatami administration had to close down. This "securitization of domestic politics" (Christensen 2017: 411) had sharp consequences for the key populations, as can be seen in Figures 8.3 and 8.4.

As can be seen from Figures 8.3 and 8.4, case registrations first peaked around 1998. This was due to the pilot studies in the three prisons. The subsequent fall was due to the overreaction of the population to the proposal of the MP from Kermanshah. The second peak in new case findings around 2004 was due to the increase in testing and the establishment of trust. During the eight years of the Ahmadinejad presidency (2005–2013), the number of new registered cases fell significantly, since the key populations were too fearful to access AIDS services. The officials misinterpreted the data, claiming that the decrease in the number of new cases showed that they had been able to control HIV, a claim that is not sustainable.

The approach to women, for example, was impacted by the reversal of the family planning policies impacting access to condoms (Famili 1386/2007). The approach to drugs also turned from *demand reduction* (treat drug users; if they are treated, they won't seek drugs) to *supply reduction* (close borders, etc.). The harm-reduction programs, for example needle exchange, were negatively affected in terms of accessibility, quantity, and quality. Regarding drug users, the approach turned from a *harm-reduction approach*, favored under the Khatami administration and supported in the Shahroudi Executive Order of January 2005, to a punitive or *national security approach*. Though methadone treatment did not diminish throughout Ahmadinejad's presidency (Ghiabi 2018: 285) the objectives of the National Strategic Plan to expand *harm reduction* slowed down dramatically.

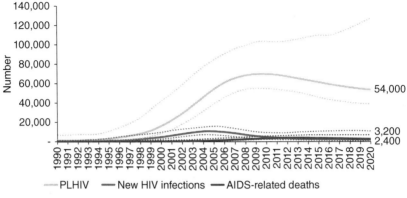

Figure 8.3 Estimated number of people living with HIV, new HIV infections, and AIDS-related deaths, 1990–2020
Source: UNAIDS (2021b).

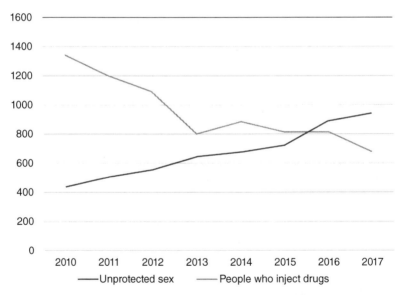

Figure 8.4 HIV population by mode of contraction, 2010–2017
Source: Figures are reproduced from the UNAIDS website.[27]

[27] (In Persian): "Report on AIDS Monitoring Control in the Islamic Republic of Iran," Secretariat of the National AIDS Working Group, Ministry of Health and Medical Education, Esfand 1395/February 2017: www.unaids.org/sites/default/files/country/documents/IRN_2017_countryreport.pdf, accessed March 15, 2020.

The approach of the new presidency also impacted the appointments at the Iranian Drug Control Headquarters. General Esmail Ahmadi-Moghaddam – head of law enforcement and a member of Sepah (the Revolutionary Guards) – took over at the helm, and was followed in 2010 by General Mohammad Najar. Furthermore, Ayatollah Sadegh Amoli Larijani, formerly of the Guardian Council, was appointed as the head of the judiciary in August 2009, marking a conservative turn. In what Ghiabi (2018: 283) has referred to as an "institutional response," drug users were once again arrested, sent to prison, or forced into compulsory treatment camps more akin to prisons (Ghiabi 2018: 284). The number of executions of drug traffickers rose very sharply, with drug smugglers "accounting for approximately 75% of annual executions during the last three years of Ahmadinejad's presidency" and "reaching a record-setting 509 drug-related executions in 2011" (Christensen 2017: 412). Though the law itself had not changed, the approach to drug users had shifted from a harm-reduction approach to a coercive and punitive approach.

Just before the Ahmadinejad presidency, a joint Russian–Iranian research project with Dr. Mohammad Farhadi as head of the Ministry of Health, claimed an Iranian herbal drug was a cure for AIDS.[28] This research project intended to put patients, including late-stage patients whose life would be at immediate risk, on this treatment plan,[29] despite the gold standard antiretroviral therapy being widely available due to budgetary support from the Global Fund to Fight HIV, Tuberculosis and Malaria.[30] This research did not emerge from academia or private research centers. It emerged from very well-funded research from the Office of the Research and Innovation of the Presidency. It was this center that had, for example, employed the Russian scientist. This claim had little traction until the Ahmadinejad presidency, at which time the president himself came to the fore, adopting this as part and parcel of a number of astonishing scientific claims.

In September 2007, during the United Nations (UN) General Assembly meeting in New York, President Ahmadinejad delivered a speech at Columbia University. In his address, he asserted that there is no homosexual population in Iran (Whitaker 2007). In other speeches, President Ahmadinejad made other claims in relation to nuclear

---

[28] (In Persian): Deutsche Welle Farsi, "A New Drug to Treat AIDS?," February 4, 2007: https://m.dw.com/fa-ir/ایدز-درمان-برای-جدید-دارویی/a-2398219/, accessed March 10, 2018.

[29] For another example, see World Health Net, "Iran Claims Found Herbal Cure for AIDS," February 6, 2007: www.worldhealth.net/news/iran_claims_found_herbal_cure_for_aids_a/, accessed March 12, 2018. See also Joseph (2008).

[30] The Global Fund, "United against Malaria": www.theglobalfund.org/en/, accessed May 10, 2020.

capability, an Iranian cure for paralysis, and so on. In this context, the claim of the Iranian cure for AIDS gained momentum and political weight, becoming a significant motif of the president, its political weight being evident from the fact that President Ahmadinejad made the announcement in a speech marking the anniversary of the Islamic Revolution.

All in all, the presidency ignored the key populations (or denied their existence altogether in the case of homosexuals) in Iran on the one hand and, on the other, claimed that Iran held the keys to an herbal treatment for AIDS. The president even removed the commemoration of International AIDS Day from the annual calendar. The return to the harsher policies of the past in relation to the key populations meant that patients became fearful to attend the Triangular Clinics for HIV testing and treatment. As a consequence, case findings decreased.

We objected to the claim of an Iranian herbal cure for AIDS, since the life of late-stage patients would be jeopardized. Patients had an immediate need to access antiretroviral treatment instead of placebos resulting from questionable and ineffective clinical trials. In 2007, Kamiar Alaei wrote to the Human Rights Watch about the human rights risks that would result from the president's new focus on the Iranian–Russian research project. In turn, the Human Rights Watch wrote to the World Health Assembly, which voiced its objections to the Iranian Ministry of Health. The Ministry gave no response.[31] Dr. Arash Alaei (1385/2006) published an extensive article in *Shargh* newspaper outlining objections and the risk to patients. It was written as a scientific commentary for a public audience, stating that the claim that the herbal remedy cured AIDS was scientifically unproven and risked patients' lives.[32] We were arrested the following year and sentenced to six and three years in prison respectively.[33]

4.7 The Rouhani Presidency

The Rouhani presidency (August 2013–August 2021) claimed the mantle of a middle way, neither conservative nor reformist. By this time,

---

[31] Human Rights Watch, "Iran: Guarantee Protections for HIV Patients," November 27, 2007: www.hrw.org/news/2007/11/27/iran-guarantee-protections-hiv-patients, accessed May 15, 2020. Also see Amnesty International, "Iran Resorts to Mass Executions to Deal with Its Drug Crisis," December 16, 2011: www.amnestyusa.org/iran-resorts-to-mass-executions-to-deal-with-its-drug-crisis/, accessed February 10, 2018.

[32] (In Persian): BBC Persian, "Testing a New Drug to Treat AIDS," Mordad 2, 1389/July 24, 2010: www.bbc.com/persian/iran/2010/08/100811_l07_iran89_aids_hiv_aimod, accessed March 12, 2018.

[33] See "Free the Iranian HIV/AIDS Doctors!," October 30, 2008. Physicians for Human Rights: https://i-base.info/htb/140, accessed September 3, 2023.

trust had already been severely broken amongst the key populations, the restrictive birth control policy was still in place, and the purview of the Revolutionary Guards rather than the Ministry of Intelligence over national security could not be reversed. The role of the Basij forces had also been strengthened during the Ahmadinejad presidency, for example in the severity of restrictions over sex workers. The new presidency was ineffectual in intervening to open this space.

Despite the potential of the new presidential rhetoric regarding the key populations, it was not impactful. For example, the right to health was included in the Citizenship Rights Charter,[34] but did not lead to tangible results. It may be said that no concrete shifts can be observed in any direction in relation to the key populations and their access to treatment.

President Rouhani's appointee as secretary of the Drug Control Headquarters was Abdolreza Rahmani-Fazli, who also served as the minister of interior. Due to his workload, Rahmani-Fazli appointed Police Chief Brigadier General Eskandar Momeni as his successor. The head of the judiciary remained a conservative, with Ayatollah Sadegh Amoli Larijani in the post until March 2019 and then the ultraconservative hojjatoleslam Ebrahim Raisi. This did not allow amenability to any flexibility or new legal breakthroughs. This contrasts with a neutral stance to key populations by the Ministry of Health. The Ministry of Health has made a few announcements about countering the spread of AIDS. The Ministry has neither sought to engender fear amongst the key populations, but nor has it offered much support. There have, however, been some supportive public education campaigns and announcements by the Ministry. The services have continued, and case findings have increased, but detection still falls very short and the overall rate of findings has not improved. As one 2018 article reports, there remains "a remarkable gap," with only 30–40 percent of those living with HIV being aware of their status – highlighting lost opportunities as "numerous people receive their HIV diagnosis at a late stage of the disease" (Joulaei and Zaraei 2018: 33). This 60–70 percent gap of those who are not aware of their HIV status has remained consistent over the last three presidencies and remains an ominous challenge.

Overall, the administration has been ineffectual on these issues because of contrasting stances taken by the Drug Control Headquarters, Prisons Organization, Ministry of Health, and the head of the judiciary. However, the criteria for the application of the death penalty were revised in relation to the weight of drugs traffickers carried. This

---

[34] For an English translation of the charter, see: http://president.ir/en/96865.

has resulted in a reduction in the numbers sentenced to death for drug trafficking.[35] The fact that the Speaker of Parliament, the head of the judiciary, and the head of the High Council on Human Rights were all brothers at that time (the Larijani brothers), could well have facilitated the brokering of this decision in light of international pressure. The inconsistency of the treatment by the authorities of drug traffickers versus drug users (there having been minor reduction in the instances of arrest or imprisonment for drug users which have changed over time) shows that the impetus has not been a comprehensive concern but a knee-jerk reaction to pressure.

5   Conclusion and Lessons Learned for Other Issues and in Similar Settings

As we have seen, where Iranian law followed the specific and clear determination of shari'a – for example, in regulating sex workers and MSM – this was consolidated in the Iranian constitution and resulted in specific criminal penalties in the law, leaving little flexibility for reinterpretation and little room for legal reform. As a consequence, sex workers and MSM have been left with extremely poor access to AIDS services throughout the decades since 1979. Other than the partial protection that could accrue to sex workers contracting a *sigheh* (temporary) marriage, no other means of legal protection were available to them.

The matter was quite different, however, when it came to drug users. Since there was no explicit shari'a-inspired policy on drugs, the response to it was not specified in the constitution or in other laws. In this instance, governmental authorities exhibited some openness to a pragmatist approach. The political outlook and tone of the country's presidency were key in this regard, as, depending on who was president at a given time, one of two approaches would be taken. Where the revolutionary "war on drugs" and policing (or armed forces) approach dominated, the focus was on countering trafficking, criminalizing addiction, and enforcing drug bans. Where the Ministry of Intelligence approach dominated, by contrast, *amniyat* or national security would be prioritized, resulting, perhaps counterintuitively, in a softer national security and harm-reduction approach, for example, the offering of methadone treatment and needle exchanges.

---

[35] For a discussion of these changes (in Persian), see Iranian Students News Agency (ISNA), "Which Traffickers Will Not Be Executed under the New Law," Day 20, 1396/ January 10, 2018: https://tinyurl.com/2xcucye8, accessed May 15, 2019.

The flexibility of the law and susceptibility to modification could only find opportunity where there was no explicit shariʿa-inspired prohibition at play. The impossibility of basing a drugs policy on shariʿa allowed for the formulation of a harm-reduction approach facilitating access for concerned populations to HIV services. Though a principled human rights-centered discussion would not have succeeded in changing the drug policy toward a harm-reduction approach, the approach was able to proceed "when advanced as a part of projects seeking practical solutions, which address local social concerns" (Christensen 2017: 431). An examination of the challenges faced by those seeking to provide health access to the key populations reveals that success not only depends on identifying legal loopholes, but also on taking part in a masquerade with many participants, all of whom know what lies under each mask.

Even where there *was* the window of opportunity, as in the case of drug users, there was still the need for innovative professional intermediaries to put forward solutions, as the government remained inactive on the issue. Our case study illustrates the significance of *intermediaries* as a channel from the grassroots to the *negotiators* who have access to those that hold the reins of power, the political *leadership*. Experts with wide-ranging cultural capital and informed by evidence-based learning could act as intermediaries between the grassroots and the political leadership (Aman and Maher 2006). The intermediaries from the grassroots cannot access the leadership directly. They therefore stand in need of negotiators, who can act as a bridge between the service providers and the leaders and who can also persuade the leadership. The grassroots, alone, are unable to reach the negotiator. They stand in need of intermediaries. In turn, the intermediary is unable to reach or persuade the leadership directly but stands in need of negotiators. When the three actors (intermediaries, negotiators, and those in leadership) are informed and connected to the grassroots and can use specific language acceptable to the leadership (i.e., Islamic legal concepts pursuant to the desired legal initiative), the opportunity of changed interpretations and applications in the law can be brokered. Without these actors and the mastery of pertinent Islamic legal concepts, the challenges prove insurmountable. This is the method required to change the interpretation and application of the law. In such contexts, the rule of law can be abrogated by the power of such key persons (intermediaries, negotiators, and those in leadership) and their networks, rather than merely by the mandate or competence of these individuals as pursuant to their position within the political or legal system. That is, the informal power of these agents and networks can override any formal rule of law.

Bibliography

Alaei, Arash. "Reflections on the Discovery of the AIDS Drug [in Persian]," *Shargh*, Vol. 855, September 11, 2006 [Shahrivar 20, 1385], pp. 28. www.magiran.com/npview.asp?ID=1201562, accessed September 3, 2023.

Alaei, Kamiar and Alaei, Arash. "The History of HIV/AIDS in Iran: From a Long Denial to Breaking the Silence," *Epidemic Proportions* (John Hopkins Undergraduate Public Health Journal), 4 (1), 2007. https//pages.jh.edu/ep/Downloads/Issues/Vol4Issue1.pdf, accessed March 15, 2020.

Alaei, Kamiar and Arash Alaei. "The assessment of epidemiologic status of mortality among HIV infected patients from April 2000 until Nov 2001." *XIV International AIDS Congress*, July 2002. Barcelona, Spain. Abstract (WePeF6875).

Aman, Fatemeh and Heather Maher. "Iran: Brothers Change Face of HIV, Drug-Addiction Treatment," *Radio Free Europe*, October 3, 2006. www.rferl.org/a/1071768.html, accessed March 15, 2020.

Amon, Joseph H. "Dangerous Medicines: Unproven AIDS Cures and Counterfeit Antiretroviral Drugs," *Global Health*, 4 (5), February 27, 2008. www.ncbi.nlm.nih.gov/pmc/articles/PMC2291042/, accessed September 3, 2023.

Asadi, Heshmatollah, Mohammad Hassan Imani-Nasab, Ali Garavand, Mojtaba Hasoum, Abdollah Almasian, Behzad Haghi, and Fatemeh Setoodehzadeh. "HIV Positive Patients' Experience of Receiving Health Care Services: A Phenomenology Study in Iran," *The Open AIDS Journal*, 12, 2018, pp. 150–161.

Behrouzan, Orkideh. "An Epidemic of Meanings: HIV and AIDS in Iran and the Significance of History, Language and Gender," in Nguyen Vinh-Kim and Jennifer F. Klot (eds.), *The Fourth Wave: Violence, Gender, Culture & HIV in the 21st Century*, Social Science Research Council; UNESCO, 2010, pp. 319–346.

Christensen, Janne Bjerre. "Human Rights and Wrongs in Iran's Drug Diplomacy with Europe," *Middle East Journal*, 71 (3), Summer 2017, pp. 403–432. www.jstor.org/stable/90016471, accessed September 3, 2023.

Claeson, Mariam. "Reaching Women Drug Users with Methadone Treatment and Other HIV Prevention Services in Tehran," *Journal of Public Health Policy*, 32 (2), 2011, pp. 231–233.

Dahl, Fredrik. "'Iranian Wall' Seen Hindering Drug Smugglers: UN," *Reuters*, May 13, 2007. www.reuters.com/article/us-iran-drugs/iranian-wall-seen-hindering-drug-smugglers-un-idUSDAH33724920070513, accessed September 3, 2023.

Famili, Shireen. "Ahmadinejad's Two Year Record: Women and Two Tumultuous Years [in Persian]," *Radio Farda*, July 21, 2007 [Tir 30, 1386]. www.radiofarda.com/a/o1_wemen_after_ahmadinejad/399214.html, accessed September 3, 2023.

Ghiabi, Maziyar. "Maintaining Disorder: The Micropolitics of Drugs Policy in Iran," *Third World Quarterly*, 39 (2), 2018, pp. 277–297.

Ghiabi, Maziyar, Masoomeh Maarefvand, Hamed Baheri, and Zohreh Alavi. "Islam and Cannabis: Legalisation and Religious Debate in Iran," *International Journal of Drug Policy*, 56, 2018, pp. 121–127.

Jafari, Siavash, Richard Mathias, Ronald S Joe, Souzan Baharlou, and Ashkan Nasr. "Effect of Law Enforcement on Drug Abuse: A Comparison of Substance

Use in Pakistan, Afghanistan, Iran and Turkey," *Journal of Substance Use*, 20 (4), 2015, pp. 295–300.

Joulaei, Hassan and Nooshin Zarei. "An Analytic Approach to HIV Testing and Counselling Services in Iran," *Journal of HIV/AIDS & Social Services*, 17 (1), 2018, pp. 32–34.

Kermanian, Sara. "Creation of Subjectivity in Spaces of Crisis: A Case Study of Daneshjoo Park, Tehran, Iran," (Master's thesis). University of British Columbia, Vancouver, CA, 2014. https://open.library.ubc.ca/cIRcle/collections/ubctheses/24/items/1.0167227, accessed September 3, 2023.

Khazaei, Salman, Ensiyeh Jenabi, and Shahab Rezaeian. "Practical Approaches for Size Estimation of High-Risk Groups in HIV/AIDS Control Program in Iran," *Iran Journal of Public Health*, 48(2), 2019, pp. 357–358.

Najmabadi, Afsaneh. *Professing Selves: Transsexuality and Same-Sex Desire in Contemporary Iran*, Duke University Press, 2013.

Nayyeri, Mohammad Hossein. "New Islamic Penal Code of the Islamic Republic of Iran: An Overview," University of Essex, Human Rights in Iran Unit, Research Paper, 2012. www1.essex.ac.uk/hri/documents/HRIU_Research_Paper-IRI_Criminal_Code-Overview.pdf, accessed September 3, 2023.

Samiei, Mercedeh, Afsaneh Moradi, Roya Noori, Sepideh Aryanfard, Rafiey, Hassan, and Naranijiha, Hooman. "Persian At-Risk Women and Barriers to Receiving HIV Services in Drug Treatment: First Report from Iran," *International Journal of High Risk Behaviours and Addiction*, 5 (2), 2016, p. e27488. doi: 10.5812/ijhrba.27488

Shadloo, Behrang, Masomeh Amin-Esmaeili, Abbas Motevalian, Minoo Mohraz, Abbas Sedaghat, Mohammad Mehdi Gouya, and Afarin Rahimi-Movaghar. "Psychiatric Disorders among People Living with HIV/AIDS in IRAN: Prevalence, Severity, Service Utilization and Unmet Mental Health Needs," *Journal of Psychosomatic Research*, 110, 2018, pp. 24–31.

Small Media. "Breaking the Silence, Digital Media and the Struggle for LGBTQ Rights in Iran." 2018. https://smallmedia.org.uk/media/projects/files/BreakingTheSilence_2018.pdf, accessed March 15, 2020.

UNAIDS (Joint United Nations Programme on HIV/AIDS). "HIV and AIDS Estimates." *AIDS Info 2021 Country Factsheets: IRAN*, 2021a. www.unaids.org/en/regionscountries/countries/islamicrepublicofiran, Accessed September 3, 2023.

UNAIDS (Joint United Nations Programme on HIV/AIDS) *Estimated people living with HIV, new HIV infections and AIDS-related deaths, 1990–2020*. 2021b. www.aidsinfo.unaids.org, accessed September 3, 2023.

Whitaker, Brian. "'No Homosexuality Here,'" *The Guardian*, September 25, 2007. www.theguardian.com/commentisfree/2007/sep/25/nohomosexualityhere, accessed September 3, 2023.

9 Reform from Within? *Hākemiyat-e Qānun* from the Reformist Era to 2022

Mirjam Künkler

Iran's judiciary is often portrayed as a monolith that fundamentally enforces the interests of the regime against all attempts at reform. This perception stems not least from the fact that the head of the judiciary is directly appointed by the Supreme Leader and all top judges are in turn appointed by committees consisting of the Supreme Leader, the head of the judiciary, and others directly appointed by the Supreme Leader. During the reformist era under President Khatami (1997–2005), the judiciary seemingly served as the primary bulwark by which conservatives suppressed dissent, neutralized a burgeoning press, immobilized a young protest movement, and silenced opposition figures. Upon closer scrutiny, one will discover, however, that friction and tensions inside the judiciary complicate the picture. This chapter sheds light on the reforms and discussions taking place inside the judiciary from 1999 onward, particularly the important reformist period when sustained efforts were undertaken to structurally democratize the Islamic Republic from within. Even though the reformist project under President Khatami failed to achieve its agenda, it did succeed in popularizing notions of the rule of law, accountability, and transparency. These notions were not lost on the head of the judiciary at the time, Mahmoud Shahroudi (1999–2009), who has undertaken the most far-reaching reforms inside the judiciary to date, notably by developing a new Code of Criminal Procedure (CCP), by attempting to close extrajudicial detention centers, and by strengthening the rights of political detainees. As will be seen in this chapter, Shahroudi's reforms had to be carefully justified with reference to reinterpretations of Islamic penal law, in the definition of political crimes, for example, and of bodily harm. Meanwhile, Shahroudi was not able to sideline key personnel spearheading the judiciary's repression of all political opposition, at the forefront of which was Saeed Mortazavi, a protégé of Supreme Leader Khamenei, who headed the press court in the early 2000s and from 2003 to 2009 served as prosecutor-general of Tehran. The chapter also reviews the tenures of the heads of the judiciary who succeeded Shahroudi, and who have spectacularly fallen short of strengthening the accountability, efficiency, and general elements of the rule of law in the justice system. Whereas Shahroudi aimed to establish a modicum of judicial independence, his successors have, by and large, returned the judiciary to its previous function – to serve as an arm of the Supreme Leader's office.

1   Khatami's Reform Politics and the Rule of Law

The Khatami presidency stands out in the history of the Islamic Republic as a period of systemic attempts at political and economic reform. It was marked by a burgeoning public sphere with a proliferation of independent news magazines and other media, the emergence of a panoply of political parties and civil society organizations, the strengthening of local democracy through the introduction of municipal elections in 1999, and recurrent public mobilization by students, workers, and human rights activists. In the realm of foreign policy, Iran aggressively pursued reintegration into the international order with Khatami's program "Dialogue among Civilizations" (taken up by the United Nations [UN], which declared 2001 the year of such dialogues), the reopening of embassies across Europe, strategic cooperation with the United States in Afghanistan, and an attempt at a trade and nuclear agreement with the European Union (EU) in the early 2000s.

Retrospective accounts of the period are overwhelmingly cynical, however, characterizing the reform era as a failure by and large. Such assessments foreground the high levels of repression that marked Khatami's presidency, the imprisonment and torture of protestors, the closures of long-standing newspapers, the persecution of artists, and the continued state-sponsored assassination of intellectuals (1988–1998), commissioned by the Ministry of Intelligence and condoned by the Supreme Leader himself. Internationally, a nuclear agreement failed to materialize largely due to the refusal of US backing, Khatami's call for a dialogue among civilizations amounted to little, and US President George W Bush's inclusion of Iran in the so-called Axis of Evil in January 2002 signified a new low in Iran's relations with the West. As voters expressed their disillusionment with the lack of tangible results from reformist policies, Iranian politics moved markedly toward the right. Hardliners and principalists overwhelmingly won the 2003 municipal elections, then the 2004 parliamentary elections, and with Mahmoud Ahmadinejad the 2005 presidential elections. Despite the reform movement's almost comprehensive policy failures, it did change the popular discourse in favor of the rule of law, however, in a manner that Iran's judiciary could no longer afford to ignore.

1.1 Advocating for the Rule of Law

When Mohammad Khatami put his candidacy forward for the 1997 presidential election, he was an unlikely contender. Khatami had been minister of culture and Islamic guidance for almost a decade (1983–1992) but retreated from politics in 1992 to become director of the National Library. He enjoyed a reputation as a politician on the sidelines, an intellectual rather than a power broker, writing books on the role of the clergy in public life, political thought, and political development. The regime's favorite for the presidency, Ali Akbar Nateq Nouri, had enjoyed generous airtime on the state-sponsored media, and Supreme Leader Khamenei had missed no opportunity praising Nateq Nouri's many skills and multifaceted political experience. But when Iran went to the polls in May 1997, voters overwhelmingly elected Khatami: With 20 million votes (nearly 70 percent of ballots cast), Khatami trounced his rival by 13 million. Remarkably, even the rank and file of the Revolutionary Guard Corps overwhelmingly lent him support (Buchta 2000) and Khatami also won majorities in Iran's clerical center, Qom. Thus, Khatami seemed to enjoy support from Iranians of all walks of life, from lower-ranking clergy to workers, artists and intellectuals, members of the armed forces, rural and urban voters, and both the younger generation and older.

Khatami had run on the slogans of strengthening the rule of law (*hākemiyat-e qānun*) and civil society (*jāme 'eh-ye madani*), and furthering political development through public participation (*moshārekat*). His inaugural speech in parliament on August 4, 1997 marked a significant shift in Iranian public policy:

> Protecting the freedom of individuals and the rights of the nation, which constitute a fundamental obligation of the President upon taking the oath [of office], is a necessity deriving from the dignity of man in the divine religion … [It requires] provision of the necessary conditions for the realization of the constitutional liberties, strengthening and expanding the institutions of civil society […] and preventing any violation of personal integrity, rights and legal liberties. The growth of law-abidingness (*qānun-mandi*) and the strengthening and consolidation of a society based on a legal framework for conduct, interactions and rights, will provide a favourable framework for the realization of social needs and demands […]. In a society well acquainted with its rights and ruled by law, the rights and limits of the citizens (*shahrvandān*) are recognized. (Khatami 1997: 81–82)

The catchwords accompanying his campaign were "law-orientedness" (*qānun-garā'i*), "law-abidingness" (*qānun-mandi*), and "pluralism/plurality/variety" (*plurālizm, chand-arzeshi, takkathurgarā'i*). Against *hokumat-e islāmi* (Islamic government), which had been the slogan of the 1979 Revolution, Khatami invoked and popularized the idea of *hokumat-e qānun*: Law-oriented government (Arjomand 2000; Tabari 2003).

During the first three years of his tenure (1997–2000), before the newly elected, overwhelmingly reformist, parliament began its work in May 2000, Khatami faced a conspicuously hostile environment. The other branches of power were dominated by conservatives and half the administration was under the direct or indirect influence of the Supreme Leader (who appoints the Expediency Council, half of the Guardian Council, the head of the judiciary, the head of television and broadcasting, and the heads of the armed services, and has personal representatives in all major state institutions). Even in his own cabinet, the president does not control all appointments, as, in the three areas of defense, judicial affairs, and intelligence, he must choose candidates from a list provided by the Supreme Leader's office or the judiciary.

Thus, Khatami's election did not translate into reformist legislation until after the 2000 parliamentary elections. Instead, during the first three years of his tenure, Khatami's efforts focused on establishing an instrument to sanction violations of the constitution by other state authorities. In accordance with his emphasis on *hākemiyat-e qānun* and *qānun-mandi* (rule of law and law abidingness), one of his first actions as president was the establishment of a commission overseeing the implementation of the 1979 constitution, which states in Article 113 that it is the responsibility of the president to "implement the Constitution and act as the head of the executive, except in matters directly concerned with (the office of) the Leadership." This article had never led to concrete measures on part of the presidency and Khatami now aimed to fill it with meaning by establishing a commission seeing to its realization. As he had emphasized in his inaugural speech, he expected "the honourable judiciary to assist the executive branch in the management of a safe, secure and just society based on the rule of law" (Khatami 1997: 76). Yet, although once established the commission received over four hundred complaints in the first two years, its hands were tied: It could point to transgressions and violations of the law but had no power to prosecute them.[1] The judiciary, at this time still headed by Ayatollah Yazdi (1989–1999), entirely ignored

---

[1] The commission, headed by law professor Dr. Hossein Mehrpour, pointed to eight articles of the constitution which had been violated and six others that had not been fulfilled. Violations concerned the competence of courts, legislation, inquisition, court proceedings, and the use of torture. Islamic Republic News Agency (IRNA), November 10, 2000. See also Hashemi (1375).

the commission. In particular, its recommendations to curb the power of the Guardian Council in screening electoral candidates went unheard.

Khatami's calls for the implementation of the constitution had been accompanied by a vigorous dissemination campaign of related concepts in public debate, including accountability (*mas'uliat*), transparency (*shaffāfiat*), and civil society (*jāme'eh madani*). This discourse was widely disseminated by a burgeoning press, which benefited from the fact that Khatami's minister of culture and Islamic guidance, Ataollah Mohajerani, removed many restrictions on the press, the arts, and culture (as reviewed in Chapter 13 of this volume). The Association of Iranian Journalists (Anjoman-e Senfi-ye Ruznamehnegaran-e Iran) was founded in 1997, the first professional organization pursuing the interests of journalists, and between 1998 and 2000, thirty new dailies were established in Tehran alone, carrying in their titles the reformist movement's key political ideals, such as *Hamshahri (Fellow-Citizen)*, *Jāme'eh (Society)*, *'Asr-e Azadegān (Age of the Freed)*, and *Moshārekat (Participation)*. As analyzed succinctly by Farideh Farhi (2003), the flourishing independent press led a democratic conversation "that eschewed conspiracies and understood politics to be about making claims" and which carried both improvisational as well as transgressive aspects.[2] These newspapers had a wide readership and because they reported with unprecedented scrutiny on those in power, they fed daily conversations to a point where it became a status symbol to be well informed about the latest columns and opinion pieces. The newspaper *Hamshahri* quickly eclipsed the state-owned *Keyhān* as the highest-circulation paper in Iran. The hardliners' reaction to this awakening of a vibrant press led to the closure of 87 newspapers and magazines and the imprisonment of 250 journalists during the first four years of Mohammad Khatami's government. In May 2000, the press court ordered the suspension of eighteen newspapers and magazines with a total circulation of more than one million, after Supreme Leader Khamenei had referred to the press as "an enemy base" in the Friday prayer. Nearly a thousand journalists and technical and administrative staff lost their employment overnight. Yet even though it was short-lived, the consequences of Iran's "Newspapers' Spring" were long-lasting. It brought about a new public consciousness, popularized a new participatory and empowering 'citizen discourse' and generally politicized the public: The public debates that ensued forced people to clarify to themselves and others what kind

---

[2] As Farhi (2003: 160) clarifies, it was not transgressive in the sense of "playing uncontrollably or with total license, but about constraints revealing themselves in the process of the act and not beforehand."

1.2 Legal Reforms of the Reformist Parliament (2000–2004)

The situation changed for Khatami and his supporters when a reformist alliance won a parliamentary majority in 2000. Over the next four years, the reformists drafted and passed numerous laws aimed at strengthening political, social, economic, and cultural rights and improving accountability in government. But of forty-one cultural bills and twenty political bills addressing freedom of expression, for example, almost all were rejected by the Guardian Council.[3] When the reformist majority in parliament tried to amend the press law, it was withdrawn from the relevant committee by direct intervention of Supreme Leader Khamenei. In the realm of labor law, the labor movement had long campaigned for the right to independent unionization. Yet several drafts were vetoed by the Guardian Council and the law that was ultimately passed did not grant the right to independent representation.

Reformists were more successful in commercial law and regarding some health policies. In the economic realm, they aimed to open Iran to international markets and to attract foreign and local private investment. In 2002, the Foreign Investment Promotion and Protection Act (FIPPA) was passed, which no longer distinguished between domestic and foreign investments in regard to rights, protections, facilities, or capital market transactions.[4] This was extraordinary in light of Article 81 of Iran's constitution, according to which "The granting of concessions to foreigners for the formation of companies or institutions dealing with commerce, industry, agriculture, services or mineral extraction, is absolutely forbidden." Foreign investments were subject to a flat 25 percent corporate income tax, but with many possibilities for exemptions and tax holidays. Investment in agricultural projects was made 100 percent tax exempt, permanently. Investments in industry and mining were subject to 80-100 percent tax exemption (see Chapter 12).

In family law, the reformist parliament raised the minimum marriage age to 13 years for girls and 15 for boys, up from 9 and 11, although exceptions continue to be possible if the marriage guardian agrees. In the realm of minority rights, some policies were more

---

[3] Report of the Performance of the Sixth Islamic Consultative Assembly (2000–2004), Center for Research of the Islamic Consultative Assembly: https://rc.majlis.ir/fa/report/show/728932, accessed June 24, 2022.

[4] Indeed, the law was repeatedly vetoed by the Guardian Council, but eventually passed by the Expediency Council to respond to the severe economic crisis at the time.

generously implemented, which resulted in temporary improvements of the rights of certain minorities, such as the Bahá'í. Until 2004, the application to sit the national university entrance examination asked applicants to indicate their religion. Those who self-identified as Bahá'í, a faith that is not legally recognized, were not permitted to register (see Chapter 10). During President Khatami's term, the question was omitted from the entrance examination registration form, with the result that many Bahá'ís entered university at that time. Relatedly, Bahá'ís' burial rights were strengthened when Bahá'ís were permitted to mark their graves.

In hindsight, the reformist movement under Khatami achieved significant reform in the realm of investment law, but fell short of systemic and lasting reforms in most other areas of law. In the area of media freedoms and minority rights, the advances achieved early during the reformist era were quickly reversed through interference by agencies under the direct command of the Supreme Leader, such as the Special Courts for the Clergy and the Ministry of Intelligence.

2 The Tenure of Mahmoud Hashemi Shahroudi (1999–2009)

Khatami's presidency overlapped with the tenure of Mahmoud Hashemi Shahroudi as head of the judiciary. From 1999 to 2009, Shahroudi pursued his own reform agenda inside the judiciary, which included major reforms of the criminal code and the CCP, as discussed in Chapters 2 and 3 in this volume. Unlike the reformists, Shahroudi was not driven by considerations of citizen empowerment and universal human rights standards. Instead, he sought to institutionalize clear competencies between offices, incentivize standards in sentencing, and insulate the judiciary from interference by the minister of intelligence and the revolutionary guards. But while the reform initiatives of Khatami and his administration have received ample attention in the relevant literatures, a critical assessment of Shahroudi's initiated reforms and their legacy is, to date, lacking.

When tracing the arenas in which judicial reform was initiated, eight stand out, falling into the two broad areas of judicial organization, and criminal law and procedure. It is striking that these reform initiatives were, if implemented at all, often ultimately watered down and partly reversed through intervention by the Supreme Leader's office and Shahroudi's successors.

When he was appointed head of the judiciary in 1999, Shahroudi had already served in the Guardian Council since 1995. Still, as someone who had grown up in Iraq (his family, although Iranian, had lived in Najaf for three generations), he was not considered a regime insider. In fact, Shahroudi had only come to Iran in 1980 after having been exiled, together with his family, by Saddam Hossein due to his activities in the Iraqi Shi'i opposition movement. Once in Iran, he concentrated on his scholarship and, having been educated in the 1960s by Khomeini and Baqer al-Sadr in Najaf, became Khamenei's main teacher of fiqh. Khamenei still lacked jurisprudential credentials, even once he ascended to the Supreme Leadership in 1989, and Khamenei appointed Shahroudi as one of four individuals to lead his office (edāreh-ye rahbari). Critics of Khamenei allege that his resā'le-ye 'amaliye, the key work of legal exegesis a Shi'i authority must produce in order to qualify for elevation to the marja'iyya (the highest level of Shi'i authority), consisted largely of Persian translations of Shahroudi's Arabic-language works.[5] For sure, his status as a teacher of Khamenei and a scholar of note afforded Shahroudi more leeway and more certainty in conviction working toward institutional reform than his successors ever mustered.

2.1 Judicial Organization

In terms of judicial organization, Shahroudi initiated four pathbreaking reforms, although the last two were ultimately not implemented: Reestablishing the prosecutorial office, creating dispute resolution councils, integrating the Special Court for the Clergy into the regular judiciary institutionally and financially, and prohibiting extrajudicial detention centers.

First, under his predecessor Mohammad Yazdi, a 1994 Law on the Formation of General and Revolutionary Courts had given the head of the judiciary the power to abolish the office of the prosecutor. Conservative jurists described the office as being "un-Islamic" and pointed to the fact that in premodern courts, judges themselves undertook the task of

---

[5] Khamenei was a *hojjatoleslām*, a mid-ranking cleric, when he was elected to become Iran's next Supreme Leader in 1989 and his authority has suffered due to his lack of theological and jurisprudential credentials ever since. After all, the 1989 constitutional amendment eliminated the requirement of being a *marja'* for the position of Supreme Leader, because Khamenei did not fulfill the requirement at the time. But even later, the Qom-based commission putting forward candidates for the *marja'iyya* refused to include his name on several occasions, until in 1994 he was recommended as a *marja'* for Shi'is outside Iran, but not in the country. His critics insist that Khamenei's only scholarly output in the field of jurisprudence was one article on *rijāl* (the study of the individuals in a hadith's chain of narration). See for example Kadivar 2014.

conducting investigations, questioning the accused and witnesses. Yazdi dissolved the office of the prosecutor the following year.

The abolition of the office of the prosecutor had resulted in a lack of impartiality on the part of the courts and in high rates of appeal (70 percent of all trials) (Mohammadi 2008: 175), prompting Shahroudi to note he had inherited a wreck (*virāneh*) of justice rather than a house (*khāneh*) of justice.[6] In close collaboration with the judiciary, in 2002 the reformist-dominated Majles passed an amendment to the 1994 law reinstating the office of the prosecutor.[7] Shahroudi reintroduced in 2002 the division of courts into criminal (*keifari*), family and personal (*madani*), civil and commercial (*hoquqi*) courts.[8] He also introduced to parliament separate laws of procedure (*dādrasi*) for each, and reintroduced for all courts an appellate system.

Second, Shahroudi worked with the Majles to create dispute resolution councils which would work toward reaching settlements of minor civil, criminal, and commercial cases through mediation before their referral to the higher courts. As part of the 2001 Development Plan (Article 189), three-member dispute-resolution councils were created, responsible for the settlement of minor civil and criminal cases.[9] The councils, designed to reduce the backlog of cases in the judiciary, were placed on permanent institutional footing with a law that eventually passed in May 2008.

Third, Shahroudi worked to integrate the Special Courts for the Clergy into the judiciary. These courts were created ad hoc in the early 1980s and rose to prominence in 1987 when the son-in-law of Khomeini's designate successor Montazeri was tried and convicted in such a special court (Künkler 2013). While they were initially set up to prosecute financial crimes and minor transgressions of the clergy, they became a major tool for the repression of non-conformist clerics in the late 1980s. Khomeini's successor Khamenei expanded their jurisdiction in 2005 by setting up full-time Special Courts for the Clergy in ten major cities of Iran and appointed senior intelligence officials to the prosecution in

---

[6] *Ettelā'āt*, 11/23/1999.

[7] The October 2002 Amendment to the Law of Formation of General and Revolutionary Courts (1994), dated Mehr 28, 1381) reestablished the office of the public prosecutor for general and revolutionary courts in every urban jurisdiction. According to the Official Gazette (Ruznāmeh-ye Rasmī), No. 16823, November 2002/Adhar 7–9, 1381, the prosecutor was only reestablished for the lower criminal courts.

[8] *Ettelā'āt*, October 7, 2000.

[9] These concern civil cases with damages of up to about 1,500 USD but also higher values if both parties agree. Dispute-resolution councils may also decide criminal cases for which the maximum penalty is ninety-one days imprisonment or fines of up to about 600 USD. The councils are not bound by the Codes of Civil and Criminal Procedure. Their decisions may be appealed in the general courts.

these courts. He also endowed the courts with a statute, which, however, was not debated in and passed by parliament but implemented by decree. Even today, the courts operate under the direct authority of the Supreme Leader's office. They are funded through his office and all staff appointments are directly made by him. Their processes take place behind closed doors and they run their own prison sections; whatever rule-of-law standards apply in the judiciary, the special courts regard themselves as exempt from these. In the late 1990s, the special courts tried several high-profile clerics who sympathized with the reform project. The highly politicized processes led to renewed calls for the closures of the courts, which the reformist parliament was not able to effectuate, however. In the early 2000s, Shahroudi distributed a circular, according to which the special courts were to be integrated into the judiciary (Künkler 2013). All Special Courts for the Clergy received the relevant missive and some of their personnel prepared for their transfer into the administration of the judiciary. Intelligence Minister Reyshahri intervened, however, and ordered the circular null and void. The courts continue to operate today, and the head of the judiciary still does not hold any authority over them.

Fourth, and in a struggle that defined his tenure for several years, Shahroudi worked to reign in the Intelligence Ministry and other security agencies by undercutting their practice of creating detention centers outside the purview of the Prisons Organization. Following the 1986 Law on the Organization of State Prisons and Security and Corrective Measures, the oversight of all prisons, detention centers, and their affiliate bodies falls under the purview of the Prisons Organization, which is a unit under the aegis of the judiciary. Despite the law, however, secret detention centers run by security and intelligence bodies have remained prevalent.

In 1999, Shahroudi issued a decree prohibiting detention facilities controlled by bodies other than the Prisons Organization.[10] In line with existing law, the detention of political prisoners would be separate, but strictly within the remit of the Prisons Organization. Only one such center would be permitted per province. The intelligence department of the police forces was mentioned as a unit with which the Prisons Organization would need to "coordinate" regarding this particular area (the detention of political prisoners), but the administration of the detention centers of political prisoners and the appointment of staff would

---

[10] See Prohibition of Forming Special Detention Centers and Allocation of One Detention Center for Security Crimes in Provinces, December 3, 1999, available on the website of the Islamic Parliament Research Center at https://rc.majlis.ir/fa/law/show/131562, last accessed June 26, 2022. Shahroudi's decree allowed for armed forces to continue maintaining their disciplinary detention facilities.

be undertaken by the Prisons Organization alone. Under the reformist Majles, a 2001 law on prisons reaffirmed in Article 18 that all detention centers, without exception, had to be placed under the oversight of the Prisons Organization.

In part, these attempts to integrate all detention facilities into the Prisons Organization were motivated by sustained reports of maltreatment and torture in the facilities run by the security services.[11] It was unusual for judges to speak out in public about cases of maltreatment, but Shahroudi's efforts were given unexpected support when the conservative *Bāztāb* website published on May 7 and 10, 2005 two letters written to Shahroudi by an unnamed judge. In the first, the author wrote,

> One of the incidents which I have personally witnessed as a judge is the case of an illegal arrest and torture of a young man in one of the cities of the South. [He] was arrested by the police, accused of robbery and was tortured in the Agahi detention center. I observed this person in the course of an inspection of the detention center and immediately ordered him to be taken to hospital. In hospital it became clear that he had numerous injuries [...] and was put under medical care. A file was opened with the military prosecutor for those who had inflicted the torture.[12]

Shahroudi himself raised attention to this letter in the media, only to be contradicted by a senior police commander who claimed reports of torture were entirely invented. *Bāztāb* then published a second letter by the same unnamed judge three days later, corroborating his criticism:

> The Commander of the Law Enforcement Forces has challenged the head of the judiciary to bring examples of torture and of the illegal acts of the disciplinary forces. I can say that, as a judge of thirteen years experience' in various parts of the country, I can produce numerous examples of such wrongdoing.... One of these is a recent case of a 27-year-old man in a southern city accused of a very petty offence. He was brought to my courtroom after three days of illegal detention and had clearly been severely beaten. I have kept photographs of his state.[13]

Despite the public debate provoked by the publication of these letters, penned not by human rights organizations but by officials inside the judiciary itself, security agencies failed to fall in line with the 1999 decree and the 1986 and 2001 laws. Shahroudi then passed a bylaw in November 2006 revoking all previous agreements between the Prisons

---

[11] Payvand. "Iran's Judiciary Chief Admits Human Rights Violations in Detention Centres," May 5, 2005. www.payvand.com/news/05/may/1044.html.

[12] See www.baztab.com/news/23986.php, Ordibehesht 15, 1384/May 7, 2005, accessed May 6, 2016.

[13] See www.baztab.com/news/23986.php, Ordibehesht 18, 1384/May 10, 2005, accessed May 6, 2016.

Organization on the one hand and security forces on the other, including the Ministry of Intelligence, the intelligence departments of the Revolutionary Guards, the police forces, and the armed forces, in an effort to remove all remaining obstacles to the full integration of extra-legal detention centers into the remit of the Prisons Organization. The bylaw reaffirmed that only one detention center for political prisoners was permitted per province and further stipulated that these had to be established inside the provincial prisons. Only in cases where this was not possible due to lack of space or "appropriate conditions," could security bodies, with the approval of the Prisons Organization, allocate a suitable space in their own facilities. These spaces would then operate under the supervision of the Prisons Organization and require regular inspection by judicial authorities, including judges and prosecutors. Officials running detention facilities for political prisoners had to be appointed from among the employees of the Prisons Organization (Article 4). Yet, despite Shahroudi's decrees and bylaw, the situation remained largely unchanged. Presumably Supreme Leader Khamenei could have intervened to insist that the directives of the head of the judiciary be obeyed and implemented by the intelligence services and Revolutionary Guard Corps, but he chose not to.

2.2 Criminal Law and Procedure

In the realm of criminal law, Shahroudi's reform initiatives addressed the problems emanating from the use of *ʿelm-e qāzi* ("knowledge" or "insight" of the judge), the punishment of stoning, the criminal responsibility of juvenile offenders, public executions, and the CCP, which urgently required reform and updating.

First, Shahroudi aimed to drastically limit the wide use of *ʿelm-e qāzi*. According to Article 167 of the Iranian constitution, in the absence of codified law on a given case, judges must deliver the judgment "on the basis of authoritative Islamic sources and authentic fatwas." Some have interpreted this article as supporting the use of *ʿelm-e qāzi* when deciding a case for which clear laws are not applicable or are nonexistent. Such an interpretation was seemingly supported by Article 160 of the Penal Code and Article 214 of the 1991 CCP. Yet juristic opinions vary not only as to whether *ʿelm-e qāzi* is valid proof but also concerning its nature. Some jurists regard it as appropriate only in cases of civil law, whereas others extend its validity to criminal law. Among the latter, many consider it applicable only in cases of *taʿzir* (punishment for offences at the discretion of the judge), while a minority also consider it valid in *hodud*. Further, some jurists believe that in the context of the contemporary

Iranian legal system, it is applicable to the interpretation of codified legal provisions only, while others, again referring to Article 167 of the constitution, believe the opposite, that is, that it can be the basis for offences and punishments not provided for in codified law. Despite the fact that its use is controversial, ʿelm-e qāzi is widely applied by judges and frequently invoked in the abstract when judges decide a case in seemingly idiosyncratic ways.

Shahroudi was strongly opposed to the use of ʿelm-e qāzi and exhorted judges to use it sparingly. In *hodud*, he argued, it was certainly inadmissible, since only confession and testimony were considered valid proof. Moreover, he outlined that since only *mojtahed*s had proper training to understand when and how it would be appropriate to invoke ʿelm-e qāzi, only judges who were also *mojtahed*s should feel qualified to use it. Since only about 20 percent of judges in Iran are *mojtahed*s, the use of ʿelm-e qāzi should therefore be out of the question for most judges. In an essay he dedicated to the topic, he reminded his audience that this had also been the position of Khomeini.[14] Moreover, he pointed out that some Islamic jurists believed that only the Imam was infallible (*maʿsum*) and therefore only he could invoke ʿelm-e qāzi, suggesting that unless a given judge could claim to be at the level of the Imam in the realm of certainty of judgment, ʿelm-e qāzi had in fact no place at all in the Iranian justice system.

As the reform of the Penal Code was under way, Shahroudi worked toward inserting the conditionality of being infallible (*maʿsum*) into the draft but failed. In fact, its applicability was expanded when the code was finalized under Shahroudi's successor Sadegh Larijani. Whereas in the Islamic Penal Code (IPC) of 1991, ʿelm-e qāzi was only admitted as evidence for theft, illegal sexual intercourse, and homicide (Articles 199, 105, and 231), in the new code it is admitted as evidence for all offences, including *hodud*. Article 220, which is contained in the second book on *hadd* punishments, states: "regarding the *hadd* punishments that are not mentioned in this law, article one hundred and sixty-seven (167) of the Islamic Republic of Iran's Constitution shall be applicable."

Some observers, such as Silvia Tellenbach in Chapter 2 in this volume, point out that this expansion of the applicability of ʿelm-e qāzi allows for a much broader category of permissible evidence, including expert opinions, visual inspection, forensic evidence, and police reports, which may all inform ʿelm-e qāzi (Article 211). Others, such as Fraser Fujinaga (2013) regard this as subverting the originally limited nature of ʿelm-e qāzi and as increasing the scope for arbitrary and subjective verdicts.

---

[14] Shahroudi, "'Elm-e qāzi," in *Bāyestehā*.

Critics further point out that in most cases *'elm-e qāzi* appears to be used to circumvent due process instead of collecting additional evidence that could mitigate the application of harsh punishments.[15]

Second, in December 2002 Shahroudi issued a moratorium on stoning, although between 2002 and the end of his tenure in 2009 at least six people were nevertheless stoned to death (Fraser Fujinaga 2013: 119f.), and the practice is ongoing.[16] When judges ignored the head of the judiciary's directive, they could legitimize their actions by referring to Article 170 of the constitution, which prohibits judges from following regulations (including those by senior judicial officials) which contradict Islamic law.

Shahroudi first campaigned in favor of eliminating stoning altogether as a punishment in the new Penal Code, then later changed his strategy and argued in favor of it being conditionally commutable to flogging or hanging.[17] In the end, years after Shahroudi's tenure, the Majles took the relevant clause out of the draft Penal Code to avoid another veto by the Guardian Council and so the 2013 Penal Code only stipulates the penalty for illicit sexual relations among unmarried people (*zinā'*), but stays silent on the punishment for adultery, which in classical *fiqh* is stoning. On the one hand, this silence allows Iranian officials to claim that stoning is no longer on the books for adultery, contrary to the previous Penal Code. However, since the law also does not stipulate any alternative punishment for adultery, judges are still able to (and may even feel required to) apply stoning, as Article 220 of the new Penal Code requires them to refer to Article 167 of the constitution, according to which they must apply Islamic law when positive law is silent. The same rule also applies to the case of apostasy, which is not mentioned as a crime in the Penal Code. On the basis of Article 220, judges must apply their understanding of the appropriate *hodud* punishment in this case. In classical

---

[15] Apart from his efforts to limit the possibilities of the death penalty for juveniles, Shahroudi also placed injunctions on execution sentences against underage offenders. Many times, these were ignored and executions went ahead regardless. A case in point is that of Makwan Moloudzadeh, who was accused of having committed sodomy at the age of 13. The sentence was based not on confession or testimony but on *'elm-e qāzi*. Shahroudi had placed an injunction on the sentence, arguing that in classical fiqh *'elm-e qāzi* is not applicable in *hodud*. The injunction was ignored and Moloudzadeh was executed in December 2007. See http://iranhr.net/en/articles/57/, accessed June 27, 2022.

[16] Notably, the witness and judge must be present during the stoning and, depending on whether the sentence is based on testimony or confession, either of the two needs to cast the first stone. DIRS293/82: Directive on the Implementation Regulations for Sentences of *Qesās*, Stoning, *Qatl* (execution), Crucifixion, *E'dām* (execution) and Flogging, [being] the Subject of Article 293 of the Procedural Code for the General and Revolutionary Courts in Criminal Matters (2003).

[17] This position is shared by some conservative jurists, such as Naser Makarem Shirazi.

Shi'i law, male apostates have to be sentenced to death and female apostates to imprisonment, which will only end when they reconvert to Islam. There are mitigating factors and strict rules of evidence from classical Shi'i law that could be applied to allow the judge to arrive at a lenient judgment, but since the new Penal Code is silent on these, judges are unlikely to apply them.

Third, Shahroudi worked to put an end to the execution of offenders who at the time of the offense were under the age of 18. According to classical Islamic law, children become criminally responsible (*bolugh*) at the age of 8¾ for girls and 14½ for boys and are thereafter treated in criminal law as adults, which explains why Iran leads the world in underage death sentences. Shahroudi issued several internal directives to judges urging them to refrain from issuing death sentences to defenders under 18. But these directives, too, were largely ignored. The new Penal Code of 2013 retained the same regulations on *bolugh* but made changes in the punishments for defendants under 18. If the offender has not yet reached the age of 15 (for both sexes), and if the court (consulting specialists if necessary) finds that the mental maturity of the accused is/was insufficient for full awareness of the crime (Article 90), he or she will be sentenced to educational measures. If the offender is between 15 and 18 years old, the usual *hadd* and *qesās* punishments apply. Tellenbach, implicitly connecting the requirement of sufficient mental maturity to *'elm-e qāzi*, in Chapter 2 in this volume observes that "This provision allows the judge to collect information by asking family members, teachers, neighbors, and other persons in the social environment of the perpetrator and to base his decision on this information. This provision grants the judge quite a broad discretion in his decision-making and gives him the possibility of avoiding applying the severe *hadd* and *qesās* punishments to juveniles." (p. 53). Critics of these provisions, by contrast, point out that the two elements of possible lenience (i.e., to have physical and mental maturity, and to have grasped the meaning of the offence) were always there as requirements in *hadd* and present nothing new. Since judges routinely ignore these possibilities to apply lenience, critics regard the new code as a missed opportunity to effectuate real reform in the realm of juvenile penal law.

Relatedly, Shahroudi issued decrees against carrying out the death penalty in public and in cases of amputations in favor of using anesthetics. He also wrote an essay on the reattachment of limbs after *qesās-e 'ozv* (retribution in kind for injuries), pointing out that classical law mentioned no restrictions against it (Shahroudi 1999: 311–147). Nevertheless, numerous cases of public executions and of amputations without anesthetics are known to have occurred during his tenure.

Fourth, Shahroudi worked toward reform of the CCP. The 1999 code (Code of Criminal Procedure for General and Revolutionary Courts), which had been drafted prior to his appointment as head of the judiciary, was passed into law for a trial period of three years. In the year 2000, Shahroudi initiated a process for drafting a new code to address the "ambiguities and mistakes of existing laws" and ensure consistency with "scientific developments."[18] In contrast to his predecessors, he ensured that the drafting process would not rely exclusively or predominantly on experts in *fiqh* but also brought in experts in criminology and comparative law. One important area concerned pretrial detention (PTD), whose length the 1999 code failed to limit, with the consequence that individuals could be detained for months, even years, often without being informed of the charges against them. Another aspect the 1999 code failed to guarantee was access to a lawyer from the time of arrest. As with the new Penal Code, the draft of the CCP (prepared in the judiciary, edited by parliament's Judicial Affairs Committee, and placed to a vote in the plenary) was repeatedly delayed due to Guardian Council vetoes. In light of the delays, Shahroudi aimed to solidify some improvement in due process by issuing a fourteen-point Charter on Citizens' Rights in April 2004, which became the basis for the Law to Respect Legitimate Freedoms and Citizens' Rights, ratified by parliament one month later. It prohibited the use of torture and outlined examples of intimidation which it also prohibited (such as the interrogator wearing a mask or sitting behind the accused without the accused being able to see the interrogator). The law also prohibited the posing of questions that were irrelevant to the charge and the confiscation of property of the accused during the investigation. It reiterated that the accused must have access to a lawyer from the moment of arrest and that any accused was to be considered innocent until proven guilty. The law also gave the head of the judiciary a mandate to appoint a committee overseeing the implementation of the law in all institutions of law enforcement.

In general, Shahroudi changed the way the judiciary and the parliament worked together, hiring for the first time independent legal researchers and law professors who drafted bills in cooperation with the parliament's Judicial Affairs Committee based on findings of criminology and comparative law, both secular and Shi'i. He also strengthened the legal office (*edāreh-ye hoquqī*) of the judiciary and instituted a Research Center in

---

[18] Meanwhile, the trial period of the 1999 CCP for general and revolutionary courts was repeatedly extended. In March 2010, the Supreme Leader, using his authority as the head of state, renewed the 1999 CCP until further notice. The code remained operational until the entry into force of the new CCP on June 22, 2015.

Jurisprudence (Markaz-e tahqīqāt-e fiqhi) that would answer enquiries from the courts and provincial branches of the Ministry of Justice. The research center would also keep a registrar of the most important fatwas of those *marāje'* (sources of emulation, the highest religious authorities in Shi'i Islam) that are officially recognized by the regime. A given judge might then compare the fatwas of the highest Shi'i authorities in the country and, if no positive law exists to be applied on a given case, invoke one of the listed fatwas.

To reduce incarceration rates, Shahroudi was also in favor of a harm-reduction rather than punitive approach to people living with HIV/AIDS, an issue that in Iran frequently overlaps with drug use. As the Alaei brothers document in Chapter 8, in January 2005 Shahroudi issued a decree explicitly endorsing increased access to needles, syringes, and methadone, "and other material used individually by drug addicts and AIDS patients." (p. 249). The decree specifically noted that some judicial authorities "have considered [the availability of needles, syringes, and methadone] as tantamount to a crime, subject to punitive action, thus unintentionally impeding the implementation of health and treatment programs."[19]

2.3 Criticism of Shahroudi

Despite many attempts at reform on various levels, the changes initiated by Shahroudi were repeatedly curtailed by the Ministry of Intelligence or the Guardian Council (both with support by the Supreme Leader's office) and his decrees were often ignored by the country's judges. The new CCP was ultimately ratified in the summer of 2015, six years after Shahroudi's tenure had ended. The ratified version did not establish access to a lawyer from the time of arrest in cases concerning national security, and did not improve standards of PTD. Moreover, Shahroudi did not initiate or aim to implement rule-of-law-oriented reforms on all fronts. In three areas, his tenure was particularly corrosive of rule-of-law standards: First, with regard to a key appointment, second, with regard to the Bar Association, third, with regard to torture.

Early in his tenure, Shahroudi had appointed as prosecutor-general of Tehran the hardliner Saeed Mortazavi. The latter led the judiciary's

---

[19] Protocol concerning penalties for narcotics, cheques and debt offences, *Islamic Parliament Research Centre of the Islamic Republic of Iran*, Mehr 5, 1381 = October 7, 2002: https://perma.cc/FYS2-EQ2S; Seyyed Mahmoud Hashemi Shahroudi, Head of the Judiciary, Executive Order to all Judicial Authorities, January 24, 2005, Reference 1-83-14434.

onslaught against reformist politicians, including sitting parliamentarians, who, per Article 86 of the constitution, should have enjoyed legal immunity. Shahroudi was able neither to stop Mortazavi's indictments of the sitting MPs, nor to dismiss him. When President Khatami addressed Shahroudi in a letter protesting the courts' prosecution of the MPs, Shahroudi's response disappointed especially lawyers and legal scholars in the country. To their surprise, the head of the judiciary wrote "Since judges, according to the constitution and ordinary laws as well as the principles of [Shi'i] jurisprudence, are independent in their interpretation of the law and issuing verdicts, nobody – not even the judiciary chief – has the right to impose their interpretation of the law on judges."[20] What then, would preclude judges from applying the death penalty against minors or death by stoning if even the head of the judiciary or the constitution had no legal power to place limits on judges' verdicts? The way Shahroudi had phrased his response also undermined Khatami's efforts to establish himself as the guardian of the constitution (per Article 113) and to solidify the constitution as the highest law of the land, which could not be abrogated by judges invoking Shi'i fiqh. Mortazavi, who also became known as the "butcher of the press" for persecuting journalists and closing some 120 newspapers while serving as the head of Iran's Press Court,[21] was also later held personally responsible for the death in custody of Canadian-Iranian photojournalist Zahra Kazemi in 2003, as well as the torture and death in custody of activists following the 2009 protests. Under Shahroudi's tenure, Mortazavi was never prosecuted, although he was arrested and charged for corruption in April 2018 (which fell far short of trying him for his role in torturing and killing protesters).[22] And even though she did not refer to Shahroudi as being personally implicated in systematic violations of fundamental human rights, Shirin Ebadi, Iran's first female judge and

---

[20] Letter of October 13, 2001. Cited in RFE/RL: *Iran Report*, Vol. 4, No. 41, October 29, 2001. www.rferl.org/a/1342852.html, accessed October 13, 2021.

[21] Ironically, Mortazavi applied the pre-revolutionary "Prevention of Crimes and Probation Act" of 1339 (1960), which targeted dangerous professional criminals, to close down reformist newspapers.

[22] Shahroudi could also have transferred Mortazavi, since per Article 164 of the constitution, the head of the judiciary can transfer or reassign judges without their consent if he considers it to be in the public's interest. Furthermore, the Judges' Disciplinary Court and the General Inspection Office could have been mobilized to prosecute Mortazavi. That none of this happened is widely interpreted as a clear signal that Mortazavi enjoyed the personal protection of the Supreme Leader. In one case, the so-called Blogger Case of 2004, Shahroudi, defying Mortazavi, put three independent judges in charge of the case, after he had heard witness statements implicating Mortazavi in torture during pre-trial interrogation sessions. It appears that after one of the judges ominously died in a car crash, Shahroudi no longer tried to sideline Mortazavi.

Nobel Peace Prize Laureate of 2003, protested in a letter that he was nevertheless indirectly culpable: "Mr. Shahroudi is directly responsible for the appointment of judges and prosecutors that have been responsible for persecutions and systematic violations of fundamental human rights. He must be held accountable."[23].

Shahroudi's reputation as a reasonable head of the judiciary also took a hit when twelve intellectuals were prosecuted and accused of having "conspired to overthrow the system of the Islamic Republic" after taking part in an international conference in Berlin in April 2000.[24] Most were tried by the revolutionary court in Tehran and sentenced to multiyear prison terms.

Although he made some improvements to the efficacy of the judiciary by reconstituting the office of the prosecutor in many courts and by partly reestablishing the appeals procedure, his position vis-à-vis the Bar Associations was ruinous. The outgoing conservative parliament had in 2000 attached a regulation to the Third Development Plan (2000–2005) establishing an accreditation process for lawyers rivaling that of the Bar Associations (see Chapter 5 in this volume). This allowed the judiciary to accredit as so-called 'legal advisors' candidates who had not passed the Bar (because they lacked a law degree for example, had failed the exam, or fell short on other criteria). With the end of the five-year plan in 2005, this parallel accreditation process should have expired but instead was retained under Shahroudi. When the Central Bar Association issued a critical assessment in the spring of 2009, he responded with a draft amendment to the Executive Regulations of the Law of the Bar Associations on June 17, 2009 (that is, five days after the consequential presidential elections that resulted in unprecedented countrywide protests due to alleged vote rigging) that would have effectively dissolved the associations by stripping them of any rights, functions, and responsibilities.[25] The proposed amendment would have de facto eradicated the independent certification process through the Bar Associations by moving the mandate to certify lawyers and legal advisors to a new "selection committee" appointed entirely by the judiciary. The amendment would also give the Ministry of Intelligence the right to keep under surveillance the defense lawyers of political activists and to

---

[23] Iranian Human Rights Organizations File Motion in Germany Against Ayatollah Shahroudi for Crimes Against Humanity, January 10, 2018, https://iranhumanrights.org/2018/01/iranian-human-rights-organizations-file-motion-in-germany-against-ayatollah-shahroudi-for-crimes-against-humanity/, accessed June 25, 2022.

[24] HRW, Report 0501-05. *Silencing Critics.* www.hrw.org/reports/2001/iran/Iran0501-05.htm, accessed June 27, 2022.

[25] *E'temād*, No. 1993, July 5, 2009/Tir 14, 1388.

Table 9.1 *Heads of the Judiciary, 1989–2022*

Name	Tenure
Mohammad Yazdi	August 15, 1989–August 14, 1999
Mahmoud Hashemi Shahroudi	August 14, 1999–August 14, 2009
Sadegh Larijani-Amoli	August 14, 2009–March 7, 2019
Ebrahim Raisi	March 7, 2019–July 1, 2021
Gholam-Hossein Mohseni-Eje'i	July 1, 2021–present

Note: Prior to 1989, the judiciary was led by a five-member high council.

pull their credentials if deemed "necessary." The draft amendment also comprised a catalogue of "professional ethics" that compromised the defense counsel in criminal cases by suggesting, per Article 44, that lawyers would abet a sin if they endorsed the plea of a client they knew to be false. As shown in Chapter 5, while the amendment underwent multiple revisions with alternating rejections by the Guardian Counil and the parliament's Judicial Commitee, some of the amendments' propositions were realized in other legislation, such as the revised CPP.

With regard to corporal punishment and the persistence of show trials, too, Shahroudi's record disappointed reformers. Throughout his tenure, Shahroudi remained a defender of the punishment of whipping over that, for example, of imprisonment. In a 2002 circular, he instructed judges not to convert a sentence of lashes to fines or imprisonment, justifying his decision with reference to the negative social consequences of imprisonment, such as absence from the core family and the loss of income.[26] The end of Shahroudi's tenure coincided with the street protests against the contested June 2009 presidential elections, which many considered rigged (Ahmadinejad instead of Mir Hossein Mousavi was declared the winner) along with the court processes against those arrested. Even though Shahroudi had spoken out against show trials, the judiciary conducted a number of such trials against citizens participating in these protests. Ayatollah Mostafa Mohaqqeq-Damad, a former head of the General Inspection Office,[27] wrote an open letter criticizing Shahroudi:

---

[26] See "Hashemi Shahroudi in the Majles: The Benefits of Flogging Outweigh Imprisonment," *ISNA*, Aban 10, 1384 = November 1, 2005: https://perma.cc/YX2C-5LRZ. Compare also the survey Ghassem Ghassemi (2009: 159–180) conducted in Iran on the perceptions of flogging among legal professionals and the general public.

[27] The General Inspection Office is a unit inside the judiciary which, per Article 174 of the constitution, may audit and may investigate all state institutions "to supervise the proper conducting of affairs and the correct implementation of laws by the administrative organs of the state."

Table 9.2 *Prosecutors general, 1979–2022*

Name	Tenure
Fathollah Banisadr	1979–1980
Abdolkarim Mousavi-Ardabili	February 23, 1980–June 29, 1981
Mohammad-Mehdi Rabbani-Amlashi	June 29, 1981–January 6, 1983
Yusuf Sane'i	January 9, 1983–July 10, 1985
Mohammad Mousavi-Kho'iniha	July 10, 1985–August 1989
Mohammad Reyshahri	August 21, 1989–1991
Abolfazl Mousavi-Tabrizi	1991–1994
Morteza Moqtada'i	August 28, 1994–1998
Abdolnabi Namazi	1998–August 14, 2004
Qorbanali Dorri-Najafabadi	August 15, 2004–August 25, 2009
Gholam-Hossein Mohseni-Eje'i	August 25, 2009–August 23, 2014
Ebrahim Raisi	August 23, 2014–March 6, 2016
Mohammad Jafar Montazeri	April 3, 2016–August 6, 2023
Mohammad Movahedi-Azad	August 6, 2023–present

In my opinion, the greatest and the most prevalent transitions for modern human beings in this century are linked to public rules of justice and the due processes of criminal law. Moreover, the world's legal experts agree that the evaluation of a society's system of justice and lawfulness is based on its public rules of justice and due processes of law. This is not an exaggeration by any means ... Please bear with my directness when I inform you that in your time as head of the judiciary, not only was this basic pillar of social security trembling, it was in fact completely destroyed publicly. The Iranian nation has not paid a small price by any means.[28]

3 The Judiciary after Shahroudi

In 2009, Khamenei appointed as Shahroudi's successor Sadegh Larijani, the fourth of five brothers who have been highly influential in the history of the Islamic Republic. Sadegh's older brother Ali had served as head of state broadcasting from 1994–2004 and between 2008 and 2020 as Speaker of Parliament. Sadegh's oldest brother Mohammad Javad has been a long-standing foreign policy advisor to both Supreme Leaders and was a chief negotiator in the 1988 ceasefire of the Iran–Iraq War. Before his appointment as head of the judiciary, Sadegh Larijani had served on all three of Iran's major councils: He was part of the twelve-member Guardian Council for eight years (2001–2009), he has continuously

---

[28] Mohaqqeq-Damad's letter to Ayatollah Shahroudi, *Ettelā'āt*, August 4, 2009. "Khatāb be Shahroudi: Kāsh dar hawza māndeh budid."

served on the Expediency Council since 2009 (and became its chair in 2018), and he has repeatedly been elected into the Assembly of Experts since 1999 (Boroujerdi and Rahimkhani 2018: 565).

Larijani did not continue Shahroudi's program of judicial and penal law reform. During Larijani's tenure (2009–2019), death sentences doubled and then tripled compared to average rates under Shahroudi. There were forty-two executions of juvenile offenders between 1990 and the end of Shahroudi's tenure,[29] but at least seventy-nine under Larijani.[30] Lawyers' access to revolutionary courts deteriorated: While lawyers had always faced restrictions in entering the revolutionary courts, such as when accessing relevant files or meeting with officials relevant to the case, they were at least permitted to attend court. After Larijani assumed office, lawyers had to obtain approval from the branch to be permitted to enter the court building, something that has been denied on many occasions.

The rights of the political opposition continued to be violated.[31] Shortly after Larijani assumed his new role at the helm of the judiciary, Iranian police, with authorization from the judiciary, raided the offices of several prominent civil society organizations, specifically several dedicated to the rights of political dissidents and victims of torture in Iranian prisons. Larijani promoted to the post of deputy prosecutor-general of Iran the notorious Saeed Mortazavi, who had served as prosecutor general of Tehran from 2003 to 2009.

During the decade of Larijani's tenure, incarceration and execution rates rose once again, in part due to harsher sentencing of drug possession and dealing. By the early 2010s, the execution of drug smugglers accounted for 75 percent of annual executions, "reaching a record-setting 509 drug-related executions in 2011" (Christensen 2017: 412). Though the law itself had not changed, the approach to drug users had shifted from a harm-reduction approach to a coercive and punitive approach (as documented in Chapter 8). After much domestic and international pressure over the issue, the Iranian parliament finally amended the drug trafficking law in 2018, which replaced the death

---

[29] Radio Free Europe/Radio Liberty (RFE/RL), "Iran Lawyer Seeks Cash to Spare Young on Death Row": www.rferl.org/a/Iran_Lawyer_Seeks_Cash_To_Spare_Young_On_Death_Row/1858467.html, last accessed June 23, 2022.

[30] IranWire, "Execution of Juveniles: Amnesty International Reports on Cover-Ups by the Iranian Government," February 26, 2016: https://justice4iran.org/persian/wp-content/uploads/2018/02/Larijani-13.pdf, accessed June 23, 2022; Amnesty International, "Iran: 17-Year-Old Boy at Risk of Imminent Execution," Press Release, October 13, 2017.

[31] In May 2012, the EU sanctioned Larijani for the many human rights abuses that were occurring during his tenure, including his signing off on harsh and inhuman sentences, the rise of arbitrary arrests and executions, and, more generally, for the overall systematic violations of due process by the judiciary.

penalty for possession of drugs with life imprisonment or fines. This led to a marked reduction in executions, which dropped from 507 in 2017 to 253 in 2018[32]

Overall, Larijani's tenure was seen as a regression in terms of the rule of law. Whereas under Shahroudi a notable improvement had taken place regarding the clarification of competencies between the judiciary and other state institutions, the boundaries of competencies once again appeared rather ill-defined as Larijani was widely seen as a stooge of Supreme Leader Khamenei. Shahroudi had also introduced higher standards of due process, which, under Larijani, were eroded as far as political cases were concerned (see Chapter 3).

Ebrahim Raisi was appointed as the new head of the judiciary in 2019, after having served from 2016 to 2019 as custodian of the Astan Quds Razavi endowment, one of Iran's wealthiest religious endowments, which manages the Imam Reza shrine in the holy city of Mashhad.[33] Raisi, a former student of Khamenei's, had previously served in the judiciary, as prosecutor general (2014–2016) and first deputy to the chief justice (2004–2014), and before that as the director of the General Inspection Office (1994–2004), the most powerful oversight body under the judiciary (Tables 9.1 and 9.2). He also served as chief prosecutor of the Special Court for the Clergy from 2012 until 2021. Since 2007, he has been a member of the Assembly of Experts, and since 2017 also a member of the Expediency Council. During his time as deputy prosecutor general of Tehran (1985–1988), Raisi was involved in the 1988 mass executions of 4,500–5,000 political prisoners. Specifically, he had been appointed to the four-member special committee that, following two fatwas by Ayatollah Khomeini, conducted the interrogations on the basis of which thousands of members of the Mojahedin-e Khalq opposition group as well as several hundred so-called apostates were executed (Abrahamian 1999).

Raisi's term was meant to last for five years but was cut short by his election to Iran's presidency in 2021. Into his two-year tenure fell the winter 2019–2020 protests, during which more than 1,500 people died,

---

[32] See www.amnesty.org/en/latest/news/2020/04/death-penalty-in-2019-facts-and-figures/#:~:text=Executions%20in%20Iran%20fell%20slightly,at%20least%20251%20in%202019.&text=At%20the%20end%20of%202019,penalty%20in%20law%20or%20practice, last accessed May 5, 2022.

[33] The Astan Quds Razavi endowment has thousands of employees as well as its own institutions, landholdings, and businesses throughout the country: www.bbc.com/persian/iran/2016/03/160306_l26_l45_astan_ghods_razavi_chart_business_activities, last accessed June 6, 2022.

including dozens of children. Security forces fired live ammunition at demonstrators, allegedly authorized to do so with impunity by the head of the judiciary. Families of the bereaved were forced into silence, with many not even permitted to view and bury the bodies. Meanwhile, the persecution of political activists continued. Many faced heavy prison sentences or even the death penalty. Activists who were released after serving their sentence were rearrested and given new sentences based on dubious charges. For example, the human rights activist (and later Nobel Peace Prize Laureate) Narges Mohammadi was released from prison in October 2020 after serving five and a half years, only to be given a new charge in June 2021 of thirty months' imprisonment, eighty lashes, and a fine.

Under Raisi's tutelage, a sixty-nine-page document on "judicial development" was issued, which laid out as top priorities the fight against corruption and increasing the efficiency of the judicial system. Raisi called, in particular, on the Ministry of Intelligence, the Audit Office, and the General Inspection Office to be more active in the fight against corruption.[34] A subsequent high-profile case indicted Akbar Tabari, the first deputy under Raisi's predecessor, Sadegh Larijani, for corruption and money laundering. The accused was given a lengthy prison sentence of thirty-one years. Critics view Raisi's fight against corruption as primarily an instrument to limit the influence of his political opponents, however. In this case, Tabari's conviction severely weakened Sadegh Larijani's potential candidacy to become the next Supreme Leader, and it also undermined the ambitions of his brother Ali Larijani to run for president in the 2021 elections.

Yet Raisi also initiated reforms in penal law. As discussed in Chapter 3, under his tenure, many punishments were commuted from prison terms into fines.[35] This included relatively minor misdemeanors such as the issuance of dud checks and the inability to pay dowry. But punishments for some graver crimes, such as drug trafficking, were also lightened, in a return to some of Shahroudi's reforms that Larijani had reversed. Nevertheless, 2020 witnessed a new spike in executions, rising to 267 (10 percent more than in 2019), partly due to the new levels of

---

[34] Iran ranks 149th among 180 countries in Transparency International's Corruption Perceptions Index (2023), with a score of 25 out of 100, indicating that the Islamic Republic is among the most corrupt countries in the world. By comparison, the average score of countries in the Middle East is 39.

[35] See www.mehrnews.com/news/4947930/کاهش ۶۸درصدی محکومان مهریه/آخرین آمار زندانیان کشور, last accessed June 21, 2023.

repression following the 2020 protests.[36] Among the 267 people executed in 2020 were also four minors, who according to Islamic law had reached the age of criminal responsibility. A new law was passed the same year, the Child and Adolescent Protection Law, aiming to end the execution of minors by recognizing as children all those under the age of 18, thus improving upon the 2013 Penal Code that had limited the applicability of criminal responsibility for children under 15 years of age.

In July 2021, Gholam-Hossein Mohseni-Eje'i was appointed the new head of the judiciary, replacing Raisi after the latter won the presidential elections. Mohseni-Eje'i had been a longtime prosecutor of the Special Clerical Court and was a high-ranking official in the Ministry of Intelligence during the time of the so-called chain murders between 1990 and 1998, when more than eighty-eight intellectuals and artists were assassinated, most likely at the behest of the Ministry of Intelligence. (Mohseni-Eje'i has been accused of personally being responsible for the murder of Pirouz Davani in 1998, editor and owner of *Pirouz* magazine). Mohseni-Eje'i also served as the judge in one of the reformist era's highest-profile cases, that of Tehran mayor Gholam Hossein Karbaschi, a staunch supporter of President Khatami. Karbaschi was arrested in 1998 on corruption charges and sentenced in a trial broadcast live on Iranian television to two years imprisonment (but pardoned by Khamenei after 9 months). The trial propelled Mohseni-Eje'i to public notoriety.

Since 2007, Mohseni-Eje'i has served on the Expediency Council, which advises the Supreme Leader and is appointed by him. From 2005–2009, he served as minister of intelligence but was dismissed in July 2009 by President Ahmadinejad due to his criticism of the president's chief of staff and first vice president Esfandiar Rahim Mashaei. Soon thereafter, the head of the judiciary at the time, Sadegh Larijani, appointed Mohseni-Eje'i prosecutor general, a role in which he became highly involved in the crackdown against the Green Movement (2009). Hundreds of journalists and demonstrators were detained, and activists given heavy sentences, some in widely broadcast show trials. The presidential candidates Mir Hossein Mousavi and Mehdi Karroubi were placed under house arrest, which in 2021 reached its decennial. The newspapers which the two candidates had cofounded long ago remain banned (Mousavi's *Kalām-e Sabz* and Karroubi's *Eʿtemād-e Melli*). In 2014, Mohseni-Eje'i rose to become the judiciary's spokesman and was then appointed first deputy of the judiciary under Larijani, who delegated

---

[36] See https://iranhr.net/en/articles/4311/, accessed June 19, 2021.

to Mohseni-Eje'i significant authority, including the power of deciding whether to execute defendants in drug cases.

Like Raisi, Mohseni-Eje'i was involved in the mass killings of 1988 (he was the judiciary's representative in the Intelligence Ministry from 1985 to 1988). Both men were also members of a committee charged with investigating reports of torture and sexual assault against protesters who had taken part in the Green Movement demonstrations in 2009. Lawyers involved in the investigations at the time claim that both men brushed aside overwhelming evidence incriminating security officials.

Unlike Raisi, Mohseni-Eje'i is known to be cruel and unscrupulous. Lawyers have drawn comparisons of Mohseni-Eje'i to Mohammad Mohammadi Reyshahri, minister of intelligence between 1984 and 1989, who later became attorney general. Reyshahri created a security- and espionage-heavy atmosphere in the courts and some already see the tenure of the new head of the judiciary as having a similar effect: Under Mohseni- Eje'i's tenure, executions have risen from 267 in 2020, to 333 in 2021, 582 in 2022, and 853 in 2023.[37]

4 Conclusions

What are the prospects for the rule of law in the Islamic Republic? Can any meaningful reform take place within the current constitutional and judicial structure? The reform movement which underpinned the Khatami presidency (1997–2005) was the most sustained attempt at achieving this objective. Whilst it was in some respects an elite-managed initiative emanating from the "Islamic leftist" cum intellectual and artistic elite, it nevertheless appealed to broad constituencies. Indeed, the slogans of rule of law (*hākemiyat-e qānun*), equal citizenship (*shahrvandi*), and civil society (*jāme'eh-ye madani*) temporarily helped forge an unanticipated coalition encompassing elements of the political elite and various social and subaltern groups who were willing to pursue their interests through the electoral process and bequeath trust to the executive – subject to the rule of law (Künkler 2012; Sadeghi-Boroujerdi 2019: 54–55). Khatami's presidency ushered in a critical transition in postrevolutionary Iran by attempting to set the country on the course of the "politics of normalcy." As Ervand Abrahamian (2008: 186–188) has pointed out, one of Khatami's most important successes

---

[37] See the annual reports of the World Coalition against the Death Penalty. https://worldcoalition.org, and the annual reports by Human Rights Watch, www.hrw.org/world-report/2024/country-chapters/iran, last accessed May 6, 2023.

was his ability to change the tone of public discourse from "revolution," "jihad," "imperialism," "the down-trodden," and "Westoxification" to "democracy," "pluralism," "equality," "civil society," "human rights," "political participation," "dialogue," and "citizenship." The fact that Khatami was re-elected in 2001 – the fourth reformist election victory in a row after his first election in 1997, municipal elections in 1999, and parliamentary elections in 2000 – further affirmed that segments of the population yearned for systemic change, an important development in and of itself, transforming the polity in those years into a diarchy, with the elected institutions on the one side facing the Supreme Leader and the clerical councils which have ultimate veto power over policy on the other. Ultimately, most of the policy reforms of the reform movement failed due to the veto of the Guardian Council and progressions in the rule of law were usually achieved, if at all, by changes in the interpretation and application of law, not through law reform. This also made advances in the rule of law easily reversible under the next president.

Yet, somewhat unexpectedly, the reformists' efforts were accompanied by a separate rule-of-law agenda at the top of the judiciary itself, led at the time by Mahmoud Shahroudi. Unlike the reformists, Shahroudi was not driven by considerations of citizen empowerment and universal human rights standards. Instead, he sought to institutionalize clear competencies between offices, incentivize standards in sentencing, and insulate the judiciary from interference by the ministry of intelligence and the revolutionary guards. Among Shahroudi's initiatives, eight stand out, falling into the two broad areas of judicial organization, and criminal law and procedure. In terms of judicial organization, they include re-establishing the prosecutorial office, creating dispute resolution councils, integrating the Special Court for the Clergy into the regular judiciary, and prohibiting extrajudicial detention centers. In terms of criminal law and procedure, they concern limiting the application of *'elm-e qāzi*, putting an end to the punishment of stoning, revising criteria for criminal responsibility among the youth, and reforming the CCP. While Khatami's reform initiatives were overwhelmingly stifled by interference from the Ministry of Intelligence and the Special Court for the Clergy (which is not under the aegis of the judiciary; Künkler 2013), the reform initiatives inside the judiciary were for the most part eventually implemented, but summarily watered down and partly reversed through intervention by the Supreme Leader's office and Shahroudi's successors.

Whilst the reform program of Khatami's administration ultimately failed as far as legal policy is concerned, the goals and aspirations of the reform movement found expression in 2009 in the Green Movement, which constituted a major ideological and discursive assault on the official ideology of the Islamic Republic, exposing its brutality and severely undermining its legitimacy (Alimagham 2020: 17). Since then, the political and ideological red lines of the regime have been narrowed further and reformists largely purged and prevented from running in elections. In the face of severe economic and political pressure, the country has experienced violent and deadly crackdowns on largely peaceful protests in 2018, 2019, 2020 and 2022. Opposition is increasingly being expressed in more revolutionary and extraconstitutional terms. The brief moment under the early years of the Rouhani presidency (2013–2021), during which the Joint Comprehensive Plan of Action (JCPOA) was passed, triggered hope that reformists might be able to reassert themselves at both the level of state and civil society. This hope was quickly extinguished with growing internal repression, the unilateral withdrawal of the Trump administration from the agreement, and the imposition of third-party sanctions. If it had proceeded as designed, the JCPOA would have triggered the structural economic reforms needed to uncouple the current political elite from its economic power – including the military-industrial complex of the Islamic Revolutionary Guard Corps (IRGC). Given Iran's recent trade deal with China along with the current domestic and geopolitical climate, this uncoupling has now moved into a distant future. This, combined with the subjugation of the legal profession and the ascendance of some of Iran's most notorious human rights offenders to the posts of president and head of the judiciary in 2021, does not bode well for those struggling to improve rights in Iran, be they political, social, cultural, or economic.

Bibliography

Abrahamian, Ervand. *Tortured Confessions Prisons and Public Recantations in Modern Iran*. Los Angeles: University of California Press, 1999.

Abrahamian, Ervand. *A History of Modern Iran*. New York: Cambridge University Press, 2008.

Alimagham, Pouya. *Contesting the Iranian Revolution: The Green Uprisings*. New York: Cambridge University Press, 2020.

Arjomand, Saïd Amir. Civil Society and the Rule of Law in the Constitutional Politics of Iran under Khatami. *Social Research*, 76 (2), 2000, pp. 283–301.

Boroujerdi, Mehrzad and Kourosh Rahimkhani. *Postrevolutionary Iran: A Political Handbook*. Syracuse: Syracuse University Press, 2018.

Buchta, Wilfried. *Who Rules Iran: The Structure of Power in the Islamic Republic*. Washington, DC: Washington Institute for Near East Policy, 2000.

Christensen, Janne Bjerre. "Human Rights and Wrongs in Iran's Drug Diplomacy with Europe," *Middle East Journal*, 71 (3), Summer 2017, pp. 403–432. www.jstor.org/stable/90016471, accessed September 3, 2023.

Farhi, Farideh. "Improvising in Public: Transgressive Politics of the Reformist Press in Postrevolutionary Iran," in Negin Nabavi (ed.), *Intellectual Trends in Twentieth-Century Iran: A Critical Survey*, Gainsville: University of Florida Press, 2003.

Fraser Fujinaga, Antonia. *Life and Limb. Irreversible hadd penalties in Iranian criminal courts and opportunities to avoid them.* Doctoral Dissertation, Islamic Studies, The University of Edinburgh, 2013.

Fraser Fujinaga, Antonia. "Islamic Law in Post-revolutionary Iran," in Anver M. Emon and Rumee Ahmed (eds.), *The Oxford Handbook of Islamic Law*, Oxford: Oxford University Press, 2016.

Ghassemi, Ghassem. "Criminal Punishment in Islamic Societies: Empirical Study of Attitudes to Criminal Sentencing in Iran," *European Journal on Criminal Policy and Research*, 15, 2009, pp. 159–180.

Hashemi, Said Mohammad. *Hoquq-e asāsi-ye jomhuri-ye eslāmi-ye Irān*. 2 vols., Qom, 1375/1996.

Kadivar, Mohsen. *Ebtedhāl-e marjaʿiyyat-e shīʿa: estizāh-e marjaʿiyyat-e maqām-e rahbari, hojjat al-islām waʾl-muslimin Khāmenehʾi* (2014). Electronically available at http://kadivar.com/wp-content/uploads/2014/03/%D8%A7%D8%A8%D8%AA%D8%B0%D8%A7%D9%84-%D9%85%D8%B1%D8%AC%D8%B9%DB%8C%D8%AA-%D8%B4%DB%8C%D8%B9%D9%87.pdf (Accessed: May 11, 2021).

Khatami, Mohammad. *Hope and Challenge: The Iranian President Speaks.* Institute of Global Cultural Studies, Binghamton: Binghamton University, 1997.

Künkler, Mirjam. "Electoral Victory, Political Defeat: The Elimination of Zones of Autonomy in Khatami's Iran," in Douglas Chalmers and Scott Mainwaring (eds.), *Problems Confronting Contemporary Democracies*, Notre Dame: Notre Dame University Press, 2012, pp. 166–202.

Künkler, Mirjam. "The Special Court of the Clergy (*dādgāh-e vīzhe-ye rūhānīyat*) and the Repression of Dissident Clergy in Iran," in Said Arjomand and Nathan Brown (eds.), *The Rule of Law, Islam, and Constitutional Politics in Egypt and Iran*, Albany: SUNY Press, 2013, pp. 57–100.

Mohammadi, Majid. *Judicial Reform and Reorganization in 20th century Iran State-Building, Modernization and Islamization.* Abingdon: Routledge, 2008.

Sadeghi-Boroujerdi, Eskandar. *Revolution and its Discontents: Political Thought and Reform in Iran.* New York: Cambridge University Press, 2019.

Shahroudi, Mahmoud Hashemi. *Bāyestehā-ye Feqh-e Qazāʾ*. Tehran: Nashr-e Mizan, 1378/1999.

Tabari, Keyvan. 'The Rule of Law and the Politics of Reform in Post-Revolutionary Iran', *International Sociology*, 18 (1), 2003, pp. 96–113

10 Iran's Religious and Ethnic Minorities in the Eyes of the Judiciary and the Security Apparatus

Shahin Milani

1 Introduction

The constitution of the Islamic Republic of Iran was drafted and subsequently ratified in a referendum in 1979. In 1989, the constitution was amended and ratified by another referendum. Article 4 of the constitution declares:

> All laws and regulations pertaining to civil, penal, financial, economic, administrative, cultural, military, political and other spheres must be based on Islamic criteria. This article governs absolutely and generally all articles of the Constitution, as well as all other laws and regulations, and the duty to ascertain this matter devolves on the [Islamic] jurists of the Guardian Council.[1]

The term "jurists" refers to six Islamic jurists appointed by the Supreme Leader. Thus, Article 4 of the Iranian constitution effectively states that all laws and regulations must conform to Islamic principles as determined by six clerics selected by the Islamic Republic's highest political authority. Furthermore, Article 12 declares that Twelver Shi'ism is Iran's official religion, and that this principle is "eternally immutable."

These two constitutional provisions delineate the broad context within which the Islamic Republic's treatment of religious minorities should be assessed. By contrast, providing an analysis of the situation of ethnic minorities in Iran is much less straightforward. The laws of the Islamic Republic do not explicitly discriminate on the basis of race or ethnicity. Nevertheless, many ethnic minorities are, in fact, religious minorities as well. Baluchis, Kurds,[2] and Turkmens constitute most of Iran's Sunni population.

I thank the anonymous reviewers and editors for their helpful comments on earlier versions of this chapter.

[1] Iran Data Portal: https://irandataportal.syr.edu/constitutions-and-constitutional-debates.
[2] While the majority of Iranian Kurds are Muslim, official statistics do not distinguish between Shi'i and Sunni Kurds. Yildiz and Taysi (2007: 5) estimate that about half of Kurdish Iranians are Sunni, while the remainder are Shi'i or Yarsan. Sunni Kurds reside across Kurdish regions, but Shi'i Kurds are centered in Kermanshah.

Moreover, with respect to Shi'i ethnic minorities, too, the Iranian government has committed human rights abuses against political dissidents and activists advocating for the rights of their respective ethnic or linguistic groups.

This chapter examines the rights situation of religious and ethnic minorities in the Islamic Republic. The chapter begins by discussing how the Iranian government views different belief systems broadly classified as "religious minority faiths." Understanding how the Iranian government treats various religious communities in contemporary Iran is predicated on understanding the underlying view of the religious Shi'i establishment toward the belief systems of these communities. After discussing the situation of religious minorities, the chapter proceeds to analyze the rights situation of ethnic minorities.

While official policies are often not at all indicative of how the Shi'i Persian majority of the country views minorities, religious and ethnic minorities suffer significant discriminations at the hands of the state. It is suggested that the actions taken by the Iranian government should be seen in the context of the perceived threats posed by ethnic and religious minorities to the Islamic Republic. The more a religious belief system is seen as a threat to the Shi'i clerical establishment, the more likely it is that its adherents are faced with discriminatory state action. As this chapter will demonstrate, the degree to which the Iranian government engages in repressive actions increases as the challenge to its authority is more strongly perceived.

The analysis of the chapter is based on cases of human rights abuses against religious and ethnic minorities as documented by human rights organizations and media reports. Drawing on specific cases, the chapter seeks to identify patterns in human rights abuses committed against religious and ethnic minorities. As the situation of minorities has been well documented up until the early 2000s, the chapter focuses on the post-2000 period. Where appropriate, detailed information on individual cases is presented to show the extent and depth of discriminatory state practices.

2 Different Categories of Religious Minorities

The term "religious minorities" captures a myriad of relationships between the Iranian state and various religious communities in Iran. Broadly speaking, there are three different categories of religious minorities in the country. The first category, whose members are the largest numerically, is comprised of Sunni Muslims and Shi'is who are not considered mainstream adherents of Twelver Shi'ism. Gonabadi Dervishes are an example of the latter.

Iran's Religious and Ethnic Minorities

Table 10.1 *Minorities in the Iranian census of 2016*

Religion	Number of Citizens	Percentage of Total Population
Muslim	79,598,054	99.59%
Christian	130,158	0.16%
Jew	9,826	0.012%
Zoroastrian	23,109	0.029%
Other	40,551	0.051%
Unspecified	124,572	0.16%

The second category comprises non-Muslims who are recognized under the Iranian constitution. These include Armenian and Assyrian/Chaldean (but not other) Christians, Jews, and Zoroastrians. While the members of these religious minorities do not have equal rights compared to Twelver Shi'i Muslims, they are nevertheless free to practice their respective faiths under the Iranian constitution. In addition, the Iranian constitution provides them with representation in the national parliament, with two seats for Armenian Christians, one seat for Assyrian/Chaldean Christians, one seat for Jews, and one seat for Zoroastrians. Other Christians, such as evangelical Christians and Christian converts, are not included in this category and, as such, do not enjoy legal protection. They can, in fact, face harsh sentences, including the death penalty on the charge of apostasy if they are Muslims who have converted to Christianity. The third category includes non-Muslims who do not enjoy legal recognition. This category includes atheists, Bahá'ís, and those who convert from Islam to any other religion (including Christianity, but also Hinduism, Buddhism, and other religions). Iranians who fall into this category may also face the death penalty, and otherwise are likely to face systematic persecution and deprivation of their rights.

Iran's census only provides data for constitutionally recognized religious communities. Sunni Muslims are simply counted as "Muslims." The census also does not provide the number of Gonabadi Dervishes and other Sufi groups.[3] Bahá'ís, of course, are not considered a recognized minority and are also not separately counted. While Bahá'ís are considered Iran's largest non-Muslim religious minority, their exact number remains unknown. Table 10.1 provides the population of religious groups based on Iran's 2016 census. It should be noted that these figures may not reflect the actual religious identification of citizens, as openly discussing one's religious affiliation could have adverse consequences for respondents.

[3] See Statistical Center of Iran, Census.

2.1 Muslim Religious Minorities

In this section, human rights issues relating to Muslim minority groups will be discussed.

2.1.1 Sunni Muslims

With the exception of Article 115 of the constitution, which explicitly states that the president of the Islamic Republic must be an adherent of Shi'i Islam, and the implied understanding that the Supreme Leader should be a senior Shi'i cleric, the Islamic Republic does not explicitly discriminate against Sunnis in its laws. While Article 12 of the Iranian constitution declares Shi'i Islam Iran's official state religion, the same article also states that adherents of the four major Sunni schools are free to practice their faiths, and that in localities where they are in the majority, local ordinances should be in accordance with their religious beliefs.

In practice, however, Sunnis have been subject to discriminatory treatment. Since the early days of the revolution the clerical establishment has been suspicious of Sunni leadership (Dudoignon 2017: 220) and Sunnis are often barred from the competitive examinations required for some universities and civil service employment (Dudoignon 2017: 162). To date, no Sunni has been appointed to high-level government positions such as minister or provincial governor. In 2013, Ali Younesi, President Rouhani's assistant for the affairs of ethnic and religious minorities, stated that President Rouhani "did not succeed" in appointing religious and ethnic minorities as ministers or provincial governors, which should be interpreted to mean that he was not able to overcome the resistance of regime conservatives, particularly in the Supreme Leader's office (BBC Persian 2013). After his reelection in 2017, President Rouhani did not appoint a Sunni to high office either, disappointing supporters such as Molavi Abdolhamid (Radio Farda 2019a), who has been the Sunni Imam Jom'eh of Zahedan since 1987 (Dudoignon 2017: 93) and is a rare voice occasionally raising Sunni minority concerns. Appointment of Sunnis to mid-level government positions is also reportedly rare. Two exceptions are Saleh Adibi, who in 2015 was appointed Iran's ambassador to Vietnam and Cambodia (Radio Farda 2015), and Homeira Rigi, who in 2019 was appointed Iran's ambassador to Brunei (Mashregh News 2019).

Despite the fact that the majority of Iranians residing in Sistan and Baluchistan province are Sunni, only a small minority of employees at governmental offices in this province are Sunni (Dudoignon 2017: 93). Due to a lack of economic opportunities in the region, many local residents engage in smuggling of consumer goods across the Iran–Pakistan border. Former President Hashemi Rafsanjani is reported to have cited Sunni leaders' refusal to issue religious rulings to prohibit smuggling of consumer goods as partial justification for denying governmental jobs to Sunni Baluch residents (Shahi and Abdoh-Tabrizi 2019: 322).

In addition to discrimination in hiring, Sunnis also face discrimination with respect to the free exercise of religion. The Iranian government bars Sunnis from building new mosques in Tehran, Mashhad, and other major cities (Iran Human Rights Documentation Center 2019b: 2). Furthermore, Iranian authorities have demolished a number of Sunni mosques and religious seminaries over the past years. In 1994, the Sheikh Fayz Mosque in Mashhad was demolished and a garden was created on its site (Dudoignon 2017: 223). On the same day, assailants used machine guns to fire at the façade of the Makki Mosque in Zahedan. In 2008, the Imam Hanifeh School in Zabol, in Sistan and Baluchistan province, was demolished. The reason given by the authorities was reportedly the school's failure to obtain the required permits, despite the fact that the school had operated for seventeen years prior to its demolition (Iran Human Rights Documentation Center 2019b: 22). In addition to closing Sunni religious institutions, the Iranian government has also taken restrictive measures on Sunni publishing houses, such as banning them from book fairs (Dudoignon 2017: 254).

Numerous Sunni clerics and Islamic scholars have been killed or have disappeared since 1979 (Dudoignon 2017: 174), including Ahmad Moftizadeh, a prominent Sunni religious leader who had initially supported the establishment of the Islamic Republic (Kadivar 2018). Moftizadeh had founded Maktab-e Qur'an, a religious movement in Iranian Kurdistan. He was held in prison until August 1992, and died six months later (Iran Human Rights Documentation Center 2019: 22). Many adherents of Maktab-e Qur'an were imprisoned and expelled from their jobs (Dudoignon 2017: 191f.). Nasser Sobhani, another prominent Sunni cleric, was executed in March 1990 (Justice for Iran 2016). Ahmad Mirin Sayyad Baluchi, a Sunni cleric who had studied in Saudi Arabia, was arrested and imprisoned in 1988 (Dudoignon 2017: 224). After his release in 1994, he settled in the United Arab Emirates. During a trip to Iran in 1996, however, Sayyad Baluchi disappeared. His corpse was later found in Minab, Hormozgan province (Alavi 2019). Another Sunni cleric, Sheikh Mohammad Ziaei, was killed in 1994 (Dudoignon 2017: 224). These two murders took place during the period in which Iran's intelligence apparatus assassinated numerous dissidents, intellectuals, and journalists, raising the possibility that these murders were also carried out by intelligence agents.

In recent years the Iranian government has imposed travel restrictions on senior Sunni clerics. In 2018, for example, Abdolhamid was barred from traveling to Qatar (BBC Persian 2018c). He has also faced restrictions on traveling inside Iran, even to neighboring Kerman province (BBC Persian 2018c). Kak Hasan Amini, a Sunni cleric from Kurdistan, has also been barred from leaving Iran, reportedly because he had spoken with media outlets based outside Iran, including NourTV, a channel that reflects Sunni views (HRANA 2016a). The Iranian government has also detained several Shi'is who have converted to Sunni Islam (Center for Human Rights in Iran 2014). These measures, taken together, indicate the extent to which security concerns inform the Islamic Republic's actions against Iran's Sunni population.

2.1.1.1 Execution of Sunni Prisoners on National Security Charges
Executions of Sunni prisoners on national security charges have been among the most egregious human rights abuses of the Iranian government in recent years. Numerous Sunni Iranian citizens have been arrested and charged with national security crimes, including *mohārebeh*, or waging war against God.[4]

The Iranian government has alleged that these individuals had ties with extremist militant Sunni groups. Many of the Sunni prisoners, however, have maintained their innocence and insisted that they were targeted because of their religious activities (Iran Human Rights Documentation Center 2014c). These prisoners were denied adequate access to counsel and were tried in trials closed to the public in violation of Iran's regulations on criminal procedure.[5] Many of the Sunni defendants were tried by Judge Mohammad Moghiseh, known for issuing harsh sentences to political prisoners.[6] Given the fact that the government does not allow its allegations against Sunni defendants to be publicly scrutinized in any meaningful judicial process, it is reasonable to conclude that the measures taken against Sunnis serve a security purpose rather than a judicial one.

---

[4] These executions have not been adequately documented, so providing adequate figures for them is very difficult. The following draws on a selection of reported cases.
[5] Judge Mohammad Moghiseh, serving at Branch 28 of the Tehran Revolutionary Court, for example, has not allowed defense attorneys to speak at the trial but only permitted them to provide a legal brief, or not speak at all.
[6] Judge Moghiseh has issued harsh sentences to many political prisoners and prisoners of conscience. For instance, he sentenced Nasrin Sotoudeh, an internationally renowned Iranian lawyer, to thirty-three years' imprisonment in March 2019. He also sentenced seven Bahá'í leaders to twenty years' imprisonment in August 2010. This sentence was later reduced to ten years.

On August 2, 2016, the Iranian government executed twenty-five Sunni prisoners.[7] These prisoners were often detained in solitary confinement for prolonged periods and were subjected to torture in order to confess (HRANA 2017c). The Iranian government alleged that the defendants were members of an extremist group named Tawhid and Jihad (ISNA 2016), but many of them maintained that they were nonviolent religious activists (HRANA 2017c).

While in prison, Shahram Ahmadi, one of the individuals later executed, spoke with numerous human rights organizations and media outlets. According to his lawyer's appellate brief before Iran's Supreme Court, Ahmadi, a Sunni preacher, was the driver of a vehicle that carried a number of armed assailants to a place where they attacked Iranian police. Ahmadi maintained that he was not aware of the intent of the assailants, and that he had driven them to that location in exchange for a fare (HRANA 2016b). Under Iran's Islamic Penal Code (IPC) of 2013, the crime of *mohārebeh* requires the actual drawing of a weapon by the defendant.[8] Ahmadi, who was arrested in 2009, was convicted while the previous version of the IPC was in effect. Under that version, mere membership in an armed group could result in conviction on the charge of *mohārebeh* whether or not the defendant had personally drawn a weapon.[9] Nevertheless, Article 10(b) of the 2013 IPC declares that if a new law is more favorable to a convicted defendant, the court is required to reduce the punishment in favor of the convicted individual in accordance with the new statute.[10] Therefore, even assuming that Ahmadi

---

[7] HRANA 2017c. The names of the executed individuals were Kaveh Veisi, Keivan Momenifard, Adel Barmashti, Behrouz Shanazari, Edris Nemati, Taleb Maleki, Voria Qaderifard, Keyvan Karimi, Shahram Ahmadi, Farzad Honarjou, Bahman Rahimi, Mokhtar Rahimi, Yavar Rahimi, Kaveh Sharifi, Arash Sharifi, Ahmad Nasiri, Mohammad Gharibi, Omid Mahmoudi, Omid Peyvand, Amjad Salehi, Pouria Mohammadi, Shahou Ebrahimi, Ali Araqi, Hekmat Araqi, and Hamze Araqi.

[8] Article 279 of the IPC of 2013 states, "Mohārebeh is defined as drawing a weapon on the life, property or chastity of people or to cause terror as it creates the atmosphere of insecurity. When a person draws a weapon on one or several specific persons because of personal enmities and his act is not against the public, and also a person who draws a weapon on people, but, due to inability does not cause insecurity, shall not be considered as a *mohāreb* [i.e., a person who commits enmity against God, *mohārebeh*]." Islamic Penal Code 2013.

[9] Article 186 of the previous version of the IPC stated: "All the members and supporters of a group or an organized association which have waged armed rebellion against the Islamic State, whilst the core of that organization or group exists, shall be regarded as mohārebs provided that they know the stance of that group or organization and have effective activities and efforts in support of its aims; even though, they are not engaged in the military subdivision. Note – A united front composed of various groups and individuals shall be regarded as one [organization]." See Islamic Penal Code (1991).

[10] Article 10(b) of the IPC of 2013 states: "In case the punishment of an offense is reduced under a subsequent law, the enforcement judge is obliged, before, or during, the execution, to ask the court which has issued the final judgment to correct it according the

was aware of the plans of the assailants or that he was a member of the Tawhid and Jihad group, an allegation that he denied, his conviction for the crime of *mohārebeh* should have been reversed based on Article 10(b) of the IPC of 2013. Disregarding this provision and other legal issues, Iran's Supreme Court affirmed Ahmadi's death sentence in June 2016 and he was executed on August 2, 2016.

In violation of Iranian law, which requires that the attorney for a person who is being executed should be notified at least forty-eight hours prior to the execution, the attorneys for the twenty-five Sunni prisoners were not notified of their impending execution in time.[11] Their families were not notified in time either, and, as a result, they were not able to have a farewell visit (HRANA 2017c). In addition, in a manner similar to other executions for national security crimes, the bodies of the executed Sunni prisoners were not returned to their families for burial, and the families were not allowed to hold memorial services for them (HRANA 2017c).

2.1.2 Gonabadi Dervishes

Gonabadi Dervishes are Twelver Shi'is, but they do not adhere to the mainstream clerical Shi'i order. Instead, they follow their spiritual leader, referred to as a Qotb. The current Qotb or spiritual leader of Gonabadi Dervishes is Alireza Jazbi Tabatabaei. The Iranian government has taken numerous actions against Gonabadi Dervishes over the years. As hardline vigilantes have attacked their places of worship, the state's security apparatus has arrested numerous Gonabadi Dervishes and the judiciary has sentenced them to imprisonment and internal exile. Taken together, the Iranian government's policy toward Gonabadi Dervishes appears to be aimed at both denying their right to freedom of religion and neutralizing their capacity as an organized network.

Invidious state actions against Gonabadi Dervishes began shortly after the 1979 Islamic Revolution, with a *hosseinieh* in Kerman being the first place of worship to be attacked (Deutsche Welle Persian 2018). In November 1979, the Moshir al-Saltaneh Hosseinieh, also known as Amir-Soleimani Hosseinieh, was burned down (van den Bos 2013:

---

subsequent law. The convict, too, may apply for the commutation of the punishment from the issuing court. The issuing court, considering the subsequent law, shall reduce the previous punishment. The same rules mentioned in this paragraph shall be applicable on security and correction measures imposed on minor offenders. In such cases, the natural or judicial guardian of [the minor offender], too, can apply for the commutation of the security and correction measures." See Islamic Penal Code (2013).

[11] Regulatory Code on Sentences of Qisas, Stoning, Crucifixion, Execution, and Flogging, Article 7(8): https://iranhrdc.org/english-translation-of-regulatory-code-on-sentences-of-qisas-stoning-crucifixion-execution-and-flogging/.

150). Revolutionary groups also destroyed the tomb of a Gonabadi Dervish spiritual leader in the Shah Abdul Azim area in Shahr-e-Rey, south of Tehran (Iran Human Rights Documentation Center 2020). In 1981, however, Ayatollah Khomeini approved the reconstruction of the Amir-Soleimani Hosseinieh (Ansari 2018). Khomeini also instructed the head of Tehran's revolutionary court to issue an official letter safeguarding the security of the site. The letter also guaranteed the Gonabadi Dervishes' leader's freedom to travel across the country. Following Khomeini's death in 1989, however, the government renewed its persecution of Gonabadi Dervishes. A section of the Amir-Soleimani Hosseinieh was burned in 1991, another was taken over by Meʿraj-e Shohada, the Committee for Finding Missing Soldiers in the Iran–Iraq War (Iran Human Rights Documentation Center 2020). Also, in the 1990s the government started funding institutions tasked with conducting research and confronting "misguided sects," which included Gonabadi Dervishes.

A new wave of repressive measures against the Gonabadis began after President Ahmadinejad assumed office in 2005. In February 2006, Iranian authorities closed down the Dervishes' *hosseinieh* in Qom, demolished it, and turned the space into a parking lot (BBC Persian 2006; Radio Farda 2007). About seven hundred Gonabadi Dervishes were reportedly detained during protests against the demolition. In December 2008, intelligence agents attacked Gonabadi Dervishes in Kish Island in the Persian Gulf as they were performing congregational prayer in front of their *hosseinieh*, which had also been closed by the authorities (Radio Farda 2008). A number of dervishes were arrested and transferred to a Ministry of Intelligence detention facility. Those arrested were subsequently charged with acting against national security, but were eventually acquitted (Radio Farda 2011). Two lawyers representing these detainees, however, were later charged with and convicted of disseminating propaganda against the Islamic Republic. Separately, Mostafa Daneshjou, a Gonabadi Dervish attorney who had represented Gonabadis in Neka, Mazandaran province, was sentenced to seven months' imprisonment on the charge of disseminating falsehoods and disturbing public opinion (Radio Farda 2011).

In February 2009, Gonabadi Dervishes' *takia* in Isfahan was destroyed (van den Bos 2013: 151).[12] A building in Karaj was attacked in 2010 while another one in Shahr-e Kord was damaged in January 2013. In 2011 a Gonabadi Dervish named Vahid Banani was fatally shot by a

---

[12] Similar to a *hosseinieh*, a *takia* is also used for mourning rituals for Hossein, Prophet Mohammad's grandson.

police officer (Majzooban Noor 2018). Although the evidence indicated that the shooting was intentional, it was prosecuted as an unintentional manslaughter (Majzooban Noor 2018).

Torture, denial of due process rights, and unfair trials are human rights violations that Gonabadi Dervishes have endured as well. Dervishes have generally avoided the charge of *mohārebeh* as there is no indication that any Dervish has ever taken up arms against the Islamic Republic. Nevertheless, clashes between unarmed Dervishes and security forces have led to other national security charges against a large number of Dervishes.

2.1.2.1 Arrest and Imprisonment of Gonabadi Dervishes in 2018
The Iranian government's decades-long confrontation with Gonabadi Dervishes reached its climax in 2018, when Iranian security forces clashed with a number of Gonabadi Dervishes who had gathered in front of the residence of Noor-Ali Tabandeh, the spiritual leader of Gonabadi Dervishes at that time.[13] His followers had assembled there anticipating that security forces were going to move into Tabandeh's home. More than three hundred were detained, according to a police commander (Tasnim 2018). One, named Mohammad Raji, died while in police custody (Radio Farda 2018b). According to his daughter, the police stated that he had died because of the injuries he had sustained. She added that she had seen her father on the night of the clashes, and that he had been beaten severely (Radio Farda 2018b). On the same night, one bus and one car rammed into police officers in the area. Both attacks were captured on video by local residents. The bus attack killed three police officers, while the car reportedly injured one person (Radio Farda 2018a). Iranian authorities arrested Mohammad Salas, a Gonabadi Dervish, for carrying out the bus attack. In a video released by state-run media, an injured Salas was shown confessing to ramming the bus into police officers (Mashregh News 2018). Salas was lying on a hospital bed as he made these statements. He added that he did not intend to kill anyone, and that he acted out of instantaneous rage (Mashregh News 2018). Salas was tried in March 2018 and sentenced to death (Center for Human Rights in Iran 2018a). In his trial he stated that he had been injured in the eye and in the head when driving the bus, and that he was trying to escape as he was scared of being beaten by agents if he were to be arrested (Center for Human Rights in Iran

---

[13] BBC Persian 2018a. His Sufi name is Majzubalishah. He had been a judge on the Supreme Court, and he is also active as a lawyer and activist. He translated Frantz Fanon's *Sociologie d'une révolution* into Persian. One of his main works is *Collection of Jurisprudential and Social Essays* (Majmu'eh-ye Maqālāt-e Feqhi).

2018a). Salas's lawyer stated that he had been tortured into confessing and requested a new trial (Center for Human Rights in Iran 2018b). In an audio recording released by the lawyer, Salas stated that he was not the driver of the bus that killed the police officers, and that he had confessed under torture and the influence of methadone (Center for Human Rights in Iran 2018b). Despite strong objections to his unfair trial by human rights organizations, including Amnesty International and Human Rights Watch, the Iranian government executed him on June 18, 2018 (BBC Persian 2018b).

The Iranian government also sentenced at least 208 Gonabadi Dervishes to prison terms and other punishments after trials that violated Iran's own regulations on criminal procedure as well as its international obligations (Human Rights Watch 2018). Prison terms ranged from four months to twenty-six years. Numerous reports indicate that Gonabadi Dervishes were mistreated in prison (Radio Farda 2018c). Other sentences included flogging, internal exile, and travel bans as well as bans on membership in social and political groups (Radio Farda 2018c).

While the security forces and the judiciary clamped down on Dervishes and other minorities, the Iranian parliament complemented their actions by enhancing legal provisions targeting religious minorities. This effort, as many before, was pursued under the guise of confronting "misguided sects."

2.1.3 The 2021 Amendments to the Islamic Penal Code

On January 13, 2021, the parliament passed a law amending the Islamic Penal Code (Laws and Regulations Portal of Iran (February 18, 2021)). This law was approved by Guardian Council on February 3, 2021. This law added two articles to the statute. The articles are denoted as Article 499 *bis* and Article 500 *bis*. Section 2 of Article 500 *bis* criminalizes "any deviant educational or promotional activity that is contradictory or disruptive to the sacred Islamic shariʿa through publicizing baseless and false claims in religious matters, including claims of being a deity, a prophet or an Imam or being in communication with Prophets or Holy Imams (Peace Be Upon Them)." Anyone convicted of this crime can be sentenced to two to five years' imprisonment. This change will likely be used to prosecute individuals who may have previously been prosecuted under the dissemination of propaganda against the Islamic Republic under Article 500, which could carry a sentence of three months to one year's imprisonment. This change effectively means that persons accused of disseminating religious content contrary to Islamic Republic's norms will face a harsher sentence than individuals accused of disseminating political propaganda against the government.

Previously, the latter would have been charged and sentenced under Article 500, which would only carry a sentence of three months to one year's imprisonment. Article 500 *bis*, however, carries a sentence of two to five years' imprisonment.

2.2 Non-Muslim Religious Minorities Recognized under the Iranian Constitution

As mentioned, Christianity, Judaism, and Zoroastrianism have been recognized under the Iranian constitution. In fact, when Iranian officials use the term "religious minorities," they are exclusively referring to these three communities. Under Islamic jurisprudence, Christians and Jews are considered Ahl-e Ketab or "People of the Book" and afforded certain rights. Zoroastrians, that is, adherents to Persia's main pre-Islamic religion, are also treated as People of the Book by the Islamic Republic.[14] Article 13 of the Iranian constitution states:

> Zoroastrian, Jewish, and Christian Iranians are the only recognized religious minorities, who, within the limits of the law, are free to perform their religious rites and ceremonies, and to act according to their own canon in matters of personal affairs and religious education.[15]

In addition, Article 64 of the Iranian constitution provides for representation of these minority groups in the Iranian parliament. Jews and Zoroastrians each have one representative. Christians are divided into three groups: (1) Assyrians and Chaldeans, (2) Armenians in northern regions, and (3) Armenians in southern regions. Each group has 1 member of parliament, which means that, overall, there are 5 members of parliament (out of 290) representing recognized religious minorities. Religious minorities must vote for candidates for their allotted seat, and Muslim parliamentary candidates cannot compete for religious minority votes, which also means the latter are institutionally discouraged from thinking about religious minority affairs.

Despite the recognized status of Christians, Jews, and Zoroastrians, they are not equal to Muslims under the law. One example of inequality is that non-Muslims are barred from employment in the Iranian military.[16] Another is the application of *qesās* or retributive punishments.

---

[14] Mandaeans (concentrated mainly in Khuzestan province) also are a religious minority not officially recognized under the Iranian constitution, but, according to a fatwa by Supreme Leader Khamenei, they are considered People of the Book and are afforded some protections. See Yjc.ir (2015).

[15] Constitution of the Islamic Republic of Iran (1979): https://irandataportal.syr.edu/wp-content/uploads/constitution-english-1368.pdf.

[16] Islamic Republic of Iran Military Law, Article 2(a).

Under Article 301 of the IPC of 2013, if a Muslim kills a non-Muslim, he or she will not be subject to *qesās*. In other words, he or she will not receive the death penalty and at most could be sentenced to ten years' imprisonment. But if a non-Muslim kills a Muslim, he or she will be subject to *qesās* and could be executed.[17] In 2013, a Muslim man who had killed a Jewish man was sentenced to thirteen years' imprisonment for murder and other crimes despite the fact that the Jewish man's next of kin had requested the death penalty (IranWire 2013). Another discriminatory policy affecting Iran's non-Muslim religious minority is Iran's inheritance laws. Under Article 881 ("repeated")[18] of Iran's Civil Code, if a non-Muslim has a Muslim heir, the decedent's non-Muslim heir will not inherit at all.[19] Therefore, if, for example, one heir converts to Islam, he or she can prevent other heirs from receiving any inheritance.

The *gozinesh* (selection) law of 1996 enshrines discrimination in hiring on the basis of ideology.[20] In January 1983, Ayatollah Khomeini issued a directive to streamline the process of selecting candidates for government employment. This directive issued broad guidelines and was meant to restrain the massive purges that were taking place in the aftermath of the 1979 Revolution. In 1995, the Iranian parliament passed a law on the basis of this directive and delineated the selection process for the Ministry of Education employees. A year later the parliament passed another law and made the requirements for employment at the Ministry of Education applicable to all government agencies.[21] While recognized religious minorities can be hired by state agencies under this law, they are still required to abstain from practices that would openly violate Islamic norms. Belief in and acceding to *velāyat-e faqih*, an Islamic precept, is also required of all state employees, whether or not they are Muslim. As such, the *gozinesh* law creates an impediment for employment of religious minorities, particularly because the public sector controls a large share of the Iranian economy.

In a similar vein, a new discriminatory policy was announced in May 2019. In a directive, an official with Iran's Social Welfare Organization announced that religious minorities were barred from employment

---

[17] See https://irandataportal.syr.edu/penal-code.
[18] When a law is amended by the addition of a new provision, the term "repeated" (*bis*) is used to denote the new provision inserted in the middle of the law in order to avoid the need to change the numbers of articles following the added provision.
[19] Civil Code (1928): https://rc.majlis.ir/fa/law/show/97937, accessed 15th March 2021.
[20] On this, see Amnesty International's concerns relevant to the 91st session of the International Labor Conference, June 3–19, 2003, AI Index: IOR 42/003/2003: https://perma.cc/C5UU-ERP2, accessed 16th March 2021.
[21] Law of 14 May 1996 (Expansion of Teachers and Ministry of Education Employees Selection Criteria to Employees of Other Ministries, and State Organizations, Institutions, and Companies): https://rc.majlis.ir/fa/law/show/92657, accessed 16th March 2021.

in kindergartens in any capacity, except for kindergartens that exclusively served minority children (Iran Human Rights Documentation Center 2019a). After human rights organizations and media outlets publicized this directive, the Zoroastrian member of parliament wrote a letter of protest to the minister of labor, whose Ministry oversees the Social Welfare Organization ('Asr-e Iran 2019). Following the public outcry, the Social Welfare Organization issued another directive, slightly moderating its policy to the effect that the restriction on religious minority employees pertained only to "general" and religious instruction positions, but not teaching positions for arts and sports (Behzisti.ir 2019).

There are instances when discriminatory verdicts issued by the Guardian Council, the body charged with interpreting the constitution and ensuring that all laws comply with Islam, have been overruled by the Expediency Council. In 2017 the Guardian Council ruled that Sepanta Niknam, a Zoroastrian member of the Yazd city council, could not serve as a city council member, arguing that under Islamic law a non-Muslim could not "reign" over Muslims. The Guardian Council issued this opinion despite the fact that Niknam was directly elected by Yazd residents. Under applicable law, members of recognized religious minorities were allowed to run for city councils. The Iranian parliament amended the law, adding a proviso reiterating that religious minorities could run for city council seats where they reside; in other words, they were allowed to represent Muslims. The Guardian Council rejected this amendment. The parliament insisted on the amendment, and, as a result, the dispute was referred to the Expediency Council, a body appointed by the Supreme Leader to resolve disputes between the parliament and the Guardian Council. Eventually, on July 21, 2018, the Expediency Council ruled that religious minorities could represent Muslims in city councils, which meant that Niknam could return to his seat on the Yazd city council (BBC Persian 2018c). While the Islamic Republic insists on implementing Islamic law, the Expediency Council is empowered to overrule the Guardian Council's decisions, citing vital national interests.

2.2.1 Non-Muslim Religious Minorities Not Recognized under the Iranian Constitution

Religious minorities that are not officially recognized under the Islamic Republic's constitution are in a more precarious legal position. They do not enjoy the right to exercise their religion and they may be deprived of other basic rights solely on the basis of their religious faith. Accordingly, human rights abuses committed against these religious minorities are more systematic compared those committed against other minority groups.

2.2.1.1 Bahá'ís

Founded in the nineteenth century in Iran, the Bahá'í faith has been faced with vigorous opposition from Shi'i *'ulamā'* and the Iranian government since its inception. Bahá'ís were often accused of conspiring against the state in both the Qajar and Pahlavi eras, but human rights abuses against the Bahá'ís sharply increased after the establishment of the Islamic Republic in 1979. Since then, more than two hundred Bahá'ís have been executed, killed, or abducted (Bahá'í International Community 2017). Another fourteen have died in prison (Bahá'í International Community 2017). The vast majority of executions and killings occurred in the first years following the Islamic Revolution. Bahá'ís across Iran were arrested and tried on baseless and unspecific charges. The trials were held in secret without basic human rights protections, including the right to be represented by counsel. Bahá'ís were often put under intense pressure to recant their faith (Bahá'í International Community 2016: 65), demonstrating that the charges brought against them were solely motivated by their religious beliefs. The authorities often buried those executed in unmarked graves.[22]

In 2015 a leaked video of the 1981 trial of seven Bahá'í leaders was released on media outlets operating outside Iran. The men were members of the National Spiritual Assembly of the Bahá'ís of Iran, the elected governing body of Iran's Bahá'í community. An eighth member, a woman, was not tried with the men. The trial, which was held in secret, shows the seven Bahá'í leaders being questioned by a judge whose image is never shown (BBC Persian 2015). As the video demonstrates, there was no attorney present to defend the Bahá'ís. In a manner similar to trials of dissidents in the Islamic Republic, the defendants were subjected to a mass trial, without any distinction among them that would show their individual responsibility for their alleged crimes. The Bahá'í leaders were accused of cooperating with Israel and other foreign nations; insulting sacred Islamic values, senior clerics, and Ayatollah Khomeini; supporting terrorist attacks; sending news from Iran to foreign adversaries; and supporting Iraq in its war against Iran (Aasoo 2015). No credible evidence was proffered to support these charges. Instead, communications from the Bahá'í leaders with the Bahá'í World Centre in Haifa, Israel, and attempts to draw the attention of Western diplomats to human rights abuses against Bahá'ís in Iran were cited as evidence of their guilt. It is not clear whether this was the only trial session for the seven Bahá'í leaders or whether other sessions were held afterwards.

---

[22] The bodies of those who died from natural causes or accidents are usually buried in proper graves.

The date of the trial is not mentioned in the video. The seven men, along with the woman who was not present in the trial, were executed on December 27, 1981, in Tehran (Bahá'í International Community 2017). The video is remarkable because it is the only publicly available audiovisual record of a judicial proceeding against Bahá'ís in Iran. Furthermore, it may indicate some degree of debate within the Iranian government regarding how to publicize its treatment of the Bahá'ís. The production of this video indicates an intention to air it for propaganda purposes. The video, however, was never aired. In fact, the executions were carried out in secret and the news that they took place was discovered accidentally (Universal House of Justice 1981).

After the 1980s, killings of Bahá'ís became more sporadic. The reduction in the killing of the Bahá'ís in the 1990s corresponds with the adoption of the 1991 secret memorandum (discussed later in this chapter), which did not stop the killings but also did not explicitly include it as part of the government's policy against them (Yazdani 2018: 164f.). The last time a Bahá'í is known to have been executed by the state was in 1998, although several have since died in prison or have been killed otherwise.[23]

In addition to executions and killings, hundreds of Bahá'ís have been imprisoned since 1979. Between 2005 and 2019 at least 1,234 Bahá'ís were arrested and 275 served prison sentences (Bahá'í International Community 2016: 6). As of August 2018 there were seventy-eight Bahá'ís in prison, according to the Bahá'í International Community (Bahá'í International Community 2019). Seven Bahá'i leaders, arrested in 2008, served ten years in prison.

Restrictions to Access of Education The execution and imprisonment of Bahá'ís have been part of a much broader governmental campaign against Iran's Bahá'í community. Following Iran's Cultural Revolution, which involved closure of the country's state-run university system from 1980 to 1982, Bahá'ís were barred from Iran's universities. This ban has continued to the present.

---

[23] Universal House of Justice 1981. On August 23, 2013, a Bahá'í man named Ataollah Rezvani was killed in the southern port city of Bandar 'Abbas. See Bahá'í World News Service (2013). Prior to his murder, Rezvani had been dismissed from his work due to pressure from the Ministry of Intelligence, and he had also received threating phone calls from anonymous callers. No culprit was ever identified. In 2016 a Bahá'í man named Farhang Amiri was murdered by two Muslim men in Yazd. The men, who are brothers, reportedly admitted that they had killed Amiri because he was a Bahá'í. See BBC Persian (2017). In 2017, a court in Yazd sentenced one of the men to eleven years' imprisonment and the other to five and a half years. See Bahá'í World News Service (2017).

The way in which the ban has been imposed has changed, however. Until 2004 the application to sit for the national university entrance examination asked applicants to indicate their religion, with four acceptable answers: Christianity, Judaism, Islam, or Zoroastrianism. Bahá'ís, whose faith requires them to disclose their religious beliefs when asked, left this question blank or otherwise indicated that they were Bahá'ís. Consequently, they could not register to sit for the examination (Bahá'í International Community 2008: 39). During President Khatami's term, the question was omitted from the form. Nevertheless, with few exceptions, Bahá'í students were still not able to complete their studies. This situation has persisted until the present. Every year many Bahá'í students are told that their files are "incomplete" and are subsequently prevented from enrolling. A small number of Bahá'í students are allowed to enroll, but most have been expelled from their respective universities before graduation (Yazdani 2018: 166). Between 2005 and 2016, at least 240 Bahá'ís were expelled from university (Bahá'í International Community 2016). In 2018, at least fifty-one Bahá'í students were not allowed to enroll after they were told that their files were "incomplete" (HRANA 2018b).

Economic Pressure In addition to restrictions on access to education, Bahá'ís are also often deprived of the right to employment. After the 1979 Revolution, Bahá'ís were expelled from all state institutions. According to the Bahá'í International Community, at least 15,000 Bahá'ís were expelled or lost their sources of income between 1979 and 2008 (Bahá'í International Community 2008: 35). In 1979, the Iranian authorities expropriated the Nonahalan Company and the Omana Corporation, two financial institutions that managed the assets of the Bahá'í community. As a result, about 15,000 Bahá'ís were deprived of their savings and pensions (Zabihi-Moghaddam 2016: 131).

In addition to the ban on employment in the public sector, Bahá'ís have also faced increasing restrictions with regard to private sector employment. The Iranian government has closed Bahá'í-owned shops across Iran, often on the pretext of violations of trade association rules as Bahá'ís temporarily close their businesses to observe religious holidays. Between 2005 and 2006 there were at least 950 incidents in which the economic rights of Bahá'í citizens were violated due to closure of shops, dismissals, actual or threatened revocation of licenses, and destruction of properties used for business (Bahá'í International Community 2016: 12). In 2007, Iranian police were officially ordered to identity Bahá'í-owned businesses and close those "in the categories of culture, advertising and commerce" as well as those that involved handling food, as the handling of food by Baháʾís could "contaminate" Muslims' food. The police were also instructed to close down all successful and highly profitable businesses (Yazdani 2018: 168). In November 2016 the Iranian government closed down more than one hundred Baháʾí-owned businesses across several Iranian cities, including Bandar ʿAbbas, Sari, and Qaemshahr (Baháʾí World News Service 2016). Destruction of Baháʾí cemeteries and vandalizing of Baháʾí homes are other examples of human rights abuses against Iran's Baháʾí community.

The 1991 Secret Memorandum The actions taken against Iran's Baháʾí community are not random. In fact, they follow policies delineated in a secret 1991 memorandum by the Supreme Cultural Revolution Council and approved by Iran's Supreme Leader, Ayatollah Ali Khamenei.[24] The memorandum explicitly declares "the government's dealings with them [Baháʾis] must be in such a way that their progress and development are blocked." The policy of the Iranian government on Baháʾís' access to higher education is also clear: "They must be expelled from universities, either in the admission process or during the course of their studies, once it becomes known that they are Baháʾís." The memorandum also delineates the policy regarding Baháʾís' employment and societal advancement: Those identifying as Baháʾí should be denied employment and any position of influence (Baháʾí International Community 2016: 94).

The Iranian government has not published this secret memorandum, and the memorandum cannot be found on searches of government databases of laws and regulations. But in a May 2018 ruling, the Court of Administrative Justice cited this memorandum as applicable law and dismissed legal cases brought by a Baháʾí student who had been denied admission to Iran's state-run university system (IranWire 2018). Meanwhile, the memorandum's lenient provisions, such as the provision stating that Baháʾís should not be arrested or imprisoned without reason, are, in fact disregarded, as the high number of detentions and prosecutions of Baháʾí citizens indicates.

The Baháʾí Institute for Higher Education In 1987 Iran's Baháʾí community established an educational institute to serve students who were deprived of higher education due to the government's policy. This institute, which was later named the Baháʾí Institute for Higher Education (BIHE), originally offered courses via correspondence and

---

[24] See www.bic.org/sites/default/files/pdf/iran/1991%20Bahai%20Question%20Memo%20ENG.pdf and www.legal-tools.org/doc/6dfdef/pdf/.

some in-person classes held at private homes. Although the BIHE degrees are not recognized by the Iranian government, many BIHE graduates have been admitted to graduate programs outside Iran. The Iranian government took action against the BIHE in 1998, raiding more than five hundred homes and detaining thirty-six instructors and administrators (*Washington Post* 1998). Those arrested, however, were soon released without being charged. In 2011 the Iranian government again took action against the BIHE, arresting nineteen educators (Bahá'í International Community 2016: 34). Of those, seventeen received sentences of four to five years' imprisonment on the charge of conspiring against national security (Bahá'í International Community 2016: 34). Despite the Iranian government's crackdown, the BIHE is continuing to provide educational opportunities to Bahá'í youth in Iran.

Recent Court Rulings There have been a few instances of court ruling in favor of Bahá'ís. In January 2019, a revolutionary court in Shiraz acquitted thirteen Bahá'ís charged with disseminating propaganda against the Islamic Republic (HRANA 2019c). In a significant development, the same month an appeals court in Alborz province ruled that proselytizing the Bahá'í faith cannot be classified as disseminating propaganda against the Islamic Republic (HRANA 2019a). Again in the same month, a Bahá'í woman in Kurdistan province was acquitted of the charge of disseminating propaganda against the Islamic Republic (HRANA 2019b). In July 2019, Fars Province Court of Appeals reversed the conviction of Yekta Fahandej, a Bahá'í woman who had been sentenced to eleven years' imprisonment. She had received ten years' imprisonment for conspiring against national security and one year for disseminating propaganda against the Islamic Republic (HRANA 2019d). In August 2019, an appeals court in East Azerbaijan province reversed the convictions of six Bahá'ís who had been sentenced to six months' imprisonment each on the charge of disseminating propaganda against the Islamic Republic (HRANA 2019g). The court declared that "disturbing national security cannot be discerned from the nature of the Bahá'í religion and sect." The court also stated that mere belief in the Bahá'í faith does not constitute a crime, but it nevertheless ruled that the Bahá'í literature discovered by the authorities should be destroyed in order to prevent the dissemination of the "ideas of the Bahá'í sect."

It should be clarified that despite their relative leniency these rulings do not signify a meaningful change in the government's policies against Bahá'ís. In July 2019, the revolutionary court in Birjand sentenced nine Bahá'ís to six years' imprisonment on charges of acting against national security and disseminating propaganda against the Islamic Republic

(HRANA 2019f). In November 2019, a court in Mazandaran province ruled that all properties belonging to Bahá'ís in the village of Ivel should be confiscated (Iran International 2020). In the court's opinion, the presiding judge accused the Bahá'ís of "seizing" ten hectares of land in the area during the Pahlavi era without providing any evidence (Iran International 2020). Referring to fatwas by senior clerics, including Supreme Leader Khamenei, the court opinion stated that the Bahá'ís do not have property rights (Iran International 2020). On June 15, 2020, twenty-six Bahá'ís appeared at the Shiraz Revolutionary Court to provide their defense arguments against national security charges, being in contact with foreign enemy states, and disseminating propaganda against the Islamic Republic (HRANA 2020).

The cases discussed show that there is some degree of variance within the Iranian judiciary in how national security charges against the Bahá'ís are adjudicated. Given that the state's policies on the Bahá'ís have been set at the highest levels, and that the Supreme Leader himself has issued a fatwa on the matter, a major change in the Islamic Republic's treatment of the Bahá'ís is unlikely. Nevertheless, reducing the number of imprisoned Bahá'ís is not without precedent. While in 1986 about 747 were imprisoned, by the end of 1989 that number had declined to just 13, perhaps in response to international pressure (Zabihi-Moghaddam 2016: 133). Since arrests and imprisonments tend to generate a higher level of international condemnation, judges might increasingly opt for economic sanctions in the future.

Issuance of National Identity Cards In January 2020 the Bahá'í International Community reported that new applicants for national identification cards were required to select one of the four officially recognized religions – Islam, Christianity, Judaism, or Zoroastrianism – in their applications (Bahá'í International Community 2020). This means that the Bahá'ís and other unrecognized minorities either have to lie about their religious beliefs or forego having national identity cards, which will create numerous obstacles for daily transactions and for obtaining social services. Previously, the application had contained an "other" option. In March 2020, in response to a complaint filed by a Bahá'í citizen, the Court of Administrative Justice issued a preliminary ruling in favor of the Bahá'í plaintiff. In this ruling, the court held that having Iranian citizenship was enough to receive a national identity card.[25] The Civil Registration Organization, which issues national identity cards, may appeal this ruling.

---

[25] Unpublished Court of Administrative Justice opinion.

2.2.1.2 Christian Converts

As indicated earlier, while the Iranian constitution provides some protection for certain Christians as recognized religious minorities (Assyrian and Armenian Christians), this does not extend to Muslims who convert to Christianity. A Muslim who converts to another religion can be considered an apostate (*murtad*) and thus may be sentenced to death. Few persons have been executed for apostasy, however. One of the most well-known apostasy cases was that of Hossein Soodmand, a Christian pastor who was executed in 1990. Soodmand had converted to Christianity in 1960, when he was only 13 years old (Palmer 2008). This occurred despite the fact that neither the 2013 IPC nor its predecessor, which was in effect at the time of the trial, had codified the crime of apostasy. In other words, apostasy is not explicitly mentioned as a crime in Iran's Penal Code. Yet, Article 167 of the Iranian constitution declares:

> The judge is bound to endeavor to judge each case on the basis of the codified law. In case of the absence of any such law, he has to deliver his judgment on the basis of authoritative Islamic sources and authentic fatwas. The judge, on the pretext of the silence of or deficiency of law in the matter, or its brevity or contradictory nature, cannot refrain from admitting and examining cases and delivering his judgment.

This article effectively permits the Iranian judiciary to make legal findings outside of codified law. To ensure the application of this principle, the 2013 IPC features a new article (220) which states that when the law is silent on a *hadd* crime, Article 167 of the constitution will apply. *Hadd* crimes are those crimes for which specific punishments have been provided in shari'a. There is some degree of disagreement among Islamic jurists regarding what constitutes apostasy and how it should be punished (Iran Human Rights Documentation Center 2014a: 4–10). Therefore, it is not surprising that the crime of apostasy is not explicitly defined in Iranian law. This lack of clarity violates the principle of legality, which holds that criminal sanction is only permissible when an act has been explicitly and clearly defined as a crime. Article 15.1 of the International Covenant on Civil and Political Rights, to which Iran is a party, states, "No one shall be held guilty of any penal offence on account of any act or omission which did not constitute a penal offence, under national or international law, at the time when it was committed." According to the United Nations (UN) Human Rights Committee, criminal liability and punishment should be limited to instances where "clear and precise provisions in the law that was in place and applicable at the time of the act or omission took place" (United Nations Human Rights Committee 2001: Paragraph 7)

Youcef Nadarkhani is another Christian convert who was found guilty of apostasy and sentenced to death (United States Commission on International Religious Freedom n.d.). He was later acquitted of the apostasy charge, but he received a three-year sentence on the charge of conspiring against national security (HRANA 2012). In July 2017, Nadarkhani received another prison sentence. Along with three other Christian converts, he was sentenced to ten years' imprisonment on the charge of acting against national security by "establishing a home church" and promoting "Zionist Christianity" (HRANA 2017a). Perhaps due to the international outcry against death sentences for Christian converts, Iran's security apparatus resorts to national security charges, rather than apostasy, to take legal action against Christian converts. Several Christian converts have been arrested and imprisoned on national security charges over the past decades.[26] It is furthermore conspicuous that the murder of converts is seldom successfully prosecuted.[27]

Assassinations of Christian Pastors Three Christian pastors were assassinated by unidentified assailants in 1990s, raising the suspicion that their assassinations were carried out by Iranian intelligence agents. On January 20, 1994, Haik Hovsepian Mehr, an Armenian Protestant minister, was found dead. Another assassinated pastor was Mehdi Dibaj, a Christian convert who had been imprisoned from 1984 to 1994. Dibaj was sentenced to death on charges of apostasy in December 1993, but was released from prison in January 1994 (Amnesty International 1994). His body was found on July 5, 1994 (Abdorrahman Boroumand Center n.d.). It should be noted that Hovsepian Mehr had campaigned for Dibaj's release. Another Christian pastor killed in the same period was Tatavous Michaelian, who disappeared on June 2, 1994. On July 2, 1994, the authorities called his son to identify his body. Michaelian had been shot several times in the head (Amnesty International 1994). The Iranian government blamed these assassinations on three female

---

[26] In July 2017, Hadi Asgari was sentenced to ten years' imprisonment for "acting against national security by establishing home churches and promoting Christianity." See HRANA (2018a). Victor Bet-Tamraz, an Assyrian pastor, and Kavian Fallah Mohammadi, a Christian convert, were both sentenced to ten years' imprisonment in June 2017. See HRANA (2017b). Ebrahim Firouzi, another Christian convert, was sentenced to five years' imprisonment in 2014 for acting against national security. See Center for Human Rights in Iran (2018c).

[27] The convert Qorban Tordi Tourani was assassinated in 2005. Two other Christian converts, Mohammad Jaberi and Mohammad Ali Jafarzadeh, were murdered in 2007. Abbas Amiri, another convert, was murdered in 2008. The culprits in these cases were never identified. See VOA News (2012).

members of the Mojahedin-e Khalq (MEK) (VOA News 2012). In 1996 the body of Mohammad Baqer Yousefi, an Assemblies of God pastor, was found hanged in a wooded area in Mazandaran province (Peace Mark 2013).

The large number of assassinations of Christian converts in the 1990s should be seen in the context of a broader assassination campaign by the Iranian government. During the 1990s, Iran was witness to a series of assassinations that later became known as "chain murders." During this period, more than eighty writers and dissidents were assassinated. In 1998, Iran's Ministry of Intelligence announced that "rogue agents" within the Ministry had committed the murders. In a 2013 interview, Esmail Ahmadi-Moghaddam, the former commander of Iran's police force, made a stunning admission when he stated that in the 1990s there were "spontaneous groups" who believed that the judiciary had not taken swift action against common criminals. Therefore, these "groups" would take matters into their own hands and assassinate these "criminals" (ISNA 2013). While this admission by Ahmadi-Moghaddam was not directly about murders of Christians or dissidents, it showed that the assassination campaigns were a well-known fact within the ruling class. Although Ahmadi-Moghaddam did not specify whom he was alluding to as the culprit of these assassinations, it is generally believed that he was referring to Iran's intelligence apparatus.

2.2.1.3 The Yarsan
The Yarsan, also known as Ahl-e Haqq, are a religious minority with roots in the Kurdish provinces of Lorestan and Kermanshah in western Iran as well as Iraqi Kurdistan (Halm 2011). The territory on which the Yarsan reside roughly corresponds to areas populated by Kurds who speak the Guarani language, but a large number of Yarsan also live in the country's major cities like Tehran, Karaj, and Tabriz. The Yarsan are not a recognized religious minority under the Iranian constitution. While their religion shares some characteristics with Shi'i Islam, Islamic influence has been described as minimal, and Yarsanis consider themselves members of an independent religion (Hosseini 2020: 117). Although most identify themselves as Muslims on official forms (due to a lack of alternatives), they are still subject to discriminatory treatment, as Yarsani men can easily be recognized due to their distinctive mustaches (according to Yarsani tradition, men should not cut their mustaches) (Yousefi 2013). Aside from public identification, Yarsanis do not seek to promote their faith through winning new adherents. Therefore, they are not seen as a challenge to the state in the same manner as Bahá'ís or Christian converts.

Nevertheless, due to their unwillingness to assume mainstream Shiʻi identities, Yarsani are subject to discriminatory practices. For example, senior Shiʻi clerics, such as Ayatollah Makarem Shirazi, have issued fatwas indicating that some Yarsan do not believe in Islamic principles, and that associating with them is not permissible (Makarem.ir n.d.).

In 2015 a member of the Iranian parliament from Kermanshah province wrote a letter to President Rouhani, asking him to address human rights violations against Yarsani citizens. In particular, the letter mentioned that Yarsanis are not selected for government jobs due to their faith (despite the fact that the 1990 labor law forbids discrimination based on "age, gender, race, ethnic origin and political and religious convictions"), and that their testimony is not accepted in court (HRANA 2015). Other discriminatory acts include being banned from running for office, even locally,[28] and having their leader under house arrest.[29]

In 2004 a police commander in West Azerbaijan province ordered the trimming of the mustache of a soldier serving in the police. Subsequently, a number of residents of the soldier's village put up signs protesting the police commander's action. When the police attempted to remove the signs, clashes erupted in which six police officers and six residents were killed (Yousefi 2013). In the end, two Yarsani citizens were sentenced to death and two others to thirteen years' imprisonment to be served in exile in Yazd (Yousefi 2013).

3 Ethnic Minorities

Human rights violations against members of ethnic minority groups are, to a great extent, different from those committed against religious minorities. Unlike explicitly stated and codified policies implemented against religious minorities, the Islamic Republic's ideological framework is not based on racial or ethnic supremacy. In practice, however, ethnic discrimination overlaps with religious discrimination to a large extent because Iran's Sunni citizens are overwhelmingly ethnic minorities as well. (For the ethnic makeup of Iran, see Map 10.1.) The public order is based on the exclusive recognition of Persian as the official language as well as the language of instruction under Article 15 of the

---

[28] In 2017, twenty-eight out of thirty Yarsani candidates who had registered to run in the municipal elections in the town of Hashtgerd, Alborz province, were disqualified from running. Center for Human Rights in Iran 2017.

[29] In 2013, Dr. Ahmed Shaheed, the UN Special Rapporteur on the situation of human rights in Iran, reported that the leader of Yarsan, Seyyed Nasreddin Heydari, was under house arrest. See Shaheed (2013).

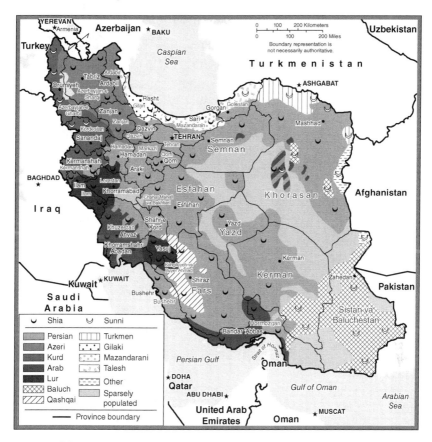

Map 10.1 Geographic distribution of religious and ethnic minorities in Iran
Source: http://ontheworldmap.com/iran/map-of-ethnic-groups-in-iran.html.

constitution. In this section, discriminatory practices impacting four ethnic minority groups are discussed. One underlying issue with discussing discrimination against ethnic minorities is the lack of reliable data. The Iranian government has never conducted a census that records information regarding the country's ethnic makeup.

Article 15 of the Iranian constitution declares that Persian is Iran's official language as well as the language of instruction. This article permits the teaching of the literature of ethnic and local languages and their use in the media. In practice, however, the realization of these rights has been very limited. In 2014, high schools in Saqez, Kurdistan province, began offering a limited Kurdish literature course (Mostafaei 2019). In 2019, an official with the Ministry of Education announced that a pilot program in East Azerbaijan province will provide two hours of Azeri Turkish instruction per week in some schools (Mostafaei 2019). The implementation of these limited programs has not yet led to widespread instruction of mother tongues in Iran. The situation of minority-language media is no better. Independent ethnic-language media are subject to censorship and repression (Elling 2013: 52). As a general rule, when political demands are framed in ethnic terms, they are seen as preliminary steps toward separatism (Elling 2013: 61).

3.1 Arabs

Arab Iranians are mostly Shi'i and generally reside in the provinces of Khuzestan, Bushehr, and Hormozgan. Poverty, high unemployment rates, and environmental problems have caused discontent within Iran's Arab minority. In addition, in oil-rich Khuzestan, the hiring of workers from other regions and their settlement in Khuzestan is seen by many locals as an attempt to change the ethnic makeup of the province in favor of Persian speakers. In December 2002, during a parliamentary question and answer with the minister of agriculture, a representative from Khuzestan province quoted a letter by a government official stating that the ethnic makeup of the region should change, and that Persian speakers should be settled in the border areas of Khuzestan province (Parliamentary Debates 2002: 29). In 2016, Arab activists released a document ostensibly prepared by the Ministry of Interior in which settlement of Persian speakers in Khuzestan province is mentioned as a component of the government's plan to ensure the province's security (Al-Arabiya 2016).

In April 2005, a memorandum ostensibly drafted by Mohammad Ali Abtahi, President Khatami's vice president for legal and parliamentary affairs, was leaked, which discussed a policy aimed at changing the ethnic makeup of Khuzestan province through settlement of Persian-speaking and Azeri Iranians in the province. Abtahi disputed the document's authenticity and stated that it was forged (Iran Human Rights Documentation Center 2014b: 11). Nevertheless, protests in Khuzestan province erupted quickly and spread to several towns, resulting in between thirty and fifty people being killed through excessive use of force or extrajudicial execution (Elling 2013: 75).

In June 2005 a series of bombs went off in Ahvaz, targeting government buildings and homes of state employees. Eleven people were killed in the bombings. A bomb also went off in Tehran, killing two persons. The Iranian government made numerous arrests. Many of those arrested were detained without credible evidence against them and reportedly subjected to physical and mental torture (Iran Human Rights Documentation Center 2014b: 12). After more bombings in Ahvaz in 2005 and 2006, nineteen persons were sentenced to death for their alleged involvement. Confessions from two of those executed were aired on Iranian TV, indicating that they were likely tortured (Iran Human Rights Documentation Center 2014b: 18).

In 2011, five members of the al-Hiwar Cultural Institute were arrested. Registered with the National Youth Organization, al-Hiwar organized cultural events in Arabic. Two of the founders were charged with *mohārebeh*, and were executed in 2014 (Iran Human Rights Documentation Center 2014b: 21). The Iranian government's English-language TV channel, Press TV, broadcast their confessions in 2011, but one of the founders later indicated that the confessions were extracted under severe torture. In addition, their trials were closed to the public. In 2012, four Arabs from the town of Shadegan were sentenced to death on the charge of *mohārebeh*. Like similar cases, the defendants reported that they were tortured (Iran Human Rights Documentation Center 2014b: 22). In addition, they stated that their trial only lasted two and a half hours. The men were executed in December 2013.

In May 2020 Amnesty International released detailed information about 304 protesters killed during the November 2019 nationwide protests. Noting that the real number of the dead was probably higher, the report indicated that Khuzestan province had the highest number of killed protesters after Tehran province, with a total of fifty-seven confirmed fatalities (Amnesty International 2020b: 5, 12–149). The ethnicities of those killed were not listed. Amnesty International also quoted Ahwazi Arab sources as saying that hundreds of children between the ages of 9 and 17 had been detained in the city of Ahvaz during the protests (Amnesty International 2020c: 22).

In May 2020 Amnesty International issued a statement expressing concern about three Arab prisoners sentenced to death. Iranian officials had charged Hossein Silawi, Ali Khasraji, and Naser Khafajian with involvement in an attack on a police station in Ahvaz in 2017 that resulted in the death of two law enforcement officers (Amnesty International 2020a: 2). The three individuals were reportedly subjected to torture in order to make self-incriminating confessions. The men were secretly executed on February 28, 2021 (Amnesty International 2021a).

3.2 Azeri Turks

Azeri Turks are Iran's largest ethnic minority, mainly residing in northwestern Iran but also in other provinces. As Shi'i Muslims, Iran's Azeri Turk population is not subject to religious discrimination. In fact, many high-level government officials, including Supreme Leader Khamenei, are of Azeri Turk origin. Nevertheless, tensions over ethnicity have erupted on several occasions. In addition, some political activists calling for autonomy have been detained.

In May 2006 a cartoon in the daily *Irān* was widely perceived as offensive to Iran's Azeri-speaking population, and protests erupted across Iran's northwestern provinces, even reaching Tehran, where a protest was held in front of the parliament buildings (Elling 2013: 78). The newspaper was temporarily shut down, and the newspaper's editor and the cartoonist were detained. On May 23, 2006, Iran's police chief stated that fifty to sixty people were arrested during the protests (ISNA 2006). Huge protests were held in Tabriz on May 23–24, with widespread clashes between security forces and protesters. There were mass arrests and reports of fatalities. The Iranian government took measures, such as offering an apology by the minister of culture to placate the protesters. Meanwhile, however, government officials also claimed that foreign governments had infiltrated the protests (Elling 2013: 78).

As mentioned, Article 15 of the Iranian constitution declares that Persian is Iran's official language and exclusive tongue of instruction, but teaching on the literature of ethnic languages is permissible in schools. Activists in Azerbaijan region and other areas have demanded broader recognition of ethnic languages in Iran, including instruction in their mother tongues. The Iranian government has arrested several activists campaigning for this issue. On February 20, 2014, Iranian authorities arrested more than fifty people at an event held in Ahar, East Azerbaijan province, to celebrate International Mother Tongue Day (Radio Farda 2014). Thirteen individuals detained at this event faced national security charges, but were eventually acquitted by the Ahar Revolutionary Court. The same court, however, convicted seven individuals on the charge of conspiring against national security because of their participation in a protest against a program broadcast on Iranian state TV that was offensive to Azeri Turks. Three persons were sentenced to ten months' imprisonment and another four to seven months. The court opinion did not base its ruling on any violent acts perpetrated by the defendants; instead, it cited distribution of a newsletter and statements made against the government and in favor of "separatism" as evidence of their guilt (HRANA 2017d).

Many advocates of autonomy for Iranian Azerbaijan have been subject to arrest and prosecution. For instance, in 2013, five Azeri political activists were sentenced to nine years' imprisonment. They were charged with acting against national security by forming an illegal group and disseminating propaganda against the Islamic Republic (HRANA 2014). This sentence was issued in response to activities that were of a nonviolent nature.

In June 2019, Kazem Safabakhsh, an Azeri Turk activist, was convicted of establishing a group with the aim of disturbing national security and sentenced to thirteen years' imprisonment. The court found him guilty of "forming and administering a separatist group (telegram channel) and inviting people to engage in riots and fighting on the streets" (HRANA 2019e). He was also convicted of disturbing public opinion and disseminating propaganda against the Islamic Republic. Under Iranian law, he will likely only serve the prison term for the crime that carries the longest sentence, which means that he will serve ten years in prison.

Another issue that surfaces from time to time is the prohibition of Turkish names. While this practice seems to be based on ad hoc decision-making at the local level rather than a national policy, it nevertheless reflects ethnic discrimination against Azeri Turks. In January 2021, it was reported that local offices of the National Organization for Civil Registration in Tabriz and Ardabil had refused to issue birth certificates for three children with Turkish names (HRANA 2021).

3.3   Baluchis

Iran's Baluch population, which is mostly Sunni, mainly resides in Sistan and Baluchistan province, one of Iran's most impoverished regions (Sabermahani et al. 2013: 149). Religious tensions in the region predate the 1979 Revolution, as Shi'i clerics have attempted to proselytize Sunni Baluchis for many years (Boyajian 2016: 401

Clashes between Baluch citizens and the Iranian government were reported from the early days after the 1979 Revolution (Dudoignon 2017: 186). Several Baluch groups and organizations sought autonomy while the Baluchistan Liberation Front called for separation from Iran (Elling 2013: 49). Clashes escalated after many Baluch groups boycotted the December 1979 referendum on the newly drafted constitution. Clashes were also reported between the Baluchis, who are mostly Sunni, and Sistanis, who are Shi'i (Elling 2013: 49).

Tension between Baluch communities and the Iranian government has continued to the present, documented in the province having one of the highest execution rates in the country (Iran Human Rights

Documentation Center 2019b: 20). In October 2013, the Iranian judiciary executed sixteen prisoners held in Sistan and Baluchistan province in response to an attack on a military outpost by armed militants. The attack had resulted in sixteen deaths, and the Iranian judiciary responded by executing an equal number of prisoners (BBC 2013). Contravening its own laws, the Iranian judiciary did not release the charges against the executed individuals, nor did it explain how they were implicated in the armed attack. Numerous Baluch citizens have been subjected to torture to confess to violent acts they have not committed (Iran Human Rights Documentation Center 2019b: 28).

In addition to executions for national security charges, many Baluchis have also been executed for drug offenses. In February 2016, Shahindokht Molaverdi, President Rouhani's vice president for women and family affairs, made news when she mentioned that all men in a village in Sistan and Baluchistan province had been executed. Molaverdi made this statement in the context of calling for government support for families of executed individuals. She added that if the government does not provide assistance to children of executed individuals, they can become smugglers themselves in order to take vengeance for their fathers' deaths as well as to earn a livelihood (Radio Farda 2016). As fuel is much cheaper in Iran than neighboring Pakistan, smuggling fuel across the border into Pakistan has become the means of earning a livelihood for many Baluchis, given the scarcity of economic opportunities in the province.

3.4 Kurds

The Islamic Republic's human rights abuses against Kurds began shortly after the establishment of the new revolutionary government. Just three weeks after Ayatollah Khomeini's return from exile in February 1979, Islamist forces and Kurdish fighters clashed. As disputes about autonomy between Kurdish political parties and the central government led to armed conflict, Sadegh Khalkhali, a notorious revolutionary judge, went to Kurdistan province and ordered the executions of numerous prisoners in summary trials. Jahangir Razmi's Pulitzer-winning picture of a firing squad executing several prisoners in Sanandaj Airport was circulated in international media in 1979.

Abdul-Rahman Ghassemlou, the leader of the Democratic Party of Iranian Kurdistan, was elected to the Islamic Republic's constituent assembly. The government, however, did not allow him to attend this assembly (Elling 2013: 47). Likewise, the government voided the parliamentary election results of March 1980 in Kurdish areas (Akbarzadeh 2019: 1149).

Concerns about separatism and Iran's territorial integrity have been dominant features of the government's relationship with Iranian Kurds. In 2017, for example, more than sixty people were arrested in Iran's Kurdish regions for participating in peaceful street celebrations held in the aftermath of the Iraqi Kurdistan independence referendum (Radio Farda 2017).

It should be noted that there is a critical sectarian element in the Iranian government's treatment of its Kurdish citizens as well as in the attitude of Kurdish Iranians toward the government. Sunni Kurds have borne the brunt of the Islamic Republic's discriminatory treatment. In turn, Kurdish anti-government insurgencies have been mostly observed in areas where Sunni Kurds reside. Kurdish nationalists have not been able to recruit Shiʻi Kurds as much as Sunni Kurds (Tezcür and Asadzadeh 2019: 658). In fact, anti-government Sunni Kurds and pro-government Shiʻi Kurds fought each other in March 1979. An in-depth 2019 study indicated that Sunni Kurds were much more likely to support Partiya Jiyana Azad a Kurdistanê (Kurdistan Free Life Party: PJAK), a secular Kurdish armed opposition group, compared to Shiʻi Kurds (Tezcür and Asadzadeh 2019: 667). While Sunni Kurds have been excluded from high-level government positions, a number of Shiʻi Kurds have served in critical state posts. For example, Oil Minister Bijan Zanganeh and former Vice President Mohammad Reza Rahimi are Shiʻi Kurds.

Shooting of cross-border porters known as *kulbars* is another major human rights concern in Iran's Kurdish regions. Iranian police and border guards regularly fire at unarmed *kulbars* whom they suspect of illegally importing consumer goods. According to one report, seventy *kulbars* were fatally shot by Iranian armed forces between March 2011 and April 2012. Some *kulbars* also die due to avalanches, landmines, and cold weather (Center for Human Rights in Iran 2012: 14). Killings of *kulbars* have not abated in recent years. From March 20, 2016 to March 20, 2017, seventy-six *kulbars* reportedly died while sixty-four suffered bullet injuries (Tribune Zamaneh 2017). In May 2019, Qasem Rezaei, the commander of Iran's Border Guard, defended firing at *kulbars*, describing them as smugglers. While Iranian law allows the armed forces to use weapons against those illegally crossing the borders, it qualifies this authorization with the requirement that using weapons must only be a last resort.[30] Iranian authorities rarely conduct investigations to determine whether shootings of *kulbars* were justified as a last resort.

---

[30] The Law on Use of Weapons by Members of Armed Forces When Necessary (January 8, 1995), Article 3, Note 3: https://rc.majlis.ir/fa/law/show/92500, accessed September 11, 2019.

Iran's Kurdish areas were the scene of large demonstrations during the November 2019 protests. According to the list compiled by Amnesty International at least thirty persons were killed in Kermanshah province while another seven were killed in Kurdistan province (Amnesty International 2020b). A video widely distributed on social media showed security agents firing at demonstrators from the roof of the Ministry of Justice building in Javanroud, Kermanshah province (Radio Farda 2019b). In addition to protesters killed by gunshot during the protests, the bodies of a number of protesters were found in dams and rivers. On December 16, 2019, BBC Persian reported that the bodies of five individuals had been retrieved from Vahdat lake in Sanandaj (BBC Persian 2019).

3.5 Disproportionate Share of Casualties from Sistan and Baluchistan Province and Kurdish-Majority Areas in 2022 Protests

Iran became engulfed in protests in the aftermath of the custodial death of Mahsa Jina Amini on September 16, 2022. Amini, a 22-year-old woman from Saqez, Kurdistan Province, was visiting Tehran when she was arrested for inadequate veiling. Her death in the custody of the Islamic Republic's guidance police (*gasht-e ershād*) was followed by months of nationwide protests. According to the UN Special Rapporteur on the situation of human rights in Iran, at least 476 persons were killed between September 16 and December 31, 2022 (Rehman 2023: 3).

The deadliest day of the protests was September 30, 2022, during which at least ninety-four persons were killed in Zahedan, the capital of Sistan and Baluchistan Province. Security forces had opened fire at protesters who had gathered in front of police station #16 to protest the killing of Mahsa Jina Amini and the alleged rape of a teenager in Chabahar, a port city in the same province. Security forces also fired at congregants who had gathered at the Great Prayer Hall for Friday Prayer. Most of the casualties are reported to have taken place at the Prayer Hall. Security forces also shot protesters at the Makki Grand Mosque (Iran Human Rights Documentation Center 2022).

On November 4, 2022, sixteen protesters were reported to have been killed in Khash, Sistan and Baluchistan Province (BBC Persian 2022). Added to those killed in Zahedan on September 30, 2022, the total number of individuals killed in Sistan and Baluchistan Province stands above one hundred. Overall, about a fifth of protest casualties of 2022 occurred in Sistan and Baluchistan Province.

Iran's Kurdish region also saw a disproportionate share of casualties. Given that Mahsa (Jina) Amini was a Kurdish woman, cities and towns in Kurdistan, West Azarbaijan, and Kermanshah provinces were scenes of numerous protests. Overall, at least 121 Kurds were reported to have been killed during the fall of 2022 (Iran Human Rights Documentation Center 2022). This number also represents about a fifth of all fatalities across the country. Combined, the number of Baluch and Kurd citizens killed during the protests of 2022 is about 40 percent of all those who lost their lives during the 2022 protests. This figure far exceeds the proportion of Baluchis and Kurds in relation to the entire population of Iran. The combined populations of the four provinces of Sistan and Baluchistan, Kurdistan, Kermanshah, and West Azarbaijan constitute just 12 percent of Iran's population, per the 2016 census data.[31]

4   Conclusions

The policies of the Iranian government toward religious and ethnic minorities are best explained in the context of the perceived ideological or security threat posed by minority communities to the clerical establishment and the Islamic Republic as a whole. The government's approach toward Christians is illustrative. While evangelical Christians who seek converts are often arrested and prosecuted, the Assyrian and Armenian communities, who do not attempt to promote Christianity beyond their own membership, are not generally subject to such measures. This does not suggest that they are equal under the law; it merely means that they are not legally pursued like evangelical Christians.

As the Islamic Republic defines itself as the vanguard of Shi'i Islam, any belief system that is perceived to be at odds with the official state ideology is seen as a threat and dealt with accordingly. Even demonstrations of secular nationalism could be punished if deemed contrary to the Islamic Republic's founding principles.[32] It follows that Bahá'ís, Sunni Muslims, and Gonabadi Dervishes are also persecuted, as their belief systems are seen as rivals to that of the Islamic Republic.

With respect to ethnic minorities, governmental discrimination has a different quality from that committed against religious minorities, as the Islamic Republic's does not derive its legitimacy from ethnic or racial identity. In reality, however, ethnic discrimination is inextricably intertwined with religious discrimination because Iran's Sunni citizens overwhelmingly belong to ethnic minority groups. Separately, when ethnic

---

[31] See Statistical Center of Iran, Census.
[32] For example, in 2016 the Iranian government sentenced seventy-four persons to prison terms ranging from one to eight years for assembling at the tomb of Cyrus the Great to commemorate him: IranWire 2016.

identity fosters political dissent, ethnicity can also be the basis for invidious state action on its own. Numerous sympathizers of ethnic opposition groups and activists advocating for the rights of ethnic minorities have received harsh sentences, including the death penalty, after grossly unfair trials.

All state institutions are responsible for enforcing the Islamic Republic's discriminatory policies. The intelligence and security apparatus intimidates and arrests members of religious and ethnic minority groups, and the judiciary usually issues harsh sentences against them. The executive branch also engages in discriminatory action, such as denying higher education and public sector employment to minorities, especially the Bahá'í. Parliament, having passed discriminatory laws, does not hold other state organs responsible for extralegal actions against minorities. Nor has it conducted investigations necessary to determine the extent of discriminatory policies in the country.

Bibliography

Aasoo. *Trial of National Assembly Members 1981* [in Persian], November 10, 2015. www.youtube.com/watch?v=rQx2-vaa5UM, accessed November 15th, 2021.

Abdorrahman Boroumand Center. *Mehdi Dibaj*, (n.d.), www.iranrights.org/memorial/story/12920/mehdi-dibaj, accessed September 6, 2019.

Akbarzadeh, Shahram, Zahid Shahab Ahmed, Costas Laoutides, and William Gourlay. "The Kurds in Iran: Balancing National and Ethnic Identity in a Securitised Environment," *Third World Quarterly*, 40 (6), 2019, pp. 1145–1162.

Al-Arabiya. *'Comprehensive Security Plan for Khuzestan' Leaked* [in Persian], April 2, 2016. https://farsi.alarabiya.net/fa/iran/2016/04/02, accessed September 23, 2020.

Alavi, Shahed. "State Murders in the Islamic Republic According to Statistics; Names that Will Not Be Forgotten" [in Persian], *Aasoo*, February 1, 2019. www.aasoo.org/fa/articles/1807, accessed March 2, 2021.

Amnesty International. *Fear for the Lives of Church Leaders*, July 6, 1994. www.amnesty.org/download/Documents/184000/mde130071994en.pdf, accessed September 6, 2019.

Amnesty International. *Iran: Fears of Secret Execution Mount for Disappeared Prisoners from Minority Groups*, May 12, 2020a. www.amnesty.org/download/documents/mde1323092020english.pdf, accessed September 24, 2020.

Amnesty International. *Iran: Details of 304 Deaths in Crackdown on November 2019 Protests*, May 20, 2020b. www.amnesty.org/download/documents/mde1323082020english.pdf, accessed September 24, 2020.

Amnesty International. *Trampling Humanity: Mass Arrests, Disappearances and Torture since Iran's November 2019 Protests*, September 2. 2020c. www.amnesty.org/download/documents/mde1328912020english.pdf, accessed September 24, 2020.

Amnesty International. *Iran: Four Ahwazi Arab men secretly executed*, March 18, 2021. www.amnesty.org/en/documents/mde13/3864/2021/en/, accessed September 12, 2023.

Ansari, Nazenin "The Gonabadi Dervishes: Gnostics, Royal Advisors, Political and Religious Adversaries," *Kayhan Life*, March 20, 2018, https://kayhanlife.com/people/the-gonabadi-dervishes-gnostics-royal-advisors-political-andreligious-adversaries/, accessed December 15, 2020.

'Asr-e Iran. *Protest by Zoroastrians' Representative in Parliament against Social Welfare Administration's Directive* [in Persian], June 3, 2019. www.asriran.com/fa/news/671447, accessed August 28, 2019.

Bahá'í International Community. *The Bahá'í Question*, 2008. http://dl.bahai.org/bwns/assets/documentlibrary/TheBahaiQuestion.pdf, accessed August 30, 2019.

Bahá'í International Community. *The Bahá'í Question Revisited: Persecution and Resilience in Iran*, 2016. www.bic.org/sites/default/files/pdf/iran/thebahaiquestionrevisited_final_160839e.pdf, accessed January 2, 2019.

Bahá'í International Community. *Bahá'ís Killed in Iran since 1978*, August 10, 2017. www.bic.org/sites/default/files/pdf/iran/bahais_killed_since_1978_180329a.pdf, accessed March 1, 2019.

Bahá'í International Community. *The Bahá'ís of Iran: A Persecuted Community*, January 2019. www.bic.org/sites/default/files/pdf/iran/overview_of_persecution-0119_2.pdf, accessed August 30, 2019.

Bahá'í International Community. *Bahá'ís Punished for Being Truthful about Their Faith*, January 27, 2020. www.bic.org/news/bahais-punished-beingtruthful-about-their-faith, accessed March 19, 2020.

Bahá'í World News Service. *Reports of the Killing of an Iranian Bahá'í Received*, August 25, 2013a. https://news.bahai.org/story/965/, accessed August 29, 2019.

Bahá'í World News Service. *Forced Closure of Shops in Iran on an Unprecedented Scale*, November 7, 2016. www.bic.org/news/forced-closureshops-iran-unprecedented-scale, accessed September 22, 2020.

Bahá'í World News Service. *Religious Discrimination Explicit in Iran's Penal Code*, July 24, 2017. https://news.bahai.org/story/1182/, accessed August 30, 2019.

BBC. *Iran Hangs 16 Rebels 'in Reprisal for Border Deaths'*, October 16, 2013. www.bbc.com/news/world-middle-east-24682729, accessed September 13, 2023.

BBC Persian. *'Raid' on Gonabadi Dervishes in Qom and Demolition of their Hosseinieh* [in Persian], February 14, 2006. www.bbc.com/persian/iran/story/2006/02/060214_mf_qom.shtml, accessed August 15, 2019.

BBC Persian. *Younesi: The Government Was Not Able to Give Provincial Governorships or Ministries to Ethnic or Religious Minorities* [in Persian], December 4, 2013. www.bbc.com/persian/iran/2013/12/131204_l39_younesi_minorities_appointments, accessed August 8, 2019.

BBC Persian. *Iranian Revolutionary Justice* (English language version), October 20, 2015. www.youtube.com/watch?v=DdsFrwJb8NM&feature=youtu.be.

BBC Persian. *Two Individuals Suspected of Murdering a Bahá'í Citizen 'Freed'* [in Persian], June 13, 2017. www.bbc.com/persian/iran-40269097, accessed August 30, 2019.

BBC Persian. *Mohammad Salas Was Executed* [in Persian], June 18, 2018a. www.bbc.com/persian/iran-44517462, accessed August 16, 2019.

BBC Persian. *Clashes between Police and Dervishes in Tehran; Three Police Officers Are Killed in a Bus Attack* [in Persian], February 20, 2018b. www.bbc.com/persian/iran-43115597, accessed August 15, 2019.

BBC Persian. *Molavi Abdolhamid: They did not let me go to Qatar to visit my relatives* [in Persian], July 21, 2018c. www.bbc.com/persian/iran-44910355, accessed September 27, 2020.

BBC Persian. *Sepanta Niknam Returned to Yazd City Council* [in Persian], July 21, 2018d. www.bbc.com/persian/iran-44909976, accessed August 28, 2019.

BBC Persian. *Iran Protests; Reports about Finding Corpses in a Number of Dams and Lakes* [in Persian], December 16, 2019. www.bbc.com/persian/iran-50817346, accessed September 25, 2020.

BBC Persian. *Reactions to the killing of "16 persons" during shooting of protesters in Khash* [in Persian], November 5, 2022. www.bbc.com/persian/iran-63531073, last accessed July 28, 2023.

Behzisti.ir. *Social Welfare Organization's Clarification on Restrictions on Employment of Religious Minorities in Kindergartens* [in Persian], June 3, 2019. www.behzisti.ir/news/343, accessed August 28, 2019.

Boyajian, Vahe S. "Is there an Ethno-Religious Aspect in Balochi Identity?", *Iran & the Caucuses*, 20 (3–4), 2016, pp. 397–405.

Center for Human Rights in Iran. *Dangerous Borders, Callous Murders*, August 2012. www.iranhumanrights.org/wp-content/uploads/kulbar-_full_report-_for_-web.pdf, accessed September 11, 2019.

Center for Human Rights in Iran. *Detention of Twenty Ahwazi Arab Sunni Converts* [in Persian], March 6, 2014. https://persian.iranhumanrights.org/1392/12/arab-ahvaz/, accessed February 1, 2021.

Center for Human Rights in Iran. *Most Yarsani Religious Minority Candidates Disqualified from Iran's 2017 Councils Elections*, May 18, 2017. www.iranhumanrights.org/2017/05/most-yarsani-religious-minority-candidatesdisqualified-from-irans-2017-councils-elections/, accessed September 6, 2019.

Center for Human Rights in Iran. *Mohammad Salas: I was Tortured and Beaten to Death* [in Persian], May 15, 2018a. https://persian.iranhumanrights.org/1397/02/i-was-tortured-and-beaten-to-death/, accessed August 15, 2019.

Center for Human Rights in Iran. *Attorney Publishes Salas Audio: I Am Not the Driver of the Bus that Killed People, I Am Not a Murderer* [in Persian], May 24, 2018b. https://persian.iranhumanrights.org/1397/03/mohammad-salas-said-he-wasdetained-before-the-deadly-bus-attack/, accessed September 13, 2019.

Center for Human Rights in Iran. *Iranian Authorities' Refuse to Allow Christian Convert Ebrahim Firoozi to See Dying Mother*, December 17, 2018c. https://iranhumanrights.org/2018/12/iranian-authorities-refuse-to-allow-christianconvert-ebrahim-firoozi-to-see-dying-mother/, accessed September 4, 2019.

Deutsche Welle Persian. *What's the Islamic Republic's Problem with Gonabadi Dervishes* [in Persian], February 20, 2018, https://bit.ly/382iDy8, accessed December 14, 2020.

Dudoignon, Stéphane. *The Baluch, Sunnism and the State in Iran: From Tribal to Global*, London: Hurst Publishers, 2017.

Elling, Rasmus Christian. *Minorities in Iran: Nationalism and Ethnicity after Khomeini*, New York: Palgrave Macmillan, 2013.

Guardian Council. *Letter of the Speaker of the Parliament to the Secretary of the Guardian Council on the Bill to Add Two Articles to the Fifth Book of the Islamic Penal Code* [in Persian], May 20, 2020a. http://nazarat.shora-rc.ir/Forms/FileLoad.aspx?id=Ax40bI2L3/4=&TN=l7tLyhyOobj0SooAFUE3m68PnpG7MruN&NF=bHiIRfspeW0=, accessed December 30, 2020.

Guardian Council. *Opinion of the Guardian Council on the Bill to Add Two Articles to the Fifth Book of the Islamic Penal Code* [in Persian], June 15, 2020b. www.shora-gc.ir/fa/news/6980, accessed September 27, 2020.

Guardian Council. *Letter of the Deputy Secretary of the Guardian Council to the Speaker of the Parliament* [in Persian], November 28, 2020c. http://nazarat.shora-rc.ir/Forms/FileLoad.aspx?id=QYNKKIr3jn0=&TN=l7tLyhyOobj0SooAFUE3m5rC3iufWLR1csaqpt/F9Oo=&NF=bHiIRfspeW0=, accessed December 30, 2020.

Halm, Heinz. "Ahl-e ḥaqq," in *Encyclopaedia Iranica*, available online at www.iranicaonline.org/articles/ahl-e-haqq-people, 2011, accessed September 6, 2019.

Hosseini, Behnaz S. *Yārsān of Iran, Socio-Political Changes and Migration*, Singapore: Palgrave Macmillan, 2020.

HRANA. *Yousef Nadarkhani, Christian Citizen, Detained to Serve Sentence* [in Persian], December 25, 2012. www.hra-news.org/2012/hranews/1-13221/, accessed September 3, 2019.

HRANA. *Mahmud Fazli Has Gone on Hunger Strike in Tabriz Prison* [in Persian], April 11, 2014. https://tinyurl.com/28hepxtj, accessed September 9, 2019.

HRANA. *Lack of Attention to Fundamental and Civil Rights of Religious Minorities and Esteemed Ahle Haq People* [in Persian], July 2015. www.hra-news.org/wp-content/uploads/2015/07/yarsan-tazakkorenamayandegan.jpg, accessed September 6, 2019.

HRANA. *Kak Hasan Amini: I am still barred from leaving the county and I am still being Threatened* [in Persian], February 4, 2016a. www.hra-news.org/2016/hranews/a-4334/, accessed February 1, 2021.

HRANA. *Appellate Brief and Opinion of Supreme Court Denying the Petition for a New Trial*, August 4, 2016b. www.hra-news.org/wp-content/uploads/2016/08/Shahram-Ahmadi-Case-Doc.pdf, accessed February 1, 2021.

HRANA. *Shahram Ahmadi; Rejection of Petition for a New Trial and Imminent Threat of Execution* [in Persian], August 4, 2016c. www.hra-news.org/2016/hranews/a-6363, accessed February 3, 2021.

HRANA. *Sentence of 40 Years' Imprisonment for Pastor Nadarkhani and Three Other Christian Converts* [in Persian], July 7, 2017a.www.hra-news.org/2017/hranews/a-11358/, September 3, 2019.

HRANA. *Long Prison Sentences Issued for 'Pastor and another Christian Convert* [in Persian], July 8, 2017b. www.hra-news.org/2017/hranews/a-11361/, accessed September 3, 2019.

HRANA. *Execution of 25 Prisoners; A Look Back at Black Monday after One Year* [in Persian], August 2, 2017c. www.hra-news.org/2017/hranews/a-11765/, accessed August 14, 2019.

HRANA. *Sentence of 58 Months' Imprisonment for 7 Activists at the Same Time as Acquittal of Those Detained during the International Mother Tongue Day* [in Persian], October 22, 2017d.www.hra-news.org/2017/hranews/a-12883/, accessed September 9, 2019.

326 Shahin Milani

HRANA. *Hadi Asgari, Christian Convert, Released on Bail* [in Persian], April 11, 2018a. www.hra-news.org/2018/hranews/a-14880/, accessed September 3, 2019.

HRANA. *Entrance Exam 2018: Number of Bahá'í Students Deprived of Education Increases to 51* [in Persian], August 18, 2018b. www.hra-news.org/2018/hranews/a-17045/, accessed September 4, 2019.

HRANA. *Appeals Court: Promoting Bahá'í Faith Is Not Disseminating Propaganda against the Islamic Republic; Liza Tebyanian Acquitted* [in Persian], January 9, 2019a. www.hra-news.org/2019/hranews/a-18684/, accessed September 2, 2019.

HRANA. *Appeals Court: Maria Kosari, Bahá'í Citizen, Acquitted* [in Persian], January 13, 2019b. www.hra-news.org/2019/hranews/a-18750/, accessed September 3, 2019.

HRANA. *Shiraz Revolutionary Court Acquitted 13 Bahá'í Citizens of the Charge of Propaganda Activity against the Islamic Republic* [in Persian], January 14, 2019c. www.hra-news.org/2019/hranews/a-18761/, accessed September 2, 2019.

HRANA. *Appeals Court: Yekta Fahandezh Sa'di, Bahá'í Citizen, Acquitted* [in Persian], July 14, 2019d. www.hra-news.org/2019/hranews/a-21003/?tg_rhash=22a41dd9689763, accessed September 3, 2019.

HRANA. *Kazem Safabakhsh Sentenced to 13 Years' Imprisonment* [in Persian], June 24, 2019e. www.hra-news.org/2019/hranews/a-20727/, accessed March 20, 2020.

HRANA. *Birjand Revolutionary Court Sentenced 9 Bahá'ís to 54 Years' Imprisonment* [in Persian], July 8, 2019f. www.hra-news.org/2019/hranews/a-20919/, accessed March 19, 2020.

HRANA. *Appeals Court: Six Bahá'í Citizens in Tabriz Acquitted* [in Persian], August 4, 2019g. www.hra-news.org/2019/hranews/a-21337/, accessed September 3, 2019.

HRANA. *Court Session to Address Charges against 26 Bahá'í Citizens Held in Shiraz Revolutionary Court* [in Persian], June 15, 2020. www.hra-news.org/2020/hranews/a-25207/, accessed September 26, 2020.

HRANA. *Continued Opposition of National Organization for Civil Registration Offices to Naming and Registration of Three Children on the Pretext of Having Non-Persian First Names* [in Persian], January 27, 2021. www.hra-news.org/2021/hranews/a-28552/, accessed February 1, 2021.

Human Rights Watch. *Iran: Over 200 Dervishes Convicted*, August 29, 2018. www.hrw.org/news/2018/08/29/iran-over-200-dervishes-convicted, accessed August 27, 2019.

Iran Human Rights Documentation Center. Apostasy in the Islamic Republic of Iran, July 2014a. iranhrdc.org/wp-content/uploads/reports_en/Apostasy_in_the_Islamic_Republic_of_Iran_104287928.pdf, accessed May 27, 2021.

Iran Human Rights Documentation Center. *A Framework of Violence: Repression of the Arab Ethnic Minority in the Islamic Republic of Iran*, September 2014b. https://iranhrdc.org/wp-content/uploads/reports_en/A-Framework-of-Violence.pdf, accessed May 27, 2021.

Iran Human Rights Documentation Center. *New Reports of Difficult Conditions for Sunni Prisoners in Rajaee Shahr Prison*, September 11, 2014c. https://iranhrdc.org/new-reports-of-difficult-conditions-for-sunni-prisoners-inrajaee-shahr-prison/, accessed August 14, 2019.

Iran Human Rights Documentation Center. *Regulatory Code on Sentences of Qisas, Stoning, Crucifixion, Execution, and Flogging,* August 29, 2014d. https://iranhrdc.org/english-translation-of-regulatory-code-on-sentences-of-qisasstoning-crucifixion-execution-and-flogging/, accessed December 16, 2023.

Iran Human Rights Documentation Center. *Directive by Social Welfare Organization Bans Employment of Religious Minorities in Most Child Care Centers,* June 2, 2019a. https://iranhrdc.org/directive-by-social-welfareorganization-bans-employment-of-religious-minorities-in-most-child-carecenters/, accessed August 28, 2019.

Iran Human Rights Documentation Center. *Extreme Inequality: The Human Rights Situation of Iran's Baluch Minority,* July 2019b. https://iranhrdc.org/en/wp-content/uploads/Baluch-Report-IHRDC-EN.pdf, accessed August 28, 2019.

Iran Human Rights Documentation Center. *Living under Suppression: The Situation of Gonabadi Dervishes in Iran,* November 5, 2020. https://iranhrdc.org/living-under-suppression-the-situation-of-gonabadi-dervishes-in-iran/, accessed December 15, 2020.

Iran Human Rights Documentation Center. *Bloody Friday in Zahedan,* October 19, 2022. https://iranhrdc.org/bloody-friday-in-zahedan, accessed July 28, 2023.

Iran Human Rights Documentation Center. *Unleashed Violence: Repression of Protests in Kurdish Areas of Iran,* June 30, 2023. https://iranhrdc.org/protests-in-the-kurdish-areas-of-iran/, accessed September 13, 2023.

Iran International. *Confiscation of Properties in Iran for Being a Bahá'í* [in Persian], January 1, 2020. shorturl.at/wBSW9, last accessed March 19, 2020.

IranWire. *Murderer of a Jewish Youth Was Sentenced to Imprisonment and Payment of Diya Because the Victim Was Not a Muslim* [in Persian], November 18, 2013. https://iranwire.com/fa/news/tehran/10704, accessed August 27, 2019.

IranWire. *Interview with the Families of Individuals Detained at the Pasargad Gathering: The Judge Said They Are Moharebs* [in Persian], December 18, 2016. https://iranwire.com/fa/features/19885, accessed September 25, 2020.

IranWire. *Bahá'í University Student: They Said Your Registration for Continuing Your Education Was Illegal* [in Persian], July 27, 2018. https://iranwire.com/fa/features/27024, accessed August 30, 2019.

Islamic Penal Code 1991. Available at https://iranhrdc.org/islamic-penal-codeof-the-islamic-republic-of-iran-book-one-book-two/#31, accessed September 13, 2023.

Islamic Penal Code 2013. Available at https://iranhrdc.org/english-translationof-books-i-ii-of-the-new-islamic-penal-code, accessed September 13, 2023.

Islamic Republic of Iran Military Law 1987. Available at https://rc.majlis.ir/fa/law/show/91404. www.isna.ir/news/95050107910, accessed September 13, 2023.

Iran Student News Agency (ISNA). *Police Commander Announced Arrests of 50 to 60 People during Recent Unrests* [in Persian], May 24, 2006. www.isna.ir/news/8503-02181, accessed September 9, 2019.

Iran Student News Agency (ISNA). *From Mining the Borders to the Police Force's Squabbles with the Ahmadinejad's Administration in His Second Term* [in Persian], November 18, 2013.

Iran Student News Agency (ISNA). *Statement of the Ministry of Intelligence on the Actions of the "Oneness and Jihad" Group* [in Persian], August 3, 2016. www.isna.ir/news/92082716428, accessed March 20, 2020.

Justice for Iran. *Reyshahri: We executed Nasser Sobhani because his pen was more effective than any weapon* [in Persian], February 24, 2016. https://justice4iran.org/persian/reports/rayshahrisobhani, accessed September 13, 2020.

Kadivar, Mohsen. *The Islamic Republic's Mistreatment of Ahmad Moftizadeh* [in Persian], April 29, 2018. https://kadivar.com/16486, accessed September 13, 2020.

Laws and Regulations Portal of Iran. *The law to add two articles to the Fifth Book of the Islamic Penal Code (Tazirāt and Preventative Punishments)* [in Persian], February 18, 2021. https://dotic.ir/news/8540, accessed July 26, 2023.

Majzooban Noor. *Seven Years Later/A Review of the Murder Case of Vahid Banani, the Dervish Who Died in the 2011 Incident in Kavar* [in Persian], September 18, 2018. www.majzooban.org/fa/17736, accessed September 13, 2023.

Makarem.ir. *Rule for Associating with Ahle Haq* [in Persian], (n.d.), https://makarem.ir/main.aspx?typeinfo=21&lid=0&catid=44744&mid=255164, accessed September 6, 2019.

Mashregh News. *Video/ Interview with the Murderer Dervish Bus Driver* [in Persian], February 20, 2018. www.mashreghnews.ir/news/833226, accessed August 15, 2019.

Mashregh News. *Homeira Rigi has been appointed Iran's Ambassador to Brunei* [in Persian], January 22, 2019. www.mashreghnews.ir/news/930842, accessed February 1, 2021.

Mostafaei, Mahdieh. "The Beginning of the Academic Year and Uncertainty regarding Bilingual Students" [in Persian], *Persian Independent*, September 10, 2019. www.independentpersian.com/node/19541, accessed September 22, 2020.

Palmer, Alasdair. "Hanged for Being a Christian in Iran", *The Telegraph*, October 11, 2008. www.telegraph.co.uk/news/worldnews/middleeast/iran/3179465/Hanged-for-being-a-Christian-in-Iran.html, accessed September 3, 2019.

Parliamentary Debates. *Debates of December 17, 2002*, p. 29, available at www.ical.ir//UploadedData/284/Contents/636790157044261296.pdf, accessed September 23, 2020.

Peace Mark. *Assassinating Christian Converts after the Revolution* [in Persian], October 7. 2013. www.peace-mark.org/ghatlenokishane-masihi-pas-az-enghelab, accessed March 20, 2020.

Radio Farda. *Demolition of Khānqāhs; the End of Coexistence between Clerics and Dervishes?* [in Persian], November 14, 2007. www.radiofarda.com/a/o2_daravish/421153.html, accessed August 15, 2019.

Radio Farda. *Arrest of Gonabadi Dervishes in Qom* [in Persian], December 29, 2008. www.radiofarda.com/a/f3_dervish_kish/478909.html, accessed August 15, 2019.

Radio Farda. *Prison Sentences for Three Gonabadi Dervishes' Attorneys* [in Persian], January 23, 2011. www.radiofarda.com/a/f12_three_lawyer_of_gonabadi_dervishes_in_iran_receive_prison_sentences/2284325.html, accessed August 15, 2019.

Radio Farda. *Tens of Activists in the Town of Ahar* [in Persian], February 20, 2014. www.radiofarda.com/a/f8-iran-azariactivists-detention/25271496.html, accessed September 6, 2019.

Radio Farda. *Rouhani Administration Selected Iran's First-Ever Sunni Kurd Ambassador* [in Persian], September 2, 2015. www.radiofarda.com/a/f4_iran_appointed_first_sunni_ambassador/27222704.html, accessed February 1, 2021.

Radio Farda. *Molaverdi: All Men in One Village in Sistan and Baluchistan Have Been Executed* [in Persian], February 24, 2016. www.radiofarda.com/a/o2-molaverdi-execution-in-iran/27570491.html, accessed September 11, 2019.

Radio Farda. *Arrest of Tens of Kurdish Citizens after Demonstrations Related to the Iraqi Kurdistan Referendum* [in Persian], September 30, 2017. www.radiofarda.com/a/dozen-arrested-linked-to-gatherings-after-Kurdish-referendum/28766263.html, accessed September 24, 2020.

Radio Farda. *Tehran Prosecutor: Interrogation of the Driver of the Samand that Injured one Basij Member* [in Persian], March 2, 2018a. www.radiofarda.com/a/29075578.html, accessed August 15, 2019.

Radio Farda. *Mohammad Radi, a Gonabadi Dervish, Died while in Detention* [in Persian], March 4, 2018b. www.radiofarda.com/amp/one-of-gonabadidervishes-died-of-injuries-sustained-during-his-arrest/29078030.html, accessed August 15, 2019.

Radio Farda. *Human Rights Watch Criticizes Beating of Imprisoned Dervishes in Fashafoyeh* [in Persian], August 29, 2018c. www.radiofarda.com/a/human-rights-watch-abour-devishes-in-iran/29459316.html, accessed August 27, 2019.

Radio Farda. *Molavi Abdolhamid: The Situation of Sunnis Has not Changed under Rouhani's Administration* [in Persian], July 21, 2019a. www.radiofarda.com/a/29381116.html, accessed August 8, 2019.

Radio Farda. *10 Days of Silence on Statistics of Those Killed in Iran's Protests; Protesters Were Fired at "from close range"* [in Persian], November 24, 2019b. www.radiofarda.com/a/ten_days_silence_killing_protesters_iran_fadavi/30289418.html, accessed September 25, 2020.

Rehman, Javaid, *Report of the Special Rapporteur on the situation of human rights in the Islamic Republic of Iran*, February 7, 2023, U.N. Doc. A/HRC/52/67, available at www.ohchr.org/en/documents/country-reports/ahrc5267-situation-human-rights-islamic-republic-iran-report-special, accessed September 2, 2020.

Sabermahani, Asma, Mohsen Barouni, Hesam Seyedin, and Aidin Aryankhesal. "Provincial Human Development Index, a Guide for Efficiency Level Analysis: The Case of Iran," *Iranian Journal of Public Health*, 42 (2), 2013, pp. 149–157, available at www.ncbi.nlm.nih.gov/pmc/articles/PMC3595646, accessed September 6, 2020.

Shaheed, Ahmed. *Report of the Special Rapporteur on the situation of human rights in the Islamic Republic of Iran*, February 28, 2013. http://impactiran.org/2013/03/28/special-rapporteur-s-february-2013-reporton-the-situation-of-human-rights-in-the-islamic-republic-of-iran/, accessed September 6, 2019.

Shahi, Afshin and Ehsan Abdoh-Tabrizi. "The Shi'i State and the Socioeconomic Challenges of the Sunni Communities in Iran: Historical and Contemporary Perspectives," in Firat Oruc (ed.), *Sites of Pluralism: Community Politics in the Middle East*, Hurst Publishers, 2019.

Statistical Center of Iran. *Census 2016: Detailed Results*, www.amar.org.ir/Portals/0/Files/fulltext/1395/n_ntsonvm_95-v2.pdf, accessed January 12, 2021.

Tasnim. Dastgirie. *300 Rioters Arrested on Pasdaran Street/Drivers of Vehicles of Death among those Arrested* [in Persian], February 20, 2018. www.tasnimnews.com/fa/news/1396/12/01/1661860/, accessed August 15, 2019.

Tezcür, Güneş Murat and Peyman Asadzade. "Ethnic Nationalism versus Religious Loyalty: The Case of Kurds in Iran," *Nations and Nationalism*, 25 (2), 2019, pp. 652–672.

Tribune Zamaneh. *Statistics of Killed Kulbars in Iranian Year 1395* [in Persian], March 14, 2017. www.tribunezamaneh.com/archives/117319, accessed September 11, 2019.

United Nations Human Rights Committee. *General Comment No. 29, 2001*, UN Doc. CCPR/C/21/Rev.1/Add.11. https://digitallibrary.un.org/record/451555?ln=en, accessed September 17, 2023.

United States Commission on International Religious Freedom. *Pastor Youcef Nadarkhani*. (n.d.), www.uscirf.gov/youcef-nadarkhani, accessed September 3, 2019.

Universal House of Justice. *Message to All National Spiritual Assemblies*, December 28, 1981. www.bahai.org/library/authoritative-texts/the-universalhouse-of-justice/messages/19811228_001/1#922510771, accessed September 20, 2020.

van den Bos, Matthijs. "Gunābādiyya," in Kate Fleet, Gudrun Krämer, Denis Matringe, John Nawas, and Everett Rowson (eds.), *Encyclopaedia of Islam III*, Leiden: E. J. Brill, 2013. http://dx.doi.org/10.1163/1573-3912_ei3_COM_27547, accessed June 20, 2019.

VOA News. *Christianity in Iran: A Political and Security Crime* [in Persian], June 23, 2012. https://ir.voanews.com/a/iranian-converts-to-christianity-increase-house-churches-threat-islam/1246195.html, accessed September 6, 2019.

Washington Post. *Iran's Crimes at Home*. October 25, 1998. www.washingtonpost.com/archive/opinions/1998/10/25/irans-crimes-at-home/93435bd4-8db9-44ed-8ad1-b27c66ceb41f/?noredirect=on, accessed September 2, 2019.

Yazdani, Mina. "Quiet Strangulation: Islamic Republic's Treatment of Bahá'ís since 1991," *Tiempo Devorado: Revista de Historia Actual*, 5 (2), 2018, pp. 156–181.

Yildiz, Kerim and Tanyel B. Taysi. *The Kurds in Iran: The Past, Present and Future*, Pluto Press, 2007.

Yjc.ir. *Younesi: Considering the Supreme Leader's Fatwa, the Mandaean Religion Could be Included among Recognized Religions* [in Persian], December 22, 2015. www.yjc.ir/fa/news/5435926, accessed September 6, 2019.

Yousefi, Firouz. "Yarsan in Fire, the Story of Ahl-e Haq People Deprived of their Rights" [in Persian]. *BBC Persian*, August 4, 2013. www.bbc.com/persian/blogs/2013/07/130729_l10_nazeran_yarsan_yousefi, accessed September 6, 2019.

Zabihi-Moghaddam, Siamak. "State-Sponsored Persecution of Baha'is in the Islamic Republic of Iran," *Contemporary Review of the Middle East*, 3 (2), 2016, pp. 124–146.

11 Labor Rights in Postrevolutionary Iran

M. Stella Morgana

1 Introduction

Before taking the helm of the Iranian presidency in 2013, Hassan Rouhani published a book entitled *National Security and the Economic System of Iran*. While stressing the importance of investments, efficiency, and production, he deplored the rigidity of Iran's labor laws and regulations. In particular, he expressed his concerns over "the heavy costs for employers" imposed by Iran's current labor law (Rouhani 2010: 336–337). Rouhani argued that increasing the annual labor costs and improving on workers' rights would obstruct further job creation. The logic behind Rouhani's words indicated an idea of labor legality that – using his own words – would neither compromise productivity understood as "the relationship between efficiency and wages," nor "leave employers behind" or undermine "investment security" (Rouhani 2010: 336–337). Following this line of reasoning, workers' rights were conceived as an obstacle to prosperity, and he demanded that wage earners should be more flexible toward employers. This framework implies an unequal relationship between workers and "job creators." The private sector, which is estimated to have a share of between 20 percent and 30 percent of the economic activity, has created the majority of jobs in the past few years.[1] Nevertheless, the public sector has an enormous presence in the Iranian economy (estimated between 60 and 80 percent),[2] meaning that most of the enterprises are state-owned, parastatal, or state-affiliated (Khajehpour 2000). Therefore, those who create jobs here are to be understood in many cases as closely connected to the Islamic Republic apparatus and interests.[3]

---

[1] See (in Persian) Chamber of Commerce, "The Private Sector Has Created Four Times More Employment than the Public," mccima.com/?id=1549. Accessed August 31, 2023.
[2] Also see Central Bank of Iran (CBI), Economic trends, fourth quarter 1398 (2019/2020): www.cbi.ir/category/EconomicTrends_en.aspx.
[3] According to the International Labour Organization (ILO) data on Iran's financial system, the private sector share reached a peak between the mid-1990s and the early 2000s,

In order to understand how the politics of labor legislation evolved in postrevolutionary Iran, this chapter examines labor rights and reforms from the 1990s until today, aiming at showing where Rouhani's conception of labor originates. Besides discussing the formal legal procedures through which the labor law has been implemented, the chapter also sheds light on the informal loopholes by which regulations are circumvented. First, it traces the path that led to the promulgation of the current labor law, which was eventually approved in 1990. Second, it discusses the law in detail through the analysis of two crucial attempts to amend it (only one of which was successful) during President Mohammad Khatami's reformist administration. Third, it explores the complex role of the central formal mediation mechanism between workers and employers, that is, the Workers' House (Khāneh-ye Kārgar), its attitude toward reforms, and the legal obstacles to forming independent unions. Fourth, it shows the contradictions of Mahmoud Ahmadinejad's policies of conservative populism, by analyzing his labor politics and the proposed amendments to the law in 2006. Finally, it delves into Hassan Rouhani's presidency (2013–2021) and the impact of labor deregulation and casualization processes on workers' conditions. The chapter ends with reflections on the limits of labor legislation in protecting labor rights.

A key argument of the chapter is that the existent labor law offers far-reaching exemptions and loopholes that make it possible to circumvent it. Thus, some categories of workers – in particular those working in small factories and those under temporary contracts – lack decent legal protection and are exposed to severe exploitation. In fact, 96 percent of Iranian workers are under temporary contracts, meaning that workers are victims of a massive casualization of labor and job insecurity.[4] The minimum wage, which is set annually by the Supreme Labor Council according to the inflation, is generally insufficient to provide an adequate standard of living for workers. As the chapter argues, starting from the 1990s onward, the introduction of temporary contracts was a key turning point spiraling large sections of workers into precarity. In this regard, there was a systematic erosion of workers' rights from one president to another. This does not mean that the different presidents' policies were equally detrimental, because of two main factors. First, the general economic context matters: That is, Rafsanjani carried the burden of the

---

accounting for 40 percent in 1996 and increasing to 65 percent in 2002. See ILO (2003: 19–22): As Kevan Harris has documented, since 2009, the Islamic Republic engaged in a complex process of pseudo-privatization, resulting in a "sub-contractor state." See Harris (2013: 45–70).

[4] Interview with Gholam Reza Abbasi (Supreme Labor Council), Mehr News Agency, November 1, 2017.

postwar era and the reconstruction of the country, Khatami coped with the youth unemployment and oil price fluctuations, Ahmadinejad failed at controlling Iran's soaring inflation, Rouhani faced unprecedented pressure from international sanctions. Second, the values fostering each administration's discourse shaped the context in which certain policies came to get accepted, from Rafsanjani's market-oriented rhetoric to Khatami's participative narrative of civil society, from Ahmadinejad's conservative populism to Rouhani's business-friendly pragmatism.

Furthermore, prohibitions on independent unions deprive workers of the legal tools to claim their rights. Only through the establishment of independent unions would it be possible to strengthen collective bargaining and significantly improve workers' conditions, in order to deliver on the 1979 Revolution's promise of social justice. As the chapter shows, only during Khatami's presidency and in a context of increasing – yet limited – space for criticism was there an attempt to create the legal conditions for the establishment of independent unions. Beyond the reformist administration, no other president has dared so far to revamp workers' collective bargaining, and labor activism has been systematically discouraged and repressed, with a peak during Ahmadinejad's presidency.

The chapter is based on primary research and interviews with industrial workers, scholars, and legal experts, which were conducted by the author in Iran between January 2018 and October 2019.

2 A Labor Law for the Islamic Republic: An Endeavor Taking Eleven Years

In December 1982, three years after the revolution, the country's parliament (Majles) discussed the first draft of the new labor law. Although the majority of seats in the legislature were won by members of the leftist branch of the Islamic Republican Party (IRP), the cabinet of prime minister Mir-Hossein Mousavi included the conservative hardliner Ahmad Tavakkoli as minister of labor.[5] Tavakkoli submitted to the Majles a draft law that defined the worker as a commodity (for further analysis of the draft, see Bayat 1991: 183; Amuzegar 1997: 66–67; Zubaida 2003: 204). This conception differed from Khomeini's frequent reference to workers as "manifestations of God" and "the country's backbone," references

---

[5] Tavakkoli started his political career as a member of the Islamic Coalition Party (ICP), founded in the early 1960s and absorbed by the IRP after the 1979 Revolution. The ICP, which was renamed *Mo'talefeh*, was considered close to the bazaaris. See also Keshavarzian (2009: 225–246).

which had raised great expectations among workers.[6] Tavakkoli's proposed draft was based on the Islamic notion of *ijāreh*, which evokes a concept of rent in hiring processes. It defined bargaining rights as individual as opposed to collective rights. Labor was conceived in terms of a service rendered in exchange for a given rent. The draft law implicitly suggested that the worker "rented himself out." According to Tavakkoli, labor contracts related to the private sphere (Niknam 1999: 17–21). Article 10 of the draft law stated that labor contracts were to be considered an obligation, a commitment (*taʿahhod*). The worker was defined as *kārpadhir* (someone who accepts or agrees to work) and not *kārgar* (lit.: bearer of labor).[7] Therefore, the draft contained no concept of "employment," but rather of "hiring" (of workers). Interestingly, as Asef Bayat has noted, the word used for payment was not wage (*dastmozd*), but rather *ojrat*, which is used for objects or animals (Bayat 1991: 191–192). The text was strongly opposed by the leftist branch and was never voted on in the Majles. Eventually, Tavakkoli was ousted from the cabinet (Barsaghian 1387/2008).

In the following years, the government worked to enhance the state's role in the economy. Wide-scale nationalization of the main sectors, as well as control over the production and redistribution of wealth were at the top of the agenda. In 1987, a new and fervent debate concerning labor legislation set in. The regime's narrative toward laborers had changed since 1979 and the importance of May Day in the regime's calendar of festivities, once so prominent, had become minimal (Morgana 2019: 133–158). The times when Ayatollah Khomeini directly addressed crowds praising workers and promising a route to social justice belonged to the past.[8] Factional struggle had reached its peak. The IRP was close to its dissolution, and the Islamic Republic had to deal with a deep internal crisis. For this reason, between 1987 and 1989, Ayatollah Khomeini intervened with various decrees. In December 1987, he replied to a letter from Abol-Qasem Sarhaddizadeh, the minister of labor at that time, who had asked for Khomeini's help on a controversial passage in the new draft labor law. The respective passage called into question the relations between the state and the private sector.[9] The Council of Guardians rejected the text, as it argued a wage contract should be considered a private issue between employer and worker, and that the state therefore had no business regulating it. In a terse response, Khomeini suggested

---

[6] Ruhollah Khomeini, May Day speech, *Ettelāʿāt*, May 2, 1979.
[7] *Kayhān*, February 22, 1982.
[8] *Jomhouri-e Eslāmi*, May 2, 1981.
[9] *Kayhān* Havaʾi, December 16, 1987.

that the state may ask the private sector for obedience in exchange for services. At the beginning of 1988, the Council of Guardians refused to approve a new draft labor law. The disputes over state intervention in labor, social, or family policies did not stop. Attempting to end the crisis, Khomeini prompted the government to revoke any lawful provisions against the interests of Islam. This last of Khomeini's tactical moves enabled the labor law to conclude its legislative path without the Council of Guardians' final approval. After several amendments were made by the newly established Expediency Council, the new text was eventually approved and became law in 1990.[10]

3   The New Labor Law and the Challenges of the 1990s under President Rafsanjani

The new labor law was finalized almost eleven years after the 1979 Revolution. The Islamic Republic eventually provided a legal framework for workers under the auspices of Islamic law. Tavakkoli's conception of *kārpadhir* was abandoned and replaced by that of *kārgar*. As Asghar Schirazi notes, the new law gave more advantages to workers, at least compared to the previous Labor Code of 1958 (Schirazi 1997: 214). Nevertheless, it was far from being "revolutionary" in the interests of the economically marginalized masses in whose name the 1979 Revolution was carried out.[11]

A closer look at the text of the 1990 law indicates that the new law made dismissals more difficult for employers, at least on paper, than they were in the previous legislation. Furthermore, it increased the amount of money given as compensation at the end of a labor contract (Articles 29–33) (Nomani and Behdad 2004: 102; Moghissi and Rahnema 2006: 207–208). Weekly working hours were reduced from forty-eight to forty-four, or thirty-six in specific cases (Articles 51–52). Wage discrimination based on "age, gender, race, ethnic origin and political and religious convictions" was prohibited (Article 38). Article 77 recognized maternity leave for ninety days. To fight child labor, the new law made employment of children under the age of 15 illegal (Article 79). Despite these steps forward, the drafters of the new law crystallized their reticence toward collective bargaining rights and workers' organizations by excluding the words *sandikā* (syndicate), *ettehādieh* (union), or *e'tesāb* (strike) from the law.

---

[10] The Expediency Council was an organ created ad hoc, in order to unlock the impasse between the Majles and the Guardian Council.
[11] Ayatollah Ruhollah Khomeini referred to the "downtrodden" (*mostaz'afin*). See also Saffari (2017: 287–301).

According to the 1990 labor law, "a worker is someone who works at the demand of an employer in any way in exchange for the receipt of compensation for his efforts, including salary, wages, shares, or any other benefits" (Article 2), and "all employers, workers, and productive, industrial, service, and agricultural institutions are obliged to follow" the law's regulations (Article 1). Despite this broad mandate, Article 188 states that "people covered by the National Employment Law or other special laws or provisions, as well as workers in family workplaces whose completion of their job is entirely done by the proprietor, the spouse, or a relative of first degree and first class thereof *shall not be included* in the provisions of this law" (emphasis added). This means that employees of arms factories, revolutionary foundations (such as Mostazʿafin Foundation or Martyr Foundation), workers situated in free trade zones (such as Kish Island), relatives employed in family businesses, and foreign nationals are all excluded from the protection of the labor law, and are subject to other regulations.[12]

The new labor law came into existence at a crucial moment for the history of the republic. The Iran–Iraq War (1980–1988) had devastated the country and left the economy in tatters. After Khomeini's death in 1989 a period of political transformation set in. With Hashemi Rafsanjani's election as president in 1989, the government started a program of reconstruction (*sāzandegi*). According to official data, the war resulted in 300,000 casualties and the displacement of 2.5 million people (Amirahmadi 1990a, 1990b: 242). Under Rafsanjani, class inequalities were exacerbated, and technocrats increasingly jockeyed for political space. As Kaveh Ehsani has pointed out, they were ready to make the dominant discourse shift from revolutionary commitment (*taʿahhod*) to praising professionalization and expertise (*takhassos*) (Ehsani 2009: 26–33). It was in this context that Rafsanjani's government sought to implement neoliberal policies to revive the economy, although, as documented by Mohammad Maljoo and Parviz Sedaghat, among others (Davari et al. 2019), neoliberalism in the Iranian context took a more diminished form, in between welfare policies and neoliberal measures.[13] The reconstruction era started with a Five-Year Development Plan (1989/1990–1993/1994) pledging the implementation of neoliberal measures (without ever calling them such), along with reforms aimed at boosting productivity, efficiency, and growth, and meant to encourage private capital and privatization policies, stimulate new investments,

---

[12] See also Islamic Republic of Iran, Ministry of Cooperatives, Labor and Social Welfare: www.mcls.gov.ir/en/rules/regulations. Accessed July 15, 2020.
[13] Maljoo and Sedaghat 2019. See also Valadbaygi (2020).

reform currency exchange rates, reduce oil dependency, and ease the state's control of economic sectors. Deregulation of economic activities and denationalization of the industries represented the main policy proposals of the pragmatist faction supporting Rafsanjani. Key car industries were included in the plan of privatization: Iran Kaveh, Iran Khodro, Iran Vanet, Khavar, Khodrowsazan, Moratab, Pars Khodro, SAIPA, Shahab Khodro, and Zamyad (Ehteshami 1995: 27–44). The First Five-Year Development Plan was approved under the auspices of achieving an average annual growth rate of 8 percent in GDP and reducing fluctuations in oil revenues from 21 billion to 6 billion US dollars.[14]

Boosting productivity and production became a mantra in the official president's speeches to attract investments. The mantra shifted focus from the workers and peasants to the new middle classes as the bearers of reconstruction. For these new subjects the mantra was produce and consume (*towlid va masraf*) (Morgana 2020: 340–344). The Islamic Republic's narrative toward labor transformed, focusing now on the youth and promoting the aspirational myth of the winner, concerned with collecting "successes" (*movaffaqiat-hā*) and "progress" (*pishrafteh-hā*). In this sense, the following headlines are emblematic: "A New Road [Different] from the Past" has to be taken.[15] "Big Successes of Our Economy."[16] Iran's "New Goals Are: Development, Growth, Efficiency."[17]

This drive to reconstruct the country's economy marginalized workers further, both discursively and legally, as they were referred to as mere instruments of production. In fact, the context provided a breeding ground for the casualization of labor that would become prevalent in the following years. Contracts represented the fulcrum of this transformation. Article 7 of the labor law stipulates: "A labor contract is composed of a written or oral contract according to which the worker will provide labor on a temporary or non-temporary duration for the employer, in exchange for receiving compensation for his efforts." The formulation is vague. The maximum temporary duration is not determined. As note 1 to the same article clarifies, "it will be determined by the Ministry of Labor and Social Affairs and confirmed by the Cabinet." A second note was added to minimize the abuse by employers, stating that "in jobs which by nature have a continuous duration, should the duration not be mentioned in the contract, the contract will be considered permanent." Until the

---

[14] On fiscal development strategies, see Ghasimi (1992: 599–614).
[15] *Kayhān*, May 23, 1993.
[16] *Irān*, August 1995
[17] *Irān*, August 8, 1995.

mid-1990s, it was normal to generally rely on permanent contracts. From 1995 onward, however, employers were allowed to renew short-term contracts without any limitations (Maljoo 2017: 47–63). Even though the law imposed stringent limitations for workers' dismissal, it also contained easily identifiable legal loopholes, which would allow employers to bend the rules. On the one hand, the labor law formalized the existence of temporary contracts, creating the conditions for them to become de facto permanent. On the other hand, it also facilitated workers' exclusion from the benefits of permanent contracts. Furthermore, since the law specified that a worker "is entitled to receive annual gratuity" only for temporary contracts with a duration of one year or more (Article 24), employers started to conclude and renew contracts for a shorter period, in order to avoid being locked into any obligation.[18]

Looking at the phenomenon over time can help to understand the impact of this law on increasing precarity of labor in the IRI. In 1990 only 6 percent of workers were in temporary contracts. By the end of the 2000s, temporary contracts represented 60 percent of all labor contracts.[19] Short-term contracts narrowed wage earners' space for labor protection further, as they excluded workers from the rights in the law, such as severance benefits, paid leave, and so on. Moreover, they contributed to the fragmentation of the process of solidarity building among workers, thus hindering collective bargaining.

As Section 4 will show, Mohammad Khatami tried to initiate a paradigm shift in the Islamic Republic's official discourse by stressing on the principle of the rule of law (*hākemiat-e qānun*) – which hitherto had not been at the center of the Iranian legal doctrine (Künkler, Chapter 9 in this volume; Banakar and Ziaee 2018: 717–746). Reforming the labor law was one of Khatami's core reformist objectives. The new president attempted to guarantee workers an expanded space for collective bargaining. In practice, his endeavors did not bear fruit, as workers' legal protection decreased even further during his presidency. Nevertheless, Khatami's efforts created the conditions for a more open – yet limited – space for criticism that, over the 2000s, allowed unofficial networks of labor activists to flourish.[20]

---

[18] Interview with lawyer conducted by the author, Tehran, June 6, 2019.
[19] Iranian Student News Agency (ISNA), July 20, 2010, https://shorturl.at/wzKW8. Accessed August 31, 2023.
[20] Worker and former labor activist, interview with the author, Tehran, April 29, 2019. Throughout the 2000s, numerous websites reporting workers' protests and strikes across the country emerged, such as Kargaran.org, Ehtehadchap.org, Jonbeshekargary.org, Iranlaborreport.org, and Gozaar.org. Most of these have since been shut down.

4 Khatami's Quest for the Rule of Law and Civil Society: What "Participants" Were Missing

When Khatami delivered his inaugural speech as president in May 1997 in front of the Iranian parliament, the words "rule of law," "rights," "civil society," "individual freedom," and "participation" resonated in the room several times (Khatami 1997: 70–86). While claiming to address the "people's most fundamental right, [i.e.] the right to determine their own destiny," he called for the support of "political institutions and organizations, associations, the media, scholars and researchers, academicians and educators, experts and specialists, all men and women of science, letters, culture and art, and all citizens in all walks of life." Interestingly, although he placed the individual at the center of his vision of justice, the newly inaugurated president of the Islamic Republic did not mention workers specifically (Khatami 1997: 76). He presented his plan of action by grounding it on three pillars: The rule of law, justice, and civil society participation. Khatami declared: "The overall policies of the executive branch will be based on institutionalizing the rule of law; a vigorous pursuit of justice as an exalted religious value and the pivotal factor for social trust, stability, progress and prosperity [...] Empowering the people in order to achieve and ensure an ever-increasing level of their discerning participation" (Khatami 1997: 76–77). Furthermore, he referred to the establishment of the rule of law as "an Islamic, revolutionary and national obligation, which requires a conducive and enabling environment as well as legal means and instruments coupled with public involvement and assistance" (Khatami 1997: 77). Khatami envisaged the future of the Islamic Republic as having "a morally and materially prosperous individual" at the forefront (Khatami 1997: 77–80). On the one hand, his government project was meant to "strengthen the culture of dialogue, discourse, appraisal and critique." On the other hand, his reform-oriented speech situated the concepts of law and justice within the framework of an individual's progress in the context of civil society, thus narrowing the space for redistributive social justice (Khatami 1997: 81). During his campaign, Khatami's emphasis on civil society boosted women and the youth in order to participate and engage in what was defined as a "healthy competition" and "collective cooperation."[21] As Khatami had gained about 70 percent of the votes in the May 1997 elections, analysts stressed that his victory had become possible only with the crucial support of women, young people, and the middle class, and that they had had a lower participation in previous elections (Tazmini 2009: 54–55). Those

---

[21] *Iran News Daily*, April 5, 1997.

who went to the polls followed the president's program and hopes, which were oriented toward "a more legal society with more clearly defined rights and duties for citizens" (Khatami 1997: 89). In this perspective, the ideal "citizen" was a "participant," "empowered," mastering his/her own "destiny." In fact, the liberal-legal and civil society approach in the new president's conception lacked a definite awareness of the heterogeneity of Iranian society. Indeed, in envisioning the realization of cultural and political "development" and "prosperity," it largely overlooked the structural and legal obstacles hindering workers' participation in particular, such as class, and economic and bargaining power (Khatami 1997: 70–86). Economic and labor issues were not at the center of the public debate stimulated by Khatami, as a clear economic agenda did not capture the slogans or make headlines throughout his presidency (Nomani and Behdad 2008: 377–396).

In this regard, before moving on to Section 5, which will delve into these obstacles in more depth by looking at the legal reforms relating to the realm of labor, it is essential to give a glimpse of the complexities of the context. Once at the helm of his government, the road ahead for Khatami was full of political and economic pitfalls. He was under pressure from hardliners that first feared, and later opposed, his attempts at reforming the economy by labeling his policies "Western" or "anti-Islamic," as well as by portraying them as threats "to security and order" in the country (Moslem 2002: 257–262; Arjomand 2009: 94–99).

Furthermore, when Khatami started his presidency, discontent with unemployment was very high, and the demographic pressure exacerbated the situation. In fact, during Khatami's presidency, there were about 1.2 million youth entering the job market (Salehi-Isfahani and Egel 2007: 26).

At the same time, supporters of economic liberalization kept pressing for the relaxation of regulations and a legal framework conducive to private enterprise. The reformists were more oriented to reducing the obstacles to private capital accumulation, firmly convinced that Iran's regulations were written only to protect jobs instead of facilitating their creation (Salehi-Isfahani 2005: 117–147). Therefore, temporary contracts – along with blank contracts – became widespread tools to ameliorate popular discontent, at least in the short term.[22] But

---

[22] Blank contracts are written agreements that give enormous power to employers, as workers are forced to sign these contracts prior to having specified working conditions or job duration. Although they are illegal, blank contracts represent common practice in Iran, according to what a lawyer confirmed to the author (interview conducted in Tehran, May 11, 2019).

this backfired and, between 2001 and 2004, several waves of protests erupted – harshly repressed by the security forces – mostly because of unpaid or delayed wages.

The factional struggle reached its peak in February 2004, when many reformists (including eighty sitting MPs) were barred from running in elections where the conservatives made a net gain of two-thirds of the seats: A harsh setback for what had been deemed by then the "Tehran Spring" (Saghafi 2004: 16–23). Regarding the economy, part of the Second Development Plan (1995–1999) – approved during Rafsanjani's term – coincided with the initial phase of Khatami's administration. By then, Khatami had inherited high inflation, growing social inequalities, rising youth unemployment, a substantial budget deficit, low crude oil prices, and declining non-oil exports (Amuzegar 2006: 57–74). Thus, the expectations in terms of GDP growth were not realized. When Khatami's administration launched the Third Development Plan (2000–2005), it was in the spirit of "progress" and, de facto, rapid growth aimed at privatizing several industries, reorganizing bureaucracy and subsidies, and reducing poverty, along with the creation of the Oil Stabilization Fund.[23] Boosted by external factors (such as the rising oil prices during Khatami's second term), Iran enjoyed a phase of economic growth. Indeed, the overall situation in terms of wages and unemployment improved, though not for all social classes (Salehi-Isfahani 2002: 142–157; 2009b: 3–37). According to the calculations of Djavad Salehi-Isfahani, during the eight years of Khatami's administration, poverty decreased by more than 2 percentage points each year (Salehi-Isfahani 2009a). Yet, a look at the difference between minimum nominal wages and minimum real wages accounting for inflation between 1997 and 2002 can better explain how the overall situation was still critical for workers. The minimum nominal wage increased from 207,210 rials in 1997 to 458,010 rials in 2002, while the minimum real wage rose only from 242,919 to 286,794 rials during the same period.[24]

5 Unprotected Ergo Invisible: Cornering Workers While Seeking to Reform the Labor Law

Understanding the disjuncture between Khatami's discourse drawing on participation and rule of law on the one hand, and its effects on workers on the other requires investigating the gaps between the de jure and de facto situation. What has remained unwritten so far in the analysis of the

---

[23] *Hamshahri*, November 2, 2004; *Donya-ye Eqtesad*, May 24, 2005.
[24] CBI.

reformist period is, indeed, twofold. The first part of the untold story is how reformist policies narrowed workers' space for legal protection. The second part concerns the government's failure to enhance the mediation between the IRI and wage earners through (the unfulfilled promise of) the legalization of independent trade unions. In fact, it was at the legal level that the reforms did not succeed in turning workers into participant citizens.

As a result of the labor law amendments drafted and approved during Khatami's administration between 1999 and 2003 – amid much criticism of the Workers' House (the key official mediation body between workers and employers) – approximately 3 million wage earners remained legally unprotected and mostly unrepresented.[25] The Majles passed the provisions exempting small enterprises and workshops with five or fewer workers from part of the labor protections. Initially, it approved the amendment as temporary, in the context of the administration's efforts to reduce bureaucracy and boost the private sector (ILO 2003: 31–37). The amendments were designed to last for three years, but eventually they were extended. In 2003, small firms with ten or fewer workers were exempted – de jure and de facto – from complying with thirty-seven articles of the labor law. The wording of the amendment, especially regarding exemptions, was vague because the text referred to "particular circumstances" and "exceptional cases," upon consideration of the Council of Ministers.[26] The provision was renewed after two years and was largely enacted.[27] The amendment resulted in a considerable deterioration in working conditions and contractual guarantees for workers, as incorporated in Article 191. This limitation of legal labor protection paved the way for the deregulation of working conditions and workers' casualization. It impacted overtime pay, additional night remuneration, paid leave, and employers' duties related to job classification or severance pay. The relation between employers and employees began to diverge from its initial definition in the 1990 labor law, further shifting in favor of employers. Larger enterprises began to benefit from the

---

[25] As reported by the ILO in a document on Convention No. 111 on Labor Discrimination, citing a worker member of the Islamic Republic of Iran. Available here: www.ilo.org/dyn/normlex/fr/f?p=NORMLEXPUB:13100:0::NO::P13100_COMMENT_ID,P13100_LANG_CODE:2555743,en.

[26] Iran labor law, miscellaneous provisions. English translation is available here: www.ilo.org/dyn/natlex/docs/WEBTEXT/21843/64830/E90IRN01.HTM#c12.

[27] The widespread diffusion and the strategies of circumnavigating the new regulation have been discussed and confirmed to the author during several interviews with workers between January 2018 and October 2019, as well as interviews with a lawyer and employment law expert (Tehran, June 6, 2019), and a labor economist (Tehran, January 18, 2018 and June 11, 2018).

amendment to bypass the law through the use of different contractors.[28] In June 2003, when the ILO assessed the situation of employment in Iran, it recommended the country "improve compliance of the labour laws by micro and small enterprises since the growth of small enterprises is often constrained by their inability to comply" (ILO 2003: 74). The provision, which exempted small workshops from compliance to part of the labor law, suited a context where a plethora of temporary contracts was expanding. As a result, most workers lacked employment protection and were excluded from legal coverage, in a general context where the enforcement of the labor law was already weak.

Though it would ultimately prove to be a losing battle, Khatami sought to facilitate workers' articulation of their collective demands. In 2003, by cooperating with the ILO and paving the way for Iran to join the World Trade Organization (WTO), Khatami considered new changes in the labor law. In particular, he attempted to reform chapter VI of the law, dealing with labor organization, freedom of association, and collective bargaining. The negotiations lasted for seven months. According to the ILO's report, the existing labor regime in the Islamic Republic was "deficient," and deemed as "undermining confidence in collective bargaining." The organization made a series of recommendations to the Iranian government. It advised it to reform the law to, first, "respect freedom of association and facilitation of collective bargaining" (ILO 2003: 60) and, second, strengthen workers' and employers' organizations "to fully participate in social dialogue" (ILO 2003: 72). The key lever was editing note 4 of Article 131, by adding independent organizations beyond state-affiliated Islamic councils and workers' representatives. Additionally, the reformist administration was advised to ratify Article 87 of Convention 1948, which concerned the Freedom of Association and Protection of the Right to Organize. Article 2 stipulates that "workers and employers, without distinction whatsoever, shall have the right to establish and, subject only to the rules of the organization concerned, to join organizations of their choosing without previous authorization." In May 2003, ILO's Bernard Jernigan triumphantly declared the meeting with Iranian officials from the Ministry of Labor a success. "From now on, the syndicates are authorized to represent labourers, while the Islamic Labour Councils will act as consultants in the welfare affairs of guild units [...] Guild associations will be registered by the Ministry of Labour and Social Affairs, while this does not mean that the ministry has the right to interfere with their affairs," he said.[29]

---

[28] Legal expert, interview with the author, Tehran, May 11, 2019.
[29] Islamic Republic News Agency (IRNA), Ordibehesht 24, 1382. English translation available via Payvand, May 15, 2003 (retrieved August 31, 2023): https://web.archive.org/web/20040110192520/www.payvand.com/news/03/may/1084.html.

Nonetheless, free and independent unions became victims of deadlocked negotiations and factional struggles. The Guild Union Act of May 2004 did not garner the expected results and various stumbling blocks brought Khatami's endeavors to a political impasse.[30] A determined and decisive opponent of these reforms was the Workers' House. Section 6. will investigate its complex role as a key official mediation body between workers and employers and as a method of control over workers.

6 The Workers' House and the Limitations to Independent Workers' Organizations

The Khāneh-ye Kārgar, "Workers' House," has a unique status in Iran. It is not a fully independent trade union nor a worker's council; neither is it a non-governmental organization (NGO) nor a party in the conventional sense.[31] Self-defined as "an organization believing in *velāyat-e faqih* and adhering to the Constitution [...] defending the rights of the deprived and the oppressed,"[32] it constitutes de facto the most influential workers' organization in Iran, and it operates as a confederation. Financially, logistically, and politically, it is supported by the Islamic Republic. Articles 130 and 131 of chapter VI of the labor law stipulate that workers can be represented by: (1) Islamic labor councils (that can exist in every workplace with more than thirty-five employees) along with Islamic societies; (2) guild societies (*anjoman-e senfi*); and (3) representatives (*namāyandegān-e āzād*), nominated by the workers. Islamic labor councils, guild societies, and workers' representatives all function de facto under the Workers' House umbrella, although there is no explicit mention of the organization's role in the labor law. These institutions are explicitly conceived to "propagate and spread Islamic culture and defend the Islamic Revolution's achievement" in the workplace (Article 130). They are free to exist, according to Article 26 of the Iranian constitution, on the condition that they do "not violate the principles of independence, freedom, national unity, Islamic standards, and the foundation of the Islamic Republic." Procedures, duties, and powers, as well as their activities, must be supervised by the Ministries of the Interior and Labor and Social Affairs and the Organization of Islamic

---

[30] Majles, Esfand 24, 1382/March 14, 2004. See (in Persian) ILO: www.ilo.org/dyn/natlex/docs/ELECTRONIC/91489/106120/F2053865805/IRN91489.pdf.

[31] Alireza Kheirollahi defines it as an "ideological party that has a not clear and not democratic legal and political structure" (Kheirollahi 1398/2010). Abbas Khalegi defines it a "party organization" (Khalegi 1389/2010: 99–22).

[32] Khāneh-ye Kārgar, "*Dar bāreh-ye mā*": http://workerhouse.ir/subject.aspx?groupid=18.

Propaganda. The IRI controls them, as the law requires "a representative on behalf of the *velāyat-e faqih*" to be present on their boards (Article 138 labor law). Therefore, the modalities of access and participation are top down and they do not directly involve workers. Despite this lack of worker participation, the Workers' House has managed to expand its room for manoeuvre, claiming to be independent from the government. This section asks where the status of the Workers' House originated? And further, how did it impact Khatami's quest for civil society in the context of labor relations?

The Khāneh-ye Kārgar was formed in 1967 (Habibzadeh 1387/2010: 90–92).[33] As a secular entity, it played a crucial role in fostering workers' collective demands during the revolutionary agitation. It became a point of reference for the working poor and unemployed, influenced by the leftist group Peykār (Bayat 2011: 104–106). In the aftermath of the 1979 Revolution, following a struggle for hegemony with leftist groups that were purged by the newly born Islamic Republic, the Workers' House was politically aligned with the IRP. After the IRP's dissolution in 1987, it was considered close to Rafsanjani's faction, as it openly supported it during the fifth Majles vote in 1996 (Tazmini 2009: 54–55). The Workers' House did not endorse Khatami's presidential bid in May 1997 and indeed announced that it would not be backing any of the candidates.[34] Although gravitating to the Islamic left, it distanced itself from Khatami from the beginning of the reformist era. Nevertheless, its leadership started to benefit from the open-door policy toward political parties promoted by Khatami (which resulted in an increase in the number of parties in Iran from thirty-five to ninety-five between 1997 and late 2000s) (Bayat 2007: 109). In fact, in October 1998, the Islamic Labor Party was officially registered in Tehran. Among its key members figured Alireza Mahjoub, the secretary-general of the Khāneh-ye Kārgar, as well as Hossein Kamali, already minister of labor in Rafsanjani's cabinet. In the words of another of its members, Abdol-Qasem Sarhaddizadeh, the party aimed to boost "workers' participation" in public life and protect their rights.[35] These developments provide an opportunity to evaluate the actual connections between the Workers' House and the political sphere of the state, despite its claims of being independent and nongovernmental. This tension could be understood through the lens of the discursive – as well as instrumental – use of "participation." Indeed, *mōsharekat* (participation) represented a key notion for the encounters

---

[33] Also see http://mworkerhouse.ir/about-khanehkargar.
[34] *Irān News*, May 8, 1997.
[35] *Irān*, Bahman 19, 1377/February 8, 1999.

between the top-down and bottom-up dynamics during Khatami's era on several levels. First, as far as this chapter is concerned, the Workers' House appropriated the terminology of the reformists. Second, it exploited the more extensive – yet limited – political space for criticism, to engage in a campaign against Khatami's government. In particular, it took a critical stance against the exemption of small workshops from the labor law and low wages. In the newspaper *Kār-o-Kārgar*, the Workers' House claimed to protect workers' rights.

Exploitation was widespread in workplaces in Iran by the early 2000s. About 53 percent of workers spent more than twelve hours per day toiling.[36] Thousands of workers in state-run factories were still waiting to be paid.[37] Those in the factories who were getting their wages were complaining about being underpaid. *Kār-o-Kārgar* described the situation as the "tragedy of wages."[38]

Despite its claims to protect workers' rights, the Khāneh-ye Kārgar acted ambiguously when Khatami's team, in cooperation with the ILO, proposed to reform chapter VII of the labor law on collective bargaining. In fact, it opposed the changes regarding the establishment of free unions in order to maintain the status quo. Independent workers' organizations would have threatened the power of the Workers' House as a labor stronghold, which was engaged in: (1) advocating for workers' justice and challenging government's policies, while (2) acting as part of the state apparatus, thus contributing to investigate workers' activities in the workplace, in order to isolate potential conflicts arising and step in to quell further outbreaks of protest.[39]

An editorial of *Kār-o-Kārgar* in April 2000 commented on the exemption of small enterprises from the labor law by constructing it as a binary opposition between the government's quest for job creation through private entrepreneurship and the demolition of workers' legal protection. Titled "Job Creation or Elimination of Workers' Rights," the Op-Ed argued that the new provisions paved the way "to unjust, illegal developments and will lead to chaos."[40] The metaphor of chaos evoked a blurred reality of disorder and confusion. Without any further detail, it mirrored a sense of discomfort due to perceived lawlessness. The editorial piece continued with a bitter equation projecting the workers as victimized: "It is interesting that they say that workers and their low wages were

[36] *Kār-o-Kārgar*, May 23, 2000/Khordad 3, 1379.
[37] *Kār-o-Kārgar*, May 4, 2000/Ordibehesht 15, 1379.
[38] *Kār-o-Kārgar*, April 5, 2000/Farvardin 17, 1379.
[39] These activities have been reported to the author by workers and legal experts interviewed in Tehran during her research stay between January 2018 and October 2019.
[40] *Kār-o-Kārgar*, April 5, 2000/Farvardin 17, 1379.

an obstacle to job creation, in other words, workers caused the unemployment." Hence, it formulated explicit accusations, by targeting the reformist government and referring to "the weakness of strategic planning, lack of organization and incapacity of realization."

Moreover, by rhetorically questioning the government, the editorial reinforced its bond with the readers: "Establishing law in support of the capitalists, and reducing legal support to workers where do they want to go? Doesn't this expand illegality?" Within this framework, threatening strike action beyond mere protests represented a way to up the ante. Yet, using the word "strike" (*e'tesāb*) as a very useful scare tactic did not mean that the Workers' House, through its columns, was campaigning for the right to strike. Headlines such as "Strikes are the Last Option for Workers" or "Strike: Its Legal Aspect," introduced commentaries that delved into formulations (and omissions) in the labor law, and eventually discouraged workers from considering strike action as an option.[41] In this regard, it is fundamental to clarify two aspects. The first one is legal: The labor law does not recognize the right to strike, but it vaguely refers to "work interruption."[42] Moreover, in the legal formulation listing the Islamic labor councils' role and duties, it can be deduced that the labor councils are meant to be the first official channel for any quarrels occurring in the workplace.[43] The second point concerns control and the use of force. As emerged from the author's interviews with workers, labor activists, and legal experts, any action potentially leading to "work interruption" could be monitored, reported to the Ministry of Intelligence, and repressed.[44]

7 The Politics of Labor and Labor Legislation under Ahmadinejad's Populist Administration

When Mahmoud Ahmadinejad won the presidential elections in 2005, he pledged to fulfill "the people's" desires and "give back the revolution to the oppressed." Social justice (*edālat-e ejtemā'i*)-related slogans permeated his speeches. On May Day 2006 he declared: "Solving the economic problem and creating job opportunities is the absolute goal of my government. Our government is here for workers, and it is honored

---

[41] *Kār-o-Kārgar*, April 9–10, 2000/Farvardin 20–21, 1379, May 13, 2000/Ordibehesht 23, 1379.
[42] For a broader discussion on the legal formulation of work stoppage in the Iranian labor law, see Khcirollahi (1398/2010: 73–74).
[43] Islamic Labor Councils Law, Majles: https://rc.majlis.ir/fa/law/show/91022.
[44] Interviews with the author: legal expert, Tehran, May 11, 2019; worker and labor activist, Tehran, April 30, 2019; scholar and labor expert, Tehran, October 25, 2018.

to be at your service, dear workers."[45] Nevertheless, his government sought to amend the labor law with a series of measures that would have seriously threatened to further erode workers' job security, by eliminating restrictions on workers' dismissal in case of a decrease of productivity or alleged misconduct. Ironically, Mohammad Jahromi, the then labor minister, campaigned for reforming the legislation claiming to increase job security in the Iranian labor market. He argued that trying to ameliorate the code's rigidity was the only way to boost productivity and foster job creation.[46] At the core of the proposed draft were Articles 21 and 27 of the labor law. The first stipulates: "The labor contract may be terminated by one of the following causes: a) The worker's death; b) The worker's retirement; c) The worker's complete inability to work; d) The determination that the labor contract is temporary in duration and that it contains no clear rehiring or guaranteed renewal; e) The worker's resignation" (labor law, chapter II). Jahromi suggested that two further conditions had to be included to facilitate workers' dismissal: A contraction of the enterprises' productivity, and a (deemed) necessary staff restructuring, due to stringent economic or political reasons (Maljoo 2007: 1–14).[47] In case of workers' misconduct, Article 27 obliges the employer to "to pay them not only their benefits and back wages but a month's salary for each year of work based on the last month of the worker's wages as the annual benefit and dissolve the contract." According to the proposed draft, the contract's termination could occur after only two warnings and with reduced severance pay.[48] The plan aroused anger and discontent, and the Workers' House openly attacked the draft, accusing the government of enabling employers to easily fire workers and dismantling workers' rights protections.[49] The draft did not manage to gain a majority vote in the Majles.

Another discrepancy between the discourse claiming to defend the poor and the toilers, on the one hand, and the political decisions, on the other hand, manifested itself again when the populist president's administration submitted a draft to reform the subsidy system. The first proposal was presented in the Majles in 2008 and approved two years later, reducing government subsidies on fuel and food. The announced goal was to ease pressure on the IRI's finances, but the policy contributed to higher inflation in the country (Habibi 2014: 1–20).

---

[45] *Ettelā'āt*, Ordibehesht 11, 1385/May 1, 2006.
[46] *Irān*, September 13, 2006.
[47] *Kayhān*, September 13, 2006,
[48] *Irān*, September 13, 2006.
[49] Mahjoub openly confronted Ahmadinejad's policies from the columns of *Kār-o-Kārgar* and *Mardom-Sālāri* between 2006 and 2007.

A third policy area in which Ahmadinejad aimed for significant reform concerned the minimum wage. In 2007, his administration received harsh criticism from the Workers' House for pushing the Supreme Labor Council to set the minimum wage at 1.80 million rials, which was considered close to the "poverty line."[50] In fact, minimum wages are regulated by Article 41 of the labor law, which stipulates that "the Supreme Labor Council should annually determine the minimum wages of the workers in different parts of the country or in various industries in accordance with the following criteria: 1) The minimum wages of workers in consideration of the percentage of inflation announced by the Central Bank of the Islamic Republic of Iran. 2) The minimum wages, without considering the physical and mental characteristics of the workers and the specificity of the work assigned to them must be at a level that it may support a family whose average number shall be announced by official authorities." In 2009 the minimum wage was raised to 2.75 million rials and in 2013 it stood at 4.9 million rials. Meanwhile, Iranians' purchasing power decreased by almost 40 percent in only two years, between 2007 and 2009 (CBI).

Furthermore, Ahmadinejad's administration tightened up the security apparatus, targeting workers' protests, and thus brutally ended the reformist era and the spirit of "political participation." Between 2005 and 2007, labor activism mobilized to claim the right to form independent unions. In 2005, the Sherkat-e Vāhed of the Tehran Bus Company collected about 9,000 signatures to establish a new independent union. Its members organized two strikes, but they faced harsh repression as the government responded with a crackdown and arrests. Labor activists were accused of conspiring against the Islamic Republic and threatening national security.[51] In 2007 and 2008 the workers at Haft Tapeh Sugar Factory in Khuzestan and the Free Union of Iranian Workers protested, claiming their right to exist as a syndicate beyond the Islamic Council. Interestingly, when the state apparatus confronted the demonstrators with violence and suppressed any illegal workers' network, the Workers' House did not support these expressions of dissent.

The government also continued to oppose the formation of free unions. Ahmadinejad's presidency exemplified that, without a determined political will to reform both the law and ease the security response, there are no legal and practical possibilities to overcome the obstacles to establishing independent workers' organizations.

---

[50] *Kār-o-Kārgar*, May 5, 2007.
[51] *Akhbar-e Rooz*, Dey 22, 1391/January 11, 2013: www.akhbar-rooz.com/article.jsp?essayId=50292.

8 Cheapening Labor, Weakening Workers' Conditions: Risks and Challenges under Rouhani

Even after Ahmadinejad left office, a political project supporting workers' participation and empowering the labor force de jure and de facto did not surface. In 2013 Hassan Rouhani won the presidential elections, pledging economic recovery and lifting the grip of international sanctions on Iranians. As mentioned in Section 1, his pragmatist temper and neoliberal doctrine toward labor relations was already manifest. Once in power, Rouhani's policies on labor were oriented toward meeting economic needs, mostly favoring employers, instead of focusing on creating employment and improving workers' conditions. Boosting domestic production, growth and industry development, restructuring the job market, removing legal limitations on workers' dismissals, and supporting job creators in the private sector represented the top priorities of the new president's first term (Hossein-Zadeh 2014). Nevertheless, these market-oriented choices under the auspices of "moderation," as he repeated fifteen times in his inaugural speech,[52] undermined – along with harsh international sanctions – workers' living conditions. "People want a better life, they want dignity and a decent life," Rouhani said in August 2013. How did this call for dignity translate into policy? Between 2011 and 2014 wages did not increase proportionally to the rising living costs.[53] In 2014, the official increase approved by the Supreme Labor Council took the minimum wage from 4,870,000 rials (by then nearly 195 dollars) to 6,090,000 rials (nearly 248 dollars), 25 percent less than labor activists and experts had been expecting (Ramazani 2014). Nonetheless, the minimum wage set by the Labor Council during Rouhani's first years as president did not guarantee basic financial security for workers. Furthermore, many employers did not respect the contracts' conditions, as they did not adjust the wages to the new standards set annually.[54] Legally, workers should be protected, as a note to Article 41 clarifies: "The employers shall be duty-bound to pay to the workers an amount not less than the newly announced minimum wages against the performance of work during the official working hours. In case of violation, the employer shall be obligated to guarantee payment of the difference between the wages paid and the new minimum wages." Yet, in practice what *Kār-o-Kārgar* defined as "the tragedy of wages" in early 2000s cast a long shadow, obscuring Iranian workers'

---

[52] *Irān*, Mordad 13, 1392/August 4, 2013.
[53] *Kār-o-Kārgar*, Esfand 22, 1392/March 13, 2014.
[54] Legal expert, interview with the author, Tehran, May 11, 2019.

lives more than ten years later. Even though the law obliged employers to guarantee workers' wages, in reality workers did not receive their pay for months. As a result of both these practices and the deteriorating situation of Iranian economy suffocated by international sanctions, in 2016 more than 7 million workers received wages below the legal standards and lived under the poverty line.[55] In 2019, 15 million Iranians lived on the brink, despite the government's attempt to improve the population's health and economic conditions, such as by health sector reform.[56] Although the difficulties of the Iranian economy under Rouhani's presidency were not exclusively a result of his policies (they were rooted in both structural domestic problems and international sanctions), it can be argued that since 2013 workers' rights and plight have not significantly improved. The deteriorated economic conditions, in particular since the beginning of Rouhani's second term, provoked several waves of workers' unrest. Nevertheless, workers' protests have been mostly scattered, and lacked leadership and coordination, mostly because of strict control in the workplaces, fear, and actual repression. The systematic repression of both independent labor activism perpetrated by the IRI's security apparatus during Rouhani's presidency shows that there are no political conditions for reopening the debate on reforming the labor law's chapter in order to facilitate the establishment of independent unions.

9   Conclusion

This chapter analyzed labor rights in Iran under the Islamic Republic through the lens of labor law reform. Whereas Ayatollah Khomeini characterized labor as a "manifestation of God," casting it under the Islamic umbrella while pledging social justice, since the 1979 Revolution this discourse has significantly transformed and has not been fully matched by policy. The ideological importance of workers as the IRI's backbone has become marginalized over the years, both in discourse and in practice. The Islamic conceptualization of labor did not play a central role after Khomeini's death. How has this transformation occurred? Rafsanjani's neoliberal turn was permeated by the fetishization of economic growth. Workers became marginalized in the dominant narrative and referred to as mere instruments of production. Under Rafsanjani's administration, temporary contracts were introduced. From 1995 onward, these

---

[55] Tasnim Agency, Ordibehesht 17, 1395/May 6, 2016: https://shorturl.at/chK45. Accessed August 31, 2023.
[56] *Hamshahri*, Azar 25, 1398/December 16, 2019: https://shorturl.at/sIWX6. Accessed August 31, 2023.

short-term contracts started to threaten job security and paved the way for job precaritization. Khatami's reformist administration tightened its focus on civil society, participation, and rule of law, but overlooked workers and labor in its dominant discourse. During the reformist era, the Majles passed an amendment exempting small enterprises and workshops with five or fewer workers (the majority in the Iranian industrial landscape) from part of the labor protections. This amendment exposed workers to further exploitation. At the same time, Khatami tried to improve workers' bargaining power. In fact, in 2003 he attempted – without success – to reform the labor law with regard to promoting more independent unions. Ahmadinejad's conservative populism pledged to give the revolution back to the people and promised full support to workers, but his rhetoric actually translated into more repressive actions against workers. Furthermore, his administration proposed to reform the labor law by eliminating restrictions on workers' dismissals in case of a decrease of productivity, stirring up unrest and discontent among workers. Rouhani's assertions against the rigidity of labor regulations fostered an employer-friendly agenda, while workers' living conditions deteriorated further under his rule, partly as a result of international sanctions.

Overall, it can be argued that workers' rights and conditions have not been at the core of the IRI's presidents' policies, especially from the 1990s onward. Although efforts to fight child labor and reduce working hours found their way in the labor law of 1990, and improvements of safety regulation have been made, particularly during Rouhani's presidency (ILO 2014–2018), three main aspects of labor regulations remain critical: Contracts, wages, and workers' bargaining power. The economic project of cheapening labor, which started in the mid-1990s with the first wave of temporary contracts, has created a long-lasting legacy. The labor law not only formalized the conclusion of temporary contracts (which were boosted from the mid-1990s by Rafsanjani's business-friendly policies), but in practice facilitated the exclusion of workers in temporary contracts from broader legal protection. Specifically, short-term contracts provoked a contraction in wages amount, depriving workers of fundamental access to housing, insurance rights, severance pay, payment of overtime rates, and rights on annual leave. Furthermore, minimum wages – which are determined annually by the Supreme Labor Council and fixed by taking account of inflation announced by the CBI – fall short of guaranteeing a fair standard of living to most Iranian working families. Although the Workers' House has conducted a long fight over this issue, it is the only official workers' organization in the country. Despite its claims to be independent from the government, it has played a major role in opposing the establishment of free unions in the country – particularly during the reformist era. In this context, with weakened bargaining power, due to legal conditions, and without free and independent trade unions' interlocutors, caused by a lacking political will to engage in legal reform, the IRI has left workers behind.

Bibliography

(1)   General Literature

Amuzegar, Jahangir. *Iran's Economy under the Islamic Republic*, London: I. B. Tauris, 1997.
Amirahmadi, Hooshang. "Economic Reconstruction of Iran: Costing the War Damage," *Third World Quarterly*, 12(1), January 1990a, pp. 26–47.
Amirahmadi, Hooshang. *Revolution and Economic Transition: The Iranian Experience*, Albany: State University of New York Press, 1990b, pp. 240–242.
Amuzegar, Jahangir. "Khatami's Legacies: Dashed Hopes," *Middle East Journal*, 60(1), Winter 2006, pp. 57–74.
Arjomand, Said Amir. *After Khomeini: Iran under His Successors*, New York: Cambridge University Press, 2009.
Banakar, Reza and Keyvan Ziaee. "The Life of the Law in the Islamic Republic of Iran," *Iranian Studies*, 51(5), 2018, pp. 717–746.
Barsaghian, Serge. "Dowlat-e Por Raft-o-Āmad," *Shahrvand*, 43, 1387/2008. http://ensani.ir/fa/article/47736/%D8%AF%D9%88%D9%84%D8%AA-%D9%BE%D8%B1-%D8%B1%D9%81%D8%AA-%D9%88-%D8%A2%D9%85%D8%AF.
Bayat, Asef. "Historiography, Class, and Iranian Workers," in Zachary Lockman (ed.) *Workers and Working Classes in the Middle East. Struggles, Histories, Historiographies*, New York: Zed Books, 1991, pp. 91–114.
Bayat, Asef. *Making Islam Democratic: Social Movements and the Post-Islamist Turn*, Stanford: Stanford University Press, 2007.
Bayat, Asef. "Workless Revolutionaries: The Unemployed Movement in Revolutionary Iran," in S. Cronin (ed.), *Subalterns and Social Protest. History from Below in the Middle East and North Africa*, London: Routledge, 2011, pp. 104–106.
Davari, Arash, Peyman Jafari, Ali Kadivar, Zep Kalb, Arang Keshavarzian, Azam Khatam, Saira Rafiee, and Eskandar Sadeghi-Boroujerdi. 'Roundtable: Iran's Domestic Politics and Political Economy,' *Jadaliyya*, November 26, 2019. www.jadaliyya.com/Details/40287/Roundtable-Iran%E2%80%99s-Domestic-Politics-and-Political-Economy-Part-1.
Ehsani, Kaveh. "Survival through Dispossession: Privatization of Public Goods in the Islamic Republic," *Middle East Report, No. 250*: The Islamic Revolution at 30 (special issue), Spring 2009, pp. 26–33.
Ehteshami, Anoush. *After Khomeini: The Iranian Second Republic*, New York: Routledge, 1995.
Ghasimi, Mohammad Reza. "The Iranian Economy after the Revolution: An Economic Appraisal of the Five-Year Plan," *International Journal of Middle East Studies*, 24(4), November 1992, pp. 599–614.

Habibi, Nader. "Economic Legacy of Mahmoud Ahmadinejad," Working Paper Series, Brandeis University, 2014, pp. 1–20.

Habibzadeh, Afshin. *Moshārekat Siyāsi Tabaqeh-ye Kārgar dar Irān* [*Political Participation of the Working Class in Iran*], Tehran: Enteshārat Kavir, 1387/2008, pp. 90–92.

Harris, Kevan. "The Rise of the Subcontractor State: Politics of Pseudo-Privatization in the Islamic Republic of Iran," *International Journal of Middle East Studies*, 45(1), 2013, pp. 45–70.

Hossein-Zadeh, Ismael. "Neoliberal Economics Come to Iran," Counter-Punch, October 17, 2014.

Keshavarzian, Arang. "Regime Loyalty and Bāzārī Representation under the Islamic Republic of Iran: Dilemmas of the Society of Islamic Coalition," *International Journal of Middle East Studies*, 41(2), May 2009, pp. 225–246.

Khajehpour, Bijan. "Domestic Political Reforms and Private Sector Activity in Iran," Iran Chamber Society, 2000. www.iranchamber.com/government/articles/political_reform_private_sector_iran.php.

Khaleji, Ali. "Tahavvol Māhiat va Kārkard Tashakkol-hāye Kārgari dar Irān pas az Enqelāb-e Eslāmi," *Motaleʿāt-e tārikhi nezāmi* (nos. 8–9), 1389/2010, pp. 99–22.

Khatami, Mohammad. *Hope and Challenge: The Iranian President Speaks*, Binghamton, NY: Institute of Global and Cultural Studies, 1997, pp. 70–86.

Kheirollahi, Alireza. *Kārgarān bi Tabagheh: Tavān-e Chānehzani Kārgarān dar Irān pas az Enqelāb* [*Workers without Class: Bargaining Power in Iran after the Revolution*], Tehran: Agah, 1398/2010.

Maljoo, Mohammad. "The Lose–Lose Game for the Iranian Workers: A Critical Evaluation of the Proposed Draft of Labor Law in Iran," University of Nairobi, working paper, August 2007, pp. 1–14.

Maljoo, Mohammad. "The Unmaking of the Iranian Working Class since the 1990s," in P. Vahabzadeh (ed.), *Iran's Struggles for Social Justice. Economics, Agency, Justice, Activism*, New York: Palgrave Macmillan, 2017, pp. 47–63.

Maljoo, Mohammad and Parviz Sedaghat. "Neoliberalism dar Iran: Afsaneh ya Vāqey'at? [Interview]," *Akhbār-e Rooz*, December 14, 2019. https://shorturl.at/ctU57.

Moghissi, Haideh and Ali Rahnema. "The Working Class and the Islamic State in Iran," in Cronin, S. (ed.), *Reformers and Revolutionaries in Modern Iran*, London: Routledge, 2004, pp. 280–302.

Morgana, M. Stella. "'Produce and Consume' in the Islamic Republic: The 1990s Myth of the Winner in the Iranian Public Sphere and Its Impact on Workers," *International Journal of Middle East Studies*, 52(2), 2020, pp. 340–344.

Moslem, Mehdi. *Factional Politics in Post-Khomeini Iran*. Syracuse, NY: Syracuse University Press, 2002.

Niknam, Azadeh. "The Islamization of Law in Iran," *Middle East Report*, 29(212), 1999, pp. 17–21.

Nomani, Farhad and Sohrab Behdad. *Class and Labor in Iran: Did the Revolution Matter?* Syracuse, NY: Syracuse University Press, 2006.

Nomani, Farhad and Sohrab Behdad. "The Rise and Fall of Iranian Classes in the Post-Revolutionary Decades," *Middle Eastern Studies*, 44(3), 2008, pp. 377–396.

Ramazani, Alireza. "Raise in Minimum Wage Not Enough for Iranian Workers," *Al-Monitor*, March 18, 2014. www.al-monitor.com/pulse/originals/2014/03/iran-wages-inflation-economy-law-protest.html.

Rouhani, Hassan. *Amniat-e Melli va Nezām-e Eqtesādi-ye Irān [National Security and the Economic System of Iran]*, Tehran: Markaz-e Tahqiqāt Estrātezhik, 1389/2010.

Saffari, Siavash. "Two Pro-Mostazafin Discourses in the 1979 Iranian Revolution," *Contemporary Islam*, 11(3), 2017, pp. 287–301.

Saghafi, Morad. "The New Landscape of Iranian Politics," Middle East Report No. 233 (Winter), 2004, pp. 16–23.

Salehi-Isfahani, Djavad. "Population, Human Capital and Economic Growth in Iran," in I. Sirageldin (ed.), *Human Capital: Population Economics in the Middle East*, Cairo: American University of Cairo Press, 2002, pp. 142–157.

Salehi-Isfahani, Djavad. "Human Resources in Iran: Potentials and Challenges," *Iranian Studies*, 38(1), 2005, pp. 117–147.

Salehi-Isfahani, Djavad. "Irani: Poverty and Inequality since the Revolution," *Brookings Institute*, January, 2009.

Salehi-Isfahani, Djavad. "Oil Wealth and Economic Growth in Iran," in Ali Gheissari (ed.), *Contemporary Iran: Economy, Society, Politics*, Oxford: Oxford University Press, 2009, pp. 3–37.

Salehi-Isfahani, Djavad. and Daniel Egel. "Youth Exclusion in Iran: The State of Education, Employment and Family Formation," Wolfensohn Center for Development and Dubai School of Government, No. 3(26), 2007.

Schirazi, Asghar. *The Constitution of Iran: Politics and the State in the Islamic Republic*, London: I. B. Tauris, 1997.

Stella, M. "Talking to Workers: From Khomeini to Ahmadinejad, How the Islamic Republic's Discourse on Labor Changed through May Day Speeches (1979–2009)," *Iranian Studies*, 52 (1–2), 2019, pp. 133–158.

Tazmini, Ghoncheh. *Khatami's Iran: The Islamic Republic and the Turbulent Path to Reform*, London: I. B. Tauris, 2009.

Valadbaygi, Kayhan. "Hybrid Neoliberalism: Capitalist Development in Contemporary Iran," *New Political Economy*, February 20, 2020.

Zubaida, Sami. *Law and Power in the Islamic World*, London: I. B. Tauris, 2003.

(2) Laws, Regulations, Agreements

ILO (International Labour Organization). *Freedom of Association and Protection of the right to organize Convention 1948 (no. 87)*. www.ilo.org/dyn/normlex/en/f?p=NORMLEXPUB:12100:0::NO::P12100_INSTRUMENT_ID:312232.

ILO (International Labour Organization). *An Employment Strategy for the Islamic Republic of Iran*. 2003. www.ilo.org/newdelhi/whatwedo/publications/WCMS_124326/lang--en/index.htm.

ILO (International Labour Organization). Labour *Law and Safety Regulations*, 2014–2018, in particular: 2018-08 (IRN-2018-R-107694) Safety in Working with Pressure Die-Casting Machines (16/5/1397); 2018-02-26 (IRN-2018-R-108520) Safety in Working with Hand Tools and Power Tools, 2018; 2016-11-14 (IRN-2016-R-108710) Regulation on Safety in Electric

Power Transmission Operations; 2015-09-07 (IRN-2015-R-108521) Regulations on Technical Protection and Safety Services Advisers, 2015; 2014-03-04 (IRN-2014-R-108585) Safety Regulations in the Casting Industry (shape and pipe castings), 2018. www.ilo.org/dyn/natlex/natlex4 .detail?p_lang=en&p_isn=21843&p_country=IRN&p_classification=01.02.

Islamic Republic of Iran. The Constitution of the Islamic Republic of Iran (1979, amended 1989). (1979/1989). English translation available at Iran Data Portal: https://irandataportal.syr.edu/wp-content/uploads/constitution-english-1368.pdf

Islamic Republic of Iran. Labor Law of 1990. (1990). Available in Persian at: https://rkj.mcls.gov.ir/fa/moghararaat/ghavanin/ghanoonkar. English translation, Iran Data Portal, https://irandataportal.syr.edu/labor-law.

Islamic Republic of Iran. First Five-Year-Development Plan. (1989). https://irandataportal.syr.edu/annual-budgets-development-plans.

Maljles. Amendments of Labor Law as approved January 27, 2003 [Bahman 7, 1381]. https://rc.majlis.ir/fa/law/%20show/122666.

Majles. Islamic Labor Councils Law. https://rc.majlis.ir/fa/law/show/91022.

12 The Effects of the Joint Comprehensive Plan of Action (JCPOA), and Subsequent US Withdrawal, on Iranian Law

Faezeh Manteghi and Seyed Emadeddin Tabatabaei

1 Introduction

On July 14, 2015, the Islamic Republic of Iran and six world powers known as the EU/E3+3 (France, the United Kingdom, Germany, plus the United States, Russia, and China) reached an agreement, the Joint Comprehensive Plan of Action (JCPOA), that limited Iran's enrichment activities and implemented enhanced monitoring of Iran's nuclear program in exchange for relief from all United Nations (UN) and European Union (EU) nuclear-related economic and financial sanctions.[1] UN Resolution 2231 was adopted, which provided for the termination of the provisions of the previous (seven) Security Council resolutions on the Iranian nuclear issue. As a result, from the JCPOA's "Implementation Day" (January 16, 2016) onward, financial transactions and a whole range of other associated service sectors were opened up for international trade. These included banking and insurance; oil, gas, and the petrochemical sector; shipping, shipbuilding, and transport sectors; gold, other precious metals, banknotes, and coinage; metals and software. Some restrictions remained in force, however, including restrictions on the transfer of sensitive goods, arms, and ballistic missiles,[2] as well as restrictive measures against certain listed persons and entities.

---

[1] EU nuclear-related economic and financial sanctions consist of implementing regulations for the member states of the EU in line with UN Security Council resolutions. It is noteworthy that EU human rights-related sanctions, apart from JCPOA, remain in place. Concerning restrictive measures directed against certain persons, entities, and bodies in view of the situation in Iran, Council Regulation (EU) No. 359/2011 of April 12, 2011, states that Decision 2011/235/CFSP provides for the freezing of funds and economic resources of certain persons and entities responsible for serious violations of human rights in Iran (listed in the Annex to the Decision). This was amended on May 22, 2023. See https://eur-lex.europa.eu/legal-content/EN/TXT/?uri=celex%3A32023R0986.

[2] In line with Annex B, Paragraph 5 of UN Security Council Resolution 2231, the five-year period of arms embargo on Iran ended in October 2020.

The JCPOA also allowed foreign subsidiaries (but not branches) of US companies to carry out activities as non-US persons. These had since 2012 been restricted by primary sanctions. US sanctions (which are imposed by Congress) were not lifted, but US president Obama was able to abrogate US sanctions for 90- and 180-day periods by executive decree. In line with his presidential campaign promise, Donald Trump, once elected US president, quickly withdrew from the JCPOA. Following Trump's announcement on May 8, 2018: (1) entities previously removed from the Specially Designated Nationals and Blocked Persons List (SDN list) (section 4.1.1, Annex II, JCPOA) were redesignated, (2) the scope of US primary sanctions changed and the exemption for overseas subsidiaries of American companies was cancelled, and (3) US departments and agencies began the process of implementing 90-day and 180-day wind-down periods for activities involving Iran that were consistent with the US sanctions relicf specified in the JCPOA. At the end of the 90-day and 180-day wind-down periods, the applicable sanctions came back into full effect in accordance with regulations of the US Department of Treasury.[3]

In this chapter, we examine the effects of the JCPOA, as well as of the US withdrawal from the JCPOA, on Iranian law. There is no question from the perspective of international law that the withdrawal of the United States from the JCPOA and the reimposition of sanctions severely undermined the rule of law in international law. The US decision weakened international law and reinforced the view of those who believe that international law is in fact not law but rather politics, and consists of recommendations and nonbinding agreements without any independently guaranteed enforcement. But this chapter addresses in particular the domestic arena of law. The position of the government of Iran is that the Trump administration's sanctions amounted to a "full-fledged economic war" and it has designated this "economic terrorism." This has led to the creation of several mechanisms, in particularly in the banking sector, to facilitate international trade in spite of revived US sanctions, and has overall increased the state's involvement in the economy. While the first part of this chapter will review the foreign investment and economic climate prior to the JCPOA, the second will provide an overview of the legal and economic consequences of the agreement. The third part will discuss the reactions of the Iranian state in terms of economic and trade policy to the US withdrawal from the JCPOA.

---

[3] The issues of secondary sanctions and extraterritoriality are explained in detail in Sections 3.1 and 3.2.

Apart from the fact that the rule of law is an integral part of liberal-democratic practices,[4] of which the Iranian system is not an example, the most important elements of the rule of law in terms of economic and business relations are security and predictability (Tamanaha 2004: 97). One goal of the JCPOA was to ensure these two elements for Iranian markets and foreign investment in Iran. But the US withdrawal from the JCPOA and the reimposition of US sanctions on Iran has increased market risk and undermined both security and predictability. The US government's so-called maximum pressure policy has contributed to a lack of normality for the Iranian economy.[5] The proliferation of sanctions is leading the Iranian government to interfere in the economy and adjust its regulatory framework, which is damaging both the security and predictability for the private sector and for foreign investment. It is notable that, as we will see in following episodes of significant reform regarding economic and financial policy, arguments referencing Islamic law played no role in any of these legal remedies, either in justifying them or in stymying their implementation.

2   The Economic and Foreign Investment Climate Prior to and Following the JCPOA

Ten years of international nuclear-related sanctions (2006–2016) slowed the performance of Iran's economy and caused a decline in foreign investments due to lack of accountability and security in Iran's markets (Mraz et al. 2016: 24). Seven UN resolutions were enacted under chapter VII of the UN Charter to address Iran's nuclear and ballistic missile programs. In 2006, UN Resolution 1696 demanded that Iran suspend all enrichment-related and reprocessing activities and urged all states to "exercise vigilance" and prohibit the transfer of any materials that could contribute to Iran's nuclear and ballistic missile programs. In the same year, UN Resolution 1737 imposed a freeze on those assets supporting or associated with Iran's proliferation of nuclear activities. A year later, UN Resolution 1747 tightened the sanctions imposed on Iran in connection with that nation's nuclear program and resolved to impose a ban on arms sales and to step up the freeze on assets already in place. In 2008, UN Resolution 1803 required Iran to stop any research and development

---

[4] Tamanaha (2004: 97) pointed out that in Hayek's notion "capitalism, liberalism, and the rule of law are tightly wrapped together" and adds that Hayek's notion cannot operate in other economic contexts.
[5] Hayek made the argument that in "normal times" a society need not be managed but should be governed – and its people largely left to their own devices – within a framework of general rules laid down in advance. See Waldron (2020).

associated with centrifuges and uranium enrichment. Then in 2010, UN Resolution 1929 imposed a fourth round of sanctions against Iran over its nuclear program to prevent Iran from rendering any international financial services – including insurance or reinsurance – and to freeze any asset that could contribute to Iran's nuclear proliferation. It also prohibited all states from new banking relationships with Iran, including the opening of any new branches of Iranian banks, joint ventures, or correspondent banking relationships on their territories. Though these resolutions were meant to address Iran's nuclear and ballistic missile programs, they increased investment risk and complicated trade with Iran. Nevertheless, the Iranian private sector could still entertain certain financial relations with partners abroad and develop its businesses, albeit with higher costs.

The initial implementation of the JCPOA and the lifting of nuclear sanctions in 2015 considerably improved the prospect for foreign investment in Iran.[6] According to a study carried out by the global consultancy firm McKinsey in June 2016, Iran could be a "one trillion-dollar growth opportunity" (McKinsey & Company 2016). The lifting of sanctions provided a boost to the country's outlook, generating some USD 250–300 billion investment opportunities within its transport infrastructure sector alone (McKinsey & Company 2016). Based on the World Bank's Ease of Doing Business Report, Iran's ranking climbed to position 120 in the world in 2017, up from 145 five years earlier (Tsui 2016). Thus, the JCPOA was an ideal opportunity for Iran to develop its economy after years of sanctions, but it did not last long enough to change the legal climate for investment significantly. Nevertheless, preexisting laws that were relevant to foreign investment became more relevant once again. For example, in 2003, under reformist president Khatami, the Islamic Republic had adopted a national twenty-year vision document outlining a comprehensive strategy toward development. The post-sanction era was a distinct opportunity for the Islamic Republic to return to this twenty-year plan and realize its developmental goals through planning, allocation of funds, and the removal of trade obstacles. However, some regulations needed changes or amendments in order to make the best use of this opportunity provided by the JCPOA. In Sections 2.1 and 2.2, we will discuss in detail the impact of the JCPOA on the Iranian legal system. Section 2.1 will lay out the legal situation as relevant to investment and business prior to the JCPOA; Section 2.2 will focus on the legal changes brought about as a consequence of the JCPOA.

---

[6] Separate sanctions have been imposed on Iran by the United States, EU, and UN respectively. UN sanctions are mentioned in No. 18 of the JCPOA, and EU sanctions in No. 19: www.europarl.europa.eu/cmsdata/122460/full-text-of-the-iran-nuclear-deal.pdf.

2.1 The Foreign Investment Climate Prior to the JCPOA

In the early 2000s, during the reformists' dominance in parliament and under Mohammad Khatami's presidency, many reforms were undertaken in Iran's general macroeconomic framework. These economic reforms were aimed at stimulating and benefiting both foreign and local investments but could not take full effect due to the international sanctions regime imposed. The most important laws and regulations concerning foreign investments and business in Iran prior to the introduction of the JCPOA fall into two main categories: Foreign investment promotion and protection, and special and free zones.

2.1.1 The 2002 Foreign Investment Promotion and Protection Act

To enhance the legal framework and the operational environment for foreign investors in Iran, the Foreign Investment Promotion and Protection Act (FIPPA)[7] was ratified by the Iranian parliament in 2002 and its Implementation Regulations approved in the same year. FIPPA replaced a 1955 law called Attraction and Protection of Foreign Investment. After economic sanctions against Iran began to take effect in 2006, however, the impact of FIPPA was limited, since Iran was considered a relatively high-risk market for foreign investment. Following FIPPA, Iranian law no longer distinguished between domestic and foreign investments in rights, protections, and facilities, and capital market transactions.[8] This was extraordinary in light of Article 81 of Iran's constitution,[9] according to which "The granting of concessions to foreigners for the formation of companies or institutions dealing with commerce, industry, agriculture, services or mineral extraction, is absolutely forbidden."[10] Some specific developments introduced by FIPPA for foreign investment included the guarantee of several noncommercial

---

[7] The official translation of this law is published by the Organization for Investment, Economic and Technical Assistance of Iran (OIETAI), Ministry of Economic Affairs and Finance (2005).

[8] According to Article 8 of FIPPA, "Foreign investments subject to this Act shall enjoy the same rights, protections and facilities available to domestic investments in a non-discriminatory manner."

[9] The government submitted the bill to parliament, which approved it and sent it to the Guardian Council. The Guardian Council objected to the bill, which contradicts Articles 44 and 45 of the constitution (the articles restrict foreign dominance on national resource). Finally, this law was approved by the Expediency Council due to the severe problems of the Iranian economy and the urgent need for foreign investment.

[10] Also note Article 82: The employment of foreign experts is forbidden, except in cases of necessity and with the approval of the Islamic Consultative Assembly.

risks, such as restrictions on currency transfers, nationalization and expropriation, government intervention, and breach of contract by the government. Foreign investments were made subject to a flat 25 percent corporate income tax, but with many possibilities for exemptions and tax holidays. Investment in agricultural projects was made 100 percent tax exempt, permanently. Investments in industry and mining were made subject to 80 percent tax exemption for four years, which were to upgrade to 100 percent for twenty years if located in less-developed regions.[11] The full consequences of the improved business climate began to unfold once nuclear program-related sanctions were lifted following the JCPOA in 2015. Iran's Foreign Investment Board reported that it approved 179 foreign direct investment (FDI) projects worth 10.640 million dollars during the year 1396 (Iranian calendar, i.e., March 21, 2017–March 20, 2018).[12] Based on data published by the World Investment Report 2018, Iran's FDI inflow was $5.01 billion in 2017, an increase of 48.8 percent compared to 2016, when it was $3.37 billion (UNCTAD 2019).

2.1.2 Special and Free Trade Zones

"Free trade and industrial zones" as well as "special economic zones" were established in Iran in the early 1990s. The purpose of these zones was to accelerate the implementation of infrastructure and development projects, enhance economic growth and progress, raise the level of investment and public income, create sound and productive employment, regulate the labor and product market, actively participate in regional and international markets, produce and export industrial and processed goods, and provide public services.[13] In short, free trade and industrial zones have been specifically set up to support economic activities and facilitate international trade relations. They help to offer attractive guarantees and protections for foreign investors. In this area

---

[11] Article 4(a) of the law stipulated that foreign investors should enjoy the same protection as domestic investors and that foreign capital be guaranteed against nationalization and expropriations – in these cases, the foreign investor may receive compensation. Nevertheless, the law created some restrictions for foreign investors and did not achieve to ensure the transparency required to guarantee investment security in the country. See Brexendorff and Ule (2004: 1–2) and also Tabatabaei (2016).

[12] Mohammad Adli, "Lovely Coward; How important is foreign investment in the Iranian economy?," Tehran Chamber of Commerce, Industries, Mines and Agriculture, http://tccim.ir/News/PrintPage.aspx?nid=62649.

[13] Article 1 of the 1993 Law on the Administration of Free Trade-Industrial Zones of the Islamic Republic of Iran, Passed on 1993-08-29 with Further Adjustments and Extensions. The law has been published (in Persian) on the official website of the Islamic Parliament Research Center of the Islamic Republic of Iran: https://rc.majlis.ir/fa/law/show/92283. The text has been translated by the authors.

too, however, the effects of sanctions severely impeded achieving the said objectives. Article 19 of the First Development Plan, passed in 1990, comprised the first law related to free zones. The article authorized the government "to establish Free Trade-Industrial Zones in border regions of Iran." Subsequently, with the 1993 Law on the Administration of Free-Trade Industrial Zones, three free trade zones were opened. The Law of Establishment of Free Trade-Industrial Zones of Abadan and Khorramshahr, Jolfa and Bandar-e Anzali, passed in 2003, added three more free trade areas. Finally, a seventh free trade zone was established in Maku with the Law of Establishing One Trade-Industrial Free Zone and Thirty-Three Special Economic Zones in 2010.

Free trade zones benefited from the privileges offered by the law. Incentives and advantages for investment in these areas include tax exemption, freedom of entry and exit of capital and profits, protection and guarantees for foreign investments, facilitated regulation on labor relations, employment, and social security, and so on. Moreover, several "special economic zones," where business and trade laws differ from those of the rest of the country, have been established. To facilitate export and import in these areas, they have been exempted from the country's customs regulations.[14] Although there are similarities between free trade zones and special economic zones, investment facilities in free trade zones are generally more expansive than in special economic zones. For example, in the free zones there is a tax exemption for fifteen years, while tax exemptions in the special economic zones are subject to national regulations. Also, the issuance of visa for foreigners in the free zones is done at the point of entry, while visas in the special economic zones are based on domestic regulations.

2.2 *New Legal Approaches Following the JCPOA*

In 2015, in anticipation of an improved economic situation following the JCPOA, the Iranian government drafted budget laws, approved by the legislature, along with a new Five-Year Development Plan. These laws were drafted on the assumption of increasing oil sales and foreign investment in the post-sanction era. Additionally, Iranian policymakers began to issue compliance regulations for the banking system and prepared the ratification of Iran's membership in international conventions on financial transactions and money-laundering prevention. The latter was necessary

---

[14] Article 5 of the Law on the Administration of Free Trade-Industrial Zones of the Islamic Republic of Iran, 1993.

for the Iranian banking sector to reintegrate with the rest of the world,[15] lest noncompliance would have hindered trade and transactions with foreign countries and prevented Iran from fully benefiting from the JCPOA.

2.2.1 Budget and Development Laws

According to the International Monetary Fund (IMF), Iran's economic conditions were improving substantially in 2016/2017.[16] Since sanctions eased after the implementation of the JCPOA, real GDP rebounded over the first half of 2016. Also, oil production and exports rebounded quickly to pre-sanction levels, helping cushion the impact of low global oil prices. In the nonoil sectors, increased activity in agriculture, automobile production, trade, and transport services led to recovery in growth. Real GDP was projected to grow by at least 4.5 percent in 2016/2017,[17] "up from a 0.5 percent average in 2013–2015."[18] This projected recovery was expected to be driven by: (1) a significant growth in the energy sector, (2) increased inflows of foreign investment, and (3) lower trade and financing costs to help the nonoil sectors contribute significantly to overall growth and job creation. The expected pick-up in economic activities was to translate into better fiscal and external balances, despite lower oil prices.[19] As the IMF concluded, "The [Iranian] government has implemented far-reaching, ambitious, reforms to support a sustained acceleration in growth."[20] Based on this perspective, the Sixth Five-Year Development Plan ("Iran Economic Monitor: Towards Reintegration"), covering the 2017–2021 period and budget law for the year 1395 (March 21, 2016–March 20, 2017), was drafted. President Rouhani also acknowledged in his speech that "Much of this year's government funding has come from the implementation of the JCPOA."[21]

A large structural reform agenda was designed to move toward an ambitious growth target under the new development plan.[22] The primary

---

[15] Global Practice for Macroeconomics and Fiscal Management Middle East and North Africa Region, "Iran Economic Monitor: Towards Reintegration," Open Knowledge Repository, World Bank, Washington, DC, 2016, p. vii: openknowledge.worldbank.org/handle/10986/25865.

[16] IMF, "Iran: Concluding Statement of an IMF Staff Visit," October 3, 2016: www.imf.org/en/News/Articles/2016/10/03/MS100316-Iran-Concluding-Statement-of-an-IMF-Staff-Visit.

[17] Ibid.

[18] See note 15.

[19] Ibid., p. 8.

[20] See note 16.

[21] Fars News Agency, "کسب و کار و بسیاری از بودجه‌های دولت در سایه اجرای برجام تأمین شده است," September 24, 2016.

[22] The Sixth Development Plan aimed for an annual growth rate of 8 percent and a reform agenda built on a gradual but sustained transformation of the economy toward a

assumptions of the 1395 Budget Law were that oil exports would rise from 1.4 million barrels per day (mbpd) at the end of 2015 to 2.25 mbpd in 2016, and that oil exports would be at an average of USD 40 per barrel in 2016.[23] These predictions proved to be broadly correct when the revenues increased to 589.6 trillion rials in the first six months of 2016 from 464.8 trillion rials in the same period of the previous year, while expenditures grew by close to 200 trillion rials during this period. As a result, the operating budget of the government increased by 17 percent in the first six months, as compared to the same period of 2015.[24]

2.2.2 Banking Regulations

The initial goal of the JCPOA in terms of economic development was to remove security barriers. The removal of international sanctions had to be met on the Iranian side by the removal of two such barriers: The first concerned restrictions on Iran's international financial transactions. This was made possible through compliance with the recommendations of the Financial Action Task Force (FATF).[25] This was the first condition for the World Bank's cooperation with Iranian banks, without which there was no possibility of international transactions. The second concerned Iran's debts to export credit agencies, including SACE of Italy, Coface of France, Hermes of Germany, and others, amounting to just under 2 billion euros. Complying with these two issues was a demonstration of Iran's goodwill and fulfillment of its commitment to provide financing for large-scale projects (Akhoundi 2019).

In the FATF list regarding the regulations of "Anti-Money Laundering" (AML) and "Combating the Financing of Terrorism" (CFT), released in 2015, Iran and North Korea were listed as dangerous countries.[26]

---

resilient, stable, productive, open, knowledge-based, and just economy. The plan envisaged the implementation of reforms of state-owned enterprises, and the financial and banking sector, and a greater emphasis on the allocation and management of oil revenues to productive investments among the main priorities of the government during the five-year period.

[23] See note 15, p. 6.
[24] Ibid.
[25] The FATF is an intergovernmental organization developing policies to combat money laundering and terrorism financing (TF). The organization maintains a blacklist of uncooperative nations, and a gray list of "monitored jurisdictions." Iran is included on the blacklist.
[26] The reason why domestic Iranian banks do not have unrestricted access to global financial markets lies in their de facto or alleged role in financing the Islamic Revolutionary Guards Corps (IRGC). By contrast, financial relations with militant movements outside Iran have rarely taken place through banking systems, as there are various alternative mechanisms for such financial relations. Both Lebanon and Iraq are fully compliant with the FATF and such transactions could not have been conducted through the banking systems for years.

After the JCPOA implementation, the blacklisting of Iran was suspended, due to Iran's engagement for ratification of related regulations. According to the IMF, the implementation of the FATF plan would bolster Iran's AML/CFT framework and facilitate the reintegration of domestic banks into the global financial system because lack of integration with the global banking system was a major impediment to foreign investment.[27] In June 2016, the FATF welcomed Iran's adoption of, and high-level political commitment to, an action plan to address its AML/CFT deficiencies, and its decision to seek technical assistance in the implementation of the action plan. The FATF urged Iran to fully address its AML/CFT deficiencies, in particular those related to TF, and it wanted to continue to engage with Iran and closely monitor its progress.[28]

Apart from these measures, the government took several steps to improve the performance of the financial and banking sectors, conducting a financial health review of the banking system. It took measures to reform the sector to support the mobilization of national savings in anticipation of the lifting of sanctions. The Central Bank of Iran (CBI) requested banks to prepare their financial statements using International Financial Reporting Standards (IFRS), which would increase transparency in the financial system.[29] Since 2016, all banks have been required by the CBI to issue their financial statements based on IFRS. In 2017, the Central Bank focused on increasing transparency and upgrading disclosure items in financial statements. The next step was the capital requirement, which involves raising the capital ratios of Iranian banks in order to fulfill the Basel II or III requirements.[30] In the most important banks of Iran, compliance departments were established for this purpose. The government also tried to enhance the supervisory role of the CBI and worked to address the linkages between government arrears, non-performing loans, and public debt to banks. Two new bills on the Central Bank and commercial banking were drafted to enhance CBI's

---

[27] See note 15, p. 8.
[28] FATF, "Public Statement," June 24, 2016: www.fatf-gafi.org/publications/high-risk-and-other-monitored-jurisdictions/documents/public-statement-june-2016.html.
[29] See note 15, p. 8.
[30] Basel II is a set of international banking regulations put forth by the Basel Committee on Bank Supervision, which leveled the international regulation field with uniform rules and guidelines. It includes rules for minimum capital requirements, a framework for regulatory review, and disclosure requirements for assessment of capital adequacy of banks. Basel III is a 2009 international regulatory accord that introduced a set of reforms designed to mitigate risk within the international banking sector by requiring banks to maintain proper leverage ratios and keep certain levels of reserve capital on hand. See, in this context, Export Development Bank of Iran, "Chabahar Port and Infrastructure Key to Increasing Exports": https://thebusinessyear.com/interview/pillar-of-support/.

mandate and strengthen banking sector governance and supervision.[31] These bills have not been enacted to date (September 2023).

3 The Effects on Iranian Law of the US Unilateral Withdrawal from the JCPOA

The US withdrawal from the JCPOA on May 8, 2018, and the subsequent reimposition of US comprehensive sanctions on Iran, have made most banking and financial transactions with Iran impossible. There are different kinds of US sanctions against Iran, comprising primary and secondary sanctions, as well as the inclusion of Iran on the SDN list.

a. Primary Sanctions: This is a domestic trade embargo which places far-reaching restrictions on transactions by individuals and entities under US jurisdiction, that is, any US citizen, permanent resident alien, entity organized under the laws of the United States, or any jurisdiction within the United States (including foreign branches), or any person in the United States (even if in the United States temporarily). The penalties could be both civil (e.g., up to $250,000 or double the transaction value and addition to the SDN list) and criminal (e.g., up to twenty years in prison).[32] It is also notable that after the US withdrawal from the JCPOA, the exemption from sanctions of overseas subsidiaries of US companies was canceled, and they are dealt with under domestic US jurisdiction again, which means they can be held subject to sanctions.

b. Secondary Sanctions: These apply to non-US individuals and entities, worldwide and irrespective of their nationality. Engaging in certain Iran-related transactions is subject to this type of restrictions, and the consequences of violating such sanctions are prohibition from accessing the US financial system and being placed on the SDN list. These types of sanctions create extraterritoriality of US sanctions in third-party jurisdictions, including on EU soil, which the EU finds unacceptable. Prohibitions include the purchase or acquisition of US dollar banknotes by the government of Iran; trade in gold or precious metals; direct or indirect sale, supply, or transfer to or from Iran of graphite, raw, or semifinished metals such as aluminum and steel, coal, and software for integrating industrial processes; significant transactions related to the purchase or sale of Iranian rials, or the maintenance of significant funds or accounts

---

[31] Ibid.
[32] OFAC Regulations for the Financial Community, p. 2, available online: www.treasury.gov/resource-center/sanctions/Documents/facbk.pdf.

outside the territory of Iran denominated in the Iranian rial. In addition, they apply to the purchase, subscription to, or facilitation of the issuance of Iranian sovereign debt; the automotive sector; port operators, and shipping and shipbuilding sectors, including the Islamic Republic of Iran Shipping Lines (IRISL), South Shipping Line Iran, or their affiliates; petroleum-related transactions with, among others, the National Iranian Oil Company (NIOC), Naftiran Intertrade Company (NICO), and National Iranian Tanker Company (NITC), including the purchase of petroleum, petroleum products, or petrochemical products from Iran. Finally, they apply to transactions by foreign financial institutions with the CBI and designated Iranian financial institutions under section 1245 of the National Defense Authorization Act (NDAA) for Fiscal Year 2012; the provision of specialized financial messaging services (such as SWIFT, which is the world's largest electronic payment messaging system) to the CBI and Iranian financial institutions described in section 104(c)(2)(E)(ii) of the Comprehensive Iran Sanctions and Divestment Act of 2010 (CISADA); the provision of underwriting services, insurance, or reinsurance; and the energy sector.

c. SDN List: Hundreds of individuals and entities are blacklisted on the US Treasury Department's Office of Foreign Assets Control's (OFAC's) list of Specially Designated and Blocked Nationals.

It must be kept in mind that from the perspective of international law, the JCPOA is an international and multilateral treaty. Only one party, the United States, withdrew from the JCPOA; therefore, the treaty is still in force for all the other signatories. Furthermore, the International Atomic Energy Agency (IAEA) has repeatedly – and based on repeated and comprehensive inspections – confirmed that Iran was implementing its nuclear-related JCPOA commitments. Therefore, from the viewpoint of international law, the US administration is not only breaching the UN Security Council's resolutions but is also infringing on other countries' legal sovereignty.

Irrespective of their illegality, the sanctions have been effective in preventing individuals and other entities from doing business with Iran. The reason is not only the US economy's dominance of the world economy but, more importantly, first, the comprehensiveness of the sanctions and, second, deliberate ambiguities in the sanctions' framework. The US sanctions aim at all dimensions of the Iranian economy comprehensively, while the UN sanctions were aimed at Iran's nuclear and ballistic missile programs. The ambiguities as well as the heavy-handed approach to enforcement of US sanctions cause foreign companies to fall in line with the US sanctions framework in anticipatory obedience (Geranmayeh and Rapnouil 1970). This means that any transaction with Iran can be interpreted broadly by the US government and the US courts, which is officially an isolated position internationally, but in fact has largely impeded transactions with Iran.

From the Iranian leadership's vantage point, a significant distinction between the past UN sanctions and the present US sanctions is that new sanctions are imposed by the United States unilaterally, while European initiatives can help Tehran to continue selling oil and provide a channel for money transfers (though this has not happened in practice) (Hoorozan 2019). Most of Iran's trade partners implement the AML regulations, which makes money transactions more difficult for Iran since the country has not yet been removed from the FATF's black list.[33] According to the FATF public statement on October 2019, Iran should fully address:

a. adequately criminalizing terrorist financing, including by removing the exemption for designated groups "attempting to end foreign occupation, colonialism and racism";
b. identifying and freezing terrorist assets in line with the relevant United Nations Security Council resolutions;
c. ensuring an adequate and enforceable customer due diligence regime;
d. clarifying that the submission of Suspicious Transactions Reports (STRs) for attempted Terrorist Financing (TF)-related transactions are covered under Iran's legal framework;
e. demonstrating how authorities are identifying and sanctioning unlicensed money/value transfer service providers;
f. ratifying and implementing the Palermo and TF Conventions and clarifying the capability to provide mutual legal assistance; and
g. ensuring that financial institutions verify that wire transfers contain complete originator and beneficiary information.[34]

In addition, on February 21, 2020, the FATF stated that, given Iran's failure to enact the Palermo and TF Conventions in line with the FATF Standards, the FATF fully lifts the suspension of countermeasures and urges all jurisdictions to apply effective countermeasures, in line with

---

[33] FATF describes itself as a "global money laundering and terrorist financing watchdog. The intergovernmental body sets international standards that aim to prevent these illegal activities and the harm they cause to society. As a policymaking body, the FATF works to generate the necessary political will to bring about national legislative and regulatory reforms in these areas." For more information see: www.fatf-gafi.org.
[34] www.fatf-gafi.org/en/publications/High-risk-and-other-monitored-jurisdictions/Call-for-action-october-2022.html

Recommendation 19, which states that countries should be able to apply appropriate countermeasures when called upon to do so by the FATF.[35] This means "Iran will remain on the FATF statement on High Risk Jurisdictions Subject to a Call for Action until the full Action Plan has been completed."[36] According to the FATF,

> if Iran ratifies the Palermo and Terrorist Financing Conventions, in line with the FATF standards, the FATF will decide on next steps, including whether to suspend countermeasures. Until Iran implements the measures required to address the deficiencies identified with respect to countering terrorism-financing in the Action Plan, the FATF will remain concerned with the terrorist financing risk emanating from Iran and the threat this poses to the international financial system.[37]

Until September 2023, Iran had not taken any new action in this regard.

3.1 Increased State Intervention in the Economy

In the remainder of this chapter, we will demonstrate how Iranian laws and regulation changed after the US withdrawal from the JCPOA. The Iranian state has characterized the new US sanctions as amounting to "economic warfare by the Trump administration" and significantly increased state intervention in the economy. Meanwhile, the Islamic Republic is trying to identify some remedies to reduce the effects of the reimposition of sanctions. These remedies are mainly targeted toward making trade with other countries possible again. The most important of these is a mechanism called the Instrument in Support of Trade Exchanges (INSTEX), though there are also other mechanism and alternatives to achieving the said goal. Moreover, by changing its laws, Iran is trying to return to the situation it was in prior to the imposition of sanctions.

To attract investment, for example, Iran has set up more facilities and has modified its own budgetary rules. To counter what the Iranian governments terms "economic war" or "economic terrorism" (terms that underpin Iran's international law claims), the Iranian government, using market control policies, is working to improve its economic situation or at least prevent its further deterioration. This means that the state is intervening in the economy by imposing many regulations, such as restrictions on imports and exports and the pricing of goods.

---

[35] See www.fatf-gafi.org/countries/d-i/iran/documents/call-for-action-february-2020.html.
[36] Ibid.
[37] Ibid.

3.1.1 Import Substitution

To control the foreign currencies in the country, Iran, in July 2018, imposed an import ban on 1,339 products, which are to be produced domestically instead.[38] This list has since been amended. President Rouhani considered the government decision to ban imports, aimed at supporting and protecting Iranian goods, as a great opportunity for domestic producers to develop and boost domestic production.[39]

3.1.2 Setting the Exchange Rate

An important effect of the US withdrawal from JCPOA on Iran's economy has been exchange rate fluctuations. Hence, one of the main attempts to decrease the pressure on Iran's economy is a reform of its exchange rate system. The value of the rial has fallen dramatically since 2018 as the United States ramped up pressure before ultimately imposing additional sanctions that went into effect in November 2018 (see Figure 12.1). The Islamic Republic has long contended with sanctions that have eroded the rial's value. It has struggled to try to maintain the currency's value as it manages multiple exchange rates, including the fixed rate for essential imports, and official and black-market rates.[40]

The Iranian government has been reluctant to let its currency devalue and maintained the official exchange rate at 42,000 rials per USD since mid-2018. As supplies of foreign exchange in the banking system dried up, Iranians increasingly turned to an unregulated black market to pay for everything from imported cars to overseas college fees. To tame the black market, in April 2018 the government introduced a currency-trading platform for local businesses known as NIMA, where exporters could sell their foreign currency earnings to importers at a market-determined rate, which was lower than the black-market rate but higher than the official rate.[41] The plan succeeded in bolstering the rial on the unregulated market. In 2019, it appreciated more than 30 percent, aligning the unregulated with the NIMA rate (Wallace 2019). While NIMA initially

---

[38] See www.s-ge.com/en/article/news/20183-import-ban-iran.
[39] See www.president.ir/fa/104974.
[40] Starfor, "Why Iran's Government Will Bear the Weight of U.S. Sanctions," November 21, 2018:https://worldview.stratfor.com/article/why-irans-government-will-bear-weight-us-sanctions#/entry/jsconnect?client_id=633726972&target=%2Fdiscussion%2Fembed%3Fc%3D1565868975341%26vanilla_category_id%3D1%26vanilla_identifier%3D292748%26vanilla_url%3Dhttps%253A%252F%252Fworldview.stratfor.com%252Farticle%252Fwhy-irans-government-will-bear-weight-us-sanctions.
[41] NIMA is an abbreviation for the "integrated foreign exchange trading system." The NIMA exchange rate is determined by the supply and demand of foreign currency on the NIMA platform, where Iranian exporters can sell their foreign currency earnings for Iranian rials (www.al-monitor.com/originals/2021/10/irans-plan-get-rid-subsidized-exchange-rate).

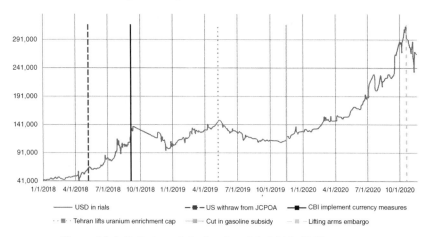

Figure 12.1 Inflation of the Iranian rial, 2018–2020
Source: TGJU – Financial Markets Network: www.tgju.org.

helped stabilize the rial and reduce inflation in late 2018 and 2019, over time it faced political interference and manipulation by various actors who sought to influence exchange rate movements. As a result, NIMA ultimately failed to ensure fair and efficient allocation of foreign currency and created new distortions, inefficiencies, and uncertainties in the foreign exchange market. Inflation has remained high, with annual inflation rates between 30 and 40 percent in 2020–2023 (inflation rates in Iran, worlddata.info). In early 2022, parliament decided to remove NIMA from the 2022 budget and replace it with a new foreign exchange system, the Integrated Foreign Exchange Market (IFEM). The IFEM is supposed to be more transparent and competitive than NIMA, partly by involving more participants, including banks, exchange bureaus, and non-oil exporters and importers. It is also supposed to be aligned with other macroeconomic policies and reforms that could enhance its performance and credibility. However, at the time of writing, the details and implementation of the IFEM are still under development.

3.1.3 Increasing Tax and Cutting Energy Subsidies

As a result of the reimposition of sanctions, the Iranian government was faced with a sharp decline in oil exports and needed to reduce its reliance on the oil sector. Increasing taxes and cutting energy subsidies have been the government's solutions, designed to cushion the effects of sanctions (Table 12.1). The revenue from oil sales in the budget bill for the 1399 Iranian fiscal year (March 21, 2020–March 20, 2021) decreased to 48,000 billion toman (one toman equals ten rials) compared to the

The Effects of the JCPOA on Iranian Law 373

Table 12.1 *State intervention, the Joint Comprehensive Plan of Action (JCPOA), and sanctions*

Decreased State Intervention in the Economy as an Effect of the JCPOA on Iranian Law	Increased State Intervention in the Economy after Reimposition of Sanctions

1. Making existing liberalizing laws effective:
  a. FIPPA
  b. Special and Free Zone Acts
2. Moving forward to the international standards
  a. Engagement to implement the FATF plan
  b. Fulfill the Basel II and III Banking requirements
3. Expansionary fiscal policy
	1. New controlling regulations
	  a. Import substitution
	  b. Setting the currency exchange rate
	2. Resistance to international standards
	  a. Suspending the implementation of FATF
	  b. Keeping banking information hidden against the sanctions
	3. Contractionary fiscal policy
	  a. Increasing tax and cutting energy subsidies

revenue from oil sales in the previous year of 153 billion toman. Under the budget bill for the 1399 Iranian fiscal year, taxes were raised by 23 percent (March 21, 2020–March 20, 2021).[42] In fact, the government estimates that in fiscal year 1402 about 261 trillion tomans, or nearly 54 percent of total revenue, will be obtained from tax revenues.[43]

3.2 Legal Reactions to Decrease the Effects of Sanctions

To reduce the pressures of sanctions, Iranian authorities have introduced several legal remedies, including alternative financial mechanisms, efforts to ratify FATF regulations, and new incentives for foreign investment.

3.2.1 Alternative Financial Mechanisms

One significant option for Iran is trading with companies untouched by or indifferent to the US sanctions because they do not have any transactions with the United States. Among these was Zhuhai Zhenrong Company from China, which accounted for more than 60 percent of China's trade with Iran (He 2019) until in July 2019, the United States imposed sanctions on it.

Besides small businesses which are not exposed to US sanctions, there have been some alternative trade facilitation mechanisms, both on governmental and private levels. These mechanisms consist of the following forms:

---

[42] See Budget Law Bill for the Year 1399 and its appendixes: www.mporg.ir/Portal/View/Page.aspx?PageId=37cd6f7f-f233-4584-9c0c-fbd09ccfb3ba.
[43] https://donya-e-eqtesad.com/بخش-بانک-بیمه-16/3602537-غلظت-نفت-در-بودجه.

First, the INSTEX was created. INSTEX, which was independent of the SWIFT system, was designed to make it possible for Iran to have direct access to foreign exchange resources derived from exports. Instead of transferring earnings of exports to Iran, the funds would remain in Europe to finance Iran's import needs from Europe. The corresponding vehicle to INSTEX in Iran was the Special Trade and Finance Institute (STFI). A European company indebted to Iran paid its debt to INSTEX, and the company, on behalf of Iran, transferred the money in the form of a transfer or credit allocations to companies that export goods to Iran. The fact is that neither the Islamic Republic nor the EU wanted the JCPOA to become ineffective, and INSTEX seemed to be a mechanism to facilitate trade without violating US sanctions. The Islamic Republic cooperated with the EU's attempt to implement INSTEX, although it was never fully satisfied with the EU's attempt to do so. The initial scope of INSTEX was confined to humanitarian goods (such as medicine, medical devices, and food) which were never directly targeted by US sanctions. Finally, on March 31, 2020, and only after the World Health Organization (WHO) made the assessment that COVID-19 could be characterized as a pandemic,[44] France, Germany, and the United Kingdom confirmed that INSTEX had successfully concluded its first transaction, facilitating the export of medical goods from Europe to Iran: "These goods are now in Iran. INSTEX aims to provide a sustainable, long-term solution for legitimate trade between Europe and Iran as part of the continued efforts to preserve the JCPOA. [...] INSTEX and its Iranian counterpart STFI will work on more transactions and on enhancing the mechanism."[45] Ultimately, by March 2023, European countries announced their decision to dissolve INSTEX, through which only that single transaction had been made.[46]

Second, an additional method to facilitate trade relations is to design the trade settlement system using a local or common currency unit. This currency unit consists of a basket of international currencies similar to special drawing rights (SDR) to conduct barter transactions.[47] Calculating the currency unit value is based on international currency,

---

[44] On March 11, 2020: www.who.int/news-room/detail/27-04-2020-who-timeline---covid-19.
[45] See www.auswaertiges-amt.de/en/newsroom/news/instex-transaction/2329744.
[46] On March 9, 2023: apnews.com/article/europe-iran-trade-system-nuclear-deal-e250566e291e5aa4a70515c5414ac510.
[47] According to the IMF website, the SDR is an interest-bearing international reserve asset created by the IMF in 1969 to supplement other reserve assets of member countries. It is not a currency, nor a claim on the IMF, but is potentially a claim on freely usable currencies of IMF members: www.imf.org/external/np/exr/faq/sdrallocfaqs.htm.

such as the US dollar or the euro. The Asian Clearing Union (ACU) is one of these types of unions (Kiani-Rad et al. 2017: 147).

Third, Iran has championed the instrument of bilateral monetary treaties with currency swap agreements (Kiani-Rad et al. 2017: 147). A currency swap agreement between states can lessen the US dollar's influence on global energy and other markets. For instance, the currency swap between Iran and Turkey entered into force in April 2018, with the opening of the first letter of credit by Bank Melli Iran.[48] Negotiations on monetary treaties with Turkey, Russia, China, the Republic of Azerbaijan, India, and some other countries are underway.[49] In December 2018, India and Iran agreed to revive their 2012 rupee–rial payment mechanism to receive payments in Indian rupee, where half of the payments would be used to import products from India. The said transaction is supervised by the major state-run United Commercial Bank (UCO Bank) of India, and the National Iran Company has been exempted from "withholding tax," which is imposed on the profit of a foreign company in India. Further, Iranian banks such as Pasargad and Parsian were given permission to open branches in Mumbai to back transactions between India and Iran (Sagar and Pednekar 2019). As of 2023, Iran is still considering an alternative banking mechanism to promote trade with India.[50]

Fourth, barter trade is an efficient way to do business in Iran. It is trading in which goods or services are exchanged without the use of cash. For example, negotiations for exporting Iran's oil to Russia began in 2014, in which Russia would buy Iranian oil in exchange for Russian equipment and supplies.

Fifth, another option to evade US sanctions is cryptocurrencies (Tassev 2018). The Iranian government's Economic Commission (one of the eight permanent commissions in the president's cabinet) approved a regulation regarding cryptocurrency mining in the country on July 22, 2019.[51] According to Iran's minister of information and communications, Said Azari Jahromi, "Cyber Currencies are effective in bypassing sanctions when it comes to small transactions, but not as mega-transactions are concerned; they can hardly go around international transactions."[52]

---

[48] Central Bank of the Islamic Republic of Iran, "Iran–Turkey Currency Swap Entered into Force, with the Opening of the First Letter of Credit by Bank Melli Iran": www.cbi.ir/showitem/17705.aspx.
[49] Mehr News Agency, "Talks Underway for Signing Bilateral Monetary Treaties: Iran's Zarif," June 23, 2019: english.almanar.com.lb/765547.
[50] www.thehindubusinessline.com/news/iran-is-exploring-an-alternative-banking-mechanism-to-promote-trade-with-india/article65511630.ece.
[51] ISNA News Agency, "مصوبه جدید برای بیت‌کوین ابلاغ می‌شود," July 12, 2019.
[52] Mohammad-Javad Azari Jahromi, Iran's minister for information and communications technology, on the Radio Tehran Channel, July 14, 2019.

Finally, those countries benefiting from trade with Iran may negotiate with the United States for sanction waivers. For example, South Korea's Deputy Foreign Minister for Economic Affairs Yoon Kang-Hyun and other leaders met with US State Department officials in March 2019 to discuss the waiver issued in November to keep buying Iranian oil in exchange.[53] Also, some companies asked for the US Office of Foreign Asset Control (OFAC) permission regarding specific deals with Iran. For example, Aerei da Trasporto Regionale, better known as Franco-Italian plane maker ATR, has been granted permission to supply parts to Iran by OFAC.[54] According to reports in *Air Transport World*, OFAC has given ATR permission to supply spares to Iran (Dron 2019).

It is notable that the strategic Chabahar port project, being developed by India in Iran, is an exception and was impacted neither by former US president Donald Trump's decision not to renew exemptions that let eight countries, including India, buy Iranian oil without facing tough American sanctions, nor by the administration of President Joe Biden.[55]

3.2.2 Attempt to Ratify the Financial Actions Task Force

President Rouhani's administration proposed four bills to the Iranian parliament for approval to fulfill the FATF requirements, while Iranian anti-JCPOA hardliners opposed passing legislation toward compliance with the FATF,[56] arguing it could disclose sensitive security information and would run against the country's interests.[57] Iran's parliament finally passed the AML bills, two of four amendments Iran needs to implement to meet FATF requirements. The Guardian Council, as a

---

[53] Reuters, "South Korean Officials to Press for Iran Sanctions Waiver in United States," March 25, 2019: www.reuters.com/article/us-iran-nuclear-usa-southkorea/south-korean-officials-to-press-for-iran-sanctions-waiver-in-united-states-idUSKCN1R61Z0. Fars News Agency, "Lawmaker: Linking INSTEX to FATF New Plot to Pressure Iran," February 3, 2019: www.farsnews.ir/en/news/13971114001032/Lawmaker-Linking-INSTEX-FATF-New-Pl-Pressre-Iran.

[54] The permission was granted back in April 2019 but has been kept pretty quiet since then. It began to be reported by the world's media in August 2019.

[55] "US Says Chabahar Project Won't Be Impacted By Iran Sanctions," *The Economic Times*, April 24, 2019: //economictimes.indiatimes.com/articleshow/69019491.cms?from=mdr&utm_source=contentofinterest&utm_medium=text&utm_campaign=cppst.

[56] In particular the political group Front for the Stability of the Islamic Revolution (Jebheh-ye pāydārī-e enqelāb-e eslāmī), which consists partly of former ministers of President Ahmadinejad. Although this could convince the wide range of principalists (*osul-garāyān* or conservatives) against the FATF regulations, it is noteworthy that the principalists have the majority in the Expediency Council.

[57] Fars News Agency, "FATF Extends Iran's Suspension for 4 More Months to Enforce Recommendations," October 18, 2019: www.farsnews.ir/en/news/13980726000477/FATF-Exends-Iran39-s-Sspensin-fr-4-Mre-Mnhs-Enfrce-Recmmendains.

vetting supervisory body, rejected them.[58] Parliament insisted on its version of the bill and sent it to the Expediency Council for a final decision.[59] But the Expediency Council, dominated by hardliners, was in no hurry to approve these two bills. The legal moratorium ended, and the bills did not pass. As a result, the suspension of Iran's inclusion on the black list has been lifted, and Iran is included on the list once again. This means that, as a result of enhanced due diligence and probable countermeasures in the most serious cases, banking activities have become even more restricted, which is particularly damaging to the private sector.

3.2.3 New Incentives for Foreign Investment

In May 2019, President Rouhani ordered executive bodies to undertake immediate steps to remove obstacles to domestic and foreign investment in the country. The decisions came as the United States introduced the harshest sanctions against Iran yet, in line with the Trump administration's "maximum pressure" policy, a policy that Trump advisors hoped will strangle the Islamic Republic.[60] In reaction, a bylaw was passed by the Supreme Council of Economic Coordination to provide incentives to foreign investors and secure foreign revenues for the national economy.[61] These incentives include guaranteed five-year residency permits for those who invest at least 250,000 euros (or equivalent in other currencies), accepted by the CBI. The targets of this investment opportunity are Iran's neighboring countries suffering from instability. The new law authorizes foreign investment to take shape in the form of opening

---

[58] The Guardian Council argued that the bills violate paragraph 2 of Article 110 of the Iranian constitution, which states supervising the proper implementation of the general policies of the system is the authority and responsibility of the Supreme Leader. The Guardian Council has also argued that in accordance with paragraph 2 of Article 158, the AML Bill should have been referred to parliament by the judiciary, not the government.

[59] The Iranian parliament is a unicameral legislative body whose 290 members are publicly elected every four years. It drafts legislation, ratifies international treaties, and approves the country's budget. The Guardian Council examines all laws passed by parliament to determine their compliance with the constitution and Islamic law. The Expediency Discernment Council is an assembly appointed by the Supreme Leader and was created to resolve conflicts between the parliament and the Guardian Council. It means this council can make a final decision in those cases where the legislative drafts of the parliament are not approved by the Guardian Council, and the members of parliament decide to pass the draft legislation on to the Expediency Council.

[60] "Rouhani Orders Facilitating Investment," *Tehran Times*, May 20, 2019, www.tehrantimes.com/news/436151/Rouhani-orders-facilitating-investment.

[61] The Supreme Council of Economic Coordination of Iran's three branches of power formed in June 2018 based on the Supreme Leader's order to decide on economic matters. The council has enabled the government to have all the necessary powers to prevent the direct impact of US economic sanctions on the nation's economy and livelihoods.

accounts in Iranian banks, and buying investment bonds and securities, as well as investment in the housing sector. Moreover, in June 2019 Rouhani ordered the interior minister to arrange exemptions to visa-stamping and not to mark passports of foreign nationals visiting the country.[62] The decision is deemed to facilitate travel to the country without fear of possible US penalties; Washington announced that travelers who visited certain countries, including Iran, would face restrictions entering the United States.[63]

3.2.4 Strict Criminal Policy against Economic Crimes

The Iranian currency sharply devalued after the US withdrawal from the JCPOA and the reimposition of economic sanctions. The CBI stated that the price increases in the foreign exchange and gold markets were mostly due to concerted efforts by enemy countries to exacerbate Iran's economic problems and cause public anxiety. In August 2018, special anti-corruption courts were established to take "fast and just" legal action against "those who are guilty of corrupt economic practices."[64] The courts sentenced dozens of people to up to twenty years in prison for paying bribes, embezzlement, and damaging the economy. An "Economic Security Police" was established in several Iranian provinces in April 2019, with the aim of tackling economic crimes, including the smuggling of fuel and livestock, and combatting hoarding.

4   Conclusion

Despite the many encouraging results Iran had experienced in various economic fields after the initial removal of UN and EU sanctions under the JCPOA in 2015, the subsequent reimposition and expansion of US sanctions in 2018 have badly hit Iran's economy on a large scale (compare Figures 12.1 and 12.2). The decline in Iran's economy is a result, however, of sanctions, along with internal corruption and mismanagement. According to the economic indicators released by the IMF and the World Bank, 2019 was one of the worst years for Iran's economy since 1984.[65] In its "Overview" of the Islamic Republic of

---

[62] "No More Passport Stamps for Foreign Nationals Visiting Iran," *Tehran Times*, June 24, 2019: www.tehrantimes.com/news/437345/No-more-passport-stamps-for-foreign-nationals-visiting-Iran.

[63] www.cbp.gov/travel/international-visitors/visa-waiver-program.

[64] www.leader.ir/fa/content/21858/نامه-رئیس-قوه-قضائیه-به-رهبر-انقلاب-برای-اقدامات-ویژه-در-برخورد-با-اخلالگران-اقتصادی.

[65] See www.dw.com/en/irans-economy-plummets-under-weight-of-sanctions/a-50950471.

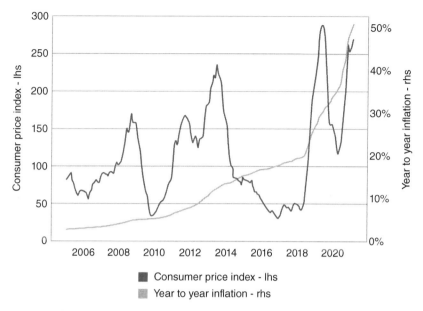

Figure 12.2 Development of consumer price index in Iran, 2005–2021

Iran, updated on October 1, 2020, the World Bank stated that "high inflation, increased gasoline prices in 2019, economic slowdown, and the economic shock caused by COVID-19 have given rise to concerns about household welfare and poverty."[66] Nevertheless, Iran's economy has not collapsed despite the expectations and goals of the "maximum pressure" policy. Well-integrated economic relations with regional partners, steering away from sole reliance on oil, and increasing diversification of the economy are some of the characteristics that have empowered the Iranian economy to resist the US policy of "maximum pressure."[67]

The rial stabilized in November 2019 after losing more than half its value. According to the president of the Central Bank (October 2019), the national currency strengthened by 21 percent compared to October of the previous year.[68] Iran managed to export a million barrels of oil a day

---

[66] See www.worldbank.org/en/country/iran/overview.
[67] See www.npr.org/2020/01/16/796781021/why-irans-economy-has-not-collapsed-amid-u-s-sanctions-and-maximum-pressure?t=1580069324746&t=1580093891565.
[68] See www.mehrnews.com/news/4762991/http://www.mehrnews.com/news/4947930/ افزایش ۲۱ درصدی قدرت پول ملی در یکسال اخیر, accessed June 21, 2021.

despite the US effort to drive Iranian crude oil off world markets.[69] It has also improved in some other respects. A foremost example is the total market capitalization of Iran's four bourses (Tehran Stock Exchange,[70] Iran Fara Bourse, Iran Mercantile Exchange, and Iran Energy Exchange), which reached 12,282 trillion rials ($102.3 billion) during June 2019 – up 106.5 percent compared to the corresponding period in the previous fiscal year.[71] According to the minister of economic affairs and finance, nonoil exports rose 20 percent in the first ten months of the Persian year 1398 (March 21, 2019–January 21, 2020).[72] Exports to the members of the Eurasian Economic Union (EAEU) rose by $783 million in the first nine months (March 21–December 22, 2019), a 116 percent increase in weight and a 72 percent increase in value.[73] FDI in the same period increased 32 percent compared to the previous year.[74]

In 2021, the ultra-conservative Ebrahim Raisi was elected president; he has adopted a more confrontational stance toward the West and rejected direct negotiations with the United States on the nuclear deal. This has had detrimental consequences for the Iranian economy, including escalating inflation and the devaluation of the Iranian rial, partly due to the mismanagement of the new government. European countries have been trying to save the JCPOA. Unfortunately, their attempts to use various financial mechanisms (such as INSTEX) as a means to facilitate trade with Iran have proven unsuccessful. The breakdown of the nuclear deal has coincided with a remarkable shift in Iran's foreign policy toward non-Western powers, especially Russia, China, and India. In line with this strategic reorientation, Iran has joined the Shanghai Cooperation Organization (SCO), engaged in the BRICS (Brazil, Russia, India, China, and South Africa) group, and held de-escalation talks with Saudi Arabia, with China acting as a mediator.

Looking ahead, the Islamic Republic faces two possible future scenarios:

(1) If the JCPOA were revived and becomes effective, or if other agreements between Iran and the United States that could de-escalate

---

[69] See http://intellinews.com/iran-exporting-million-barrels-of-oil-a-day-tracking-firm-data-indicates-175930/.
[70] See www.mql5.com/en/charts/11859578/6-w1-mofid-securities-co.
[71] "Iran Capital Market Worth $102 Billion," *Financial Tribune*, July 21, 2019: https://financialtribune.com/articles/business-and-markets/99045/iran-capital-market-worth-102-billion.
[72] See www.tasnimnews.com/fa/news/1398/11/02/2187523/رشد-32-درصدی-سرمایه-گذاری-خارجی-در-کشور-با-وجود-تحریم-های-آمریکا.
[73] See https://donya-e-eqtesad.com/بخش-سایت-خوان-62/3617166-رشد-چشمگیر-صادرات-به-اوراسیا.
[74] See www.tasnimnews.com/fa/news/1398/11/02/2187523/رشد-32-درصدی-سرمایه-گذاری-خارجی-در-کشور-با-وجود-تحریم-های-آمریکا.

Iran–Western animosities and provide security and predictability for businesses, this would have profound repercussions for the Iranian economy and the rule of law foundations in the realm of commercial law. The latter would be strengthened by improving legal certainty, ensuring that government in its actions is bound by predetermined rules. The long-term impact of such commercial arrangements might have a liberalizing effect on the political system because of the strengthening of contract and property rights in light of greater foreign investment and the growth of the private sector. However, this scenario needs to be viewed in light of the fact also that the Islamic Republic has laid out five steps to reduce and eventually suspend all of its obligations under the JCPOA,[75] claiming that these steps are not intended to harm the JCPOA but to create a balance in commitments.[76] The fact that the IAEA inspectors still have access to most of Iran's nuclear facilities, despite occasional conflicts with the Atomic Energy Organization of Iran, is a major reason why the other signatories have remained in the JCPOA.[77] The resolutions by the IAEA Board of Governors in recent years also did not formally

---

[75] On the anniversary of the US withdrawal, Iran gave the remaining signatories sixty days to protect Iran from US sanctions. After this period, Iran began enriching uranium above a concentration of 3.67 percent and continued to reduce its commitment under the JCPOA every sixty days. See BBC News, "Iran Nuclear Deal: Government Announces Enrichment Breach," July 7, 2019: www.bbc.com/news/world-middle-east-48899243.

These five steps were as follows: (1) beginning to enrich uranium to purity rates beyond the JCPOA limit of 3.76 percent; (2) increasing enriched uranium stockpile to beyond the 300 kilograms set by the JCPOA; (3) starting up advanced centrifuges to boost the country's stockpile of enriched uranium and activating twenty IR-4 and twenty IR-6 centrifuges for research and development purposes; (4) beginning to inject gas into centrifuges at the Fordow Plant; (5) no longer considering itself bound to restrict the overall number of centrifuges. For more information see: Arms Control Association, "Timeline of Nuclear Diplomacy with Iran": www.armscontrol.org/factsheets/Timeline-of-Nuclear-Diplomacy-With-Iran.

According to the Associated Press on November 11, 2020, "the International Atomic Energy Agency (IAEA) reported in a confidential document distributed to member countries [...] that Iran as of Nov. 2 had a stockpile of 2,442.9 kilograms (5,385.7 pounds) of low-enriched uranium, up from 2,105.4 kilograms (4,641.6 pounds) reported on Aug. 25": https://apnews.com/article/europe-iran-united-nations-de8772e3b88bdcbacbe98d1062d25c15.

[76] The Congressional Research Service, as a public policy research institute of the United States Congress, confirmed this in "Iran's Nuclear Program: Tehran's Compliance with International Obligations," Updated April 12, 2023: https://fas.org/sgp/crs/nuke/R40094.pdf. The report notes the IAEA Board of Governors resolution of November 2022 does not contain a formal finding of noncompliance but states that "'it is essential and urgent' that Iran take 'without delay' several actions to resolve the outstanding safeguards matters," p. 16

[77] Associated Press on November 11, 2020: https://apnews.com/article/europe-iran-united-nations-de8772e3b88bdcbacbe98d1062d25c15.

stipulate non-compliance.[78] However, this puts pressure on other signatories of the JCPOA to deliver on their obligations and to keep the deal alive. While President Biden's appointment of a new Iran envoy signaled efforts toward de-escalation between Iran and the United States,[79] the assassination of Iranian senior nuclear scientist Mohsen Fakhrizadeh in November 2020, following the earlier assassination of Major General Qasem Soleimani in January of that year, created significant new obstacles against a return to the negotiation table.[80] The August 2023 prisoner swap bodes well for future de-escalatory measures, as the West is also keen to dissuade Iran from continuing supplying Russia with armed drones.[81]

(2) If US economic sanctions remain in place or are further tightened, state involvement in the economy will increase. The Islamic Republic, which interprets the sanctions regimes as economic warfare, is likely to adopt domestic laws and regulations supporting increased state involvement, such as more control over currency assets, exchange rate fixing, more import restrictions and export obligations, and higher taxes, which enable a greater scope for corruption and economic crimes. Time has shown that neither INSTEX nor the recently established Swiss Humanitarian Trade Arrangement (SHTA) were sufficiently effective to be an alternative for the supply of humanitarian medicines during the COVID-19 pandemic: "The payment channel for the delivery of humanitarian goods and pharmaceuticals to Iran could only be launched with the agreement of the US."[82] Instead, "rather than easing sanctions to help Iran manage the pandemic better, if only to stop the spread of the virus in the region, the U.S. piled on more sanctions, and chose to ignore calls from world leaders,[83] former U.S. diplomats, and the United Nations to ease

---

[78] IAEA, "NPT Safeguards Agreement with the Islamic Republic of Iran: Resolution adopted by the Board of Governors," June 19, 2020: www.iaea.org/sites/default/files/20/06/gov2020-34.pdf. Note though that the IAEA Board of Governors report of February 2023 states that Iran's reduced implementation of its nuclear-related commitments under the JCPOA since May 8, 2019 "has seriously affected the Agency's verification and monitoring in relation to the JCPOA" (GOV 2023/8).

[79] Joe Biden, in a commentary published in CNN on September 13, 2020, said: "I will offer Tehran a credible path back to diplomacy. If Iran returns to strict compliance with the nuclear deal, the United States would rejoin the agreement as a starting point for follow-on negotiations": https://edition.cnn.com/2020/09/13/opinions/smarter-way-to-be-tough-on-iran-joe-biden/index.html.

[80] See www.aljazeera.com/news/2020/11/28/iranian-nuclear-physicist-kiiling-world-reaction.

[81] www.ft.com/content/12a725cb-ee9a-469a-b20e-a0c3556e7056

[82] As a Swiss diplomat explained to swissinfo: www.swissinfo.ch/eng/switzerland-expands-trade-relations-with-iran/46160178.

[83] See www.rollcall.com/2020/04/09/calls-grow-for-trump-to-relax-humanitarian-sanctions-on-iran/.

sanctions."[84] All this pushed Iran's economic relations eastwards, of which the process of negotiating a twenty-five-year strategic agreement between Iran and China is an example.[85]

Bibliography

(1)   General Literature

Akhoundi, Abbas. "JCPOA and Current Situation," June 2019, www.abbasakhoundi.ir/archive/ID/1341/برجام-و-موقعیت-کنونی, accessed August 31, 2019.

Brexendorff, Alexander and Christian Ule, "Changes Bring New Attention to Iranian Buyback Contracts," *Oil & Gas Journal*, November 1, 2004, pp. 1–2.

Dron, Alan. "US Agrees to Lift Sanctions for Iran Air ATR Spares," *Air Transport World*, August 13, 2019: https://atwonline.com/government-affairs/us-agrees-lift-sanctions-iran-air-atr-spares accessed September 9, 2023.

Geranmayeh, Ellie and Manuel Lafont Rapnouil. "Meeting the Challenge of Secondary Sanctions," ECFR.EU, June 25, 1970: www.ecfr.eu/publications/summary/meeting_the_challenge_of_secondary_sanctions accessed September 9, 2023.

He, Laura. "US Sanctions Chinese Company for Buying Iranian Oil: Beijing Slams 'Bullying' Behavior," CNN, July 23, 2019: edition.cnn.com/2019/07/23/business/zhuhai-zhenrong-company/index.html accessed September 9, 2023.

Hoorozan. "Making Sense of Iran's Economy Once All US Sanctions Resume," Atlantic Council, September 25, 2018: www.atlanticcouncil.org/blogs/iransource/making-sense-of-iran-s-economy-once-us-sanctions-resume accessed September 9, 2023.

Kiani-Rad, Minoo, Reza Tehrani, Akbar Komijani, Mohammad Javad Iravani. "Investigating the Effect of Monetary Treaty on Trade between Iran and Major Trading Partners," *Journal of Money and Economy* 12 (2), Spring 2017.

McKinsey & Company. "Iran: The $1 Trillion Growth Opportunity?" June 2016, McKinsey Global Institute. www.markteintritt.ir/wp-content/uploads/Iran_Report.pdf, last visited: 5 December 2019.

Mraz, Stanislav, Ludmila Lipkova, and Katarina Brockova. (2016). Economic Sanctions against Iran and Their Effectiveness. *Actual Problems of Economics* 182 (2) (January 1), pp. 22–28.

Sagar, Faraz Alam and Samiksha Pednekar. "India: US Sanctions on Iran and their Impact on India," Mondaq, August 8, 2019, www.mondaq.com/india/x/834158/Export+controls+Trade+Investment+Sanctions/US+Sanctions+On+Iran+And+Their+Impact+On+India

---

[84] Seewww.brookings.edu/opinions/iran-the-double-jeopardy-of-sanctions-and-covid-19/.

[85] See Deutsche Welle, "Without the West, Iran looks to China" August 1, 2020: www.dw.com/en/iran-china-25-year-deal/a-54403582.

Tabatabaei, Seyed Hossein. "Analyse comparative des contrats pétroliers iraniens et des contrats de partage de production," Thesis, June 20, 2016, École Doctorale Droit et Sciences Politiques, Économiques et de Gestion (Nice), Université Nice Sophia Antipolis.

Tamanaha, Brian Z. *On Rule of Law: History, Politics, Theory.* Cambridge: Cambridge University Press, 2004.

Tassev, Lubomir. "Iran Considers Using Cryptocurrencies to Evade US Sanctions." *Bitcoin News*, July 17, 2018, news.bitcoin.com/iran-considers-using-cryptocurrencies-to-evade-us-sanctions/ accessed August 31, 2019.

Tsui, Winnie. "Iran Unbound: Opportunities in the Special Economic and Free Zones." Hong Kong Means Business, December 12, 2016, hkmb.hktdc.com/en/1X0A8CT7/hktdc-research/Iran-Unbound-Opportunities-in-the-Special-Economic-and-Free-Zones, accessed December 5, 2019.

UNCTAD (United Nations Conference on Trade and Development). "General Profile: Iran (Islamic Republic of)." UNCTADstat, November 4, 2019, unctadstat.unctad.org/CountryProfile/GeneralProfile/en-GB/364/index.html. accessed December 5, 2019.

Waldron, Jeremy. (2020), "The Rule of Law," *The Stanford Encyclopedia of Philosophy*, ed. Edward N. Zalta: https://plato.stanford.edu/archives/sum2020/entries/rule-of-law/ accessed May 1, 2023

Wallace, Paul. "How Iran Is Using Currency Reforms to Withstand Trump," Bloomberg, August 20, 2019: www.bloomberg.com/news/articles/2019-08-20/how-iran-is-using-currency-reforms-to-withstand-trump-quicktake accessed August 20, 2019

(2)   Laws, Regulations, Agreements

1395 Budget Law of Islamic Republic of Iran, available in Persian at: https://rc.majlis.ir/fa/law/show/967556

Establishing One Trade-Industrial Free Zone and Thirty-Three Special Economic Zones', available in Persian at: https://rc.majlis.ir/fa/law/show/99646FIPPA (Foreign Investment Promotion and Protection Act) (2002), available in Persian at: https://rc.majlis.ir/fa/law/show/133816

NPT safeguards agreement with the Islamic Republic of Iran, Resolution adopted by the Board of Governors on 19 June 2020: www.iaea.org/sites/default/files/20/06/gov2020-34.pdf accessed August 20, 2023.

Sixth Development Plan available in Persian at: https://rc.majlis.ir/fa/law/show/1014547?keyword=%D8%A8%D8%B1%D9%86%D8%A7%D9%85%D9%87%20%D8%B4%D8%B4%D9%85 accessed August 20, 2023.

(3)   Organizations and News Websites

www.swissinfo.ch
www.dw.com
www.rollcall.com
www.brookings.edu

www.aljazeera.com
https://edition.cnn.com
https://apnews.com
www.bbc.com
www.armscontrol.org
www.investiniran.ir
https://donya-e-eqtesad.com
www.investiniran.ir
www.worldbank.org
www.npr.org
www.mehrnews.com
http://intellinews.com
www.tehrantimes.com
https://en.farsnews.com
https://de.reuters.com
https://atwonline.com
https://economictimes.indiatimes.com
www.cbi.ir
https://english.almanar.com.lb
www.mondaq.com
www.atlanticcouncil.org

13 Multilayered Mechanisms of Control and Censorship of Arts and Culture in the Islamic Republic of Iran

Roozbeh Mirebrahimi and Azadeh Pourzand

1 Introduction

In the Islamic Republic of Iran, freedom of expression is subject to severe and multifaceted restrictions. Article 24 of the constitution enshrines the right to freedom of publication "except when it is detrimental to the fundamental principles of Islam or the rights of the public. The details of this exception will be specified by law" (Iran Data Portal). The key institution established to regulate this particular "right" is the Supreme Council of the Cultural Revolution (SCCR), the highest body of cultural policy, which Ayatollah Khomeini authorized to issue guidelines and make decisions in matters related to cultural, educational, and research activities. The SCCR also dictates limitations on free speech, in particular pertaining to literary, artistic, and cultural activities and publications. Additionally, the Ministry of Culture and Islamic Guidance (MCIG), popularly known as Ershād), regulates and monitors artistic expression. For example, the MCIG reviews, censors, and approves or rejects every book manuscript before publication or reprint. It is also in charge of issuing licenses for art exhibitions, concerts, and film shoots.

Despite the structurally rigorous apparatus of censorship in place in the Islamic Republic, Iran's factional politics have at times allowed limited breathing room for artists, creative professionals, writers, and journalists; a phenomenon best manifested in 1997–2005 during the presidency of Mohammad Khatami, otherwise known as the "reform era."[1] Specifically, artistic expression and the press experienced a phase

---

[1] We refer to political factions and camps in postrevolutionary Iran the way they are domestically commonly labeled (i.e., reformists, hardliners, etc.). In doing so, we do not wish to imply that any political faction in postrevolutionary Iran has proven respectful of freedom of expression. On the contrary, as they remain adherent to the country's censorship apparatus, the said factions all endorse – but with varying intensity – repressive measures of the Islamic Republic that are inherently at odds with free expression and press.

of permissiveness in the licensing regime within the established system of censorship during this period. Yet, even though factional politics have at times helped to relax the freedom *pre-expression*, freedom *post-expression* has continued to remain in the hands of the judiciary. The judiciary, whose head is appointed by the Supreme Leader, commonly sides with the hardline factions of the state in its persecution of artists, writers, and journalists. Thus, regardless of the faction to which each president has belonged, artists and writers have experienced persecution under all presidents since 1979. Moreover, irrespective of the president in power at a given point in time, they have often been charged with ill- or vaguely defined crimes that involve threatening national security and insulting Islamic principles, for which the Islamic Penal Code (IPC) specifies harsh punitive measures.

This chapter examines both the regulatory and judicial aspects of expression in the Islamic Republic of Iran, in an attempt to illustrate the fragility of the rule of law pertaining to art and culture in theory and practice. In order to demonstrate the nature of the judiciary's verdicts in light of the defendants' artistic expression, the chapter also introduces brief examples of the cases of artists and writers prosecuted for their work both offline and online.[2] Besides providing brief examples of ways in which Iranians have worked around censorship in order to produce art and culture, the chapter lays out the plethora of limitations on cultural and artistic expression and creativity. It also provides a brief historic overview of censorship since the 1979 Revolution, capturing the relative fluctuations in the application of the law depending on the approach taken by those in charge in the executive and judiciary. In Section 2, the chapter will lay out the institutions tasked with regulating freedom of expression in the arts and provide a historical overview of the trends in regulation and censorship since the founding of the Islamic Republic. Section 3 will review the regulations and censorship practices in place prior to publication in every genre of the arts, while Section 4 will review the post-expression regime of criminalizing and securitizing arts and culture.

The paradoxical nature of contemporary Iran is that it remains a highly creative society within a culturally repressive state. While contemporary Iranian arts and culture are among some of the most dynamic in the Middle East, recognized for their accomplishments internationally, artists, musicians, writers, and journalists face continuous state-led harassment and persecution. Not a month goes by without them being called to court, detained, and sentenced for charges often tied to national

---

[2] In the following, we highlight not necessarily the most recent, but instead particularly insightful cases to illustrate and characterize the censorship apparatus at play.

security. As Annabelle Sreberny-Mohammadi and Ali Mohammadi write, "From its establishment in 1979, the Islamic Republic has engaged in a totalizing project of cultural hegemony that dictates what counts as acceptable 'cultural expression' and the forms this may take" (Sreberny-Mohammadi and Mohammadi 1994: 1).

Exploring the complex artistic and creative dynamics in contemporary Iran with a focus on censorship should not be viewed, however, as implying an underestimation of important cultural and artistic work produced amid all the limitations. Many Iranian artists, writers, journalists, and others are taking immense risks to maintain the integrity of their work amid limiting circumstances, while also challenging the status quo.

This chapter was first drafted prior to the historic and nationwide Woman, Life, Freedom (WLF) protests, sparked by the death in custody of the young Kurdish woman Jina Mahsa Amini, who had been detained for "un-Islamic attire."[3] Her death shook the country in September 2022, with masses of protesters demanding not only an end to the country's compulsory Islamic veil for women but also accountability, justice, and fundamental changes in governance. While the structural and procedural pathways of censorship remain unreformed and continue to violate Iran's domestic and international human rights commitments, the WLF protests revealed the inability of the Islamic Republic to contain and homogenize arts and culture exclusively at the service of state propaganda and repression. Well-known as well as anonymous artists and journalists,[4] and the wider cultural milieu of Iran, played key roles in these protests, making creative political expression a central feature of uprising. In their aftermath, hundreds of Iranian journalists and artists were detained and/or called to court due to their writing, art, and activism in support of the protests. Among the most prominent were the musician Shervin Hajipour,[5] whose song "Barāye" emerged as the iconic song of solidarity among protesters, and Niloufar Hamedi and Elahe Mohammadi, two investigative journalists who first reported in detail on Mahsa Jina Amini's death in custody, and who were subsequently charged with "crimes against national security" and sentenced to twelve and thirteen years in prison respectively.[6]

---

[3] See www.britannica.com/topic/Woman-Life-Freedom.
[4] Katayoun Vaziri, "How Anonymous Artists Built a Visual Language of Resistance during Iran's Woman, Life, Freedom Uprising," Ajam Media Collective, September 19, 2023, https://ajammc.com/2023/09/19/iranian-art-resistance-uprising/.
[5] See https://time.com/collection/100-most-influential-people-2023/6269445/shervin-hajipour/.
[6] See https://cpj.org/2023/10/iranian-journalists-niloofar-hamedi-and-elahe-mohammadi-sentenced/.

2 Censorship Laws and Practices in the Islamic Republic of Iran

2.1 The Establishment of the Supreme Council of the Cultural Revolution

Almost immediately after the establishment of the Islamic Republic in 1979, large-scale political repression and brutality was instigated by its founder Ayatollah Ruhollah Khomeini and his followers. Universities across the country were shut down for two and a half years while a "cultural revolution" (1980–1983) was organized from above to Islamize curricula and teaching staff. The key institution tasked with this cultural transformation was the Cultural Revolution Headquarters, established by Ayatollah Khomeini on June 12, 1980. During this time, many university professors and students were purged and curricula across all levels of education were made to conform to Islamic and revolutionary values.

The Cultural Revolution imposed limitations on artists, writers, journalists, and others in the names of anti-westernization and Islamization. As Ameneh Youssefzadeh writes for the case of music, "[a]ll concerts, and especially all radio or television broadcasts of foreign and Iranian, classical and popular music were banned" (Youssefzadeh 2000: 38). Other genres of arts and culture also experienced similar restrictions, justified by the demonization of Western influence and ideologization of what was left as acceptable.

In December 1984 the Cultural Revolution Headquarters were turned into the SCCR, which Ayatollah Khomeini authorized to introduce guidelines and make decisions in all matters related to cultural, educational, and research activities.[7] In this context, the regulations of the SCCR provide the grounds for limiting freedom of expression in the Islamic Republic. The SCCR consists of twenty-nine members, ten of whom serve on the council ex officio, including the heads of the three branches of power as well as several cabinet ministers. The Supreme Leader chooses the rest.[8] If reformist groups dominated all seats on the council that consist of elected ex officio members, they could control a maximum of six of the twenty-nine positions.[9]

The SCCR has, since its founding, been the most important institution in policymaking on issues related to culture and art, as well as in the

---

[7] See the council's official website at https://sccr.ir/pages/1/1.
[8] See https://sccr.ir/members/2.
[9] These are ten members of the elected executive and four heads of parliamentary commissions. Therefore, the Supreme Leader's appointees are always in a position to dominate the council and its policy and regulations.

regulation and restriction of freedom of expression in these areas. The regulations that the council prepared and approved over the years create critical limitations on freedom of expression in arts and culture. Some of the key regulations cover areas such as: (1) policies for the distribution and screening of movies and audiovisual material; (2) policies to combat Western cultural influence; (3) policies for publishing rules and regulations; and (4) criteria for supervising theater performances and issuing licenses. The application of such rules, regulations, and policies leads to limiting and filtering artists and cultural productions through the prism of state-led religious norms, excluding a large range of artists and creative productions that do not align with the ideological vision of the Islamic Republic.

Although, according to Article 58 of Iran's constitution, legislative authority rests with the national parliament, the Islamic Consultative Assembly (Majles), this is not the case in the regulation of arts and culture, where the legislative authority of the SCCR supersedes that of the Majles. Its resolutions are implemented by the order of the Supreme Leader.[10] At present, the council has twenty-three functions,[11] the implementation of which involves various institutions, including the MCIG.[12]

The SCCR focuses on the Islamization of all spheres of culture and the arts, and its remit includes: (1) preparation and approval of the goals and principles of the country's cultural planning policies; (2) preparation of the cultural mapping and planning of the country; (3) determining the media policies of the Islamic Republic; (4) determining ongoing necessary policies to expand and strengthen the cultural sovereignty of Islam; and (5) policymaking for the production of cultural work based on national and Islamic values. As evident from the list, the council focuses on the Islamization of all cultural and artistic aspects.

---

[10] The measures passed by the SCCR are called "resolutions" (*mosavvabeh*) (e.g., Resolution of the Council regarding the criteria for book publishing). These resolutions can either be regulations (*āyin-nāmeh*) or policies (*siyāsat-hā*). That the Supreme Leader orders the implementation of the resolutions was clarified in Ayatollah Khomeini's response to then *hojjatoleslam* Khamenei in 1985 (at the time president of Iran), regarding the legal guarantee of implementation of the council's resolutions and guidelines. Published on February 25, 1985: *SCCR's Resolutions*, vol. 1, Tehran: Publishing House of the SCCR's Secretariat, 1397/2018, p. 4. This was reaffirmed and recalled in Ayatollah Khamenei's speech in the meeting with the members of the SCCR on January 24, 1998, in response to questions raised in the media during the reformist era about the necessity of implementing the resolutions of the SCCR.

[11] *SCCR's Resolutions*, pp. 5 and 6.

[12] Duties of the SCCR, Session 633 of the Council, latest update on October 14, 2008: http://sccr.ir/.

2.2 Other Bodies Influencing and Implementing Censorship Laws in Arts and Culture

The most important institution responsible for the enforcement of the SCCR's policies and regulations is the MCIG.[13] Additionally, the Broadcasting Organization of the Islamic Republic of Iran (IRIB),[14] and a number of religious organizations that operate directly under the Supreme Leader, such as the Islamic Development Organization (Sāzemān-e Tablighāt-e Eslāmi) and the Qom seminaries,[15] exert influence over restrictions of freedom of expression in arts and culture.

The MCIG serves as a body of the executive branch that essentially regulates and monitors artistic expression.[16] Even though the Ministry is part of the cabinet led by the president's mandate, it remains one of the Ministries over whose leadership the president has restricted authority. Prior to proposing the minister of culture and Islamic guidance for the parliamentary vote of approval, the president has to receive the Supreme Leader's approval of the nominee. (This is also the case for the nominated ministers of defense, foreign affairs, and information and security.)

The MCIG reviews, censors, and approves or rejects every manuscript before publication or reprint. It is also in charge of issuing permits for art exhibitions, concerts, filmmaking, and other activities of artistic expression. Apart from being responsible for issuing permits, the Ministry is also responsible for overseeing compliance. Several layers of supervision are embedded within each area of art and culture to ensure the application of all the said restrictions. For example, publishers should first send a manuscript they intend to publish to the MCIG where its content will be reviewed, and print permission will be issued or denied, or propositions for censorship will be offered for conditional print permission. When and if the book is printed, it requires another review and permission by the MCIG for distribution. Similarly, a filmmaker who intends to produce a film must first obtain permission based on a script review from the Ministry to begin the work. Subsequently, upon completing the production of the film, the filmmaker must apply for a screening or a distribution permit, at which point further issues may be flagged and requirements for censorship imposed by the Ministry.

---

[13] Official website of the Ministry of Culture and Islamic Guidance: www.farhang.gov.ir/en/home.
[14] Official website of the IRIB: www.irib.ir/.
[15] Official website of the Islamic Development Organization, in charge of crafting and disseminating state propaganda: http://ido.ir/en/.
[16] For the Ministry of Culture and Islamic Guidance's structure and duties, see www.farhang.gov.ir/fa/intro/duty.

The IRIB is also one of the key institutions in the implementation of laws and regulations pertaining to culture and art, especially in the fields of film, TV series, and music (IRIB bylaws). The head of IRIB is also appointed (and dismissed) by the Supreme Leader (per Article 175 of the constitution).[17] IRIB is responsible for the production of TV content through its technical facilities and capabilities. Additionally, its music production unit is one of the main music production and distribution units in the country.[18] Essentially all content produced by and passing through IRIB is subject to policies and restrictions that are formulated and issued by the SCCR.[19]

In addition to MCIG and IRIB, there are religious and military institutions that are influential in restricting freedom of expression in arts and culture due to their direct affiliation with the office of the Supreme Leader. The Islamic Development Organization (Sāzemān-e Tablighāt-e Eslāmi),[20] Headquarters for Promoting Virtue and Preventing Vice (Setād-e Amr-e beh Ma'rouf va Nahy-e az Monkar),[21] the religious seminaries, the Basij Force, provincial representatives of the Supreme Leader, as well as the political and cultural division of the Islamic Revolutionary Guard Corps (IRGC) are among the institutions that act independently to strictly enforce censorship laws and regulations.[22]

Due to their direct affiliation with the Supreme Leader, these religious and paramilitary (Basij) institutions also consider themselves responsible for implementing restrictive cultural and artistic policies. In recent years, for example, some of these groups have repeatedly blocked the cinema release of some films that have received legal licenses by complying with all existing terms and conditions.[23] Similarly, there have been concerts

---

[17] Article 175 of the Islamic Republic's constitution: https://irandataportal.syr.edu/wp-content/uploads/constitution-english-1368.pdf.

[18] A prominent company affiliated with the IRIB is the Soroush Audio and Video Company, which has been active in the field of artistic and cultural productions since 1987. The company has played a significant role in the field of advertising, supporting IRIB's commercial operations within the framework of cultural and ideological policies of the Islamic Republic. Gradually, it expanded its operation across Iran, opening thirty provincial offices and establishing an office in Dubai to liaise with foreign companies. See www.soroush.tv/page/view/29.

[19] Strategies for Promoting the Activities of the Broadcasting Organization of the Islamic Republic of Iran: Approved by the SCCR, October 4, 2005.

[20] Official website of the Islamic Development Organization, in charge of crafting and disseminating state propaganda: http://ido.ir/en/.

[21] Official website of the Headquarters for Promoting Virtue and Preventing Vice: https://setad-abm.com/.

[22] Bylaws of the IRGC: https://rc.majlis.ir/fa/law/show/90595.

[23] A few examples of films that were banned vis-à-vis pressure groups include, but are not limited to, *Monshi-ye Makhsus-e* (*My Private Secretary*) by Saleh Deldam (in 2014),

whose organizers had obtained all the necessary permits, and which were canceled by intervention of military forces, affiliated with the IRGC or the Basij, or the representative of the Supreme Leader in the provinces. The same applies to some books that were initially licensed to be published and distributed, but were ultimately banned through the intervention of religious and military institutions. As such, given that they share the same strict ideological outlooks as the SCCR, these institutions essentially act as supplementary mechanisms that ensure the full implementation of state censorship.

2.3 The Historical Trajectory of Censorship in the Islamic Republic of Iran

As evident in the early formation of the SCCR, censorship has a long history in the Islamic Republic, having emerged in tandem with the ideological apparatus of the current political institutions.

The Pahlavi dynasty (1925–1979), whilst permitting important contributions to the advancement of the arts (Hossein-Rad and Khalili 2012), also institutionalized state-led censorship. For example, the Office of Book Writing, established in 1941 and active until the final days of the Pahlavi era, would screen all books prior to publication (Mollanazar 2010; Small Media 2015: 12). Similarly, according to the Regulations for Supervision of Film and Slide Screening (approved in 1968), films that, in the opinion of the Supervisory Council, contained insults to the Shah, the royal family, high-level governmental and military officials, or portrayed diminishing images of Iran (among other disqualifying factors mentioned in the regulation) were to be censored or banned (Mehrabi 1992).[24] Moreover, the state intelligence service SAVAK also surveilled and imprisoned some of the high-profile writers of the time, especially those with Communist or Islamist inclinations (Sandler 1986: 246–251; Small Media 2015: 12).

Immediately after the overthrow of the Pahlavi dynasty, the first signs of the Islamic Republic's now systematic and aggressive censorship and restrictions regime appeared. The earliest bans on the press came about in the summer of 1979, with the Revolutionary Court Prosecutor's Office

---

Khāneh-ye Pedari (Father's Home) by Kianoush Ayari (in 2010), and *Zendegi-ye Khosusi (Private Life)* by Mohammad Hossein Farahbakhsh (in 2012): www.radiofarda.com/a/movies-which-dropped-after-screening/29886764.html.

[24] Movies such as *Dāyereh-ye Minā (Circle of Mina)* by Dariush Mehrjui, *Ārāmesh dar Hozur-e Digarān (Peace in the Presence of Others)* by Nasser Taghvaei, and *Gavazn-hā (The Deer)* by Masoud Kimiai are among the films that were banned or censored before the Islamic Revolution of 1979.

becoming a censorship body throughout the country.[25] Soon after, the Islamic Republic began calling for the purge of all manifestations of the Pahlavi era. Popular genres of arts such as cinema and music were among the first targets of censorship under the pretext of Islamization of the nation. As a result, many artists were banned, with the Islamic Republic authorities dubbing them as sources of corruption in society. While some managed to find their way back into arts production, others were forever deprived of their profession.

In the years of the consolidation of the Islamic Republic, the Iran–Iraq War (1980–1988) profoundly shaped the political, social, and cultural mentality of the Islamic Republic. During this time, the Islamic Republic took arts and culture hostage to the environment of the war, further institutionalizing restrictive measures against westernization and toward Islamization of the country's cultural affairs. It was during this time that the SCCR's restrictive measures became widespread, contributing to the creation of a state-led environment of ideology, war, martyrdom, and resistance.

The post-war government, led by then President Akbar Hashemi Rafsanjani (1989–1997) prioritized the reconstruction of the country, marginalizing cultural affairs in its national development plans. Still, during this era, there were relative openings for some to engage in small-scale cultural and artistic activities without crossing ideological and religio-political red-lines. For example, several magazines were licensed, and, despite the many restrictions in place, emerged as hubs for intellectuals who had lived in isolation for years.[26] Nevertheless, during this time, Iranian intellectuals, writers, and artists also faced harsh consequences for their activism promoting freedom of expression, and their work more broadly. In 1994, members of the Writers' Association of Iran wrote an open letter against censorship that came to be known as the 134 Letter for its 134 signatories.[27] Not only did the Islamic Republic

---

[25] On May 10, 1979, *Ayandegan* newspaper published a translation of Ayatollah Khomeini's interview with *Le Monde*. Following the publication of this translation, Ayatollah Khomeini's office issued a statement calling the translation a distortion of Khomeini's words, condemning the newspaper's action. Two days later, the newspaper was published with several blank pages, protesting censorship. On August 7, 1979, the newspaper was banned, and its building sealed by order of the Revolutionary Prosecutor's Office. Along with this newspaper, other publications and magazines were shut down. This was prior to the formation of the Islamic Republic's judiciary as we know it today, given that the new constitution was not yet approved. During this time, the Revolutionary Court's Prosecutor's Office emerged as one of the first and key censorship bodies of the newly established Islamic Republic, putting on trial, sentencing, and arresting the "violators" with charges such as corruption or being anti-revolutionary.

[26] Examples of these publications include *Adineh*, *Gardun*, *Payam-e Emruz*, and *Kian*.

[27] Open Letter by 134 Writers, November 12, 1994, Abdorrahman Boroumand Center for Human Rights: www.iranrights.org/library/document/255/open-letter-by-134-writers.

dismiss the demands of this letter, there emerged even more targeted attacks against the signatories and other writers and intellectuals alike. In 1996, an attempt to kill a bus full of writers, journalists, and intellectuals failed (Fowler 2018).

With the victory of Mohammad Khatami in the presidential elections in 1997, the Islamic Republic entered an eight-year period which came to be known as the reform era. During this time, some artists and intellectuals found slightly more room to engage with their work, albeit still within the red lines and restrictions of the Islamic Republic. As stated in the report "Unveiled: Art and Censorship in Iran," published by the organization ARTICLE 19, "During this period, political debate was relatively unbridled, revolutionary dogma was more openly challenged and the nation was able to demand greater intellectual and artistic freedoms with less fear of punishment."[28] Nevertheless, this relative and minimalistic opening of space did not result in any structural reform or the elimination of censorship laws and regulatory bodies. There are cases of filmmakers, authors, and other artists alike who were faced with charges and prison sentences at the revolutionary court during this time (Fathi 2001).

Moreover, during this time the country witnessed the "chain murders" (as they became widely known) of a number of intellectuals, writers, and translators. Even though the Islamic Republic claimed that the murders were undertaken by rogue members of the intelligence community, it is clear that they were initiated by the Ministry of Intelligence (Rastgoo 2018).[29] Thus, despite a cautious opening that emerged for arts and culture during the presidency of Mohammad Khatami, artists and intellectuals remained under much pressure. Khatami was unable to bring about fundamental reforms to alleviate censorship substantially and in a lasting manner, while also failing to ensure the safety of the country's artistic

---

[28] ARTICLE 19, "Unveiled: Art and Censorship in Iran," September 2006, p. 11: www.article19.org/data/files/pdfs/publications/iran-art-censorship.pdf.

[29] What follows are the examples of books whose authors have investigated the chain murders of intellectuals in Iran and the role of security forces in these murders. It should be noted that all these books were licensed for publication and reprinted several times during the presidency of Mohammad Khatami. However, with the change of administration, they did not receive permission for reprint and were banned: (1) Akbar Ganji, *Tārikkhāneh-ye Ashbāh* (*The Darkhouse of Ghosts*), 1st ed., Tehran: Tarh-e No Publications, 1999; (2) Akbar Ganji, *Talaqi-ye Fāshisti az Din va Hokumat* (*Fascist Interpretation of Religion and Government*), 1st ed., Tehran: Tarh-e No Publication, 1999; (3) Akbar Ganji, *ʿĀlijenāb-e Sorkhpush va ʿĀlijenābān Khākestari* (*The Red-Clad Highness and the Gray-Clad Highnesses*), 1st ed., Tehran: Tarh-e No Publication, 1999; (4) Emaddedin Baghi, *Trāzhedi-ye Demokrāsi dar Irān* (*The Tragedy of Democracy in Iran*), Tehran: Nashr-e No Publication, 2000; (5) Hamid Kaviani, *Dar Jostojuy-ye Mahfel-e Jenāyatkārān* (*In Search of the Criminal Circle*), Tehran: Negah-e Emrooz Publications, 1999.

and cultural community in light of political backlashes by hardliners and their allies. Similarly, during this time the sixth Islamic Consultative Assembly (Majles), which had a reformist majority (2000–2004), was unable to reform laws pertinent to the censorship of arts and culture, as well as the persecution of artists, writers, and journalists, due to repeated vetoes by the Guardian Council. Indeed, it rejected almost all of the forty-one cultural bills and twenty political bills addressing freedom of expression that had been passed by the Majles.[30] For example, the amendment to the Objectives and Duties of the Ministry of Science and Research, and the Assessment and Admission of Students in Universities Bill were rejected by the Guardian Council. The council argued that the proposed amendments were not congruent with the rulings and regulations of the SCCR, which it considered *as important as the opinions of the Supreme Leader* (Abolfazl et al. 1397/2018: 25–50).

The end of Mohammad Khatami's second term in office and the election of Mahmoud Ahmadinejad in 2005 ushered in an even more difficult period for artistic and cultural expression. Ahmadinejad's MCIG took a radical approach toward the censorship of arts and culture, especially after he appointed Hossein Saffar-Harandi, the then editor-in-chief of the hardline *Keyhan* newspaper,[31] as his minister of culture and Islamic guidance. The announcement of his victory in the 2009 election leading to his second term in office was met with mass protests, otherwise known as the Green Movement, disputing the accuracy of vote count. The Islamic Republic responded to these protests with state violence and major crackdowns and followed this with even more restrictive measures over society at large.

As Hashemi and Kalb (2020: 119) observe, the level and intensity of censorship varies depending on which administration is in power, and softens with more moderate administrations. When looking at the implementation of regulations for book licensing, the study of available statistics provides a useful starting point for the analysis of the performance of different administrations, including different ministers of guidance and Islamic culture.[32]

For example, from the beginning of the Islamic Revolution in 1979 until 1988, when the first book publishing regulations were approved by

---

[30] Report of the Performance of the Sixth Islamic Consultative Assembly (2000–2004), Center for Research of the Islamic Consultative Assembly: https://rc.majlis.ir/fa/report/show/728932. During this time also, the amendment of the press law was withdrawn due to the direct intervention of Supreme Leader Ali Khamenei.

[31] *Keyhan* is a newspaper that represents an ultraconservative approach toward cultural, political, and social issues, and its management is directly appointed by the Supreme Leader.

[32] All of the data have been gathered from the Ministry of Cultural and Islamic Guidance annual statistic books.

the SCCR, a total of 35,434 books were permitted: 15 percent of these books were in the field of literature and fiction, 23 percent in the field of religious and Islamic studies, 2.96 percent in the field of philosophy, and 9 percent in the field of social sciences. Since the first version of the Regulation of the Objectives, Policies and Criteria for Publication of Books was approved and implemented in 1988 until 2010, when the new version replaced the previous one, a total of 582,022 titles of books were permitted, 13 percent of which were in the field of literature and fiction, 19 percent in religion and Islamic studies, 3.83 percent in philosophy, and 9 percent in social sciences.[33]

Easing or tightening the rules in implementation can impact the total number of licenses issued for book publishing. During the entire period of Ali Khamenei's presidency (1981–1989), a total of 41,497 books were permitted. A total of 82,303 books were permitted during Akbar Hashemi Rafsanjani's presidency (1989–1997), increasing to 261,335 during Mohammad Khatami's presidency (1997–2005). The number of books permitted reached 260,498 during the presidency of Mahmoud Ahmadinejad (2005–2013), but, thematically, the percentage of literature and fiction decreased from 13.44 percent to 12.22 percent. Additionally, at the level of the ministers of culture and Islamic guidance, the share of literature and fiction decreased from 17 percent during the time Mohammad Khatami was in that role (1982–1991) to 13 percent during the time of Mostafa Mirsalim (1994–1997).[34]

Looking closely at the numbers of films permitted under different administrations in the Islamic Republic also reveals varying approaches to the implementation of regulations. In this context, comparing statistics from the second term of Mohammad Khatami's presidency (2001–2005) with the first term of Mahmoud Ahmadinejad's presidency (2005–2009) illustrates an insight into the approach of the two administrations in licensing films. While there was a slight increase in film production during the first term of Ahmadinejad's presidency as compared to the number of films produced during Khatami's second term in office, the screening of films decreased. The total number of films produced in the second term of Khatami as president was 309, and the number of films produced in the first term of Ahmadinejad in

---

[33] The genres of literature and fiction as well as translated work on social sciences and political science are among key topics that have faced varying approaches by auditors under different administrations. As such, we have chosen these topics to briefly assess the varying approaches in the implementation of the same regulation within different administrations.

[34] These statistics have been compiled from reports of the Ministry of Culture and Islamic Guidance: www.farhang.gov.ir/ accessed 23rd Jan 2023.

office was 345. However, while a total of 55 percent of films produced in the second term of Khatami as president were released within the first year after their production, a lower percentage (42 percent) produced in Ahmadinejad's first term in office were screened within the first year of their production. As such, despite the fact that hundreds of films were able to receive licenses for production, many did not receive screening permissions within an adequate period of time.[35]

The dark years of Ahmadinejad's presidency were followed by the presidency of the "moderate" Hassan Rouhani as president in 2013. Throughout Rouhani's presidential terms, censorship of arts and culture as well as the harassment and persecution of artists remained prevalent. Iranian artists remained at risk; they were frequently called to court, detained, persecuted, and forced into exile. For example, in July 2019 two members of an Iranian heavy metal band called Confess, who were charged with crimes such as "insulting the sacred" and "propaganda against the state," fled Iran to Norway in order to avoid persecution, flogging, and multiple years of imprisonment for their music.[36] Similarly, Mohammad Rasoulof, one of Iran's renowned film directors known in international film circles such as the Cannes Film Festival, was charged with propaganda against the state and sentenced to prison.[37]

In 2021, the hardliner Ebrahim Raisi assumed the presidency, bringing about a further deterioration of freedom of expression in the arts and culture. Already prior to his appointment, he had criticized the state of the arts at the time, emphasizing the negative ramifications of the "production of anti-value, non-revolutionary and non-moral films with the license of the MCIG, the lack of a clear and explicit stance against the activities of those with security charges against them and cinematic figures in line with the enemy, as well as the granting of financial support to cinematic productions misaligned with the Islamic Republic."[38] His statement was met with collective objection by members of the cinematic community in Iran. His appointment of Mohammad Mehdi Esmaili as Minister of Culture and Islamic Guidance (MCIG) in 2021

---

[35] These statistics have been compiled from reports of the Ministry of Culture and Islamic Guidance: www.farhang.gov.ir/ accessed 23rd Jan 2023.

[36] Center for Human Rights in Iran, "Iranian Heavy Metal Band Members Escape to Norway After Receiving Prison Sentences," July 30, 2019: https://iranhumanrights.org/2019/07/iranian-heavy-metal-band-members-escape-to-norway-after-receiving-prison-sentences/.

[37] Center for Human Rights in Iran, "Cannes Film Festival, Iranian Filmmakers Condemn Sentence Against Colleague Mohammad Rasoulof," July 26, 2019: https://iranhumanrights.org/2019/07/cannes-film-festival-iranian-filmmakers-condemn-sentence-against-colleague-mohammad-rasoulof/.

[38] Ali Mosleh. "Criticism of Artists of the Exasperation of Censorship and Limitation in Raisi's Cabinet" [translation from Persian], BBC Persian, December 27, 2021: www.bbc.com/persian/arts-59801749.

and his explicit plans to further censor and limit the production and staging of licensed arts fanned further fears among the cultural community.

With the eruption of the Woman, Life, Freedom protests in September 2022, Iran's political authorities feel ever more threatened by the nation's demands for change. Fearful of losing power, they rely on the censorship apparatus to preempt any coalescence of grievances and demands, whether in the form of artistic and cultural production or otherwise. According to PEN America, Iran is "among the most inhospitable places in the world for free expression" next to China.[39] In 2021, Iran jailed the fourth highest number of writers and public intellectuals in the world.[40] As of 2022, it is also the largest jailer of women writers globally.[41]

3 Restrictions to Pre-Expression: Examples of Genre-Specific Censorship Regulations and Practices

As is evident from the foregoing analysis, the censorship of arts and culture is a systematic and widespread practice in the Islamic Republic. The following sections highlight the specific surveillance and censorship regulations and practices per genre. To this end, we briefly explore existing regulations and practices in book publishing, cinema and theater, as well as the music industry. In each of these areas, we examine the various layers of oversight and control by the government, while reviewing relevant regulations, in order to characterize the overall approach to genre-specific censorship. Such restrictions constitute the foundations for the imposition of arbitrary and ideological layers of censorship, undermining freedom of expression in theory and practice.

3.1 Censorship in Book Publishing

The criteria for book publishing in the Islamic Republic have thus far been determined by two regulatory texts, approved by the SCCR in 1988 and 2010. What follows entails a quick overview of these two regulations, and their implications. The first regulation, entitled "Objectives, Policies and Criteria for Book Publishing," was adopted in

---

[39] "China and Iran: Protests are Last Resort for Those Whose Freedom Has Been Curtailed," PEN America 2023: https://pen.org/report/freedom-to-write-index-2022/.

[40] "Pen Networks Welcome the Release of Iranian Writers Arash Ganji and Rezaa Khandan Mahabadi, Calls for Release of Other Members of the Iranian Writers; Association," PEN America, February 27, 2023: https://pen.org/press-release/pen-network-welcomes-release-of-iranian-writers-arash-ganji-and-reza-khandan-mahabadi-calls-for-release-of-other-members-of-the-iranian-writers-association/.

[41] See the 2022 Freedom to Write Index. For examples of recent cases, see www.bbc.com/persian/articles/c3g7e8jdx2vo.

May 1988. Article 4 of this regulation designated a "supervisory board" to implement it. The supervisory board, consisting of five experts, is appointed by the minister of culture and Islamic guidance after approval of candidates by a body inside the SCCR.[42] Article 3 specified at least seven categories for books that were "not worthy of publication." These included books (1) propagating atheism and the denial of the principles of religion; (2) promoting prostitution and moral corruption; (3) encouraging society to rise up against the Islamic Republic; (4) promoting and propagating the ideals of armed and illegal groups and heretical sects, as well as defending monarchical, authoritarian, and global arrogant systems; (5) creating chaos and conflict among ethnic and religious groups,[43] or disrupting the unity of society and the territorial integrity of the country; (6) mocking and weakening national pride and the spirit of patriotism, and humiliation and weakening of national spirit, lowering self-confidence and pride in the face of Western and Eastern culture and civilization and colonial systems; and (7) promoting dependence on one of the world powers and opposing a policy based on maintaining national independence.[44]

The strictness of the interpretation and implementation of this regulation, which was in effect until April 2010, varied depending on the hardline or reformist orientation of each administration. For example, when the conservative hardliner Mostafa Mirsalim was minister of culture and Islamic guidance (1994–1997), the Ministry's censors considered many of the long stories and novels by Iranian and non-Iranian authors to be promoting corruption, and thus withheld authorization for their publication. A case in point was a collection of poetry by the sixteenth-century poet Vahshi Bāfqi, which was banned from being reprinted on the grounds that some of its verses were considered excessively romantic, after having been previously reprinted six times. Similarly, a book discussing the history of the Ottoman Empire, *Commanders of the Golden Horn*, underwent licensing issues at its seventh reprinting request (Nazari 2017). Notably, the same regulation was implemented less strictly when Mohammad Khatami was minister of culture and Islamic guidance (1982–1992), and even less so during his presidency. When he took over the presidency in

---

[42] The minister of culture and Islamic guidance proposes his candidates for the Supervisory Board to the Council of Public Culture, which is part of the SCCR. Once the Council of Public Culture vets and approves these candidates, the minister is able to appoint them to the Supervisory Council. For the Council of Public Culture, see www.farhang.gov.ir/fa/intro/subordinate/culturalcouncil.

[43] The text of the regulation refers to ethnic and religious groups as ethnic and religious "tribes."

[44] Article 3 of the Resolution of the SCCR on "Objectives, Policies and Criteria for Publication of Books," 1988: https://ketab.farhang.gov.ir/fa/principles/bookprinciples67.

1997, 14,386 book titles were published per year. By the end of his term in 2005, the number had risen to 38,991.[45]

The next iteration of the SCCR book publishing regulations, which remain in place today, was passed under the same title during the second term of Ahmadinejad's presidency in 2010. It identifies twenty-eight categories for the prohibition of book publication,[46] leaving little room for the less strict interpretation and implementation of book censorship.[47]

3.2   Censorship in Cinema and Theater

In the field of cinema and theater, the Islamic Republic has restrictive regulations that create the legal grounds for censorship, as well as mechanisms that influence the nature of production at different stages (see SCCR 2012). According to the Law Regarding Screenwriting and Licensing promulgated in 1989 and amended in 1998, every script must be reviewed by the Evaluation Council of the MCIG, and a filming license obtained from the Ministry. After the film is completed, it must be submitted to the Review Council at the MCIG. Upon the approval of this council, the screening license will be issued.

According to Article 2 of the aforementioned law, a council called the Evaluation Council, consisting of five experts, are appointed by decree of the deputy minister of cinema affairs of the MCIG to screen and comment on submitted scripts, ultimately issuing or denying film production licenses.[48] The nominated members of the council must be approved by the deputy minister for culture and Islamic guidance.

---

[45] Ibid.

[46] As mentioned earlier, the first version of this regulation (1988) has determined seven categories of book publication prohibition.

[47] Examples of additional criteria in the new resolution include, but are not limited to: (1) promoting and propagating deviant and obsolete religions and sects, distorted and heretical; (2) promoting superstition and tarnishing the image of Islam; (3) disseminating images in a way that promote prostitution (e.g., dancing, drinking, and immoral gatherings); (4) promoting propaganda against the constitution and the Islamic Revolution and opposition to them; (5) promoting propaganda against national interests and security and making the Islamic Republic system appear inefficient; and (6) promoting the destruction of national language identity: https://ketab.farhang.gov.ir/fa/principles/principles89.

[48] The five members originally had to include a professional filmmaking expert, an expert in film production and management, an expert familiar with cultural and artistic policies, a representative of the General Directorate of Monitoring and Evaluation, and a member of the general management of monitoring and evaluation. The amended article identifies the following as the members of the Evaluation Council: (1) two individuals suggested by the Ministry's Department of Monitoring and Evaluation, (2) two individuals suggested by the House of Cinema, and (3) the director general of the

The filmmaking license is valid for three months from the date of issue, and for every renewal the Evaluation Council's approval needs to be secured once again. The council also has the authority to suspend the film at any stage of production if it detects scenes diverging from the approved script.[49] The basis for evaluating the content of all works of art, including film and theater, are two major documents issued by the SCCR, namely the "Principles of the Country's Cultural Policy" of 1992,[50] and the "Policies to Counter Cultural [Western] Aggression" of 2001.[51] One of the expert members of the Evaluation Council responsible for evaluating scripts was specifically tasked with reviewing compliance with the framework of the country's cultural policies stated in the aforementioned documents. Following the 1998 amendment, there is no designated member for this specific task, yet all members must comply with policies directed by the SCCR.[52]

The next stage of government oversight of the film industry is the requirement for filmmakers to seek a screening license. In order to issue this license, the completed film has to be reviewed by the General Directorate of Monitoring and Evaluation of the MCIG.[53] The members of the Review Council are appointed by the deputy minister of cinema in the MCIG, with the approval of the minister. The Review Council members include: (1) an Islamic cleric familiar with artistic matters; (2) three individuals with political, social, and Islamic insights, familiar with the film industry; (3) an expert in domestic and foreign film and cinematic affairs; and (4) a member of the General Directorate of Monitoring and Evaluation Unit without the right to vote.[54] As evident from the descriptions of its members, the composition of the Review Council is based on governmental and ideological grounds, with even the nomination of

---

Supervision and Evaluation Department, or his authorized representative. In addition, in the amended version of this document, the responsibility for issuing appointments of these members was handed over to the deputy minister of cinema of the Ministry of Culture and Islamic Guidance, instead of the minister himself.

[49] Article 9 of the Law Regarding Screenwriting and Licensing.
[50] Principles of the Country's Cultural Policy, adopted on August 11, 1992: https://rc.majlis.ir/fa/law/show/100172.
[51] Policies to Counter Cultural [Western] Aggression," adopted on March 14, 2001: https://rc.majlis.ir/fa/law/show/100703.
[52] Article 2 of the Law Regarding Screenwriting and Licensing. See also Mehr News Agency, "Response to Ambiguities Regarding the Issuance of Production License," April 9, 2019: www.mehrnews.com/xNYs2.
[53] Law Regarding Supervising the Screening of Films, Slides and Videos, and Issuing Their Screening Licenses of 1982 (https://rc.majlis.ir/fa/law/show/106928) and its amendment of 1985 (https://rc.majlis.ir/fa/law/show/108946).
[54] Per Article 5 of the Law Regarding Supervising the Screening of Films, Slides and Videos and Issuing Their Screening Licenses.

experts who take part in the council requiring internal nomination and the approval of the Ministry.

The process and criteria for issuing theater production and staging performances is similar to that of film and cinema. According to Article 2 of the regulation titled "Criteria for the Oversight of Screening and Issuance of License,"[55] adopted in 2000, the performance of any play requires the issuance of a license. The play license is issued after the play is reviewed and approved by the Play Supervision Council, which sits under the supervision of the MCIG. The composition of the council also gives the government maximum oversight over the content of the plays under review.

The aforementioned lengthy and restrictive processes and review criteria ensure strict oversight over the production and staging of film and theater within the Islamic Republic's religious and ideological red-lines. Nevertheless, even when films and plays finally pass the difficult approval process and receive the required screening and staging licenses, at times radical religious and ideological pressure groups and institutions (including intelligence services) intervene and ensure that public viewings and screenings are discontinued.[56]

---

[55] Article 2 of Criteria for the Oversight of Screening and Issuance of License: https://rc.majlis.ir/fa/law/show/100686.

[56] A few examples of films that were banned due to the influence of pressure groups and extra-governmental institutions in the last two decades (these films were either banned temporarily or permanently): (1) *Seh Rokh* (*Three Faces*) by Jafar Panahi –2018 (the director made this film when he was banned from professional activity; as a result, it was not permitted to be screened in Iran); (2) *Rahmān 1400*, made by Manouchehr Hadi – 2018 (this film was screened in cinemas for twenty days; however, it was later banned by MCIG, given that some of its scenes had not been sufficiently edited to meet the instructions of the Ministry); (3) *Lord* by Mohammad Rasulov – 2016 (this film was not allowed to be screened in Iran); (4) *Kānāpeh* (*A Couch*) by Kianoush Ayari – 2016 (this film was not allowed to be screened in Iran); (5) *Panjāh Kilu Albālu* (*Fifty Kilos of Sour Cherries*) by Mani Haghighi – 2016 (this film was not allowed to be screened in Iran); (6) *Neveshtan bar Shahr* (*Writing on the City*) by Keyvan Karimi – 2015 (this film was not allowed to be screened in Iran); (7) *Monshi-ye Makhsus-e Man* (*My Private Secretary*) by Saleh Deldam – 2014 (this film was not allowed to be screened in Iran); (8) *Taxi* by Jafar Panahi – 2014 (the director made this film when he was banned from professional activity; as a result it was not permitted to be screened in Iran; however, the director sent it to international festivals, including the Cannes Film Festival, and it was ultimately shown outside of Iran); (9) *Dastneshteh hā Nemisuzand* (*Manuscripts Don't Burn*) by Mohammad Rasoulov – 2013 (this film was not permitted to be screened in Iran; however, it was screened abroad); (10) *Mehmuni-ye Kāmi* (*Kami's Party*) by Ali Ahmadzadeh – 2013 (this film was banned due to the loose form of veiling (*hejab*) of the actresses); (11) *Mosalas-e Vāzhegun* (*Inverted Triangle*) by Hossein Rajabian – 2013 (this film was banned due to the loose form of veiling of the actresses; upon receiving a prison sentence, the director released the full film on YouTube in protest against his sentence); (12) *Man 'Asabāni Nistam* (*I Am Not Angry*) by Reza Darvishian – 2013 (this film was banned due to the fact that it addresses the atmosphere in Iranian society after the 2009 Green Movement unrest; however, in

3.3 Censorship in Music

Similar to other genres of art, music is also subjected to surveillance and censorship in the Islamic Republic of Iran. In line with the oversight and control over the book publishing and film industries described, the entire supply chain and production, dissemination, and staging of music are subject to restrictive measures and various approval requirements by the MCIG.

Currently, the Office of Music Affairs, a unit under the remit of the Ministry's deputy for arts, is in charge of licensing music recordings and performances.[57] Article 2 (paragraphs 22 and 23) of the mentioned "Objectives and Duties of the Ministry of Culture and Islamic Guidance (MCIG)" assigns the responsibility for issuing licenses and the supervision of the music industry at large to the MCIG. This Ministry is also in charge of implementing the regulations approved by the SCCR in regard to music production oversight, in particular, the council's Rules and Regulations for the Establishment of Cultural Centers, Institutions, and Associations, and the Oversight of their Activities, as approved on September 18, 1996.[58]

The review process for music licensing slightly differs depending on whether the music being produced is considered instrumental music or whether it involves vocals. If the music is instrumental only, the Music

2018, the ban was lifted under a different administration, and the film was screened for a short time); (13) *Gasht-e Ershād (Guidance Patrol)* by Saeed Soheili – 2012 (this film was not allowed to be screened in Iran); (14) *Āshghāl-hā-ye Dust Dāshtani (Lovely Trash)* by Mohsen Amiryoussefi – 2012 (this film was banned due to the fact that it addresses the atmosphere of Iranian society after the 2009 Green Movement unrest; however, in 2018, the ban was lifted under a different administration, and the film was screened for a short time); (15) *Rastākhiz (Resurrection)* by Ahmad Reza Darvish – 2012 (this film was initially screened in cinemas; however, given that the face of a religious Shi'i figure was shown in the film, religious pressure groups protested against it, resulting in it being ultimately banned); (16) *Nimeh-ye Penhān (The Hidden Half)* by Tahmineh Milani – 2000 (the film was banned, and the director was arrested for a while; however, it was later allowed to be screened for a limited period); (17) *Dāyereh (Circle)* by Jafar Panahi – 1999 (this film was not allowed to be screened in Iran); (18) *Dah (Ten)* by Abbas Kiarostami – 2001 (after the film's production was completed, the Review Council requested the removal of some scenes due to the lack of acceptable veiling of the actresses, which was not accepted by the director; the film was ultimately banned and not allowed to be screened in Iran); (19) *Beh Rang-e Arghavān (In Purple)* by Ebrahim Hatamikia – 2004 (the film was banned due to a complaint filed by the Ministry of Information; however, in 2009 it was permitted to be screened under the new administration); and (20) *Offside* by Jafar Panahi – 2005 (the film was not allowed to be screened in Iran due to the sensitivity of the subject revolving around women's struggle to gain access to sports stadiums in the IRI).

[57] Previously, this was the responsibility of the Center for Revolutionary Hymns and Songs.
[58] See https://rc.majlis.ir/fa/law/show/100438.

Council conducts the review and issues licenses. If the music involves vocals, in addition to the Music Council, the Poetry Council of the Ministry will also provide feedback and comments. Both councils are formed and function under the supervision of the Music Office in the MCIG, which is in charge of implementing the regulations of the SCCR and the directives of the minister. The number of council members, the composition of the members, the term of membership, and the manner of appointments are unknown and vary depending on the practice of the Ministry or the approach of the presidential administration in power. This contributes to inconsistencies in the outcome of rulings regarding licensing approvals and rejections during various political periods in the Islamic Republic. Notably, even when a music production obtains the required licensing under one administration, it may require another review and licensing under a different administration. In this context, a music production that receives licensing today may be rejected under a different presidential administration tomorrow.[59]

Types of state-approved music have evolved over the decades. In the early years of the Islamic Republic, only traditional music was considered legitimate. Other genres such as pop, rock, and hip-hop were banned. Gradually, small openings emerged for non-traditional music, until Mohammad Khatami's administration issued licenses also for some pop music productions, and later for other genres such as hip-hop.[60] This trend has continued to date, even though the auditing and censorship of music and lyrics have fluctuated under each administration.[61]

Meanwhile, the female solo voice has remained consistently banned throughout the rule of the Islamic Republic. The prohibition of women solo singers from performing for coed audiences or releasing songs and albums has no legal basis in the Islamic Republic, and it is solely based on the religious fatwas of a number of grand ayatollahs, including the current and the former Supreme Leader.[62] Most of these fatwas have declared women's solo singing be forbidden, while Ayatollah Khomeini and Ayatollah Khamenei banned such singing if it led to "corruption."[63]

---

[59] See, for example: www.magiran.com/article/3372019, www.honaronline.ir/fa/tiny/news-128818, www.eghtesadnews.com/fa/tiny/news-232846, and www.ilna.news/fa/tiny/news-546526.
[60] In 2015, a hip-hop album was finally released for the first time: https://p.dw.com/p/1FNge.
[61] See, for example: www.iranart.news/fa/tiny/news-40734 and www.tabnak.ir/001gOj.
[62] Khabar Online, "Is Woman's Singing Haram? The Opinion of Ayatollah Khamenei and Ayatollah Makarem": www.khabaronline.ir/news/320418.
[63] Ayatollah Khomeini, "Opinions on Music," Imam Khomeini's Official Website: www.imam-khomeini.ir/fa/n144616/.

Regardless, thus far in the history of the Islamic Republic no permits have been issued for women's solo singing, except in the cases of all-women private concerts.[64]

Live music performances also face numerous auditing and restrictive measures in the Islamic Republic. There are two types of licenses required, issued by the MCIG, for live performances and music concerts. The first license allows for the first performance of a music band, while all subsequent performances require a second license. According to the Regulations for the Oversight of the Execution of Stage Music Programs and the Issuance of Performance and Advertising Licenses, the first stage of music concert licensing entails a long list of requirements such as, but not limited to, the audit of the CD of the sample performance, the review of the lyrics by the Poetry Council, the review of the music by the Music Council, and the review of the submitted group photography of the band, which audits the appearance of the band members, as well as their gender composition.[65] The second license required for subsequent performances entails an enquiry from the Security Office (*Herāsat*), a subsidiary of the Ministry of Intelligence, with a permanent office in all governmental offices responsible for security and intelligence oversight of personnel and managers.

In addition to the many aforementioned barriers in the way of licensing music concerts, even when licenses have been obtained, concerts may still be cancelled ad hoc by the judiciary. For example, in March and April 2015 alone, coinciding with the annual Persian New Year's celebrations, Salar Aghili's concert in Sabzevar, Hamid Asgari's concert in Mashhad, Parvaz Homay's concert in Golbahar city, and Alireza Ghorbani's concert at Shahid Beheshti University in Tehran were all canceled after intervention by local judicial authorities.[66] It is important to note that the same musicians have received licenses to perform in some other parts of the country, including the capital city of Tehran.

---

[64] ISNA, "We Don't Have Legal Restrictions for Joint Singing of Women and Men/ We Didn't Issue Permit for Women's Solo Singing," February 1, 2015: www.isna.ir/news/93111206883/.

[65] Regulations for the Oversight of the Execution of Stage Music Programs and the Issuance of Performance and Advertising Licenses, approved by the minister of culture and Islamic guidance on October 28, 2000: www.farhang.gov.ir/fa/servicedesk/honari/h23.

[66] See, for example: www.baharnews.ir/news/66894/, https://ir.voanews.com/persian newsiran/iran-music-restrictions, and www.bbc.com/persian/arts/2015/03/150320_141_yearender_93_music.

4 Restrictions to Freedom of Post-Expression: Criminalizing and Securitizing Expression

Article 9 of the Islamic Republic's constitution, which addresses freedom, independence, and unity in the Islamic Republic, also emphasizes the following: "No individual, group, or authority, has the right to infringe in the slightest way upon the political, cultural, economic, and military independence or the territorial integrity of Iran under the pretext of exercising freedom." Additionally, Article 23 forbids the investigation of individuals' beliefs, emphasizing that "no one may be molested or taken to task simply for holding a certain belief." Article 24 also considers that "Publications and the press have freedom of expression except when it is detrimental to the fundamental principles of Islam or the rights of the public." Moreover, according to Article 4 of the Press Law, "No governmental or non-governmental official has the right to put pressure on the press to publish an article or to censor and control publications."[67] From the aforementioned excerpts of the law it can be inferred that there is a basis in the constitution of the Islamic Republic that supports, even if conditionally, freedom of expression, prohibiting censorship.

Moreover, as described earlier, there are a range of domestic laws and regulations that restrict freedom of expression for artists and others. As we have seen, one of the ways in which the restriction of free expression manifests itself in today's Iran is the requirements and processes that stand in the way of artists and writers obtaining production and distribution licenses. Another key manifestation of obstacles consists of the restrictions and punitive measures prescribed by law and implemented by the judiciary against artists, authors, and intellectuals. This section addresses the role of the judiciary and the punitive measures frequently taken against artists in Iran, further substantiating some of the aforementioned charges commonly used against artists.

Artists and writers frequently face security charges such as "acting against national security," "disturbing the public," and "promoting propaganda against the Islamic Republic." Many of these charges are prescribed in Articles 498 to 512 of the IPC, which deal with crimes against domestic and foreign security.[68] These laws also criminalize insulting political and religious figures, including the Supreme Leader, and include a number of broad and vague offenses criminalizing free

---

[67] Article 4 of the Press Law (adopted on March 17, 1986 and amended on April 26, 2000), Iran Data Portal.
[68] Fifth Book of the IPC on *Ta'zirāt* and Deterrent Punishments of January 22, 1997: https://shenasname.ir/laws/4475-ghanon-mojazat.

expression, such as "propaganda against the Islamic Republic" (Article 500 IPC), "*mohārebeh*" (enmity against God) (Articles 279–285 IPC), or "sowing corruption on earth" (Article 286 IPC).

There are plenty of cases of artists facing the aforementioned legal obstacles in contemporary Iran. For example, Athena Farghadani, a young painter, was detained and tried during the Green Movement protests of 2009 after the release of some of her paintings, including an art project that was critical of members of parliament (Majles). She was charged with "promoting propaganda against the Islamic Republic," "insulting the leadership, the president, and members of parliament." She was sentenced to a total of twelve years and nine months in prison in 2015, reduced to eighteen months on appeal.[69] Similarly, the well-known filmmaker Jafar Panahi, winner of the festivals of Venice and Berlin, was detained during the Green Movement protests in 2009, ultimately receiving a six-year prison sentence, and a twenty-year ban on filmmaking. The charge of "promoting propaganda against the Islamic Republic" was among one of the charges against him for his attempt to make a film about the Green Movement protests.[70]

In recent years, there have also been cases of Instagram celebrities such as fashion artists being summoned to the Islamic Revolutionary Court due to allegations that include "promoting prostitution" and "promoting propaganda against the Islamic Republic."[71] Similarly, in 2019, actress Matin Sotudeh was summoned to court for the loose attire she wore at the premiere of a film called *A Hairy Affair* held in Tehran on October 10, 2019. Subsequently, the MCIG announced that it would draft guidelines for the way those belonging to the country's film industry should present themselves in public.[72] Moreover, in August 2019 satirist Kiomars Marzban was sentenced to twenty-three years and nine months in prison for "contact with U.S. enemy state," "insulting the sacred," "insulting the Supreme Leader," "propaganda against state," and "insulting officials."[73]

---

[69] "Coverage of painter Atena Farghadani's Trial," Radio Farda, May 23, 2015: www.radiofarda.com/a/f35_reactions_atena_farghadani/27032269.html.

[70] Deutsche Welle, "Heavy Sentence against Jafar Panahi," December 20, 2010: https://p.dw.com/p/Qh0F.

[71] We refrain from using specific names of some of these artists due to security considerations.

[72] Center for Human Rights in Iran, "Iranian Actress Matin Sotudeh Summoned to Court for Red Carpet Attire: 'The Reaction Shocked Me,'" October 21, 2019: https://iranhumanrights.org/2019/10/iranian-actress-matin-sotudeh-summoned-to-court-for-red-carpet-attire-the-reaction-shocked-me/.

[73] Center for Human Rights in Iran, "Iran Sentences Satirist Kiomars Marzban to 23 Years Imprisonment," August 26, 2019: https://iranhumanrights.org/2019/08/iran-sentences-satirist-keyomars-marzban-to-23-years-imprisonment/; and Deutsche Welle

Articles 513 and 514 of the IPC address punitive measures regarding "insulting religious sanctities," the interpretation of which can result in arbitrary implementation of the law against all, including artists, writers, journalists, and intellectuals. For example, Pouyan Khoshhal, a reporter for the *Ebtekar* newspaper, used the term "death" of Imam Hossein instead of the word "martyrdom" in his report in 2018; subsequent to the publication of this report, he was detained and charged with "insulting religious sanctities."[74]

Additionally, some articles of the IPC, such as Articles 498 to 500, are written in such a way that allow the formation of organizations and groups that are critical of government policies – even if a small group of peaceful artists gathered to create a video clip on social issues – to be construed as a security offense. For example, in October 2019 the Revolutionary Court of Tehran charged a group of six women and eight men with "unauthorized audiovisual activity" for producing and disseminating a music video without seeking the necessary licenses. All six were sentenced to one year's imprisonment.[75] In another example, the Baha'i painter Shahriar Cyrus was detained in 2015 and sentenced to five years in prison for alleged "assembly and conspiracy against the Islamic Republic" during his painting classes, a charge Cyrus denies. He stated that his classes were merely painting lessons with no political motivation behind them whatsoever.[76]

As described briefly in this section, some of the key restrictions against freedom of expression in Iranian law are found in the IPC, specifically prohibiting insulting Islamic sanctities and desecration of individuals (Articles 513, 514, 515, 608, 609, 697, 698, and 700);[77] prohibiting conspiracy and attempts to overthrow the Islamic Republic (Articles 498, 512, 610, and 611); preserving religious principles, values, and moral standards (Article 639); avoiding inciting ethnic and religious

---

Farsi, "Confirmation of Kiomars Marzban: 23 Years of Imprisonment for Authorship," October 13, 2019: https://bit.ly/3nj2OrO. The sentence was later reduced to six years and Marzban released early after two years and six months in prison.

[74] Radio Farda, "A Reporter is Detained for Insulting the Shiite's Third Imam," October 25, 2018: www.radiofarda.com/a/iranian-journalist-arrest-over-insult-to-imam-pouyan-khoshhal/29563735.html. Pouyan Khoshhal's arrest was announced on October 23, 2018. He spent two months in detention, and was released on bail, during which he left Iran. The court convicted him on July 9, 2019, in absentia, sentencing him to six years of imprisonment: https://iranwire.com/fa/jinac/34756.

[75] BBC Persian, "One Year Imprisonment Sentence was Confirmed for Six Women Singers and Eight Men," October 15, 2019: www.bbc.com/persian/iran-50061770.

[76] Iran Press Watch, "Baha'i Artist Shahriar Cyrus Sentenced to Five-Year Imprisonment," November 3, 2016: http://iranpresswatch.org/post/15952/bahai-artist-shahriar-sirous-sentenced-to-five-year-imprisonment/.

[77] Also Article 26 of the Press Law.

differences (Article 512);[78] and respecting the security and the independence of the country, as well as national interests and the interests of society (Article 500). The text of the law, as well as the vagueness of the concepts that allow for an expansive interpretation of the alleged "crimes" by the judiciary, result in a wide range of legal challenges for artists in Iran. Indeed, these laws and punitive measures hang like a sword over the heads of artists and intellectuals, instilling fear of a constant threat that can result in self-censorship and systematic censorship of art and culture.

5 Conclusion

From the foregoing analysis, it is evident that the elaborate censorship apparatus of the Islamic Republic of Iran severely restricts freedom of expression, and the rights of artists, writers, musicians, and filmmakers. Legal restrictions are enforced through an ideological multi-layered system of monitoring and control mechanisms, imposed in the form of production and dissemination licensing of the arts. This process ensures that any work of art outside of this system of control is considered unlawful, leading to criminalization and the conviction of the artist(s) in question. Meanwhile, successfully completing the licensing processes and obtaining official permits does not guarantee freedom from post-expression persecution by the judiciary either. As described in the chapter, artists and intellectuals face the constant fear of facing heavy criminal charges under the pretext of security crimes such as "promoting propaganda against the Islamic Republic." There are varying degrees of censorship at the level of the MCIG, some of which can be intensified or minimally relaxed within the realm of the authority of the president of the Islamic Republic and his appointed minister of culture and Islamic guidance. Nevertheless, the violation of freedom of expression is often undertaken by state institutions and entities whose control is outside the scope of the authority of the president of the country at all times, such as the IRGC, the Basij (paramilitary organization), the judiciary, and intelligence entities.

In spite of all the attempts of the IRI to control, mainstream, and censor the production of arts and culture in the country, Iranian artists and writers remain known internationally for their resilience and vibrant creativity. While they often pay a high price for their courage and art, many continue to seek ways to produce and present their work beyond the limits of the Islamic Republic's censorship apparatus. There are also others who, while trying to resist propaganda, are careful not to cross the

---

[78] Also Article 6 (note 4) of the Press Law.

red lines of censorship regulations and work lawfully within the restrictions. Meanwhile, there are also those artists who fully align themselves with the regulations and the propaganda of the IRI, and do not seek to further the independence of arts and culture.[79]

In the field of book publishing, some authors wait for years to go through all the stages of auditing and censorship by MCIG and in the end publish their books lawfully in Iran, while others take the risk of seeking alternative ways (e.g., online publication or publication outside the country with or without pseudonyms). In the music industry, as Nahid Siamdoust (2017: 27) writes, "New media fundamentally transformed the framework for the production, distribution, and consumption of music in Iran." In this context, while there are musicians who seek licensing for the production, live presentation, and distribution of their art, others take the risk of taking offline and online underground means to produce and/or present their work.[80] In cinema, too, if the films are not allowed to be screened, their directors may eventually take the risk of screening them outside the country or via online means.[81] The field of theater, by contrast, hardly has any online alternative means at its disposal, and thus is fully exposed to the rigid and unpredictable licensing regime.

While working hard to seek appropriate ways to produce and showcase their art, many Iranian writers and artists have courageously emerged as vocal advocates of freedom of expression and against censorship in the IRI. For example, in November 2019 two hundred film personalities, including writers, directors, producers, actors, and others with a range of expertise in the film industry who make documentaries, fictional movies, and animations, wrote and published a letter to condemn censorship, stating that "Our Profession Has Been Under Attack."[82]

---

[79] Artists who fully align themselves with the propaganda of the IRI, or state artists, and their ways of working closely with the authorities are not the focus of this chapter, nor do any of our examples cover this category of artists.
[80] "Underground Music in Contemporary Iran" (3 episodes), *People of the Underground Podcast Series*, Siamak Pourzand Foundation, 2016: https://soundcloud.com/pourzand-foundation/people-of-the-underground-episode-2-underground-music-in-contemporary-iran-part-i,https://soundcloud.com/pourzand-foundation/people-of-the-underground-episode-2-underground-music-in-contemporary-iran-part-ii, and https://soundcloud.com/pourzand-foundation/people-of-the-underground-episode-6-underground-music-in-contemporary-iran-part-iii.
[81] "Underground Cinema in Contemporary Iran," *People of the Underground Podcast Series*, Siamak Pourzand Foundation, 2016: https://soundcloud.com/pourzand-foundation/people-of-the-underground-episode-7-underground-cinema-in-contemporary-iran.
[82] Center for Human Rights in Iran, "200 Film Personalities Condemn Censorship in Iran: 'Our Profession Has Been under Attack'," November 2019: https://iranhumanrights.org/2019/11/200-film-personalities-condemn-censorship-in-iran-our-profession-has-been-under-attack/.

Despite the continuous peaceful efforts of many Iranian artists, writers, and advocates of freedom of expression over the decades, the situation of censorship and persecution of artists remains as grim as ever in contemporary Iran. The numerous attempts to reform censorship laws and regulations have remained largely unsuccessful. Meanwhile, many artists and writers continue to work tirelessly and pay a high price to maintain integrity while producing and showcasing creative works of culture and contributing to the vibrant visual and performing arts of contemporary Iran.

Bibliography

(1)   General Literature

Darvishvand, Abolfazl, Ahmad Fazaeli, and Hamidreza Esmaili Givi (1397/2018). "Barrasi-ye jāygāh-e mosavabāt-e Shorā-ye 'Āli-ye Enghelāb-e Farhangi dar nezārat-e Shorā-ye Negahbān" (Study of the status of the resolutions of the Supreme Council of the Cultural Revolution in the views of the Guardian Council), *Quarterly Journal of "Knowledge of Public Law,"* Vol. 7, Fall, No. 21, pp. 25–50.

Fathi, Nazila. "Court in Iran Detains Filmmaker on Charges of Political Crimes." *New York Times*, September 1, 2001: www.nytimes.com/2001/09/01/world/court-in-iran-detains-filmmaker-on-charges-of-political-crimes.html

Fowler, Sarah. "Iran's Chain Murders: A Wave of Killings that Shook a Nation." BBC, December 2, 2018: www.bbc.co.uk/news/world-middle-east-46356725.

Hashemi, Masoumeh and Zep Kalb. "Tehran's Universal Studios." *New Left Review* 121, January–February 2020, pp. 109–131.

Hossein-Rad, Abdolmajid and Maryam Khalili. "Barrasi-ye naghsh-e jaryān-hā-ye fekri va hokumati dar ruykard-e melli-gerāyaneh naqāshi nogerā-ye Irān dar dorān-e Pahlavi" [Study of the role of thought and the state in the nationalist approach of modernist Iranian painting in the Pahlavi era] *Journal of Fine Arts-Visual Arts* 49 (4), Spring 1391 (2012), pp. 5–17. https://jfava.ut.ac.ir/article_28516_b203c4d0d0366b63d24cfe712bfda449.pdf

Mehrabi, Masoud. *Tārikh-e sinemā-ye Irān az ebtedā' tā Enghelāb-e 1357 [The History of Iran's Cinema, from the Beginning till the 1979 Revolution]*. Tehran: Nazar Publication, 1992.

Mollanazar, Hussein. *Text Screening (Censorship) in Iran: A Historical Perspective*. Tehran: Allameh Tabatabai University, 2010.

Nazari, Fahimeh. "The Legacy of Mirsalim in the Ministry of Culture and Islamic Guidance: Censorship of Love and Friendship." *Iran's History* (website), May 6, 2017: https://bit.ly/2GpVkmb

Rastgoo, H. *Decoding Iran's Politics: The Chain Murders of Dissidents*, IranWire, November 30, 2018: https://iranwire.com/en/features/5674

Sandler, Rivanne. "Literary Development in Iran in the 1960s and the 1970s prior to the 1978 Revolution," *World Literature Today* 60 (2) (1986), pp. 246–251.

Siamdoust, Nahid. *Soundtrack of the Revolution: The Politics of Music in Iran.* Stanford: Stanford University Press, 2017.
Small Media. *Writer's Block: The Story of Censorship in Iran*, Small Media, May 2015: https://smallmedia.org.uk/writersblock/file/Writer%27s%20Block.pdf.
Sreberny-Mohammadi, Annabelle and Ali Mohammadi. *Small Media Big Revolution: Communication, Culture and the Iranian Revolution.* NED new ed., University of Minnesota Press, 1994. *JSTOR*, www.jstor.org/stable/10.5749/j.ctttbf8.
Youssefzadeh, Ameneh. "The Situation of Music in Iran since the Revolution: The Role of Official Organizations." *British Journal of Ethnomusicology* 9(2) (2000), pp. 35–61.

(2)   Laws, Regulations, Agreements

Islamic Republic of Iran. (1990). Constitution of the Islamic Republic. Iran Data Portal: https://irandataportal.syr.edu/wp-content/uploads/constitution-english-1368.pdf
Islamic Republic of Iran. (year). The Broadcasting Organization of the Islamic Republic of Iran (IRIB) Bylaws: https://rc.majlis.ir/fa/law/show/90402
Islamic Republic of Iran. (1989). Law Regarding Screenwriting and Licensing (adopted August 5, 1989) https://rc.majlis.ir/fa/law/show/112323 and its amendment (adopted June 10, 1998) https://rc.majlis.ir/fa/law/show/118563
Islamic Republic of Iran (year). Bylaws of the IRGC: https://rc.majlis.ir/fa/law/show/90595
SSCR (Secretariat of the Supreme Council of the Cultural Revolution). *Collection of Rules and Regulations in the Field of Film and Cinema*, 2012: https://sccr.ir/Files/11513.pdf
SSCR (Secretariat of the Supreme Council of the Cultural Revolution). *Resolution on Objectives, Policies and Criteria for Publication of Books*, 1988: https://ketab.farhang.gov.ir/fa/principles/bookprinciples67

14 The Legal Situation Regarding Assisted Reproduction in Iran
Current Developments and Concerns

Shirin Naef

1 Introduction

The legal regulation of assisted reproductive technologies (ART) in Iran has emerged within and across a variety of institutions and actors, particularly involving medical, legal, and religious scholars. Since the first IVF birth in Iran in 1990, the Iranian medical community has not only given full support to the use and development of ART but has aided the emergence of a powerful, locally trained body of medical practitioners and biomedical researchers. At the same time, from a religious and legal point of view, most Shi'i religious authorities and legal scholars – differences of opinion notwithstanding – have taken a relatively permissive view and generally support ART, including paid surrogacy arrangements that are highly controversial elsewhere in the world. The perspective of Shi'i law is a significant element in regulating ART within the national context.

As a general term, ART refers to a variety of medical procedures primarily used for infertility treatments. It includes procedures such as IVF (in vitro fertilization), ICSI (intracytoplasmic sperm injection), and gamete and embryo donation in order to establish a pregnancy.[1] In these procedures, which are designed to help infertile couples to conceive a child, fertilization takes place outside the woman's body. ART procedures may also involve surrogacy arrangements in which a woman agrees to carry another couple's embryo to term. Some forms of ART are also used with regard to fertile couples for genetic diagnosis and sex selection. What makes all these techniques ultimately similar are the common acts

---

The author is grateful to the German Research Foundation (Deutsche Forschungsgemeinschaft, DFG) for their generous doctoral fellowship at the International Center for Ethics in the Sciences and Humanities (IZEW), and to Mirjam Künkler and Hadi Enayat for their very helpful comments on this chapter. All errors remain my own responsibility.

[1] Gamete donation refers to giving sperm, eggs, or both, to another person/couple so that another person/couple may have a child.

of releasing eggs, obtaining sperm samples, fertilizing the eggs outside of a woman's body in a lab setting, developing an embryo, and finally embryo transfer or freezing. Meanwhile, a variety of legal issues are raised by ART. For example, what is the legal relationship between the egg, sperm, and embryo contributors and recipients as well as the surrogates? How does the marital status of the donors and recipients affect their rights as well as that of the embryo? Will the resulting embryo be carried by the gamete owners or will another woman be involved as gestational carrier, and if the latter, what are the rights of the gestational carrier toward the child and when and where do they end?

Despite more than forty years of experience with ART since IVF was first pioneered in England in 1978 (Louise Brown was the world's first "test-tube baby"), the legal practices vary widely across countries, largely because of differences in the cultural, religious, and legal norms surrounding sexuality, conception, and the family. Many countries have, over time, legalized some forms of ART. Some countries prohibit egg donation and surrogacy arrangements while permitting other forms of ART. Others have no legislative regulation at all (Boele-Woelki et al. 2014; Eekelaar and George 2020). Japan, for example, has no laws or regulations regarding surrogacy; while in Germany and Switzerland surrogacy is strictly prohibited. In the UK and Canada, it is permitted if altruistic with no commercial payment involved, whereas in India, Israel, Russia, and some US states, commercial surrogacy is also permitted. In Iran, surrogacy is regulated via contract law, the law of embryo donation to infertile couples enacted in 2003, and the issue of birth certificates. Each regulatory situation creates specific legal challenges, especially when it comes to the legal issues related to birth registration and the cross-border recognition of parental rights in surrogacy arrangements (Ditzen and Weller 2018; Sayani et al. 2018).

This chapter reviews the regulation of ART – surrogacy in particular – in Iran. It also explores the main legal issues related to the law of filiation (the child's descent from his or her parents, *nasab*) and the recognition of parenthood as a consequence of third-party reproduction. In 2003, the first Iranian law concerning ART was passed in the Iranian parliament, permitting embryo donation to infertile married couples. The law also implicitly recognized the permissibility of surrogacy and embryo-carrying agreements. The Iranian regulation of ART has been viewed as rather permissive, allowing almost every infertile married couple wanting to have a child of their own through assisted reproduction to fulfill their dream. As we will see, Shi'i jurisprudence has played a decisive role in shaping this permissive legal framework. Furthermore, the Iranian medical community has played an important role in pressing for more permissive regulations (Inhorn and Tremayne 2012), not least because some of the main IVF infertility clinics are owned and run by physicians who are also employed in the health and medical system. Finally, academics who have elaborated on the ethical and legal aspects of assisted reproduction have influenced the debate.

Whereas in Sunni Muslim countries, procedures such as gamete donation and surrogacy arrangements are religiously controversial and, therefore, usually not allowed, Iran is the only Muslim country where the legislative work has been done by the state and local agencies, such as health departments, hospitals, and medical schools, to facilitate assisted reproduction via embryo donation and surrogacy arrangements as a means of helping infertile married couples conceive children (Inhorn and Tremayne 2012).

Embryo donation is the only form of third-party reproduction to be regulated through its own law. The law, formally titled the Act Concerning Embryo Donation to Infertile Couples (known as "the embryo donation law"), also implicitly recognizes the permissibility of surrogacy and embryo-carrying agreements. All other reproductive technologies are legalized in Iran through the regulations issued by the Ministry of Health and Medical Education (MOHME) and the National Organization for Civil Registration (Sāzemān-e thabt-e ahvāl-e keshvar).

In my previous research on the relationship between kinship, law, and religion in the context of ART in Iran (Naef 2017a; 2017b), I have argued that ART do not necessarily displace foundational Iranian beliefs and practices about kinship and reproduction. Rather, many of these beliefs and practices – mostly reconciled with Shi'i doctrines – are being reinforced and refashioned by these technologies. Family (*khānevādeh*), religion (*din*), and the government (*hokumat*) are the three dominant social institutions that shape Iranian economic, social, and political life. The representatives of these institutions, as I have discussed, have come together to form an Iranian coalition model in support of ART, even including procedures that involve gamete and embryo donation or surrogacy. In particular, the legal opinions on kinship of the Shi'i religious authorities are the foundation on which Iran's permissive approach toward reproductive technologies and advanced biomedicine has been constructed.

Complementing this discussion, this chapter argues that Iran has a family-oriented approach to the regulation of ART. From a legal point of view, the rules and guidelines governing assisted conception and surrogacy present one central aspect of Iranian family ideology, that is, continuity of genealogical kinship and procreation within the legal union of husband and wife; in other words, the legitimacy of offspring. Of course, it is not suggested here that having children is the only purpose of getting married in today's Iranian society. Family as a social institution has undergone many changes throughout Iranian history, and today, in the struggle between modernity and tradition, the concepts of family, marriage, and gender relations have undergone many changes and there are different attitudes to these.[2] Many Iranian families today are single-child, and voluntarily childless families are also seen in today's society. But concerning family as a legal concept, when it comes to childbearing (*farzand-āvari*) and the production of genealogical continuity (*baqā-ye nasl*), this is recognized only in the context of legal marriage between a man and a woman in Iranian culture, law, and religion.

In the following, I will first present how kinship relations and reproduction are reflected in Iranian family law, and then provide a detailed overview of Shiʻi religious-legal perspectives on the construction of motherhood and fatherhood and the concept of legitimacy in the context of law and assisted reproduction. I will then move to show how assisted reproduction and surrogacy are regulated by the Iranian state and its institutions and policies.

2 Reproduction, Kinship, and Parenthood in Iranian Family Law

The Constitutional Revolution of 1905–1911 that led to the promulgation of the first Iranian constitution (*qānun-e asāsi*) and the establishment of the first Iranian national parliament (*majles-e shorā-ye melli*) in 1906, triggered a process of state-formation which led to the establishment of a modern legal system by the 1940s.[3] Since the Iranian Revolution of 1979 and the subsequent referendum on the establishment of the Islamic Republic of Iran, Shiʻi jurisprudence (*fiqh*) has been considered the most prominent resource for legislation, although it should be noted that the transforming of religious juridical rules (*ahkām-e fiqhi*) into positive laws (*hoqūq-e mozuʻeh*) had already been attempted in Iran before the establishment of the Islamic Republic. The Iranian Civil Code (ICC, *qānun-e*

---

[2] In his book on the Iranian family, the Iranian sociologist Taghi Azad Armaki (2014: 195) considers *hamkhānegi* (cohabitation) in which a woman and a man live together without marriage as a new form of family in Iran, especially among young Iranian adults in the city of Tehran. He believes that the main desire of the Iranian family is the collapse of the extended family system and the formation of the nuclear family in its various forms. The discussion around this new form of male–female relationship has recently gained popularity under the term *ezdevāj-e sefid* (white marriage). However, having children, at least for now, is not the goal of couples who engage in this kind of relationship. See also Rodziewicz (2020), on the issue of white marriage and its legal dimension in Iran.

[3] For a historical–sociological analysis of the development of the modern legal system in Iran, see Enayat 2013. On Islamic constitutionalism in Iran, see Künkler and Law (2022).

madanī), devised in 1928, was partly based on Shi'i jurisprudence, although it also demonstrates many similarities with the Civil Code of France in terms of structure and subject arrangement (Herissinejad 2010). Under contemporary Iranian law, many areas of Iranian family and personal status law are under the authority of Shi'i clerics, so are treated according to *fiqh*. The word *fiqh* – literally meaning "deep understanding" – refers to the overall system of religious law, or to the Islamic science of jurisprudence, and like any other system of jurisprudence it is local, contextual, and subject to change in its premises.

Issues pertaining to kinship are addressed in two ways in Iranian legal writings: First, in legal texts (*motun-e hoquqi*) that are mostly associated with civil law and the nation-state and are characterized by a more homogenous pattern, and second in legal texts (*motun-e fiqhi*) written by Shi'i religious scholars and legal experts in fiqh that are more inclusive and diverse in subject matter.[4] *Khishāvandi* is the best equivalent term for kinship in the Persian language. It derives from the root *khish* or *khod*, meaning either "oneself" and "one's own," or "kindred" and "relative." The Iranian legal experts consider *khishāvandi* as equal to the Arabic term *qarābah*, the root meaning of which is "closeness." *Khānevādeh* (family) is another word close to the root *khish* in meaning. It stems from the word *khāneh* (house) and includes such members as father, mother, children, brother, and sister. *Khishāvandi* and *khānevādeh* are two major terms in modern Persian used to refer to kinship and family. The ICC, in accordance with Shi'i law, acknowledges three ways of reckoning kinship: First in terms of filiation, second in terms of affinity, and third in terms of suckling. In the course of the development of the family law in Iran, Iranian lawmakers have added adoptive parenthood to these three traditional sources for the establishment of kinship relations (see e.g., Safai and Emami 2007).

---

[4] Elsewhere, I have discussed at length some of the most recent work published in Iran on the relationship between fiqh and *hoquq*, or between religious law and law (Garmaroudi Naef 2015). This relationship – both conceptual and institutional – is crucial to understanding the formation of laws and regulations on a diverse array of bioethical issues in Iran. The first generation of nonclerical lawmakers in Iran had received their academic training in Western countries such as France, Switzerland, and Belgium. The appearance of the term "hoquq" in the modern Persian legal language is the result of the translation of the French "droit" (meaning "law") by these Iranian lawmakers (Forughi 2010). *Hoquq* is the plural form of "haqq," which is indeed the equivalent of the word "droit" in the sense of "right." *Haqq* is used in the Qur'an, hadith (traditional sayings), and Islamic jurisprudence (*fiqh*) and mysticism (*'erfān*) with a variety of meanings. It embraces a wide range of implications in ethics, law, philosophy, and politics that have recently become the subject of lively intellectual and academic debate in Iran. *Hoquq*, on the other hand, refers to the wide array of legal regulations and codes in a society, as well as the legal system and legal science.

2.1 Kinship Relationships that Exist Through Ties of Filiation (Khishāvandi Nasabi)

The analysis of kinship relations in the Islamic legal tradition is associated with the notion of *nasab*, an Arabic term variously translated as "consanguinity," "genealogy," "lineage," "descent," "kinship relations," or "relations of filiation." When it comes to ART, *nasab* is a concept of fundamental importance. Shiʿi scholars justify assisted reproduction on the basis of the need to define kinship relations (*nasab*, both agnatic and uterine) resulting from the use of ART.[5] The primary definition of *nasab* in the Iranian legal literature is that of the natural relationship of a child to its parents through procreation.[6] Iranian legal experts – both in religious and civil matters – consider this definition as the most commonly understood conception of *nasab* (*nasab-e sharʿi*). The ICC acknowledges *nasab* as legitimate (*mashruʿ*; that is to say, having religious legitimation) and lawful (*qānuni*; that is to say, having civil legitimation) only if the father and the mother of the child are within a valid marriage contract at the time of conception (*enʿeqād-e nutfeh*). As such, the primary concept of *nasab* in the Iranian legal discourse is that of relations of bilateral filiation based on a married union, both de facto and de jure.

Hence, if conception takes places as a result of illicit sexual intercourse (*zenāʾ*), it is not possible to acknowledge the child's *nasab* as legitimate. According to Article 1167 of the ICC, a child born out of wedlock is not attached to the *zāni* (fornicator, both man and woman in Shiʿi law), is not recognized as legitimate, and is the subject of an illegitimate *nasab* (*nasab-e nāmashruʿ*). According to Article 884 of the ICC, a child who is the result of illicit sexual intercourse is not attached to either of its biological parents (*pedar va mādar-e tabiʿi*) and does not inherit from them or their relatives (Safai and Emami 2007: 338–339). In other words, the establishment of legal filiation (*nasab-e mashruʿ*) and the right of inheritance is based on legal paternity and maternity, and not just a natural bond between parents and children. In Sunni law, if conception takes place as a result of *zenāʾ*, the child is considered illegitimate with no paternal relations, although she/he is still related to the mother and is entitled to receive inheritance from her side (Shabana 2015).[7] As will be seen in this chapter, whereas in Shiʿi law the definition of maternity is a legal act, in Sunni law maternity is determined primarily on the basis

---

[5] Agnatic means patrilineal (through the father), uterine matrilineal (through the mother).
[6] See, for example, *mafhum-e nasab* (concept of *nasab*) by Hamdollahi and Roshan (2009: 160–165) and by Safai and Emami (2007: 288–292).
[7] For more on the question of kinship and filiation in Sunni Islam, see Eich (2012).

of the biological relationship between a mother and her child through pregnancy and birth.

It should be noted that Iranian law treats legitimate (born inside marriage) and illegitimate children (born outside marriage) equally except when it comes to inheritance rights (*erth*); the rights and obligations remain the same in matters of custody, guardianship, and alimony. Also, in order to protect illegitimate children, the uniformity vote of the National Supreme Court in 1997 requires the birth of the child to be reported to the National Organization for Civil Registration and the birth certificate to be issued under the name of the father. According to Ayatollah Khomeini, the Islamic Republic's Supreme Leader during its first decade (1979–1989), the fornicator (the biological father) is recognized as the child's social father (*pedar-e 'orfi*) and it is a legal duty of the father to obtain the birth certificate for his child (Safai and Emami 2007: 339–342). In cases where the mother of the child is known but not the father, the birth certificate is issued under the mother's name and the father's name is specified with a hypothetical name.[8] As we will see, the regulation of adoption and embryo donation shows the same legal pattern.

2.2 Kinship Relationships that Exist Through Ties of Marriage (Khishāvandi Sababi)

Sabab is an Arabic term used in Persian as "a cause of something." *Khishāvandi sababi* refers to kinship relations created through marriage. Iranian law requires the existence of a marital relationship, whether permanent or temporary, between a man and a woman at the time of conception as a condition of acknowledging the legitimate filiation. Whereas the importance of marriage and legitimacy has decreased significantly in Western countries, legitimacy takes precedent over all other principles in many Muslim countries, especially when inheritance and citizenship are at stake. Legitimacy and the important of the matrimonial union also continue to be relevant in the context of assisted reproduction. In the Iranian context, the religious-legal permissibility of assisted reproduction is available, as long as it is only accessible for infertile couples that are married. "Intended couples" (*zojeyn-e motaqāzi*) – rather than "intended parents" – is a term that is often used in Iran to refer to couples who intend to use assisted reproduction. Couple (*zojeyn*) is defined as a man and woman who are bound together by marriage,

---

[8] Hamshahri online, August 22, 2020: www.hamshahrionline.ir/news/549723/فرزند-در-ایرانرای-نامشروع-هم-شناسنامه-صادر-می-شود-روش-گرفتن.

Artificial Reproduction in the Rule of Law 421

which indicates the importance of matrimonial union in the context of kinship and reproduction.

In the Islamic legal tradition, social and sexual interactions are defined by the division of men and women into two reciprocal categories of *mahram* and *nāmahram*. The rules on marriage and its prohibition, incest and adultery, adoption, veil, and dress result from such reciprocal categories. *Mahram* is an unmarriageable member of kin with whom having sexual intercourse is taboo and would be equated with "incest" (*zenā'-ye bā mahārem*). *Nāmahram* are potential marriage partners with whom sexual relations without having a marriage contract – permanent or temporary – is forbidden. In Iranian family law (Safai and Emami 2007: 112–115), a *mahram* relationship (*mahramiyat*; intimacy) is established through consanguinity, marriage, and milk-suckling.

Temporary marriage (*ezdevāj-e movaqqat*; *mut'a* in Arabic) is a form of marriage which is only recognized by Shi'i Islam and is practiced in Iran and other parts of the Shi'i world. *Mut'a* is a legal personal contract. It refers to a union between an unmarried woman and a married or unmarried man for a limited period of time, and usually in exchange for a set amount of money (*mehriyeh*) to be paid by the man. Under Islamic law in Iran, marriage is considered a civil contract, and *mehriyeh* is a mandatory payment, in the form of money or possessions, by the husband to the wife at the time of marriage and is reflected in the marriage contract. *Mehriyeh* becomes legally the woman's separate property and is usually only asked for at the time of divorce or the husband's death. According to Article 1095 of the ICC, one of the conditions that makes a temporary marriage contract valid is the determination of the *mehriyeh*, so if the *mehriyeh* is not mentioned in the contract, that marriage is void. The time agreed could be from one hour to several years. However, Sunni law does not recognize temporary marriage, considering it illicit sexual intercourse and therefore forbidden. Temporary marriage is not subject to dissolution by divorce. At the end of the contracted period, both parties may decide to terminate the relationship or to transfer their temporary union to a permanent one. Furthermore, this type of marriage does not entail the mutual right of inheritance between the temporary spouses, although children born as a result of temporary marriage are recognized as legitimate offspring (Safai and Emami 2007: 24–29).[9] In the context of egg donation, some Shi'i scholars have proposed that the husband of the woman who is going to receive the egg enter a temporary marriage with the egg donor in order to

---

[9] For an anthropological study of temporary marriage in Iran with a feminist approach, see Haeri (1989). For a critical discussion with a sociolegal approach, see Safai and Emami (2007: 28–29).

legitimize the egg donation. In this case, at the time of insemination both women, the egg donor, and the egg recipient, would be in a marriage – temporary or permanent – with the producer of the sperm (the biological father). Other Shi'i scholars, however, argue that temporary marriage is not required for donation or for the offspring to be legitimate.

According to the ICC, if a man or woman is barren, either of them is eligible to file for divorce. It is worth noting that a man can also seek a second (permanent) wife, since polygamy is permitted in Islam for up to four wives. In addition, a man may enter an unlimited number of contracts of temporary marriage, whereas a woman may only enter one marriage at a time, whether temporary or permanent. A man cannot take an additional permanent wife without permission from the family court and the consent of his first wife (Safai and Emami 2007: 99–106). Taking an additional permanent wife is frowned upon in Iranian society and overall a rare phenomenon, but entering a temporary marriage is not unusual for a man. Further, it is still hard for a man or woman to remarry after divorce or the death of a spouse, although the conditions vary greatly when various factors such as family background, financial status, and social status come into play.[10]

Meanwhile, taking a temporary wife – in order to avoid polygamy and divorce – has become an accepted way of resolving the issue of infertility in Iranian society. In this particular situation, the first wife or the husband's (close) relatives find a woman – usually from a lower-class family or a remote village – prepared to marry him temporarily for an agreed amount of compensation, in order to bear him a child. The temporary wife must then leave the child in the care of the man and renounce all rights over the baby. Consequently, the man and his first wife will have offspring.[11] It is in this context that surrogacy and egg donation have become culturally accepted. In fact, the concept of assisted reproduction already existed in the culture in a way, and has not come into existence through technology alone.

2.3 Kinship Relationships Created or Existing Through Milk-Suckling (Khishāvandi Rezā'-i)

The issue of breastfeeding holds a special position in Islam. Besides the continuing importance attached to the mother's milk as the best and

---

[10] For a critical discussion of polygamy with a sociolegal approach, see Safai and Emami (2007: 94–97).
[11] The movie *Leila* by the renowned Iranian filmmaker Dariush Mehrjui is a great example of this genre.

most perfect food for an infant, the breastfeeding of another woman's child, or wet-nursing, either in charity or for payment, has also been given much attention by jurists and religious scholars. Attention has also been given to the methods and the length of breastfeeding, the breastfeeding wage (*mozd*), the weaning of the child from the breast, and both father's and mother's duties during the breastfeeding period. Questions around the selection of the wet nurse have elicited much debate. Besides the ability to breastfeed, other factors such as mental and physical health, chastity, and even beauty have been taken into consideration (Nazari Tavakkoli 2006: 17–148). Islamic legal sources recognize children who have suckled from the same woman as "milk siblings" and prohibit their marriage to one another for reasons of incest. In other words, the milk bond created between the infant and the wet nurse constitutes the basis for kinship relations other than those created through ties of filiation (*nasabi*) and marriage (*sababi*). The milk bond constitutes a marriage prohibition and establishes permanent legal relations between the child and the woman who suckles the child and subsequently between all the other members of the milk mother's kin, including her husband and his kin, with no inheritance rights.[12]

The Shi'i consensus regarding milk kinship, which is codified in Book VII of the ICC (Article 1046), stipulates that kinship relations created by the act of suckling (*reza'-i* in Arabic, *shir khordan* in Persian), not by the milk as substance, are equivalent to kinship relations created by *nasab* as far as impediments to marriage are concerned. Furthermore, Shi'i scholars add many more conditions and rules, which are very detailed and complex arguments in their own right. For example, two of the prevalent opinions among Shi'i scholars, which are also part of Article 1046, are that the milk of the woman must be generated by a legitimate conception (*haml-e mashru'*), and that the milk must be received directly from the breast and should not be taken, in particular, from a bottle (Safai and Emami 2007: 274–276). This implies that what is important is the matrimonial union and the legitimacy of sexual relations as well as physical act of suckling (the physical connection between the milk mother's nipple and the child) in the constitution of kinship relationships, rather than simply the transmission of bodily substances (Héritier 1999; Fortier 2007).

Nevertheless, although milk kinship may have lost its sociocultural importance in today's society, its transformative mechanism to establish

---

[12] See Nazari Tavakkoli (2006: 17–148) for a detailed discussion of the issue of breastfeeding in Shi'i jurisprudence.

other types of kinship relations (both in legal and moral terms) is still apparent, as we will see in the context of assisted reproduction.[13]

With the introduction of surrogacy as a form of assisted reproduction, the issue of milk kinship has once again gained prominence and many articles have been published in this regard. In fact, making the comparison between the surrogate mother and milk mother may be one of the reasons that has made surrogacy a more acceptable type of assisted reproduction in Iran. For instance, based on the information available on the website of one of the main Iranian infertility clinics and IVF research centers, the infertile couple can either introduce a volunteer to the infertility treatment center to perform the surrogacy, or they can seek help from the center. Furthermore, from the religious perspective, the surrogate is considered like a milk mother and it is acceptable for the infertile couple to compensate her financially. And from the legal perspective, the surrogate mother and the child are not the subject of any maternal rights, responsibilities, and inheritance like those of real mother and her child.[14]

2.4 Kinship Relationships Following Adoption

The ICC, in accordance with Islamic law, does not acknowledge adoption as such. But a 1974 law created some of the legal effects and social functions of adoption (*farzand-khāndegī*). Following the Act of Protection of Children Without Guardians, infertile Iranian couples residing in Iran could adopt children without any guardian (*sarparast*) under certain conditions, whereby the child is given the name of the adoptive parents (forbidden in other Islamic normative settings). According to this law, the responsibilities of the adopting couple and the adopted child are the same as those of "real parents" (*pedar va mādar-e vāqeʿī*) and their child in terms of custody, education, alimony, and respect; but this adoption does not include inheritance rights and does not affect the legal consequences of the natural relationship between the child and its biological parents (Safai and Emami 2007: 277–285).[15]

Although Iranian law endorses adoption as a way of establishing the guardianship of minor children for the good of children, child adoption is less common in Iranian culture. This, as I have argued elsewhere

---

[13] See also Clark (2007), on the modernity of milk kinship in the context of reproductive technologies in Islam.
[14] See, for example, the Royan Institute's website: www.royaninstitute.org/cmsfa.
[15] For the content of the law, see the Iranian National Organization for Civil Registration's website: www.sabteahval.ir/Default.aspx?tabid=174, accessed June 10, 2015.

(Naef 2017b), is mostly due to uncertainty about the legitimate filiation of adoptive children and the complexity of legal procedures for adoption in Iran. In addition, another important problem is that adoption does not constitute a biological relationship and is thus not subject to *mahramiyat* (marriage prohibition; intimacy) between an adopted child who is male and the adopting mother or where the adopted child is female between her and the adopting father.[16] As will be seen, the legal regulation of embryo donation is very similar to regulations concerning adoption in Iran, except that the regulations for embryo donation have alleviated some of these adoption problems.

More recently, in 2013, a new adoption law, entitled the Act of Protection of Children and Adolescents Without Guardians or With Irresponsible Guardians, was approved to facilitate the conditions of adoption in Iran, giving, for example, Iranian couples living abroad and single Iranian women over 30 the right to adopt a child (in the latter case only a female child, to whom the name of the adoptive mother is given).[17] The law includes conditions for the protection of adoptive children and covers issues pertaining to inheritance and marriage in Islamic law. After single women were authorized to apply for adoption, the number of applications for adoption increased.[18]

3 Shiʻi Religious-Legal Perspectives on Assisted Reproduction and Legal Parenthood

Shiʻi jurists evaluate modern medical technology in terms of its permissibility within the principles and reasoning procedures of Islamic jurisprudence. The majority of jurists consider assisted reproduction as a viable and legitimate option to have a child, as long as it is only accessible for infertile heterosexual couples that are married. Due to the multicentric nature of religious authority in Islam, however, there is no one particular authority on Islamic ethics or legal norms that governs everyday practice. Rather, Shiʻi scholars' responses to the appropriate uses of these technologies are very broad, complex, and controversial, yet morally binding on the individual believer (in Shiʻi Islam, each believer should follow one of the highest religious authorities, of whom there have been about ten to twenty in recent decades). Opinions range from the permissibility

---

[16] For more details on the religious legal and civil legal aspects of child adoption in Iran, see Shariati Nasab (2011). See also Sardoueinasab (2013).
[17] For the content of the law, see www.dastour.ir/brows/?lid=386544, accessed September 27, 2020.
[18] KhabarOnline, August 8, 2019: www.khabaronline.ir/news/1287758/-شرایط-جدید-فرزندخواندگی-اعلام-شد.

of artificial insemination by the husband's sperm to the permissibility of embryo and gametes donation as well as surrogacy arrangements. All of these arrangements are generally forbidden in Sunni *fiqh* (as well as by the Catholic Church), although it should be noted that there are large minorities amongst Shi'i scholars who reject the majority opinions (Inhorn and Tremayne 2012).

The Islamic approach to medical ethics has historically been pragmatic. The guiding principle has generally been that as long as the basic Islamic principles are not violated, a compromise can be reached between the Islamic heritage and the achievements of modern medicine (Rispler-Chaim 1993; Brockopp and Eich 2008). In general, in Islamic normative debates those applications of science and technology that can maintain and improve the health and wellbeing of individuals and families are generally accepted (Atighetchi 2007; Naef 2017c). However, with regard to ART and donor procedures in particular, the major religious concerns are the offspring's legitimacy and the determination of filiation (Clarke 2009; Inhorn and Tremayne 2012; Naef 2017a). From this standpoint, most contemporary Shi'i scholars adopt a pragmatic and permissive approach to ART and tend to consider it as supportive of preserving filiation (Naef 2017a), whereas Sunni Muslim scholars tend to put emphasis on the dangers it introduces into the marital relationship and the family order, such as confused genealogy (*nasab*) and the anonymity of the mother (various authors 2003: 409–412), and thus reject the use of donor gametes and surrogacy arrangements in the reproductive process (Houot 2012; Shabana 2015).

As I have discussed elsewhere, this is because of the two traditions' different representations of lineage and legitimacy: Whereas Sunni (and to a large extent Arab) notions of filiation place more importance on the male line (agnatic filiation, having means of heritage and genealogy pass through the male line), Shi'i (and to a large extent Iranian) notions take a more gender-balanced approach under which maternal and paternal filiation are clearly distinguished and are, in many regards, viewed as complementary and symmetric (bilateral filiation). This leaves room for the legal permissibility of adoption by conferral of the adoptive parents' name and for third-party reproduction, including egg donation and surrogacy, namely situations in which the question of maternal identity arises. Accordingly, most Shi'i authorities (though not all) argue that legal maternity, like paternity, is solely determined on the basis of the genetic potential embedded in the female's seed from which the fetus comes into existence (*takavvon*) and not through gestation and birth (*velādat*). They give equal emphasis to both the maternal and paternal seed in the procreation of a child and argue that the principle whereby paternity is ascribed to the contributor of the sperm is also applicable to ascribe maternity to the contributor of the egg. In other words, the sources of the child's being are a man's sperm and a woman's egg. According to this line of legal reasoning, both maternity and paternity are established at conception. The emphasis is on the bringing into existence and not on gestation and birth. They support this view with Quranic verses that indicate the constitution of *nasab* (both agnatic and uterine) and the origins of the human being. Although a group of Shi'i scholars argues that the maternity of the child should be assigned to the woman who carries the pregnancy and gives birth to the child, the consensus of Shi'i opinion is that a maternal filiation is generated between the mother and the child by conception alone. There is also a minority view that argues that maternity is established by two principles: One through bringing into existence and one through gestation and birth (Garmaroudi Naef 2012). Whereas in Shi'i legal discourse the construction of maternity is a legal act, in Sunni law maternity is determined primarily on the basis of the natural connection between a mother and her child through birth (Shabana 2015).

Another religious concern involves the question of a *zenā'*-like relationship (illicit sexual relations including adultery and incest). In Sunni Islam, the use of donor gametes and surrogacy is unacceptable and is regarded as analogous to *zenā'*-like relationships. Many Shi'i authorities disagree with this Sunni consensus and follow the reasoning that assisted reproduction does not involve the physical act of sexual intercourse, and assisted reproduction involving a third party is therefore not analogous to adultery or incest. With regard to male-factor infertility, the idea of using donor sperm, however, is controversial. Most Shi'i authorities raise moral objections against the insertion of the donor sperm into the woman's uterus. Nevertheless, without a sexual act involved, most scholars consider the offspring to be legitimate, and the originator of the sperm as the biological father (*pedar-e tabi'i*) of the child. However, Shi'i authorities recognize other possibilities for the treatment of male-factor infertility: Most authorities prefer IVF, ICSI, and the use of embryo donation in which an embryo created by the gametes of another married couple is donated to an infertile couple; and a minority permit the insemination of the woman's egg with the donor's sperm under laboratory conditions, and then the implantation of the fertilized egg into the wife's uterus, as long as no forbidden act, such as gaze or touch, has taken place. For example, according to the fatwa of Ayatollah Khamenei, the Supreme Leader of Iran (Samadi Ahari 2004: 33), in the case of the husband's infertility, fertilization of the woman's egg with the sperm of a man other than her husband is allowed. However, the consensus of Shi'i opinion is that the artificial insemination of a married woman with donor sperm from a third party does constitute adultery and must be prohibited.

Clearly, a distinction can be made in the Shi'i context between the act of placing sperm directly into the woman's uterus, which, according to the majority of religious scholars, is not allowed, and the act of implanting an embryo formed in the lab from egg and sperm of a married couple into the uterus of a woman – whether a surrogate or the intended mother – for which there is religious moral permissibility. The in vitro embryo in this context is the result of a legal union and not the result of an illicit or impure (*nāpāk*) sexual act. Following this line of legal reasoning, the consensus of Shi'i opinion considers the use of donated embryo formed with the egg and sperm of a married couple for the purpose of infertility treatment and establishing a family as legitimate. The biological father and the mother (*pedar va mādar-e tabi'i*), accordingly, are the two donors of the genetic material (Naef 2017a).

The use of donated eggs raises the same concern as the use of donor sperm. As mentioned, to legitimize egg donation some Shi'i scholars have proposed that the donor-egg recipient's husband and the egg donor enter a temporary marriage. In this way, at the time of insemination, both the egg donor and the egg recipient would be in a marriage – temporary or permanent – with the producer of the sperm (the father). However, as noted, there is no uniform viewpoint among religious scholars. For example, many scholars who permit sperm donation also permit the insemination of the donor's egg in a petri dish, no matter whether the egg donor is married or single at the time of insemination. In this case, the use of temporary marriage to religiously legitimate egg donation is not required. Other scholars compare egg donation with organ donation, and regard the act of transferring the egg from one woman's body to another woman's uterus as constituting a reassignment of maternity from one woman to the other. Yet other scholars suggest that the donor's relinquishment of his/her gamete and its anonymous donation to a sperm, egg, or embryo bank is an indication of obliterating the ties of *nasab* from the gamete owners. These interpretations permit egg donation even among close kin, for example between two sisters.

Another important issue for understanding the relatively permissive Shi'i views on this issue is Shi'i interpretation of the moral status of the human embryo. Unlike the position of the Catholic Church, for example, which gives full moral status as a person to the embryo from the moment of conception (Banchoff 2011), in the Shi'i tradition, the newly formed fetus does not have the same moral status as a person, and gradually increases in moral status according to its physical maturation during the pregnancy (Naef 2017b). According to this position, which stems from theological interpretations of Quranic references to the stages of human embryonic development (Eich 2008), human life starts with the infusion of the soul (*ruh*) into the fetus in the fourth month of pregnancy. Hence, ensoulment makes a distinction between the biological life that begins at conception and the human life that begins at ensoulment. Within this perception, medical manipulations of the in vitro embryo before implantation is not considered equivalent to abortion, which involves the medical termination of pregnancy. However, Shi'i scholars, in general, do not permit abortion under unnecessary conditions and ascribe a moral juridical status to human embryos from the moment of conception as well. From their legal standpoint, when abortion takes place during any stage of an embryo's development, *diyeh* (monetary compensation) is determined for it depending on the embryo's growth and the stage it was at. Consequently, Shi'i jurisprudence considers embryonic stem cell research for therapeutic purposes permissible only in pre-ensoulment stages of fetus development. Following the same reasoning, if the mother's life is at stake, or the fetus is diagnosed with birth defects such that caring for it will burden the mother with extreme hardship, therapeutic abortion is permissible before the ensoulment (various authors 2007; Aramesh 2009).

Traditional surrogacy, which involves the insertion of sperm from a man other than the husband into the woman's uterus, is not allowed according to the majority of Shi'i scholars. In contrast, the practice of gestational surrogacy, in which the surrogate woman carries the embryo of a married couple, is, among the majority of Shi'i authorities, an accepted form of assisted reproduction. They argue that the implantation of the fertilized egg of a married couple into another woman's uterus is allowed, and the legal father and mother of the child (*pedar va mādar-e vāqe'i*) are the couple who are the recipients of the donated embryo (*sāhebān-e janin*). According to the majority opinion, it is both permissible to employ a surrogate and to serve as a surrogate. Again, a clear distinction can be made here between the act of placing sperm directly into the female's uterus, which is not allowed according to the majority of Shi'i scholars, and the act of implanting an embryo into the womb of a woman, a new technological procedure in which the sperm and egg of a married couple are combined outside the woman's body and the resulting embryo is placed in a surrogate woman's womb, for which there is religious permissibility (Garmaroudi Naef 2012).

For example, in an interview I conducted with the late Ayatollah Sadeqi Tehrani in 2006, a distinguished scholar of the Qom seminary and a Shi'i *marja'* in Qom, he explained to me that a third-party donation in the form of sperm and egg donation is not permissible. In these forms of third-party donation, according to him, "another man's sperm" or "another woman's egg" enters a place in which it does not belong. Such procedures are against Quranic Sura 23:5–7, which, in the eyes of Ayatollah Sadeqi Tehrani, gives strong clarification about the immorality of such actions. His opposition to sperm and egg donation, however, does not extend to embryo donation involving an embryo from another married couple or gestational surrogacy, which involves the uterus of another woman. In other words, he separates the status of egg and sperm from the status of the embryo and identifies embryo donation as a fully legal religious act. He does this by considering the embryo as the result of a legal marriage between a man and a woman. Following his arguments, both embryo donation and gestational surrogacy are allowed in order to overcome either male or female infertility in another married couple. According to him, it is even necessary (*vājeb*) for an infertile married couple, who would like to have a child and do not have another way to attain true parenthood, to take gestational help into account (Garmaroudi Naef 2012).

Most Shi'i authorities who regard surrogacy as permissible allow the surrogate to be compensated monetarily (*ojrat*), and the gesture is considered appropriate. Since the human act is respectable, the woman who endures the hardships of pregnancy is entitled to receive money for her pains. Thus, the response of Shi'i legal authorities to ART is very complex, yet exceptionally sensitive to social realities. Their response is not limited to the definition of bodily substances such as sperm, eggs, or milk; these are analyzed and defined in a legal context, which furthermore paves the way to produce and establish more legal and social relations instead of reducing these to biological relations.

4   Iran's National Guidelines and Regulations on ART: A Combination of Family Law and Contract Law

4.1   *Iran's Embryo Donation Law*

Both religious and civil legal debates about reproductive technology in Iran began in the 1960s with debates about the determination of filiation in the context of artificial insemination. For example, in 1966, Mehdi Shahidi, one of the distinguished Iranian jurists trained both in law and in the religious seminary, published an article about the legal determination of filiation in the context of donor insemination (Shahidi 2013). Sustained efforts to discuss legal and ethical issues only started in the late 1980s, however, and were directly linked to the establishment of biomedical institutions and IVF clinics. The Avicenna Research Institute, today one of the best-known reproductive biotechnology research centers, and the first of its kind to be established in Iran, organized a conference in 1999, in cooperation with the Faculty of Law and Political Sciences of Tehran University, on "Jurisprudential and Legal Issues Concerning Embryo Donation." One outcome of the conference was the publication of the book *Modern Human Reproductive Techniques from the View of Jurisprudence and Law* (*Ravesh-hā-ye novin-e towlīd-e methl-e ensāni az didgāh-e fiqh va hoquq*). After the conference, Iranian legislators, taking advantage of the conference's achievements to bridge the gap between scholars of *fiqh* and *hoqūq* to find the appropriate model for a law, proposed a bill to parliament concerning embryo donation. Following years of intense medical, theological, and legal debates, and both regional and national scientific conferences and workshops, in 2003 the Iranian parliament approved the Act Concerning Embryo Donation to Infertile Couples (known as "the embryo donation law"). After its passage through the Guardian Council, the Act became law in 2005.[19]

According to its Article 1, upon receiving the written consent of the embryo owner couple (*zojeyn-e sāheb-e janin*), all specialized and licensed centers for infertility treatment are authorized to transfer embryos resulting from IVF of a married couple to the uterus of married women whose infertility or whose husband's infertility (or that of both) has been confirmed. This transfer should be carried out in compliance with shari'a and with conditions set forth in the law. In other words, the donated embryo must arise from the gametes of a legally married couple, and only a legally married couple can ask to receive such an embryo. Further, according to the law and its bylaw, approved in 2005, donor couples must be in a good state of physical and mental health. In the law, embryo (*janin*) refers to the fertilized egg outside the uterus up to five days after retrieval. The donated embryo can be used either fresh or frozen (Safai and Emami 2007: 330–335). The donation must be voluntary and free of charge. The recipients must be infertile, married, Iranian couples who have previously submitted their request to the civil court. Receiving, preserving, and transferring donated embryos must be done under a system of confidentiality. Last but not least, the infertility treatment centers must preserve the embryos of Muslim and non-Muslim donors separately to later match the religion of the infertile couples with that of the donated embryo.

As mentioned, the legal regulation of embryo donation is very similar to regulations concerning adoption in Iran. According to Article 3 of the

---

[19] For the content of the law and the bylaw, see the Iranian National Organization for Civil Registration's website: www.sabteahval.ir/tehran/default.aspx?tabid=30424.

embryo donation law the duties and responsibilities of the married couple receiving the embryo and the resulting child would be the same as those of real parents and children in terms of custody (*negāhdāri*), education (*tarbiat*), alimony (*nafaqeh*), and respect (*ehterām*). Regarding filiation (*nasab*) and inheritance rights (*erth*), the article remains silent. As I mentioned earlier, the majority of Shi'i authorities agree that embryo donation is legitimate from the viewpoint of Islamic law, although, according to most of them, "the true parents of the child" (*pedar va mādar-e hokmi*) are the providers of the egg and sperm, no matter who may raise the child. In other words, most Shi'i scholars regard the donors of the embryo as the biological parents of the child. As a consequence, in these scholars' view, the child should inherit from the donating couple, and not the recipients of the embryo with whom the child grows up. But social and legal practice appears to be different from this Shi'i scholarly opinion. In practice, and indeed in Iranian law, through the institution of confidentiality (*mahramānegi*) the recipients will be treated as the child's real parents. In addition, the child will be *mahram* (non-marriageable member of kin) to the recipient woman, if it is a boy, since she carries the embryo in her uterus and breastfeeds the baby after birth; hence, if it is a girl it will also be *mahram* to her husband. This is like the *rabiba* principle in Islamic jurisprudence, according to which the daughter of the woman from the previous marriage will become *mahram* to her new husband (Naef 2017b). Thus, a child born as a result of embryo donation has a legal relationship with the recipient couple, and the natural lineage (*nasab-e tabi'i va hokmi*) does not always have to correspond to the legal lineage (Samadi Ahari 2012).

The issue of confidentiality has elicited a legal theoretical discourse of its own. For example, in a symposium on confidentiality in infertility treatment held in 2009 in Tehran, Seyyed Taha Merghati-Khoei, a cleric and expert in Islamic jurisprudence and member of the ethical department of the Royan Institute stated: "I am one of the supporters of confidentiality in infertility treatment. In our country, favouring non-confidentiality will face us with numerous problems that arise due to the culture and shar'i (religious legal) regulations and we'll be unable to find a solution for them." He elaborated further: "If we reveal the information, it is possible that the egg and sperm donor claims inheritance from the child. This will lead to setbacks in issues pertaining to inheritance; therefore, the foundation [*mabnā*: basis, principle, here in reference to the definition of filiation] must be altered which is not an easy task on itself" (various authors 2009: 18). Similarly, at the same symposium, a lawyer and legal expert in bioethical issues, claimed: "Currently, confidentiality is of utmost importance to both donors and recipients due to various reasons. It may change in the future. But considering the present conditions, they ask for confidentiality" (various authors 2009: 30). In the meantime, some make arguments about "the right to know one's biological parents" (various authors 2009: 20) or, as suggested by Mohammad Rasekh, a leading jurist in the field of law and bioethics, "the right to know the genetic roots or history" (various authors 2009: 23). At the same time, Iranian legislation has shown considerable support for this approach. According to Article 10 of the bylaw of the Embryo Donation Law, donor and recipient information must be kept confidential and only accessible to competent authorities under special legal conditions.

4.2 Iran's Surrogacy Regulations

Surrogacy has been practiced openly in Iran for more than a decade, and surrogacy arrangements, in which a surrogate woman agrees to carry another married couple's embryo to term, is legal and both privately regulated (per contract) and state-regulated. As in the case of embryo donation regulation, Shi'i tradition exerts a decisive role in shaping Iranian regulation on surrogacy. Thus, paid surrogacy arrangements are both permissible from the perspective of Shi'i law and socially accepted (Garmaroudi Naef 2012; Naef 2017a). Iran's embryo donation law of 2005 not only legalized embryo donation but also surrogacy arrangements. The law does not explicitly mention the permissibility of surrogacy. It concerns the permissibility of embryo transfer and carrying agreements, which are, however, relevant to surrogacy arrangements as well.[20] From the legal point of view, in both procedures a woman is carrying the embryo of a married couple that was fertilized outside her body. In the case of embryo donation, a woman is carrying the embryo of another married couple for herself; in the case of surrogacy, a woman (surrogate) is carrying the embryo of an infertile married couple for them.

As seen, there is no consensus against surrogacy arrangements among Shi'i authorities; rather, according to the majority opinion, it is permissible from the viewpoint of Shi'i law. Almost all Iranian lawmakers

---

[20] In a legal situation similar to Iran (the surrogacy arrangement is legal), in 1996, the Israeli government legalized surrogacy arrangements under a law titled the Embryo Carrying Agreements Law. This law makes surrogacy permissible for heterosexual Israeli married couples. Single women, single men, and homosexual couples are not allowed to contract a surrogate, and only single, divorced, or widowed women are allowed to become surrogates (see, e.g., Weisberg 2005). Rabbinic attitudes toward reproductive technologies have been crucial for the permissive regulation of ART in Israel (Kahn 2000). For a recent analysis of the Israeli surrogacy and egg donation legislation, see Rimon-Zarfaty (2018).

support this position and agree on the permissibility of surrogacy.[21] For example, the Ahl al-Bayt World Assembly, an Iranian-led Shi'i umbrella organization comprised of a number of senior clerics and established by Ayatollah Khamenei in 1990 in order to address and reflect on modern issues, issued a legal statement supporting surrogacy arrangements (Hamdollahi and Roshan 2009: 86–87). The Iranian Research Center for Ethics and Law in Medicine sought the standpoint of this assembly on surrogacy and embryo transfer to which the following statement is the answer: "the implantation of an embryo [of a married couple] in another woman's uterus is permissible; however, the mother of the child is considered to be the woman whose egg has generated life in the embryo" (Hamdollahi and Roshan 2009: 398).

According to Article 19 of the Civil Registration Law, the midwife or doctor who is present at the time of birth and participates in the delivery is obligated to issue the birth certificate under the name of the woman giving birth. In the early stages of surrogacy, this matter was one of the legal roadblocks in surrogacy arrangements, although, in the absence of a codified law, it is possible to seek advice from authentic fatwas and legitimate Islamic resources (Article 167 of the Iranian constitution) as well as the law for embryo donation and other general laws to resolve disputes concerning surrogacy. In the first interdisciplinary national conference on surrogacy in 2007, participating jurists and lawmakers proposed a suggestion that the following sentence should be added to Article 19 of the Iranian Vital Records Law as an amendment (*tabsareh*):

> The physician or midwife who in accordance with Article 19 of the Vital Records Law is authorized to issue the birth certificate [under the name of the woman who has delivered the child], must issue the birth certificate – subject of Article 19 – under the name of the infertile couple [not the surrogate] referred to by one of the accredited infertility treatment centers, upon receiving the written confirmation from such centers endorsing the surrogacy as the recommended treatment procedure. (Milanifar 2008: 87)

While the majority of Shi'i scholars approve of surrogacy arrangements, and despite the popularity of such arrangements, the proposed bill did not get a hearing in parliament. This could be due to disagreements between the politicians and officials of the administrative bodies. In an interview, a member of the Iranian parliament's Health Committee (Komisiyon-e behdāsht va darmān-e majles) stated that parliament had

---

[21] On the legal issues relating to children born through surrogacy, see Ayatollah Mousavi Bojnordi (2007: 102–124); for more on civil legal and religious legal arguments in Iran concerning surrogacy arrangements, see Hamdollahi and Roshan (2009) and various authors (2007: 35–168).

not seen a necessity to devise a law for surrogacy.[22] By contrast, a medical doctor and legal expert in medical issues and bioethics who was also one of the contributing writers of the proposed bill indicated that it was not surrogacy itself which the bill was intended to regulate, since surrogacy was "already a legitimate procedure from the Shi'i legal point of view." Rather, "the proposed bill was meant to resolve two issues: accommodating intending couples in their efforts to obtain a birth certificate for the newborn; and protecting physicians against accusations of issuing false birth certificates."[23]

The latter was one of the legal obstacles to the seamless practice of surrogacy, and was finally resolved in 2018 after almost a decade of de facto practices in surrogacy arrangements as well as years of scientific seminars and meetings between lawmakers, physicians, heads of infertility clinics, and state/government officials. Currently, in surrogacy births at hospitals or clinics, the hospital birth certificate is issued under the surrogate mother's name, and in case she is married, under the name of the surrogate mother's husband as well. This hospital birth certificate, which also bears the name of the intended parents, is given to the intended parents. In order to get an identity card (*shenās-nāmeh*) for a child born from a surrogate mother, the intended parents submit the hospital birth certificate to a branch of the National Organization for Civil Registration. The organization then issues the identification booklet of the newborn under the intended parents' name – who are the legal parents – after confirming the data with the hospital and the treatment center, without any reference to the surrogacy. In other words, in this type of birth, the civil legal system does not recognize the woman who has given birth as the legal mother, and does not issue the identity card under her name. In fact, the birth certificate issued by the hospital in the name of the surrogate mother only serves the purpose of holding the surgeon or midwife present at the time of birth accountable and ensuring they do not deviate from Article 19 of the Civil Registration Law.

Moreover, based on my research in 2019, a court's permission is not required for surrogacy. Infertile couples may seek relief through surrogacy to address their infertility if all other possibilities have been exhausted. After deciding to try surrogacy, the infertile couple either finds a surrogate on their own or will be introduced to reliable surrogate candidates by infertility treatment clinics or hospitals. Once a (suitable) surrogate is identified, with the help of a lawyer a contract will be signed by the

---

[22] Entekhab, February 6, 2012: www.entekhab.ir/fa/print/52004.
[23] Khabaronline, September 22, 2013: http://khabaronline.ir/(X(1)S(daimlyoa5a432 sdl4j3zll2r))/detail/314135/society/health.

couple and the surrogate (and her husband if she is married) where the terms and conditions of contract are outlined, including the expenses such as costs of carrying the baby for nine months, how the payment will be transferred, and expenses to cover the surrogate's living essentials, such as food, clothes, and treatment procedures during pregnancy. The main legal aspects of surrogacy in Iran are thus regulated by both family law and contract law.

4.3 On Eggs and Sperm Donation: Between Regulations and Restrictions

Although sperm donation is legal in many countries of the world, the use of donated eggs in infertility treatment is strictly regulated, and in some countries, like Germany, Italy, and Switzerland, it is forbidden by law. The differential treatment of egg and sperm donation exists also in the Iranian regulations; however, as opposed to many countries, in Iran permitting egg donation has proven less problematic than sperm donation. This can partly be explained by the fact that the religious-legal and cultural meanings ascribed to eggs and sperm are grounded in different normative ideas about kinship and reproduction. The Iranian medical experts' understanding of gamete donation and its biological and health effects are also important factors in this differential infertility treatment.

Unlike embryo donation and surrogacy arrangements, Iranian law is silent on the subject of egg and sperm donation. However, according to Article 167 of the Iranian constitution, in the absence of codified law it is possible to seek advice from authentic fatwas and other legitimate Islamic sources.[24] When it comes to issues involving third-party donation of eggs and sperm, as we have seen, from a religious-legal point of view a distinction is made between the use of donor egg and donor sperm. This distinction also exists in the clinical regulations and in the Iranian Ministry of Health guidelines on gamete donation. With respect to egg donation, most Shi'i authorities consider the act permissible and the offspring to be legitimate. The temporary marriage of the donor-egg recipient's husband and the egg donor has been proposed by some Shi'i scholars as a religious-legal solution to legitimize egg donation. Other scholars, on the contrary, following the principle of the absence of sexual act, consider the insemination of the donor's egg with the sperm of a man other than her husband outside of the woman's body and then the implantation of the fertilized egg into the uterus of the man's wife religiously permissible. In their view, the use of temporary marriage is not required. Regarding

---

[24] Notably, only in civil matters, not in criminal cases.

the legal definition of motherhood, there is no uniform viewpoint among religious scholars. Most conclude that the egg owner is the legal mother. Others ascribe maternity to the woman who gives birth to the child, and some suggest that the child should be considered to have two real mothers. While a wide range of opinions exists, Iranian regulations and medical guidelines adopt a flexible view of motherhood and define motherhood according to the context of the cases and the intention of the parties involved in these procedures. According to this approach, in the case of egg donation, the carrying mother is considered the legal mother of the child, while in the case of surrogacy the mother will be the intended mother who cannot conceive or carry a pregnancy to term.

The divergence of religious legal opinions, however, has not prevented the practice and regulation of egg donation in Iran. In its early stages, with the establishment and development of the research and clinical centers for infertility treatment in different cities of Iran since the late 1990s, and based on the fatwas issued by religious authorities, most of the IVF and infertility clinics have provided egg donation; the regulations of each clinic, however, differed. Some clinics left it to the infertile couples to find their own egg donors, which often led them to ask a close relative or friend to become a donor. A few clinics had their own egg donors available. Some clinics kept the identity of both donors and recipients confidential and the matching of donors and recipients was carried out by the clinic staff. A donor must provide identifying information, and this information was kept confidential in some clinics while in others it was made accessible to the recipient couple. Others left it to the donors and recipients to decide whether they wish to remain anonymous. And some clinics advocated using donor eggs in combination with temporary marriage and therefore looked for a donor who was divorced or widowed. The compensation for egg donors was, from the beginning of the practice, permissible. In fact, the legality of egg donation at the time was based on religious permissibility. However, after more than a decade of experience of egg donation for female infertility treatment as well as following many national conferences and internal meetings and discussions among legal experts, medical associations, Ministry of Health staff, and hospital and IVF clinic directors, these different regulations have been harmonized through MOHME guidelines.

Currently, IVF centers are authorized to perform egg donation in Iran; all donations must be kept confidential and anonymous, although each clinic can establish their own regulations regarding payment for donors. Any woman, married or unmarried, between the ages of 21 and 35 years, may donate her eggs. All donors must first undergo medical and genetic evaluations; they must provide identifying information, and this information is kept confidential. The recipients should remain anonymous to the donors. Most clinics look for egg donors who have ideally had a child of their own. Married women who have not become pregnant after repeated IVF procedures and suffer from a form of infertility that makes their eggs unviable are entitled to seek treatment using donated eggs. The donor egg program is also available to married cousins (still not infrequent in Iran across both the paternal and maternal lines) with a family history of genetic disorder as well as married women undergoing cancer treatment. Egg donation includes preparing and collecting eggs from donors, fertilizing eggs with the recipient male sperm, and transferring the embryos to the recipient's uterus. In fact, in the Iranian context, the regulation of compensating egg donation has emerged through clinical practice and later through the development of professional guidelines. The positive response of religious authorities has been an important factor behind this regulation.

And yet, whereas the use of donor eggs for female fertility problems is now a routinized practice in Iran, the social acceptability and routine practice of sperm donation is far from a reality. There are many objections to the use of donor sperm for male infertility treatment. From a religious-legal perspective, as noted, a distinction can be made between the act of placing sperm directly into the woman's uterus, which, according to the majority of religious scholars, is not allowed, and the act of implanting the donated embryo of a married couple into the uterus of another woman, for which there is religious moral permissibility. Most Shi'i scholars consider the embryo as a legal entity resulting from a matrimonial union between a man and a woman. The other man's sperm, in contrast, is impure and contaminates the woman's uterus and thereby the purity of genealogical continuity and kinship relations. Alternatively, the use of donated embryos is allowed in order to overcome male infertility. This means, however, that the healthy wife gets pregnant with an embryo not stemming from her own eggs, but another woman's eggs (together with the sperm of that woman's husband). From a social perspective, too, for many Iranian couples – both religious and nonreligious – sperm donation is not an option for the treatment of male infertility. As my research has shown, despite the involvement of another man's sperm in embryo donation, many couples refer to the distinction between legitimate embryos and impure sperm and prefer embryo donation (involving neither the recipient couple's egg nor sperm) over sperm donation.[25]

---

[25] As mentioned, a minority of Shi'i scholars, comprising the most high-ranking authorities, permit the use of sperm donation in the case of the husband's infertility. As a result of this religious permissibility, sperm donation is offered in some private infertility clinics in Iran. However, the medical and national guidelines do not support this practice.

In fact, since the donor couple are connected through marriage the sperm is not considered impure. The superiority of the matrimonial relationship and legitimacy in this procedure is certainly a considerable factor here. In addition, there are also medical concerns about the use of donor sperm for infertility treatment in Iran. Problematizations of sperm donation in medical discussions seem to focus overwhelmingly on issues of genetic and sexually transmitted diseases, the future possibility of incest between siblings, and the lack of national and reliable data banks to store the medical histories of donors (Naef 2017a).

5 Conclusions

This chapter has provided an account of how ART are regulated in Iran, where legal reasoning and rhetoric are mainly informed by Shi'i juridical discourse (*fiqh*). Taking family as a legal concept, I have argued that the Iranian family beliefs and values play a crucial role in shaping Iran's permissive policy toward reproduction. Certain procedures such as embryo donation and surrogacy arrangements have been legislated by the state through family law, contract law, and other forms of national regulation. And when a civil law is silent on a procedure, such as gamete donation, national and institutional guidelines and policies attempt to regulate the practice and in some cases place limits on access to procedures such as sperm donation.

In looking at the legislative history, it can be argued that the legal regulation of reproductive technologies in Iran has emerged within and across a variety of institutions and settings and is not something that has been imposed by state authorities. Its implementation has thus come about through the involvement and contributions of several relevant stakeholders – particularly reformist parliamentarians, and medical, legal, and religious scholars.

By taking advantage of medical and technological advances, the confluence of religious and secular forces has provided a means to develop legal regulations and national guidelines as well as critical insights to deal with biomedical issues in Iranian society, a society which is comprised of both secular and religious values (not in terms of faith and political ideology but rather in terms of cultural and historical aspects) that are expressed in different places to different degrees. In this context, both religion (not as a political force but as source of law) and culture have a significant impact on the rational development of law. This type of bottom-up approach to innovation in legislation throws light on the possibilities of forming new capacities in the Iranian legislative system in order to provide solutions to the sociolegal demands of the Iranian people.

However, this approach does not exist in most cases and circumstances in the Islamic Republic of Iran. Regarding reproduction, and sexual and reproductive health, for instance, in an attempt to increase fertility rates the Iranian parliament in 2014 voted to pass legislation including the banning of permanent forms of birth control such as vasectomies. The proposed bill, which includes punitive charges, was hastily formed and attracted much controversy and critiques from both public and academics in the country. Finally, soon after the 2021 presidential election, the Islamic government of Iran, in entering into the most intimate boundaries of Iranian men and women, passed a new law titled "Rejuvenation of the Population and Protection of the Family," which severely restricts women's access to reproductive health services and contraceptives.

In fact, the 1979 Iranian Constitution has major contradictions that make it difficult to understand the idea of rule of law and the definitions of key terms such as freedom and rights. Theoretically, according to Article 4 of the constitution, all civil, penal, financial, economic, administrative, cultural, military, political laws, and regulations must be in compliance with Islamic criteria (*mavāzin-e eslāmi*); Article 6 states that in the Islamic Republic of Iran, the affairs of the country must be administered on the basis of public opinion, like the election of the president and members of the parliament; and according to Article 57, the executive, judicial, and legislative branches are separate powers supervised by the absolute leadership of the *umma* (Muslim community). According to the theory of *velāyat-e faqih* – or guardianship of the Islamic jurist – developed by Ayatollah Khomeini, the leader of the Islamic government should be an expert in Islamic laws and regulations (a *faqih*) and the implementation of all public matters and laws related to the functioning of state institutions is the responsibility of the Supreme Leader (*rahbar*). With the revolution of 1979 and the subsequent referendum on the Islamic Republic, the first *rahbar* was Khomeini himself.

But in practice, a look at the development of the legislative process in Iran indicates that the Islamic Republic has been faced with numerous challenges and undermined by many weaknesses and failures since its formation. The principle of people's sovereignty contradicts the doctrine of divine sovereignty and the guardianship of the jurist. During the forty-year history of the Islamic Republic, these principles have undergone transformation, but their major foundations have always been at the centre of political and social dilemmas. The conflict between the rule of shari'a (God's law) and the rule of law, in fact, the battle between orthodoxy and the rational development of law, prevents the consolidation of a rule of law state in Iran.

Bibliography

Aramesh, Kiarash. "Iran's Experience on Religious Bioethics: An Overview." *Asian Bioethics Review* 1(4), 2009, pp. 318–328.

Aramesh, Kiarash. "Population, abortion, contraception, and the relation between biopolitics, bioethics, and biolaw in Iran." *Developing World Bioethics* 2023. 10.1111/dewb.12386.

Atighetchi, Dariush. *Islamic Bioethics: Problems and Perspectives*. New York: Springer, 2007.

Azad Armaki, Taqhi. *Khānevādeh-ye Irani [Iranian Family]*. Tehran: Nashre Elm, 2014.

Boele-Woelki, Katharina, Nina Dethloff, and Werner Gephart. *Family Law and Culture in Europe: Developments, Challenges and Opportunities*. Cambridge: Intersentia, 2014.

Banchoff, Thomas. *Embryo Politics: Ethics and Policy in Atlantic Democracies*. Ithaca: Cornell University Press, 2011.

Brockopp Jonathan. E. and Thomas Eich. *Muslim Medical Ethics: From Theory to Practice*, Columbia, SC: University of South Carolina Press, 2008.

Clarke, Morgan. "The Modernity of Milk Kinship." *Social Anthropology* 15(3), 2007, pp. 287–304.

Clarke, Morgan. *Islam and New Kinship: Reproductive Technologies and the Shariah in Lebanon*. New York and Oxford: Berghahn Books, 2009.

Ditzen, Beate and Marc-Philippe Weller. *Regulierung der Leihmutterschaft*. Tübingen: Mohr Siebeck, 2018.

Eekelaar, John and Rob George. *Routledge Handbook of Family Law and Policy*, 2nd ed. London and New York: Routledge, 2020.

Eich, Thomas. "Decision-Making Processes among Contemporary 'Ulamaʾ: Islamic Embryology and the Discussion of Frozen Embryos." In Jonathan E. Brockopp and Thomas Eich (eds.), *Muslim Medical Ethics: From Theory to Practice*. Columbia: The University of South Carolina Press, 2008, pp. 61–78.

Eich, Thomas. "Constructing Kinship in Sunni Islamic Legal Texts." In Marcia Inhorn and Soraya Tremayne (eds.), *Islam and Assisted Reproductive Technologies. Sunni and Shia Perspectives*. New York and Oxford: Berghahn Books, 2012, pp. 27–53.

Enayat, Hadi. *Law, State and Society in Modern Iran: Constitutionalism, Autocracy and Legal Reform, 1906–1941*. New York: Palgrave Macmillan, 2013.

Fortier, Corinne. "Blood, Sperm and the Embryo in Sunni Islam and in Mauritania: Milk Kinship, Descent and Medically Assisted Procreation." *Body and Society* 13(3), 2007, pp. 15–36.

Foroughi, Mohammad Ali. "The History of Modernization of Law." *Journal of Persianate Studies* 3, 2010, pp. 31–45.

Garmaroudi Naef, Shirin. "Gestational Surrogacy in Iran: Uterine Kinship in Shia Thought and Practice." In Marcia Inhorn and Soraya Tremayne (eds.), *Islam and Assisted Reproductive Technologies. Sunni and Shia Perspectives*. New York and Oxford: Berghahn Books, 2012, pp. 157–193.

Garmaroudi Naef, Shirin. "The Iranian Embryo Donation Law and Surrogacy Regulations: The Intersection of Religion, Law and Ethics." *Die Welt des Islams. International Journal for the Study of Modern Islam* 55 (3–4), 2015, pp. 348–377.

Haeri, Shahla. *Law of Desire: Temporary Marriage in Shi'i Iran*. Syracuse and New York: Syracuse University Press, 1989.

Hamdollahi, Aasef and Mohammad Roshan. *Barrasi-ye tatbiqi-ye fiqhi va hoquqi-ye qarārdād-e estefādeh az rahem-e jāygozin* [*A Comparative Study of the Religious and Civil Legal Issues Surrounding Surrogacy Contracts*]. Tehran: Majd, 2009.

Herissinejad, Kamaladdin. "Ta'ammoli dar 'avāmel-e ta'thirpaziri-ye hoquq-e novin-e Irān az nezām-e hoquqi-ye romi-zhermani [Study of the Factors of the Roman-German Legal System's Impact on Iranian Modern Law]." *Law Quarterly* 39(2), 2010, pp. 369–382.

Héritier, Françoise. *Two Sisters and Their Mother: The Anthropology of Incest*, trans. Jeanine Herman. New York: Zone Books, 1999.

Houot, Sandra. "Islamic Jurisprudence (Fiqh) and Assisted Reproduction: Establishing Limits to Avoid Social Disorder." In Marcia Inhorn and Soraya Tremayne (eds.), *Islam and Assisted Reproductive Technologies. Sunni and Shia Perspectives*. New York and Oxford: Berghahn Books, 2012, pp. 53–69.

Inhorn, Marcia and Tremayne, Soraya. *Islam and Assisted Reproductive Technologies: Sunni and Shia Perspectives*. New York and Oxford: Berghahn Books, 2012.

Kahn, Susan Martha. *Reproducing Jews: A Cultural Account of Assisted Conception in Israel*. London: Duke University Press, 2000.

Künkler, Mirjam and David S. Law. "Islamic Constitutionalism: Iran." In David S. Law (ed.) *Constitutionalism in Context*. Cambridge University Press, 2022, pp. 449–473.

Milanifar, Alireza. "Issuing Birth Certificates and ID Cards for Newborns Following a Surrogate Birth and the Legal Ethical Responsibilities of the Medical Team." *Medical Journal of Reproduction and Infertility* 9(1), 2008, pp. 82–88.

Mousavi Bojnordi, Seyyed Mohammad. *Hoquq-e khānevādeh* [*Family Law*]. Tehran: Majd, 2007.

Naef, Shirin. *Kinship, Law and Religion: An Anthropological Study of Assisted Reproductive Technologies in Iran*. Tübingen: Francke Verlag, 2017a.

Naef, Shirin. "Legal Status, Moral Values and Cosmological Order: Embryo Politics in Iran." *Ethnologie française* 2017(3), 2017b, pp. 459–470.

Naef, Shirin. "Bioethik im Iran." In Ludwig Paul (ed.), *Handbuch der Iranistik*, vol. 2. Wiesbaden: Reichert Verlag, 2017c, pp. 174–181.

Nazari Tavakkoli, Saiid. *Hezānat- e kodakān dar fiqh-e eslāmi* [*Child Custody in the Islamic Jurisprudence*]. Tehran: Samt, 2006.

Rimon-Zarfaty, Nitzan. "Parochial Altruism: A Religion-Sensitive Analysis of the Israeli Surrogacy and Egg Donation Legislation." In Mitra Sayani, Silke Schicktanz, and Tulsi Patel (eds.), *Cross-Cultural Comparison on Surrogacy and Egg Donation: Interdisciplinary Perspectives from India, Germany and Israel*. Cham: Palgrave Macmillan, 2018, pp. 371–393.

Rispler-Chaim, Vardit. *Islamic Medical Ethics in the Twentieth Century*. Leiden: Brill, 1993.

Rodziewicz, Magdalena. "The Legal Debate on the Phenomenon of 'White Marriages' in Contemporary Iran." *Anthropology of the Middle East* 15(1), 2020, pp. 50–63.

Safai, Seyyed Hossein and Asaddolah Emami. *Mokhtasar-e hoquq-e khānevādeh* [*A Concise Family Law*]. Tehran: Mizan Publications, 2007.

Samadi Ahari, Mohammad Hashem. *Nasab-e nāshi az leqāh-e masnu'i dar hoquq-e Irān va Islām* [*Kinship Relations Resulting from Artificial Insemination in Iranian and Islamic Law*]. Tehran: Ganj-e Danesh, 2004.

Samadi Ahari, Mohammad Hashem. "*Hoquq va takālif-e farzandān-e nāshi az janin-e ehdāyi* [Rights and Duties of Children Born as the Result of Embryo Donation]." *Tahqiqāt-e hoquq-e tatbiqi-ye Irān va bein al-melal [Comparative Iranian and International Legal Research]* 18, 2012, pp. 113–138.

Sardoueinasab, Mohammad. "Child Adoption from Iranian Law View." *International Journal of Liberal Arts and Social Science* 1(2), 2013, pp. 29–38.

Sayani, Mitra, Silke Schicktanz, and Tulsi Patel. *Cross-Cultural Comparison on Surrogacy and Egg Donation: Interdisciplinary Perspectives from India, Germany and Israel*. Cham: Palgrave Macmillan, 2018.

Shabana, Ayman. "Foundations of the Consensus against Surrogacy Arrangements in Islamic Law." *Islamic Law and Society* 22(1/2), 2015, pp. 82–113.

Shahidi, Mehdi. "Talqih-e masnu'i-e ensān [Human Artificial Insemination]." In Mehdi Shahidi (ed.), *Majmu'eh maqālāt-e hoquqi-e Mehdi Shahidi* [*Collection of Legal Articles Written by Mehdi Shahidi*]. Tehran: Majd, 2013, pp. 159–179.

Shariati Nasab, Sadegh. *Farzand-khāndegi [Adoption]*. Tehran: Shahr-e-Danesh, 2011.

Various authors. *Ravesh-hā-ye novin-e towlid-e methl-e ensāni az didgāh-e fiqh va hoquq* [*Modern Human Reproductive Techniques from the View of Jurisprudence and Law*]. Tehran: Avicenna Research Institute and Samt Publication, 2003.

Various authors. *Seqt-e janin az manzar-e pezeshki, hoquqi, fiqhi, akhlāqi-falsafi, ravānshenāsi va ejtmā'i'*[*Medical, Legal, Islamic Jurisprudential, Ethical-Philosophical, Social and Psychological Aspects of Abortion*]. Tehran: Avicenna Research Institute and Samt Publication, 2007.

Various authors. *Hamneshast: mahramānegi dar darmān-e nābārvari, haqq bar shenākhtan-e pedar va mādar-e biolozhik, entekhāb-e jensiyat* [*Symposium: Confidentiality in Infertility Treatment, A Right to Know Biological Parents, Sex Selection*]. Tehran: Avicenna Research Institute, 2009.

Weisberg, Kelly. *The Birth of Surrogacy in Israel*. Gainesville: University Press of Florida, 2005.

15 Conclusions
Regressions and Progressions in the Rule of Law of the Islamic Republic of Iran

Hadi Enayat and Mirjam Künkler

As the chapters in this volume have shown, the quality of the rule of law has been anything but static in the Islamic Republic. It has varied from area to area of law and across time, with improvements being made in some years and regressions occurring in others. It is worthwhile recapitulating these progressions and regressions since the 1979 Revolution in order to render a more comprehensive picture of the quality of the rule of law in postrevolutionary Iran. Established accounts tend to either discount the dramatic erosion of the rule of law in light of the revolution's real or alleged achievements (e.g., in education and the development of the welfare state), or they paint an entirely bleak picture with gross human rights violations all around. In both cases, discussions seldom differentiate between different areas of law, or acknowledge the changes in the quality of the rule of law over time. This closing chapter aims to do so. Chapter 1 reviewed different notions of the rule of law from the most minimalist to substantive notions. While in some areas of the law only the most minimalist conditions for the rule of law are operative across most of the forty-five-year history of the Islamic Republic, in others achievements are more tangible across certain periods of time.

1 Policing

The rule of law cannot be realized without dedicated agencies to maintain law and order and enforce court judgments – police, bailiffs or marshals, and the like. Conversely, the rule of law depends on police forces and officers who are accountable and themselves subject to the law. In many countries, the police force is the first contact between citizens and the justice system and citizens often experience police forces as abusive and corrupt. In Iran, this has been a pervasive problem since the revolution and was thrown into sharp relief with the student protests in 1999, the contested elections of 2009, and protests in 2017/2018, 2020, and 2022, during which police and security forces cracked down with deadly violence. As Saeid Golkar shows in Chapter 6, the police forces have been involved in violent suppression of protests and are widely seen as corrupt. They have also played a significant role in the judiciary (often unconstitutionally) as judicial officers (*zābetān-e qazā'i*), especially in cases involving a political interest. Popular discontent and the subsequent legitimacy crisis have led to some attempts at reform, such as the 1991 administrative centralization of police forces in the Niruhā-ye Entezāmi Jomhuri-ye Eslāmi (Law Enforcement Forces – NAJA), and the stipulation of NAJA's competencies in a charter, according to which the police's core mission is to ensure public order and security by fighting crime and terrorism, providing security for authorized demonstrations, dispersing illegal gatherings, suppressing riots, protecting government buildings, protecting Iranian and foreign politicians, and controlling the country's borders. Other reforms have included anti-corruption drives, attempts to engage with civil society, and the recruitment of female police officers. During President Khatami's term (1997–2005), the Office of Public Surveillance was created, through which people could report police misconduct to the authorities. Yet, despite progress toward the rule of law at that time, Iran's police force is still not sufficiently accountable to elected institutions or subject to independent oversight. What is more, the proliferation since 2009 of (partly competing) security forces with overlapping competencies and competing channels of command have made arrests and detentions less predictable. Beside the Security and Law Enforcement Forces under the Interior Ministry, which reports to the president, the security forces also comprises forces under the aegis of the Ministry of Intelligence, and the Islamic Revolutionary Guard Corps (IRGC) Intelligence and Security Organization (created in 2009). The latter is directly under the command of the Supreme Leader and is now Iran's most powerful intelligence organization. It is not at all unusual for political detainees to be released by one security agency only to be re-arrested hours later by another. Suppression of protests with brutality and impunity reached a zenith during the 2020 protests, during which police and security forces cracked down with deadly violence, killing up to 1,500 protesters. There has been no accountability for these killings other than offers of blood money to the families of the bereaved and threats to those who refused it and dared to speak out. In the aftermath of the death of Mahsa Jina Amini at the hands of the *gasht-e ershād* (guidance patrols) – widely regarded as an extra-judicial killing –, some 500 protestors have been killed by police and other security forces.

2 Criminal Justice

In the years immediately following the 1979 Revolution, thousands of people were arbitrarily detained, imprisoned, tortured, and summarily executed with little or no regard for due process. Gradually, from the mid-2000s to early 2010s, some degree of order and predictability was restored to the criminal justice system. The various legal reforms discussed in Chapters 2 (Tellenbach) and 3 (Dyke and Enayat), such as the restoration of the office of public prosecutor in 2004, the introduction of the new Criminal Code of 2013 and the new Code of Criminal Procedure of 2015 constitute some improvements on the previous codes and procedures. But they also contain many shortcomings which severely undermine the right to a fair trial and more generally hinder Iran's compliance with international human rights obligations. For example, while the new IPC of 2013 specified some crimes in greater detail than the previous code had done, it also expanded in general the catalogue of crimes, in particular in the realm of *hodud*. Apostasy is now indirectly punishable by death (per Art. 220). For the first time in Iranian history, this makes apostasy from Islam punishable in codified law. Blasphemy is now explicitly defined as a *hadd* crime and *mohārebeh* is defined more broadly than was previously the case. Moreover, *mohārebeh* is now exclusively punishable by death. The new CCP also contains many procedural flaws. For example, it does not expressly provide for the presence of the accused at appeals court sessions (Art. 80), leaving it to the discretion of the court itself, thus favoring the prosecution and undermining an effective right to appeal. The new CCP has also reduced the scope for retrial compared to the previous code (Art. 474). Apart from these developments in codified law, legal and judicial practice fall short in a variety of ways. Continuing violations include the interference of security officials in the judicial process, the frequent use of special courts in which rule of law standards are severely curtailed, the continued absence of lawyers during interrogation, the use of torture and extraction of forced confessions, and arbitrary judicial decisions facilitated by the application of the Shi'i principle of *'elm-e qāzi* (knowledge of the judge) employed as evidentiary proof. Knowledge of the judge is interpreted by some judges as constituting evidence in itself and it cannot be appealed on substantive grounds.

Moreover, the Islamic Republic has consistently had one of the highest execution rates globally. The majority of these executions are related to drug offences, ranging from possession to drug-dealing. Such executions are a violation of international law, which prohibits the application of the death penalty for crimes not involving intentional killing. After much domestic and international pressure, the Iranian parliament amended the drug laws in 2017, removing the death penalty for a number of drug-related crimes and replacing it with life imprisonment or fines. As Enayat and Enayat show in Chapter 7, this led to an amendment of the Anti-Narcotics Law in January 2018, which substantially raised the threshold for the death penalty for possession of drugs. With the amended law in force, the majority of those executed in 2018 had been convicted of intentional murder under the principle of *qesās* (retribution in kind). As discussed in Chapter 3, under *qesās*, the victim's heirs can seek punishments like the death penalty, blinding, or amputations, or instead forgive and reduce the sentence to the request of "blood money," in which case the judge can sentence the accused to up to ten years in prison, provided the murderer can put up the blood money (about USD 60–70,000 per life). By 2018, non-governmental organizations (NGOs) recorded 272 cases of clemency in *qesās* – almost the same as the number of recorded executions. Yet the reduction in executions did not last long. Following the appointment of the new head of the judiciary Mohseni-Eje'i in 2021, numbers shot up, with more than 580 and 850 executed in 2022 and 2023 respectively, and at least half of these on drug-related charges.

3   The Legal Profession

The independence of the legal profession suffered immeasurably when the bar associations were dissolved after the 1979 Revolution. They only gradually recuperated and reorganized in the 1990s and, once Khatami was elected president in 1997, were able to hold internal elections again. This allowed them to regain a degree of political independence and, during the first Khatami term (1997–2001), the bar associations revived their internal human rights committees and were able to publicize and speak up against human rights violations, particularly those committed in the area of criminal justice. Since the early 2000s, however, hardliners have prevented internal elections and ensured that regimist lawyers dominate the bars' boards, with the effect that the human rights work of the bar associations has come to a halt. Lawyers protested in 2009 when a law was passed to the effect that lawyers defending those accused of political crimes could be charged with being complicit in these same crimes. What has undermined the work of the bar associations most, however, is the fact that since the early 2000s, the judiciary has begun to set up parallel training and examination mechanisms for a different kind of lawyer, so-called Article 187 legal advisors, who are certified by the judiciary. With this new mechanism, Iran was able to triple its numbers of lawyers between 2005 and 2015 from 20,000 to 60,000. The Article 187 legal advisors do not take a Bar exam and also otherwise are not organized by the Bar. They are required to seek renewal of their accreditation from the judiciary every year, thus making them highly dependent on the judiciary's goodwill. After forty years of struggle between the bars and the judiciary, officials in 2023 provided a new twist to the standoff by tabling a bill that forces the bars not to submit to judicial control but to the control of the Ministry of Economics and Finance. If confirmed by the Guardian Council, the new legislation will give the ministry the power to establish a taskforce that will assume control of all training, recruitment, and certification of lawyers in the future, effectively thereby taking over all major functions of the bar associations.

Thus, the legal profession saw some improvements toward the restoration of its independence in the early Khatami years, but its decimation and the gradual displacement of independently trained and certified lawyers by judiciary-certified legal advisors ever since. The planned replacement of the bars by a regime-appointed board will incorporate the profession into the regime, akin to a *Gleichschaltung* (forced integration of societal institutions into the state).

4   Prison Reform and Decarceration

The humane and decent treatment of prisoners is central to the rule of law and here international legal covenants, such as the International Covenant on Civil and Political Rights (to which Iran is a signatory), provides a framework of norms.[1] The experience of inmates while in prison will largely determine their chances of becoming productive and law-abiding citizens after their release. But prisons are often so inadequately funded, managed, and operated that those inside them are forced to experience conditions and treatment that breach the duty of care owed by the state. This leads to a paradox in connection with the rule of law since prisons are responsible for implementing the decisions of courts, but much of what happens in prisons in not lawful. The problems of overcrowded prisons, poor prison conditions, and attendant problems such as widespread drug use and the transmission of diseases, have been pervasive in the Islamic Republic since its inception. Iranian prison officials have generally argued that this is primarily an issue of capacity, implying that the answer would be simply to build more prisons. But as Enayat and Enayat show in Chapter 7, the causes of this overcrowding include over-punitive criminal sentencing policy (especially in connection with drug offenders, but also in

---

[1] For the text of this treaty see: http://hrlibrary.umn.edu/instree/b3ccpr.htm. An additional set of guidelines flesh out how governments should comply with this convention, the most important of which is: "United Nations Standard Minimum Rule for the Treatment of Prisoners": www.unodc.org/documents/justice-and-prison-reform/Nelson_Mandela_Rules-E-ebook.pdf, accessed June 12, 2020.

the area of "non-intentional crimes") as well as problems with long delays in the justice system and pretrial detention. From the early 2000s, various initiatives and campaigns from doctors, judicial officials, Majles deputies, and to a lesser extent NGOs have tried to deal with the problem of overcrowding and worked toward improving prison conditions in various ways: through the establishment of drug camps, needle-exchange programs (see the account by Alaei and Alaei in Chapter 8), reducing the number of those imprisoned for "unintentional crimes," reduced sentencing, and, most importantly, implementing prison furlough schemes and amnesties. As a result of these reforms, the incarceration rate has generally fallen from the relatively high levels of the late 1990s and 2000s (in 2008, Iran had the 9th highest incarceration rate worldwide) to 54th on the global scale in 2022.[2] In addition, the COVID-19 pandemic led to a wave of amnesties and clemencies. Between March 2020 and March 2021, 100,000 prisoners were granted leave, the number of new jail sentences declined by 11 percent, and clemencies almost doubled compared with the previous year (see Chapter 3). Yet, the prisons' population spiked again after the protests following Mahsa Jina Amini's death in September 2022, with some 22,000 arrested since. Some of those arrested have been pardoned (see Chapter 7), but the high number of new arrests have moved Iran back into the world's top 10 by overall prison population. And although women have been at the forefront of recent protests, 97 percent of Iranian prisoners are still male.

5   Property Rights and Commercial Law

Property rights have been at the heart of ideological contention between political factions in Iran since the 1979 revolution and disagreement over the land reform characterized much of the standoff in the 1980s between the clerical Guardian Council and the left-leaning parliament. Property law does much more than protect individuals in the acquisition of their possessions and is part of a larger scheme which determines the political and economic constitution of society. In this sphere, as Kaveh Ehsani (2013: 156) has observed, the Islamic Republic "never managed to resolve its hybrid identity between contending poles of Islamism and developmentalism, social justice and cultural conservatism, representative politics and authoritarian paternalism." In 1979, substantial areas of the economy were nationalized but the issue of property rights remained the subject of ongoing political contestation. Indeed, political differences

---

[2] World Prison Brief (WPB): https://worldpopulationreview.com/country-rankings/incarceration-rates-by-country, accessed 24 March, 2023.

over the size and role of the public sector in the economy were already evident in 1979 during the heated debates over the drafting of the new constitution (see Chapter 1 of this volume). According to Article 44 of the constitution, the Iranian economy should consist of three sectors: Public, private, and cooperative. During the early days of the Islamic Republic, radical factions demanded a *dirigiste* economy with extensive land reforms, state control over public services, and industry, as well as the imposition of strict limits on the accumulation of private wealth. Conservative factions, on the other hand, insisted that *shari'a* protected private property and affirmed the Islamic legitimacy of free trade and the acquisition of wealth. Whilst Khomeini leaned toward a left-wing economic populism, he acted as a mediator who tried to forge a third way, insisting that the new Republic was "neither capitalist nor socialist but Islamic" (Ehsani 2013: 156).

After Khomeini's death, Ayatollah Rafsanjani, who had been elected president in 1989, redefined the contours of the Islamic Republic by transforming the populist redistributive state of the 1980s into a neoliberal state capitalism modeled on China and Malaysia. He did this by integrating various revolutionary institutions into the state bureaucracy and trying to force state institutions to become economically self-sufficient. Rafsanjani also introduced a five year-privatization plan (1989–1993), although this remained largely unenforced for a decade (Ehsani 2013: 159–160). The liberalizing impetus was continued under President Khatami when, between 2000 and 2004, the reformist-dominated parliament launched legislation to open Iran to international markets and to attract foreign and local private investment. In 2002, the Foreign Investment Promotion and Protection Act (FIPPA) was passed (see Chapter 12 of this volume), which, remarkably, no longer distinguished between domestic and foreign investments in rights, protections, facilities, and capital market transactions. This was extraordinary in light of Article 81 of Iran's constitution, according to which "The granting of concessions to foreigners for the formation of companies or institutions dealing with commerce, industry, agriculture, services or mineral extraction, is absolutely forbidden." Foreign investments were made subject to a flat 25 percent corporate income tax, but with many possibilities for exemptions and tax holidays.

Shortly after Ahmadinejad's electoral victory in 2005, economic reforms went further. Ayatollah Khamenei issued a directive to re-interpret Article 44 with the intent of reversing the limits set on the private sector in the constitution. This directive was accompanied by a neoliberal discourse amongst some commentators in Iran, which viewed state intervention in the economy as inherently incompatible with the rule of law (Kashani 2006: 66–84). Khamenei's directive ordered the government to reduce its share in the "non-essentials" sectors annually by 20 percent, and to privatize some 80 percent of its assets in "essential sectors," such as large-scale industries, mining, downstream oil and gas, insurance, banking, communications, energy, and some sectors of military technology (Ehsani 2013: 165). The following year, the directive was expanded into a parliamentary law, but privatization efforts stalled due to a lack of private capital investment and the government's habit of trying to interfere in the management of privatized companies.

The 2007–2008 period saw yet another wave of attempted privatization, with budget legislation designating USD 7.8 billion worth of state assets be privatized, and USD 3.3 billion be sold to "the public." The latter proved particularly thorny as Iran is notoriously short of private capital. Four decades of nationalization policies and expropriation have left their mark. Whatever private capital did not take flight abroad in 1979 gradually found its way into state coffers. All major infrastructure projects of the Islamic Republic have been state projects, and tougher sanctions since the early 2010s led to large capital transfers from the state into parastatal companies. Thus, instead of privatization, what happened was the shifting of economic ownership away from the state toward a variety of parastatal organizations, including pension funds, banks, cooperatives, foundations, and contractors linked to the military, with the Revolutionary Guards becoming the supreme dominating economic force to whose subsidiaries the state has subcontracted major economic and social responsibilities. The result is a "military/commercial/industrial complex" (Arjomand 2009: 60) that economically and financially binds political elites, the Revolutionary Guards, and the country's industry to one another, making regime survival not only a political but also supreme economic interest to those involved. As argued in Chapter 12, the growth of the private sector will be key to any political liberalization. The JCPOA, if implemented, would have, over time, significantly contributed to reestablishing private economic activity, ownership, and trade with Western partners (with immense consequences also for the implementation of property and labor law standards) instead of incentivizing Iran to reinforce parastatal economic activity with Chinese and Russian partners.

6   Workers' Rights

In connection with labor rights, the rule of law is concerned not just with the procedural fairness of the courts but with the substantive rights of collective bargaining, fair pay, minimum working hours, and safe working conditions. Political struggles between labor and capital in this sphere have often been conceived as a zero-sum game pivoting on the struggle to secure these rights against the imperatives of economic efficiency. In Chapter 11, Stella Morgana discusses how pro-market critics of the 1990 Iranian Labor Code (ILC) consistently claimed that it burdens employers and makes the labor market inflexible. This view sees the ILC as a major obstacle to economic growth and investment as well as a contributing factor to a higher unemployment rate. Conversely, left-wing critics of the ILC have highlighted its shortcomings in terms of implementation and enforcement, as well as the ambiguities and loopholes that have paved the way for employers to circumvent the law. They argue that amendments to the code have stripped the workforce of many of its constitutionally recognized rights.

As Morgana documents, the drafting of the ILC was a laborious and highly contested process, which began in 1982 and was spearheaded by the left-wing factions inside and outside the Majles. After the Iran–Iraq War (1980–1989), the conservatives who had opposed the ILC in the 1980s gained political prominence and left-wing factions were forced out of power. The ILC was finally approved by the Expediency Council in 1990 and its provisions were more progressive than the pre-1979 labor law (and the labor laws of most other Middle Eastern countries at the time). For example, working hours were reduced from forty-eight hours to forty-four hours a week and to thirty-six hours for dangerous jobs. Annual paid leave was increased to thirty days and the minimum working age raised to 15. Yet the words *sandikā* (syndicate), *ettehādieh* (union), or *eʿtesāb* (strike) remained conspicuously absent from the law – revealing the drafters' reticence toward legalizing collective bargaining.

During his term, President Khatami aimed to legalize independent trade unions, but the labor law amendments that were drafted and approved between 1999 and 2003 ultimately failed to do so. Ahmadinejad, whose administration was composed of the same conservatives who had wholeheartedly objected to the ILC in the 1980s, tabled a reform proposal which gave employers more rights to terminate contracts. Workers' organizations objected to these proposals as they saw them as giving absolute freedom to employers regarding the severance of contracts. In the end, small enterprises were exempted from part of the labor protections, as a result of which approximately 3 million wage earners remained legally unprotected.

Negotiations over the ILC continue, as employers (and to some extent the government) continue to treat the ILC as one of the main obstacles to economic growth. Moreover, as Morgana shows, circumventing the ILC altogether, by exploiting loopholes and leveraging governmental negligence in its enforcement, all to the detriment of workers' rights, has become a well-established practice in Iran. Meanwhile workers' living conditions have deteriorated further, along with general living conditions across the country, partly due to annual inflation rates of 35–45 percent. Average real compensation was lower in 2020 than twenty years prior.

7   Minority Rights

One of the central pillars of a substantive conception of the rule of law is equality before the law of all citizens, irrespective of racial, ethnic, or religious identity. But there is a deeply embedded tension between the nation-state, the rule of law, and the notion of equal citizenship. This is because states often employ law to construct frameworks of citizenship that generate forms of exclusion and hierarchy against those who do not belong to the majority nation, such as religious and ethnic minorities, migrants and indigenous peoples. This discrimination also finds expression formally and informally in various legal fora such as the courts and mistreatment by the police.

How has this issue played out in the Islamic Republic, which initially prided itself on the rejection of nationalism in the name of an Islamic solidarity that would supposedly transcend racial and ethnic divisions? On the one hand, as Elling (2013) has shown, the Islamic Republic has engaged in a project of state-building which has managed to incorporate large segments of the population who were previously marginalized under the Pahlavis. This project has included the construction of a vast infrastructure of health, education, and welfare, as well as attempts to engage the whole population in electoral politics. Even though this has not brought genuine democracy to Iran, it has provided the participatory mechanisms that eventually helped forge the late 1990s reformist wave. Moreover, it has brought many previously excluded minority voters into an arena of nationwide politics. On the other hand, as Milani shows in Chapter 10, the constitutional core of the Islamic Republic is still very much Perso-centric and Shi'i-centric, and this has structured social and political hierarchies and the rule of law in connection with minorities. Moreover, any belief system that is perceived to be at odds with the official state ideology is seen as a threat and dealt with accordingly. This has been the case particularly in connection with unrecognized religious minorities such as Sunni Muslims, Bahais, and Gonabadi Dervishes who have faced severe repression at the hands of judicial and police authorities. But even the recognized religious minorities (Jews, Christians, Zoroastrians) continue to be discriminated against in Iranian law. Their life continues to have less value in the application of *qesās* or retributive punishments, even after Penal Code reform in 2013. For example, if a Muslim kills a non-Muslim, he or she will not be subject to *qesās* and thus will not receive the death penalty and at most could be sentenced to ten years' imprisonment. If a non-Muslim kills a Muslim, by contrast, he or she will be subject to *qesās* and could be executed.[3] In criminal procedure, the testimony of religious minorities carries less value in court than that of Muslims. Inheritance law also continues to disadvantage religious minorities: If a non-Muslim has a Muslim heir, the decedent's non-Muslim heir(s) will not inherit at all.[4] Therefore, if, for example, one heir converts to Islam, he or she can prevent other heirs from receiving any inheritance. Moreover, the *gozinesh* (selection) law of 1996 that regulates employment in the public sector requires employees, whether or not they are Muslim, to believe in and commit themselves to the principle of *velāyat-e faqih*. As such, the *gozinesh* law enshrines discrimination in hiring on the basis of ideology,[5] and creates an impediment for the employment of religious minorities, particularly because the public sector controls a large share of the Iranian economy.

Unlike the formally codified policies discriminating against religious minorities, the regime's ideological framework regarding ethnic minorities is not based on assumptions of racial or ethnic supremacy. In practice, however, ethnic discrimination overlaps with religious discrimination to a large extent because Iran's Sunni citizens are overwhelmingly ethnic minorities as well. Thus, when ethnic identity fosters political dissent, ethnicity can also be the basis for invidious state action on its own (Dudoignon 2017). Numerous sympathizers of ethnic opposition groups and activists advocating for the rights of ethnic minorities have received harsh sentences, including the death penalty, after grossly unfair trials. The Iranian government's policy toward ethnic minorities could be broadly described as one of repressive securitization (Dudoignon 2017), which has been reinforced by the hegemonic expression of ethnic Iranian nationalism based on the Persian language and Shi'i exceptionalism. The civic ideals of the Khatami administration and the 2009 Green Movement – "Iran for all Iranians" – offered a more inclusive and pluralistic vision of Iranian identity, but the discourse of civic nationalism is still ambiguous on the question of tolerance and difference and has thus far failed to find expression at the level of state institutions. The Women, Life, Freedom movement and its violent repression – disproportionally felt in the Baluchi and Kurdish regions – has further highlighted the discriminatory ethnonationalism of the Islamic Republic.

---

[3] Islamic Penal Code (2013): https://irandataportal.syr.edu/penal-code, accessed 20 July, 2020.
[4] Civil Code (1928): www.refworld.org/docid/49997adb27.html
[5] On this, see Amnesty International's concerns relevant to the ninety-first session of the International Labor Conference, June 3–19, 2003, AI Index: IOR 42/003/2003: https://perma.cc/C5UU-ERP2, accessed 25 July 2020.

8 Family Law

Family law has been one of the most ideologically contested spheres of the law under the Islamic Republic. The Islamic Republic abolished the Family Protection Law (FPL) of 1967 and in doing so weakened the rule of law in a substantive sense by curtailing women's rights in the areas of marriage, divorce, child custody, and alimony. This was met with protest by women's groups, which led to the introduction of new standard marriage contracts in 1982, containing a stipulation by which the husband could authorize his wife to pronounce *talāq*, provided she could prove to the court that one of the contractual conditions according to which she may execute this right had been fulfilled. As Richter shows in Chapter 4, however, the wife could also be granted a divorce by a judge through the principle of *'osr va haraj* (hardship and suffering), acknowledged in Article 1130 of the 1982 Civil Code, if she could prove that the continuation of marriage would cause her such hardship.

The absence of legal definitions of what constituted *'osr va haraj* meant that judges had a great deal of discretion in this area. The concept was gradually clarified in legal reforms and amendments between 2002 and 2013, which reduced the discretion of the judge in this sphere. Separately, female counselor judges were introduced, who would accompany male judges in the family courts. As Richter shows, the introduction of legislation defining *'osr va haraj* indicates that codification need not bring an end to the flexibility associated with Islamic law. Legislative organs may and do respond to social needs and changes. At the same time, the examples Richter marshals also illustrate how strengthening formal legal procedures can improve women's rights substantively.

In comparing Iranian family law with its cognates in Iraq, Bahrain, and Afghanistan, Richter shows that in the latter cases demands for codification often went hand in hand with expectations of a greater, or even exclusive, role for parliament in developing legal drafts, at the expense of the involvement of religious scholars and institutions. In Iran, the process is slightly different as even parliament needs to anticipate potential vetoes by the *mojtahed*s of the Guardian Council. Here the discursive struggles revolve around gender-egalitarian *ijtihād*. To help their campaigns, those working for progressive family law reform seek religious interpretations that can buttress the intended reform, and with which they can challenge the Guardian Council's *ijtihād* in the court of public opinion. From this perspective, *ijtihād* is or can be practiced by the legislator, who might be informed by the expert opinions of *mojtahed*s outside the Guardian Council, and potentially anyone else who chooses to enter the "*ijtihādi* discourse."

9 Artistic Expression

A democratic and rights-based conception of the rule of law is, at its core, rooted in universalist humanism. When human empathy breaks down or is weakened by political and ideological polarization, it is often artistic expression and communication that reminds people of their common humanity. The rule of law can help create a sphere in which people have the freedom to engage in this dialogue and express their creativity (Aresty 2012). In the sphere of artistic expression, the rule of law has experienced some of the most striking fluctuations under the Islamic Republic. After the 1979 Revolution, political leaders were acutely suspicious of the arts, especially cinema, seeing this kind of cultural production as a conduit for capitalist or socialist influences that would "spray poison [by] corrupting people's minds and values" (Hashemi and Kalb 2020: 114). To this end, two bodies were tasked with regulating artistic and cultural production: the Ministry of Culture and Islamic Guidance (otherwise known as Ershād, established immediately after the revolution in 1979) and the Supreme Council for the Cultural Revolution (SCCR – established in 1984). Popular genres of art, such as cinema and music, were among the first targets of censorship and many artists were banned, with the political authorities dubbing them as sources of corruption in society. At the same time, Khomeini did not exclude the possibility that modern cultural production could benefit the cause of Islam. Gradually, the Islamic Republic became more aware of the potential uses of culture as state propaganda and set up institutions, such as the Farabi Cinema Foundation established in 1985, which were tasked with "managing" the industry in association with the Ershād. But at this stage the Islamic Republic was still somewhat inexperienced at regulating artistic expression such as cinema, making it the prerogative of the individual filmmaker to serve the Islamic Republic without much formal guidance. This gave film directors a small measure of autonomy from the state censor (Hashemi and Kalb 2020: 116).

As Pourzand and Mirebrahimi show in Chapter 13, toward the late 1980s a multilayered regime of control and censorship of arts and culture was established, with the Ershād and the SCCI at its apex. This regime comprised of several layers of supervision embedded within each area of art and culture, to ensure the application of the regulations issued by higher legislative and executive bodies. Additionally, paramilitary groups such as the Basij and groups linked to the IRGC acted as supplementary mechanisms for the enforcement of censorship, even when artists and writers had received legal licenses for publishing or displaying their work.

Despite the structurally rigorous censorship apparatus in place in the Islamic Republic, Iran's factional politics have at times allowed space for artists, creative professionals, writers, and journalists to thrive; a phenomenon most manifested in 1997–2005 during the presidency of Mohammad Khatami. Art, culture, and the press experienced a phase of revival during this period. Artistic expression was repressed again under the Ahmadinejad presidency, which witnessed the arrest of a number of prominent film directors and actors, including Jafar Panahi and Golshifteh Farahani. Under President Raisi there was an escalation in repression against film directors, with the arrest of Jafar Panahi (again), Mohammad Rasoulof, and Mostafa al-Ahmad in 2022.[6] Today, levels of state censorship and repression remain high in the artistic sphere but also somewhat uneven, with some artistic expressions, such as theater, being relatively open, whilst musical, literary, and film production are more strictly censored.

10 Health

The rule of law is a foundational determinant of health since health systems can only be established, financed, and monitored with accountability through processes and structures established by law. But the scope and nature of rights in this area are particularly contested in ethical, philosophical, and theological debates. For example, is there a right to procreative freedom, in particular in vitro fertilization (IVF), irrespective of whether one is fertile? Shirin Naef's Chapter (14) suggests that the Iranian regulation of assisted reproductive technologies (ART) since 2003 has been one of the most permissive in the Muslim world, allowing almost every infertile married couple wishing to have a child of their own to fulfill their dream through assisted reproduction. Shi'i scholars, along with the Iranian medical community, have played a decisive role in shaping this permissive legal framework. Further, rather than leaving this to the private sphere, Iran is the only Muslim-majority country where the state is the main actor facilitating assisted reproduction via state-run embryo donation and surrogacy arrangements as a means of helping infertile married couples conceive children.

But rule-of-law imperatives can clash sharply in the sphere of health, too. This is highlighted in Chapter 8, authored by Arash and Kamiar Alaei, which looks at the trajectory of AIDS policy in connection with drug users and sex workers, who are both defined, as in many other

---

[6] (In Persian): "Protests against the Arrest of Filmmakers," *Kayhan London*, Tir 22, 1301/ July 13, 2022: https://kayhan.london/fa/1401/04/22/291505/, accessed 15 August 2023.

countries, as "criminal" groups and are both disproportionately carriers of HIV. The chapter illustrates how the legal challenges in responding to this problem are intertwined with cultural, religious, and political responses to the HIV/AIDS pandemic in Iran – highlighting the tensions between the rule of law, security, and health imperatives in this area. In connection with AIDS amongst drug users, the chapter shows how Iran's strategy has oscillated between a "national-security" and a "harm-reduction" approach. The first decade of the Islamic Republic adopted a highly punitive approach to drug users, who were jailed in often overcrowded prisons with little or no medical care, with disastrous consequences for the spread of HIV/AIDS. This approach was gradually replaced by a more pragmatic harm-reduction approach during the Khatami years, which saw attempts to provide treatment for drug users as well as reducing their incarceration rate. This policy shift was a result of pressure by prisoners and civil society but also the coincidence of the Khatami presidency with the tenure of Mahmoud Shahroudi as the head of the judiciary, two leaders who were open to experimenting with a harm-reduction approach on a nationwide scale. The pendulum swung back again, however, under the presidency of Ahmadinejad and Shahroudi's successor, Sadegh Larijani, who encouraged imprisonment. A clear achievement of the reformist years has been the public acknowledgment of drug addiction as a widespread social problem, even if recent heads of the judiciary have abandoned more holistic harm-reduction approaches and reverted to punishment and imprisonment.

11   Judicial Reform

As Chapter 9 has shown, there have been substantial reforms inside the judiciary since the late 1990s, improving on the rule of law in some respects and for some time, while also dramatically falling short of doing so in a manner demanded by the reformist parliament (2000–2004), legal professionals, and human rights organizations. Under Head of the Judiciary Shahroudi (1999–2009), a number of important reforms were undertaken from trying to phase out special courts, to prohibiting the security services from running their own detention and prison systems, ending the death penalty for minors, ending execution by stoning, strengthening the rights of political prisoners, and reforming the Penal Code and the CCP. Many of these reforms were only implemented temporarily, or were disregarded by lower-ranking judges and the security services, were reversed under Shahroudi's successors, or, as with the reforms of the Penal Code and CCP, were later watered down. Under his successor,

Sadegh Larijani (2009–2019), death sentences doubled and then tripled compared to average rates under Shahroudi. There were forty-two executions of juvenile offenders during the decade of Shahroudi's tenure,[7] but at least seventy-nine under Larijani's.[8] His successor Ebrahim Raisi (2019–2021) revived some of Shahroudi's reforms in sentencing by commuting death sentences against drug traffickers to imprisonment and fines. Raisi also inaugurated a concerted effort to fight corruption in the judiciary, but the introduced measures appeared to apply more harshly to members of rival political factions than his own networks. Raisi's first term was cut short when he was elected president in 2021 and Gholam-Hossein Mohseni-Eje'i appointed new head of the judiciary. The appointments of both Raisi and Mohseni-Eje'i were severely tarnished by the fact that both were involved in the mass killings of 4,500–5,000 political prisoners in 1988: Raisi as a member of the four-person committee leading the interrogations and ordering the executions, Mohseni-Eje'i as the judiciary's representative in the Intelligence Ministry at the time. In the course of Mohseni-Eje'i's term since August 2021, dozens of protesters have been executed, thousands have been imprisoned, and security forces have killed on the street with impunity. In the aftermath of the Women, Life, Freedom protests, more than forty lawyers who had announced they would represent detained demonstrators for free were arrested. Overall, compared to the previous year, executions in 2023 rose by 75 percent to more than 580. The death penalty has been handed down on the basis of forced confessions in court proceedings which, under Shahroudi, would have been considered unlawful. As Chapter 9 has shown, the judiciary is not a monolith, and much of the quality of the rule of law stands and falls with its leading administrators and professionals.

12 Conclusion

Where does Iran fall on the rule-of-law continuum discussed in Chapter 1 of this volume? The answer depends very much on the realm of the law and time period under consideration. In the areas of criminal law and criminal procedure, Iran falls short of anything more ambitious than the most minimalist notion (Tamanaha 2004: 91f.), although

---

[7] Radio Free Europe/Radio Liberty (RFE/RL), "Iran Lawyer Seeks Cash to Spare Young on Death Row": www.rferl.org/a/Iran_Lawyer_Seeks_Cash_To_Spare_Young_On_Death_Row/1858467.htm, accessed October 15, 2020.
[8] IranWire, "Execution of Juveniles: Amnesty International Reports on Cover-Ups by the Iranian Government," February 26, 2016: https://justice4iran.org/persian/wp-content/uploads/2018/02/Larijani-13.pdf, accessed 15 October 2020. Amnesty International, "Iran: 17-Year-Old Boy at Risk of Imminent Execution," Press Release, October 13, 2017.

important reforms were initiated in the 2000s with the aim of rendering the law more compatible with international human rights standards and strengthening the rights of the political opposition and of dissidents (see Chapter 9). In labor and commercial law, Iran comes close to a mid-range notion (Tamanaha 2004) of the rule of law, where the law is – for the most part at least – "general, prospective, clear and certain." In the 2000s, initiatives were undertaken to grant workers the right to independent representation, but these efforts ultimately bore no fruit, and even today Iran does not allow for independent unions. In commercial law, some improvements in investment law were made that opened parts of the economy to private investment and ownership, as reformists applied for Iran to join the World Trade Organization (WTO). These efforts were shelved under Ahmadinejad's presidency and the state, through subsidiaries and parastatals, remains the predominant actor in trade and commerce. The Joint Comprehensive Plan of Action (JCPOA) would have brought about seismic changes in creating independent capital, along the way gradually decreasing the tight link between economic and political power in Iran, but, at the time of writing, it looks unlikely to be revived. Thus, in labor and commercial law, the rule of law has on the whole not improved since the 1990s. By contrast, economic crises have eroded the quality of jobs and living standards, and state-affiliated actors, at the forefront the IRGC, have increased their hold on major sectors of the economy through myriad parastatal companies that are largely shielded from market competition. In the arts, levels of state censorship and repression differ from sphere to sphere. While painting and theater are less severely monitored (perhaps partly because of high levels of self-censorship), musical, literary, and film production remain strictly censored. In this area, the rule of law meanders between Tamanaha's notion of rule by law and formal legality, the two least ambitious notions of the rule of law. If one looks at reproductive rights, where the Islamic Republic has some of the most progressive forms of regulation in the world, the rule of law fulfills many of the requirements of a more ambitious rule-of-law notion, where law is aimed at creating "the conditions in which one can live a life in dignity" (Tamanaha 2004: 91f.). In family law, by contrast, the letter of the law in the early 2020s renders Iran closer to the minimalist end of the rule-of-law continuum, even if legal and social practices alleviate some of the more draconian regulations of family law.

In 2011, the year Iran was first included in the World Justice Project (WJP), which attempts to measure the rule of law in more than 130 countries in a comparative manner, Iran ranked in the middle range of its income group. Notably, it ranked ten places higher at that time than

Turkey and Venezuela. It also at that time ranked higher than Malaysia, Mexico, and European Union (EU) member Romania. Eleven years later, Iran ranked 39 out of 40 in its income group, 7th out of 8 in the Middle East, and 119th out of 139 in total. Romania meanwhile had climbed up to rank 41 and Malaysia to 54.

A general lesson from the reformist period under President Khatami (1997–2005) was that as the reformist parliament (2000–2004) and president pointed to opportunities in the 1979 constitution to enhance the competencies and political importance of the elected institutions, and to thereby seek to democratize the political system from within, conservative factions reacted by closing up politically relevant spaces: Independent media were closed down, and civil society organizations were infiltrated by regimist agents and seemingly voluntarily brought under government control; the legal profession was sidelined; independent economic actors were forced to cooperate or cease operation; and the creation of political parties and trade unions was prohibited or made de facto impossible. Whereas many in the political opposition still believed that a rule-of-law oriented, democratic future was attainable by reforming rather than replacing the Islamic Republic, and thus by evolution rather than revolution, the conservative response to the reformist movement effectively showed the impossibility of that political project. Democratizing reform then will only occur if the Supreme Leader himself embraces such an agenda since all constitutional reform procedurally begins and ends with the Supreme Leader himself. This is unlikely to happen unless sustained levels of country-wide popular mobilization combine with fissures within the regime and force his hand. Short of this, it is difficult to envision a rule-of-law oriented, democratic Iran that will not be the outcome of yet another revolution.

Bibliography

Arjomand, Said Amir. *After Khomeini: Iran Under His Successors*, Oxford: Oxford University Press, 2009.

Aresty, Jeff. "Arts, Culture and the Rule of Law," *World Justice Project*, October 21, 2012: https://worldjusticeproject.org/news/arts-culture-and-rule-law, accessed June 15, 2022.

Dudoignon, Stéphane A. *The Baluch, Sunnism and the State in Iran: From Tribal to Global*, London: Hurst Publishers, 2017.

Ehsani, Kaveh. "The Politics of Property in the Islamic Republic of Iran," in Said Amir-Arjomand and Nathan Brown (eds.), *The Rule of Law, Islam and Constitutional Politics in Egypt and Iran*. Albany: State University of New York Press, 2013, pp. 153–179.

Elling, Rasmus Christian. *Minorities in Iran: Nationalism and Ethnicity after Khomeini*, London: Hurst Publishers, 2013.

Hashemi, Masoumeh, and Zeb Kalb. "Tehran's Universal Studios," *New Left Review*, 121, January/February 2020, pp. 109–131.

Kashani, S. H. "Privatization and the rule of law" (in Persian), *Kanun-e Vokalla*, No 96 & 97, 1386/2006, pp. 66–84.

Tamanaha, Brian Z. *On the Rule of Law: History, Politics, Theory*, New York: Cambridge University Press, 2004.

Index

Abrahamian, Ervand, 68, 102, 282, 285, 287
Administrative Justice Court (*divān-e ʿedālat-e edārī*), xxv, 7, 16, 18n9, 20, 43, 154, 156, 171, 177, 306, 308
adoption, xxiv, 420–421, 424–426, 431, 443
adultery, xxxii, 19, 48, 57–58, 71–74, 230, 236, 241, 273, 419, 421, 427–428
Āgāhī police, *see* police
Aghajari, Hashem, 24n16
Ahmadi, Nemat, 87
Ahmadi-Moghaddam, Ismail, xxi, 171–172, 174, 176, 182, 186, 226, 253, 311
Ahmadinejad, Mahmoud, xi, xxi–xxii, 21, 27, 29, 87, 112, 151, 170, 176, 190, 218, 224, 244, 251, 253–255, 258, 261, 279, 284, 297, 327, 332–333, 347, 348–350, 352, 354–355, 376, 396–398, 401, 450, 452, 457, 458, 460
AIDS, vii, viii, xix, xxi, 27, 57, 188, 224, 236–259, 276, 457–458
alternative sentences, *see* sentences
Amini, Mahsa Jina, xxviii, 79, 98–99, 178, 184, 188, 198, 202, 320, 388, 445, 449
amnesty, xxvi, 35, 49, 99, 197, 201–202, 230, 449
Amnesty International, ix, 61, 69, 72–73, 77–78, 80, 82–89, 91–92, 94–98, 102, 172, 177, 183–184, 198, 203–204, 208, 223, 226, 233, 254, 281, 299, 310, 315, 320, 322–323, 459
amphetamine, 227
amputation, *see* sentences
Anti-Drug Law, xvii, xix, xxiii, xxvii, 48, 222, 224
apostasy, x, xvii, 47, 57, 273, 282, 291, 309–310, 327

Arab, Arabs, xxiii, xxvi, 104, 107, 114, 116–117, 119, 130, 132–133, 150, 191, 267, 293, 313–315, 322–324, 327, 380, 418–423, 426
Armed Forces General Staff (AFGS, *Setād-e koll-e niruhā-ye mosallah*), xxxi, 94, 164, 175, 180, 256, 262, 269, 271, 319
armed rebellion against the state (*baghy*), *see* crimes
Ashtari, Hossein, xxiv, 176, 179
Ashtiani, Sakineh Mohammadi, xxii, 72
Assisted Reproductive Technologies (ART), 4, 31, 414–417, 419–420, 422–425, 427, 429, 441–442, 457
Azeri Turks, 98, 313–314, 316–317

Baghi, Emaddedin, 90–91, 189–190, 395
baghy (armed rebellion against the state), *see* crimes
Baháʾís, xviii, 145, 149, 215–217, 266, 291, 294, 303–308, 311, 320–324, 326–328, 331–332, 409, 453
Baháʾi Institute for Higher Education, 306
bakhshesh (forgiveness/clemency), xxxi, 69, 70, 75, 187
Baluch, Baluchis, Baluchistan, xx, xxvi, 98, 175, 209, 289, 292–293, 313, 317–318, 320–321, 325, 328, 330, 454, 461
bankruptcy, 207, 212–213, 219
Bar Association, xxxiii, 9, 16, 21, 25–26, 36–37, 42–43, 73, 91, 135–158, 185, 210n94, 276, 278, 447–448
Basij, x, 26, 31, 79, 83–84, 165–166, 171, 173–175, 177–178, 182–186, 242, 255, 330, 392–393, 410, 456
Beheshti, Mohammad, xv, xvi, 161–162
bioethics, 418, 432–435, 441
blood-money (*diyeh*), xxi, xxxii, 25, 45–46, 48, 50–51, 54–56, 60–63, 75–76, 94, 96, 187, 211, 213–218, 233

463

Index

bolugh (criminal responsibility), 34–35, 51–52, 274
bride-price (*mehrieh*), 205, 211, 212, 214, 217–220, 232–233
Broadcasting Organization of the Islamic Republic of Iran (IRIB), 96, 263, 280, 391–392, 413

censorship, 31, 41, 314, 386–413, 456–457, 460
Chastity Houses (*khāneh-ye 'efāf*), 250
cheques, 206n77, 211–213, 217, 225n153, 232–234, 276n19, 283
children
  Act of Protecting Children Without Guardians, xxiv, 424–425
  children's rights, xxiv, 35, 52, 68n6, 77, 89, 109, 121–122, 251, 274, 284, 317–318, 335, 421–425, 432, 443
Cinema, 392, 394, 398, 399, 401–404, 411–413, 456
Civil Code(s)
  Afghanistan (1977), 111, 125
  Iran (1928), xxxiii, 6–7, 9, 25, 52, 111–112, 128, 141, 217, 301, 417, 418, 454n4
    Amendments (Islamic Republic), xvi, xx, 118–124, 454–455
Code of Criminal Procedure for General and Revolutionary Courts (CCP) (*qānun-e dādresi-ye keyfari-ye dādgāhhā-ye 'omumi va enqelābi*)
  1999, xx, 38n25, 47, 69, 90, 206–209, 271, 275
  2015, xxiv, xxxi, 17, 28, 36, 38, 41, 58, 69, 83–95, 152, 175–176, 208–209, 260, 266, 271, 275–276, 286, 447, 458
confession (*eqrār*), *see* evidence
forced, *see* evidence
Constitution of 1906/constitutional revolution, 5, 6–9, 42, 77, 100, 135–136, 140, 143, 156, 234, 417, 441
Constitution of the Islamic Republic of Iran, ix, xii, xv, xvii, xxxiii, 9–23, 28, 32–36, 38, 42–48, 61–67, 78–79, 82, 84, 90, 93, 96, 100–107, 110, 112, 116, 130, 137, 140, 144, 146, 151, 154, 157–158, 184–185, 256, 262–267, 271–273, 277, 278n27, 285–292, 300, 302, 309, 311–313, 316–317, 344, 355–356, 361, 377, 386, 390, 392, 394, 401, 407, 413, 417, 423, 427, 434, 436, 440–442, 445, 450, 452–453, 461

converts, 47, 274, 291, 294, 301, 324, 454
  Christian converts, 309–311, 321, 325–326, 329, 331
Counterintelligence Organization (*sāzeman-e hefāzat-e ettelā'āt*), 164, 166–167, 174
courts
  Court of Administrative Justice, xxv, 7, 16, 18n9, 20, 43, 154, 156, 171, 177, 306, 308
  Criminal Courts, 15, 23, 41, 78, 94n82, 102, 147n20, 268n7, 288
  Disciplinary Court for Judges, 16, 20, 44, 142–143, 149, 151, 277n22
  Family Courts, xxiii, 20, 111–112, 118, 147, 455
  Revolutionary Courts, xv, xx, 15–17, 22, 29, 33n17, 38, 40, 66–69, 78–79, 83n47, 91–99, 145–147, 161–163, 174, 177, 189, 207n78, 240–242, 267–268, 273n16, 275, 278, 281, 294n5, 297, 307–308, 316, 326, 393, 395, 408–409
  Special Court for the Clergy, xxxv, 15–16, 18n10, 22, 33–34, 43, 94, 100, 138, 146, 157, 161, 167, 182, 185, 266–269, 282, 286, 288, 446, 458
  Supreme Court, xxvi, 16–18, 21, 23–24, 33, 36, 82, 94–96, 128, 142, 151, 205, 295–296, 298n13, 325, 420
crimes
  baghy (armed rebellion against the state), 38–39, 45, 48, 60, 93, 295
  drug-related, xvii, xix, xxi, xxiii, xxvii, 15, 17, 26–28, 35, 38, 48, 93, 165, 172, 175, 181, 188, 190, 192, 194, 196, 197, 203–204, 206–208, 211n98, 212, 220–230, 232–234, 236–259, 276n19, 281, 283, 285, 318, 446–448, 457–458, 459
  economic, 15, 83, 181, 378, 382
  efsād-e fel-'arz (corruption on earth), xxix, xxxii, 38, 45, 48, 57, 60, 93, 408
  financial, 15, 268
  mohārebeh, xvii, xxxiii, 38–39, 45, 48–49, 57, 59–60, 63, 93, 98, 294–296, 298, 315, 408, 446
  unintentional crimes (*gheir-e 'amdi*), 56, 60, 205, 211, 213, 217, 229, 230, 298, 449
Criminal Code, *see* penal code
Criminal Investigations Office of the Law Enforcement Forces (*edāreh-ye āgāhi-ye niruhā-ye entezāmi*), *see* police

Cultural Revolution, x, xv, 304, 389
Cultural Revolution Headquarters, 389
see also Supreme Council for the
   Cultural Revolution (SCCR)

death sentence, *see* sentences
decarceration (*zendān-zodāi*), 188, 206, 230, 448
Disciplinary Court for Judges (*dādgāh-e entezāmi-ye qozzāt*), *see* courts
divorce, xv–xviii, xxxiv–xxxv, 13, 15, 107, 109–112, 122–130, 133, 217–218, 220, 239, 421–422, 433n20, 437, 455
Drug Control Headquarters (DCHQ), 223, 242, 245, 249–250, 253, 255
drug rehabilitation camps, 192, 201n57, 223–224, 226–228, 230, 243, 253, 449
drugs, 51, 91n77, 100, 124–125, 188, 190, 192, 194, 196–197, 203, 206n77, 212, 220–229, 234–235, 237–239, 240, 242–243, 245, 251–252, 255–258, 276n19, 282, 447

Ebadi, Shirin, xxi, 20, 79, 102, 277
efsād-e fel-ʿarz (corruption on earth), *see* crimes
egg donation, 415, 421–422, 426, 428–430, 433n20, 436–438, 442–443
ʿelm-e qāzī, *see* knowledge of the judge
Embryo Donation Law, xxi, 416, 430–433, 441
Esmaili, Gholamhossein, 194–195, 199, 203, 208
Evaluation Council, *see* Ministry of Culture and Islamic Guidance
evidence
  confession (eqrār), 35–36, 55, 57–58, 66n3, 69–75, 84–90, 94, 100, 102, 174, 181, 272–273, 287, 315, 446, 459
  forced confession, 35, 69, 84–85, 87, 89, 100, 102, 446, 459
  knowledge of the judge (*ʿelm-e qāzī*), ix, xxii, xxxii, 22, 25, 36, 55–56, 70–74, 98, 100–103, 271, 272–274, 286, 446
  laws of evidence, 25, 36, 54–56, 70, 73–74, 85, 86n58, 272–274, 316
  witness testimony (*shahādat*), 56, 70, 74, 84n52, 272–273, 312, 454
Evin prison, 21n14, 86n58, 91, 150, 190n8, 196n33 and n35, 202

exile, xi, xv, 105 (n10), 144, 238, 312, 318
  coerced, 144, 244, 398
  internal, 296, 299
Expediency Council, xxvi, xxxiii, 11, 14, 17, 18n9, 20, 29, 39, 112, 129n68, 138–139, 145–147, 156, 229, 263, 265n4, 281–284, 302, 335, 361n9, 376n56, 377, 452

Fakhrizadeh, Mohsen, 101, 382
FARAJA (*Farmāndehi-ye entezāmi jomhuri-ye eslāmi*), *see* police
Fashāfuyeh prison, *see* prisons
FATA (*Polis-e fazā-ye towlid va tabādol-e ettelāʿāt*, lit: "police of the virtual space and information exchange"), Cyberspace Police, *see* police

Ganji, Akbar, 80, 150, 395n29
General Directorate of Monitoring and Evaluation, *see* Ministry of Culture and Islamic Guidance
Gonabadi dervishes, 290–291, 296–299, 321, 323–324, 327, 328, 329, 453
gozinesh (selection), ix, xix, xxxii, 301, 454
Green Movement, xxii, xxv, 5, 173–174, 176, 179, 284–285, 287, 396, 403n56, 408, 454
Guardian Council, xvii–xviii, xxi–xxv, xxvii–xxviii, 7, 9–13, 17, 18, 20, 23, 29, 37, 39, 41, 62, 75, 86n61, 92, 101, 110–112, 115–116, 129n68 and n69, 137–139, 145–146, 154, 156, 215n114, 253, 263–266, 273, 275–276, 280, 286, 289–299, 302, 325, 335n10, 361n9, 376–377n58, 396, 412, 431, 448–449, 455
guardians, guardianship (in family law), xxiv, 9–10, 34, 60, 110, 143, 150n22, 334–335, 420, 424–425, 440
irresponsible guardians, xxiv, 425

Haft Tappeh Sugar Factory, 349
hākemiyat-e qānun, xxxiii, 43, 110, 260, 262–263, 285, 287, *see also* Rule of Law
hashish, 223
hejab, xiv, xxv, xxvii, xxix, xxx, 153n33, 161, 173, 230, 403n56
hip-hop music, 405
HIV/AIDS, vii–viii, xix, xxi, 27, 188, 224, 236–259, 276, 458

Index

hodud, xvi, xviii, xxxii, xxxv, 15–17, 23, 45, 46–49, 54, 64, 70, 72, 75, 187, 241, 271–273, 446

hoquq, xxxiii, 7–8, 42, 64–65, 134, 141, 143, 157, 192n16, 234, 235, 288, 417–418, 431, 442–443

human rights, viii–xii, xvi, xxi, xxvii, xxix, xxx, xxxv, 2, 10, 23, 24n16, 33n18, 35n22, 39, 42–44, 66–68, 72–92, 97, 100–102, 109, 135–137, 143, 145–150, 153, 155, 157–160, 170, 172, 184–186, 188n4, 189n6, 190, 191n12, 198, 203n66, 204, 209n89, 234–236, 238, 240–243, 254, 256–261, 266, 270, 277–278, 281n31, 283, 285n37, 286–288, 290, 292–295, 297–299, 302–303, 306, 309, 310n26, 312, 314–315, 317–321, 324, 326, 327, 329–330, 357n1, 388, 394n27, 398n36–37, 408n72–73, 411n82, 444, 446–447, 458, 460

ijtihād, xxxiii, 19, 25, 106–108, 110, 116, 127, 129, 131, 455

incarceration rate, 27, 187n2, 190–192, 230–231, 276, 449, 458

incest, 421, 423, 427, 439, 442

insurance, 3, 13, 30, 62, 207, 214–217, 352, 357, 360, 368, 451

IRGC (Islamic Revolutionary Guard Corps), *see* Revolutionary Guards

Islamic Council of Scholar, ICS (Bahrain), 114–117, 120, 132

Islamic Development Organization (*Sāzeman-e tablighāt-e eslāmi*), xxxv, 391–392

Islamic Revolutionary Committees (*Komiteh-ye enqelāb-e eslāmi*), xviii, xxxiii, 161–164, 186

judges, xx, xxii, xxvii, 6, 8–9, 15, 19–20, 22–23, 25, 29, 35–36, 40–42, 48, 52, 67, 70–74, 78, 81–82, 85, 94–97, 99, 101, 106, 112–113, 116, 121, 129n70, 136–137, 140–145, 148, 154, 163, 177, 188, 204–211, 220, 229, 267, 270–274, 276–277, 279, 308, 446, 455, 458, *see also* knowledge of the judge
  appointment, 8, 18–19, 33, 115, 128n16, 139–140, 142, 147, 155, 161, 260, 278
  removal of, 18, 20–21, 33–34, 151, 161, *see also* Disciplinary Court for Judges

judicial divorce (*talāq tavassot-e mahkame*), 111n24, 123–124

judicial officers (*zābetān-e qazā'i*), 79, 83, 89, 96, 162, 165–167, 177, 181–182, 445

judicial personalism, 67, 70

judicial police (*polis-e qazā'i*), *see* police

judiciary
  history of [pre-1979], 6–9, 105–108, 140–144, 417–418
  independence of, 9, 20, 26–29, 33–34, 41–42, 66, 78, 95–96, 136, 139, 156, 159–160, 182, 261, 277

judicial police, *see* police

Judiciary's Intelligence Protection Organisation (*sāzman-e hefāzat-e ettelā'āt-e quwwa-ye qazā'iyeh*), xxxv, 165, 175, 184, 186

Kahrizak Detention Center, *see* prisons
Kamali, Hossein, 345
Karimi-Rad, Jamal, 73
Kazemi, Zahra, 21n14, 81, 150, 277
Khamenei, Ali, xvi–xviii, xxiii, xxvii–xxix, 13–14, 26, 43, 63, 69, 163–168, 171, 260, 262, 264–265, 267–268, 271, 280–282, 284, 300n14, 306, 308, 316, 319n10, 396n30, 405, 427, 434, 450

Khāneh-ye Kārgar (Workers' House), 332, 344–346

Khatami, Mohammad, xix–xxi, 5, 16, 27, 29, 39, 110n21, 130, 148, 150, 152, 167, 183, 224, 244, 250–251, 260–266, 277, 284–288, 305, 314, 332–333, 338–346, 352–355, 360–361, 386, 395–398, 400, 405, 445, 447–448, 450, 452, 454, 457–458, 461

khishāvandi (kinship), 418–420, 422

Khomeini, Ruhollah, xi, xv, xvi–xvii, 9–15, 22–23, 27–28, 32, 43, 59, 68–69, 71, 88, 101, 110–111, 112n25, 144–146, 161, 163, 166, 187, 221, 234, 244, 267–268, 272, 282, 297, 301, 303, 318, 324, 333–336, 351, 353, 354–355, 386, 389, 390n10, 394n25, 405, 420, 440, 450, 456, 461–462

Khuzestan, xxviii, 148n21, 199, 300n14, 313–315, 322, 349

knowledge of the judge (*'elm-e qāzī*), *see* evidence

*komiteh*s, *see* Islamic Revolutionary Committees

Kurds, Kurdish, Kurdistan, 68, 98, 116n40, 148n21, 289, 293–294, 307, 311, 313–314, 318–322, 327, 329–330, 388, 454

Index

Labour, xxvi, 77n23, 301n20, 302, 331–357, 362–363, 454n5
   activism, 265, 333, 343, 349, 350
   law, xviii, 4, 10, 13–14, 29, 265, 312, 331–338, 341–349, 351, 352, 354, 356, 451–452, 460
   rights, 4, 331–357, 451
   trade unions, 13, 39, 342, 344, 353, 452, 461
Language Rights, 17, 312–314, 316, 401n47, 454
Larijani, Sadegh Amoli, xxii, 16, 28, 88, 176, 203, 206, 216, 220, 253, 255–256, 272, 279–285, 458–459
Law of the Principle of Trials (1911), 69
lawyers, 8–9, 15, 20, 25–26, 30, 34, 36–37, 38n25, 42, 52, 54, 68, 73, 78, 80, 82, 91, 92, 97, 99–101, 135–159, 171, 185, 189–190, 204, 209–211, 213n106, 277–279, 281, 285, 297, 446–448, 459
   Article 187 legal advisors, 36–37, 150, 152–155, 447
   certification, 135, 137, 141, 150, 152, 155, 278, 448
   training, 37, 135–137, 141, 145–146, 150–151
legality, 30, 32, 135n1, 156, 460
   principle of legality, 46–47, 65, 309
Lotfian, Hedayat, 166, 168

Mahdavi-Kani, Mohmmad Reza, xxiv, 161
Mahjoub, Alireza, 345, 348n49
majles, see parliament
marriage, xvi, xxxiv, 45, 57–58, 109–111, 113n28, 119–133, 217–219, 240–241, 265, 417, 419–423, 425, 430, 432, 439, 442, 455
   mut'a marriage (*nikāh-e al-mut'a*)/ temporary marriage (*sigheh*), xxiv, xxxiv, 45, 57, 107, 112, 119, 121–123, 127–128, 130–132, 134, 250, 256, 421–422, 428, 436–437, 442
   white marriage, 417n2, 442
Maslahat Council, see Expediency Council
Milk kinship, 421–424, 430, 441
Ministry of Culture and Islamic Guidance (MCIG, or otherwise known as *Ershād*), 16, 31, 242, 386, 391n13, 397n34, 398n35, 390–392, 396, 398, 401–406, 408, 410–412, 456
   Evaluation Council, 401–402
   General Directorate of Monitoring and Evaluation, 402
   Music Council, 405–406
   Poetry Council, 405–406
   Review Council, 401–402, 404n56

Ministry of Health and Medical Education (MOHME), 199, 235, 246n16, 247–248, 252n27, 253–255, 416, 436–437
Ministry of Information and Security (Intelligence Ministry), 11, 28, 38, 67n5, 79, 83, 89, 94, 102, 145, 152, 162, 243, 245, 255–256, 261, 266, 269, 271, 276, 278, 283–286, 297, 304n23, 311, 328, 347, 395, 404n56, 406, 445, 459
Ministry of Justice, 7–9, 16, 113, 136, 140–143, 145, 148, 276, 320
   Office for Drafting Judicial Bills (*Edāreh-ye tadvin-e lavā'eh-e quwwa-ye qazā'iyeh*), xxxiv, 46
Ministry of Labour, 337, 343
Mohaqqeq-Damad, Mostafa, 88, 108, 131, 152, 157, 279–280
mohārebeh (enmity against God), see crimes
Mohseni-Eje'i, Gholam-Hossein, xxviii, 21n13, 28, 99, 145, 202, 279, 280, 284, 285, 447, 459
mojtahed, xxxi, 10–12, 18–19, 20, 22, 24, 107–108, 110, 128–129, 137, 145, 147, 272, 455
moral policing, see police (Guidance Patrols)
Mortazavi, Saeed, xxiv, xxvi, 16, 21n14, 80–82, 168, 260, 276–277, 281
Mossadegh, Mohamad, 5, 100, 143, 144, 153
Mousavi, Mir-Hossein, xvi, xxii–xxiii, 279, 284, 333
Mousavi Ardebili, Ayatollah, 162, 434n21
MSM (Men who have Sex with Men), 236, 238, 240–241, 256
mujtahid [Arabic transliteration], see *mojtahed* [Persian transliteration]
Music Council, see Ministry of Culture and Islamic Guidance
mut'a marriage (*nikāh al-mut'a*), see marriage

NAJA, see police
Narcotics, see drugs
nasab (legal filiation, lineage), 415, 419, 423, 425n16, 426–428, 432, 443
National Organization for Civil Registration (*sāzemān-e thabt-e ahvāl-e keshvar*), 308, 317, 326, 416, 420, 442n15, 431n19, 434–435

Index

National Prisons Organization (*sāzemān-e zendānhā-ye keshvar*), 19, 170, 190–197, 199–203, 205, 207–208, 210, 220, 222n146, 225–227, 231–232
National Security Council, 11, 83, 97, 101, 139
Niruhā-ye entezāmi-ye jomhuri-ye eslāmi (Law Enforcement Forces of the Islamic Republic or NAJA), *see* police
NOPO (Counter-Terrorism Special Force), *see* police
November 2019 protests, *see* protests

Office of Public Prosecutor (*dādsarā*), xviii, xx, xxxii, 23, 77–78, 80, 100–101, 147n20, 163, 179, 268n7, 446
Office of Public Surveillance (*daftar-e nezārat-e hamegāni*), 169, 183, 445
'*osr va haraj* (hardship and suffering), xvi, xx, xxxiv, 111–112, 122–124, 127–128, 455
Overcrowding, *see* prisons

pardons, xxii, xxvi, xxix, 23, 24n16, 49, 63, 73, 99, 101, 130, 197–198, 202–203, 284, 449
parenthood, 32, 415, 417–418, 425, 430
parliament (*majles*), xv, xvii–xviii, xxi–xviii, xxxiii, 6–7, 9–13, 17–18, 21, 23–24, 29–30, 32–34, 37, 39, 49, 60, 62, 69, 79, 81n39, 86n61, 105, 110n22, 112, 120, 135, 138–141, 146, 148, 150, 152–154, 156, 162, 165, 166n2, 168, 169, 170, 176–177, 194, 195n30, 199–200, 204n70, 205n72, 206n77, 207, 211–212, 213, 215n114, 216, 218–219, 229–230, 243, 244, 256, 262–263, 265, 268–270, 273, 275, 276n19, 278–281, 291, 299–302, 312, 316, 322–323, 325, 333–335, 339, 342, 344n30, 345, 347n43, 348, 352, 356, 361, 362n13, 372, 376–377, 390, 396, 408, 415, 417, 431, 434, 440, 446, 449–450, 452, 455, 458, 461
Penal Code
  1926 Penal Code, 8, 45, 141
  1991 Penal Code, xviii–xix, 28, 45–46, 48–52, 56, 58n16, 59, 61–63, 69, 71, 146, 161, 266, 272, 295n9, 327, 407
  2013 Penal Code, xxiv, 22, 35, 38, 45–66, 68, 70–71, 73–75, 100, 148, 170, 204–205, 259, 273–275, 284, 295, 296, 299, 301, 309, 323, 325, 327, 387, 408–409, 446, 453–454, 458
personal status law, 132, 133
  Afghanistan, 123n55, 131
  Bahrain, 25, 104, 105, 113–121, 124, 126–134, 455
  Iran, 105, 418
  Iraq, 117n42, 130
plays (theatre), 403
Poetry Council, *see* Ministry of Culture and Islamic Guidance
police
  Criminal Investigations Office of the Law Enforcement Forces (*edāreh-ye āgāhi-ye niruhā-ye entezāmi*), xxiv, 83, 87–88, 181, 270
  Cyberspace Police (FATA, *Polis-e fazā-ye towlid va tabādol-e ettelā'āt*), xxxii, 174
  FARAJA (*Farmāndehi-ye entezāmi jomhuri-ye eslāmi*), xxxii, 160, 164, 178, 180, 181
  general judicial officers (*zābetān-e qazā'i 'āmm*), 83, 89, 162, 165–167, 177, 177n8, 181–182, 445
  Guidance Patrols (moral policing), *gasht-e ershād*, xxxii, 98, 172–173, 179, 181, 188, 320, 404n54, 445
  judicial police (*polis-e qazā'i*), xv, xviii, 162–164, 168, 176, 185
  NAJA, *Niruhā-ye Entezāmi-ye Jomhuri-ye Eslāmi* (Law Enforcement Forces of the Islamic Republic), vii, xviii, xx, xxi, xxiv, xxviii, xxxiv, 164–179, 181–184, 186, 328, 445
  NAJA Cooperative Foundation, 166
  NOPO, *Niruhā-ye vizheh-ye pād-vahshat* (Counter-terrorism Special Force), 166–167, 173, 181–182
  Office of the Acting Commander-in-Chief on Police Affairs (*Daftar-e Jāneshini-ye Farmāndehi-ye Koll-e Qovā Dar Omur-e NAJA*), 164
  PAVA, General Public Security and Intelligence Police (*Polis-e Amniyat va Ettelā'āt 'Omumi*), xxxiv, 178
  police brutality, 79, 99, 151, 170, 173, 178, 183, 445
  police corruption, 160, 169, 176, 445
  Police Counterintelligence Organization (*Sāzeman-e Hefāzat-e Ettelā'āt-e NAJA*), 165, 167–168, 175, 186

Index

Police Electronic Services Offices, 169
Polis-e Amniyat-e Akhlāghi: moral security police, sub-branch of the PAVA, xxxiv, 179, 181
Polis-e Nizārat bar Amāken-e 'Omumi (Police for the Supervision over Public Facilities and Locations), sub-branch of PAVA, xxxiv, 179–180
Prevention and Operation Police (*polis-e pishgiri va 'amaliyyāt*, PPVA), xxxiv, 179
Protection units (*yegānhā-ye hefāzat*), 175, 181
special judicial officers (*zābetān-e qazā'i khāss*), 177, 181
volunteer policing, 174
pop music, 405
Pourzand, Siamak, xii, 411n78–79
pre-trial detention, 36, 72, 82, 84, 153, 188, 207, 209n59, 210n90, 230, 275, 449
Prevention and Operation Police (*polis-e pishgiri va 'amaliyyāt or* PPVA), *see* police
principle of legality, *see* legality
prisoners
 ordinary prisoners (*zendāniyān-e 'ādi*), 26, 188–189, 198, 230
 political prisoners, xvii, 26, 38, 39, 85n57, 90n75, 94, 144n13, 149, 188–189, 196, 198, 209–210, 230, 269, 271, 282, 294, 458–459
 security prisoners (*zendāniyān-e amniyati*), *see* political prisoners
prisons, xvii, xxviii, 99, 174, 188, 203, 205n73, 223–224, 229, 283, 304, 310, 326, 330, 395, 398n34, 403n54, 408
 budget, 188, 193, 196–201, 205
 conditions, 34, 143, 192, 198, 200n50, 220, 230
 Evin prison, 21n14, 86n57, 91, 150, 190n8, 196n33, 202
 Fashafuyeh prison, 196, 330
 Kahrizak Detention Center, xxvi, 21n14, 81, 87, 172, 173, 196, 201
 leave, 202, 203, 227
 National Prisons Organisation, *see* National Prisons Organisation
 overcrowding, 27, 49, 188–190, 196–197, 199, 205–206, 211, 213n106, 229–230, 233
 Qezel Hesar prison, 196, 201
 Rajai Shahr prison, 196

propaganda, xxix, xxxv, 16n7, 31, 34, 38, 83, 94, 99, 190n8, 297, 299, 304, 307–308, 317, 326, 327, 345, 388, 391n15, 392n20, 398, 401n47, 407–408, 410–411, 456
 see also Ministry of Culture and Islamic Guidance
protection of children, *see* children's rights Act of Protecting Children and Adolescents Without Guardians or With, xxiv, 424–425
Protection units (*yegānhā-ye hefāzat*), *see* police
protests
 1999 protests, xx, 79, 149, 168, 444, 445
 2009 protests (summer), xxii, xxvi, 21n14, 173, 210, 278, 279
 2018 protests, 177, 277, 287, 396, 408, 445
 2019/2020 protests (December-January), xxvii, 96, 153, 178, 204, 282, 284, 287, 320, 323, 445
 2022 protests (autumn), xxvii, 5, 98–99, 153, 178, 188, 198, 287, 320, 388, 399, 445, 449, 460
Public Prosecutor, xviii, xx, xxxii, 23, 77–78, 80, 100–101, 142, 147n20, 163, 168, 268n7, 446
Public Security and Intelligence Police (*polise-e amniyat va ettelā'āt 'omumi, or PAVA*), *see* police
punishments
 amputation, 17, 34, 36, 48, 59, 71, 73, 75, 92, 95, 96, 274, 447
 blood money/compensation *(diyeh, pl. diyāt)*, xxi, xxxii, 25, 45–46, 48, 50–51, 54–56, 60–61, 63, 75–76, 94n82, 96, 187, 211, 213–218, 233
 discretionary punishments (*ta'zirāt*), xvi, xix, xxxv, 45–48, 50, 64, 82, 93, 407n66
 hadd (pl. hodud), xvi, xviii, xxxii, xxxv, 15, 16, 23, 45–49, 54, 64, 70, 72, 75, 187, 241, 271–273, 328
 prison sentences, *see* sentences
 retaliation *(qesās)*, xvi, xviii, xxxii, xxxv, 25, 34, 45–46, 48, 50–52, 54–56, 60–63, 69–71, 75–77, 149, 187, 273–274, 300–301, 447, 453–454
 stoning, xx, xxii, xxiv, 17, 19, 35, 48, 55, 57–58, 61n20, 72–75, 103, 236, 241, 271, 273, 277, 286, 296n11, 327, 458
 whipping, 204, 279

Index

Qalibaf, Mohammad Baqer, xx, 168, 170
qesās (retaliation), *see* punishments
Qezel Hesar prison, *see* prisons
Qom, xvi, xxii, xxxiii, 46, 49, 96, 113n26, 133, 148n21, 216n118, 233, 262, 288, 297, 323, 330, 391, 429

Radan, Ahmad Reza, xxviii, 172, 179
Rafsanjani, Hashemi, xv, xvii, xix, 12, 26, 29, 120n50, 129n68, 136, 223, 242–243, 250, 293, 332–333, 335–337, 341, 345, 351–352, 394, 397, 450
rahbar, *see* Supreme Leader
Raisi, Ebrahim, xxv, xxvii, 18, 28, 34, 40, 154, 220, 255, 279, 280, 282, 283–285, 380, 398, 457, 459
Ramezani, Gholam Hossein, 167–168, 203
Rasekh, Mohammad, 433
Reform Movement, 148, 167, 261, 285–287
Review Council, *see* Ministry of Culture and Islamic Guidance
Revolutionary Courts, *see* courts
Revolutionary Guards (Islamic Revolutionary Guards Corps - IRGC), xxvi, xxvii, 28, 31, 83, 97, 138, 149, 162, 165–166, 168, 170, 171, 173, 176, 178, 253, 255, 266, 271, 286–287, 365n26, 392–393, 410, 413, 445–446, 451, 456, 460
Rouhani, Hassan, xxiv, xxv, xxvii, 29, 176, 186, 254–255, 287, 292, 312, 318, 329, 331–333, 350–352, 355, 371, 376–378, 398
Rule of Law, xxxiii, 1, 14, 23, 25–26, 28, 30, 43–44, 66–67, 69, 102, 104, 132–134, 157–158, 285–288, 386, 389, 442
and artistic expression, 389, 458
and Bar Association, 135–136, 140, 146, 154, 156
challenges to strengthening, 32–41
and criminal justice, 86, 89, 100, 101
different conceptions of, 1–5, 444, 461–462
and family law, 104, 106–110, 114, 118–119, 121, 122, 125, 127, 129–130, 457
and health, 459
and JCPOA, 360–361, 383
Khatami and, 260–263, 341–345
Khomeini and, 9
and police, 159–160, 183, 444–445
and prisons, 450

progression and regressions in, 446–461
and property rights, 451
Shahroudi and, 268, 276, 282
and workers' rights, 451

Sarhaddizadeh, Abol-Qasem, 334
securitization, 66, 69, 100–101, 176, 251
Security Office (*herāsat*), 406
sentences, xvii, xxvi, xxvii, xxviii, 17, 19, 23, 24n16, 28–29, 36, 49, 57, 61n20, 72–74, 99, 140, 174, 187–188, 197, 202–206, 213, 223–224, 227–229, 243, 273–274, 281, 283–284, 291, 294, 296n11, 299, 304, 307, 310, 322, 326, 327, 330, 395, 398n34, 408n71, 449, 459
alternative sentences, 204–206, 320
death sentence, 23–24, 72, 93, 98, 228, 274, 281, 296, 310, 459
drug related sentence, 17
prison sentences, xvii, xxvii, 99, 174, 188, 203, 205n73, 223–224, 229, 283, 304, 310, 326, 330, 395, 398n34, 403n54, 408
setād-e diyeh (*diyeh* task-force), 216–217
sex workers, 27, 236, 237, 238–241, 250, 255–256, 457
Shahroudi, Mahmoud Hashemi, xx, xxi, xxii, 19, 20, 22, 28, 32, 38n25, 39, 41, 44, 69, 72–73, 78, 80, 87–88, 147–148, 152, 157, 168, 170, 176, 182, 192, 202–204, 206–207, 249, 250, 251, 260–288, 458–459
Sherkat-e Vāhed, 349
Shi'i, Shi'is, Shi'ism, xxiii, xxxi, 6, 8, 11–14, 15, 19, 22–25, 31, 39, 98, 137–138, 144–146, 148, 161, 267, 274, 275–276
and assisted reproduction, 432–436, 438–439
and criminal procedure, 67–68, 70–71, 74–75
and family law, 104–134
and minorities, 289–290, 294, 296, 303, 311–312, 314, 316–317, 319, 321, 331
and the penal code, 47–48, 55–59
sigheh, 119, 250, 256
Soleimani, Qasem, 100, 382
Sotoudeh, Nasrin, xxvii, 37n24, 153n33, 294n6
special judicial officers (*zābetān-eqazā'i khāss*), *see* police
sperm donation, 428, 436, 439
stoning, *see* punishments
Stop Stoning Forever campaign, 73

Sunni, Sunnis, Sunnism, xii, 14, 28, 56n12, 57n15, 59, 60n18, 104–105, 107, 146
  and assisted reproduction, 416, 419, 421, 426–427, 441–442
  and family law, 104–105, 107, 112–115, 119–122, 124, 126–128, 130–132
  as a minority, 289–296, 312–313, 317–319, 321, 324–325, 327, 329–331, 453–454, 461
Supreme Council for the Cultural Revolution (SCCR), xviii, xxxiv, 17, 18n9, 31, 386, 389–394, 396–397, 399–404, 412–413, 456
Supreme Leader, xv, xvii, xxiii, xxvii, 20, 24n16, 26, 79–80, 93–94, 97, 99n97, 110n22, 136n4, 151, 242, 262, 264–266, 275n18, 276, 277n22, 280, 283–284, 300n14, 306, 308, 316, 332, 396, 405, 407–408, 420, 427, 461
  constitutional powers of, 10–11, 14, 15–16, 137–139, 263, 289, 292, 302, 377n58, 387, 389–390, 440, 445
  executive powers over media bodies, 391–393
  executive powers over police, 160, 163–164, 167–168, 175, 180
  powers of pardon, 23, 49, 63, 201
  relationship to judiciary, 18, 28, 31–33, 67, 69, 78, 260–261, 269, 271, 286
surrogacy, 31, 32, 414–416, 417, 422, 424, 426–427, 430, 439, 441–443, 457
  regulations, 433, 434–437
surveillance, 162, 169, 181–183, 278, 399, 404
sworn oaths (*qassāmeh* and *sogand*), 70

talāq (divorce), xxxv, 107, 111, 122, 123, 124–129, 455
Tavakkoli, Ahmad, 333–335
temporary marriage (*sigheh*), *see* marriage
theatre, *see* plays
torture, xxi, xxiv, 19, 32, 34, 42, 55, 57, 78n28, 79n29, 80n33, 98–101, 150, 167, 174, 185, 189n6, 193n20, 208n86, 235, 261, 270, 276, 277, 277n22, 281, 285, 287, 295, 298–299, 323, 325, 446
  constitutional and legal provisions against, 66n3, 84, 170, 263n1
  to extract confessions, 69, 75, 315, 318
  at Kahrizak prison, 81, 172–173
  legal and judicial flaws enabling, 83–85
  Shahroudi's 2004 Charter prohibiting, 275
Triangular Clinics (for the treatment of AIDS), xix, 27, 244, 245, 247–249, 254

UN Special Rapporteur on the situation of human rights in the Islamic Republic of Iran, 35n22, 42, 44, 67n4, 86, 89, 312n29, 320, 331
United Nations Working Group on Arbitrary Detention (WGAD), 78, 80n33, 86n58, 90, 91n77, 189

velāyat-e faqih (guardianship of the jurist), xix, xxxii, xxxv, 9–12, 34, 43, 67, 101, 110, 149, 301, 344–345, 440, 454
volunteer policing, *see* police

wages, 341, 352, 354
  in the Labour Law, 331, 336, 346, 348–351
witness testimony (*shahādat*), *see* evidence
women solo singers, 405
workers, 261–262, 314, 332–344, 349, 351–353
  health-care workers, 246–247
  social workers, 196–197, 216–217, 228, 242
Workers' House (*Khāneh-ye Kārgar*), 331–332, 342, 344–349, 351–352, 451–453
workers' rights
World Prison Brief (WPF), 190–195, 197, 207, 231, 232, 449n2
Writers' Association of Iran, 394, 399n38

Yarsan, 289n2, 311–312, 324–326, 332
Yazdi, Mohmmad, xxiv, xxvii, 147, 163, 168, 263, 267–268, 279
yegānhā-ye hefāzat (protection units), *see* police
Yesaqi, Ali Akbar, 192–193, 196–197, 202–203, 225
Younesi, Ali, 292, 323–330

zenā/zinā', *see* adultery

Printed in the United States
by Baker & Taylor Publisher Services